How Congress Works

CONGRESSIONAL QUARTERLY INC.
1414 22ND STREET N.W.
WASHINGTON, D.C. 20037

Congressional Quarterly Inc.

Congressional Quarterly Inc., an editorial research service and publishing company, serves clients in the fields of news, education, business and government. It combines specific coverage of Congress, government and politics by Congressional Quarterly with the more general subject range of an affiliated service, Editorial Research Reports.

Congressional Quarterly was founded in 1945 by Henrietta and Nelson Poynter. Its basic periodical publication was and still is the *Congressional Quarterly Weekly Report,* mailed to clients every Saturday. A cumulative index is published quarterly.

CQ also publishes a variety of books including college political science texts, public affairs paperbacks and reference volumes. The latter include the *CQ Almanac,* a compendium of legislation for one session of Congress that is published each spring, and *Congress and the Nation,* a record of government for a presidential term that is published every four years.

The public affairs books are designed as timely reports to keep journalists, scholars and the public abreast of developing issues, events and trends. They include such recent titles as *Regulation: Process and Politics* and the third edition of *The Supreme Court, Justice and the Law.*

College textbooks, prepared by outside scholars and published under the CQ Press imprint, include such recent titles as *Goodbye to Good-time Charlie: The American Governorship Transformed, Second Edition,* and *Interest Group Politics.*

In addition, CQ publishes *The Congressional Monitor,* a daily report on current and future activities of congressional committees. This service is supplemented by *The Congressional Record Scanner,* an abstract of each day's *Congressional Record,* and *Congress in Print,* a weekly listing of committee publications. CQ also publishes newsletters including *Congressional Insight,* a weekly analysis of congressional action, and *Campaign Practices Reports,* a bi-monthly update on campaign laws and developments.

CQ conducts seminars and conferences on Congress, the legislative process, the federal budget, national elections and politics, and other current issues. CQ Direct Research is a consulting service that performs contract research and maintains a reference library and query desk for clients.

Editorial Research Reports covers subjects beyond the specialized scope of Congressional Quarterly. It publishes reference material on foreign affairs, business, education, cultural affairs, national security, science and other topics of news interest. Service to clients includes a 6,000-word report four times a month, bound and indexed semi-annually. Editorial Research Reports publishes paperback books in its field of coverage. Founded in 1923, the service merged with Congressional Quarterly in 1956.

Printed in the United States of America

Library of Congress Cataloging in Publication Data

Main entry under title: How Congress Works
    Includes index.
    1. United states. Congress. I. Congressional Quarterly, inc.
JK1061.H65 1983 328.73 83-5244
ISBN 0-87187-254-4

Editor: Mary L. McNeil
Supervisory Editor: John L. Moore
Major Contributors: Tom Arrandale, Sari Horwitz, Patricia Ann O'Connor, Georgianna Rathbun, Elizabeth H. Summers, Margaret C. Thompson, Michael D. Wormser
Design: Mary L. McNeil
Cover: Richard A. Pottern
Graphics: Richard A. Pottern, Bob Redding, Cheryl Rowe
Indexer: Toni Gillas

Book Department

Congressional Quarterly Inc.

Contents

Editor's Note. Congress has undergone a number of dramatic changes since the early 1970s. Reforms enacted in the post-Watergate era included a restructuring of the committee system and the enactment of strict campaign finance laws. Members became independent of party appeals and increasingly more interested in fulfilling individual constituent demands. A revised congressional budget process, passed in 1974, shifted Congress' timetable and power centers. When President Ronald Reagan made drastic budget cutting mandatory, the budget process became the central focus of congressional action throughout each year. And since 1981 Congress' ability to legislate has been tested by divided party rule — Republican in the Senate, Democratic in the House. Descriptions of these changes, along with a clear step-by-step explanation of how laws are made, are provided in **How Congress Works**. Chapters deal with party leadership, the legislative process, the committee and seniority systems, pay and perquisites for senators and representatives, pressures on Congress, seating and disciplining of members, and ethics and criminal prosecutions. The book shows how lawmaking remains an evolving process continually affected by those who make up our legislative branch of government.

How Congress Works

Introduction

In the early 1980s, continuing a trend begun a decade earlier, the American legislative branch has undergone fundamental changes at a tempo perhaps unequalled since the Great Depression. One factor alone, the changing membership of the House and Senate, has profoundly altered Congress' view of the country's ills and of the types of remedies needed.

A significant number of the current members of both chambers have been elected since 1980. And not just the faces have changed. The new senators and representatives have given Congress a decidedly more conservative outlook on national issues. They have a different view of their role as legislators, are more impatient with the legislative process as practiced by their senior colleagues and often take issue with the way congressional leaders do business.

More permanent, perhaps, has been the effect of changes in congressional operations and procedures and in campaign laws intitiated in the early and mid-1970s. Those reforms, it is now clear, were not transient fixes of the moment. The reforms left congressional operations open to the public as never before, though in some cases their long-term impact was the reverse of what was intended by the mainly liberal bloc of senators and representatives that provided the impetus for most of them.

In any case, the reforms led to significant organizational changes, particularly in the committee system; an expanded corps of power brokers, but weaker overall leadership; and a more complex congressional-executive relationship.

The cumulative effect was to make members of Congress more independent of party appeals by their leaders and more dependent on special interests and movements back home. Party unity, at least among the ruling Democrats, collapsed in the late 1970s. The Speaker of the House, Thomas P. O'Neill Jr., D-Mass., went so far as to assert that his party had become little more than an organizational convenience. Members had become more home oriented, he lamented. "They no longer have to follow the national philosophy of the party. They can get re-elected on their newsletters, or on how they serve their constitutents." And with instant communications and the mobility of the jet age — and congressional willingness today to finance more and more special services aimed at the home folks — many members almost unquestioningly have allowed attention to local interest to dominate their congressional performance.

In 1981, with the two houses of Congress controlled by the different parties for the first time in 26 years, a new test of leadership befell the country's elected representatives: the capacity of Congress to improve its track record under divided party rule. After a year's honeymoon with Congress, in which Republicans displayed a unity of purpose unmatched at least since the Great Society years of the Johnson administration, President Ronald Reagan was in danger of becoming mired in some of the same difficulties with Congress that his recent predecessors had confronted.

In 1982 Congress was absorbed primarily in economic decisions from the time Reagan sent Congress his fiscal 1983 budget in February until it passed a stopgap funding bill in December. Many legislative decisions were collected into omnibus budget and reconciliation bills. Then, when Congress could not pass appropriations bills following these budget dictates, it wrapped most of its appropriations decisions into a series of massive continuing resolutions.

Budget Act Impact

Although omnibus bills had been used throughout U.S. history, they multiplied since enactment of the Congressional Budget and Impoundment Act in 1974. Until then, Congress received the administration's budget proposal, considered it and then went on to pass separate bills authorizing and appropriating funds for programs and providing revenues to keep the government afloat. Bills were not considered within a total budget plan.

The Budget Act required Congress to set out the nation's priorities in a spending plan for the coming fiscal year. Under the act, two budget resolutions were required each year. The first, which sets spending and revenue targets, is due May 15. The second — due Sept. 15 — updates the first and converts the targets into ceilings that Congress must live within.

Spending cuts and revenue increases mandated by the budget resolutions were achieved through a reconciliation process. Using this process, authorizing committees were required to modify their programs so that funding for them fell within the budget guidelines. The House and Senate budget committees compiled the work of the authorizing committees and took them to the floor as omnibus bills subject to single up-or-down votes.

In forcing this fiscal discipline upon itself, Congress helped to create a major shift in the institution's timetable and its power centers. During times of plenty the budget process was not particularly painful or time-consuming. In the first three years of the process, budget deadlines were met or missed by a few days as Congress divided an expanding budget pie.

But when drastic cuts in government spending were found necessary, the budget process became the central focus of congressional action throughout each year. The budget almost totally dominated the congressional schedule in 1982, and, as the year ended, members of both parties were considering changes in the budget process. Because Congress spent so much time on the budget, there was little time left for passing spending bills that actually provided the money to carry out the budget decisions. It was this lack of time that caused President Reagan to insist after the November 1982 elections that Congress reconvene in a lame-duck session to work on appropriations bills.

A consequence of this shortage of time was massive stopgap legislation, called continuing appropriations resolutions, because regular spending bills for many agencies did not clear Congress before the fiscal year began. In 1981 Congress had to approve four continuing resolutions. At one point the entire government, except for the legislative branch, was operating under temporary funding; many agencies went through all of fiscal 1982 in that status.

Congress was able to clear only three of the 13 annual appropriations bills before it adjourned Oct. 2 for the 1982 election recess. During the lame-duck session, four more of the bills were cleared, leaving six bills, including the defense and energy bills, unfinished.

Fewer Bills Originated

While it modified or rejected many of Reagan's requests, the 97th Congress (1981-83) originated little of its own legislation. As of Jan. 14, the deadline for Reagan to sign or veto bills passed before Congress adjourned, 473 bills enacted by the 97th Congress had become law, far fewer than the output of any Congress in the past 20 years. The 96th Congress in 1979-80 created 613 public laws. Filibusters in the Senate also were a regular occurrence throughout 1982, not just in the lame-duck session. In late summer, for example, the Senate spent weeks bogged down in protracted debate over amendments on abortion and school busing as part of a bill increasing the national debt limit. The bill itself passed, after the controversial amendments were stricken.

If the adjournment-delaying filibusters were not enough to make civility difficult, senators also had to debate the expulsion of one of their colleagues, Harrison A. Williams Jr., D-N.J. (1959-82), who resigned before a vote was taken to oust him over his Abscam conviction.

Senators, a handful of whom unofficially began running for president, also fought institutional battles over whether the chamber's proceedings would be televised and whether senators should get a gymnasium in the new Hart office building, which opened in November 1982. Both television and the gym were defeated, to the displeasure of many senators. The new office building, which had been politically ridiculed as a costly palace, was so unpopular that the most junior senators had to be ordered into offices there.

The 97th Congress finally adjourned Dec. 23, when the Senate cleared legislation increasing the gasoline tax to pay for highway repairs and mass transit. Senators left town feeling bitter toward a handful of their colleagues who had staged a last-ditch filibuster on the gas tax bill. The normally gentlemanly Senate turned into a collection of 100 tired men and women complaining about each other's bad behavior.

Earlier, as Congress adjourned for the elections, Senate Minority Leader Robert C. Byrd, D-W.Va., complained of the "very limited legislative focus" of the 97th Congress. "The Senate agenda has been primarily a debate on budget numbers," Byrd said. "I am certain my friends on the Republican side are as anxious as I am to use the Senate as it once was used, as a forum for full and open debate on the great issues facing the country."

Profile of 98th Congress

The 1982 congressional election delivered a promise of more disunity between the White House and Capitol Hill than there had been in the 97th Congress. Twenty-six incumbent House Republicans were defeated and some GOP senators found themselves in much tighter races than they anticipated. The 98th Congress, which had 57 new House Democrats, would be less inclined to take direction from the White House.

The election results indicated that Democrats were beginning to fight their way back into power in Congress, especially in the House where they gained a 269-166 majority over Republicans and increased their voting majority on almost every committee. The 269-166 lineup worked out to 62 percent Democrats and 38 percent Republicans. But on many panels Democrats gave themselves a better deal than that ratio would dictate. For example, the new ratio would have given Democrats a 26:16 edge on the Energy and Commerce Committee, but they took a 27:15 majority. On Foreign Affairs, the new ratio would have given Democrats a 23:14 margin, but they made it 24:13.

The sensitive political work of assigning members to committees was done behind closed doors by both parties in both chambers. In the Senate, where the Republicans continued to hold 54 of 100 seats, the process was essentially a bidding system based on seniority. In the House, particularly among Democrats, members lobbied the leadership hard for their assignments, with voting records, past favors, political need and geographical considerations coming into play.

Again in keeping with the pattern of recent years, the 98th Congress was younger and had more Roman Catholics, Jews, blacks and Hispanics than any other of the past quarter century. The number of women, 23, was the same as at the end of the 97th Congress, although it was two more than the number who took office at the beginning of that Congress.

But there were more lawyers in the 98th Congress — a departure from a recent trend toward somewhat fewer attorneys. Lawyers constituted the largest single occupation group in both the House and Senate. The second largest group consisted of businessmen and bankers.

While the U.S. population as a whole had gotten older, Congress was younger. In 1983 the average member of Congress was 47, compared with 53 in the early 1950s. The average age of Democrats was 45.8 years while Republicans were slightly older at 48.7 years. Senators were generally older than representatives, averaging 53.4 years compared with 45.5 for House members.

Because there was little new blood — only five new

members — in the 1983 Senate, the average age increased from 52.5 at the beginning of the 97th Congress to 53.4 in 1983. In the 98th Congress the oldest member was Rep. Claude Pepper, D-Fla., chairman of the House Rules Committee, who was 82. The youngest was 28-year-old Rep. Jim Cooper, D-Tenn.

Growing Independence of Senate

A growing characteristic of members of Congress, particularly senators, was their independence from party control. The Senate, in contrast to years past, was now seen as a place where individual rights and performance were more valuable to its members than were party unity and a community feeling.

An extraordinary amount of time in the 97th Senate was taken up by individuals, or pairs of competing individuals, pushing the system to see how far it could go without collapsing. Much of this had to do with the strained budget and appropriations process. The arguments over budget resolutions, continuing resolutions and supplemental appropriations had been seemingly endless, and they had been the vehicle for introduction of unrelated issues that otherwise would be crowded out of the process. Because these economic measures were so vast in scope and no one action was likely to prevent their passage, senators felt no restraint about using them for their own narrow purposes.

Serious policy implications were expected to result from a Senate where the individual was in control. The more individuals had to be personally satisfied for a policy to be enacted, the more likely it was that there would be none, or that what emerged would be the lowest common denominator. The more senators insisted on entering a debate to offer a parochial point of view, the less chance the institution had to deliberate about what it was doing for the country in the long run.

The 97th Congress may not have been the one from which to draw permanent conclusions, however. The new Republican majority had disrupted a quarter-century of Democratic control, perhaps changing the style of the place as well. The unusual number of incumbent defeats in 1978 and 1980 meant an institution dominated by junior members. At the end of the 97th Congress, 55 senators were in their first term. Some of the current problems were made worse by a transient atmosphere that itself could prove temporary.

Congressional leadership also had come to mean something entirely different from what it meant in the days when Lyndon B. Johnson ruled over the Senate Democratic majority with an iron hand. The modern leader had a sensitive constituency to protect — the members of his party expected him to schedule the chamber's actions around their personal needs.

One leader who paid attention to members' personal needs was West Virginia's Robert Byrd, who was elected secretary of the Democratic Conference in 1967. Byrd turned that once-innocuous job into a power base by performing endless favors for Senate colleagues: keeping them up to date about when a vote was to take place, for example, or postponing the vote if they could not be there. The "constituent service" that Byrd performed was largely responsible for his election as Democratic whip in 1971 over Edward M. Kennedy of Massachusetts — and for Byrd's ultimate accession as majority leader. It also imposed a burden of personal favors on all leaders in both parties since then.

Congressional Pay Raise

On Dec. 18, 1982, members of Congress voted themselves another pay raise. Breaking with nearly two centuries of tradition, the new pay scale gave House members a higher salary than senators. With the $9,138 raise, representatives began drawing an annual salary of $69,800 effective immediately. *(See Pay and Perquisites, p. 113.)*

Senators were to remain at an annual salary of $60,662.50 but would be able to earn as much as they could in outside income, including legal fees, business income and honoraria for speeches and articles. Outside earnings for representatives would continue to be limited by the House rules to 30 percent of their salary, or $20,940.

The pay raise measure also provided salary increases of up to 15 percent for about 32,000 senior government employees. The pay of Cabinet officers went from $69,630 a year to $80,100; senior bureaucrats went from $59,500 to up to $68,400. The raises also affected House and Senate staffers, although their precise pay levels are set by the members for whom they work. Because senators did not get a raise, but their staff members were eligible for increases, it was possible some aides would end up making more than the senators they worked for. Without congressional action, members would have received an automatic 27 percent raise Dec. 18, 1982, when an earlier pay cap expired. While the House was noisily voting to raise its pay, members' office accounts and travel allowances were being increased in more quiet fashion. Effective Jan. 3, 1983, House members began receiving 10 percent more for office accounts and 15 percent more in travel allowances.

The constituent problem must have flashed through Byrd's mind, however, late one summer night in 1980, his last year as majority leader. As he stood on the floor trying desperately to find a time the following Monday when the Senate could vote on the 1981 budget resolution, Byrd listened to one senator after another announce that a particular time would be inconvenient. Byrd was reduced to writing all the preferences on a long yellow legal pad, a process that made him look more like a man sending out for sandwiches than the leader of a deliberative body. The discussion on scheduling did not appear in the following day's *Congressional Record*.

Some members believed the Senate schedule itself was out of control. Even when no one person was holding up the action, important matters frequently yielded to trivial affairs. Some members insisted the real problem was the rules. Much smaller than the House and supposedly more insulated from public pressure, the Senate always had operated on the theory that it could control itself with personal norms of conduct and did not need the kind of strict regulations common in the House. There was some feeling that modern political pressures were making the Senate more like the House, that unwritten custom did not work there anymore, and that restrictions on individualism represented the only chance to re-create a deliberative body.

Changes in House Rules

Democratic leaders, claiming that changes were needed to streamline the legislative process and avoid unnecessary votes and amendments, voted in early January 1983 to revise several House rules. These changes, which the House adopted, were expected to affect legislative agendas in the 98th Congress. Republican leaders objected that the rights of the minority were being trampled.

The most contentious of the changes made it harder for members to offer "riders" to appropriations bills. Such amendments to limit government actions had become popular. For example, conservatives in recent years had attached riders on school busing and abortion to appropriations bills.

Another change allowed the Speaker to resolve the House into the Committee of the Whole without a vote. In the past, members frequently sought a time-consuming, roll-call vote on forming the Committee of the Whole, a device the House used to debate and amend bills before voting on final passage.

An additional change gave the Speaker authority to postpone for up to two legislative days a vote on approval of the previous day's *Journal,* the record of House proceedings. Republicans often forced votes on both procedures to get a quorum of members to the House floor.

And in response to concern about party loyalty, the House adopted a rule making continued assignment to committees contingent upon members being members of their party caucus. Similarly, the Democratic Caucus revised its rules in December 1982 to call for throwing a member out of the caucus if he or she switched parties.

All these Senate and House changes, big and little, were certain to affect how Congress performed in the 1980s. In some ways, Congress as an institution would be more efficient, less cumbersome and more professional. Yet Congress would continue to be essentially the same colorful deliberative body it has been since it first convened in 1789. As Roger H. Davidson and Walter J. Oleszek wrote in *Congress and Its Members,* "...Congress is, above all, a fascinating place — a 'strategic site' from which to view the varied actors in the American political drama."

It is the aim of this book to provide a strategic site for observing how Congress works — how its procedures and traditions shape the nature of our legislative system.

Party Leadership in Congress

Although the Constitution does not mention the role of political parties in the legislative process, party leadership is one of the decisive forces influencing the way Congress operates.

Since the last half of the 19th century, when the two-party system became firmly entrenched on Capitol Hill, congressional leaders have tried to develop methods that advance their party's legislative effectiveness. To that end, they have attempted — with varying degrees of success — to solidify party unity, discipline recalcitrant colleagues while rewarding the loyal, utilize and shape the rules to facilitate enactment of the party's — and the president's — legislative goals and, in the process, enhance the party's national image and electoral fortunes.

That the record has been mixed is due to a variety of circumstances that impinge upon the ability of the congressional leaders to respond to a complex and changing legislative environment. On occasion, party leaders have been able to use their authority to shape the setting and institutions in which they operate. But increasingly in recent years, party leadership has been weakened by competing influences and power centers, including a more decentralized committee and subcommittee structure and the emergence of new election laws and congressional rules and practices that reinforce the independence of individual members.

" '[T]he party principle' organizes Congress. But the 'committee principle' significantly shapes most issues Congress will debate," wrote Roger H. Davidson and Walter J. Oleszek, authors of *Congress and Its Members*. "The first emphasizes integration, the second fragmentation. Traditionally, party leaders struggle to manage an institution that disperses policymaking authority to numerous workshops." [1]

Leadership Positions

In the House, the leadership structure consists of the Speaker, who is both the chamber's presiding officer and the majority party's overall leader; the majority and minority floor leaders; the assistant floor leaders (called whips), who have numerous assistants; and a variety of supporting organizations including special committees controlled by the political parties that develop party strategy, assign party members to House committees and assist the leadership in scheduling and keeping track of legislation.

In the Senate, there is no institutional or party official comparable in power and prestige to the Speaker. The vice president of the United States is designated by the Constitution as the president of the Senate — the presiding officer. In his absence, the Senate president pro tempore presides. Neither office, however, has been endowed with commanding congressional authority or given much political power. The remainder of the Senate leadership apparatus, though, is similar in function to that of the House.

Of all the leadership positions in Congress, the only one that has functioned continuously since 1789 is the Speaker — a post established by the Constitution. Although the office of president pro tempore in the Senate also was established by the Constitution, it was not filled on a continuing basis until 1890. Before then, the Senate elected a president pro tempore only when the vice president was absent, and during some sessions of Congress the office was left vacant. All the other leadership posts in both chambers have been set up at various times by the Republican and Democratic Party caucuses.

The Leadership Role

"House and Senate leaders have basically the same job: to bring coherence and efficiency to a decentralized and individualistic legislative body," wrote Davidson and Oleszek. "Leadership duties break down into institutional and party functions. Both kinds of functions point toward the parties' objective of influencing policymaking in conformity with their political leanings." [2]

Foremost among the tasks of congressional leaders is organizing the House and Senate chambers to effectively carry out their party's programs. In that role, the leadership must decide how best to guide proposals through the various stages of the legislative process: committee action, floor action and House-Senate conference negotiations.

The task is difficult and, often, unexciting: meeting with committee chairmen on their legislative problems and priorities and resolving jurisdictional disputes; scheduling bills for floor action; knowing the rules and procedures and setting strategies employing them in a way that can help, rather than jeopardize, the party's chances of legislative success; assessing support and opposition to the leadership's positions and initiatives; and rounding up votes (a task sometimes, but not always, made easier for the majority if the White House is controlled by a president of the

Pay of Congressional Leaders

The top six leaders of Congress — the Speaker of the House, the Senate president pro tempore and the majority and minority leaders of both chambers — receive additional pay. Salaries listed below were in effect as of March 1983. (The salary of House members was $69,800. The salary of members of the Senate was $60,662.50.)

Speaker

Highest paid is the House Speaker, with a salary of $91,000. In addition to his regular pay, the Speaker received an estimated $676,000 in fiscal 1983 for office expenses and staff, including $18,000 for official expenses (with no accounting required except for income tax purposes).

The table below lists the changes in the Speaker's salary since 1789, and the dates the measures authorizing the changes were enacted:

Salary	Date Signed into Law
$12 per day in session	Sept. 22, 1789
$3,000 per annum	March 19, 1816
$16 per day in session	Jan. 22, 1818
$6,000 per annum	Aug. 16, 1856
$8,000 per annum	Jan. 20, 1874
$12,000 per annum	Feb. 26, 1907
$15,000 per annum	March 4, 1925
$20,000 per annum	Aug. 2, 1946
$30,000 per annum	Jan. 19, 1949
$35,000 per annum	March 2, 1955
$43,000 per annum	Aug. 14, 1964
$62,500 per annum	Sept. 15, 1969
$65,625 per annum	Aug. 9, 1975
$75,125 per annum	April 1, 1977
$79,125 per annum	Oct. 12, 1979
$91,000 per annum	Dec. 21, 1982

Party Floor Leaders

The pay of the majority and minority leaders of both houses, as well as the president pro tempore of the Senate was increased to $78,900 in 1983 from $65,000 in 1977. The floor leaders in both chambers receive additional appropriations for staff and operating expenses. For fiscal 1983, funding for the office of the House majority leader was estimated at $555,000 (including $10,000 for official expenses) and for the minority leader, $617,000 (including $10,000 in official expenses). The expenses of the Senate majority and minority leaders' offices were estimated at $660,000 each.

Appropriations for staff and operations of the House whips was estimated at $470,000 for the majority and $408,000 for the minority; for the Senate whips, $308,000 each. Each whip also received $2,500 in official expenses.

Source: Offices of House and Senate sergeants at arms.

same party); organizing party members through the caucus (called the conference by Senate and House Republicans and by Democrats in the Senate); consulting with and informing the president on legislative matters; and serving as congressional spokesmen for the party.

Generally, leaders represent the ideological center of their party. In this as well as in their role as mediators, they act in a sense as "middlemen" for the various factions of the party in trying to draft legislative compromises that the party and Congress will support.

Factors such as personality, geographical balance and length of service play an important part in the selection of the leadership. Once elected, however, "legislative leaders, no matter how strong their personalities, can never fully escape the constraints placed upon them by the collaborative demands of their partisan positions and the ... autonomy of their followers which, in turn, flows from their independent constituencies," observed Robert L. Peabody, professor of political science at Johns Hopkins University.[3]

Trying to Promote Loyalty

The leaders of both houses rely on a variety of methods and strategies to achieve their legislative objectives. There are few tangible rewards they can offer today: promises of support for a committee chairmanship or leadership post; their support of a public works project in a member's district; use of House and Senate election campaign funds to award loyalty — a tool of diminishing value in the 1980s — help in obtaining outside campaign contributions and promises to assist members' re-election efforts by campaigning in their behalf.

A less tangible but equally important factor is the favoritism shown to the party faithful who cooperate with the leadership and the cold shoulder given defectors. As political scientist Randall Ripley noted in a 1967 study of the House, "The party leaders are in good position to influence the attitude of the House toward a member early in his career by telling other members what they think of him. There are also visible ways, such as the Speaker's selection of members to preside over the House or over the Committee of the Whole, by which party leaders indicate the younger members whom they regard highly."[4]

In recent years, congressional leaders have relied primarily on tact and persuasion instead of rewards, threats or actual punishments to win members' support.

Leadership in the 1980s

The leadership styles used in the House and Senate today naturally reflect individual preferences and temperaments. But they also result from the changed characteristics of Congress itself. "The Congress of the 1980s is a different, more complex institution than the Congresses of the 1970s or 1960s," wrote Frank H. Mackaman, executive director of the Everett McKinley Dirksen Congressional Leadership Research Center in 1981. "Leaders confront a much less predictable environment than their predecessors did. They are elected by their colleagues but are not endowed with unrestricted power. Their tasks have become more complicated, time-consuming and tenuous.... A former Hill staff member put it this way: 'Congress gives the impression of a football team which goes to the line of scrimmage not having had a huddle. When the ball is snapped, every player runs the play he would have called if there had been a huddle.'

"Into the breech step the leaders, the would-be quarterbacks of Congress."[5]

But the task of quarterbacking the legislative game has become much more difficult. Individual members of Congress have become less bound by tradition than their predecessors. Election law reforms allow them to be less dependent on the political party apparatus for their survival. Members used to be content to bask in the reflected glory of their party's accomplishments. In turn, the party, at the local, state and national level, would lend its muscle at re-election time. But with the changes that took place inside and outside Congress in the 1970s, members found they could campaign more effectively by becoming powers in their own right.

New rules and procedures made the institution more democratic, further diminishing the power of the leadership and the political parties they led. The leaders discovered they increasingly had to give in to their colleagues' demands for greater freedom and independence within what remained of the party structure. They were required to spend more and more of their time consulting with and currying favors from their troops.

A decade of widespread turnover in membership, the emergence of new power centers that sprung up after the "democratization" of Congress and the growth in the power and influence of subcommittees all complicated the task of forging the strong leadership needed to formulate and enact a coherent legislative program.

On the other hand, some changes, especially in the House — such as reactivating the Democratic Party Caucus, giving new powers to the Democratic Steering and Policy Committee and adopting rules that reduced the often capricious and obstructive powers of committee chairmen — did serve somewhat to enhance the power of party leaders. But at the same time, power was being distributed more broadly among the members, requiring the leadership to be more responsive to them.

In her study of the Democratic leadership in the House in the 1970s, Barbara Sinclair, professor of political science at the University of California, concluded, "From the leadership's point of view, changes in the 1970s have not been detrimental. The current leadership has shown considerable skill in using the new resources available to it. Even an adroit employment of resources does not, however, always translate into victory, and sometimes the immense time pressure under which the leadership works prevents the most effective use of the tools available." [6]

HOUSE LEADERSHIP: HISTORY OF THE SPEAKER

For the first two decades of the U.S. Congress, the Speaker was largely a figurehead. But by the eve of the War of 1812 he had become the predominant elected official of the legislative branch. The power of the Speaker ebbed and flowed during most of the 19th century; then, for almost three decades beginning in the 1880s, the Speaker commanded unparalleled influence and power over the House.

The arbitrary use of power by a series of autocratic Speakers reached its peak under Joseph G. Cannon, R-Ill., Speaker from 1903 to 1911. Cannon skillfully developed a hierarchical system based on manipulation of the House's formal organizational structure and reinforced by strong party discipline. In 1910 Republicans joined Democrats in a revolt against Cannon's arbitrary rule. The Speaker was stripped of most of his power, including his authority to appoint all House members to committees and his absolute control over recognition of members wishing to speak or offer motions and amendments during House debates.

Changes in the caucus rules of the two political parties as well as in the standing rules of the House also lessened the Speaker's authority. For example, in the 1910 revolt against Cannon, the Speaker was denied a seat on the powerful Rules Committee, through which most bills must go before they can be sent to the House.

That dismantling of the Speaker's power had a long-term effect on the office. Never again was the speakership given such authority over the House. All subsequent Speakers who have been effective House leaders have achieved influence chiefly through personal prestige, persuasion, brokerage and bargaining.

Today, the Speaker's formal duties are to preside over the House and decide points of order (with advice from the parliamentarian); refer bills and resolutions to the appropriate House committees (usually upon the recommendations of the chairmen); appoint members to select, ad hoc, special and conference committees; and designate members to sit as chairman of the Committee of the Whole, the parliamentary format in which most House action is transacted. These are usually routine tasks, providing the Speaker with little real power or flexibility to shape the outcome of legislation.

Like the rest of his colleagues, the Speaker may participate in debate and vote, although recent Speakers seldom have voted except to break a tie. During the Carter administration (1977-81) Speaker Thomas P. O'Neill Jr., D-Mass., voted just three times, once to break a tie. However, with Republican Ronald Reagan in the White House, the Speaker became more partisan, voting six times in 1981 alone, primarily to oppose the administration's economic policies.

In modern times, the Speaker has not been a member of any legislative committee; nor, in general, have the House majority and minority leaders. (By contrast, the majority and minority floor leaders in the less institutionalized Senate serve on several committees.)

Beyond those formal roles, the Speaker is above all a political figure, the leader of the majority party in the House. Most 20th century Speakers have sought to apply their authority within parliamentary limits and yet aid their own party whenever possible. As former Senate parliamentarian Floyd M. Riddick noted in a 1949 book, *The U.S. Congress: Organization and Procedure*, "Tradition and unwritten law require that the Speaker apply the rules of the House consistently, yet in the twilight zone a large area exists where he may exercise great discrimination and where he has many opportunities to apply the rules to his party's advantage." [7]

One notable example of such selectivity occurred in 1941, when a ruling by House Speaker Sam Rayburn, D-Texas (1913-61), won him credit for having made possible the passage of a bill extending the military draft. After the measure had passed by a one-vote margin, 203-202, Rayburn employed a series of parliamentary maneuvers to prevent the bill's reconsideration, despite an outcry from Republican opponents that he was using his power arbitrarily. Historians have observed that the entire preparedness program for World War II might have been disrupted if the bill had not been passed in the summer of 1941.

Although the Constitution does not specify that the Speaker must be a member of the House, no non-member has ever been elected to the post. During the 20th century, only relatively senior members have been chosen. (Before 1896 the average period of previous service in the House by members who became Speaker was only seven years; since 1899 it has been more than 24 years.)

It also has become an unwritten tradition, particularly for Democrats, to elevate the party's floor leader to Speaker once an opening occurs. Thus Speaker O'Neill and his two immediate predecessors — Carl Albert, D-Okla. (1947-77), and John W. McCormack, D-Mass. (1928-71) — all moved from majority whip to majority leader to Speaker.

Since the Civil War, neither party has ousted a sitting Speaker while the party remained in the majority, and only two former Speakers — J. Warren Keifer, R-Ohio (Speaker, 1881-83), and Joseph W. Martin Jr., R-Mass. (Speaker, 1947-49, 1953-55) — have been removed from leadership positions after their party became the minority. As congressional specialist Randall B. Ripley has observed, "In general, the Speaker retains leadership status in his party as long as he remains in the House." [8]

"No other member of Congress possesses the visibility and authority of the Speaker of the House," wrote Davidson and Oleszek. "Part of the Speaker's prestige comes from the office's formal recognition in the Constitution.... As chief parliamentary officer and leader of the majority party, the Speaker is in a unique position to influence the course and record of the House. But his success rests less on formal rules than on personal prestige, sensitivity to member needs, ability to persuade and skill at mediating disputes." [9]

Framers' Intentions

The intentions of the framers of the Constitution in regard to the speakership were not set forth in either the Constitution or the records of the Constitutional Convention. The Constitution's only reference to the office is in Article I, Section 2, clause 5, which states, "The House of Representatives shall chuse their Speaker and other Officers...." There is no evidence that the provision was debated by the Founding Fathers.

Two respected authorities on the speakership, Mary P. Follett and Hubert Bruce Fuller, have suggested that the failure of the framers to elaborate on the Speaker's office indicated that the role they envisioned for the post was one similar to the speakership of the colonial legislatures — a post with which the framers were, of course, intimately familiar. In most cases, the colonial Speakers were active politicians who not only presided over the legislatures but also used their positions to further their own or their faction's legislative aims. This concept of the office differed sharply from that of the speakership of the House of Commons. The British Speaker was, and still is, a strictly non-partisan presiding officer. (The term "speaker" first appeared in the Commons in 1377, when Sir Thomas Hungerford assumed the post. Until the late 17th century, the Speaker in England was directly responsible to the Crown. The term was derived from the fact that it was the duty of the presiding officer to interpret the will of the House of Commons to the Crown.)

Follett, whose 1896 book, *The Speaker of the House of Representatives*, still is widely regarded as the authorita-

tive study of the early development of the office, maintained that a proposal put before the Constitutional Convention in 1787 for a Council of State, consisting of the Speaker, the president of the United States, the president of the Senate (the vice president of the United States), the chief justice of the United States and the heads of federal departments, further indicated that the Founding Fathers intended the Speaker's office to be an important political post. The proposal for a Council of State, though seriously considered, was rejected by the convention.

"Surely," Follett said, "those who advocated this important board could not have thought of the Speaker as a non-political moderator, as a mere parliamentary officer whom it was necessary to dissociate from politics. What they intended must be inferred from that with which they were familiar: they knew a Speaker in the colonial assemblies who was at the time a political leader; they knew a presiding officer of [the Continental] Congress who was both a political leader and the official head of the state with important administrative functions; they knew a president of the Constitutional Convention who to his power as chairman [was] added all the influence to be expected of one acknowledged as the foremost man of the nation. Few of their number had ever been in England, and there is no reason for believing, as has been frequently asserted, that they provided for a speaker similar to the presiding officer of the House of Commons." [10]

The House of Representatives spelled out the duties of the Speaker on April 7, 1789, when a select committee of 11 members reported a suggested code of standing rules and orders of procedure. The code, debated and adopted the same day by the House, assigned the following duties to the Speaker: presiding at House sessions, preserving decorum and order, putting questions to the House, deciding points of order, announcing the results of standing and teller votes, appointing select committees of not more than three members and voting in cases of a tie, a practice referred to as the Speaker's "casting" vote.

In the beginning, the Speaker was elected by secret ballot, but since 1839 his selection has been made formally by a roll-call vote of the House. (In practice, he still is chosen by secret ballot in that the nominee for Speaker is selected by the majority party in its party caucus, where voting is secret. The House roll call then is a formality.)

Because political parties had not yet been formed, Frederick A. C. Muhlenberg, Pa., the first Speaker (1789-91), was non-partisan. In the 2nd Congress, however, clearly defined party divisions had begun to develop, and Muhlenberg's successor, Jonathan Trumbull of Connecticut, displayed definite leanings toward President Washington's legislative program. Jonathan Dayton, a Federalist from New Jersey, presided over the House in the 4th Congress, even though his opponents were in the majority. [11]

Partisanship had become pronounced by 1799, when the Federalists elected Theodore Sedgwick of Massachusetts, to the Speaker's post. According to Follett, "Sedgwick made many enemies by decided and even partisan acts. He was Speaker during the debates on the repeal of the Alien and Sedition Acts, and gave his influence and cast votes in favor of the Bankrupt Act and the Sedition Acts (two important Federalist measures)." [12] In addition, Sedgwick denied a request by two reporters from the *National Intelligencer*, a leading anti-Federalist newspaper, to cover House proceedings. Sedgwick later made that decision final by exercising his "casting vote" on the matter when the reporters applied directly to the House.

Speakership of Henry Clay

One of the most important periods in the evolution of the speakership was from 1811 to 1825, during which Henry Clay, a Democratic-Republican (the Jeffersonian party) and later a Whig, held the post for six terms. Clay, a popular Kentuckian who had resigned a seat in the Senate in order to run for the House, was one of only two members ever elected Speaker during a first term in office. (The other was William Pennington, Whig-N.J., in 1859.)

Clay owed his election as Speaker in 1811 to a faction of young Democratic-Republicans known as the War Hawks, who had swept 70 House seats in the election of 1810 by advocating Western expansion and war with England over its interference with American shipping. On these and other issues, Clay sought to assert the supremacy of Congress over the other branches of government and of the speakership over affairs of the House.

In one of his first acts as Speaker, Clay stacked key House committees with proponents of his war policy. To the Foreign Affairs Committee he named three War Hawks: Peter B. Port, N.Y., who was named chairman; John C. Calhoun, S.C., and Felix Grundy, Tenn. In other important appointments, Clay named David R. Williams, N.Y., chairman of the Committee on Military Affairs, and Langdon Cheves, S.C., chairman of the Naval Affairs Committee. The newly organized House immediately set out to push the government into war with England. On Nov. 29, 1811, less than four weeks after Congress had convened, the Foreign Affairs Committee issued a report recommending war.

Although President James Madison sought a peaceful settlement with England, continuous pressure from Clay finally resulted in a declaration of war. On March 15, 1812, Clay presented the administration with a program calling for a 30-day embargo on British goods, followed by a declaration of war and the acceptance of 10,000 volunteers into the Army on short-term enlistments. Clay noted that while the declaration of war lay within the constitutional powers of Congress, he expected the administration to take the responsibility of recommending it. After considerable deliberation, Madison agreed to the embargo, and on June 1 sent Congress a war message.

According to congressional historian George Rothwell Brown, "Clay had lifted the Speakership of the House to a point of new power and responsibility, the Speaker to a place in the state where, backed by the party organization, . . . he could present to the President a program determining national policy and involving a declaration of war. . . . Mr. Clay brought to bear upon Mr. Madison . . . the influence of his great office in an appeal to arms, against the pacifist sentiment of the President and most of the Cabinet." [13]

Clay, a gifted orator, was the first House Speaker to use debate extensively as a tool to achieve his party's legislative aims. In a series of heated exchanges with Rep. Josiah Quincy, a powerful Federalist from Massachusetts who thought the war would endanger New England's foreign trade interests, Clay cast the issue in terms of patriotism. In this way he was able to mobilize national support for the war. As historian Hubert Bruce Fuller has noted, "No subject was so well suited to Clay's native talents [as debate]; he touched the keys of inspiration, and the nation echoed one strain; the boundless resources of the country, the glamor of successful war, the magic of enlarged domain, the prestige of victory. This stamped Clay [as] not the traditional moderator of the House, but rather [as] party leader who could control the House. . . . In the stirring times of his first term in the Chair, with all the bitterness of party feeling, there was scarcely a day when he did not give voice to his sentiments." [14]

Clay reinforced his control of the House by taking advantage of such rules as that governing recognition of members desiring to speak. A notable example was afforded in the debate on the proposed declaration of war when John Randolph, a Virginia Democrat who for years had intimidated other House members with his rhetoric, sought to take the floor to oppose the war policy. Clay ruled that Randolph could not speak unless he submitted a motion to the House. When the motion was submitted, Clay ruled that Randolph still could not speak until the House considered the motion. The House refused to consider it, and Randolph was denied the floor. Clay frequently resorted to such tactics on important issues. In his six terms as Speaker, none of his rulings from the Chair was overturned, though many were sustained only by strict party-line votes.

Unlike his predecessors, Clay remained a vigorous spokesman for the interests of his congressional district, despite his position as Speaker. He was the first Speaker — and one of the few in history — to vote in instances when his vote could make no difference in the result. Clay's voting practices and his participation in debate set the precedent that Speakers forfeited none of their normal privileges as members.

Notwithstanding setbacks in the war, Clay's personal popularity was not diminished. He kept his influence over the House and later attained equal or even greater influence when he returned to the Senate. Just as he had forced the war policy of the House upon Madison in 1812, Clay imposed other foreign and domestic policies upon President James Monroe after the war. Among the measures he pushed through Congress over Monroe's opposition were various internal public works projects, a protective tariff, recognition of certain South American governments and the Missouri Compromise.

In her study of the speakership, Follett concluded that Clay was "the most powerful man in the nation from 1811 to 1825." [15] According to Follett, his legacy to the House included three important elements: strengthening the Speaker's parliamentary powers, broadening the Speaker's personal influence over the House and winning new prestige for the Speaker as a legislative leader of his party.

Clay's Pre-Civil War Successors

With few exceptions, the Speakers who succeeded Clay during the period up to the Civil War attempted to follow Clay's model of the speakership. Among the most politically partisan were two Democrats, Andrew Stevenson, Va., who held the post in 1827-34, and James K. Polk, Tenn., who served from 1835 to 1839. Both gave strong backing to the programs put forth by the Democratic presidents holding office at the time.

In 1832 Stevenson cast the deciding vote against a motion that a committee to investigate the Bank of the United States (an institution strongly opposed by President Andrew Jackson) be chosen by ballot of the House. Defeat of the motion meant that Stevenson was free to appoint the committee himself. Polk, who was to become president in 1845, drew considerable criticism from former President John Quincy Adams, then a Whig from Massachusetts, who accused him of making appointments to

House committees "in favor of the administration" and of being "partial."

The main attempt at non-partisanship in this period was made in 1839-41, when Robert M. T. Hunter, D-Va., was in the Speaker's chair. Hunter, elected as a compromise candidate after Whigs and Democrats had deadlocked over their own candidates, was considered fair but indecisive as a presiding officer.

John Quincy Adams described him as a "good-hearted, weak-headed, young man." [16] In his final speech, Hunter said: "It is something if I can hope I have made it easier for those who succeed me to act on some better principle than that of giving the whole power of the House to one of the parties without regard to the rights and feelings of others. Clothe this station with the authority of justice and how much may it not do to elevate the views of parties from themselves to their country. But arm it with the mere power of numbers and administer it with an exclusive eye to the interests of a party and it may become the engine of as much fraud and oppression as can be practiced in a country as free as ours." [17]

Post-Civil War Speakers

The political character of the speakership became even more pronounced during and after the Civil War. Schuyler Colfax, R-Ind., who served in the post from 1863 to 1869, frequently left the chair to participate in House debates on party issues.

One House member said of Colfax that "he sometimes announces the passage of a bill as if it were the triumph of his own work, not as if he were merely reading the record of the House."

In April 1864, when a member advocated recognition of the Confederate states, Colfax took the floor to offer a resolution recommending the member's expulsion. "I recognize," Colfax said, "that there is a double duty incumbent upon me: first to the House of Representatives, to administer the duties of the Chair and the rules of the House faithfully and impartially to the best of my ability and judgment. But I feel that I owe still another duty to the people of the ninth Congressional district of Indiana, who sent me here as their Representative to speak and act and vote in their stead. It is in conforming with this latter duty to those who cannot speak here for themselves, and who, I believe, would endorse the sentiment of this resolution, that I have felt my duty to rise in my place as a Member of Congress from the state of Indiana and offer this resolution." [18]

The speakership of Colfax's successor, James G. Blaine, R-Maine, was more political in nature. Not since the time of Clay had a Speaker attempted so consciously to frame the organization of the House in a manner favorable to his party's program.

According to George Rothwell Brown, "Blaine created the committees as he desired them to be, ... naming as chairmen tried and trusted men ..., men of proved ability and loyalty, who owed their allegiance to him as the head of the party in the House. Through these lieutenants, occupying every strategic place in the organization, the Speaker controlled the House and made it instantly responsive to the will of the party, of which, at this period, he was one of the great leaders, if, indeed, not the greatest leader." [19] The result of this structuring of committees was a flood of Republican-sponsored legislation favorable to business — particularly railroad — interests.

Carlisle, Reed and Crisp

Dimensions of the Speaker's office were further broadened in the late 19th century under two Democrats, John G. Carlisle, Ky., and Charles F. Crisp, Ga., and one Republican, Thomas B. Reed of Maine, often called "Czar" Reed.

Carlisle, who held the post from 1883 to 1889, established the concept, which endured for more than two decades, that it was the duty of the Speaker not to follow the dictates of his party but to impose his own will on the House. Carlisle achieved that objective primarily through the power of recognition, which he used arbitrarily to further his legislative ends. Follett observed that Carlisle "considered it the Speaker's duty to be the leader of Congress, to have a definite legislative policy, and to take every means in his power to secure the accomplishment of that policy. He himself shirked neither the duty nor the responsibility; again and again he opposed the will of a large majority of the House by refusing recognition to members who wished to take up important business; his committees also, while fair and able, represented Carlisle's view more closely than anyone's else. By every other means which his office afforded, he sought, entirely regardless of his position as chairman, to impose his will on the House and to be the real source of the legislation of the United States." [20]

Carlisle's successor, Reed, who served from 1889-91 and again from 1895-99, expanded the powers of his office more than any other Speaker in history except Clay. In essence, Reed's rulings from the Chair, later formally incorporated into the rules and precedents of the House, established the absolute right of the majority to control the legislative process.

At the outset of the 51st Congress, when Reed assumed office, filibustering by the minority in the House had grown to such lengths that it had become difficult for the majority to transact business. The minority was able to paralyze the House by introducing a series of dilatory motions, such as motions to recess or adjourn, or by demanding time-consuming roll-call votes on other motions. (A provision of the Constitution provides that one-fifth of a House quorum can demand a roll-call vote on any question.)

Another method of obstruction was the tactic of "constructive absences," under which members of the minority would fail to vote on certain questions even though they were present in the chamber. Under established procedures, only those voting were counted for purposes of establishing the presence of a quorum, which is necessary for the transaction of business. Thus a minority often was able to stall action in the House simply by refusing to answer to their names on quorum calls. Reed's rulings, though attacked as arbitrary by the minority, put an end to the Democrats' obstructionist tactics.

On Jan. 21, 1890, Reed took his first major step against such obstruction by refusing to consider a member's demand for a teller vote on a motion to adjourn. Later that month he announced his intention to disregard all motions and appeals, even if procedurally correct, if they were intended simply to delay House business.

On Jan. 30, 1890, Reed made a second ruling to curb obstruction. When the yeas and nays were demanded on consideration of a contested election case, the vote came to 161 yeas, 2 nays, and 165 not voting. After the result was announced, Democrats immediately claimed that the vote was invalid because a quorum had not voted. Reed then startled the House by ruling that 130 Democrats present but not voting would be counted for the purpose of establishing a quorum. The motion thus was carried by a majority of those voting. An appeal from the decision was tabled by a majority of those voting (again with a quorum present but not voting).

On the following day, the Speaker declined to reconsider the ruling. Follett recalled that Reed was "denounced as a tyrant, despot, czar; . . . never before had the House of Representatives witnessed such a scene — its presiding officer condemned, and subjected to the most violent abuse on account of a parliamentary decision. But Mr. Reed by his calmness under personal accusations, and by the firmness with which he stood his ground against both importunity and attack, guided the House through its stormy crisis and the establishment of a more sound and salutary principle of parliamentary law." [21]

The "Reed Rules." On Feb. 14, 1890, the House formally adopted new rules incorporating Reed's rulings and other new procedures. The new code, reported by the Rules Committee chaired by Reed, provided that: 1) all members must vote unless they had a pecuniary interest in the question at issue; 2) motions to take a recess and to fix a date of adjournment would not be entertained when a question was under debate; 3) 100 members would constitute a quorum in the Committee of the Whole; and 4) no dilatory motions should be entertained by the Speaker.

In its report to the House, the Rules Committee majority stated: "The abuse has grown to such proportions that the parliamentary law which governs American assemblies has found it necessary to keep pace with the evil, and to enable the majority by the intervention of the presiding officer to meet by extraordinary means the extraordinary abuse of power on the part sometimes of a very few members." [22]

The "Reed Rules" were adopted by the House after bitter debate. The most controversial of the new provisions — counting present, but non-voting, members to make a quorum — was upheld by the U.S. Supreme Court in an 1891 test case.

Crisp, who succeeded Reed as Speaker in the Democratic-controlled House of 1891-95, contributed to the evolution of the speakership by strengthening the Rules Committee as a tool of the Speaker. Although the Reed rules were dropped in the 52nd Congress (1891-93), essentially the same powers were lodged in the Rules Committee. Speakers had sat on and chaired the Rules Committee since 1858 and had derived much of their power from that arrangement.

The rules of the 53rd Congress (1893-95) permitted the Rules Committee to meet at any time and report a motion to put an immediate stop to filibustering. Historian Hubert Bruce Fuller has noted that the expanded role of the Rules Committee was "a radical departure from the long-established rules and principles of parliamentary law and practice." Fuller added: "The tyranny of Reed seemed beneficence when Crisp ruled that not even 'the question of consideration could be raised against a report from the Committee on Rules.' This committee, dominated of course by the Speaker, became the dictator of the House, and the members were forbidden even to question its wisdom or decision. . . ." [23]

Era of Cannonism

The peak of the Speaker's power was reached during the rule of Joseph G. Cannon, R-Ill., a staunch conservative who instituted few parliamentary changes in the House but fully exploited those made by Carlisle, Reed and Crisp. Like Reed, Cannon also was known as the "czar."

"Taken individually, Cannon's powers were little different from those of his immediate predecessors," according to Davidson and Oleszek, "but taken together and exercised to their limits they bordered on the dictatorial." [24] Under his reign — from 1903 to 1911 — recognition of members was made entirely arbitrary. It was reported that when members rose without first consulting Cannon, the Speaker would say "For what purpose does the gentleman rise?" [25] If the explanation was unsatisfactory, Cannon would invariably deny the member the floor.

On days set aside for approval by unanimous consent of purely local bills of a minor nature, Cannon moved arbitrarily to reward his friends and punish his enemies. "Often on the success of these bills would depend the re-election of many men to Congress," wrote Fuller. "Each member was compelled first to consult the Speaker and secure his consent to recognition. The Speaker on these days had before him a list of the members to be recognized, and this order was scrupulously followed. Thus the Speaker's power was neither to be ignored nor defied. His smile and assent made and unmade members, accordingly, as he bestowed or withheld those powerful benefices." [26]

Under Cannon, the House Rules Committee became an even more powerful instrument of the speakership than it had been under Crisp. Before any committee could report legislation to the House, the committee was required to obtain clearance from the Rules Committee, and clearance usually was granted only for measures that met with Cannon's favor. The Rules Committee's special terms and guidelines for bills to be considered by the House — those acceptable to Cannon — usually included sharp limits on debate and foreclosure of floor amendments. The latter practice made it possible for Cannon and his associates to attach legislative "riders" (non-germane amendments) in committee that might have been voted down on the floor if brought to a separate vote. Rather than kill the entire bill, the House usually accepted such riders, which most frequently were attached to annual appropriation bills that were virtually assured of passage.

Unlike Speaker Reed, who had ruled the House alone, Cannon established a network of trusted lieutenants. Key committee assignments went to a group of Republicans who had become associated with Cannon in evening poker games: Sereno E. Payne, N.Y., John Dalzell, Pa., James R. Mann, Ill., and Nicholas Longworth, Ohio. The Speaker and his leadership group reportedly decided much of the business of the House during the after-hours poker sessions.

Revolt Against the Speaker. Cannon finally was shorn of much of his power in 1910 after insurgent Republicans joined with Democrats to force a liberalization of the rules. Changes instituted included new rules that: prohibited the Speaker from naming or serving on the Rules Committee, denied the Speaker the right to appoint members to standing committees and reduced the Speaker's power to deny recognition to members wishing to speak during a House debate or to offer motions or amendments.

The insurgents at this time also instituted the Consent Calendar and Private Bills Calendar as well as the Calendar Wednesday and Discharge Petition procedures. These innovations were designed generally to provide alternative means to expedite legislation opposed by the leadership or blocked by a hostile committee. Under the discharge procedure, for example, a bill could be forced out of a committee

Heated Contests for Speakership...

Of the top leadership positions in Congress, only the office of House Speaker is filled by a formal vote of the chamber's membership. Other posts, which are not recognized in the rules of the House or Senate (except for the Senate president pro tempore), are filled by the party caucuses. Those groups also nominate the candidates for Speaker, with the choice of the majority party caucus tantamount to election. The House then merely ratifies the choice of the party in power, usually on a straight party-line vote.

On various occasions in the past, the majority party in the House has been splintered by factions — often reflecting divisions in the country — that resulted in spirited election battles among candidates.

Pre-Civil War Era

In the years before the Civil War, regional disputes, mainly over slavery, produced at least 10 hotly contested races for the speakership. The first was in 1809, when none of the Democratic-Republican Party candidates were able to achieve a majority on the first ballot. The election finally went to Joseph B. Varnum of Massachusetts after the South's candidate, Nathaniel Macon, N.C., withdrew because of poor health. Other minor antebellum battles occurred in 1820, when an anti-slavery candidate, John W. Taylor, D-N.Y., won on the 22nd ballot; in 1821, when Philip P. Barbour, D-Va., won on the 12th; in 1825, when Taylor recaptured the post on the second ballot; in 1834, when John Bell, Whig-Tenn., won on the 10th vote; in 1847, when Robert C. Winthrop, Whig-Mass., won on the third; and in 1861, when Galusha A. Grow, R-Pa., won on the second.

There also were several instances — in 1839, 1849, 1855 and 1859 — in which the House became deadlocked for weeks or months over the election of the Speaker:

1839 New Jersey Controversy

The first of the prolonged battles over the speakership began on Dec. 2, 1839, when election of the Speaker hinged on the outcome of five contested House seats in New Jersey. Excluding the five New Jersey members, the party lineup in the House was 119 Democrats and 118 Whigs. Democrats sought to organize the House (and elect the new Speaker) before the New Jersey cases were decided. The Whigs, also hoping to win control of the House, wanted to await the outcome of the New Jersey contests.

Chaos reigned for several days while the clerk of the House, according to custom, refused to put any question to the House until a quorum was present. After four days of disorder, Rep. John Quincy Adams, Whig-Mass., took the floor and demanded that the body proceed with the roll call to establish a quorum, including a call of those members from New

Jersey whose seats were not contested. The House voted overwhelmingly that Adams should take the Chair as the temporary presiding officer; finally, on Dec. 14, the House consented to vote for Speaker, with the contested New Jersey delegations excluded from participating. Although the decision was what the Democrats had been seeking, the party's leaders were unable to hold a sufficient number of members in line to win on the ensuing votes. On Dec. 16 Robert M. T. Hunter, D-Va., who had declared himself an independent, was elected Speaker on the 11th ballot. As Adams concluded in his *Memoirs*, Hunter "finally united all the Whig votes, and all the malcontents of the Administration."

1849 Free-Soil Dispute

The next major contest for the speakership developed in 1849, when neither the Whigs nor the Democrats could achieve a majority because the so-called Free-Soil factions in both parties decided to act independently. The resulting deadlock lasted for three weeks and 63 ballots.

The main issue underlying the deadlock was the makeup of the House Committee on the District of Columbia and on Territories, which Free-Soilers contended should be organized so that a majority of its members opposed the expansion of slavery. Free-Soilers thus were against the election of the leading candidates of either party for the office: Robert C. Winthrop, Whig-Mass., who they felt had been lukewarm on the slavery issue as Speaker from 1847 to 1849, and Howell Cobb, D-Ga., a strong proponent of slavery. Each faction put up its own candidate — at one time there were 11 — preventing either Cobb or Winthrop from achieving a majority.

At various points in the controversy, compromise solutions were considered and rejected, including proposals that the Speaker be divested of his power to appoint committees (thus leaving that authority to the full House), that the Speaker be chosen by lottery and that members receive no salary or mileage reimbursement until a Speaker was elected.

Finally, after the 59th vote a motion was carried that the Speaker be elected by a plurality, provided that it be a majority of a quorum. On the 60th vote, Cobb led, on the 61st, Winthrop, and on the 62nd, the vote was tied. On the 63rd ballot the issue was finally decided when Cobb won a plurality of two votes with a quorum of members voting. The House then confirmed his election by adopting a resolution "That Howell Cobb, a representative from the state of Georgia, be declared duly elected Speaker of the House of Representatives for the Thirty-First Congress."

Commenting on the significance of Cobb's election, Mary P. Follett concluded in her book on

...Lively But Rare in House History

Speaker: "Southern suspense was now relieved. If the Whigs had elected their candidate in 1849 the Civil War might have been delayed, for the committees of this Congress effected the Compromise of 1850. It is probable that Mr. Winthrop's prestige would have carried him into the Senate and eventually have affected the makeup of the Republican Party. The choice of a very pronounced pro-slavery and southern man at this crisis undoubtedly aggravated the struggles of the following decade."

Kansas, Slavery Controversy

Six years after the Cobb-Winthrop contest, another multi-faction battle based on the slavery issue led to a deadlock in the election of a Speaker. Like the 1849 battle, the 1855 dispute focused on the question of composition of House committees either for or against slavery. The immediate concern of both sides was the effect those committees might have on the question of admission of Kansas as a free or a slave state. The dispute, which began in December 1855, lasted through 133 ballots taken over a period of almost two months.

Although anti-slavery forces held a majority of House seats, their ranks were so split by factions (mostly the new Republican Party and various Free-Soil groups) that they could not unite behind a single candidate. At the outset of the election battle, on Dec. 3, 1855, 21 candidates were nominated. After 129 ballots, the House decided that, following three more roll calls, the candidate receiving the largest number of votes would be elected. On Feb. 2, 1856, on the 133rd ballot, Nathaniel P. Banks, American-Mass., was elected with 103 votes out of 214 cast.

As in 1849, the election was subsequently confirmed by a resolution adopted by majority vote. Follett noted that "[M]r. Banks was elected above all because it was expected that he would constitute the committees in favor of the Free-Soilers. He justified the expectation by putting a majority of anti-slavery men on the Kansas Investigation Committee, which action practically delayed the settlement of the Kansas episode until after 1857, and this gave time for the anti-slavery forces to organize."

1859 Pennington Election

The last of the great pre-Civil War contests over the speakership occurred in 1859. The House took 44 ballots over a period of nearly two months to decide the question. On the first day of the session, Dec. 5, the tone was set when slavery advocates proposed a resolution that any candidate who endorsed the sentiments of *The Impending Crisis of the South: How to Meet It*, a book hostile to slavery, was not fit to be Speaker of the House. The next day, a second resolution was proposed, stating that "it is the duty of every good citizen of this Union to resist all attempts at renewing in Congress or out of it the slavery agitation, under whatever shape and color the attempt may be made. And that no member shall be elected Speaker of this House whose political opinions are not known to conform to the foregoing sentiment."

Both resolutions were directed at John Sherman, R-Ohio, who had endorsed the book opposing slavery. As Follett observed, "The ball thus set rolling, the discussion of slavery began, bitter and passionate on one side, eager and vehement on the other. The state of the country was reflected in the struggle for Speaker. The House was the scene of a confusion and uproar which the clerk could not control.... Bitter personal invectives nearly led to personal encounters.... It seemed as though the Civil War was to begin in the House of Representatives."

Sherman led in the early voting, falling only six votes short of a majority on the third ballot. By the end of January, however, Republicans saw that Sherman could not be elected and shifted their support to William Pennington, Whig-N.J., a new and unknown member. On Feb. 1 Pennington was elected with 117 votes, the minimum required to win. According to Follett, Pennington as Speaker was regarded as an "impartial" presiding officer, although "notably ignorant of the practice of the House." Pennington was the only Speaker other than Henry Clay ever elected to the speakership during his first term in the House.

1923 Progressive Insurgency

The only deadlock over the speakership since the Civil War occurred in 1923, when 20 Progressive Republicans held the balance of power in the House. (The party breakdown at that time was 225 Republicans, including the Progressives, 205 Democrats, one Independent, one Farmer-Laborite and one Socialist.) The Progressives put up their own candidate, Henry A. Cooper, R-Wis. (1893-1919, 1921-31), as a protest against House procedures. After eight inconclusive votes, Nicholas Longworth, R-Ohio (1903-13, 1915-31), the GOP leader, made an agreement with the Progressives to liberalize the rules. The next day the Progressives threw their support behind the Republican candidate, Frederick H. Gillett, R-Mass. (1893-1925), the Speaker since 1919, who was reelected.

Since 1923 there have been no other floor battles for the speakership. Over that period, one party always held a clear majority and has been able to elect its choice on the first ballot.

Source: George B. Galloway, *History of the House of Representatives* (New York: Thomas Y. Crowell Co., 1961), p. 43; Mary P. Follett, *The Speaker of the House of Representatives* (New York: Longmans, Green & Co., 1896; reprinted, New York: Burt Franklin Reprints, 1974), pp. 56, 59, 61-62, 95.

and sent directly to the floor when a majority of the House signed a petition "discharging" the committee from further consideration of the bill.

Members of all standing committees, including the Rules Committee, henceforth were to be appointed by the House, which in effect meant that each party would appoint its own members to the committees through the Democratic and Republican Committee on Committees. (Those two panels nominate members of their party to all House committees. In 1974 House Democrats transferred the selection power to the Steering and Policy Committee.

Decline of the Speaker's Power

When the Democrats won control of the House in 1911, the power of the speakership went into a decline that lasted nearly 15 years. "The Speaker became a figurehead, the [majority] floor leader supreme," according to a contemporary observer.[27] The first Speaker to preside under the liberalized rules was James Beauchamp "Champ" Clark, D-Mo., Speaker from 1911 to 1919. During this period, the real power was exercised by Oscar W. Underwood, D-Ala. (House, 1895-1896, 1897-1915), the majority leader and chairman of the Ways and Means Committee (and thus chairman of the newly established Democratic Committee on Committees made up of the Democratic members of Ways and Means).

Democrats in 1909 had adopted caucus rules that bound all party members to support any party position approved by two-thirds of the caucus, unless a member considered the position unconstitutional or had made "contrary pledges to his constituents prior to his election or received contrary instructions by resolutions or platform from his nominating authority."[28] Democrats then adopted a resolution pledging their support for all bills presented to the House by the Ways and Means Committee. These procedures produced considerable party unity and gave Democrats tight control of the House throughout the first term of President Woodrow Wilson, when a large body of domestic reform legislation was enacted.

Clark's successor, Frederick H. Gillett, R-Mass., Speaker from 1919 to 1925, attempted to diminish the position's partisan nature and restore its judicial character. With Gillett declining to assert political leadership, power in the House shifted to Majority Leader Franklin W. Mondell, R-Wyo. (1895-97, 1899-1923), and a five-member Republican Steering Committee. From 1919 to 1925, the committee met almost daily to discuss party positions and map strategy with committee chairmen and other Republican leaders. "For the most part," according to Randall B. Ripley, "the Steering Committee carried out the wishes of the Republican leaders in the House, even when these were not in accord with the Republican Administration. For example, a bill in the 68th Congress to increase civil service pensions was held up for an entire Congress and thus killed by an unfavorable Steering Committee decision, despite support for it from a unanimous House Civil Service Committee, the Senate and the [Coolidge] administration."[29]

Leadership under this system was so diffuse that House Republicans accomplished little during the period. Republicans found it difficult to achieve party unity even on such a traditionally partisan issue as the tariff. According to Ripley, the Steering Committee was plagued with "occasional lapses in communications between the various leaders," and its "communications with the White House

were even more uncertain." House members, he said, "including some committee chairmen, used the loose leadership structure to pursue legislative ends other than those officially sanctioned."[30]

New Prestige Under Longworth, Rayburn

The shortcomings displayed by the House Republican Steering Committee prompted the next Speaker, Nicholas Longworth, R-Ohio, Speaker from 1925 to 1931, to again centralize power in the Speaker's office. Upon assuming the speakership, Longworth set forth his conception of the Speaker as party leader: "I believe it to be the duty of the Speaker, standing squarely on the platform of his party, to assist in so far as he properly can the enactment of legislation in accordance with the declared principles and policies of his party and by the same token to resist the enactment of legislation in violation thereof."[31]

Like Cannon, Longworth established a small group of trusted associates to help him run the House. This group, called the "Big Four," consisted of Longworth; John Q. Tilson, R-Conn. (1909-13, 1915-32), the majority leader; Bertrand H. Snell, R-N.Y. (1915-39), chairman of the Rules Committee, and James T. Begg, R-Ohio (1919-29), a longtime personal friend of Longworth's. Longworth was able to achieve through personal persuasion what Cannon had done by arbitrary interpretation of the rules.

The prestige of the speakership was strengthened in the 1940s and 1950s during the tenure of Sam Rayburn, another master of the art of persuasion. Confronted after World War II with a party that was badly split over civil rights and other domestic issues, Rayburn found he could minimize disunity by making party decisions himself and bargaining with individuals rather than with the party as a whole.

Elected to the House in 1913, Rayburn was Speaker from 1940 until his death in 1961, except for two stints as minority leader — the 80th and 83rd Congresses (1947-49, 1953-55) — when the Republicans controlled the House.

Although many of his party's domestic programs were emasculated by a "conservative coalition" of Republicans and Southern Democrats, Rayburn was able to win enactment of an impressive amount of legislation in the field of foreign affairs as well as important domestic bills, including two far-reaching civil rights acts (1957 and 1960). In Ripley's opinion, the Speaker's record, in view of the split in his own party, was "enough to earn for Rayburn a reputation as an incomparable legislative wizard when faced with unfavorable odds."[32]

Indeed, during the 1950s and 1960s, when Rayburn and his fellow Texas Democrat, Sen. Lyndon B. Johnson (House, 1937-49; Senate, 1949-61), cracked the whip, the House and Senate jumped. (Johnson was a Rayburn protégé when he entered the House in 1937. After going to the Senate, he soon equaled his mentor's legislative prowess. Johnson was elected Senate minority leader in 1953 and became majority leader when the Democrats became the majority two years later.)

"To get along, go along," Rayburn routinely advised House freshmen who came to him for guidance. Johnson demanded a similar measure of loyalty from his Senate colleagues. And for the most part, their colleagues willingly complied. The pair's reputation for moving legislation through Congress retains mythic proportions to this day.

Nonetheless, Rayburn's style of leadership demonstrated the profound changes that had occurred in Congress in the nearly half a century between Cannon and

Rayburn. The decline in party discipline meant that in order to be effective, a leader had to rely more and more on his personal style in a political environment in which power was increasingly decentralized. "The old day of pounding on the desk and giving people hell is gone. . . ," said Rayburn in 1950. "A man's got to lead by persuasion and kindness and the best reason — that's the only way he can lead people." [33]

McCormack and Albert: Sharing Power

The mode of leadership adopted by McCormack, Rayburn's successor, was more like that of the Republican leadership of the 1919-25 era. Lacking the persuasive ability of a Rayburn or Longworth, McCormack, who served as Speaker from 1962 to 1971, placed considerable reliance on his majority leader, Carl Albert, D-Okla. (1947-77), and majority whip, Hale Boggs, D-La. (1941-43, 1947-73).

Ripley has observed that "each element of the collegial leadership had its own importance, but the lack of cohesion that had troubled the Republicans in the early 1920s was not present in this arrangement. The functions were split between the various leaders, but there were numerous integrating meetings of the three principal leaders with committee chairmen and legislative liaison officials. The unity of the Democrats was still far from perfect and some major bills were lost, especially in 1962 and 1963. But the Democrats cohered well enough in 1964, 1965 and 1966 to pass many presidential proposals." [34]

While personally popular, McCormack's successor, Albert, was generally considered by his colleagues to be a weaker leader. However, Albert's leadership — he was Speaker from 1971 to 1977 — was not usually compared unfavorably with that of his immediate predecessor. Albert's style was described by a colleague as being "accommodating, on good terms with everyone."

Before the opening of the 94th Congress (1975), the Democratic Caucus approved changes in party procedures that considerably strengthened the Speaker's position. He was given control over the selection of Democratic members of the all-important Rules Committee, subject to caucus approval. The Democratic Steering and Policy Committee, which Albert chaired, was given the authority (previously held by Ways and Means Democrats) to appoint the Democratic members to House committees.

The Speaker also was empowered to refer bills to more than one committee and to set deadlines for committee action on that legislation. And although the Speaker has not found it necessary to do so, he could use the more compliant Rules Committee to set deadlines for action by legislative committees. *(Details, see Legislative Process, The Committee System chapters.)*

During his speakership, Albert drew strong criticism from many of the younger and more activist party members in the House. By the early 1970s, the House had received a significant infusion of new blood, as a sharp increase in retirements and re-election defeats of much of the "Old Guard" changed the complexion of the House. The average age of House members crept steadily downward, and most of the new generation were liberal Democrats. With the dramatic turnover in membership came pressure for changes in House rules and practices. The once nearly absolute grip over the House held by senior members was diminished. The seniority system was cracked by subjecting committee chairmen to secret-ballot election by the Democratic Caucus. The powers exercised by the chairmen had to be shared with quasi-independent subcommittees, some of which were led by junior members, even first- and second-termers.

Many of the 75 freshman Democrats elected in 1974, as well as some of their more senior colleagues, were especially distressed when House Democrats, with a 2-1 majority over the Republicans, were unable in 1975-76 to override many of President Ford's vetoes of Democratic-backed legislation.

Some freshman Democrats talked openly of removing Albert after the House in 1975 upheld a Ford veto of a strip-mining control bill, a proposal on which the Democrats had placed considerable importance. Albert met with the dissatisfied freshmen and called for more effective work by party whips, better communication between leaders and the freshmen and improved publicity for Democratic-backed legislation. No effort was made to oust Albert, and criticism subsided by 1976.

Albert also faced obstacles that were beyond his control. One was a White House occupied by a Republican president, Richard M. Nixon, who was intent on expanding his own power and acting with minimal consultation with and concern for Congress. And the Nixon administration was committed to conservative political and economic programs opposed by the bulk of the Democratic majority. In this situation, the Democrats' first priority was to halt administration plans to revamp or terminate existing Great Society programs. A prolonged congressional-executive stalemate existed throughout the Nixon years, which gave rise to frustration in Democratic ranks that found expression, especially in the House, in criticism of the leadership.

An offshoot of the greater democracy and openness in Congress during the 1970s was that the parties became more difficult to manage. There were far fewer members who were willing to toe the party line. Consequently, the House during Albert's term had many power centers and members who were less amenable to party discipline than in the past.

O'Neill and the 'New' House

Albert's retirement at the end of the 94th Congress led to the elevation of Thomas P. O'Neill Jr., D-Mass., first elected to the House in 1952 and majority leader since 1973, to the speakership.

The election of O'Neill, a protégé of fellow Bostonian McCormack, was almost a foregone conclusion because of the House tradition in which the majority leader moves up to the speakership. Another factor in his favor was his wide appeal to the diverse groups of Democrats in the House.

"He bridges certain major Democratic elements in the House," said a high-ranking Democrat in 1976. "He draws his support from the organization Democrats who feel comfortable with his style and from the younger Democrats who like his early opposition to the [Vietnam] war and his support of House reform moves.[35] Known for his party loyalty and partisanship, O'Neill nonetheless had publicly broken with President Johnson's Vietnam policy in 1967 and denounced American involvement in Indochina.

As Speaker, O'Neill was much more activist and partisan than was his predecessor. Wrote Minority Leader John J. Rhodes in his 1976 book on the House, *The Futile System*, O'Neill was "the most partisan man I have ever known." [36] During his first two terms as Speaker, O'Neill presided over a House that had a solid Democratic majority, although more of its members were newcomers less wedded to respect the "old ways" and less inclined to follow Rayburn's admonition to "go along" with the leadership, rules and norms. O'Neill had the advantage of serving under a Democratic president — but that, too, had its troubles. Although Carter met frequently with congressional leaders, relations between O'Neill and Carter were not close, and the White House congressional liaison team drew considerable criticism for its frequent inability to sell the president's legislative packages on Capitol Hill.

"The leadership's task must have been infinitely less complicated in the days of Mr. Rayburn and Mr. McCormack," commented O'Neill's majority leader, Jim Wright, D-Texas, in 1980. "In Mr. Rayburn's day, about all a majority leader or Speaker needed to do in order to get his program adopted was to deal effectively with perhaps 12 very senior committee chairmen. They, in turn, could be expected to influence their committees and their subcommittee chairmen whom they, in those days, appointed.... Well, now that situation is quite considerably different. There are, I think, 153 subcommittees [in Congress].... We have relatively fewer rewards that we can bestow or withhold. I think that basically about all the leadership has nowadays is a hunting license to persuade — if we can. But if it makes the task harder, perhaps it also makes it more interesting. It wouldn't be any fun if it were easy." [37]

"The world wasn't so complex" during Rayburn's time, and Congress had simpler problems to deal with then," O'Neill once commented. "You didn't have the problems of the environment. You didn't have the problems of the budget." [38] The Democratic Party, he said, had become over time little more than an organizational convenience. Because 274 House members called themselves Democrats during the 96th Congress, and pledged to vote together on the first day of the new Congress, they were able to control the House and its committees. But after that, the party apparatus became more dependent on the members than the members were on the party, he said.

Members today are "more home-oriented," O'Neill explained. "They no longer have to follow the national philosophy of the party. They can get re-elected on their newsletters, or on how they serve their constituents."

Speaking of his own party in the House, O'Neill observed, "We're five parties in one. We've got about 25 really strong liberals, 110 progressive liberals, maybe 60 moderates, about 45 people just to the right of the moderates, and 35 conservatives. We have 10 fellows who haven't voted with us 10 percent of the time. We have 13 who haven't voted with us 20 percent of the time."

Difficulties in controlling the House became acutely apparent during one week in September 1979, when the House defeated a continuing appropriations bill, the second budget resolution, legislation implementing the Panama Canal treaties and a bill to hike the public debt limit. After that experience, Democratic leaders tried to crack the whip. O'Neill said he called in "a couple [of Democrats] to show them their [voting] records.... I told them that with their record of voting against us, they'd be better off joining the Republican Party." [39] Many Democrats later said the exercise in party discipline was more form than substance. Yet others maintained it worked. (Challenge to O'Neill decisions, box, p. 57)

Weakness in the House leadership's influence was evident even in such traditional strongholds as the Rules Committee. In 1980 three Democrats on that committee joined the panel's Republicans to oppose O'Neill's position on a key budget bill. Despite weeks of trying, the Speaker was unable to turn around even one of the three Democrats.

"When Sam Rayburn was around here, he could call up one person, the leader of a state delegation, and that one man could deliver the entire delegation," commented O'Neill. "Today you can't do that. The nature of the institution is not the same.... You don't have the discipline out there."

Whether discipline had eroded simply because party leaders no longer attempted to use it, or because the party was incapable of enforcing it, was debatable. In any case, O'Neill conceded that Democrats who defected knew they had little to fear. But O'Neill maintained he would not apply heavy pressure tactics even if he could. "You can't do those things by arm-twisting," he said. "I don't believe in that. You have to reason with them."

Summarizing his thoughts on the speakership during a 1977 interview, O'Neill said, "You know, you ask me what are my powers and my authority around here? The power to recognize on the floor; little odds and ends — like men get pride out of the prestige of handling the Committee of the Whole, being named Speaker for the day.... [T]here is a certain aura and respect that goes with the Speaker's

Happier times! Newly elected House Speaker Thomas P. O'Neill Jr., D-Mass., (l) and Senate Majority Leader Robert C. Byrd, D-W.Va., pose for picture in Statuary Hall in the Capitol at the start of the 95th Congress.

office. He does have the power to be able to pick up the telephone and call people. And members often times like to bring their local political leaders or a couple of mayors [to see me]. And often times they have problems from their area and they need aid and assistance.... We're happy to try to open the door for them, having been in the town for so many years and knowing so many people." [40]

Although O'Neill's description of the Speaker's job and powers was considerably understated, political science professors Joseph Cooper and David Brady said in a 1981 assessment of House leadership: "Given his sources of leverage in the formal and party systems, O'Neill has little choice but to adopt a leadership style that in many key respects is similar to Rayburn's. Yet, the greater degree of fractionalization in both systems in the 1970s, as opposed to the 1940s, reduces his overall prospects for success in passing party programs. O'Neill therefore is likely to have far less success overall than Rayburn, even though he too leads in a highly personal, informal, permissive and ad hoc manner." [41]

HOUSE HIERARCHY: DIRECTING THE TROOPS

The problems confronting the leadership in the 1970s affected not only the Speaker but the rest of the leadership apparatus as well. In a 1963 study of the House, Neil MacNeil called the chamber's leadership organizations its "priesthood." The Speaker, MacNeil asserted, "[h]as never run the House of Representatives without help. The House has been from the beginning such a sprawling, discordant mass of men that the Speaker has had to depend on lieutenants to guide and oversee its multiple operations in its committees and on the floor, and to ensure the orderly flow of responsible legislation. Indeed, over the years, a hierarchy of leaders has been constructed in the House to support the Speaker, and opposing the hierarchy has been another, created by the minority party and led by the 'shadow' Speaker, the leader of the opposition party. With the hierarchy also has been built a vast array of political and party organizations to assist the Speaker and his lieutenants in the complicated task of making the House a viable, responsible legislative body." [42]

The Speaker's principal assistant is the majority leader, or floor leader. Like the Speaker, he is nominated at the beginning of each Congress by secret ballot in the majority party's caucus and then formally elected by the House. Usually picked by the Speaker himself, the majority leader in modern times frequently has been elevated from the next-ranking party post, the majority whip.

The Majority Leader

The first House member to be officially designated majority leader was Sereno E. Payne, R-N.Y. (1883-87, 1889-1914), who assumed the post in 1899. Before then, the chairman of the Ways and Means Committee normally was looked upon as the party's floor leader, primarily because his committee handled tariff and tax measures, which were considered some of the more important measures to come before the House. Occasionally, the Speaker designated a trusted lieutenant other than the Ways and Means chairman as the party's leader. In the interest of party harmony, he sometimes named to that post his leading rival within the party.

The Speaker continued to pick the majority leader until 1911. After the revolt against Speaker Cannon in 1909-10, rank-and-file House members took it upon themselves to exercise this authority, usually through the party caucus, or conference as Republicans called their caucus.

In 1911, with the Democrats in power, the party caucus chose Rep. Underwood as majority leader. And the caucus re-elected him in 1913. When Underwood went to the Senate two years later, the caucus selected Claude Kitchin, D-N.C. (1901-23).

When the Republicans returned to power in 1919, it was their Committee on Committees that chose the majority leader, who for the 66th and 67th Congresses was Franklin W. Mondell of Wyoming. Democrats continued to use the caucus to select the party's floor leader when they regained control in 1931, and this procedure has been in use by the party ever since.

Republicans have vested the power of selection in their party conference since 1923.

The power and prestige of the post of majority leader reached new heights during President Wilson's first term, when Underwood dominated the House through the party caucus and his chairmanship of the Ways and Means Committee. According to congressional historian George B. Galloway: "As floor leader, Underwood was supreme, the Speaker a figurehead. The main cogs in the machine were the caucus, the floor leadership, the Rules Committee, the standing committees, and special rules. Oscar Underwood became the real leader in the House. He dominated the party caucus, influenced the rules, and as chairman of Ways and Means chose the committees. Champ Clark was given the shadow, Underwood the substance of power." [43]

After 1925 the speakership regained much of its prestige and some of its power. Since that time, the majority leader has been the chief lieutenant — rather than a rival — of the Speaker.

Duties of the majority and minority leaders are not spelled out in the standing rules of the House, nor is official provision made for the offices, except through periodic appropriations specifically made for their offices. (Funding, box, p. 6)

In practice, the majority leader's job has been to formulate the party's legislative program in cooperation with the Speaker and other party leaders, to steer the program through the House, to persuade committee chairmen to report bills deemed of importance to the party, and to arrange the House legislative schedule by securing agreement from key members. In the latter duty, the majority leader has a significant parliamentary advantage in that, if a member objects to his proposal to consider a given bill, the majority leader usually can achieve the same result by putting the matter to a simple majority vote. He also has the advantage of being first to be recognized on the floor.

The Minority Leader

The position of minority leader first became identifiable in 1883. Since that time, the post always has been assumed by the candidate nominated by the minority party for the speakership. As in the case of the majority leader, the selection of the minority leader is made by the Democratic Caucus or Republican Conference.

The minority leader's principal duty has been to organize the forces of his own party to counter the legislative program of the majority. Rarely has the minority offered its own legislative program. But the Republican House minority did achieve significant legislative successes in the 75th Congress (1937-39) and in the 87th Congress (1961-62), when a number of liberal proposals put forth by the Democratic majority were rejected. And during the 1st session of the 97th Congress (1981), the House GOP minority scored decisive victories when Congress — aided by a Republican Senate and a popular president of the same party — passed the Reagan administration's unprecedented budget and tax cut packages. Large-scale defections by conservative Democrats made possible the Republicans' successes.

As the titular leader of the "loyal opposition," the minority leader "is the spokesman for his party and enunciates its policies. He is required to be alert and vigilant in defense of the minority's rights. It is his function and duty to criticize constructively the policies and program of the majority, and to this end employ parliamentary tactics and give close attention to all proposed legislation," said Bertrand H. Snell, R-N.Y., minority leader from 1931 to 1939.[44]

Everyday duties of the minority leader correspond to those of his majority counterpart, except that the minority leader has no authority over scheduling legislation. The minority leader is spokesman for his party and its field general. It is his duty to consult ranking minority members of House committees and to encourage them to follow adopted party positions. If his party occupies the White House, he is likely to become the president's chief spokesman in the House.

"One of the minority leader's greatest problems," said Ripley in 1967, "is the generally demoralizing condition of minority party status. Minority members — especially those in a long-standing minority — are less likely to be informed about what the House is doing. They are on the losing side much of the time both in committee and on the floor. They have little patronage inside the Capitol. Their smaller committee staffs make it difficult to prepare legislative positions, and they usually are unable to obtain such assistance from the executive branch. Yet they want to be informed, to win, and to have patronage, committee staffs and executive branch cooperation. When they cannot gain these objectives, one target of their frustrations is the minority leader." [45]

Since Ripley made those observations, however, both organizational and electoral changes have enhanced the minority leader's position. The changes in House operations adopted in the 1970s provided additional committee staffing for the Republican minority, and the increasing turnover of House members brought with it by the end of the decade a new breed of conservative freshmen, many of whom were Republicans or Democrats disillusioned with their party's leadership and legislative record. The Republicans' 1980 election victories in the Senate and the White House paved the way for additional leverage by the House minority leadership. Nevertheless, the results were mixed. Part of the minority's difficulty lay in the need to redirect the party's philosophy and modes of action in order to provide legislative alternatives.

The November 1982 election resulted in 81 new House members — 57 of them Democrats. Only three other elections in the last 30 years had brought in as many Democratic freshmen, a factor that would affect minority leadership in the 98th Congress.

Party Whips: Massing Support

From the outset, the party leadership has relied on its more influential members to forge a consensus on important issues. During most of the 19th century members were employed in that capacity only during a particular floor fight. It was not until 1899 that one of the parties officially designated a member as a party whip. According to Ripley, the term "derives from the British fox-hunting term 'whipper-in' used to describe the man responsible for keeping the hounds from leaving the pack." [46]

Unlike the British system, where political parties are well disciplined and a whip's major concern is good party attendance, whips in the United States House have to cajole as well as count noses. For example, in the 95th Congress (1977-79), during which Democrats held almost a 2-1 edge over Republicans in the House and enjoyed the support of the Carter administration on most bills, it may have seemed unusual for the Democratic whips to be called on for more than an occasional nose count. But by May 1978 Majority Whip John Brademas, D-Ind. (1959-81), had had his assistants counting votes on 63 bills or amendments since becoming majority whip in 1977.[47]

Whips of both parties help their floor leader keep track of the whereabouts of party members, assist in exerting pressure on members to vote the party line, induce them to turn out for votes, compile lists on how they are likely to vote and arrange "pairs" between members with opposing positions on bills and amendments on which votes are expected. A whip serves as the party's acting floor leader in the absence of the regular leader (a position not to be confused with the "floor manager" of a particular bill).

The whip's office is responsible for the preparation of whip notices, which contain the schedule of upcoming legislation and identify key amendments likely to be offered on the floor. The majority and minority whips also hold weekly meetings with their assistants where party policy, scheduling and complaints are regular agenda items.

In the Democratic Party, the regional whips, of which there were 22 in 1982, are selected by the leadership from among House Democrats representing various geographical areas of the country. They usually function primarily as vote counters. In addition to the regional whips, the majority whip in 1982 was assisted by a chief deputy whip (appointed by the majority leader and approved by the party caucus), three other deputy whips and special at-large whips appointed by the Speaker and majority leader. They serve as vote seekers as well as tally-keepers.

The Republican whip organization in 1982 was headed by a minority whip elected by the Republican Conference. He was assisted by a chief deputy whip, two deputy whips and four regional whips.

Throughout the 1970s and continuing in the Reagan administration, the Democratic majority whips operated under the direction of the Speaker, the Steering and Policy Committee (chaired by the Speaker) or the majority leader. In preparing the party's strategy on controversial legislation, whip checks are conducted several days before the bill in question is scheduled for debate.

House Democratic Whips:
Preaching Party Loyalty Gets Tougher

Freshman Rep. Leon E. Panetta, D-Calif., was having a tough time finishing his phone call in the House cloakroom. First, Majority Leader Jim Wright, D-Texas, interrupted him. Wright was followed by several other Democrats, who took turns breaking in. Then a page brought Panetta a note saying Speaker Thomas P. O'Neill Jr., D-Mass., wanted to see him.

Panetta found no escape on the House floor. As he left the cloakroom and strode down an aisle into the crowded chamber, Jim Mooney, chief aide to Majority Whip John Brademas, D-Ind. (1959-81), spotted him. Mooney grabbed Norman Y. Mineta, D-Calif., and steered him toward Panetta. "Can you give us a vote on this?" asked Mineta.

Panetta said no, resisting his friend's plea to change the vote he had just cast in favor of an amendment by Joseph L. Fisher, D-Va. (1975-81), to cut about $7 billion from the first fiscal 1979 budget resolution.

Undaunted by the rejection, Mineta turned to court other Democrats who had voted for the amendment — and against the wishes of the Democratic leadership. Meanwhile, Wright wove his way through a crowd of younger members in the well of the chamber, urging them to switch their votes by signing little red cards stacked on a nearby table. O'Neill and Brademas stalked up an aisle, looking like hunters in search of prey. They, too, sought vote switches.

By the time the leaders stopped stalking — 10 minutes after the House scoreboard showed time had elapsed on the roll-call vote — 16 Democrats had trooped down to the well to change their votes. The amendment, which had been a sure winner when time ran out, instead was defeated, 195-203.

The last-minute victory was credited to the arm-twisting of the Democratic leadership — O'Neill,

Wright and Brademas. But behind that highly visible trio were Mineta and other members of the leadership's intelligence-gathering network: the Democratic whips.

While the praise or blame for the Democratic record in the House ultimately rests with the party's leaders, many of the leadership's decisions are based on information the whips gather in their monitoring of members. It is the whips' advice that helps determine whether, and when, bills should be taken to the House floor. It is also the whips, representing the leadership, who can provide some of the muscle needed to get those bills passed.

When Brademas expanded his empire by adding seven new whips in 1977, he was not featherbedding, said several experienced whips. The additional persons were needed to combat changes in the House that had made the whip's job of gathering votes for the leadership "a hell of a lot more difficult than it used to be," according to George E. Danielson, D-Calif. (1971-82), who in 1978 was serving his eighth year as a whip.

The major change cited by several of the whips is the greater independence of members elected in recent years, which makes the party loyalty appeal for votes more difficult.

"At one time you'd blow a whistle and say this is what the party wants and the members would line up and say, 'Yes sir, yes sir, yes sir,' " said Joe Moakley, D-Mass., an at-large whip in Brademas' operation and once the only Democratic whip in the Massachusetts House.

However, younger members no longer are kept meekly disciplined by a rigid seniority system. "Today they get elected on Monday and they are giving a [floor] speech on Tuesday," said Moakley.

Source: Adapted from Ann Cooper, "House Democratic Whips: Counting, Coaxing, Cajoling," *Congressional Quarterly Weekly Report*, May 27, 1978, pp. 1301-1306.

The committee chairman managing the bill usually advises the whips on controversial issues and provisions in the legislation so the whips can decide on floor tactics and questions to ask their colleagues. They must assess the opposition's strengths and weaknesses and decide where it is necessary to count votes: on adoption of the rule, on controversial amendments, on recommittal motions or on final passage of the bill.

Only a few questions are asked on a whip check because most members "don't like to be probed that much," explained an aide to Majority Whip Brademas in 1978. At the same time, "a whip check is a declaration of party

policy. These are not Gallup polls." The party position is implicit in the typical opening phrase of a whip question: "Will you vote for. . . ?" According to the aide, "The question is always phrased so the right answer is yes." On occasion, whips have been instructed to ask, "Do you intend to vote for. . . ?" in order to signal members that the leadership is neutral.

The questions and a packet of background material on the bill are given to each regional whip. The whips report their findings to the chief whip's office, categorizing each member as for or against the bill, leaning for, leaning against or undecided. Among Democrats, about two-thirds of the answers usually are a definite "yes" or "no." Members also are asked whether they will be present the day the bill is scheduled for floor action. A few members never respond to whip inquiries, while a handful of others so routinely give unreliable answers that they are not counted on when a vote is close.

Since whip polls are designed to help the leadership get an accurate assessment of the strength of the party position, information on individual members is kept confidential. Whip counts are "a very close-knit matter of trust," said one at-large whip. If individual names are given to lobbyists "it would start a stampede" of lobbying pressure on members, he said. "Once it breaks down we would not ever be trusted again."

As the information from regional whips is reported to the majority — or minority — whip's office, it is compiled and interpreted; strategies then are drawn up. On some occasions, initial checks have shown such overwhelming support for the party's position that no further action by the whips is needed. But if there is any question about the final vote, the at-large and deputy whips are called in for a briefing with the leadership. The list of undecided and "leaning" members is divided up, with the whips taking names of members they feel they can influence to vote with the leadership. Regional whips might help at this stage if they themselves support the leadership position on the bill.

The information obtained at this stage provides tips on what might turn a member around, such as an amendment or a phone call from the Speaker, the majority (or minority) leader or, if he is of the same party, the president. Depending on how soon the bill is scheduled for floor debate, those who still are undecided may get visits from other whips.

As the list of commitments is firmed up, the leaders of the majority party study the whip information to make a final determination on whether to bring the bill to the floor or postpone action. While the leadership decision on whether to schedule action on a controversial bill largely is based on the intelligence gathered by the whips, such data can prove ephemeral. For instance, some Democrats who indicated they would vote for adoption of the first fiscal 1979 budget resolution in 1978 could not be counted on to do so after the House substantially amended it. A similar breakdown occurred in both parties during consideration of the fiscal 1983 budget in the spring of 1982. As time wore on and alternative proposals multiplied, both the Democratic and Republican leaders were confronted with widespread defections that their whips seemed unable to prevent.

Once a bill reaches the floor, some whips "work the doors," lining up for one last shot at members as they enter the chamber to vote. During the vote a machine on the floor gives the whips a computer printout of members who have voted yea and nay. If a vote is close, the whips use that list as a guide to seek possible vote switches before the result of the vote is announced.

Beginning in the 95th Congress, O'Neill supplemented the Democrats' whip system by appointing task forces to work on particularly controversial or complex bills. Those ad hoc panels — established in 1977-78 for the budget resolutions and the national energy conservation and Social Security bills, as well as for other legislation — were made up of representatives who supported the leadership positions. They function like whips, asking members for commitments on votes.

During the 95th and 96th Congresses, 14 task forces were appointed. In 1982 issues dealt with by task forces included the budget, the automobile industry and the economy (the economic task force was a more permanent panel, meeting about once every two weeks). The Republicans in 1982 had no comparable panels.

One of the purposes of task forces, according to Barbara Sinclair in her study, "Majority Party Leadership Strategies," was to get junior members more involved in a bill's fate.

The first task force meeting usually begins with a "pep talk" by the Speaker. Much of the task force's activity takes place during the debate, Sinclair observed. "Because large numbers of amendments are now proposed to most controversial bills, the floor stage has become much less predictable.... Amendments can be extremely complicated and their actual effects obscure. Consequently, although vote mobilization efforts in the days before a bill reaches the floor are essential, holding the coalition together during floor consideration to ward off amendments which could seriously damage the bill is equally crucial." [48]

One leadership official characterized the role of task forces in the following manner: "The leadership is the general staff; the floor manager the battlefield general; and the task force the company commanders." [49]

Role of Party Caucuses

Use of the party caucuses — the formal organizations of House Democrats and House Republicans — dates back to the beginning of Congress. In the Jeffersonian period, the Democratic-Republicans, in conjunction with President Jefferson, used the caucus to formulate their party's legislative strategy. From 1800 to 1824 party caucuses in the House chose the nominees of the major parties for president and vice president. By the 1830s the importance of both major parties' caucuses had diminished, and they met rarely over the next 60 years except to nominate the party's candidate for Speaker at the beginning of each Congress.

In the 1890s the caucus was revived as a forum for discussing legislative strategy. Speaker Reed used the Republican caucus to a limited extent to discuss policy questions. For the most part, though, the caucus under Reed functioned only to give the party's stamp of approval to decisions Reed already had made. In the early 1900s, Speaker Cannon called caucus meetings occasionally but manipulated them in much the same manner as had Reed. It was not until Cannon's overthrow that the caucus was restored to its earlier legislative significance.

The Democratic Caucus

The Democratic Caucus has had a checkered history in the 20th century. After an active period during the Wilson administration, the caucus was little used for much of the next half-century. Its actions during this time were confined largely to nominating a candidate for Speaker, selecting floor leaders and approving proposed committee assignments.

The Democrats for many years had a rule that the caucus, by a two-thirds majority, could bind its members on a specific vote. The rule was adopted in 1909 and used effectively throughout President Wilson's first term. It was employed during Franklin D. Roosevelt's first term as well, but fell into disuse after that, when it was invoked only on procedural or party issues, such as voting for Speaker. It was last used in 1971 when Democrats were bound on a vote repealing a House rule that gave Republicans one-third of committee investigative funds for minority staff. The Democrats repealed the rule at a caucus meeting in December 1974.

Younger House Democrats, with relatively little seniority, began a campaign in the late 1960s to revitalize the caucus as a means of countering the arbitrary authority exercised by committee chairmen and other senior members. The campaign, led by the House Democratic Study Group (DSG), began when regular monthly caucus meetings were established by Speaker McCormack. They gained momentum in subsequent Congresses. The result was a basic transformation of power in the Democratic Party and, eventually, in the House.

The most important change was the modification of the seniority system by making committee chairmen subject to secret-ballot election by the caucus. This was achieved in steps and took its final form — automatic secret-ballot votes on all committee chairmen — in December 1974. Early in 1975 the caucus rejected three committee chairmen, an action that effectively changed the seniority system.

Their defeat meant that all chairmen in the future would be accountable to their colleagues and thus could never again be the absolute powers unto themselves that they had been when the seniority system all but guaranteed them tenure as chairmen.

The Democratic Caucus instituted other changes that helped transform the House by the early 1970s into a more open and accountable institution. The caucus helped enact a House rule requiring committee bill-drafting sessions to be open to the public. (Republicans played an important part in that change.) It also placed the Democratic Steering and Policy Committee firmly under the leadership's control. It limited House Democrats to one subcommittee chairmanship and guaranteed each party member an assignment on a major committee. The caucus also transferred the committee assignment power to the Steering and Policy Committee (from the Democrat members of the Ways and Means Committee).

Finally, the caucus created a "bill of rights" for subcommittees that gave them considerable independence from committee chairmen. *(Procedural changes, see Committees chapter, p. 79)*

"In these innovations, extended over Congresses, Speaker McCormack and then Speaker Albert acted as mediators between the Democratic Study Group reformers and the committee barons...," wrote Roger H. Davidson in his study, "Congressional Leaders as Agents of Change." "Of the [three Speakers in the 1970s], O'Neill was probably the most friendly, and McCormack the least friendly, to the reformers' objectives," he said. "In no case do the party leaders seem to have originated these innovations — even those that enlarged their own authority.... Perhaps the leaders were reluctant to raise the spectre of Cannonism. Perhaps they were fearful of the 'old bulls' who chaired the standing committees. Perhaps they found it more convenient to let others establish the beachheads. Perhaps they failed to appreciate fully the shift in power that offered a new leadership base in the full caucus. Whatever the reason, House Democratic leaders were content with mediating or brokerage roles, facilitating the reformers' thrusts while deflecting direct assaults on the seniority principle." [50]

Although most of the work of the rejuvenated caucuses centered on procedural reforms, attention also was given, at least temporarily, to substantive issues. For example, in 1972 the Democratic Caucus forced a House vote on a non-binding end-the-Vietnam-War resolution. In 1975 it went on record as opposing more military aid to Indochina, and it voted to order the Rules Committee to allow a floor vote on an amendment to end the oil depletion allowance. *(Details, box, p. 47)*

These forays into substantive legislation plunged the caucus into new controversy, partly because they were seen as usurping the powers of the standing committees and undermining the committee system. At least this was the argument expressed by conservative Democrats, who opposed the resolutions because they were drafted and backed mainly by the party's liberal bloc. The conservatives, joined by many Republicans on the other side of the aisle, charged that the caucus was trying to seize control of the House. Republicans began to talk about a return to "King Caucus," a pejorative term that came from the earlier period when the caucuses of both parties dominated House activities.

By the end of the 94th Congress, the controversy had subsided as fewer legislative issues were brought before the caucus. That was the result of a decision by the Democratic leadership, which conceded that the earlier caucus actions offended many in the party and threatened to harm the effectiveness of the caucus on procedural matters.

However, controversy over the role of the caucus surfaced once again, in 1978, when House Democrats, to the embarrassment of the leadership, voted 150-57 to approve a resolution urging the Ways and Means Committee to roll back a planned Social Security tax increase, an unpopular plan, particularly in an election year. (President Carter and House leaders backed the increase and succeeded in thwarting the rollback attempt.) [51]

One year later House Democrats, again opposing Carter, tried once more to use the caucus to put their imprint on legislation. The issue was the president's decision in April 1979 to end federal controls on the price of domestic oil, thus allowing U.S. supplies to rise to international levels. The president had moved to implement decontrol by issuing an executive order in April. Late in May, the caucus voted overwhelmingly, 138-69, in favor of retaining the old price controls. The caucus rejected a compromise that would have urged Carter to delay lifting controls until Congress had approved the president's plan to impose a new "windfall profits" tax on the oil companies. Despite the caucus action, a proposal to extend price controls was subsequently rejected by the full House, 135-257.

The key to the power of the Democratic Caucus remained its authority to select committee chairmen. When the caucus "urged" a committee to take action, the assumption was that the chairman would heed that recommendation, or face the consequences. Another lever was the caucus' ultimate control over Democratic committee assignments.

There was little dispute about its authority to take in-House actions such as making committee assignments, electing party leaders and recommending changes in House rules and procedures. But when the caucus tried to move into legislative policy making, such as the Social Security vote, members parted ways.

The most powerful House policy-makers — the committee chairmen and the Speaker — opposed the idea of having the caucus tell them what to do. Older members, who remembered when the caucus was moribund, said they felt a few substantive legislative issues, such as Social Security, were worthy of caucus involvement — but only in rare instances. But many younger members felt the caucus was a slumbering giant that ought to be awakened as a new voice for the party, setting broad policy and legislative priorities and occasionally endorsing specific bills.

Most Democrats by the end of the 1970s appeared content to keep the caucus in the background, leaving policy decisions to committee chairmen and the leadership. Some said the caucus was not needed as much as previously because the chairmen had become more responsive to members' interests, committee operations had become more democratic and O'Neill was a powerful Speaker who usually reflected majority thinking in the party.

O'Neill's position about caucus action on substantive issues was expressed at a press conference prior to the 1978 Social Security vote. While acknowledging that party sentiment appeared strong enough to pass a caucus resolution against a payroll tax hike, he said, "I don't like any of these matters coming from the caucus on a direct vote." Both O'Neill and Majority Leader Wright voted against the resolution.

The Republican Conference

Republicans, who never adopted a binding caucus rule for legislative proposals, nonetheless used the caucus, renamed the "conference" in 1911, in the 1940s and 1950s to achieve a consensus among party members on important issues.

The conference was dominated by the party leadership, who resorted to it much as Reed and Cannon had done to achieve party support for their own predetermined courses of action.

The conference rarely served as a deliberative body in the true sense. An exception was in the 1965-1969 period when it was used occasionally to develop policy positions for consideration by the party's leadership. With the Democrats' swollen majorities and the increasing power of the Democratic Caucus during the 1970s, House Republicans began to use the conference to publicize their objections to the actions taken by the Democratic Caucus.

Committee on Committees

After the House revolt against Cannon in 1910, the power to appoint members of standing committees was taken from the Speaker and vested in the party caucuses. In 1911 the Democratic Caucus delegated the authority to choose the party's committee members to a special Committee on Committees, which was composed of all Democrats on the Ways and Means Committee. That function remained with Ways and Means until the reorganizations of the 1970s.

In December 1974, just before the beginning of the 94th Congress, the caucus transferred that power to the Steering and Policy Committee, which is composed of the Democratic leadership and their nominees and regionally elected members. The change was part of the effort by junior and freshman Democrats to wrest power from the chairmen. The Steering and Policy Committee's recommendations, as well as those of Ways and Means in the past, are subject to ratification by the caucus. Previously, that was automatic, but once the changes in seniority were made it no longer was perfunctory.

In 1917 the Republican Conference also established a Committee on Committees, which in recent times has been

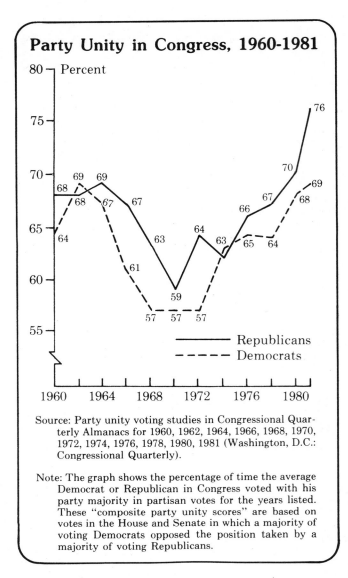

Party Unity in Congress, 1960-1981

Source: Party unity voting studies in Congressional Quarterly Almanacs for 1960, 1962, 1964, 1966, 1968, 1970, 1972, 1974, 1976, 1978, 1980, 1981 (Washington, D.C.: Congressional Quarterly).

Note: The graph shows the percentage of time the average Democrat or Republican in Congress voted with his party majority in partisan votes for the years listed. These "composite party unity scores" are based on votes in the House and Senate in which a majority of voting Democrats opposed the position taken by a majority of voting Republicans.

composed of a representative from each state having a Republican representative. It is chaired by the GOP leader in the House. Committee assignments, except for the top-ranking members, are not subject to approval by the conference.

Speakers often have exercised great influence on committee assignments, even when they were not a member of the panel making the choices. In the late 1920s, for example, Speaker Longworth had four uncooperative members of the Rules Committee replaced with his own choices.

In the 1940s and 1950s Speaker Rayburn intervened frequently to influence the makeup of the Ways and Means Committee, which he insisted had to be stacked with members sympathetic to reciprocal trade agreements and opposed to reductions in the oil and gas depletion allowance. Rayburn was from Texas, one of the largest oil-producing states.

Steering and Policy Committees

During the 20th century, both parties established groups called "steering committees" to assist the leadership with legislative scheduling and party strategy.

The Republican Steering Committee, established in 1919, dominated the business of the House until 1925, when power again shifted to the Speaker. Speaker Longworth largely ignored the Steering Committee. In 1949 the committee was renamed the Policy Committee and expanded from eight to 22 members. The committee later was increased to 35 members. The Policy Committee was considered the chief advisory board for the minority leader from 1959 to 1965, when it was replaced in that role by the GOP conference. Since 1969 the Policy Committee has focused its attention on policy research.

Democrats established a Steering Committee in 1933, abandoned it in 1956 and reconstituted it in 1962. Its duties and role in the party structure were vague. In 1973 the Democratic Caucus voted to create a new Democratic Steering and Policy Committee to give coherence and direction to the party's legislative strategy. The 24-member unit was composed of the Speaker, the Democratic floor leader, the whip, the caucus chairman, 12 regionally elected members and eight members appointed by the Speaker. The appointed members included the chief deputy whip, the three deputy whips, a freshman and usually a member of the Black Caucus and a woman. As previously noted, the committee's power was further increased in 1974 when it was given the authority to make Democratic committee assignments.

SENATE LEADERSHIP: MANY CENTERS OF POWER

The emergence of formally designated Senate floor leaders did not occur until the period 1911-13. The positions of majority and minority leaders were the logical result of an era of party dominance in the Senate that began about 1890. Before that time, leadership in the Senate, when identifiable at all, usually was vested in powerful individuals or groups who did not have formal leadership roles. As late as 1885 Woodrow Wilson could write, in his graduate thesis, *Congressional Government*: "The public now and again picks out here and there a senator who seems to act and to speak with true instinct of statesmanship and who unmistakably merits the confidence of colleagues and of people. But such a man, however eminent, is never more than *a* senator. No one is *the* senator. No one may speak for his party as well as for himself; no one exercises the special trust of acknowledged leadership. The Senate is merely a body of individual critics...."[52]

Early Senate Leadership

Until 1846 party organization in the Senate virtually was non-existent. Committee members were selected by ballot by the full Senate without formal recommendation by the political parties. And in the early days of the Senate they were appointed by the vice president of the United States (the president pro tempore of the Senate).

In 1846 parties began nominating the members of standing committees, who then were routinely approved by the Senate. Further steps toward party control were slow to develop until well after the Civil War. According to Profes-

sor David J. Rothman in his book, *Politics and Power*, party pressure on senators still was negligible as late as the 1870s: "No one had the authority to keep his colleagues in line, and positions of influence were distributed without regard for personal loyalties. Democratic and Republican organizations rarely attempted to schedule legislation or enforce unity in voting. In brief, senators were free to go about their business more or less as they pleased."[53]

The Presiding Officers

The Constitution's only references to leadership posts and responsibilities in the Senate are contained in two passages of Article I, Section 3. One clause provides that the vice president "shall be President of the Senate, but shall have no vote, unless they be equally divided" (clause 4). The other provides that the "Senate shall choose . . . a President pro tempore, in the absence of the Vice President, or when he shall exercise the office of President of the United States" (clause 5).

With few exceptions, the Senate has been reluctant to place substantial power in these positions. It has entrusted power instead to the majority and minority leaders. Thus the powers of the vice president and president pro tempore consist of little more than presiding over the Senate. Neither post has ever equalled the significance of the House speakership.

In addition to the officially elected president pro tempore, a number of senators from the majority party — usually junior members — preside over the chamber for short stints during a typical day's session. For a short period, Democrats also had a deputy president pro tempore as a way of honoring Sen. Hubert H. Humphrey Jr., D-Minn. (1949-64, 1971-78). It was created in 1977 for any senator "who has held the Office of President . . . or Vice President of the United States."

Historians and political scientists who have studied the Senate's attitude toward its top officers emphasize the disinclination of senators to delegate power to a non-member (the vice president) or to a member (the president pro tempore) who presides during the vice president's absence. If the vice president and president pro tempore are of different political parties — as has often been the case — the vice president is able to neutralize the pro tem's authority at any point by merely taking the chair. Accordingly, the Senate has vested the real power in its party floor leaders — the majority and minority leaders — who in turn attempt to persuade the presiding officers (depending upon their party affiliation) to use their parliamentary role where possible to support party goals.

Duties as Presiding Officer

Powers of the pro tempore as presiding officer differ little from those of the vice president. Powers applicable to both officers (when presiding) are: 1) recognition of members desiring to speak, introduce bills or offer amendments and motions to bills being debated; 2) the authority to decide points of order, subject to appeal to the full Senate; 3) appointment of senators to House-Senate conference committees, although it is customary for the presiding officer to appoint as conferees senators recommended by the floor manager of the bill in question, subject to the party ratios in the Senate; 4) enforcement of decorum; 5) the authority to administer oaths; and 6) appointment of members to special committees. *(Authority to appoint conferees, box, p. 83)*

Vice presidents today rarely preside, except on ceremonial occasions or when their vote may be decisive.

The major difference in the powers of the two positions is that only the Senate pro tempore may appoint a substitute to replace him in the chair. Also, the pro tempore, as a member of the Senate, may vote on all matters, while the vice president may vote only to break a tie. Since World War II, only 22 votes have been cast by vice presidents (during some of that time, however, the office of vice president was vacant).

At various times in the 19th century, the pro tempore was authorized to appoint all members of the Senate (from both parties) to standing committees. According to Walter Kravitz and Walter Oleszek, in *The President Pro Tempore of the U.S. Senate*, the pro tempore exercised that authority in the years 1823-26, 1828-33, 1838, 1841, 1843 and 1863.

The President Pro Tempore

The first president pro tempore, John Langdon of New Hampshire, was elected on April 6, 1789, before the first vice president, John Adams, had appeared in the Senate to assume his duties. On April 21 Adams took his seat as presiding officer, and Langdon's service in that capacity ended. Until 1890 the Senate continued to act on the theory that a president pro tempore could be elected only in the vice president's absence and that his term expired when the vice president returned. Unlike the modern practice, in the 19th century vice presidents frequently presided.

By 1890, when the president pro tempore first was chosen to serve until "the Senate otherwise ordered," the Senate had elected presidents pro tempore on 163 occasions. In the 42nd Congress alone (1871-73), 10 such elections (all of the same senator) were held. That procedure came under scrutiny in 1876, when the Senate directed its Committee on Privileges and Elections to make a thorough study of the matter. After considerable debate on the committee's report, the Senate adopted the panel's recommendations: 1) that the term of a president pro tempore elected at one session would extend into the next session in the continuing absence of the vice president; 2) that the death of the vice president did not automatically vacate the office of president pro tempore; and 3) that the Senate had the right to replace a president pro tempore at any time it pleased.

Fourteen years later, in 1890, the Senate gave the president pro tempore tenure of a sort by adopting a resolution stating that ". . . it is competent for the Senate elect a president pro tempore, who shall hold the office during the pleasure of the Senate and until another is elected, and shall execute the duties thereof during all future absences of the vice president until the Senate otherwise order." [54] That practice was still in use in 1982. Under its terms, the president pro tempore holds office as long as he serves in the Senate, unless the Senate elects

Senate Republican leaders Howard H. Baker Jr., Tenn. (majority leader), on the right, and Ted Stevens, Alaska (majority whip), confer in the Capitol during the 1981 session. Hill leaders always attract a contingent of reporters: note the microphone at the right side of the photo.

another in his place. Thus an election is not necessary at the beginning of every Congress, as it is for the Speaker of the House.

Under current practice, the Senate selects only members of the majority party to be president pro tempore, and their election usually is by straight party-line votes. In the postwar years, a sitting pro tempore has failed to be re-elected only when his party lost its majority in the Senate.

Since 1945 the custom has been to elect as pro tempore the most senior majority party member in terms of Senate service. Of those elected pro tempore since 1945, only one was not the highest ranking member of his party in seniority: Arthur H. Vandenberg, R-Mich. (1928-51), who was the second-ranking Republican when elected in 1947. (Strom Thurmond, R-S.C., was considered the highest-ranking Republican when he was elected pro tempore in 1981 even though one other senator had served longer as a Republican. Thurmond began his Senate service in 1956 as a Democrat, becoming a Republican in 1964. But the Republican Conference agreed to base his seniority from the date of his 1956 election to the Senate rather than from the date he switched parties.)

Before 1945 there were some notable exceptions to this custom. George H. Moses, R-N.H. (1918-33), ranked only 15th in party seniority when he was elected pro tempore in 1925, and Willard Saulsbury, D-Del. (1913-19), was still in his first term when elected in 1916.

Vandenberg was the only president pro tempore in the 20th century who exerted much political influence. He held the position during the 80th Congress (1947-49). Floyd M. Riddick, who later became Senate parliamentarian, wrote in 1949 that Vandenberg, who was both president pro tempore and chairman of the Foreign Relations Committee, "took quite an important part in the legislative program and no doubt exerted as much influence in what was done and not done as the Speaker of the House." Riddick added: "He was firm in his rulings, of which all but one or two stood as the decision of the Senate, even though several appeals were taken; he participated in discussions of the pending legislation from the chair, perhaps to an unprecedented extent during any Congress of recent years. . . ."[55]

A more recent pro tempore, Richard B. Russell, D-Ga. (1933-71), wielded power potentially equal to that of Vandenberg through his posts as chairman of the Appropriations Committee and its Defense Appropriations Subcommittee. Russell, however, was hospitalized during much of his term as pro tempore (1969-71).

Although the powers of the Senate president pro tempore are far less extensive than those of the Speaker, Majority Leader Robert C. Byrd, D-W.Va., observed in 1980 that "because of his position as a senior member of the party and often [as] the chairman of a key committee, the leadership regularly consults the president pro tempore as to his views on policies and actions of the party."[56]

On the other hand, the vice president, although he rarely presides today except for ceremonial occasions or when a close vote on a bill or amendment of interest to the administration is likely to occur, has a greater opportunity in his capacity as president of the Senate to lobby on behalf of the president's programs. Carter's vice president, Walter F. Mondale, D-Minn. (Senate, 1964-76), proved to be an effective spokesman for the White House on numerous occasions, as has Reagan's vice president, George Bush, R-Texas (House, 1967-71).

In 1981 Bush attended weekly meetings of Senate Republican committee chairmen and the luncheons of all Republican senators that followed those meetings. Participation in those sessions was useful, Bush said, "because people can come up to me and say, 'Tell the president you can't do this, or you ought to do that.' They let off steam on personnel problems and other things, and I get a pretty good sense of the mood that I can share with [President Reagan]."[57]

Development of Party Leaders

Beginning in the 1870s Republicans sought to strengthen party control of the Senate by appointing a caucus chairman, who was considered to be the party's floor leader. But the power of the GOP chairman at that time, Henry Anthony, R-R.I., was overshadowed by a Republican faction led by Roscoe Conkling, R-N.Y., that sought to develop and pursue its own policies at the expense of the interests of the party as a whole. The influence of the Conkling faction, which was never great enough to control the Senate, eventually dissipated as a consequence of a series of unsuccessful feuds with Republican presidents over patronage in New York State.

Senate Republicans

It was not until the 1890s — and the emergence of another Republican faction led by William B. Allison, Iowa (Senate, 1873-1908), and Nelson W. Aldrich, R.I. (1881-1911) — that a consistently effective leadership organization was established.

Allison derived his power from his chairmanship of the Appropriations Committee. Aldrich achieved his through force of personality. He held no formal position in the Senate until he became chairman of the Finance Committee in 1899. By pooling their influence, the two Republican leaders were able to dictate committee assignments, caucus posts, decisions of standing committees and scheduling of floor action. Like Speaker Cannon, who dominated the House for much of the same period, Allison and Aldrich were largely successful in imposing their own conservative political views upon the chamber.

According to Rothman, the Allison-Aldrich clique "instituted once and for all the prerogatives of power" in the Senate. "Would-be successors or Senate rivals would now be forced to capture and effectively utilize the party posts. Allison understood clearly that 'both in the committees and in the offices, we should use the machinery for our benefit and not let other men have it.' His heirs had no choice but to follow his dictum."[58]

In the opinion of Rothman and others, Allison and Aldrich used the tactic of after-hours poker games to cement the loyalties of key senators. (That method also was used in the House at about the same time by Speaker Cannon.

About six or eight Republican senators usually attended the sessions, which were held at the home of Sen. James McMillan, R-Mich. (1889-1902), and came to be known as the "School of Philosophy Club."[59] Eventually, two principal lieutenants emerged from the group: John C. Spooner, Wis. (1885-91, 1897-1907), and Orville H. Platt, Conn. (1879-1905). Defeats for the Allison-Aldrich group were rare until President Theodore Roosevelt was able to push through Congress a part of his progressive legislative program.

The group retained much of its power after Allison's death in 1908, but it disintegrated soon after Aldrich retired in 1911.

Senate Democrats

The evolution of a centralized Democratic organization in the Senate dates back to 1889, when Sen. Arthur P. Gorman, Md. (1881-99, 1903-06), was named chairman of the party's caucus. Like the Allison-Aldrich group, Gorman solidified his control by appointing his political allies to positions of influence. Gorman further merged his formal Senate powers with Democratic Party positions by assuming all of the party's top leadership posts himself, including floor leader, chairman of the party's Steering Committee and chairman of the Democratic Committee on Committees.

Unlike the Republicans, Democratic Party leaders served as long as they remained in the Senate and Gorman's lieutenants had clearly defined responsibilities.

Gorman is credited with contributing more to modern party organization in the Senate than did Allison and Aldrich, even though the Republican clique attained far greater political influence at the time. During Gorman's 10 years as caucus chairman, 1889-99, Democrats were in the minority for all but two years. Leadership in the party was dispersed after Gorman left the Senate.

In 1911 Democrats broke new ground by formally designating Thomas S. Martin, Va. (1895-1919), minority leader. But it was not until 1913, with the Democrats now in control of the Senate, that the party was able to create an organization as strong as the Allison-Aldrich group had been.

Democrats that year appointed John W. Kern, Ind. (1911-17), as majority leader. Kern, who worked closely with President Woodrow Wilson, mobilized solid Democratic support behind the president's tariff, currency and antitrust programs. Ripley has observed that Kern's leadership "was unobtrusive and effective. He wielded his powers of influencing committee assignments, scheduling and chairing the caucus to unite Democrats behind the New Freedom legislative program." [60]

Most students of government characterized the Senate majority leaders who served from 1919 to 1933, except Republican Henry Cabot Lodge, Mass. (1893-1924), as largely ineffective. On two occasions, Lodge, majority leader from 1919 to 1924, managed to mobilize the Senate to oppose the Treaty of Versailles, which embodied the Covenant of the League of Nations, despite enormous pressure from President Wilson. Both in 1919 and 1920 the Senate voted to reject the treaty.

President Franklin D. Roosevelt was fortunate in having effective Senate leadership in the 1930s. Majority Leader Joseph T. Robinson, D-Ark. (Senate, 1913-37), succeeded in pushing through the Senate most of the president's controversial New Deal legislative program, particularly in the early years. Robinson organized solid party support for Roosevelt's economic measures even though he sometimes disagreed personally with some of them.

Postwar Leadership

In the period from World War II to the present, two men — one of whom never became majority leader while the other never served under a president of his own party — were widely acclaimed for their legislative accomplish-

ments. They were Lyndon B. Johnson, D-Texas (1949-61), who served as minority leader from 1953 to 1955 and majority leader from 1955 to 1961, and Everett McKinley Dirksen, R-Ill. (1951-69), minority leader from 1959 until his death in 1969.

Johnson, whose entire tenure as majority leader was spent while President Eisenhower was in the White House, became a master of compromise and thus was able to win enactment of legislation satisfactory both to the Democratic majority in Congress and to the Republican president. Johnson was a highly persuasive leader. He used a variety of techniques to win the cooperation of his colleagues.

The "Johnson Treatment" was described by Rowland Evans and Robert Novak in their book, *Lyndon B. Johnson: The Exercise of Power:* "The treatment could last ten minutes or four hours. It came, enveloping its target, at the LBJ Ranch swimming pool, in one of LBJ's offices, in the Senate cloakroom, on the floor of the Senate itself.... Its tone could be supplication, accusation, cajolery, exuberance, scorn, tears, complaint, the hint of threat.... Interjections from the target were rare. Johnson anticipated them before they could be spoken. He moved in close, his face a scant millimeter from his target ... his eyebrows rising and falling. From his pockets poured clippings, memos, statistics. Mimicry, humor, and the genius of analogy made The Treatment an almost hypnotic experience and rendered the target stunned and helpless."

Another observer of the Senate, Ralph K. Huitt, noted: "As chairman of the Policy Committee [Johnson] had substantial control over legislative scheduling (in close collaboration with the minority leader), which gave him not only the power to help and hinder but an unequalled knowledge of legislation on the calendar, and who wanted what and why. A tactical power of importance was what Johnson called the 'power of recognition' — the right of the majority leader to be recognized first when he wanted the floor. He exploited this right with great skill to initiate a legislative fight and on the terms he wanted." [62]

That "one-man rule," however, came under some criticism, particularly from Johnson's liberal, younger party colleagues. "I came here and found that we had one caucus a year — to hear Lyndon Johnson's own State of the Union message," said William Proxmire, D-Wis., then a junior senator, in 1959. "Then we'd adjourn until the next January to hear Lyndon's next message. There was no debate in caucus. We were told what the program would be and that was it." [63]

Dirksen, whose party was in the minority throughout his tenure, was able to put a Republican imprint on many measures inspired by the Democrats by maintaining tight party unity. Using methods similar to Johnson's, Dirksen translated party unity into amendments and other concessions, although his party was seldom able to block important administration bills.

Mike Mansfield, D-Mont. (1953-77) and Hugh Scott, R-Pa. (1959-77), who replaced Johnson and Dirksen as Senate majority and minority leaders, were well liked by their colleagues but considered generally less effective than their predecessors. Mansfield and Scott chose to lead by "gentle persuasion" and compromise and often let their whips line up members for specific votes and take care of the political arm-twisting.

Much of the reason for the change in tactics was due to the altered environment of the Senate. "From the early 1950s to the mid-1970s, the Senate changed from a largely

Southern-dominated, senior-controlled, committee-centered institution ... to a relatively decentralized, much more egalitarian institution characterized by democratized leadership and a greatly expanded role for its junior members," Robert L. Peabody pointed out.[64] Mansfield himself viewed his position as one among equals. "I can see a Senate of real egalitarianism, the decline of seniority as a major factor, and new senators being seen and heard and not being wallflowers," he commented.[65]

Both senators occasionally were charged with not being sufficiently partisan. Mansfield encountered criticism from his party because of his willingness to compromise on some issues with Republican Presidents Nixon and Ford. Scott, on the other hand, was rebuked by some of his Republican colleagues because his moderate-to-liberal stance sometimes led him to oppose the positions taken by Nixon and Ford.

Both senators retired at the end of the 94th Congress.

Byrd: A Parliamentary Technician

While other senators built their careers on national issues and oratorical flair, Mansfield's successor, Robert C. Byrd, D-W. Va., worked quietly behind the scenes constructing a power base through favors and knowledge of Senate operations. He had spent years mastering the arcane Senate rules and then, as majority whip, made himself indispensable to the needs of his colleagues.

On his promotion to majority leader in 1977, Byrd warned his colleagues that "our problems will be as great in many ways now that we have a Democratic president as they were under a Republican president." His prediction was borne out. However, considering the Democrats' disarray and the problems the leadership had with the Carter administration, Byrd was reasonably effective as majority leader of the 95th and 96th Congresses.

Byrd on many occasions emphasized the need for strong party loyalty. "If there is to be party government in the Senate — and in the other body for that matter — senators and representatives cannot ignore their respective political parties, just turning to them for conveniences' sake," he said in 1980. "The leaders, with the aid of their whips and the whip organizations, have to reckon with all of the inconsistencies, the variances, the individual problems, the regional, parochial interests of members, and still try to hold enough supporters together to maintain a coherent and effective organization that can produce the votes when necessary in order to carry out the party's program."[66]

Byrd said that one of his goals was "to bring about a resurgence of feeling of party spirit. ... For too long, it was every man for himself, do your own thing, and not do enough for party unity." Byrd considered his personal views and ideology secondary to his leadership function. "Above all, Byrd is a process-oriented man," wrote Peabody. "Secular dates, now and in the future, are his near constant concern."[67]

Parliamentary adroitness became a hallmark of Byrd's leadership. His style was midway between the soft-spoken Mansfield and the hard-hitting Johnson. As majority leader, Johnson chose a legislative objective and pursued it relentlessly, shamelessly bullying his colleagues. Byrd, on the other hand, played the ambassador. He tended to go to his colleagues with only the hint of an objective. If a consensus could be found that would attract the necessary votes, he would take the bill under his wing. Because of his knowledge of the rules and Senate procedures, that meant the bill usually had a good chance of passage.

Byrd did not see his role as forcing an unpopular measure on his colleagues. "I talk to senators. I have meetings with senators, I try to stimulate a consensus for a party position on issues where one is necessary," he explained. "By getting a consensus first, senators are more likely to support the leadership."

Baker: Cultivating Friendships

The 97th Congress convened Jan. 5, 1981, with the Republicans in control of the Senate for the first time since the 83rd Congress of 1953-55. Unopposed as the new majority leader was Howard H. Baker Jr., Tenn., son-in-law of one of the party's most effective leaders, Everett McKinley Dirksen. Baker had led the Senate Republican minority in 1977-81.

A relaxed manner and close friendships with many of his Republican colleagues were Baker's principal assets as majority leader. He relied on these ties to win support for party positions. Byrd, on the other hand, was regarded as somewhat aloof, confining his relationships with fellow Democrats purely to matters of Senate business. He ran the Senate like a bank manager, said Sen. Mark O. Hatfield, R-Ore. "He kept a tab on bills, and kept a ledger of what favors he was owed and what favors he owed others."[68]

Although Baker might lack Byrd's almost legendary knowledge of the Senate and its rules, the strong support he received from the other 52 Republicans in 1981 enabled him to maintain control without having to resort to elaborate parliamentary maneuvering.

Baker was open and accessible to GOP senators of every ideology and was committed to protecting their rights and privileges. Among his colleagues, Baker went to extraordinary lengths to settle intra-party disputes before they came to the floor. He followed the established customs and observed proper protocol, deferring to others — whether it be a Republican committee chairman, President Reagan or the position of a majority of his own colleagues — when appropriate.

But if he felt that a chairman, or even the president, was making a mistake, Baker would not hesitate to say so. For example, when the administration announced in March 1981 that it wanted to sell expensive arms to Saudi Arabia, including sophisticated radar planes, Baker quietly advised Reagan not to move too quickly, warning that the Senate might reject the deal if it were sent to Congress right away. Reagan took Baker's advice and waited until Oct. 1 to formally submit the proposed sale to Congress, as required by law. Baker endorsed it the next day, and it was approved later that month by a margin of four votes.

Baker's overall emphasis was on making the chamber operate more efficiently. "I think one of the reasons the legislative branch has fallen into low esteem with the public is the impression that we dillydally around," he once commented.[69]

Baker started his stint as majority leader by promising to regularly schedule floor action in advance, and to stick to the schedule. He also promised to cut down on late-night sessions, Saturday sessions and roll-call votes. He assigned the task of computerizing the Senate schedule to Majority Whip Ted Stevens, R-Alaska. To coordinate Senate efforts with the leadership's goals, Baker formed a "chairman's committee" composed of himself; all the Senate committee chairmen; Stevens; GOP Conference Chairman James A. McClure, Idaho; Policy Committee Chairman John Tower,

Another Job for Leaders: Campaigning at Election Time

In addition to the various party committees that aid the majority leadership in running Congress, Republicans and Democrats have established congressional campaign committees that provide financial and other assistance to incumbents running for reelection and to each party's candidates for Congress. There are four such committees: the Democratic Congressional Campaign Committee (House), the Democratic Senatorial Campaign Committee, the National Republican Congressional Committee (House) and the National Republican Senatorial Committee. All are chaired by members of Congress.

In addition, congressional leaders maintain close liaison with the national party organization.

A great deal of the leadership's time is spent in assisting congressional candidates in election years. Well known for his deftness with the fiddle, in tune with his state's tradition, Robert C. Byrd, D-W.Va., made numerous appearances on behalf of Democratic candidates during his years as Senate majority leader from 1977 through 1980.

The electoral efforts of the leadership on behalf of fellow party members naturally provide other benefits. If the party's nominees are successful, both the leaders and the candidates they aided no doubt will remember the favor when the next Congress convenes. "I suppose that by making some contributions to colleagues, some colleagues might sense a little closer spirit of unity with the leadership program," commented House Majority Leader Jim Wright, D-Texas, in 1978.[1] Besides sponsoring his own campaign fund for party candidates, Wright visited 83 congressional districts in behalf of Democratic Party candidates during his first year and a half as majority leader.

"I have an open-door policy," commented Speaker Thomas P. O'Neill Jr., D-Mass., in 1977. "Rare is the occasion when a man has a personal fund-raiser or [is] being personally honored that I don't show up at it. . . . I'm always accessible. These are part of the duties and the obligations of the Speaker, and it shows the warm hand of friendship. . . ."[2]

1. *The New York Times*, Jan. 31, 1978.
2. Michael J. Malbin, "House Democrats are Playing with a Strong Leadership Lineup," *National Journal*, June 16, 1977, p. 942.

Texas; Paul Laxalt, Nev., one of President Reagan's closest friends in the Senate; and two representatives of the Senate Republican freshmen, who served on a rotating basis. The group met twice a week.

Baker also tried to turn ideological struggles into questions of procedure or matters of protocol. In working on the mammoth 1981 budget reconciliation bill that put in place the first year of Reagan's package of budget cuts, Senate committees could have derailed the measure by reining in the Budget Committee, which recommended where the cuts should be made. Baker convinced the various committee chairmen to work together and to defer to the budget panel. "He did an exceptional job when he convinced [Finance Chairman Robert] Dole [R-Kan.] and [Appropriations Chairman] Mark O. Hatfield [R-Ore.] to step aside and leave reconciliation to the Budget Committee," Sen. Laxalt said. "We'd still be floundering around today in a Carter-like fashion were it not for Howard's leadership on that."[70]

Laxalt said conservatives believed Baker had worked out well. "I don't think there's one of them who could say he has not been helpful to them," he said.

"It is clear Howard has subordinated his views to the views of the committee chairmen and the party," said Sen. Charles McC. Mathias Jr., R-Md., "and I think this is a necessary thing for a leader. You've got to be with your own majority a majority of the time."[71]

Senate Whip Operations

The first whips appeared in the Senate shortly after the positions of majority and minority leader were established. Democrats established the position of whip in 1913, the Republicans, in 1915. Although duties of the Senate whips essentially are the same as those of their House counterparts, the Senate whip organizations rarely achieved as much success. For one thing, the functions and duties of Senate whips are less institutionalized; for another, party leaders have chosen to assume many of the functions under the whip's auspices in the House.

Moreover, Senate whips at times have openly defied stands taken by their own party leaders. The Democratic and Republican caucuses elect their Senate leaders, including the whips, and the political maneuvering for such offices sometimes has led members to back certain senators on the basis of considerations other than leadership effectiveness.

A serious breach occurred between Majority Leader Mansfield and Russell B. Long, D-La., the Senate whip in 1965-69. Long and Mansfield clashed in 1966 over a proposal by Long for federal subsidies for presidential election campaigns. Long exacerbated the dispute in 1967 by sending a newsletter to constituents in which he listed his disagreements with President Johnson (and Mansfield) on the campaign financing issue. Mansfield sought to circumvent Long's influence by appointing four assistant whips. In 1969 Long was defeated by Edward M. Kennedy, D-Mass., a Mansfield supporter, in his bid for re-election to the whip's post.

The occasional differences majority and minority leaders have had with their whips, coupled with the fact that the Senate is smaller and less structured than the House, has led to a reluctance by the leadership to give the whips much power. As Ripley observed, the assistance of the whips has been "peripheral, not central, to the impact of the floor leaders." [72] He added that only a few whips had "developed into major influences in the party, usually through . . . persuasion." Nonetheless, a number of senators have moved rapidly from the position of whip to floor leader, among them Johnson, Mansfield and Byrd.

One notable exception was Kennedy's defeat for re-election as majority whip in 1971 at the hands of Robert Byrd. At the time, Byrd was secretary of the Democratic Conference (caucus). He had used that position shrewdly during the four years he had held it to build a broad base of support among his colleagues. This was done largely through hard work.

A key element of Byrd's success in winning the whip position was his exacting attention to detail and willingness to assist Democratic colleagues in many diverse ways that indebted them to him.

Central to Byrd's victory in the contest for majority whip was his reputation for spending hour after hour on the Senate floor carefully looking after the legislative program. This was possible because of Mansfield's willingness to delegate the task and Kennedy's apparent lack of interest in the often mundane work of managing the details of the Senate's, and the party's, legislative business. "The leadership must have the right members at the right place at the right time," Byrd commented of his job as whip in 1975. [73] In that position, Byrd was instrumental in the mid-1970s in liberalizing the cloture rule for ending Senate filibusters. Previously, the cloture procedure (Rule 22) had been of little help in ending Senate talkathons or aiding the leadership in speeding up action on controversial legislation. *(Senate cloture changes, p. 62)*

Senators are extremely busy, usually serving on several committees and subcommittees and in demand by constituents, civic associations and other groups. Byrd capitalized on this situation by seeing that the interests of senators were taken care of. For example, he made certain that bills of concern to a senator came up at the right time, that amendments on which a senator wanted to be recorded were called to the senator's attention before the vote and that accommodations and compromises were arranged. As early as 1972, Mansfield viewed Byrd as a likely successor as majority leader.

When Byrd became majority leader in 1977, Alan Cranston, a two-term senator from California with a liberal voting record, was selected majority whip. Discussing their relationship when the Democrats controlled the Senate, Peabody said, "The two men maintain a cooperative, if not especially close, working relationship. . . . Byrd seldom delegates coverage of the floor. Cranston's principal responsibilities are to prepare the whip notices and to assist Byrd in going over the votes on controversial legislation." [74]

Byrd called his majority whip "the best nose counter in the Senate" and said he was "absolutely superb" when it came "to knowing how the votes will fall in place on a given issue." [75]

Senate Party Caucuses

The development of party caucuses in the Senate paralleled that of the House. In 1846 the party caucus increased in importance by acquiring the power to make committee assignments. During the Civil War and Reconstruction era, Republicans used the caucus frequently to discuss and adopt party positions on legislation.

In the 1890s both the Republican organization of Sens. Allison and Aldrich and the Democratic organization of Sen. Gorman used the caucus extensively, with the Republican caucus achieving more control than its Democratic counterpart. As Rothman has observed in *Politics and Power*, "The Republican caucus was not binding, and yet its decisions commanded obedience, for party leadership was capable of enforcing discipline. Senators could no longer act with impunity unless they were willing to forego favorable committee posts and control of the chamber proceedings." [76]

In 1903 Senate Democrats adopted a binding caucus rule, but there is no evidence that they ever put it to use. In 1933 Democrats readopted that rule, but once again it was not employed. Since that time, neither party has seriously considered using caucus votes to enforce party support on legislative issues. In recent years, both parties have employed the caucus (now called "conference" by both parties in the Senate) to collect and distribute information to members, to perform legislative research and to ratify decisions made by the Policy Committee.

Byrd, like Johnson before him, convened the caucus only at the opening of Congress to approve the selection of party leaders. However, when Republicans captured control of the Senate in 1980, Byrd modified his operations and began holding weekly luncheon meetings of the conference. He also set up a series of issue task forces on subjects such as interest rates, housing and law enforcement, that helped spotlight the work of Senate Democrats.

The Republican Conference, which meets more frequently than its Democratic counterpart, has been used as a forum of persuasion by the leadership. After the 1980 elections, Republicans began to expand the activities of their conference organization, using its resources to launch a sophisticated nationwide public relations effort to bolster their image and publicize party positions. [77]

Under the leadership of Sen. James A. McClure, R-Idaho, the conference devoted most of its resources to providing the news media and the public with a steady flow of publicity about the views and accomplishments of Republican senators. To help a member's press secretary better publicize the senator's individual accomplishments, 10 of the 16 GOP conference staffers provided technical expertise, access to expensive electronic equipment and backup staff support in the form of ghost-writers, graphic artists and broadcast assistance. At the same time, the conference produced and disseminated nationwide its own supply of print and broadcast materials publicizing the accomplishments of the Republican Senate majority.

Funds for conference activities (of both parties) are provided, at government expense, in the annual legislative branch appropriations acts. For fiscal 1982, the Republican organization received an estimated $415,000 for staff salaries, the same amount provided the Democratic conference. Funds for office equipment, printing, telephones, postage, mail processing and office supplies for both organizations came from about $30 million set aside by the Senate in its contingent fund for the "general expenses of the Senate."

Party Control of Congress and Presidency...

Although congressional leaders as a rule naturally try to cooperate with a president of their own party, there have been numerous occasions in American history in which determined lawmakers resisted the proposals of their own president, and strong-willed presidents disregarded their party spokesmen in Congress. And congressional leaders have been known to ride roughshod over their own presidents. Congress has even drawn up its own legislative program and imposed it on the White House.

Cases in which a party's congressional leadership has cooperated in a substantial way with a president of another party are less frequent and have dealt mainly with national security and related issues. A notable exception, however, occurred in the New Deal era when House Minority Leader Bertrand H. Snell, R-N.Y. (1915-39), threw his support behind President Franklin D. Roosevelt's emergency banking bill with the statement: "The House is burning down, and the President of the United States says this is the way to put out the fire."

Lincoln, Wilson, Both Roosevelts

Many of the conflicts between the White House and Congress when both were controlled by the same party have come at times of strong presidential leadership. Lincoln, Wilson and the two Roosevelts all had difficulties with their party's congressional leaders, although all four men were largely successful in winning enactment of their programs.

The first important conflict of this kind arose during the Civil War, when Republican extremists dominated Congress and sought to interfere with Abraham Lincoln's prosecution of the war and his plans for postwar reconstruction. The Radical Republicans espoused the theory of congressional domination of the government.

The Republican-controlled Congress of 1861 created a Joint Committee on the Conduct of the War, which went so far as to intervene in military operations. In 1864 Congress sought to undermine Lincoln's liberal reconstruction program by passing the Wade-Davis bill to transfer responsibility for reconstruction from the president to Congress. Lincoln pocket-vetoed the bill and, so far as possible, ignored the extremists. He managed to hold the upper hand by the use of executive orders, but after Lincoln's assassination Congress achieved the supremacy it was seeking and retained it for more than 30 years.

The next strong president to experience difficulty with his own party's leadership in Congress was Theodore Roosevelt, who clashed sharply with Sen. Nelson W. Aldrich, R-R.I. (1881-1911), the unofficial but acknowledged leader of the Senate's Republicans. Roosevelt was able to work successfully for the most part with the powerful House leader, Speaker

Joseph G. Cannon, R-Ill. (1873-91; 1893-1913, 1915-23), by agreeing to compromise on various parts of his programs. Although Speaker Cannon had agreed to support the president's bill to regulate railroad rates in exchange for Roosevelt's agreement to drop tariff reform, Aldrich refused to go along. After relying mostly on Democrats to report the rate bill from the Senate committee, Roosevelt won agreement from William B. Allison, Iowa (1873-1908), another influential Senate Republican, to take a open-minded position on the need for judicial review of Interstate Commerce Commission adjustments of railroad rates. This maneuver split the opposition and led to passage of the bill by an overwhelming vote. Aldrich, however, continued to oppose administration measures and occasionally won important concessions from the president.

Although relations between President Woodrow Wilson and the Democratic congressional leadership generally were good, there were instances where party leaders deserted the president on foreign policy. On the eve of the opening of the Panama Canal in 1914, both Speaker Champ Clark, Mo. (1893-95, 1897-1921; Speaker, 1911-1919), and House Majority Leader Oscar W. Underwood, Ala. (1895-1896, 1897-1915), opposed Wilson's request to repeal a provision of a law exempting American coastwise vessels (those traveling between U.S. ports) from having to pay canal tolls. The exemption, which Great Britain said violated an Anglo-American treaty, eventually was eliminated despite the opposition of the congressional leadership.

In 1917, when Wilson asked Congress to declare war on Germany, he was opposed by Rep. Claude Kitchin, D-N.C. (1901-23), who had replaced Underwood as majority leader. Later, Wilson was opposed by Speaker Clark on his request for military conscription. Near the end of Wilson's second term, relations between Clark and the White House were practically nonexistent.

Although Franklin Roosevelt's overall relations with Congress were as good or better than Wilson's, the nation's 32nd president also experienced difficulties with his congressional leaders, particularly in the latter part of his administration. During Roosevelt's third term, there were desertions by the leadership on major domestic programs. In 1944 Senate Majority Leader Alben W. Barkley, Ky. (1927-49, 1955-56), resigned the post when FDR vetoed a revenue bill. Barkley was promptly re-elected by the Democrats, and the bill was passed over the president's veto.

Madison, Johnson, McKinley

Congressional leaders also frequently clashed with less aggressive presidents of their own party. This usually occurred when Congress attempted to

...No Guarantee of Legislative Success

dominate the president by initiating its own legislative programs and directives. One of the earliest examples came during the administration of James Madison, when Speaker Henry Clay forced the president into the War of 1812 against Britain. Another was Clay's successful attempt to pressure President James Monroe into a series of unwanted postwar measures, including a revision of the tariffs.

After the Civil War, the Radical Republicans in Congress were able to push through their own reconstruction policy over President Andrew Johnson's opposition. In the process, they almost managed to impeach the president.

The next major conflict came in 1898. Speaker Thomas B. Reed, R-Maine (1877-99; Speaker 1889-91, 1895-99), a strong isolationist, sought but failed to block three controversial aspects of President William McKinley's foreign policy: war with Spain, the annexation of Hawaii and the acquisition of the Philippine Islands. Reed's failure to stop McKinley, which led to his retirement from Congress, was due largely to the popularity of the president's policies, not to the successful application of pressure on congressional leaders by McKinley.

There were several policy disagreements between congressional leaders and the White House during the Republican era of Harding and Coolidge. The Washington Naval Conference of 1921-22 was thrust on an unwilling President Warren G. Harding by Sen. William E. Borah, R-Idaho (1907-40). Soon after Calvin Coolidge became president, the Republican-controlled Congress passed a veterans' compensation (bonus) bill over the president's veto and drastically amended numerous administration proposals.

Success Through Bipartisanship

In the 1950s and 1960s the congressional leadership — both Democratic and Republican — actively and willingly cooperated with the White House most of the time, regardless of the president's party affiliation. In those days, leaders of both parties enjoyed good relations with the president. Speaker Sam Rayburn, D-Texas (1913-1961; Speaker, 1940-47, 1949-53, 1955-61), who often described himself as a Democrat "without prefix, without suffix and without apology," generally acted as the president's man in the House, whether it was Democrat Truman or Republican Dwight D. Eisenhower. During Eisenhower's second term, Rayburn's liberal critics, dismayed over his seeming inattention to traditional Democratic Party causes, began referring to him as an "Eisenhowercrat."

As Senate majority leader, Lyndon B. Johnson, D-Texas (1949-61), was a firm believer in the bipartisan conduct of foreign policy. Rep. John J. Rhodes, R-Ariz., recalled Sen. Johnson sitting in on foreign aid conference committee meetings. "He was there, not to ensure the Democratic position would win, but to ensure the administration position would win. He was acting as a broker for the Eisenhower administration. More than anybody else, Eisenhower had a lot to do with it. It was often said at that time that 'the president proposes while Congress disposes.' The philosophy is not very popular today, but the people running Congress then were pretty much dedicated to that idea, no matter who the president was."

During Eisenhower's two terms, first the Republicans, then the Democrats, controlled Congress, and Eisenhower was forced to work with the leaders of both parties.

Continuing Conflict Since Vietnam

In the mid-1960s, President Johnson demanded congressional support of his military policies in Southeast Asia. Although the Democratic Congress generally went along with Johnson's conduct of the war, his majority leader in the Senate, Mike Mansfield, D-Mont. (1953-77), actively opposed the president's military venture virtually from the beginning.

Under Democrat Jimmy Carter, Congress was overwhelmingly Democratic throughout his presidency. Nevertheless, Carter's proposals — and the way they were formulated and presented to his party — received less than enthusiastic support from the leadership in Congress. Said Majority Leader Robert C. Byrd, D-W.Va, "At the leadership meetings, he [Carter] urges certain actions and says he hopes he'll have our support. But he can't force it. The president is expected to make his proposals, and we have a responsibility to him and the country to weigh them and act on them only if, in the judgment of the Senate, we should."

Carter's inept lobbying, particularly in the early years, was a key reason for his legislative failures. Problems ranged from minor, but irritating, lapses involving the White House liaison team to major communications breakdowns between the administration and party leaders.

In contrast to Carter's performance, Ronald Reagan's first year in office was marked by close consultation with a Senate in Republican hands and a more conservative House. It made possible a string of dramatic victories for Reagan, including the deepest budget cuts and largest tax reductions ever considered by Congress and a controversial arms deal with Saudi Arabia.

Sources: George B. Galloway, *History of the House of Representatives* (New York: Thomas Y. Crowell Co., 1961), p. 260; Irwin B. Arieff, "House, Senate Chiefs Attempt to Lead a Changed Congress," *Congressional Quarterly Weekly Report*, Sept. 13, 1980.

All Republican conference mailings were sent under the conference chairman's frank, the congressional mail service for which the Postal Service is reimbursed by Congress. All printing is performed by the Senate Services Office, with Senate labor, paper and ink. Conference telephones are part of the regular Senate telephone system. *(Details, see Pay and Perquisites chapter, p. 113)*

"Our goal is to get information out onto the streets on what the issues are and what are the [GOP] senators' viewpoints," said conference chairman McClure. He added that the organization's public relations activity "is not designed to promote the party as a whole. It is designed to promote only the viewpoint of individual senators."

In contrast to the Republicans, Senate Democrats' partywide public relations activities have been left to their political arm, the Democratic Senatorial Campaign Committee. Those operations were funded from campaign contributions rather than public funds. *(Box, p. 28)*

Other Senate Party Committees

The origin of the Committee on Committees in the Senate goes back to the Civil War era, when Republicans, the majority party, utilized a special panel appointed by its party caucus to make both Republican and Democratic committee assignments. After the war, Republicans gave control of the committee to the caucus chairman.

Republicans to this day have retained a Committee on Committees to make committee assignments.

Senate Democrats set up a Committee on Committees in 1879, which today is known as the Steering Committee.

Committee assignments recommended by each party's committee on committees are subject to formal ratification by the full chamber. Democratic nominations also must first be approved by the party caucus.

What was in effect the first Senate Steering Committee — a committee set up solely to handle the chamber's daily legislative scheduling and other matters — was established in 1874 by the Republicans. The GOP Conference that year appointed a special committee to prepare a schedule for Senate floor action. That committee was replaced in the mid-1880s by a Steering Committee appointed by the caucus chairman. Democrats had established a Steering Committee in 1879 but discontinued it when Republicans took control of the Senate and thus of the legislative agenda.

In 1947 both parties created Policy Committees that were assigned the scheduling functions of the old Steering Committees. At the same time, the 25-member Democratic Steering Committee, while retaining its name, was reconstituted as the party's committee on committees, chaired by the Democratic leader.

In years in which they have been in the minority, the Republicans' Policy Committee recommended party positions on legislation to the caucus and the minority leadership.

The Democratic Policy Committee did not assume an active policy-making role. Although in theory the principal function of the committee, when the party is in the majority, is to schedule legislation, in practice under Byrd its staff primarily worked for the Democratic leader's office, preparing background material on issues and legislation pending in the Senate and making voting assessments and supplying memorandums for Byrd's news conferences. Byrd and Cranston did most of the legislative scheduling themselves in the 1970s.

1980s LEADERSHIP: CAN PERSUASION WORK?

Though Democrats controlled both chambers and the White House in the 96th Congress (1979-80), the party had great difficulty retaining day-to-day control over legislation. In the House, major bills were pulled from the floor after crippling amendments sprang from nowhere and won adoption. Appropriations bills were weighted down with riders.

An Unmanageable House

The two annual budget resolutions — the first setting spending and appropriations targets for the fiscal year, the second establishing ceilings on expenditures — presented such difficulties that House Democrats in 1980 put off a vote on the final 1981 budget until after the November 1980 elections. Party leaders felt it would be politically risky to ask Democrats to approve a multibillion-dollar budget deficit just weeks before voters went to the polls.

Aggravating the situation was the erosion of party discipline. Rarely did Democratic leaders even pretend they had the power — or proclivity — to reward and punish members in order to ensure their loyalty.

While the Democrats watched their fortunes decline along with their party's unity in the late 1970s, House Republicans were increasing their effectiveness by rallying around traditional conservative issues such as defense, the economy and cutting the budget.

In earlier years, House Republicans were about as splintered as the Democrats. The number of Republicans voting with the Democrats was about the same as the number of Democrats voting with the minority. When it came down to an important vote, the Democrats usually were able to squeak through.

By 1979, however, fewer and fewer House Republicans were joining the Democratic majority on key votes, while about the same number of Democrats continued to vote with the minority. As a result, Republicans won more and more close votes. And even when they lost, they still were able to disrupt legislative business, often derailing the schedule drawn up by the Democratic majority.

The greater GOP unity was developed by a group of young, militant Republicans, who in 1979 urged their leaders to assume a new attitude toward the Democrats. When the Republicans cooperated with the opposition, their good will merely ended up contributing to the success of the Democrats' programs, they argued. This just helped the Democrats get re-elected. The younger Republicans contended that the minority should oppose the legislation submitted by the Democrats. Without GOP support the majority's programs would founder. Then the Republicans could campaign against the Democrats' failures.

Though the GOP strategy led to some major legislative victories, it also served to embitter relations between the two parties and led the House at times to the brink of total paralysis.

1981: Ideological Warfare

Although the Democrats retained control of the House for the 97th Congress, their majority was reduced considerably from that which they enjoyed in the 96th Congress. And with many of the newer members, including Democrats, more conservative than the representatives they replaced, the Republicans had an ideological majority on many issues. This was quickly borne out in 1981, when President Reagan achieved legislative successes in Congress that had not been seen since the presidency of Lyndon B. Johnson. Reagan's success in the House on a package of unprecedented cuts in government spending further undermined the Democratic leadership.

The fact that Speaker O'Neill's role in the budget fight provoked criticism from both liberal and conservative Democrats revealed the sharp differences that existed between the party's opposing wings. The Speaker was criticized by Democratic conservatives for his reluctance to go along with the Reagan administration's budget-cutting fervor. At the same time, liberals said he was not fighting hard enough to save the endangered social spending programs for which the party was best known.

O'Neill was out of the country during a critical week just before the Reagan package of budget cuts was first considered by the House. The administration, meanwhile, was busily lining up votes among Republicans as well as Democrats, particularly among the so-called "Boll Weevils," an informal group of Southern Democrats that opposed many of the party's more liberal positions on major issues. The Democratic leadership, on the other hand, had yet to begin twisting arms.

Even though a week remained before the first budget votes, O'Neill conceded that the Democrats were about to be licked. "Support the president — that's the concern out there, and Congress can read that," he said. "I've been in politics a long time, and I know when you fight and when you don't." [78]

Some House Democrats said O'Neill was just reflecting the grim reality of their party's position. But others were angry that the Speaker had jumped the gun in conceding defeat. O'Neill later reversed his earlier pessimism with a burst of enthusiastic lobbying. But his effort had little impact. The Republicans won handily.

Earlier in 1981, O'Neill probably thought he had appeased his party's conservatives by increasing their numbers on the Democrats' policy-making bodies and key committees. But despite these concessions, many of them continued to disregard the views of the House leadership and, instead, looked to the GOP for policy direction. A leading insurgent was Phil Gramm, D-Texas, who owed his newly acquired seat on the Budget Committee to O'Neill's intervention. Gramm defected from the leadership's position and negotiated an alternative budget proposal with the Republicans. Reagan ultimately adopted the plan as his own. (Gramm subsequently was not named as one of the large contingent of Democrats appointed as House conferees in the final negotiations with the Senate on the budget.)

Some Democrats argued that the conservatives should be punished for disloyalty. While liberals had agreed to certain compromises to broaden the appeal of the Democrats' version of the budget, few demands were made of conservatives, they said. But the leadership needed the Gramm faction to retain control and refused to threaten or expel them from the party.

"It will be a continuing issue of concern why members who bolt the party still are considered members of the party in good standing," said Rep. James J. Blanchard, D-Mich. "I think the issue is going to grow and build, particularly among liberals, who will continue to ask why they

have to go along with the party while the other side doesn't. . . . But I think it will ultimately turn into concern over the role of the party and its goals," he added. [79]

An outgrowth of the difficulty in maintaining party loyalty came at a Democratic Caucus meeting later that year. Majority Leader Wright said there would be "amnesty" for party members who defected to Reagan on the tax and budget votes, but he added that the Democratic Steering and Policy Committee would take members' future behavior into account in awarding committee assignments. The idea in dealing with an errant Democrat, Wright said, was "not to punish that person, but just to refrain from rewarding [him]. Nobody is going to be asked to leave the party." [80]

"Even when the Democrats are together, we're still fragmented," lamented W. G. "Bill" Hefner, D-N.C., a Southern Democrat who supported the Democratic budget in 1981. "We're a party made up of liberals, moderates and conservatives. We don't have the luxury of the Republicans, who know exactly what their constituency is and who won't let just anybody into their party." [81]

Hefner's observation about the "luxury of the Republicans" was cast in doubt the next year with the breakdown of Republican unity during the prolonged battle over the fiscal 1983 budget. With the country in economic recession and congressional elections coming up that fall, many conservative Democrats and Republicans defected from the administration on the budget and offered a plethora of substitutes. The coalition that provided the president with his victories in 1981 had been weakened.

Senate Independence

Developments on the other side of the Capitol illustrated that the Senate was not immune from the problems afflicting the House. Unanimous consent agreements — arrangements that speed up legislative business by setting deadlines on debate and proposed amendments and, normally, on final votes on a bill — had become harder for leaders to obtain. There was a greater tendency for senators to block such agreements in order to reserve the right to buck the leadership at a later date. *(Box, p. 59)*

More filibusters, roll-call votes and floor amendments provided additional signs that the same forces at work in the House in the late 1970s were consuming more of the Senate's time.

Majority Leader Byrd observed, "Going back to my earliest years in the Senate, I think there was more of an allegiance to party, more of an establishment-minded feeling. There was more cohesiveness on the part of political parties than there has been in recent years. The emergence of the 'individual' has been a kind of phenomenon." [82]

"Circumstances don't permit the Lyndon Johnson style," he said on another occasion. "What I am saying is that times and things have changed. Younger senators come into the Senate. They are more independent. The 'establishment' is a bad word. Each wants to do his 'own thing.'" [83]

"The job of forming coalitions is more difficult," agreed Minority Whip Ted Stevens, R-Alaska, in 1980. "We have to work harder to achieve a consensus than Lyndon Johnson or Everett Dirksen, who were in control of so many things that they could at least hint at retaliation" if a member balked at falling into line. "I've never even once threatened to punish a member. We probably don't even have the power to do so if we wanted to," Stevens added.[84]

Republican Unity

Although achieving a consensus became increasingly difficult for the Democrats, Senate observers cited the contributions of Majority Leader Baker to the administration's almost unbroken string of legislative victories in 1981. Although Senate Republicans had a popular president to rally around, it was Baker who worked to keep the GOP together and who devised the basic legislative strategy.

In March 1981 Baker asked his colleagues to give top priority to the president's budget and tax cuts and to postpone their own legislative goals. Otherwise, Baker explained, the crush of bills competing for the Senate's time would slow the pace of the Republican economic recovery program. To reassure conservatives pressing for action on controversial social issues, such as abortion and school prayer, Baker promised to set aside time in 1982 for those matters.

For the most part the strategy worked, although there were some lapses. Conservative Sen. Jesse Helms, R-N.C., twice forced Senate votes on those highly divisive issues. Baker later said the incidents represented a failure of his

leadership. "One of the toughest things a politician ever has to do, and particularly one who is in a leadership position, is to say you've failed, but I've flat failed to keep those social issues off the pending legislation," Baker said in August 1981.

Despite those setbacks, Baker was able to move the economic package through the Senate and on to enactment with few significant changes in the president's original proposals. The contrast with the Carter years was striking. Under the Democrats, the Senate generally marched to its own tune, even though the leadership was committed to the president's programs. Often lacking strong direction from the administration, the Republicans were able to play a significant role in legislative policy.

Under the Republicans in 1981, the Senate was transformed into a tightly knit unit that saw itself as one platoon in a Republican army. Moreover, on even the most controversial measures the GOP garnered considerable Democratic support, although it rarely needed it to secure victory.

Discussing the challenges facing congressional leaders of both parties as the nation entered a new decade, Frank H. Mackaman, executive director of the Everett McKinley Dirksen Congressional Leadership Research Center, wrote:

"[I]f leadership is indeed an organizational condition that blends expression and integration in proper propor-

Three congressional powers confer in 1949 about President Truman's request for arms assistance for foreign nations. From the left: Sen. Tom Connally, D-Texas, House Speaker Sam Rayburn, D-Texas, and Rep. (and later Speaker) John W. McCormack, D-Mass.

tion, the Congress of the 1980s has yet to strike the proper balance. There is too much emphasis on responsiveness to member demands, too little emphasis on responsible leadership. . . . [T]he leadership is often swept along by a tide over which it has little direct control. Leaders tend to be reactive, not active. . . .

"At one level, the quality of congressional leadership is linked inextricably to the public's expectations for it. If people are asked what kinds of leaders they want, they will define the qualities of boldness that include certain characteristics of a George Patton or a Vince Lombardi. On the other hand, if that kind of leadership emerges, the public tends to resist it and seldom allows it to succeed. Members of Congress are not much different. They call for strong leadership but often complain if they get it." [85]

Footnotes

1. Roger H. Davidson and Walter J. Oleszek, *Congress and Its Members* (Washington, D.C.: CQ Press, 1981), p. 197.
2. Ibid., p. 184.
3. Robert L. Peabody, *Leadership in Congress* (Boston: Little, Brown & Co., 1976), p. 7.
4. Randall B. Ripley, *Party Leaders in the House of Representatives* (Washington, D.C.: The Brookings Institution, 1967), p. 7.
5. Frank B. Mackaman, ed., "Introduction," in *Understanding Congressional Leadership* (Washington, D.C.: CQ Press, 1981), p. 2.
6. Barbara Sinclair, "Majority Party Leadership Strategies for Coping with the New U.S. House," in *Understanding Congressional Leadership*, p. 203.
7. Floyd M. Riddick, *The United States Congress: Organization and Procedure* (Washington, D.C.: National Capitol Publishers, 1949), p. 67.
8. Ripley, *Party Leaders in the House of Representatives*, p. 13.
9. Davidson and Oleszek, *Congress and Its Members*, pp. 168, 170.
10. Mary P. Follett, *The Speaker of the House of Representatives* (New York: Burt Franklin Reprints, 1974), pp. 25-26 (reprint of 1896 edition).
11. Hubert B. Fuller, *The Speaker of the House* (Boston: Little, Brown & Co., 1909), p. 26.
12. Follett, *The Speaker of the House of Representatives*, p. 67.
13. George Rothwell Brown, *The Leadership of Congress* (New York: Arno Press, 1974), pp. 37-38 (reprint of 1922 edition).
14. Fuller, *The Speaker of the House*, pp. 40-41.
15. Follett, *The Speaker of the House of Representatives*, p. 79.
16. Ibid., p. 89.
17. Ibid., pp. 89-90.
18. Ibid., pp. 99-100.
19. Brown, *The Leadership of Congress*, p. 74.
20. Follett, *The Speaker of the House of Representatives*, p. 115.
21. Ibid., p. 193.
22. *Congressional Record*, 51st Cong., 1st sess., Feb. 7, 1890, p. 1150.
23. Fuller, *The Speaker of the House*, p. 244.
24. Davidson and Oleszek, *Congress and Its Members*, p. 169.
25. Fuller, *The Speaker of the House*, p. 256.
26. Ibid., p. 257.
27. Robert Luce, *Congress: An Explanation* (Cambridge: Harvard University Press, 1926), p. 117.
28. George B. Galloway, *History of the House of Representatives* (New York: Thomas Y. Crowell Co., 1961), p. 139.
29. Ripley, *Party Leaders in the House of Representatives*, p. 101.
30. Ibid.
31. Galloway, *History of the House of Representatives*, p. 144.
32. Ripley, *Party Leaders in the House of Representatives*, p. 93.
33. *U.S. News and World Report*, Oct. 13, 1950, p. 30.
34. Ripley, *Party Leaders in the House of Representatives*, p. 102.
35. *Congressional Quarterly Weekly Report*, March 13, 1976, p. 561.
36. Quoted in *Congressional Quarterly Weekly Report*, June 12, 1976, p. 1491.
37. Quoted in Christopher J. Deering and Steven S. Smith, "Majority Party Leadership and the New House Subcommittee System," in *Understanding Congressional Leadership*, pp. 288-289.
38. Irwin B. Arieff, "House, Senate Chiefs Attempt to Lead a Changed Congress," *Congressional Quarterly Weekly Report*, Sept. 13, 1980, p. 2695.
39. *Congressional Quarterly Almanac 1979* (Washington, D.C.: Congressional Quarterly, 1980), p. 15.
40. Michael J. Malbin, "House Democrats are Playing with a Strong Leadership," *National Journal*, June 18, 1977, p. 942.
41. Joseph Cooper and David W. Brady, "Institutional Context and Leadership Style: The House from Cannon to Rayburn," in *Understanding Congressional Leadership*, p. 46. Deering and Smith note that, contrary to his image among some members and the press, O'Neill generally has not attempted to employ even the positive rewards at his disposal in order to gain cooperation of House members. In fact, some members have been critical of his lack of arm twisting. (*Understanding Congressional Leadership*, p. 287)
42. Neil MacNeil, *Forge of Democracy: The House of Representatives* (New York: David McKay Co., 1963), p. 87.
43. Galloway, *History of the House of Representatives*, p. 108.
44. Quoted in Floyd M. Riddick, *Congressional Procedure* (Boston: Chapman & Grimes, 1941), pp. 345-346.
45. Ripley, *Party Leaders in the House of Representatives*, pp. 29, 32.
46. Ibid., p. 33.
47. Much of the discussion of whips is taken from Ann Cooper, "House Democratic Whips: Counting, Coaxing, Cajoling," *Congressional Quarterly Weekly Report*, May 27, 1978, pp. 1301-1306; and Arieff, "House, Senate Chiefs Attempt to Lead a Changed Congress."
48. Barbara Sinclair, "Majority Party Leadership Strategies for Coping with the New U.S. House," p. 200.
49. Quoted in Ibid.
50. Roger H. Davidson, "Congressional Leaders as Agents of Change," in *Understanding Congressional Leadership*, p. 144.
51. The following discussion is based on "Party Caucus Role on Legislative Issues," *Guide to Current American Government*, (Washington, D.C.: Congressional Quarterly, Fall 1978), pp. 13-15.
52. Woodrow Wilson, *Congressional Government* (Cleveland: Meridian, 1956), pp. 146-147 (reprint of 1885 edition).
53. David J. Rothman, *Politics and Power: The United States Senate 1869-1901* (Cambridge: Harvard University Press, 1966), p. 4.
54. George H. Haynes, *The Senate of the United States: Its History and Practices*, vol. I, (Boston: Houghton Mifflin Co., 1938), p. 251.
55. Riddick, *The United States Congress: Organization and Procedure*, p. 66.
56. *Congressional Record*, May 21, 1980, p. S-5674.
57. *The Washington Post*, March 30, 1981.
58. Rothman, *Politics and Power: The United States Senate 1869-1901*, p. 44.
59. Ibid., p. 45.
60. Randall B. Ripley, *Power in the Senate* (New York: St. Martin's Press, 1969), p. 31.
61. Rowland Evans and Robert Novak, *Lyndon B. Johnson: The Exercise of Power* (New York: New American Library, 1966), p. 104.
62. Ralph K. Huitt and Robert L. Peabody, eds., *Congress: Two Decades of Analysis* (New York: Harper and Row, 1969), p. 146.
63. *Congressional Record*, 86th Cong., 1st sess., Feb. 23, 1959.
64. Robert L. Peabody, "Senate Party Leadership: From the 1950s to the 1980s," in *Understanding Congressional Leadership*, p. 103.

65. Quoted in Davidson and Oleszek, *Congress and Its Members,* p. 178.
66. *Congressional Record,* May 2, 1980, p. S-4493.
67. Peabody, "Senate Party Leadership," p. 77.
68. Irwin B. Arieff, "Under Baker's Leadership Senate Republicans Maintain Unprecedented Voting Unity," *Congressional Quarterly Weekly Report,* Sept. 12, 1981, pp. 1743-1747.
69. Ibid.
70. Ibid.
71. Ibid.
72. Ripley, *Power in the Senate,* p. 35.
73. *Congressional Record,* 94th Cong., 1st sess., Jan. 28, 1975, p. S-1390.
74. Peabody, "Senate Party Leadership," in *Understanding Congressional Leadership,* p. 72.
75. *The Wall Street Journal,* March 15, 1977.
76. Rothman, *Politics and Power,* p. 60.
77. Irwin B. Arieff, "Senate Republicans Using Incumbency to Advantage in Snappy Media Operation," *Congressional Quarterly Weekly Report,* June 6, 1981, p. 993-995.
78. Irwin B. Arieff, "Budget Fight Shows O'Neill's Fragile Grasp," *Congressional Quarterly Weekly Report,* May 9, 1981, p. 786.
79. Ibid.
80. Ross Evans, "Amnesty Extended to Democratic Defectors," *Congressional Quarterly Weekly Report,* Sept. 19, 1981, p. 1794.
81. Ibid.
82. Arieff, "House, Senate Chiefs Attempt to Lead a Changed Congress.
83. Ibid.
84. Ibid.
85. Mackaman, "Introduction," in *Understanding Congressional Leadership,* pp. 8-9, 18.

The Legislative Process

Article I of the Constitution vests "legislative powers herein granted" to a Congress consisting of two chambers, a Senate and a House of Representatives, and provides that proposed legislation must be passed in identical form by both chambers and signed by the president before it can become law.

The Founding Fathers did not expect the lawmaking function to be unduly burdensome because they thought Congress would confine itself chiefly to external affairs and leave most domestic matters to state and local governments. Alexander Hamilton even surmised at one point before the Constitution was approved that Congress would have little to do once the central government was established.

The First Congress (1789-91) consisted of 26 senators and 65 representatives, serving a population of about 4 million in 13 states along the Atlantic Coast. Legislating in the First Congress was limited in scope and volume, and a few simple rules were sufficient to guide its deliberations. Only a few hundred bills were introduced, and only 108 were enacted into law. Most dealt with the establishment of the new government and its relations with the states or with matters of defense and foreign relations.

Period of Congressional Supremacy

At first, members of Congress apparently expected to conduct most of their deliberations in the House and Senate chambers. In the early years the two bodies considered any question brought before them and indicated the line of action to be followed before appointing temporary select committees to work out the details of proposed legislation. In those days there were no standing (permanent) committees. As the nation grew, the volume and complexity of legislative business increased, and the recurrent nature of many questions and issues led gradually to the establishment of standing committees. At first, these bodies functioned as advisers whose reports were carefully considered on the floor, but by 1885 they had become such a powerful force in determining the shape of legislation that Woodrow Wilson could write: "It is now, though a wide departure from the form of things, no great departure from the fact to describe ours as a government by the standing committees of Congress." [1]

A succession of weak presidents in the years following the Civil War had made possible the congressional supremacy Wilson deplored, but Congress would not be able to retain its commanding role indefinitely. World War I marked the beginning of a dramatic expansion of federal authority into almost every area of human activity, and strong presidents were quick to reassert eroded executive prerogatives. Congress, operating under arduous lawmaking procedures more in keeping with a simpler era, gradually relinquished its policy-making role, and the legislative initiative shifted from Capitol Hill to the White House.

Presidential Leadership

The president's control over policy was strengthened by the Budget and Accounting Act of 1921, which enabled him to draw up a unified national budget — a detailed business and financial plan for the government that reconciled proposed spending and estimated revenues. Before 1921 no system existed, either in Congress or the executive branch, for unified consideration or control of fiscal policy.

While Congress continues to exercise significant policy-making responsibilities today, it is the executive branch that largely shapes the legislative agenda. Ventures into congressional government have had limited success at best. Congress may be able to block presidential programs, but it does not speak with a unified voice and it has few means of developing a comprehensive program of its own. This was dramatized in 1982 when Congress wrestled for months with various Democratic and Republican alternatives to President Reagan's budget recommendations.

The proposed budget, which the administration submits to Congress shortly after it assembles each January for the fiscal year beginning the following October, offers the framework of the president's program for the nation in the coming year. Together with the State of the Union address and various special messages to Congress, it forms the basis of legislative action to meet the needs of more than 226 million Americans.

In 1974 Congress took a step toward more responsible action on federal economic policy when it approved the Congressional Budget and Impoundment Control Act (PL 93-344) revising the way lawmakers consider the president's budget.

The new law, which was fully implemented in 1976, established a framework for timely and comprehensive congressional action on appropriations for government agencies and programs as well as on revenue, spending and

Congressional Terms and Sessions

The two-year period for which each House of Representatives is elected constitutes a Congress. Under the 20th Amendment to the Constitution, ratified in 1933, this period begins at noon on Jan. 3 of an odd-numbered year and ends at noon on Jan. 3 of the next odd-numbered year. Congresses are numbered consecutively, and the Congress that convened in January 1981 was the 97th in a series that began in 1789.

Under the Constitution, Congress is required to "assemble" at least once each year, and the 20th Amendment provides that these annual meetings shall begin at noon on Jan. 3 unless Congress "shall by law appoint a different day." Each Congress, therefore, has two regular sessions, each beginning in January of successive years. In addition, the president may "on extraordinary occasions" convene one or both houses in special session.

In practice, the annual sessions may run as long as a whole year. The Legislative Reorganization Act of 1970 stipulates that "unless otherwise provided by the Congress," the Senate and House "shall adjourn *sine die* not later than July 31 of each year" or, in non-election years, take a 30-day recess in August. The provision is not applicable if "a state of war exists pursuant to a declaration of war by the Congress." *Sine die* (literally, without a day) adjournment ends a session of Congress. Within a session, Congress may adjourn to a specific day, although neither house can adjourn for more than three days without the consent of the other.

In 1973 Congress, reviving a procedure that had not been used in 25 years, twice gave its leaders authority to call it back into session during an adjournment. A resolution to adjourn *sine die* was approved Dec. 22, 1973, only after the House accepted a Senate amendment permitting the leadership to reconvene Congress if there were a national emergency. A resolution earlier in 1973 providing for an adjournment from Aug. 3 to Sept. 5 also permitted the leaders to call Congress back into session.

expanded greatly, and congressional sessions have averaged close to 10 months in length since World War II. The 96th Congress (1979-81) was in session for 703 days, during which 14,594 public bills were introduced and 613 were enacted. A total of 2,304 recorded votes were taken.

Institutional Structure

As its membership grew during the 19th and early 20th centuries and as the volume and complexity of its business multiplied, Congress as an institution underwent changes. The Congress of 1982 is a very different body from that of the early years of this century, much less from the one contemplated by the Founding Fathers.

Perhaps the most noteworthy characteristic of the modern Congress is its diffusion of power. There is no unity of command. Both the Senate and House are marked by a loose and disorganized internal structure coupled with a lack of strong party control. Leadership is divided among the committee chairmen, subcommittee chairmen and the party leaders, with the increasing influence of subcommittee chairmen in the 1970s being the most dramatic recent change.

The institutional structure is decentralized through the committee system. The standing committees of Congress — 17 in the Senate (including the Select Intelligence Committee, which is a permanent committee) and 23 in the House as of the beginning of the 97th Congress — are the cornerstone of the legislative process. The committee system provides a convenient division of labor for the heavy congressional workload and makes it possible for members to develop expertise in complex fields of legislation. It also creates an independent power base for chairmen, subcommittee chairmen and other senior members.

The committees hold virtually life-or-death power over legislation. They may approve, alter, kill or ignore any measure referred to them. When a bill reaches the floor, the committee leaders are the ones who must guide it to passage. And when it goes to a House-Senate conference, senior committee members are chosen to meet with their counterparts from the other chamber to work out the final language. At every stage the committee plays a determining role.

Legislative Leadership

Until the 1970s committee chairmen held power through the seniority system — that is, by tenure in office rather than election — and therefore were not subject to direct control by the party leaders, who are elected by their party's members in the House and Senate. In the early 1970s changes in the committee assignment process and in the method of selecting committee chairmen led to some strengthening of the congressional party apparatus. Nonetheless, the party leadership structure in Congress is itself so fragmented (among the House Speaker, floor leaders, influential committee chairmen and the like) that party government is today almost impossible to achieve. *(Seniority changes p. 109)*

Leadership in Congress is difficult because in practice there are no disciplined parties to be led. Members of Congress are responsible to a local electorate and are dependent, for the most part, on local financial support. Most members, therefore, are independent of the national party and frequently are at variance with it on legislative issues,

deficit projections in the budget.

Gathered to exercise its legislative responsibilities is a Congress of 100 senators and 435 representatives elected from the 50 states, plus four elected delegates — from the District of Columbia, Guam, the Virgin Islands and American Samoa — and an elected resident commissioner from Puerto Rico. Although a part-time job for much of the 19th and early 20th centuries, the work of lawmakers today is a year-around responsibility. The concerns of Congress have

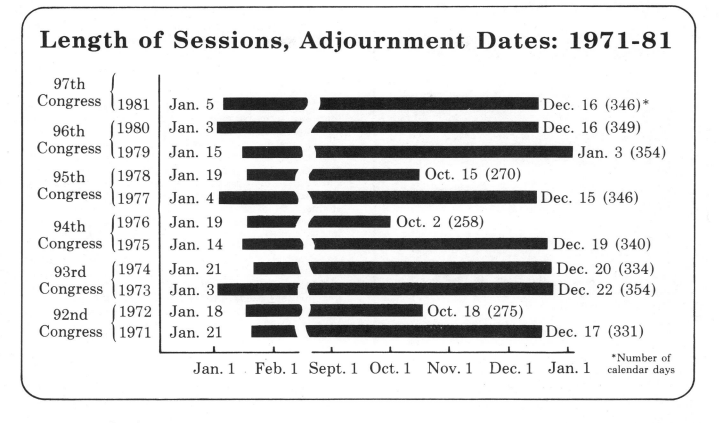

Length of Sessions, Adjournment Dates: 1971-81

97th Congress	1981	Jan. 5	Dec. 16 (346)*
96th Congress	1980	Jan. 3	Dec. 16 (349)
	1979	Jan. 15	Jan. 3 (354)
95th Congress	1978	Jan. 19	Oct. 15 (270)
	1977	Jan. 4	Dec. 15 (346)
94th Congress	1976	Jan. 19	Oct. 2 (258)
	1975	Jan. 14	Dec. 19 (340)
93rd Congress	1974	Jan. 21	Dec. 20 (334)
	1973	Jan. 3	Dec. 22 (354)
92nd Congress	1972	Jan. 18	Oct. 18 (275)
	1971	Jan. 21	Dec. 17 (331)

Jan. 1   Feb. 1   Sept. 1   Oct. 1   Nov. 1   Dec. 1   Jan. 1

*Number of calendar days

making it extremely difficult to achieve party unity. Attempts to bind members to particular positions at party caucuses are seldom made.

Voting blocs in Congress represent shifting coalitions of divergent interests that frequently cross party lines. The "conservative coalition" of Republicans and Southern Democrats voting against Northern Democrats, for example, has been a potent legislative force for years.

Although the legislative process works generally in the same way in both houses of Congress, rules and traditions vary and thus each chamber operates somewhat differently. The Senate, with only 100 members, can afford to be more relaxed in its procedures than the 435-member House of Representatives. Furthermore, each senator is an ambassador from a "sovereign" state and as such is accorded more deference, even indulgence, than a representative from a small district within a state.

Consequently, the House is more hierarchically organized, more rules are necessary and power is less evenly distributed than in the Senate, where even a freshman member occupies a position of some stature. A representative typically can expect to serve a lengthy apprenticeship before being able to rise to prominence, although this situation is less true today because of the reforms of the 1970s and the high turnover among members. Similarly, the House operates under a more rigid system of rules designed to expedite its business. Because debate is restricted and the amending process frequently curtailed, the House is able to dispose of legislation more quickly than the Senate.

By comparison, the Senate is a leisurely and informal institution. It usually operates in a spirit of comity where the prerogatives of all members are respected. In the hectic final days of the 1981 session, with Republican leaders working feverishly to complete action on priority legislation, Majority Leader Howard H. Baker Jr., R-Tenn., felt compelled to mollify senators for increasing their workload. "I apologize to senators and, more especially, to their families and friends,..," he said Dec. 2, "but I am sure all members will recall that before the Thanksgiving recess the leadership placed senators on notice that the usual arrangement of confining late hours to Thursdays only would no longer apply...." Much of the Senate's business is handled by unanimous consent, rather than by elaborate procedures spelled out in the rules.

One of the Senate's most cherished traditions is the privilege of unlimited debate — the filibuster — which cannot be employed under House rules. Another difference is that the Senate's amending powers are broader than those of the House. Given these conditions, it is not surprising that the Senate may spend days considering a measure that the House has debated and passed in one afternoon.

The legislative process is complex and varied. Experienced lawmakers know how to select the methods best suited to advance their legislative goals. As congressional specialist George B. Galloway observed, "In the end, the statutes that emerge from the travail of the legislative process reflect the influence of many forces. For better or for worse, they are affected by the way in which Congress is organized and by its rules of procedures." [2]

Bill Drafting

Legislative proposals may originate in a number of different ways. A member of Congress, of course, may

Longest Sessions of Congress

Con-gress	Ses-sion	Convened	Adjourned	No. of days
76th	3rd	Jan. 3, 1940-	Jan. 3, 1941	366
77th	1st	Jan. 3, 1941-	Jan. 2, 1942	365
81st	2nd	Jan. 3, 1950-	Jan. 2, 1951	365
80th	2nd	Jan. 6, 1948-	Dec. 31, 1948	361
88th	1st	Jan. 9, 1963-	Dec. 30, 1963	356
91st	1st	Jan. 3, 1969-	Dec. 23, 1969	355
65th	2nd	Dec. 3, 1917-	Nov. 21, 1918	354
93rd	1st	Jan. 3, 1973-	Dec. 22, 1973	354
96th	1st	Jan. 15, 1979-	Jan. 3, 1980	354
79th	1st	Jan. 3, 1945-	Dec. 21, 1945	353
80th	1st	Jan. 3, 1947-	Dec. 19, 1947	351
78th	1st	Jan. 6, 1943-	Dec. 21, 1943	350
91st	2nd	Jan. 19, 1970-	Jan. 2, 1971	349
96th	2nd	Jan. 3, 1980-	Dec. 16, 1980	349
77th	2nd	Jan. 5, 1942-	Dec. 16, 1942	346
95th	1st	Jan. 4, 1977-	Dec. 15, 1977	346
97th	1st	Jan. 5, 1981-	Dec. 16, 1981	346
40th	2nd	Dec. 2, 1867-	Nov. 10, 1868	345
78th	2nd	Jan. 10, 1944-	Dec. 19, 1944	345
90th	1st	Jan. 10, 1967-	Dec. 15, 1967	340
94th	1st	Jan. 14, 1975-	Dec. 19, 1975	340
93rd	2nd	Jan. 21, 1974-	Dec. 20, 1974	334
97th	2nd	Jan. 25, 1982-	Dec. 23, 1982	333
92nd	1st	Jan. 21, 1971-	Dec. 17, 1971	331
63rd	2nd	Dec. 1, 1913-	Oct. 24, 1914	328
50th	1st	Dec. 5, 1887-	Oct. 20, 1888	321
51st	1st	Dec. 2, 1889-	Oct. 1, 1890	304
31st	1st	Dec. 3, 1849-	Sept. 30, 1850	302

himself develop the idea for a piece of legislation.

Assistance in drafting legislative language is available from the House and Senate Office of Legislative Counsel. Special interest groups — business, labor, farm, civil rights, consumer, trade associations, and the like — are another fertile source of legislation. Most of these organizations and their lobbyists in Washington provide detailed technical knowledge in specialized fields and employ experts in the art of drafting bills and amendments. Constituents, either as individuals or groups, also may propose legislation. Frequently, a member of Congress will introduce such a bill "by request," whether or not he supports its purposes. *(Office of Legislative Counsel, box, p. 106)*

Today much of the legislation considered by Congress originates in the executive branch (although key members of Congress may participate in the formulation of administration programs). Each year after the president outlines his legislative program, executive departments and agencies transmit to the House and Senate drafts of proposed legislation to carry out the president's program or ideas. These bills usually are introduced by the chairman of the committee or subcommittee having jurisdiction over the subject involved, or by the ranking minority member if the chairman is not of the president's party.

Occasionally, committees consider proposals that have not been formally introduced. The committee then drafts its own bill, which is introduced by the chairman. This is the usual practice with appropriation and revenue bills. There also are occasions in which the chairman may introduce an alternative measure for a bill being considered by the committee.

No matter where a legislative proposal originates, it can be introduced only by a member of Congress. In the House, a member (including the resident commissioner of Puerto Rico and the non-voting delegates of the District of Columbia, Guam, Somoa and the Virgin Islands) may introduce any of several types of bills and resolutions by handing them to the clerk of the House or by placing them in a box called the hopper. He need not seek recognition for the purpose.

Senators introduce bills during the so-called "morning hour."

After it is introduced, a bill is numbered (in order of introduction), referred to the appropriate committee by the House and Senate parliamentarian, labeled with the sponsor's name and sent to the Government Printing Office (GPO) so that copies can be made for subsequent study and action.

There is no limit to the number of bills a member may introduce. House and Senate bills may have joint sponsorship and carry several members' names. (Before 1967 House rules barred representatives from cosponsoring legislation. Members favoring a particular measure had to introduce identical bills if they wished to be closely identified with the original proposal.)

The Constitution stipulates that "all bills for raising revenue shall originate in the House of Representatives," and this stipulation generally has been interpreted to include spending (appropriation) bills as well. All other bills may originate in either chamber. Major legislation usually is introduced in both houses in the form of companion (identical) bills.

Although thousands of bills are introduced in every Congress, most never receive any consideration. Of the 14,594 bills introduced in the Senate and House during the 96th Congress (1979-81), only 2,494 were reported by committees. Bills not enacted into law die with the Congress in which they are introduced and must be reintroduced in a new Congress if they are to be eligible for further consideration. Treaties are the only exception to this rule. Once introduced, they remain pending from one Congress to another.

Types of Legislation

The types of measures that Congress may consider and act upon (in addition to treaties in the Senate) include bills and various types of resolutions. The nomenclature and designations are:

Bills — prefixed with "HR" when introduced in the House and with "S" when introduced in the Senate, followed by a number assigned the measure based on the order in which it is introduced during each Congress. Bills are the legislative form used for most legislation, whether general or special, public or private. When passed by both chambers in identical form and signed by the president (or repassed by Congress over a presidential veto), they become laws.

At the beginning of a Congress, members vie to be the sponsors of the first bill introduced and to retain the same bill number in consecutive Congresses on legislation that has not been enacted. In both the 94th and 95th Congresses, HR 50 was the Humphrey-Hawkins Full Employment Act.

Joint Resolutions — designated H J Res or S J Res. A joint resolution, like a bill, requires the approval of both houses (in identical form) and the signature of the president; it has the force of law if approved. There is no real difference between a bill and a joint resolution. The latter generally is used when dealing with a single item or issue, such as an emergency appropriation bill. These funding measures even are referred to informally as continuing resolutions. Joint resolutions also are used for proposing amendments to the Constitution. Such resolutions must be approved by two-thirds of both houses. They do not require the president's signature but become a part of the Constitution when ratified by three-fourths of the states.

Concurrent Resolutions — designated H Con Res or S Con Res. They are used for matters affecting the operations of both houses, such as fixing the time of adjournment of a Congress or expressing the "sense" of the two chambers on some question. They must be passed in the same form by both houses, but they are not referred to the president for his signature and they do not have the force of law.

Resolutions — designated H Res or S Res. A simple resolution deals with matters entirely within the prerogative of one house of Congress. It is not considered by the other chamber and is not sent to the president. Like a concurrent resolution, it does not have the force of law. Most resolutions deal with the rules or procedures of one house. They also are used occasionally to express the opinion of a single house on a current issue. Special orders or rules setting the guidelines for debate on a bill, as laid down by the House Rules Committee, also are contained in simple resolutions.

Steps in Legislative Process

The House and Senate handle bills in different ways, but both employ the committee system for screening proposals and legislative calendars for listing them in order. The chambers have their own procedures for scheduling floor action on bills on various calendars.

Committee Action

Nearly all bills are sent to committees. A bill is referred to the appropriate committee by the House parliamentarian on behalf of the Speaker and by the Senate parliamentarian acting for the presiding officer. This constitutes the first reading of a bill (although the legislation is not actually read).

Generally, custom and rule govern the referral of legislation to a committee. The jurisdiction of the standing committees is spelled out in House Rule 10 and Senate Rule 25. Sometimes, however, the presiding officer has a measure of discretion — for example, in the case of new programs or bills involving overlapping jurisdictions — and bills may be drafted in such a way as to to take advantage of this situation. In 1963 a controversial civil rights bill was referred to the Senate Commerce Committee instead of the Southern-dominated Judiciary Committee because its sub-

ject matter, public accommodations, fell within the commerce clause of the Constitution.

Occasionally when problems of overlapping jurisdiction arise, bills are referred to more than one committee, or first to one committee and then re-referred to a second, and sometimes a third, committee.

The standing committees of Congress, operating as little legislatures, determine the fate of most legislative proposals.

Committee members and staff frequently have a high degree of expertise in the subjects under their jurisdiction, and it is at the committee stage that a bill comes under the sharpest congressional scrutiny.

A committee has several options with respect to a piece of legislation: it may consider it, usually after holding hearings on the measure, and then approve it (called "reporting" it), with or without amendments; rewrite it entirely; reject it; or report it unfavorably (which allows the bill to be considered by the full House or Senate, but with a recommendation that the bill be rejected); or simply refuse to consider it. In some situations, committee members who are opposed to a bill will agree to report it, either favorably or unfavorably, so as to allow the House, or Senate, to make the final judgment.

Failure of a committee to act on a bill usually is equivalent to killing it. One of the ways a measure can be taken away from the panel's purview is through a discharge petition, signed by a majority of the House membership on House bills, or by unanimous consent in the Senate. Discharge attempts rarely succeed.

When a bill reaches a committee, it is placed on the panel's calendar. (Most standing committees periodically publish cumulative calendars of legislative business, listing all action on the measures referred to them.) The committee then requests comment from interested parties, particularly agencies of government. The agencies give their views on the effects of the proposed legislation and how it would accord with the president's program and positions.

Subcommittee Hearings/Markup. A bill may be considered by the full committee in the first instance, but more often the committee chairman assigns it to a subcommittee for study and the initial hearings. Especially in the House, the power of assignment may be used to promote or impede proposed legislation. (The referral prerogatives of committee chairmen have been somewhat restricted since 1973.)

Subcommittees usually invite testimony from government officials, outside experts or scholars and special interest groups. Other interested citizens at their own request may be given the opportunity to testify or submit a statement for the record. Most witnesses offer prepared statements, after which they may be questioned by subcommittee members and even by staff members on some committees.

The hearings may be brief and perfunctory or they may go on for weeks. Because the demands on a member's time are so great, frequently only a few subcommittee members with a special interest in the subject will participate in the hearings.

Most hearings today are held in open session, although committees dealing with national security and other sensitive information must close many of their meetings. In the Armed Services committees, a combination of open and closed (executive) hearings is used, and sometimes the same hearing will be closed for part of the day but open to the public for the remainder of the hearing. Until 1971 all hearings of the House Appropriations Committee were in closed session.

In 1973 both chambers adopted new rules to encourage more open committee meetings. The House required all committee meetings to be open to the public unless a majority on the committee votes — by roll call, in open session with a quorum present — to close a meeting. Sessions on national security and internal committee business, such as budget and personnel matters, were excepted from the new rule.

The Senate rule, also adopted in 1973, was weaker. After defeating a proposal that was similar to the House version, the Senate adopted a proposal allowing each committee to make its own rules on secrecy, thereby permitting, but not requiring, open sessions. A previous Senate rule had prohibited committees from allowing the public to attend their bill-drafting sessions. Three committees chose that year to allow such meetings to be open.[3] In November 1975 the Senate adopted "sunshine" rules governing committee hearings that were similar to those in the House.

Hearings on legislation may serve a variety of purposes: to obtain information on the subject under consideration; to test public opinion; to build support for the bill; or even to delay action on it. Sometimes hearings serve primarily as a safety valve for the release of citizen or group frustrations.

After hearings have ended, the subcommittee meets to "mark up" the bill — that is, to decide on legislative language before sending the measure to the full committee. The subcommittee may approve the legislation unaltered, which is rarely the case, amend it or substitute an entirely new version. Or it can vote to reject the bill outright. The subcommittee then reports its version of the bill to the full committee.

Full Committee Action. House and Senate committees today hold most of their markups in open session.

When the full committee receives the bill, it may repeat the subcommittee procedures — including additional hearings — or it may simply ratify the action of the subcommittee, as is commonly the case in the House and Senate Appropriations committees.

When a committee votes to approve a measure, after reviewing the bill and making any additional changes, it is said to "order the bill reported." Occasionally, a committee may order a bill reported unfavorably. But most of the time the committee's report on the bill (see below), submitted by the chairman of the committee to the House or Senate before floor action is held, calls for passage because the committee can effectively kill legislation it opposes simply by failing to take action. Another reason committees usually favor passage of bills they report is that the version reported usually has been amended to satisfy a majority of the committee's members.

Frequently, the full committee will make additional amendments. If the changes are substantial and the legislation is complicated, the committee may introduce a "clean bill" embodying the proposed amendments. The original bill is then put aside and the "clean bill," with a new number, is the version reported. If the amendments are not extensive, the original bill is "reported with amendments." Later, when the bill is taken to the floor, the House or Senate must approve, alter or reject the committee amendments before the bill itself can be put to a vote.

Committee Report. When a committee sends a bill to the floor, it justifies its actions in a written statement, called a report, which accompanies the bill. The report describes the purposes and scope of the bill, explains the committee amendments, indicates proposed changes in existing law, estimates the additional costs to the government of program changes recommended by the committee and usually includes the texts of communications from department and agency heads whose views on the legislation have been solicited.

Since enactment of the Legislative Reorganization Act of 1970, committees have been required to publish in their reports all votes taken on amendments disposed of in committee as well as the vote to report the bill. Only vote totals are required, not the positions of members on roll calls, although many committees include the breakdown. (Committees are required to keep a record of all roll-call votes and to make then available to the public on request.)

Often, committee members opposing the bill, or certain sections of it, submit a minority report through dissenting, supplementary or additional views.

Reports are numbered, by Congress and chamber, in the order in which they are filed (S Rept 94-1, H Rept 94-1, etc.) and immediately printed. The reported bill also is printed, with the committee amendments indicated by insertions in italics and deletions in stricken-through type. The report number and the date the bill formally is reported also are shown on the bill. In addition, the calendar number is printed on both the bill and the committee report.

In some situations, the language of the report is as important as the bill itself. It has been common practice for committees, including House-Senate conference committees, to write instructions in their reports on how government agencies should interpret and enforce the law. And the courts have relied on these guidelines in establishing congressional intent.

Lobbyists have been vitally interested in the report language as one way of promoting or protecting their clients' interests. Many appropriation bills, for example, include only the amount of money a particular agency or department may spend. But the accompanying committee report often contains directives on how Congress expects the money to be spent or warnings to bureaucrats not to take certain actions.

In 1980 the U.S. Court of Appeals for the District of Columbia, in a case involving the authority of the Civil Aeronautics Board (CAB) to regulate the domestic air cargo industry, admonished Congress to write its directives in legislation. Explaining the legislative aspect of the case, which involved interpretations of a 1977 law deregulating the air transportation industry, Chief Judge J. Skelly Wright, writing for the court, said: "[I]nterest groups who fail to persuade a majority of the Congress to accept particular statutory language often are able to have inserted in the legislative history of the statute statements favorable to their position, in the hope that they can persuade a court to construe the statutory language in light of these statements. This development underscores the importance of following unambiguous statutory language. . . ."[4]

As of 1982, the impact on the legislative process of the court's ruling in the CAB case remained unclear.

House and Senate Calendars

After a bill is reported, it is placed on a calendar. Although bills are placed on the calendar in chronological order, usually they are not called up for floor action in that order.

House. There are five legislative calendars in the

How a Bill Becomes Law

This graphic shows the most typical way in which proposed legislation is enacted into law. There are more complicated, as well as simpler, routes, and most bills never become law. The process is illustrated with two hypothetical bills, House bill No. 1 (HR 1) and Senate bill No. 2 (S 2). Bills must be passed by both houses in identical form before they can be sent to the president. The path of HR 1 is traced by a solid line, that of S 2 by a broken line. In practice most bills begin as similar proposals in both houses.

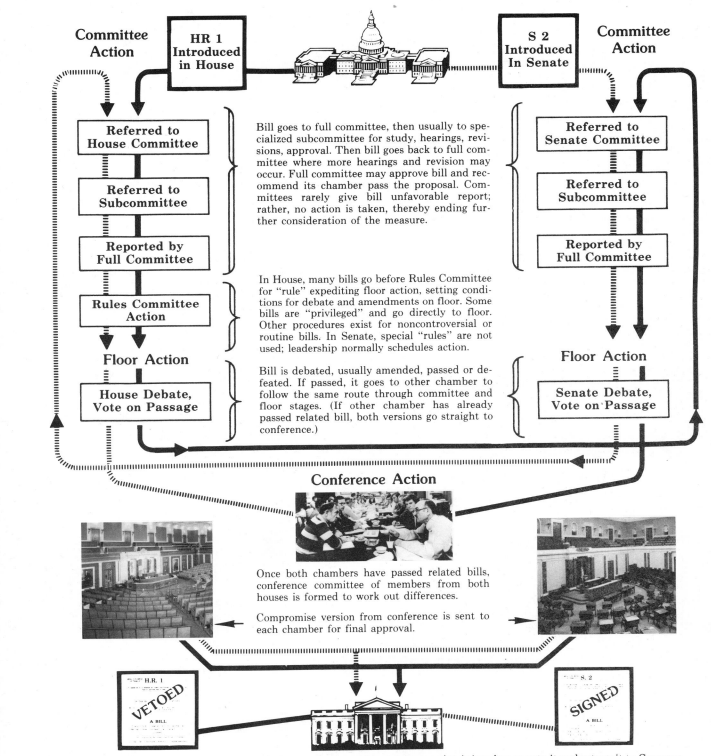

Committee Action

HR 1 Introduced in House

S 2 Introduced In Senate

Committee Action

Referred to House Committee

Referred to Subcommittee

Reported by Full Committee

Rules Committee Action

Floor Action

House Debate, Vote on Passage

Bill goes to full committee, then usually to specialized subcommittee for study, hearings, revisions, approval. Then bill goes back to full committee where more hearings and revision may occur. Full committee may approve bill and recommend its chamber pass the proposal. Committees rarely give bill unfavorable report; rather, no action is taken, thereby ending further consideration of the measure.

In House, many bills go before Rules Committee for "rule" expediting floor action, setting conditions for debate and amendments on floor. Some bills are "privileged" and go directly to floor. Other procedures exist for noncontroversial or routine bills. In Senate, special "rules" are not used; leadership normally schedules action.

Bill is debated, usually amended, passed or defeated. If passed, it goes to other chamber to follow the same route through committee and floor stages. (If other chamber has already passed related bill, both versions go straight to conference.)

Referred to Senate Committee

Referred to Subcommittee

Reported by Full Committee

Floor Action

Senate Debate, Vote on Passage

Conference Action

Once both chambers have passed related bills, conference committee of members from both houses is formed to work out differences.

Compromise version from conference is sent to each chamber for final approval.

H.R. 1 VETOED A BILL

S. 2 SIGNED A BILL

Compromise bill approved by both houses is sent to the president, who can sign it into law or veto it and return it to Congress. Congress may override veto by a two-thirds majority vote in both houses; bill then becomes law without president's signature.

House, issued in one cumulative document titled *Calendars of the United States House of Representatives and History of Legislation.* This calendar, which is printed daily when the House is in session, lists all bills in numerical order on each of the five legislative calendars. It also gives a capsule legislative history of all measures in both houses that have reached the committee report stage in the legislative process: bills ordered reported by House and Senate committees and bills on which there has been floor action. Also included is valuable reference material, and each Monday's edition carries a subject index.

The five legislative calendars are:

The Union Calendar, to which are referred "bills raising revenue, general appropriation bills and bills of a public character directly or indirectly appropriating money or property." This description means that legislation having any effect on the Treasury, including authorization bills, goes on the Union Calendar. Technically, it is the Calendar of the Committee of the Whole House on the State of the Union, so called because bills listed on it are first considered in the Committee of the Whole House *(see below)* and reported back to the House for a final vote on passage.

The House Calendar, to which are referred "all bills of a public character not raising revenue nor directly or indirectly appropriating money or property." Bills on this calendar must have no impact of the Treasury; generally, they deal with administrative and procedural matters. These measures usually are not considered in the Committee of the Whole but are taken up directly by the House.

The Consent Calendar, to which are referred bills of a non-controversial nature, is intended to expedite such legislation. Any member may request that a bill already on the Union or House calendar be placed on the Consent Calendar. The Consent Calendar is called on the first and third Mondays of each month. These bills are not debated. The first time a bill is called up any member may object to its consideration. If called up again, it requires three or more members to block floor action. When a bill is blocked twice it is removed from the calendar for the remainder of the session. Usually, if there appears to be objections, sponsors of the bill will request that it be passed over "without prejudice" so it can remain on the calendar.

The Private Calendar, to which are referred bills for the relief of individuals with claims against the United States and private immigration bills. The Private Calendar is called the first Tuesday of each month and may be called the third Tuesday.

Most private bills are passed without debate, but if two or more members object to a bill, it may be recommitted to the committee that reported it. The Judiciary Committee handles most private relief bills.

The Discharge Calendar, to which are referred motions to discharge committees from further consideration of a bill when the required number of names (a majority of the total House membership — 218) are signed to a discharge petition. A rarely used device, discharge motions may be taken up on the second and fourth Mondays of each month. Those days also are set aside for consideration of business presented by the District of Columbia Committee. *(For details of Consent Calendar and discharge procedures, see pp. 54-55.)*

Senate. The Senate has only two calendars, the *Executive Calendar,* on which treaties and nominations are listed, and the *Calendar of Business* (General Orders), to which all legislation is assigned.

A bill is brought before the Senate usually in one of two ways, either on a motion to call up a bill on the calendar, on which a vote is taken, or by unanimous consent.

Scheduling Floor Action

House. Although a variety of methods exist for bringing up legislation, for major bills the route to House floor action usually lies through the Rules Committee. This committee is empowered to report "rules" setting guidelines for floor debate on legislation. *(A history of the committee appears on pp. 96-97)*

Usually the chairman of the committee that favorably reported the bill, supported by the bill's sponsor and other committee members, appears before the Rules Committee to request a rule, technically a resolution specifying a special "order of business." The request is considered by the Rules Committee in the same fashion that other committees consider legislation. And the rule ultimately agreed to by the committee is incorporated in a House resolution. The resolution sets the time limit on general debate and governs the amending process. It may forbid all amendments or, in some cases, all amendments except those proposed by the legislative committee that handled the bill. In this instance it is known as a "closed rule," as opposed to an "open rule" permitting amendments from the floor. Some bills are given "modified closed rules" that allow specified amendments to be introduced or that permit floor amendments only to certain sections of the bill. Tax bills today often are considered under some type of modified closed rule.

The rule also may waive points of order against certain provisions of the bill or against specified amendments that are expected to be offered from the floor. This waiver permits the House to violate its own rules by barring any objection to such violation. A typical example might block objections to legislative provisions tacked onto a general appropriations bill — something not permitted under House rules.

Once the Rules Committee reports a special rule for a bill, floor action ordinarily cannot occur for at least one day. This layover period was added to the rules to give members time to prepare for floor action on the bill. When the leadership brings the bill to the floor, the rule must be debated and adopted first. Normally, rules are approved routinely; very few are rejected. Nevertheless, on some occasions the strategy of a bill's opponents is directed at defeating the rule as a way of killing the bill. If a leadership-supported rule is rejected, the committee chairman may withdraw his bill from further consideration rather than risk a worse fate on the House floor.

More often, the opponents attempt to vote down the rule and substitute one more to their liking. That occurred in June 1981 on President Reagan's program to cut the federal budget. The Democratic-controlled Rules Committee had sent the House a special rule under which members would be forced to vote separately on individual spending cuts — including some on popular social programs — proposed by the president. The Republicans wanted a single, up-or-down vote on the entire package of cuts. Democrats believed members would not vote to cut some of the programs if forced to take a stand. But 29 conservative Democrats defected and joined the Republicans to defeat the committee's rule by a seven-vote margin. They then succeeded on a 216-212 vote in amending the rule to provide for a single vote on the Reagan budget package.

There are certain limitations on the Rules Commit-

Proceedings of the House and Senate

The Senate and House normally meet at noon daily, although earlier meetings are common in both chambers. In each chamber the session opens with a prayer, followed by the "reading" and approval of the *Journal*, which comprises a record of the previous day's proceedings). The reading usually is dispensed with, but occasionally, as part of dilatory tactics, it is demanded in the Senate. Under the Legislative Reorganization Act of 1970, the House *Journal* cannot be read unless the Speaker or a majority of those present so order.

What happens next depends on whether the chamber recessed or adjourned at the conclusion of its last previous sitting. If it adjourned, a new "legislative day" — the period from adjournment to adjournment — now begins, and the rules set forth certain matters to be taken up and disposed of at the beginning of a new daily session. If it recessed, the same legislative day continues, and the chamber may move on to unfinished business without further preliminaries. The distinction is less significant in the House, which normally adjourns from day to day, than in the Senate, where a legislative day frequently extends over several calendar days. (In 1922, when the Senate was considering a controversial tariff bill, a single legislative day extended for 105 calendar days.)

Daily life on Capitol Hill is punctuated by the ringing of bells, intended to alert members not in their seats to what is going on in Senate or House. Systems of electric bells or buzzers are installed at various places in the Capitol and in the Senate and House office buildings (and even in some nearby restaurants) to summon members when their presence is required for votes or other purposes. Conveniently located wall lights show how many bells have rung. Different systems are used in each chamber. Since 1979 House members also have been able to keep abreast of floor action through live TV coverage.

Senate

Following an adjournment, the Senate sets aside the first two hours of a legislative day as a "morning hour" for the consideration of routine business. This business includes such matters as receiving messages from the president, communications from department heads, messages from the House, presentations of petitions and memorials and reports of standing and select committees. The morning hour also is used to introduce bills and resolutions. Senators are limited to brief statements, usually three minutes, to explain their bills.

During the first hour of the morning period, no motion to proceed to the consideration of bills on the Senate calendar is in order, except by unanimous consent. During the second hour, motions may be made, but they must be disposed of without debate.

At the conclusion of morning business or after the hour of 1 p.m., any senator may move to take up a bill out of its regular order on the calendar. If the bill is not disposed of by the time the Senate is ready to resume consideration of its unfinished business, the bill is held over to the next morning hour.

Although not required under the rules, a morning hour frequently is arranged by unanimous consent following a Senate recess.

At 2 o'clock, or earlier if the morning business has been completed, the Senate moves on to unfinished business or to the business planned by the majority leader for the day. Unlike the more orderly House, the Senate frequently interrupts consideration of a bill to take care of other legislation. The Senate may take up a bill, lay it aside temporarily to consider another, return to debate on the first, then pause for speeches unrelated to the subject technically under consideration. Generally, its pace is leisurely, and it may take days or even weeks to dispose of a single bill. In recent years, Senate majority leaders often have operated on a two-track system whereby a certain period of time is reserved daily for particularly controversial bills. In this way, a much-debated bill, which sometimes is being filibustered, does not interfere with other business.

House

The House tends to operate on a Monday-to-Thursday schedule, with Mondays reserved primarily for non-controversial legislation considered under special procedures.

Although the House rules provide for a morning hour, that procedure is rarely employed. After approval of the *Journal*, the Speaker recognizes members for one-minute speeches and submission of material to be inserted in the *Congressional Record*. Bills are introduced, reports filed and messages, petitions and memorials received. This constitutes the morning business of the House, after which the chamber turns to legislative business, sitting either as the House or in Committee of the Whole.

The House is able to dispose of most bills in one or two days. Once it takes up a bill, it generally sticks with it until action is completed. Stringent House rules preclude undue delay.

Typically, the House sets aside a time at the close of the day's session, after disposing of legislative business, for "special orders" and unanimous consent requests. At this time, members who have requested time in advance are permitted to make speeches on various subjects for inclusion in the *Congressional Record*. Few other members stay in the chamber to listen. Indeed, the speeches sometimes are not even delivered; only the texts of the remarks are inserted in the Record. The special orders time is followed by adjournment.

tee's power. It is not allowed to report a rule that denies the minority the right to make a motion to recommit a bill once debate is completed. That motion usually is expressly written into the rule, which will state that after all amendments have been disposed of, opponents will have one more shot to alter or reject the bill.

When the committee approves a rule, it is spelled out in the special resolution and sent to the House. Although the rule cannot be brought to the floor until the following day, the committee may wait up to three legislative days to file the resolution. If not immediately considered, the resolution goes on the calendar. If the member submitting the resolution does not call it up within seven legislative days, any member of the committee may do so. The resolution cannot be called up on the day it is reported except by a two-thirds vote of the House. This rule does not apply during the last three days of a session.

The committee at different times in the history of the House has not always been amenable to the wishes of the leadership in granting rules on bills. In the 1960s, when the committee was under the chairmanship of Rep. Howard W. Smith, D-Va. (1931-67), it regularly blocked or delayed civil rights and consumer-oriented legislation. At other times the committee has forced substantive changes in bills as the price for granting a rule allowing floor action. Since the era of Rep. Smith, however, the committee usually has done the leadership's bidding. During the chairmanship (1979-83) of Rep. Richard Bolling, D-Mo., the committee worked closely with Speaker Thomas P. O'Neill Jr., D-Mass., and it probably is fair to say that most bills it has blocked in recent years were opposed either by the leadership or by a majority of the House.

If the Rules Committee refuses to grant a rule, the bill may be brought up under alternative methods, such as suspension of the rules or the rarely successful discharge or Calendar Wednesday procedures. *(For details of alternative procedures, see p. 54)*

Another method of getting around the committee was the 21-day rule, adopted in 1965 but abandoned in 1967. Under that rule, the Speaker could recognize a committee member to call up for House consideration any bill reported by the committee that had been before the Rules Committee for 21 days. Enlargement of the committee from 12 to 15 members in 1961 and a change in 1974 that allowed the Democratic Speaker to appoint the Democratic members of the committee — subject to caucus approval — helped to strengthen the leadership's control of the panel.

Bills from certain committees have privileged status and may be considered by the House without a rule from the Rules Committee. Revenue bills originating in the Ways and Means Committee do not require a rule, but the committee usually has sought a closed rule anyway to preclude floor amendments. *(Closed rules, box, p. 47)*

General appropriations bills also are privileged, as are matters required to be reported by the Budget Committee in accordance with the Congressional Budget and Impoundment Control Act of 1974 and certain matters under the jurisdictions of the House Administration, Rules, and Standards of Official Conduct committees.

Conference reports, presidential veto messages (in which the president returns to Congress bills he has vetoed) and certain types of House amendments to Senate bills also are privileged. The member in charge of any of these legislative vehicles may call them up at practically any time, although usually this is done only after consulting with the majority and minority leaders.

Generally, a bill cannot be considered on the floor until the third day after the committee report has been filed, although this requirement can be waived by a two-thirds majority vote. House rules also require copies of the legislation to be available to members for at least two hours before the bill is considered on the floor. But again, this rule can be suspended upon approval of the Rules Committee and the House by majority vote. In such cases, the legislation can be brought up immediately, even before copies have been printed. This is most likely to occur in the hectic final days of a session. But even the two-hour requirement hardly is sufficient on complex legislation. On the huge 1981 Reagan tax bill, members of both parties decried the procedure that made most details of the tax bill available only a few hours before the vote.

Senate. Unlike the House, the Senate has few elaborate rules or procedures for bringing bills to the floor, and it has no counterpart to the House Rules Committee.

Theoretically, under Senate rules any senator at almost any time may offer a motion to call up a bill. A simple majority is sufficient to adopt the motion. During the so-called morning hour (the period before 2 p.m. at the beginning of a legislative day, assuming the Senate convenes at noon) such a motion is not debatable. At other times it is subject to debate — and thus to a filibuster, which can be stopped only by invoking cloture, a process that requires a majority vote of three-fifths of all senators — 60 votes. Occasionally, controversial bills meet defeat at this stage.

In practice, floor action is scheduled by the majority leader with the help of the majority party's Policy Committee and after consultation with the minority leader. Efforts are made to accommodate the wishes of individual senators, and action on important bills and nominations sometimes is postponed for long periods because of previously known objections.

The most common way to bring up bills in the Senate is by unanimous consent.

House Floor Procedures

The House has developed elaborate procedures for handling the hundreds of bills that committees send to the floor each year. Most substantive bills are debated under terms set forth in a resolution from the Rules Committee. But alternative methods are provided for handling other bills, mostly those of a routine nature.

Debate on the Rule

Floor action on a major House bill ordinarily begins when the Speaker recognizes the member of the Rules Committee who has been designated to call up the rule governing how the bill is to be considered. The rule may be debated for up to one hour, with half the time allotted to opponents of the bill. A typical "open rule" (allowing floor amendments) may provide:

"Resolved, That upon the adoption of this resolution it shall be in order to move that the House resolve itself into the Committee of the Whole House on the State of the Union for the consideration of the bill (H.R.—), entitled, ————. After general debate, which shall be confined to the bill and continue not to exceed — hours, to be equally divided and controlled by the chairman and the ranking minority member of the committee on —, the bill shall be read for amendment under the five-minute rule. At the

Reining-in the Rules Committee

In the heady days of the House "reform" movement in the early 1970s, the Democratic Party put through rules changes that effectively terminated the Rules Committee's power to unilaterally send bills to the House floor with closed rules — barring floor amendments.

The change was directed both at the Rules Committee, which often acted as a power unto itself, and at Ways and Means Chairman Wilbur D. Mills, D-Ark. (1939-77). Since 1932 Ways and Means had routinely sent bills to the House floor with so-called gag rules barring amendments.

The rules change, adopted by the Democratic Caucus in 1973, left it to the caucus rather than the Rules Committee or the chairman of the committee that wrote the bill to decide whether a particular amendment should be considered on the House floor.

The caucus was to convene for the purpose of judging an amendment's suitability if 50 or more Democrats petitioned it to do so. If the caucus decided the amendment should be considered, Rules Committee Democrats — who constituted a majority of the committee — were required to write a rule for the bill specifying that the amendment could be offered on the House floor.

The new caucus procedure, though rarely invoked, resulted in more and more bills coming out of the Rules Committee accompanied by open rules permitting a wide variety of amendments. It also was effective in making the Rules Committee and the committee chairmen more responsive to the will of their Democratic colleagues.

A subsequent change in caucus rules made the Rules Committee even more responsive to party concerns. The caucus in December 1974 authorized the Speaker to appoint — subject to party ratification — the Democratic members of the Rules Committee. Previously, all committee assignments had been made by the Committee on Committees, composed of the Democratic members of the Ways and Means Committee.

But a few years later, the looser controls on the number of amendments that could be offered on the House floor appeared to boomerang on the reform-minded Democrats.

During the late 1970s, a group of militant Republicans began to wage a sort of guerrilla warfare on the House floor by sniping at the Democrats' legislative initiatives with endless minor amendments.

For example, a 1979 debate on a bill to establish a separate Department of Education spanned six days, during which 19 Republican amendments were considered. One of those amendments proposed to change the name of the agency to the Department of Public Education — thus changing its acronym to DOPE.

To counteract the militants' attack, the Rules Committee under Chairman Richard Bolling, D-Mo., began to rely on "modified closed rules," permitting only certain amendments, specified in advance, to come to a floor vote. This allowed the leadership to narrow the points of disagreement by bargaining with various factions wanting to offer amendments, while keeping some control over the bill.

The tactic subsequently met with considerable success in limiting debate on hotly contested bills. On President Reagan's 1981 tax cut proposal, for example, only two recorded votes occurred on amendments. One vote was on a substitute to the Ways and Means Committee bill backed by Democratic liberals, and the other was on the substitute put forward by the Reagan administration.

---

conclusion of the consideration of the bill for amendment, the committee [of the whole] shall rise and report the bill to the House with such amendments as may have been adopted and the previous question shall be considered as ordered on the bill and amendments thereto to final passage without intervening motion except one motion to recommit with or without instructions."

"Closed rules" or "modified closed rules" usually are more complex. An extreme example was the modified closed rule to the aforementioned 1981 tax bill, which took nearly a page of the *Congressional Record*, in small type, to explain. After the rule has been adopted, the House resolves itself into the Committee of the Whole House on the State of the Union (working title: Committee of the Whole) for preliminary consideration of the bill. A 1983 change in House rules allowed the Speaker to resolve the House into the Committee of the Whole without a vote.

Action in Committee of the Whole

Although only bills on the Union Calendar must be considered in Committee of the Whole, other bills may be so considered. In practice, most important bills are considered in Committee of the Whole. If a bill is considered in the House, rather than in the Committee of the Whole, the amount of time for debate is determined either by a special rule, by the so-called hour rule or by unanimous consent.

The Committee of the Whole procedure goes back to a period in English history when the Speaker of the House of Commons was regarded as an agent of the King. The Committee of the Whole was devised so that during periods of strained relations between the King and the Commons members could elect a chairman of their own and proceed to discuss matters, particularly matters pertaining to the King's household expenses, without the normal restrictions of a House of Commons session.

House Takes the Initiative ...

Gavel-to-gavel television coverage of the House had its public debut on March 19, 1979. Floor proceedings were televised by the House's own $1.2 million system operated by House employees.

The House had begun experimental closed-circuit, black-and-white telecasts of its debates in March 1977. In 1979 it installed high-quality color cameras for public viewing. The new system began operating Feb. 19, with broadcasts sent initially only to Capitol Hill offices. But in March the telecasts were made available to broadcast and cable systems.

On April 3, 1979, the Cable-Satellite Public Affairs Network (C-SPAN) went on the air, sending live coverage of all House sessions to its commercial cable system subscribers. Some public television stations also carried selected live coverage of major House action, while the networks used brief recorded segments for their evening news programs. By the end of 1980, C-SPAN was telecasting House proceedings to more than 1,200 cable television systems with the potential of reaching 10 million homes in all 50 states.

The Senate moved much more slowly. In the early 1970s it appeared that senators might be more receptive than representatives to television. But enthusiasm waned abruptly after the chamber endured many weeks of bitter debate and roll-call votes over a disputed election for a Senate seat from New Hampshire. The experience was an embarrassment to senators and made them leery of televising such displays directly into voters' homes.

The Senate leadership, then in the hands of Sen. Robert C. Byrd, D-W.Va., resisted televising floor action. It was only in 1981, after the Republicans were in the majority, that televised coverage was made a priority matter. But influential senators in both parties continued to resist it. Although Senate Majority Leader Howard H. Baker Jr., R-Tenn., who favored the idea, brought the proposal to the floor early in 1982, the debate was inconclusive. With a filibuster on the issue looming, and time needed for more pressing legislation, Baker took the television plan off the Senate agenda.

House TV Coverage

The idea of televising congressional floor action surfaced in the 1940s, but it began to be discussed seriously only in the early 1970s. In 1944 then-Sen. Claude Pepper, D-Fla. (1936-51), introduced the first resolution calling for televising floor proceedings. In 1947 the House let television cameras record its opening session. But after that initial experiment, House leaders pulled the plug on broadcasting anything other than special joint sessions such as the president's annual State of the Union message.

Except for a brief interlude in the Republican-controlled 80th and 83rd Congresses, the House shunned televised committee hearings until the Legislative Reorganization Act of 1970 sanctioned live coverage of hearings under strict standards. One of the best known televised hearings was the House Judiciary Committee's impeachment proceedings against President Richard Nixon in 1974.

Also in 1974, the Joint Committee on Congressional Operations recommended gavel-to-gavel coverage of both chambers. But a major sticking point developed over who would control and operate the live TV broadcasts. The television networks and some members of Congress maintained that technical control of the cameras and of the programming should be given to commercial broadcasters. But Speaker Thomas P. O'Neill Jr., D-Mass., argued that the House, not the networks, should control the telecasts' contents, while members generally were concerned about TV cameras scanning the House chamber and focusing on empty seats or on members reading papers and recording their expressions.

These problems delayed further progress in televising the House until the 95th Congress. In 1977 the Democratic leadership directed the Select Committee on Congressional Operations to conduct a 90-day experiment using closed-circuit telecasts of House floor proceedings to members' offices. In addition, the leadership studied the broadcasting system used in Canada's House of Commons and held tests of broadcasting equipment. The experiment was labeled a success, and the select committee recommended gavel-to-gavel coverage, with the House retaining control over the operation and the cameras focused only on members participating in the debates.

Later in 1977 the Rules Committee endorsed the recommendation for gavel-to-gavel coverage, but left unresolved the question of who would control the broadcasts. In October the House tentatively endorsed the committee's recommendation by a 342-44 vote, despite warnings that broadcasts would expose members to embarrassment or grandstanding.

The issue of who would control the operation, including the cameras, was resolved in June 1978 when the House rejected a move to bar funding of a House-controlled television system and then endorsed a House-run operation. Fear that commercial broadcasters would show members of the House in an unflattering light tipped the scale toward in-House

...In Televising Floor Debates

control. Under the system finally adopted, only the Speaker's rostrum and the majority and minority tables from which members often address the House would be televised. No shots of the representatives sitting in the chamber or of the public galleries were allowed. Use of the broadcasts, either live or recorded, was prohibited as was commercial use "except as part of bona fide news programs and public affairs documentary programs." All broadcasting services and accredited correspondents were given access to the live coverage.

After another delay in 1978 to develop a more sophisticated system than the House originally had planned, televised coverage finally began in 1979.

A group of young Republicans quickly took advantage of the daily opening period when members were allowed to give one-minute speeches. The televised period proved ideal for attacks on Carter administration policies that were short enough for network newscasts to pick up. The Republican speeches so annoyed the Democratic House leaders that for a brief time the leadership moved the one-minute speeches period to the end of the day's business.

A sensitive issue related to the telecasts was member use of the television tapes of the floor proceedings to promote themselves with the folks back home. Playing to the television audience had been one of the arguments raised by opponents of televising the House. The House leadership told members they could tape floor speeches broadcast into their offices and send the tapes to television stations in their districts, so long as they were not put to commercial or political use.

Rep. John B. Anderson, R-Ill. (1961-81), attacked the tapes policy. In a letter to O'Neill in 1979 he charged that the policy allowed the House-controlled system to become "one more incumbent protection device at taxpayers' expense." Anderson's complaint was aimed at a Democratic decision permitting members to use their official expense accounts to buy the broadcast tapes for distribution to local television stations. Some Democrats expressed the same concern.

Senate Television Debate

The Senate had a long tradition of allowing telecasts of committee hearings. In the early 1950s the Kefauver hearings on organized crime and the Army-McCarthy hearings intrigued millions of television viewers. In the 1960s the Foreign Relations Committee chaired by Sen. J. William Fulbright, D-Ark. (1945-74), brought television into his hearings on the Vietnam War.

In the early 1970s, the Senate appeared more inclined to allow broadcast coverage than the House. Among those who endorsed the idea at 1974 hearings before the Joint Committee on Congressional Operations was Sen. Robert Byrd, then the majority whip. Byrd leaned toward a system giving the Senate control over the cameras "to avoid the possibility of media-provoked theatrics."

But two events considerably dampened senators' enthusiasm for television on their side of the Capitol. The first event was the swearing-in ceremony for Vice President Nelson A. Rockefeller in December 1974. The ceremony marked the first time television cameras had been allowed in the Senate chamber. And those who were in the chamber at the time remembered how hot it was under the hastily assembled lights.

The other event came in 1975, when the Senate faced the bitter, divisive issue of settling the outcome of the 1974 New Hampshire Senate election. Republicans offered a resolution calling for broadcast coverage of the debate. Although the resolution was not enacted, it started some members thinking about the potential embarrassment of having such a bitter partisan dispute aired to voters back home.

In 1978 the Senate allowed the National Public Radio network to carry verbatim the lengthy debate on the Panama Canal treaties. But proposals to televise the debate were never acted upon.

A resolution to provide gavel-to-gavel coverage was introduced by Sen. Baker early in the 97th Congress. The Baker measure (S Res 20) proposed that the broadcast be continuous, as in the House, but it left unresolved the question of media or Senate control and when coverage would begin. The Rules Committee had approved the resolution in July 1981.

As soon as Baker brought the resolution before the full Senate, in February 1982, the proposal was threatened with a filibuster by Sen. Russell B. Long, D-La. Long argued that to bring television into the Senate would be "a very great mistake and a net minus to the Senate." He said it would result in senators giving more frequent and longer speeches and would attract senators to the floor when they should be attending committee sessions. A revised TV measure was approved by the Rules Committee in July 1982, and sponsors were optimistic the Senate would approve it.

Rules Committee Chairman Charles McC. Mathias Jr., R-Md., disputed Long's argument, saying, "I do not think we are 100 moths fascinated by the candle of television."

Architect George M. White estimated the cost of the broadcast equipment at between $2.5 million and $3.5 million and the cost of operating and maintaining the system at $500,000 a year.

Methods of Voting in the House and Senate

House

The House has four methods of voting, one or more of which may be used in deciding the outcome of an issue. Occasionally, the House takes several votes on the same proposition, using first simple and then more complex voting methods, before a decision is reached.

Voice Vote. This is the usual method of voting when a proposition is first put to the House, although the other methods also are in order. The presiding officer calls for the "ayes" and then the "noes," members shout in chorus on one side or the other, and the chair decides the result.

Division (Standing) Vote. If the result of a voice vote is in doubt or a further test is desired by any member, a division, or standing vote, may be demanded. In this case, members stand up and are counted, first those for a proposal and then those against. Only vote totals are announced; there is no record of how individual members voted. Few issues are decided at this stage because division votes do not allow enough time for many absent members to reach the floor.

Teller/Recorded Teller Votes. A teller vote may be ordered upon demand of one-fifth of a quorum (20 in the Committee of the Whole and 44 in the House). Traditionally, the chair appointed tellers from opposite sides on a measure and directed members to pass between them up the center aisle to be counted — ayes first, then the nays.

Before 1971 only vote totals were announced on teller votes, but a provision of the Legislative Reorganization Act of 1970 opened the way for "tellers with clerks," or recorded teller votes. This procedure, for the first time in the Committee of the Whole, made it possible to record the votes of individual members. When the change first went into effect, members were required to write their names on red or green cards, which they handed to tellers.

After the electronic voting system was installed in 1973, the recorded teller vote process became known simply as a recorded vote. In January 1979 the quorum required to demand a recorded vote in the Committee of the Whole was raised to 25, or one-fourth of a quorum, instead of one-fifth (20). The one-fifth quorum requirement remained for teller votes and for recorded votes requested when members are sitting as the House.

Yea and Nay Votes. Yeas and nays are ordered by one-fifth of those present. They are not taken in the Committee of the Whole. Before the installation of the electronic voting system, roll calls were a time-consuming process in the 435-member House, with each roll call taking about a half hour. The Speaker still retains the right to call the roll rather than use the electronic voting system.

During roll calls, members are required to vote yea or nay. Members who do not wish to vote may answer "present." The Speaker's name is called only at his own request. He is required to vote only if his vote would be deciding.

The Constitution requires yea-and-nay votes on the question of overriding a veto. Under House rules, the yeas and nays are required automatically whenever a member objects to holding a non-record vote when a quorum is not present.

Senate

Like the House, the Senate uses voice, division (standing) and roll-call votes. It does not employ the teller vote, and it does not have an electronic voting system. Vote totals are seldom made public on division votes; usually only the result is announced.

The Senate seldom follows the House practice of voting on a single proposition by several different methods. Once the result of a vote has been announced, the demand for another type of vote is not in order. When the Senate reconsiders an earlier vote, the same result usually occurs. But on a closely contested issue it gives the Senate an opportunity to change its mind.

Roll calls are easier to obtain in the Senate than in the House. As in the House, they are available upon demand of one-fifth of those present (a minimum of 11 is required), but in practice a senator seldom is denied a roll-call vote if he insists on one. Yeas and nays are required on a vote to override a veto.

Pairs

Pairs are "gentlemen's agreements" that House and Senate members use to cancel out the effect of absences on recorded votes. A member who expects to be absent for a vote pairs off with another member, both of them agreeing not to vote. Pairs are not counted in vote totals, but their names are published in the *Congressional Record*, along with their stands, if known. If the vote is one that requires a two-thirds majority, a pair requires two members favoring the action and one opposed to it.

A *live pair* covers one or several specific issues. A member who would vote "yea" pairs with a member who would vote "nay." Thus both announce their stands. Live pairs may determine the outcome of a vote if a member who is present withholds his vote because he has a pair with one who is absent.

A *general pair* is widely used in the House. No agreement is involved, and the pair does not tie up votes. A member expecting to be absent may notify the House clerk that he wishes to make a general pair. His name is then paired with that of another member desiring a pair, and the list is printed in the Record.

The Committee of the Whole procedure differs in several ways from the parliamentary procedure used when the House of Representatives is not operating as a committee. The Speaker does not preside but appoints a chairman — a member of his own party — to take his place. A quorum consists of 100 members, rather than a majority of the entire House (218 if there are no vacancies). Amendments are debated under the so-called five-minute rule rather than the hour rule. And although the method used is the same, electronic votes taken in the Committee of the Whole are referred to as recorded votes; when taken in the House they are known as roll-call votes. *(Use of electronic voting, box, p. 55)*

The Committee of the Whole debates and amends bills, subject to approval by the full House before a final vote on passage is taken, but it cannot pass them. It cannot itself recommit a bill, although it may report back to the House with a recommendation that the enacting clause be stricken — a parliamentary motion that, if adopted, kills the measure. Recommittal as well as other motions must be voted on in the House rather than in the Committee of the Whole. When such a motion is offered during a floor debate, the Committee of the Whole must interrupt its work and go through the formal step of rising and returning to the House to dispose of the motion. It then reconvenes as the Committee of the Whole.

In a rule change incorporated in January 1983, the only way a rider to an appropriations bill can be offered is for the House to reject a motion to rise out of the Committee of the Whole after all other work on the bill has been completed. If that motion were defeated, one rider could then be offered. The same process would have to occur again before any subsequent riders could be considered.

Role of Floor Managers. House floor action is guided by the legislative committee, or committees, that reported the bill. The committee members occupy seats at tables on either side of the center aisle. Ordinarily, the committee chairman (or someone designated by him) acts as floor manager for the proponents of the bill, while the ranking member of the minority party theoretically leads the opposition, even if he supports the bill. On some House (and Senate) committees, particularly at times when most of the membership generally shares the same perspective on the policies and programs within the committee's jurisdiction, the ranking minority member more often than not will side with the chairman in support of the bill. In such cases, the ranking minority member usually will allocate some of his debate time to members opposing the bill.

Cannon's Procedure describes the floor manager's role: "A chairman directed to report a bill to the House ceases to function individually so far as that measure is concerned and becomes the representative of the committee in charge of the bill. Although he may have opposed the bill or parts of it in committee, he either steps aside and permits the next ranking member of the committee to take charge of the bill on the floor or subordinates his personal views and devotes every effort to securing its consideration and passage in the form in which reported to the House. He is precluded from accepting modifications and is under the obligation of interposing points of order against vulnerable amendments although personally he may approve of them. If for exceptional reasons he deems it necessary to offer an amendment or digress from the instructions under which the bill was reported, he should yield his seat to the next ranking member and explain unequivocally that the action is taken in his individual capacity. . . ."[5]

Knowing the Rules

The penalty for speaking out without knowing just what is involved can be more than acute embarrassment, as a bit of inspired congressional doggerel suggests:

"The Clerk's reading a bill
when an eager young pill
bounces up and moves to amend,
which all comes to naught,
he didn't move when he ought,
and all that he did was offend."

Source: Donald G. Tacheron and Morris K. Udall, *The Job of the Congressman* (Indianapolis: Bobbs-Merrill, 1966), p. 193.

The rule under which the bill is considered provides for a certain number of hours of general debate, to be divided equally between the chairman and ranking minority member of the committee that reported the bill. The chairman controls time for supporters of the bill, the ranking minority member for the opponents. Usually, each of these floor managers opens and closes the debate for his or her side, yielding the rest of the time first to other committee members and then to other representatives who wish to speak. No amendments may be offered during general debate.

Voting on Amendments. At the conclusion of general debate on a bill given an open rule, the measure is read for amendment under the five-minute rule. This constitutes the second reading of the bill. (The first reading occurs when the bill is introduced and assigned to a committee.) The special rule granted by the Rules Committee usually specifies that each part of a bill must be considered in sequential order. The bill may be read paragraph by paragraph, section by section or title by title, in which case amendments are offered to each part as it is read (once the reading of that part is completed, amendments no longer can be offered to it). On occasion, however, the special rule drafted by the Rules Committee may waive the House rule on sequential order and allow the bill to be considered as read and open to amendment at any part. Alternatively, the floor manager may make a unanimous consent request that the bill be open to amendment.

Debate on an amendment is limited to five minutes for supporters and five minutes for opponents, but additional time may be obtained by offering pro forma amendments to "strike out the last word." In contrast to Senate practice, amendments in the House must be germane, not only to the bill but also to the section to which they are offered. *(Germaneness, box, p. 67)*

Committee amendments always are taken up first on the floor, but they may be further amended, as may all amendments, up to the second degree. An amendment to an amendment to an amendment is not in order as this would be an amendment to the third degree. Although such amendments are not permitted, it is common for four

Using the Rules to Obstruct the House

Obstructionist tactics in Congress change with the years. When an abused loophole in the rules is plugged up, ingenious members are able to devise new ones that serve the same purpose.

House members bent on blocking legislation have had to be more imaginative than their colleagues in the Senate, where the filibuster always has been available to those wishing to delay congressional action. Stringent House curbs on debate preclude a filibuster in the Senate mold, and in recent years the House has closed other avenues of delay, for example, by giving the Speaker additional authority aimed at speeding up legislative business and severely curbing the use of quorum calls.

Until the late 1970s the quorum call was one of the most useful delaying devices. A dramatic example, which became the equivalent of a Senate filibuster, occurred on the eve of adjournment of the 1968 session. At issue were bills on legislative reorganization, campaign spending reform and televising the presidential candidates' debates. All three bills failed to win approval before Congress went home.

The stalling began in earnest on Oct. 8 when House Republicans, saying they sought action on the first two reform bills, forced the House to stay in session for more than 32 hours before it passed the television debate bill. When Senate Republicans, also using dilatory tactics, succeeded in killing that measure, a group of House Democrats then employed stalling tactics of their own to hold up adjournment from Oct. 10 to Oct. 14 in an effort to force the Senate to accept the television bill.

On Oct. 8 the House Republicans combined a demand for the full reading of the *Journal*, 33 quorum calls, three roll-call votes and other procedures to delay the day's proceedings for 20 hours before the House was able to consider the television bill. Democrats charged that Republican presidential candidate Richard Nixon did not want to debate his Democratic opponent, Vice President Hubert H. Humphrey, while the Republicans responded that they were concerned about the two reform measures.

During the Oct. 8-9 House session — lasting 32 hours and 17 minutes — there were 37 quorum calls and eight roll-call votes. And in those days, before the advent of electronic voting, a single roll-call vote took between 30 and 45 minutes to complete. According to the Congressional Research Service of the Library of Congress, that session was surpassed in length only twice: by a 48-hour, 25-minute session in 1875 on a civil rights bill, and by a 35-hour, 30-minute session in 1854 on the Kansas-Nebraska bill repealing the Missouri Compromise of 1820.

As seen by the 1968 example, it is much easier for obstruction to succeed near the end of a session when usually there is not enough time to counter repeated delaying tactics. Another example occurred 10 years later, at adjournment time of the 95th Congress. This time, obstructionists employed the "disappearing quorum" to defeat a water projects development bill. Opposed by environmentalists, the bill was hurriedly brought to the floor by its sponsors under a shortcut procedure, known as suspension of the rules, that required a two-thirds vote for passage.

It was the last day of the session, and members already had started to leave for home. The previous roll call had drawn only 11 more votes than were necessary for a quorum (218). Opponents knew the popular water projects bill had overwhelming support in the House. Because their only hope was to prevent a quorum from voting, they mobilized like-minded colleagues to stay away from the chamber. On the final tally, the bill was backed by a 129-31 vote, but this was more than 50 short of a quorum. The House then was forced to adjourn, ending any chance of reviving the water bill.

At other times, dilatory tactics merely delay legislation, presenting scheduling irritations for the leadership. For example, on April 23, 1975, House members opposed to quick action on a Ford administration aid bill for Vietnamese refugees used the one-minute-speeches period at the opening of the day's session, along with demands for roll calls on normally routine motions, to delay the bill's consideration.

These one-minute speeches also gave members an opportunity to vent their frustrations with other aspects of America's Vietnam policy, including the administration's belated evacuation of U.S. and high Vietnamese government personnel from South Vietnam. In all, 26 members used the period to attack the bill and U.S. Southeast Asia policies.

In 1980, on the eve of a July recess, approval of a crucial emergency appropriations bill was in jeopardy because of differences over budget priorities and the eagerness of members to leave town. Conservatives were critical of providing aid to Nicaragua, and there was much opposition to Senate cuts in revenue sharing. It appeared that a delicate compromise could unravel.

At one point Rep. Robert E. Bauman, R-Md. (1973-81), a leading foreign aid opponent, refused to relinquish the floor despite entreaties from Speaker Thomas P. O'Neill Jr., D-Mass. When the presiding officer permitted O'Neill to proceed anyway, Bauman charged the chair's action was based on partisan politics. In a rare move, Bauman appealed the ruling to the full House. Though the rules appeared to support Bauman, the House supported O'Neill, 199-163. Eventually, the pending recess worked to the congressional leaders' advantage. They hinted members would be called back to Washington if the measure was not passed. This convinced lawmakers to stop stalling and clear the bill.

amendments in the first and second degree to be pending at the same time: an amendment to the bill, an amendment to that amendment, a substitute for the original amendment and an amendment to the substitute. They are voted on in the following order, as diagrammed in *Cannon's Procedure.*[6]

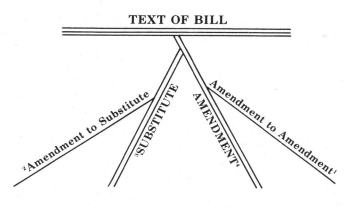

TEXT OF BILL

Amendment to Substitute

"SUBSTITUTE"

"AMENDMENT"

Amendment to Amendment

If the substitute is agreed to, the fourth vote technically is on the amendment as amended by the substitute. In fact, the substitute, if adopted, entirely replaces the original amendment.

Some amendments that are offered are labeled "amendments in the nature of a substitute," which seek to replace the entire text of the bill.

More than one vote may be taken on a given amendment. The Committee of the Whole may first take a voice vote, then move on to standing, teller or recorded votes before finally deciding the question. Amendments adopted in the Committee of the Whole are subject to roll-call votes after the committee rises and the chamber resumes sitting as the full House. Few separate votes actually are taken, and rarely are amendments rejected once they have been adopted. Amendments previously defeated in the Committee of the Whole cannot be offered again at this stage.

The mark of an accomplished floor manager is his ability to get his bill through the House generally intact. In voting on amendments, representatives — at least of the majority party — are under considerable pressure to support the actions of the committee that reported the bill. Expressing the traditional view of the House hierarchy, Cannon gives the following advice to members:

"Generally speaking, and in the absence of convictions to the contrary, members are justified in voting with the committee. Committees are not infallible, but they have had long familiarity with the subject under discussion, and have made an intimate study of the particular bill before the House and after mature deliberation have made formal recommendations and, other considerations being equal, are entitled to support on the floor. *Members should be particularly wary of proponents of amendments disapproved by the committee who station members or employees at the doors to accost members arriving in response to the bells and who have not heard the debate.* It is a questionable practice and should serve to put members on their guard until they have ascertained the committee's point of view." (Cannon's italics).[7]

Under the Legislative Reorganization Act of 1970, 10 minutes of debate are guaranteed on any amendment that has been published in the *Congressional Record* at least one day before it is offered on the floor — even if debate

has been closed on the section of the bill to which the amendment is proposed. Previously, an amendment received no explanation at all if the Committee of the Whole voted to cut off further debate on the bill or on the section to which the amendment applied.

Action by the Full House

When the Committee of the Whole has completed its work, it "rises," according to the House's parliamentary terminology. The Speaker returns to the chair, and the erstwhile chairman of the Committee of the Whole formally reports the bill to the House with or without amendment, in effect announcing that action on the bill has been completed.

If the "previous question" has been ordered — the usual procedure — the full House then votes immediately on amendments reported (adopted) in the Committee of the Whole. (The previous question motion is a device to cut off debate and force a vote on the subject under consideration. Unless it is ordered, the bill would be subject to further debate and amendment. The previous question is not used in the Senate.) Members at this point may demand a roll call on any amendment adopted in the Committee of the Whole. If there are no requests for separate votes on any amendments, the House then approves all amendments en masse by a pro forma voice vote. There is no way to obtain another vote on an amendment rejected in the Committee of the Whole unless it can be incorporated in a recommittal motion.

Once the amendments have been disposed of, the question is on engrossment and third reading (by title only) of the bill. A member opposed to the bill may offer a motion to recommit the measure to the committee that reported it. There are two kinds of recommittal motions: a simple motion to recommit, which kills the bill if it is adopted; and a motion to recommit with instructions, in which case the motion contains language instructing the committee to report the bill back with amendments forthwith, or after a study is completed or by a certain date, etc. Usually, such instructions present one last chance to offer an amendment to the bill. If adopted, the instructions automatically become part of the legislation; the bill is not literally recommitted to the committee that reported it.

The motion to recommit with instructions, on which 10 minutes of debate is allowed under the 1970 act, is frequently used by the minority to present an alternative program. Although recommittal votes seldom succeed, they sometimes provide a better indication of members' views than a vote on final passage. Some members, for instance, may prefer a different approach while generally supporting the purposes of the bill. In such cases, they may vote to recommit but then turn around and vote for the measure on passage. Or, it may be an example of politics coming into play, with a member simply wanting to be recorded on both sides of the bill.

If the recommittal motion fails, the next step is the vote on final passage. After the vote is taken, and the bill is passed, there usually is introduced a pro forma motion to reconsider the final vote. Then proponents offer a counter motion to kill reconsideration — to "lay the motion on the table," thus safeguarding final passage. With that, the bill has been formally passed by the House. While a motion to reconsider is pending, the bill cannot be sent to the Senate.

At this point, the bill officially becomes an "act," although it generally still is referred to as a bill. An engrossed copy of the bill as passed by the House, certified by the clerk of the House, is printed on blue paper and transmitted to the Senate for its consideration.

Alternative House Procedures

The procedures discussed above describe the usual route of a major bill through the House, but certain alternative methods also are available.

Consent Calendar

Members of the House may place on this calendar any bill on the House or Union Calendar that is considered to be non-controversial. Bills on the Consent Calendar normally are called up on the first and third Mondays of each month. On these days, immediately after the reading of the *Journal*, the Speaker directs the clerk to call the bills that have been on the Consent Calendar for at least three legislative days in the order of appearance on that calendar.

When a bill is called for the first time, its consideration may be blocked by the objection of a single member. If objection is made, the bill is carried over on the calendar to the next day when the Consent Calendar is called. If the bill is called for a second time, and there are three objections to it, the bill is stricken from the Consent Calendar. If there are fewer than three objections, the bill is passed without debate. Ordinarily the only amendments considered are those sponsored by the committee that reported the bill.

Official objectors — three from each party — are appointed at the beginning of each Congress to guard against passage of important measures on which there may be substantial opposition or, because of the complexity of

the legislation, a full debate is thought to be necessary. Objectors police the bills on the Consent Calendar and act for absent members.

A bill on the Consent Calendar may be postponed in another way. A member may ask that the measure be passed over "without prejudice." In that case, no objection is recorded against the bill and its status on the Consent Calendar remains unchanged.

A bill stricken from the Consent Calendar remains on the Union or House Calendar.

Suspension of the Rules

This is often a time-saving procedure for passing bills in the House. The wording of the motion, which may be made by any member who is recognized by the Speaker (arrangement for recognition must be made in advance) is: "I move to suspend the rules and pass the bill. . . ." Before it is considered by the House, the motion must be seconded by a majority of the members present, by teller vote if requested. A second is not required if printed copies of the measure brought up under the suspension procedure have been available for one legislative day. Debate is limited to 40 minutes. The motion, usually made by a committee chairman, may not be amended, effectively barring amendments from the floor.

The rules may be suspended only by affirmative vote of two-thirds of the members voting, with a quorum present. If a two-thirds favorable vote is not obtained the bill may be considered later under regular House procedures. In 1979 the House added to its rules a provision providing for cluster voting when numerous bills are considered under the suspension procedure. The Speaker was given the discretion of delaying final votes on suspension bills until all the measures have been debated. The bills

The House's electronic voting system is operated by a member inserting a plastic card into one of several boxes located in the chamber and pressing the proper button to indicate a "yea," "nay" or "present" vote on a roll call.

then may be called up the next day and voted on in rapid succession, without interruption. The Speaker also was given the discretion of shortening the time for each recorded vote from 15 minutes to five minutes.

Suspension of the rules is in order on Mondays and Tuesdays of each week as well as during the last six days of a session, when normally there is a backlog of legislation awaiting House action.

The suspension procedure generally has been reserved for non-controversial bills, although in the late 1970s under Speaker O'Neill House rules were revised to allow greater use of the procedure. Republicans charged that Democrats were abusing the short-cut procedure to push through some complex and controversial legislation without adequate debate or the opportunity to offer amendments. A study made by the Congressional Research Service showed that in the 95th Congress (1977-79) the House considered 449 bills under suspension of the rules compared with 167 in the 90th Congress. Of the 449 considered in the 97th Congress, 31 were rejected — a very large number for a procedure intended only for non-controversial legislation.

The procedure itself by 1978 had become almost as much of an issue as the bills themselves. A major embarrassment to Democrats occurred that year on a suspension vote when a controversial education aid bill backed by President Jimmy Carter as an alternative to tuition tax credits was soundly defeated, 156-218, in part because of members' anger over the plethora of suspension bills. In one week alone in September 1978, 35 bills were considered under suspension.

In reaction to the increased burden placed on members through use of the procedure, the Democratic Caucus in 1979 formalized guidelines that prohibited any bill with an estimated cost of more than $100 million in a single year from being placed on the suspension calendar, unless the Democratic Steering and Policy Committee granted a request from the Speaker to waive the rule.

Nevertheless, some major legislation is passed under suspension because there is substantial bipartisan support for it or an emergency situation warrants it.

Discharge Petition

The discharge petition is a little-used device designed to permit a majority of the House to bring to the floor legislation blocked by a recalcitrant legislative committee or by the Rules Committee.

The modern discharge rule was first adopted in 1910.[8] The existing form of the rule, in use since 1935, enables a majority of the membership — after a complicated series of parliamentary steps — to bring before the House: 1) any public bill that has been before a standing committee of the House for 30 days; or 2) any committee-approved bill that has been before the House Rules Committee for seven legislative days without receiving a special rule for floor debate. In addition, the discharge rule may be used to dislodge from the Rules Committee a special rule for debate on any bill that has been before a standing committee for 30 days — a combination of the first two procedures.

This is how the procedure works: If a bill has been before a legislative committee for 30 days, or the Rules Committee for seven days, any member may file a discharge motion, popularly called a discharge "petition." When 218 members, a majority of the House, have signed the petition, it is placed on the Discharge Calendar where it must remain for seven legislative days before it can be called up. This seven-day "grace period" makes it possible

Electronic Voting

The House began taking votes electronically at the start of the 93rd Congress. The first recorded vote using the system was taken Jan. 31, 1973. The rules require the use of an electronic voting system for quorum calls and all recorded votes unless the Speaker invokes a call of the roll.

Members have 15 minutes to answer quorum calls and recorded votes on legislation and other substantive matters. In some instances where a series of votes is called for — for example, when several bills are brought up under the suspension of the rules procedure and the final votes are postponed until the following day — only five minutes are allowed per vote.

Members are able to vote at any of more than 40 consoles in the House chamber by inserting a plastic card and pressing a button to indicate a yea or nay. Boards installed on the walls of the chamber show instantly how each member voted as well as a running breakdown of votes cast.

The leadership tables on the majority and minority sides of the House floor are equipped with consoles to allow the leadership to see how members have voted.

for the committee, if it chooses, to act on the bill before the discharge petition is considered. On the second and fourth Mondays of each month, except during the last six days of a session, any member who has signed the petition may be recognized to move that the committee be discharged. Debate on the motion is limited to 20 minutes, equally divided between proponents and opponents, and if the motion carries, consideration of the bill becomes a matter of high privilege. The House may consider the measure immediately or place it on one of the calendars.

Although the discharge method is seldom used successfully, the threat of such a move may be used to spur committee action. (Discharge petitions since 1910, box, p. 56)

In 1979 opponents of school busing to achieve racial integration used the discharge procedure to dislodge the House Judiciary Committee from an anti-busing constitutional amendment. It was the first successful use of a discharge petition since 1971 and only the 26th since the procedure was instituted. (Supporters of a constitutional amendment to permit prayer in the public schools had succeeded in 1971 in bringing that issue to the floor for a vote.) But anti-busing supporters, like the school prayer proponents eight years earlier, failed to win approval of their constitutional amendment in the House. The House vote was 209-216, not even a simple majority. (Constitutional amendments need a two-thirds majority to win approval.)

Obviously, not all of the 218 representatives who signed the discharge petition voted for the anti-busing

Discharge Petition

The discharge petition is a little-used House device that enables a majority of representatives to bring to the floor legislation blocked by a legislative committee or the Rules Committee.

The following table shows the frequency with which the discharge petition has been employed between its adoption in 1910 and the close of the 1st session of the 97th Congress in December 1981. Although 26 bills were pried loose from committee by the discharge route and 20 of them ultimately were passed by the House, only two were enacted: the 1938 Fair Labor Standards Act and a 1960 federal pay raise bill.

Congress	Petitions Filed	Bills Discharged	Discharged Bills That Passed House
61 (1909-11)	223	figures not	
62-67 (1911-23)	241	available	
68 (1923-25)	4	1	0
69 (1925-27)	4	0	0
70 (1927-29)	2	0	0
71 (1929-31)	5	0	0
72 (1931-33)	12	1	1
73 (1933-35)	31	1	1
74 (1935-37)	33	2	0
75 (1937-39)	43	3	2
76 (1939-41)	37	2	2
77 (1941-43)	15	1	1
78 (1943-45)	21	3	3
79 (1945-47)	35	1	1
80 (1947-49)	20	1	1
81 (1949-51)	34	3	3
82 (1951-53)	14	0	0
83 (1953-55)	10	1	1
84 (1955-57)	6	0	0
85 (1957-59)	7	1	1
86 (1959-61)	5	1	1
87 (1961-63)	6	0	0
88 (1963-65)	5	0	0
89 (1965-67)	6	1	1
90 (1967-69)	4	0	0
91 (1969-71)	12	1	1
92 (1971-73)	15	1	0
93 (1973-75)	10	0	0
94 (1975-77)	15	0	0
95 (1977-79)	11	0	0
96 (1979-81)	14	1	0
97 (1981-83)	9	0	0
(first session)	0	0	0
Total	909	26	20

amendment. In all, 31 members (14 Democrats and 17 Republicans) who signed the petition later voted against the amendment. The reasons varied; in some cases members said they felt the issue needed to be aired in the House, but that they did not support the constitutional amendment approach. Others said they never expected the petition sponsors to be successful.

In 1980 sponsors of a bill to protect certain exclusive soft drink bottling franchises from antitrust prosecution succeeded in obtaining the necessary 218 signatures on a discharge petition. But before the committee could be discharged from the bill — it was subject to the seven-day layover requirement — the committee went ahead and reported a version of the bill, which subsequently was passed by the House, under suspension of the rules, and enacted into law.

Calendar Wednesday

This is a method for bringing to the House floor a bill that has been blocked by the Rules Committee. Under the procedures, each Wednesday committees may be called in the order in which they appear in Rule 10 of the Standing Rules of the House (that is, alphabetically), for the purpose of bringing up any of their bills on the House or Union Calendars except bills that are privileged. General debate is limited to two hours. Bills called up from the Union Calendar are debated in the Committee of the Whole, with amendments considered under the five-minute rule. Since the Calendar Wednesday procedure requires action to be completed in the same legislative day, it is vulnerable to dilatory action by opponents of the bill in question.

Calendar Wednesday is not observed during the last two weeks of a session and may be dispensed with at other times by a two-thirds vote. In practice, it usually is dispensed with by unanimous consent. Use of this procedure is even more rare than the other alternative methods already listed.

Built-in hindrances make the procedure cumbersome:

● Because the committees must be called in alphabetical order, those at the end of the list may have to wait 15 to 20 weeks before they are reached.

● Many delaying tactics are available to opponents of any bill called up because the procedure requires that it be disposed of in one day.

● If a committee has had one opportunity to call up a bill, it cannot have another bill considered until all other committees have been called.

● Only the chairman is authorized to call up a bill reported by the committee.

Between 1950 and mid-1982, the Calendar Wednesday procedure was used successfully only twice: on Feb. 15, 1950, on the Fair Employment Practices Act, and on May 4, 1960, on the Area Redevelopment Act. It had not even been attempted since 1968.

Other Methods

Special legislative days are set aside twice each month for the consideration of private bills and District of Columbia business.

The so-called "21-day rule," a device under which legislative committees could bring to the floor bills that had been blocked by the Rules Committee, was in force in the House in the 81st (1949-51) and 89th (1965-67) Congresses. The 1965 rule permitted the chairman, or any

Parliamentary Decisions Challenged

The second session of the 96th Congress witnessed an increase in partisanship, particularly in the House. Though not uncommon in election years, some partisan outbursts in 1980 were unusual in that the House presiding officer's procedural rulings were challenged.

Appeals of the chair's rulings are common in the Senate, but seldom made in the House. And extremely rare are requests for recorded votes on appeals. During the 50 years from 1931 until July 1980 there were only six demands for recorded votes on appeals of rulings of the chair. But in a two-month span in 1980 three votes were demanded on the rulings of Speaker Thomas P. O'Neill Jr., D-Mass., and Majority Leader Jim Wright, D-Texas.

With the Democrats holding a comfortable majority, the chair was upheld on all three occasions, although 44 Democrats voted against the chair on one of the votes. The last time a Speaker was overruled by his colleagues was in 1931 when Nicholas Longworth, R-Ohio (1903-13, 1915-31), requested that one of his own rulings be reversed to correct an error.

The 1980 challenges came from two Republicans — Robert E. Bauman, Md. (1973-81), and John M. Ashbrook, Ohio (1961-82).

On July 2, during House action on a fiscal 1980 emergency funding bill, Bauman appealed a ruling that made in order a motion by Speaker O'Neill appropriating foreign aid funds for Nicaragua. The ruling enabled the Speaker's motion to supersede Bauman's own motion denying aid to that country. The House upheld the chair's ruling by tabling Bauman's appeal, 222-140, with two Democrats siding with Bauman.

A second Bauman appeal occurred on July 25 when Majority Leader Wright ruled out of order a resolution by Bud Shuster, R-Pa., asking the Speaker to reinstate one-minute speeches at the beginning of each House meeting. Once again the House voted to table Bauman's appeal. This time the vote was 233-129, with a unified Democratic Party joined by two Republicans. *(One-minute speeches controversy, box on televised sessions, p. 48)*

The Ashbrook appeal took place Aug. 19 during debate on an appropriation bill for the Treasury-Postal Service. Ashbrook proposed an amendment barring the Internal Revenue Service from using funds in the bill to issue rules depriving segregated private schools of their tax-exempt status. A Democrat, Louis Stokes of Ohio offered an objection, maintaining the amendment constituted legislation in an appropriation bill, a violation of House rules. When the chair upheld Stokes' position, Ashbrook demanded a recorded vote on the ruling. On the vote, the chair's ruling was upheld 214-182. (Ironically, Ashbrook's amendment was passed by the House in slightly altered form later the same day.)

Generally, the presiding officer's rulings are based on the advice of the House parliamentarian, who is considered a non-partisan House employee. Such rulings, however, play an important role in shaping legislation. Their impact is never neutral in the sense that procedural decisions favor one side or the other. The parliamentarian's rulings are based on precedents, but skillful selectivity of the precedents, which go back to the first Congress, often can provide the basis for siding with either side of a parliamentary question.

After the August challenge to the chair's ruling, O'Neill sent a letter to the 44 Democrats who defected, saying he was "extremely disappointed to note that you voted against a motion to uphold the ruling of the chair.... It is elementary to our procedural control of the House that the chair be supported by members of our party. That is basic to a parliamentary body. In other countries, if such a vote were lost, the government would fall."

The Republicans, as could be expected, saw the issue differently. "I have a very stern view of appealing a ruling of the chair," said Bauman. "I have often discouraged a member from such an appeal." However, he said the rulings he had appealed were based on "crass politics."

other member of a committee that had favorably reported a bill, to bring to the floor a rule authorizing House action on the bill. The rule then would need to win approval by majority vote just like any other rule.

The procedure was permitted on the second or fourth Monday of the month for legislation on which the Rules Committee had not granted clearance to a bill within 21 calendar days from the date a resolution to call up the bill had been filed by the legislative committee. Discretion remained with the Speaker to recognize a member from the committee. Thus it was highly unlikely, if not impossible, for a bill to be successful under this procedure without leadership approval. (The 1949 rule required the Speaker to recognize a member wishing to call up a 21-day resolution.)

The 21-day rule was employed successfully on eight occasions in the 89th Congress.

Senate Floor Procedures

Although the Senate has an elaborate framework of parliamentary machinery to guide its deliberations, in practice its procedures are far more flexible than those of the House. Almost anything can be done by unanimous consent, and the rules can be suspended by a two-thirds vote.

Bills may be brought to the Senate floor on the call of the calendar (a process described below), or they may be called up through adoption, by majority vote, of a motion to consider a particular measure. A motion to consider a bill is not debatable if it is made during the so-called "morning hour" — the portion of the daily session before 2 p.m. (assuming the Senate meets at noon). After that hour it is subject to debate, which can be limited only by invoking cloture if a senator wishes to engage in a filibuster against the matter. In practice, most major bills are taken up by unanimous consent in accordance with a schedule worked out by the majority and minority leaders.

Unlike the House, the Senate does not consider bills in Committee of the Whole, and it does not set aside a specific period for general debate before the amending process begins.

Once a senator is recognized by the presiding officer, he may speak virtually as long as he likes and on any subject he chooses, unless he violates the rules of the Senate. He may yield temporarily for the consideration of other business, or he may yield to another senator for a question, but he may not parcel out time to other members as is the practice in the House.

Under the rules, no senator is permitted to speak more than twice on the same subject in the same legislative day. However, since each amendment is considered a different subject, this is not an effective limit on debate. Under a rule adopted in 1964, debate is required to be germane for three hours following the morning hour, but this stricture usually is ignored.

The previous question as a device for bringing debate to a close is not used in the Senate. The only bar to unlimited debate (filibusters) in the rules of the Senate is the cloture rule (Rule 22), which requires the assent of three-fifths of the entire Senate membership to cut off debate on regular legislation and a two-thirds majority to invoke cloture on proposals to change the Senate's rules. However, debate is restricted in other ways in certain situations. Some statutes with deadlines for congressional action, such as the 1974 budget act and the 1976 foreign arms sales act, contain provisions that in effect prohibit filibusters and other unlimited dilatory tactics. A section of the arms sales law, for instance, states: "Debate in the Senate on a [arms sales] resolution, and all debatable motions and appeals in connection therewith, shall be limited to not more than 10 hours, to be equally divided between, and controlled by, the majority leader and the minority leader or their designees.... A motion in the Senate to further limit debate on a resolution, debatable motion, or appeal is not debatable." Unanimous consent agreements and tabling motions also restrict debate. *(Cloture rule, p. 62; previous questions, see House procedures, p. 53)*

The Senate could not operate with unlimited debate if senators frequently abused it.

In the past, when a consensus developed that freedom of debate had gone too far, Rule 22 usually was modified. The last change (as of 1982) was made in 1979. *(Changes, p. 62)*

Unanimous Consent Agreements

In practice, unanimous consent agreements are widely used to expedite business. The majority leader, or another member of the leadership, usually initiates the proposal. This may occur before a bill is brought to the floor — a method often employed by Sens. Mike Mansfield, D-Mont. (1953-77), who was majority leader from 1961 to 1977, and Robert C. Byrd, D-W.Va., who held the post from 1977 to 1981 — or after debate on a bill, controversial amendment or motion has gone on for some time.

The majority leader will consult with the minority leader and other interested senators in an effort to work out an agreement on controlling further debate and reaching a final resolution of the issue, sometimes including a specific time for conducting roll calls.

Because a single objection blocks a unanimous consent request, care is taken to protect the rights of all senators and to assure that those who wish to speak, or in some cases offer amendments, will have an opportunity to do so. The majority leader then seeks Senate approval of the arrangement.

With the end of the 1981 congressional session approaching, Majority Leader Howard H. Baker Jr., R-Tenn., was anxious to keep debate moving on the multibillion-dollar fiscal 1982 Defense Department appropriation bill. Hoping to avoid the everyday parliamentary obstacles that can be thrown in the way of a Senate bill, Baker drafted a unanimous consent agreement covering two pending amendments by Sen. Ernest F. Hollings, D-S.C. The agreement called for "a 15-minute roll call on the first Hollings amendment, to be followed immediately, without intervening motion, debate appeal or point of order, by a second vote of 10 minutes duration" on the second amendment. *(Unanimous consent agreements, box, p. 59)*

Senate Amendment Procedure

When a bill is taken up, it is open immediately to virtually unlimited amendment. Committee amendments are taken up first and, like other amendments, may be amended to the second degree. *(See diagram, p. 53)*

Frequently, the Senate by unanimous consent first agrees to the committee amendments en bloc, particularly if the amendments are extensive, and then provides that the bill as amended is to be "considered as an original text for the purpose of further amendment." This facilitates amending the bill from the floor. Substitute amendments are in order, in which case both the committee-approved version of the bill and the substitute are open to amendment at the same time. The text of one bill may be offered as a substitute for another.

Except in the case of general appropriations bills, bills on which cloture has been invoked, concurrent budget resolutions and measures regulated by unanimous consent agreements, amendments need not be germane. *(Germaneness, box, p. 67)*

An amendment may be modified or withdrawn by its sponsor before action has been taken on it. (In the House this requires unanimous consent.) Once adopted, a floor amendment generally is not subject to further amendment unless a motion to reconsider the previous action is approved. Occasionally, a bill's floor manager will agree to accept an amendment on which he has reservations, saying he will "take it to conference." These are likely to die there.

Voting on amendments, politically sensitive ones in particular, sometimes is avoided at all costs. It is possible to defeat an amendment and still not be recorded on it. This is accomplished by voting to table the amendment instead of voting to reject it outright. A member can mask a policy objective or claim he has not taken a position on the

Drafting a Unanimous Consent Agreement

Following are excerpts from the Senate session of March 17, 1982, in which a unanimous consent agreement covering several bills and days of debate was arranged by Sen. Ted Stevens, R-Alaska, the majority whip

Mr. STEVENS. Mr. President, I ask unanimous consent that any roll-call votes ordered today in connection with S. 391 [the Intelligence Identities Protection Act] be postponed to begin back-to-back at 2 p.m. tomorrow, with the first roll-call vote to occur in connection with the [Sen. Bill] Bradley [D-N.J.] amendment No. 1339.

The PRESIDING OFFICER. Without objection, it is so ordered.

Mr. STEVENS. Further, Mr. President, I ask unanimous consent that no additional amendments will be in order to S. 391 tomorrow; that following the final passage of S. 391 or its companion measure, H.R. 4, the Senate proceed to a vote immediately on the [Sen. Gary] Hart [D-Colo.] resolution as just introduced by the distinguished acting minority leader.

The PRESIDING OFFICER. Without objection, it is so ordered.

Mr. STEVENS. Mr. President, I ask unanimous consent that following the disposition of S. 391 or its companion measure, H.R. 4, and the Hart resolution dealing with Libyan oil, the Senate proceed to the consideration of S. 1080, the regulatory reform bill. It is my understanding that it does require unanimous consent in order to displace the television resolution [S Res 20]. Is that correct?

The PRESIDING OFFICER. The Senator is correct.

Mr. STEVENS. I do ask that unanimous consent.

The PRESIDING OFFICER. Without objection, it is so ordered.

Mr. STEVENS. Mr. President, I ask unanimous consent, further, that not earlier than the disposition of S. 1080, or, in any event, not earlier than 1 p.m. March 29, 1982, the Senate resume the consideration of Senate Resolution 20 [to permit Senate sessions to be televised] when the majority leader, after consultation with the minority leader, so indicates.

Mr. [WENDELL H.] FORD [D-KY.]. Mr. President, reserving the right to object — and I do not believe I will object — in order to be sure that I am clear for my side, in the consideration of S. 1080, we hope there will be no votes on Friday with respect to regulatory reform.

Mr. STEVENS. It is my understanding that the majority leader has so indicated, and I state that that is the policy of the majority leadership, that there will be no votes on S. 1080, the regulatory reform bill, on Friday.

Mr. FORD. I have no objection.

The PRESIDING OFFICER. Without objection, it is so ordered.

Mr. STEVENS. Mr. President, I further ask unanimous consent, with respect to the measures on which we have just had unanimous consent, that no call for the regular order serve to take the measure off the floor.

The PRESIDING OFFICER. Without objection, it is so ordered.

Source: U.S., Congress, Senate, *Congressional Record*, daily ed., 97th Cong., 2d sess., March 17, 1981, p. S 2301.

---

amendment. And sometimes an opponent can round up more votes against an amendment by promising a tabling vote. On the other hand, this procedure can prevent sponsors of an amendment from forcing the Senate, or House, to go on record on a particular issue.

The tabling strategy was summed up by Sen. Byrd in 1975, when he was majority leader: "A motion to table is a procedural motion. It obfuscates the issue, and it makes possible an explanation by a Senator to his constituents, if he wishes to do so, that his vote was not on the merits of the issue. He can claim that he might have voted this way or . . . that way, if the Senate had voted up or down on the issue itself. But on a procedural motion, he can state he voted to table the amendment, and he can assign any number of reasons" for doing so.[9]

Pro forma amendments, used in the House to gain additional speaking time, are not offered in the Senate because debate is unlimited anyway.

Voting in the Senate is by voice, division (standing) or roll call. There is no teller vote, and unlike the House the Senate typically uses only one method of voting on a single question. Senate roll-call votes, required when requested by one-fifth of senators present, are easily obtained. *(Description of House, Senate voting procedures, box, p. 50)*

When action on amendments is completed, the bill is ready for engrossment and a third reading (usually by title only), followed by a vote on final passage. A motion to reconsider may be offered by any senator on the winning side, or by anyone who did not vote, within two days of the passage vote. If the bill is passed without a roll-call vote having been taken, any senator may make the motion. In practice, a pro forma motion to reconsider usually is offered at the time the bill is passed in order to nail down the final result. These motions rarely succeed.

Motions to recommit are seldom used in the Senate,

Senate Cloture Attempts, 1917-81...

Between 1917, when Senate Rule 22 was adopted, and the end of 1981, 168 cloture votes were taken; 53 (in **bold type**) were successful.

Cloture efforts through March 7, 1975, required a two-thirds majority vote to win approval. (Figures in the right-hand column through that date are hypothetical: the vote majorities that would have been needed to invoke cloture had Rule 22 required only a three-fifths majority of senators present and voting, as reform advocates wanted. Italic lines show votes that would have succeeded under that standard.) In 1975, Rule 22 was changed so that three-fifths of the full Senate (60 votes) was required for cloture after March 7.

Issue	Date	Vote	Yeas Needed 2/3 Majority	Yeas Needed 3/5 Majority
Versailles Treaty	Nov. 15, 1919	78-16	63	57
Emergency tariff	Feb. 2, 1921	36-35	48	43
Tariff bill	July 7, 1922	45-35	54	48
World Court	Jan. 25, 1926	68-26	63	57
Migratory birds	June 1, 1926	46-33	53	47
Branch banking	Feb. 15, 1927	65-18	56	50
Disabled officers	Feb. 26, 1927	51-36	58	52
Colorado River	Feb. 26, 1927	32-59	61	55
D.C. buildings	Feb. 28, 1927	52-31	56	50
Prohibition Bureau	Feb. 28, 1927	55-27	55	49
Banking Act	Jan. 19, 1933	58-30	59	53
Anti-lynching	Jan. 27, 1938	37-51	59	53
Anti-lynching	Feb. 16, 1938	42-46	59	53
Anti-poll tax	Nov. 23, 1942	37-41	52	47
Anti-poll tax	May 15, 1944	36-44	54	48
Fair Employment Practices Commission	Feb. 9, 1946	48-36	56	50
British loan	May 7, 1946	41-44	55	49
Labor disputes	May 25, 1946	3-77	54	48
Anti-poll tax	July 31, 1946	39-33	48	43
Fair Employment	May 19, 1950	52-32	64*	58*
Fair Employment	July 12, 1950	55-33	64*	58*
Atomic Energy Act	July 26, 1954	44-42	64*	58*
Civil Rights Act	March 10, 1960	42-53	64	57
Amend Rule 22	Sept. 19, 1961	37-43	54	48
Literacy tests	May 9, 1962	43-53	64	58
Literacy tests	May 14, 1962	42-52	63	57
Comsat Act	Aug. 14, 1962	63-27	60	54
Amend Rule 22	Feb. 7, 1963	54-42	64	58
Civil Rights Act	June 10, 1964	71-29	67	60
Legislative reapportionment	Sept. 10, 1964	30-63	62	56
Voting Rights Act	May 25, 1965	70-30	67	60
Right-to-work repeal	Oct. 11, 1965	45-47	62	55
Right-to-work repeal	Feb. 8, 1966	51-48	66	59
Right-to-work repeal	Feb. 10, 1966	50-49	66	59
Civil Rights Act	Sept. 14, 1966	54-42	64	58
Civil Rights Act	Sept. 19, 1966	52-41	62	56
D.C. Home Rule	Oct. 10, 1966	41-37	52	47
Amend Rule 22	Jan. 24, 1967	53-46	66	59
Open Housing	Feb. 20, 1968	55-37	62	55
Open Housing	Feb. 26, 1968	56-36	62	55
Open Housing	March 1, 1968	59-35	63	57
Open Housing	March 4, 1968	65-32	65	58
Fortas Nomination	Oct. 1, 1968	45-43	59	53
Amend Rule 22	Jan. 16, 1969	51-47	66	59
Amend Rule 22	Jan. 28, 1969	50-42	62	55
Electoral College	Sept. 17, 1970	54-36	60	54
Electoral College	Sept. 29, 1970	53-34	58	53
Supersonic transport	Dec. 19, 1970	43-48	61	55
Supersonic transport	Dec. 22, 1970	42-44	58	52
Amend Rule 22	Feb. 18, 1971	48-37	57	51
Amend Rule 22	Feb. 23, 1971	50-36	58	52
Amend Rule 22	March 2, 1971	48-36	56	50
Amend Rule 22	March 9, 1971	55-39	63	57

Issue	Date	Vote	Yeas Needed 2/3 Majority	Yeas Needed 3/5 Majority
Military Draft	June 23, 1971	65-27	62	55
Lockheed Loan	July 26, 1971	42-47	60	54
Lockheed Loan	July 28, 1971	59-39	66	59
Lockheed Loan	July 30, 1971	53-37	60	54
Military Draft	Sept. 21, 1971	61-30	61	55
Rehnquist nomination	Dec. 10, 1971	52-42	63	57
Equal Job Opportunity	Feb. 1, 1972	48-37	57	51
Equal Job Opportunity	Feb. 3, 1972	53-35	59	53
Equal Job Opportunity	Feb. 22, 1972	71-23	63	57
U.S.-Soviet Arms Pact	Sept. 14, 1972	76-15	61	55
Consumer Agency	Sept. 29, 1972	47-29	51	46
Consumer Agency	Oct. 3, 1972	55-32	58	53
Consumer Agency	Oct. 5, 1972	52-30	55	49
School Busing	Oct. 10, 1972	45-37	55	49
School Busing	Oct. 11, 1972	49-39	59	53
School Busing	Oct. 12, 1972	49-38	58	53
Voter Registration	April 30, 1973	56-31	58	53
Voter Registration	May 3, 1973	60-34	63	57
Voter Registration	May 9, 1973	67-32	66	59
Public Campaign Financing	Dec. 2, 1973	47-33	54	48
Public Campaign Financing	Dec. 3, 1973	49-39	59	53
Rhodesian Chrome Ore	Dec. 11, 1973	59-35	63	57
Rhodesian Chrome Ore	Dec. 13, 1973	62-33	64	57
Legal Services Program	Dec. 13, 1973	60-36	64	58
Legal Services Program	Dec. 14, 1973	56-29	57	51
Rhodesian Chrome Ore	Dec. 18, 1973	63-26	60	54
Legal Services Program	Jan. 30, 1974	68-29	65	58
Genocide Treaty	Feb. 5, 1974	55-36	61	55
Genocide Treaty	Feb. 6, 1974	55-38	62	56
Government Pay Raise	March 6, 1974	67-31	66	59
Public Campaign Financing	April 4, 1974	60-36	64	58
Public Campaign Financing	April 9, 1974	64-30	63	57
Public Debt Ceiling	June 19, 1974	50-43	62	56
Public Debt Ceiling	June 19, 1974	45-48	62	56
Public Debt Ceiling	June 26, 1974	48-50	66	59
Consumer Agency	July 30, 1974	56-42	66	59
Consumer Agency	Aug. 1, 1974	59-39	66	59
Consumer Agency	Aug. 20, 1974	59-35	63	57
Consumer Agency	Sept. 19, 1974	64-34	66	59
Export-Import Bank	Dec. 3, 1974	51-39	60	54
Export-Import Bank	Dec. 4, 1974	48-44	62	55

...53 of 168 Votes Were Successful

Issue	Date	Vote	Yeas Needed 2/3 Majority	Yeas Needed 3/5 Majority
Trade Reform	Dec. 13, 1974	71-19	60	54
Fiscal 1975 Supplemental Funds	Dec. 4, 1974	56-27	56	50
Export-Import Bank	Dec. 14, 1974	49-35	56	50
Export-Import Bank	Dec. 16, 1974	54-34	59	53
Social Services Programs	Dec. 17, 1974	70-23	62	56
Tax Law Changes	Dec. 17, 1974	67-25	62	55
Rail Reorganization Act	Feb. 26, 1975	86-8	63	57
Armed Rule 22	March 5, 1975	73-21	63	57
Amend Rule 22	March 7, 1975	73-21	63	57
Tax Reduction	March 20, 1975	59-38		60
Tax Reduction	March 21, 1975	83-13		60
Agency for Consumer Advocacy	May 13, 1975	71-27		60
Senate Staffing	June 11, 1975	77-19	64**	
New Hampshire Senate Seat	June 24, 1975	57-39		60
New Hampshire Senate Seat	June 25, 1975	56-41		60
New Hampshire Senate Seat	June 26, 1975	54-40		60
New Hampshire Senate Seat	July 8, 1975	57-38		60
New Hampshire Senate Seat	July 9, 1975	57-38		60
New Hampshire Senate Seat	July 10, 1975	54-38		60
Voting Rights Act	July 2, 1975	72-19		60
Voting Rights Act	July 23, 1975	76-20		60
Oil Price Decontrol	July 30, 1975	54-38		60
Labor-HEW Appropriations	Sept. 23, 1975	46-48		60
Labor-HEW Appropriations	Sept. 24, 1975	64-33		60
Common-Site Picketing	Nov. 11, 1975	66-30		60
Common-Site Picketing	Nov. 14, 1975	58-31		60
Common-Site Picketing	Nov. 18, 1975	62-37		60
Rail Reorganization	Dec. 4, 1975	61-27		60
New York City Aid	Dec. 5, 1975	70-27		60
Rice Production Act	Feb. 3, 1976	70-19		60
Antitrust Amendments	June 3, 1976	67-22		60
Antitrust Amendments	Aug. 31, 1976	63-27		60
Civil Rights Attorneys' Fees	Sept. 23, 1976	63-26		60
Draft Resisters Pardons	Jan. 24, 1977	53-43		60
Campaign Financing	July 29, 1977	49-45		60
Campaign Financing	Aug. 1, 1977	47-46		60
Campaign Financing	Aug. 2, 1977	52-46		60
Natural Gas Pricing	Sept. 26, 1977	77-17		60
Labor Law Revision	June 7, 1978	42-47		60
Labor Law Revision	June 8, 1978	49-41		60
Labor Law Revision	June 13, 1978	54-43		60
Labor Law Revision	June 14, 1978	58-41		60
Labor Law Revision	June 15, 1978	58-39		60
Labor Law Revision	June 22, 1978	53-45		60
Revenue Act of 1978	Oct. 9, 1978	62-28		60
Energy Taxes	Oct. 14, 1978	71-13		60
Windfall Profits Tax	Dec. 12, 1979	53-46		60
Windfall Profits Tax	Dec. 13, 1979	56-40		60
Windfall Profits Tax	Dec. 14, 1979	56-39		60
Windfall Profits Tax	Dec. 17, 1979	84-1		60
Lubbers Nomination	April 21, 1980	46-60		60
Lubbers Nomination	April 22, 1980	62-34		60
Rights of Institutionalized	April 28, 1980	44-39		60
Rights of Institutionalized	April 29, 1980	56-34		60
Rights of Institutionalized	April 30, 1980	53-35		60
Rights of Institutionalized	May 1, 1980	60-34		60
Bottlers' Antitrust Immunity	May 15, 1980	86-6		60
Draft Registration Funding	June 10, 1980	62-32		60
Zimmerman Nomination	Aug. 1, 1980	51-35		60
Zimmerman Nomination	Aug. 4, 1980	45-31		60
Zimmerman Nomination	Aug. 5, 1980	63-31		60
Alaska Lands	Aug. 18, 1980	63-25		60
Vessel Tonnage/Strip Mining	Aug. 2, 1980	61-32		60
Fair Housing Amendments	Dec. 3, 1980	51-39		60
Fair Housing Amendments	Dec. 4, 1980	62-32		60
Fair Housing Amendments	Dec. 9, 1980	54-43		60
Breyer Nomination	Dec. 9, 1980	68-28		60
Justice Department Authorization	July 10, 1981	38-48		60
Justice Department Authorization	July 13, 1981	54-32		60
Justice Department Authorization	July 29, 1981	59-37		60
Justice Department Authorization	Sept. 10, 1981	57-33		60
Justice Department Authorization	Sept. 16, 1981	61-36		60
Justice Department Authorization	Dec. 10, 1981	64-35		60
State, Justice, Commerce Judiciary Appropriations	Dec. 11, 1981	59-35		60

* Between 1949 and 1959, the cloture rule required a two-thirds majority of the Senate membership, rather than two-thirds of senators who voted.

** In 1975, Rule 22 was changed to require a three-fifths majority of the Senate membership for cloture except for changes in Senate rules, in which a two-thirds majority of senators voting still would be required.

partly because the amending process is so much more flexible than it is in the House.

Alternative Senate Procedures

Because the normal Senate procedures are so flexible, there is less need than in the House for alternative methods of bringing bills to the floor. In the Senate, bills reported by committee usually can be taken up without difficulty. Legislative obstruction is more likely to occur on the floor in the form of a filibuster.

Bills that have been reported may be taken up on the call of the calendar, which is used for non-controversial legislation similar to bills on the Consent Calendar in the House. Although the Senate calendar may be called following the conclusion of morning business on any day and is privileged on Mondays, it usually is called only once or twice a month. When the calendar is called, bills on which there are no objections are taken up in order, and each senator is limited to five minutes' debate on each bill. If objection is raised, the bill either is passed over or, upon the adoption of a motion, considered. If the Senate votes to consider the bill, the five-minute rule no longer applies.

Under the Senate's discharge rule, any senator during the morning hour may offer a motion to discharge a committee from further consideration of a bill. The motion must lie over for one legislative day. It then may be brought up; a simple majority vote is sufficient to discharge the committee. This procedure is rarely used. A more common method of forcing action on a measure is by offering it as a floor amendment to a pending bill.

Except in the aforementioned cases, there is no Senate rule requiring amendments to be germane to the bill to which they are offered. Thus, this offers an easy way to bring controversial legislation to the floor.

An outstanding example occurred in 1960 when the Senate leadership made good on a promise to act on civil rights legislation, although no bill had been reported by the Judiciary Committee. It did so by calling up a minor House-passed bill to which civil rights amendments were added. In 1965 Sen. Everett McKinley Dirksen, R-Ill. (1951-69), brought to the floor a minor sports bill and substituted a proposed constitutional amendment on state legislative apportionment that had been blocked by the Judiciary Committee.

The prohibition on non-germane amendments, or riders, to appropriation bills may be suspended upon adoption by a two-thirds majority vote of a motion to permit consideration of the rider. Senate rules also require one day's notice, in writing, to the Senate of the sponsor's intention. However, when the House decides to open its doors to non-germane amendments, as occurred in the 1970s with the plethora of anti-abortion proposals, the Senate may also.

Tax legislation frequently is subject to non-germane riders for a special reason: the Constitution requires revenue measures to originate in the House, which means in the Ways and Means Committee. The Senate is restricted to amending House-passed tax bills. The Senate does not load a bill with unrelated amendments as a regular practice, but when it does, usually at the end of a session, the results can be spectacular and often are dubbed "Christmas tree bills." *(Non-germane amendments, box, p. 67)*

In 1977 a major Social Security financing bill was passed by the House and sent to the Senate Finance Committee, chaired by Russell B. Long, D-La. His committee proceeded to attach several non-germane welfare provisions from another bill after it became apparent that the welfare measure would not be enacted. Among those provisions was one authorizing special work projects on an experimental basis — a pet project of Long's. When the bill reached the full Senate, other riders were added, including a proposal opposed by President Carter providing tax credits against college tuition expenses. The final bill, cleared on the last day of the session, included the Finance Committee's welfare provisions but not the tuition tax credits.

In 1978 a $19 billion tax cut bill was in jeopardy in the Senate because a host of expensive non-germane amendments had been introduced. But this time Majority Leader Byrd offered a cloture motion, which the Senate adopted. Under cloture, non-germane amendments are out of order. (The cloture rule is discussed below.)

Senate riders sometimes are the result of logrolling, sometimes are accepted out of courtesy to the sponsoring senator who has a strong interest in the proposal, and sometimes are approved simply because they are popular but with the knowledge that they quietly will be dropped in conference later.

Another method of bypassing Senate committees also is available. Senate rules provide that House- or Senate-passed bills may be placed directly on the Senate calendar without being referred to committee. This method was used to keep the civil rights bills of 1957 and 1964 out of the hostile Senate Judiciary Committee.

Senate Cloture Rule

A unique characteristic of the Senate is the right of members to extended — virtually unlimited — debate. Continuing debate designed to prevent Senate passage of a bill is known as a filibuster. Even the threat of a filibuster can be effective in deterring action on legislation.

Rule 22. The Senate for many years has had a rule by which it can end filibusters, but until the early 1970s the rule rarely was used successfully, and even then it remained a difficult instrument to employ. That method is known as the cloture rule — Senate Rule 22.

From 1917, when it was established, until 1975, Rule 22 provided that a filibuster could be stopped by a two-thirds majority vote. For most of that period, this meant two-thirds of the senators present and voting, but during some years the rule was strengthened to require a two-thirds vote of the full Senate. Once cloture has been invoked, the filibuster is ended. *(Cloture votes, box, p. 60)*

The cloture rule was revised in 1975 to make it easier to cut off filibusters. The vote needed to approve a cloture resolution was reduced to a three-fifths majority of the Senate membership — 60 votes if there are no vacancies — instead of two-thirds of senators present and voting (except for measures proposing to change the standing rules of the Senate, where the two-thirds majority still is required to end a filibuster).

A cloture vote is taken two days after a cloture motion has been filed by 16 senators. Once a cloture motion is adopted, each senator is limited to one hour of debate on the bill and on all motions and amendments affecting it. No new amendments may be offered except by unanimous consent. Only those amendments formally before the Senate when cloture was invoked may be considered. Amendments that are not germane to the pending business and amendments and motions clearly designed to delay action are out of order.

Changes in the Cloture Rule. The Senate had

adopted Rule 22 in 1917 following a furor over a filibuster against President Woodrow Wilson's proposal, before America entered World War I, to arm U.S. merchant ships against the German submarine menace. In its 1917 form, Rule 22 required two-thirds of the senators present and voting to invoke cloture.

In 1949, when the Truman administration was seeking enactment of a civil rights measure, the rule was changed to require two-thirds of the entire Senate membership to invoke cloture, but it allowed cloture to operate on all pending business or motions, except on motions to change Senate rules.

In 1959 the rule was changed again, largely at the instigation of Majority Leader Lyndon B. Johnson, D-Texas (1949-61). Under the 1959 rule, the cloture requirement was returned to two-thirds of those present and voting, but this time it applied to all legislative action including motions to change the Senate rules. At the same time, however, language was added to Senate Rule 32 (now Rule 5) to specify that: "The rules of the Senate shall continue from one Congress to the next unless they are changed as provided in these rules."

The language added to Rule 32 in 1959 was aimed at a key question with which the Senate had wrestled for years: Was the Senate, because one-third of its membership is elected every two years, a continuing body that should operate under rules carried over from Congress to Congress, or should it be able to adopt new rules by general parliamentary procedure — by majority vote — at the beginning of each Congress? The House, all of whose members are elected every two years, adopts its rules by majority vote at the beginning of each Congress. Proposed rules changes, if the Senate is considered a continuing body, can be talked to death unless two-thirds of the entire membership supports a change and votes for cloture. If the Senate is considered a new body after every election, a filibuster can be stopped by majority vote at the beginning of a new Congress, making it much easier for proposed changes in the rules to be voted on and adopted.

The new language in Rule 32 buttressed the position of those who maintained that the Senate is a continuing body, but opponents of the filibuster never conceded the point. For 16 years they tried without success to make it easier to cut off filibusters. Attempts to change the rule were made at the beginning of every Congress between the 86th and the 94th, except the 93rd in 1973, but all efforts were thwarted by the filibuster itself until 1975.

Proponents of a rules change renewed their effort in 1975 with a proposal to require a three-fifths majority of senators present and voting to invoke cloture. A compromise finally was reached in March to require a three-fifths majority of the entire Senate membership, except for proposals to change the rules.

Between 1917 and the 1975 modification of Rule 22, only 24 of the 103 cloture votes taken were successful.

A further change in the rule was made in 1979 after senators found ways to continue to bottle up legislation despite the 1975 change. The Senate imposed a 100-hour cap on all action on a bill once cloture has been invoked and deadlines for submitting proposed amendments. The 100-hour limit included the time spent on all types of procedural motions and voting on amendments as well as on debate. Before the change, Rule 22 had applied only to further debate on a bill; it was powerless to stop dilatory tactics involving procedural motions and requests for roll calls. The change that was made in 1979 effectively cur-

tailed this practice, which was referred to as the post-cloture filibuster.

Action in Second Chamber

After a bill has been passed by one house, an engrossed copy is transmitted to the other chamber.

When the Senate receives a House-passed bill, the measure usually is referred to the committee having jurisdiction. Frequently, that committee already is considering the same legislation. On proposals initiated by the executive branch, identical legislation (called companion bills) normally is submitted to the House and Senate.

On rare occasions a House-passed bill is referred directly to the Senate calendar.

A bill passed by the Senate and transmitted to the House usually goes to committee, unless a House bill on the same subject already has been reported from committee and placed on the calendar.

Under normal procedure, therefore, a bill passed by one chamber and transmitted to the other is referred to the appropriate committee, from which it must follow the same route to passage as a bill originating in that chamber.

Amendments may be offered at both the committee and floor action stages, and the bill as it emerges from the second chamber may differ significantly (even radically) from the version passed by the first. A frequently used procedure when this occurs — or even when the differences are minor — is for the chamber that acts last to bring up the other chamber's bill and substitute its own version (replacing the text of the other chamber's bill), thus retaining only the latter's bill number. That numbered bill, containing both the House and Senate versions, then is sent to a conference committee to resolve all differences.

This normally is a routine step to expedite conference action. But the way it is arranged is a good example of parliamentary legalese. Here is an example, as published in the Daily Digest of the *Congressional Record* for July 16, 1981: "By a yea-and-nay vote of 354 yeas to 63 nays, the House passed HR 3519, the Department of Defense Authorization Act for fiscal year 1982. Subsequently, this passage was vacated and S 815, a similar Senate-passed bill, was passed in lieu, after being amended to contain the language of the House-passed bill. . . . The House then insisted on its amendment to S 815, and asked for a conference." The Digest then listed the House conferees appointed to negotiate with the Senate.

Whenever House and Senate versions are not identical, the differences must be reconciled before the measure can be sent to the president.

When a bill is passed in identical form by both the House and Senate, no further legislative action is required. But this is seldom the case for major legislation.

If the second house has made changes in the bill, it may return it to the chamber of origin, which then has the option of accepting the second chamber's amendments, accepting them with further amendments or disagreeing to the other version and requesting a House-Senate conference. Or the second house itself may request a conference. The chamber must have possession of the "papers" — the engrossed bill, engrossed amendments and messages of transmittal — to request a conference committee. If the amendments are of a minor or non-controversial nature, they usually are agreed to without a conference.

Recorded Votes: 1947-81

The 95th Congress (1977-79) took 2,691 recorded votes, the highest number for an entire Congress. The high for a single year was in 1978 when 1,350 recorded votes were taken. That year also was the high mark for recorded votes in the House — 834. The high for the Senate was 688 recorded votes in 1976. Following is a list of the total number of votes taken each year from 1947 through 1981.

Year	House	Senate	Total
1981	353	483	836
1980	604	531	1,135
1979	672	497	1,169
1978	834	516	1,350
1977	706	635	1,341
1976	661	688	1,349
1975	612	602	1,214
1974	537	544	1,081
1973	541*	594	1,135
1972	329	532	861
1971	320**	423	743
1970	266	422	688
1969	177	245	422
1968	233	281	514
1967	245	315	560
1966	193	235	428
1965	201	258	459
1964	113	305	418
1963	119	229	348
1962	124	224	348
1961	116	204	320
1960	93	207	300
1959	87	215	302
1958	93	200	293
1957	100	107	207
1956	73	130	203
1955	76	87	163
1954	76	171	247
1953	71	89	160
1952	72	129	201
1951	109	202	311
1950	154	229	383
1949	121	227	348
1948	79	189	268
1947	84	138	222

 * Electronic voting in the House began Jan. 31, 1973.
** Recorded teller votes in the Committee of the Whole first authorized at the start of the 1st session of the 92nd Congress, Jan. 21, 1971.

Major amendments made in one chamber sometimes are accepted by the other to avoid further floor action that might jeopardize the bill. That occurred on the Alaska lands bill in the post-election second session of the 96th Congress. Democratic sponsors of the House-passed bill, facing the political realities of the Republican election landslide that November, grudgingly accepted the less-environmentally-protective Senate version rather than risk a conference version or perhaps no bill at all.

Several rules changes adopted in the 1970s made it possible to get a separate House vote, upon the request of any member, on non-germane amendments added by the Senate to a House-passed bill.

Conference Committee Action

Sen. Joel Bennett "Champ" Clark, D-Mo. (1933-45), once introduced a resolution providing that "all bills and resolutions shall be read twice and, without debate, referred to conference." He was joking, of course, but his proposal highlights the crucial role of conference committee negotiations in drafting the final form of complex and often controversial legislation.

As noted, minor legislation usually does not go to conference. Where one house makes few changes in a bill passed by the other chamber, the house that passed the bill initially usually will agree to the changes and clear the bill for the president's signature. But seldom does legislation of any consequence or controversy escape the need for a conference. Over one-quarter of all public bills enacted during the 96th Congress — including all of the annual appropriations bills — were products of conference deliberations. Many other bills that were not enacted also ended up in conference committees.[10]

Calling a Conference

Either chamber can request a conference once both have considered the same legislation. Generally, the chamber that approved the legislation first will disagree to the amendments made by the second body and request that a conference be convened. Sometimes, however, the second body will ask for a conference immediately after it has passed the legislation, assuming that the other chamber will not accept its amendments. *(See also The Committee System chapter, box, p. 83)*

A conference cannot take place until both chambers formally agree that it be held. The Senate usually requests or agrees to a conference by unanimous consent. In the House this action generally is taken by unanimous consent, by motion or by adoption by majority vote of a rule from the Rules Committee providing for a conference on a particular bill. Before 1965 the House could bypass the Rules Committee only by unanimous consent or by suspension of the rules, for which a two-thirds majority is required. Since 1965 it has been possible to send a bill to conference by majority vote — without recourse to the Rules Committee — if the committee with jurisdiction over the bill approves.

Selection of Conferees

The selection of conferees, who formally are called "managers" of the bill, in the past often caused as much controversy and criticism as the actions they took on legislation.

The two chambers have different rules for selecting conferees, but in practice both follow similar procedures. Senate rules allow the chamber as a whole to elect conferees, but the body rarely does so. The common practice is for the presiding officer to appoint conferees on the recommendation of the chairman of the committee having jurisdiction over the legislation.

House rules grant the Speaker the right to appoint conferees, but he usually does so only after consultation with the appropriate committee chairman or chairmen.

Each house's delegation to a conference can range in size from three to an unlimited number, depending on the length and complexity of the legislation involved. On the massive 1981 omnibus budget reconciliation bill, there were more than 250 conferees from the two houses. This was an exception made necessary by the budget cuts, which reached almost all agencies of government and thus involved almost all House and Senate committees. (Most of the 250 conferees dealt with only a part of the bill.)

There may be five senators and three representatives on a conference committee, or the reverse (although the Senate usually sends larger groups than the House). But whatever the size, a majority in each delegation must be from the majority party in the chamber. Each delegation votes as a unit on issues in dispute, with the majority position in the delegation determining how the whole delegation will vote in negotiations with its counterpart.

Seniority ordinarily governs the selection of conferees, but it is quite common today for junior members in each chamber to be named conferees. On a major bill, the chairman of the committee that handled the legislation usually selects himself, the ranking minority member — the most senior member on the committee from the minority party — and other senior members of the committee. Where a subcommittee has exercised major responsibility for a bill, its senior members may be chosen. Only rarely will a conferee be appointed who is not a member of the committee that originally worked on the bill.

Few legislative committees have hard and fast rules guiding the chairman on his selection of conferees, although most chairmen consult with and take the advice of the ranking minority member in choosing conferees from the minority party. The lack of guidance frequently has led to charges that sometimes committee chairmen stack conferences with members favoring their own positions rather than the will of the chamber.[11]

There also is the question of whether conferees are likely to uphold their chamber's position on key points in conference deliberations. Precedent in both the House and the Senate indicates that conferees are expected to support the legislative positions of the chamber they represent. The Legislative Reorganization Act of 1946 stipulated that conferees must have demonstrated support for the bill in the form it was passed by their chamber, but this provision is difficult to enforce.

In an effort to ensure that its conferees would uphold its position, the House in 1974 modified its rules on conferee selection. The revised rule said that in making appointments to conferences, "the Speaker shall appoint no less than a majority of members who generally supported the House position as determined by the Speaker."

Instructing Conferees

Either chamber may try to enforce its will by instructing its conferees on how to vote when they go to conference, but the conferees are not obligated by the rules to follow

Open Conferences Have Become the Rule

House-Senate conference committees, which traditionally carried on their legislative work in secret, began to open their doors to the public in the mid-1970s. Before then, conferees almost always met privately to forge the concessions and compromises that blended differing House and Senate versions into a single bill.

Beginning in the early 1970s, Congress came under increasing pressure to admit the press and public to more of its proceedings. In 1974 12 conferences voluntarily opened their sessions. A rules change to require open conferences was adopted by the House in January 1975. The new rule required open sessions unless a majority of either chamber's conferees voted in public to close a meeting. Senate Democrats and Republicans in caucus endorsed the change, and the Senate formally approved it in November 1975.

In 1977 the House amended its rules to require open conference meetings unless the full House voted to hold conferences in secret session. Since that time most conferences, except those dealing with national security legislation, have remained open. The Intelligence Committee is exempt from the rule.

Some members, aides and lobbyists had feared that the openness might lead some conferees to make long speeches explaining their actions, while others would hold out stubbornly on issues of particular interest to their constituents.

Open conferences were an issue as far back as the first session of Congress in 1789. The first conference, on import and tonnage legislation, was held in open session. Members who were not conferees wandered in and out of the meeting room, and the Senate finally had to adjourn for the day because its members, distracted by the conferees, were paying little attention to regular business. The next open conference was not recorded until 1911.

While their advocates have argued that open conferences make conferees more accountable to their chamber and the public, opponents questioned how openly conference decisions really are made.

"Sunshine laws kid the public," said Rep. Richard Bolling, D-Mo., in 1975. "They imply a total openness and there never will be." Bolling, a chief advocate of institutional change in the House and an author of several books on Congress, maintained that openness was healthy. But he cautioned that some compromises and accommodations have to be made in secret if certain types of legislation are to win enactment.

the instructions. Nevertheless, efforts by members to instruct conferees sometimes does reflect the degree of support for their chamber's position on major provisions or amendments. Votes to instruct may act as warnings that conferees better not stray too far from the language adopted by the chamber in the disputed provision or amendment.

In seeking to instruct House conferees on the fiscal 1982 Defense Department appropriations bill, Rep. Marge Roukema, R-N.J., noted that although such instructions were not binding, "they do put the full moral suasion of the House behind its own committee's work." Her motion was intended to strengthen the hand of the House in bargaining with the Senate by helping "the conferees make a very strong case for supporting these carefully calculated spending levels." The House accepted her motion by voice vote.

A year earlier, in 1980, divisions on defense spending within the House were reflected in a motion to instruct conferees on the first budget resolution for fiscal 1981. Republicans and conservative Democrats succeeded in having House conferees instructed to accept a level of defense spending ($153.7 billion) opposed by President Carter, Speaker O'Neill and liberal House Democrats. This occurred after the House had rejected, 123-165, a motion to table, or kill, the "instructions" to conferees.

In 1974 the House on three separate occasions instructed conferees on that year's elementary and secondary education bill to insist on the House language limiting school busing for the purpose of achieving racial integration. The House conferees nevertheless agreed, with some modifications, to the much weaker Senate version.

Authority of Conferees

The authority given House and Senate conferees theoretically is limited to matters in disagreement between the two chambers. They are not authorized to delete provisions or language agreed to by both the Senate and the House or to draft entirely new provisions. When the disagreement involves numbers, such as the level of funding in appropriations bills, conferees are supposed to stay within the amounts proposed by the two houses.

In practice, however, the conferees have wide latitude, except where the matters in disagreement are very specific. In considering legislation on the floor, if one house deletes the entire contents of its bill (in parliamentary terminology: "striking out everything after the enacting clause") — and inserts a substitute version approved by the other house, the entire subject technically is in disagreement, and the conferees may draft an entirely new bill if they choose to do so. In such a case, the Legislative Reorganization Act of 1946 stipulates that they may not include in the conference version of the bill (technically, their changes are contained in a conference report until the report is approved by each house) "matter not committed to them by either house." But they may include any "matter which is a germane modification of subjects in disagreement."

The Legislative Reorganization Act of 1970 reinforced this provision. It amended House rules to provide that any language dealing with "a specific additional topic, question, issue or proposition" not approved by either chamber before the bill was sent to conference "shall not constitute a germane modification of the matter in disagreement." It also forbade House conferees to modify any topic beyond the scope of the differing versions of the bill sent to conference.

Conference Bargaining

Some of the hardest bargaining in the entire legislative process takes place in conference committees, and frequently the conference takes days and even weeks. Conferences on complex, multibillion-dollar appropriation bills sometimes are particularly drawn out.

In conference, conferees attempt to reconcile their differences, but generally they try to grant concessions only insofar as they remain confident the chamber they represent will accept the compromises. Sometimes, on particularly sensitive political issues, this is not possible. Unwanted amendments that were hard to oppose publicly on the floor may be quietly weeded out. The threat of a Senate filibuster on the conference version may influence House conferees' deliberations. Time also may be a factor, especially at the end of a Congress when delay may cause a bill to die in conference.

If the conferees find they are unable to reach agreement, they may return to their respective chambers for instructions. Or they may simply report their failure to reach agreement to the parent chamber and allow the full House or Senate to act as it wishes.

Under the rules, House conferees may be instructed or discharged and replaced by new conferees if they fail to reach agreement within 20 calendar days (or within 36 hours of their appointment during the last six days of a session). This rule, adopted in 1931, is rarely invoked.

The Conference Report

When the conferees have reached agreement on a bill, conference committee staff write a conference report indicating changes made in the bill and explaining each side's actions. One or more of the amendments in the House or Senate version may be "reported in disagreement." These amendments are acted upon separately following floor action on the conference report.

The 1970 Reorganization Act prohibited House conferees from agreeing to non-germane Senate amendments unless authorized to do so by a vote of the House. The House had often been forced to vote on the bill as a whole, with members having to choose whether to accept the measure with the non-germane amendments or reject the entire bill. The 1970 change applied the same rules to non-germane Senate amendments as were already applicable to legislative amendments offered to appropriation bills. In practice, conferees usually report such amendments in disagreement and move for a House vote on accepting them once the conference report itself is approved by the House. Each amendment in disagreement must be voted upon separately.

The conference report must be signed in duplicate by a majority of conferees from each chamber and submitted in document form to each house for approval. Minority reports are not permitted. Traditionally, the conference report was printed only in the House, together with an explanation by the House conferees, but under the 1970 act an explanatory statement has to be prepared jointly by the House and Senate conferees. The conference report is supposed to be printed in the Senate as well as in the House, but this requirement frequently is waived by unanimous consent. The report always is published in the *Congressional Record* when each chamber considers the conference version of the bill.

Once a conference committee completes its work, the House may send the report to the Rules Committee before

Non-germane Amendments: Potent Policy Tool

A legislative custom practiced at the end of almost every congressional session is the introduction of the so-called "Christmas tree bill." Although the term often is used disparagingly, even in Congress, most members are devoted followers of the custom. Enactment of these bills often comes as Congress is preparing to adjourn for Christmas.

A Christmas tree bill usually is a minor House-passed measure onto which the Senate has attached a variety of non-germane special-interest amendments, often dealing with special tax or trade treatment. One of the most famous bills of that type was passed in 1966, when Sen. Russell B. Long, D-La., was in his second year as chairman of the Finance Committee. The bill's original purpose was to help the United States solve its balance-of-payments difficulties, but Long's committee transformed it into a gem of legislative logrolling and congressional accommodation aiding, among others, presidential candidates, the mineral ore industry, large investors, hearse owners and Scotch whisky importers.

Artful Rider Writing

Non-germane amendments, also known as riders, generally are defined as provisions that are not germane, or pertinent, to the bill they are tacked on to. The Christmas tree bill is perhaps the most lavish legislative vehicle for the rider.

Riders have a long and colorful history in both houses. They are commonly used in the Senate, where non-germane amendments are considered fair play, especially by the Finance Committee. The Constitution says tax legislation must originate in the House, but the Finance Committee has learned how to initiate major tax proposals by attaching them to minor House-passed tax bills. It has used riders in other areas as well. In 1969, for example, the committee added to a House-passed securities tax bill a controversial rider repealing a provision of the 1968 Gun Control Act requiring sellers of shotgun and rifle ammunition to register all purchasers.

House rules prohibit non-germane amendments on most bills, but loopholes provide ways to skirt such restrictions. By waiving the rule against nongermane provisions, House members, like their Senate colleagues, often have created strange legislative bedfellows. A 1980 House bill simultaneously set new nutritional requirements for infant formulas and increased federal penalties for marijuana trafficking.

Uses of the Rider

Riders are an important weapon in the congressional arsenal. They have been used to slip legislation past a hostile president by hitching it to a more favored bill. President Franklin D. Roosevelt in 1938 denounced this practice, charging that it "robs the executive of legitimate and essential freedom of action in dealing with legislation."

After President Jimmy Carter in 1980 vetoed a pay increase for Public Health Service doctors, Congress stuck the raise on a mental health services bill, a pet project of first lady Rosalynn Carter. The president signed the bill in spite of the pay hike.

On the other hand, riders sometimes are offered on the Senate or House floor to bypass unsympathetic committees. That was the technique used in 1960 by Senate Majority Leader Lyndon B. Johnson, D-Texas (1949-61), to bring up a controversial civil rights bill. Johnson offered the bill as an amendment to an obscure piece of legislation aiding a federally impacted school district in Missouri.

Riders to Appropriations Bills

In the late 1970s, riders proved to be a powerful weapon in the hands of conservatives, who had little influence in many of the most important committees. House rules requiring that floor amendments be germane encouraged the use of riders to the annual appropriations bills, which touch on almost every government program and agency and often provide the only opportunity to enact legislation on controversial issues. This was the form in which conservatives first raised many politically sensitive social issues such as anti-abortion provisions (the so-called Hyde amendment), anti-busing legislation and school prayer amendments. In 1983 the House incorporated a rules change that would make it more difficult to attach riders to appropriations bills. (See p. 51.)

Appropriations riders help Congress avoid vetoes. The president is empowered to reject entire bills only. He has no "item veto," as do some state governors, that would allow him to strike just the disagreeable portions of bills. Thus he cannot kill a rider without also endangering the funds for an entire department or groups of independent agencies.

Politics provides another impetus for appropriations riders. They often are the best way to dramatize issues, especially just before an election.

There are two types of appropriations riders:

● Limitation riders, which merely restrict the use of funds appropriated by the bill and are considered germane amendments and therefore permissible in both the House and Senate. These riders do not actually change existing law, although they often have the effect of legislation.

● Legislative riders, which change existing law or put new duties on government agencies. Generally, they are not allowed on money bills under either chamber's rules, but the rules may be waived by unanimous consent or a two-thirds vote of the House.

the legislation goes to the floor for a final vote. This frequently occurs when conferees add new language to a bill that might make the conference report subject to a point of order or if any provision in the bill for any reason violates House rules. The Rules Committee then may grant a rule waiving points of order against the report.

Adoption of Conference Report

In both chambers, debate on conference reports is highly privileged and can interrupt most other business. The house that agreed to the other chamber's request to go to conference on a bill acts first on the conference version. This procedure is followed by custom rather than by a requirement of the standing rules and occasionally is altered, as was the case on the conference report on the big 1981 Reagan tax cut bill. The Senate had requested the conference, and it acted first on the conference report.

Final Approval. Approval of the conference report by both houses, along with any amendments in disagreement, constitutes final approval of the bill.

Under the 1970 act, conference reports were supposed to be available for three days before the House could consider them. (In 1972 this was changed to allow House action on the third day. The Senate does not have a layover requirement for considering conference reports.) Debate on a conference report is equally divided between the majority and minority parties in each chamber.

The conference version of the bill must be approved or rejected in its entirety by both bodies. Exceptions are made only for non-germane Senate amendments, which may be deleted by the House, and for certain other amendments that are reported "in technical disagreement" — because they do not conform with House rules. Conferees are not in disagreement on such amendments, but because of House rules they must be considered separately and cannot be added to the conference version. For those situations, the House conferees indicate in the joint explanatory statement accompanying the report that particular amendments were reported in technical disagreement but that they will offer a motion "to recede and concur in the amendment of the Senate," either as the Senate passed it or as modified by the conference committee.

Disposing of Non-germane Amendments. The 1970 rules change allowing separate votes in the House on non-germane Senate amendments failed to achieve the desired result, partly because it did not spell out the procedure under which the separate votes could be taken, and partly because the new rule appeared to conflict with a House rule requiring an up-or-down vote on the entire conference report.[12] In 1972 the House again amended its rules to allow members to make points of order against conference reports. If any portion of a report is ruled non-germane, that portion is immediately subject to 40 minutes of debate and a separate vote. If no points of order are sustained or if the House accepts all non-germane amendments, the House then votes on the conference report as a whole.

If any of the non-germane amendments are rejected, the conference report is considered rejected. In that case, the House can accept the Senate version with an amendment, the amendment consisting of all provisions of the conference version not rejected by the House. If adopted, the House version is sent to the Senate, which can approve it (with the non-germane amendments deleted), or request a new conference.

The procedure was employed during the 1974 session. The House had approved a bill calling for a White House symposium on libraries. The Senate added two non-germane amendments, one clarifying a law on the privacy of student records, the other exempting certain organizations from compliance with federal sex non-discrimination regulations. The provisions were retained in the conference report, and when the bill reached the House floor Rep. William A. Steiger, R-Wis. (1967-78), raised a point of order against the provision dealing with sex discrimination. The point of order was sustained, but the House on a 37-102 standing vote rejected the motion to delete the non-germane provision. Thus the bill was accepted as it had been approved by the conference committee.

Conference Disputes

The conference machinery does not always work smoothly. In 1962 a classic feud between the Senate and House Appropriations committees blocked conference action on major appropriation bills for months, and in 1981 conference disputes delayed final approval of an omnibus farm bill for a month and a half and nearly led to rejection of the bill.

One of the most frequently voiced complaints about the conference system is the charge, raised from time to time in both chambers, that conferees often are not in sympathy with the position taken by their own chamber on key issues between the two bodies and do not sufficiently defend their chamber's position against opposition from the other chamber's conferees.[13]

In 1972 a major controversy developed over conference action on a bill raising the hourly minimum wage. A coalition of House Republicans and Southern Democrats objected so strenuously to the House conferees that they blocked the bill from going to conference. Generally regarded as more liberal than the rest of the House, the Education and Labor Committee had approved the minimum wage bill in 1971. When the bill came to the floor in May 1972, after a long delay in the Rules Committee, the House approved a substitute version offered by John N. Erlenborn, R-Ill. Erlenborn's bill made the increase more gradual, deleted a proposed extension of coverage to additional workers and added a controversial provision that allowed employers to hire youths under 18 at a subminimum wage.

Subsequently, the Senate passed a version of the bill that was even more generous than the House committee's original version. The committee chairman, Rep. Carl D. Perkins, D-Ky., then requested unanimous consent to send the bill to conference. Asked by Erlenborn who he had recommended to be conferees, Perkins said they would come from the General Labor Subcommittee, which originally considered the bill (six Democrats and four Republicans). Ten of the 11 Democratic members of the subcommittee had voted against the Erlenborn substitute.

Erlenborn objected to the unanimous consent request, thereby blocking it. He said it was unfair to send to conference a delegation whose majority voted against the House-passed version of the bill.

Certain that a second unanimous consent request would be objected to, Perkins offered a motion that the House disagree with the Senate version and request a conference to resolve the differences. Only a simple majority was needed to pass the motion. But Erlenborn again objected: "If we refuse to send the bill to conference at this time, then we may receive assurances in the future that when the bill does go to conference a majority of the managers [conferees] on the part of the House will fight for the position the House has taken."

Perkins' motion was defeated, 190-198. Later the House killed the bill by voting 188-196 against another Perkins motion to request a conference. "All too often," Erlenborn said, summing up his opposition to the motion, "the House speaks its will by amending legislation . . . or adopting substitute bills and sending the legislation to the other body. All too often the other body passes a bill very similar to that rejected by the House. And almost without exception the conference committee members appointed by the House accede more to the provisions of the other body than they try to protect the provisions which the House had adopted." [14]

The 1981 farm bill was buffeted by conflicting demands from a divided farm constituency, by proposed Reagan administration budget cuts and by the deteriorating state of the economy. These adversities were reflected in attempts by House and Senate conferees to win final agreement of a farm bill that would be acceptable to both houses as well as the president. House conferees, in particular, balked at having to accept lower Senate-passed farm support prices for certain commodities than those approved by the House. Reflecting the bitterness in the House, seven conferees, including Thomas S. Foley, D-Wash., the majority whip and former chairman of the Agriculture Committee, refused to sign the conference report on the bill, and two House Agriculture subcommittee chairmen urged members to vote against the bill. The conference bill ultimately survived on a 205-203 vote.

Final Legislative Action

After a bill has been given final approval by both houses, the original papers are sent to the enrolling clerk of the chamber in which the bill originated. The clerk then prepares an enrolled bill, which is printed on parchment. After the bill has been certified as correct by the secretary of the Senate or the clerk of the House, depending on which chamber originated the bill, it is always signed first by the Speaker of the House (regardless of whether it is a House or Senate bill) and then by the president of the Senate. It then is sent to the White House to await action by the president.

The president has 10 days (Sundays excepted) from the time he receives the bill to act upon it. If he approves the measure, he signs it, dates it and usually writes the word "Approved" on the document. Under the Constitution, however, only his signature is required.

Veto Powers

If the president does not want the bill to become law, he may veto it by returning it to the chamber in which it originated without his signature and with a message stating his objections. If no action on the message is taken there, the bill dies.

When a bill is returned to Congress unsigned, an attempt may be made to override the president's veto and, as stated in the Constitution, enact the bill into law "the objections of the president to the contrary notwithstanding." A veto override requires a two-thirds vote of those present and voting in both chambers. There must be a quorum present for the vote, which must be by roll call.

Debate may precede the vote, with motions permitted to lay the message on the table, to postpone action on it or to refer it to committee.

If a vote to override a veto succeeds in the first house, the measure is sent to the second house. If the veto is overridden there by a two-thirds vote, the bill becomes law without the president's signature; otherwise the veto stands, and the bill is dead. Senate or House action on a veto can be taken at any time during either session of the Congress in which the veto is received.

Under the Constitution, a bill may become law without the president's signature in one way other than through an overridden veto: It becomes law if the president does not sign it within 10 days (Sundays excepted) from the time he receives it, provided Congress is in session. Presidents occasionally permit enactment of legislation in this manner when they want to register their disapproval but do not feel their objections warrant a veto. However, if Congress adjourns before the 10 days expire, a bill not signed by the president does not become law. Such bills become pocket-vetoed.

Congress does not have an opportunity to override a pocket veto because it has adjourned *sine die* (for the remainder of the session). The question of whether a president can pocket veto legislation during a congressional recess became an issue when President Nixon used that method during a six-day recess in 1970. He was challenged in court by Sen. Edward M. Kennedy, D-Mass. The pocket-vetoed measure, a medical training bill, had passed both houses by nearly unanimous votes, indicating that a regular veto would have been overridden in Congress. The U.S. Court of Appeals for the District of Columbia on Aug. 14, 1974, upheld Kennedy's challenge and declared that Nixon had improperly used his pocket veto power. That bill became law.

The court in the Nixon case did not indicate whether it considered any adjournment or recess shorter than a *sine die* adjournment as grounds for a pocket veto, but through informal agreement between Congress and the White House pocket vetoes since then have been used only during *sine die* adjournments.

Public and Private Laws

When bills are passed and signed, or passed over a veto, they are given numbers in numerical order as they become law by the archivist of the United States. There are two series of laws, one for public bills and one for private bills, starting with number "1" for each two-year term of Congress. They then are identified by law number and by the Congress in which they were approved: Private Law 45, 97th Congress; Public Law 245, 97th Congress, or simply PL 97-245. A few laws are popularly referred to by their public law number, such as PL-480, the Food for Peace program.

The Legislative Veto

In the mid-1970s Congress turned increasingly to the so-called legislative veto as its primary method of exercising greater control over administrative decisions and regulations issued by the executive branch.

Every president since Herbert Hoover denounced the veto mechanism. President Jimmy Carter, for example, said in 1978 that the veto infringed "on the executive's constitutional duty to faithfully execute the laws. . . ." Nevertheless, most White House occupants since World War II willingly accepted the veto as a necessary component of legislative compromises.

Although there are many varieties of legislative vetoes, also called congressional vetoes, all share a common feature: They permit Congress to block an executive action — in some cases with, in other cases without, the president's approval. Regardless of the method used, the veto forces the affected government agency to delay carrying out its regulation, usually for 30 or 60 days.

Although the first bill to contain a legislative veto provision was enacted in 1932, its use did not become a major controversy until late in the Ford administration when Congress, in a single session, added veto language to several key bills.

Increased Usage

The legislative veto attracted considerable support in Congress in the 1970s in part because of citizen unhappiness with the performance of government and public opposition to what was seen as excessive government regulation.

Use of the veto mechanism multiplied rapidly during the Carter presidency. By the time President Reagan took office in January 1981 there were about 200 statutes in force containing one or more legislative veto provisions, according to the Congressional Research Service. Of that number, at least a third had been enacted between 1976 and 1981. One law, the Energy Security Act of 1980, contained more than 20 veto provisions.

Despite a record of executive acquiescence in legislation containing the veto, presidents since Franklin D. Roosevelt have questioned the constitutionality of the procedure. Roosevelt, for example, after signing the Lend Lease Act of 1941, which contained a veto clause, wrote to Supreme Court Justice Robert H. Jackson setting forth his constitutional objections to the provision.

In 1976 President Gerald R. Ford dramatized his objections by vetoing a pesticides control bill that contained a version of the veto. That was one of the few instances in which a president had directly challenged Congress on the issue.

It appeared initially that Reagan would be the first president not to oppose the veto. As a presidential candidate he had endorsed its use by Congress. But once in office he changed his position. Reagan's attorney general, William French Smith, announced early in 1981 that the administration considered the veto unconstitutional if it "intrudes on the power of the president to manage the executive branch."

After some modifications, the Reagan administration said it opposed legislative vetoes of executive branch decisions but would accept them for actions taken by independent regulatory agencies. And it agreed not to oppose them for executive branch actions when a veto required approval by both houses as well as the president's approval. However, in 1982 the Reagan administration gave its blessings to a regulatory reform bill approved by the Senate that contained a two-house veto provision without a presidential sign-off clause. The veto applied across-the-board to all federal agencies except the Defense Department, the Internal Revenue Service and certain types of regulations.

Types of Legislative Vetoes

Under one form of the legislative veto, a single house of Congress can veto a federal department's regulation or an independent agency's ruling. This method was employed in the 1974 Congressional Budget and Impoundment Control Act as a way of giving the president limited authority to defer previously appropriated funds. Another version, which was used for major arms sales such as the controversial 1981 AWACS radar planes deal with Saudi Arabia, requires approval by both houses to block a sale or executive action. A third type allows reconsideration of executive regulations already in effect.

In a few cases, congressional committees alone have been given veto authority over executive actions, or the right to review them. This usage came as a shock to the Eisenhower administration in the 1950s when it discovered that certain federal agencies had to obtain advance clearance from congressional committees before taking specified actions.

Background

The first legislative veto clause drafted by Congress was incorporated in a bill allowing President Hoover to reorganize the executive branch. Hoover signed the bill, but the following year (1933), at the urging of his attorney general, he vetoed an emergency appropriation bill that included a provision giving a single committee, the Joint Committee on Taxation, power to veto certain tax refunds.

Hoover's change of position set the pattern for the on-again, off-again attitude of his successors toward legislation containing the veto.

Congress made use of the veto during World War II to provide a check on the broad war-making powers it had delegated to the Roosevelt administration. Use of the veto then declined in the 1950s and 1960s.

In the 1970s Congress began adding veto provisions to a wide range of bills, primarily those relating to defense, foreign policy, public works, energy and environment issues. Examples included the 1973 War Powers Act, the 1974 Congressional Budget and Impoundment Control Act, the pesticides bill vetoed by Ford and the 1974 Federal Election Campaign Act. Provisions of the War Powers Act served as a model for a 1976 bill empowering Congress, through concurrent resolution, to terminate any future national emergency proclaimed by the president.

Not all legislative veto provisions apply to agency rules. Under a 1976 amendment to the Arms Control Act, Congress has the right to veto major arms sales abroad. The 1981 arms sale to Saudi Arabia provided a dramatic example of this type of veto. The Reagan administration notified Congress Oct. 1 of its intention to sell that Mideast country the sophisticated AWACS radar planes. Under the 1976 veto provision, the arms deal could have been blocked if each house, by majority vote, had passed a resolution of disapproval within 30 days of receiving Reagan's formal notice of the sale, worth $8.5 billion. The House voted 301-111 in favor of the disapproval resolution, but the Senate, on a dramatic 48-52 vote, then rejected it, allowing the sale to take place.

General Veto Power Sought

The Senate initially resisted the 1970s demands for greater controls on the federal bureaucracy. Those pressures came primarily from the House, which added variations of the veto to numerous bills. And in 1976 the House came within two votes of passing a sweeping bill that would have made most agency regulations subject to congressional review and rejection.

Symbols of Authority: Mace and Gavel

Mace in the House

The most-treasured possession of the House of Representatives is the mace, a traditional symbol of legislative authority. The concept, which the House borrowed from the British House of Commons, had its origin in republican Rome, where the fasces — an ax bound in a bundle of rods — symbolized the power of the magistrates.

The mace was adopted by the House in its first session in 1789 as a symbol of office for the sergeant-at-arms, who is charged with preserving order on the House floor. The first mace was destroyed when the British burned the Capitol in 1814, and for the next 27 years a mace of painted wood was used. The present mace, in use since 1841, is a replica of the original mace of 1789. It consists of a bundle of 13 ebony rods bound in silver, terminating in a silver globe topped by a silver eagle with outstretched wings, and is 46 inches high in all. It was made by William Adams, a New York silversmith, for the sum of $400.

The sergeant-at-arms, custodian of the mace, is charged with its use when necessary to preserve order. There have been a number of occasions in the history of the House when the sergeant-at-arms, on order of the Speaker, has lifted the mace from its pedestal and "presented" it before an unruly member. On each such occasion, order is said to have been promptly restored. At other times the sergeant-at-arms, bearing the mace, has passed up and down the aisles to quell boisterous behavior in the chamber.

The mace also serves a second purpose. When the House is in regular session, it rests on a tall green marble pedestal at the right of the Speaker's desk, but when the House is sitting as the Committee of the Whole it is moved to a low white marble pedestal nearby. Thus, upon entering the chamber a representative can tell at a glance whether the House is meeting in regular session or as the Committee of the Whole.

Gavel in the Senate

The Senate has no mace, but it cherishes another symbol — a small silver-capped ivory gavel that Vice President John Adams is believed to have used in calling the first Senate to order in 1789. Evidence exists that it was in use at least as early as 1831, and it remained in use until 1954 when it began to disintegrate beyond repair. It has no handle.

A replica of the old gavel, a gift of the government of India, was presented to the Senate on Nov. 17, 1954. Since that time a case containing both the old and the new gavels is carried into the Senate chamber and placed on the vice president's desk just before the opening of each Senate session. The new gavel is removed from the case for use by the presiding officer. The old gavel is not used but remains on the desk in its case, a symbol of the continuity of the Senate.

Efforts to win approval of the general legislative veto bill were intensified during the Carter years. Proponents said lawmakers should be able to block "bad" regulations. As the number of vetoes attached piecemeal to bills increased, the need for a uniform approach to reviewing all agency regulations also increased, they said.

"The legislative veto will make certain that the people who are elected make the laws — not unelected bureaucrats who are obviously not accountable," said Rep. Elliott H. Levitas, D-Ga., the chief House champion of the veto. And according to Sen. Harrison "Jack" Schmitt, R-N.M., Congress has written legislation so broadly that agency officials have been free to formulate "many of the essential principles in the law" without any congressional oversight.

Those who argued against a general legislative veto said it would place a heavy burden on congressional committees forced to review some 10,000 regulations generated annually by federal agencies. And Congress already had ways to let agencies know when it felt a regulation did not reflect the congressional intent of the law, they said.

In 1980 lawmakers took a step toward providing Congress with blanket veto authority when they passed a Federal Trade Commission (FTC) authorization bill. That measure was the first to give Congress comprehensive veto power over all regulations issued by a single agency.

The agency's increasingly aggressive regulatory stance in the late 1970s under Chairman Michael Pertschuk mobilized the business community to lobby vigorously for a congressional check on the FTC. Congress appeared to be sympathetic to such pleas, but disagreement over how to remedy the problem led to a prolonged funding dispute. Beginning in 1977, the agency's operations had to be funded through an emergency money bill. The regular authorization-appropriation process was blocked by the House's insistence on attaching a veto provision.

The stalemate continued until 1980, when key House members announced they would not allow any funding of the FTC until the veto issue was settled. In April 1980 the Senate finally gave in to House demands by accepting a two-chamber veto for FTC rulings — without needing the president's approval.

Efforts by the House to pass a comprehensive veto measure as part of governmentwide regulatory reform continued into the 1980s.

Court Rulings

With so many constitutional questions raised by opponents of the veto, it was only a matter of time before the courts were asked to intervene. In October 1981 the Supreme Court agreed to decide whether a single house of Congress, through use of the veto, could nullify executive branch regulations.

The case before the court, *Immigration and Naturalization Service (INS) v. Chadha, U.S. House of Representatives v. Chadha, U.S. Senate v. Chadha,* arose after the House in 1975 vetoed an INS decision not to deport Jagdish Rai Chadha, a Kenyan student who had overstayed his visa. The House had acted under a provision of the 1952 Immigration and Nationality Act giving either chamber the power to veto an INS decision blocking an individual's deportation.

After he was ordered deported in 1976, Chadha appealed, challenging the constitutionality of the one-house veto. In December 1980 the 9th U.S. Circuit Court of Appeals struck down the provision and canceled Chadha's deportation. The court said the one-house veto conflicted with both the separation of powers doctrine and the constitutional requirement that both houses must act on legislation, in effect ruling that the veto was an unconstitutional intrusion by Congress into the domain of the executive branch and the courts.

In a separate and considerably broader case, a three-judge panel of the U.S. Court of Appeals for the District of Columbia ruled on Jan. 29, 1982, that the legislative veto "contravenes the constitutional procedures for making law." That decision was expected to be considered by the Supreme Court, but not before a decision was handed down on the immigration case.

The 1982 ruling came on an appeal brought by consumer groups who were challenging a 1980 House veto of Federal Energy Regulatory Commission (FERC) natural gas pricing regulations. The veto was exercised under a provision of the Natural Gas Policy Act of 1978. In an opinion written by Judge Malcolm Wilkey, the court said: "In effect, Congress is able to expand its role from one of oversight, with an eye to legislative revision, to one of shared administration. This overall increase in congressional power contravenes the fundamental purpose of the separation of powers doctrine. Congress gains the ability to direct unilaterally, and indeed unicamerally, the exercise of agency discretion in a specific manner considered undesirable or unachievable when the enabling statute was first passed."

If Congress decides it has given an agency too much power, the court said, "it may by statute take it back or may in the future enact more specific delegations." The court acknowledged the ramifications of its ruling: "We are aware that our decision today may have far-reaching effects on the operation of the national government. Yet this cannot deter us from finding the one-house veto unconstitutional."

The Parliamentarian

Two of the most influential — and publicly unnoticed — Capitol Hill officials are the parliamentarians of the House and the Senate. Their roles extend far beyond that of mere arbiters of parliamentary practice.

Consulted by White House legislation-drafters, relied upon heavily by congressional leaders, and sought out for advice by members of both parties and — even more frequently — by their staffs, the parliamentarians' influence is greatest in the guarded, private, behind-the-scenes pro-cedural mechanics that transform an idea into a piece of legislation.

The parliamentarians, serving unbroken terms in Congress after Congress, become masters of the procedural and technical skills that are the backbone of successful legislating. They are at home in the specialized congressional world of bills, resolutions, amendments, rules, motions, precedents and parliamentary maneuvering. And they are acknowledged experts in suggesting ways to route legislation to a sympathetic committee, preparing it for floor debate and protecting it from opposition attacks.

Long-Term Nature of the Job

Parliamentarians are appointed by the leadership of the House and Senate, but because of their highly skilled, technical functions they normally remain in office regardless of changes in political control of the two chambers.

The acquired experience of the parliamentarians admits them to the innermost political councils. Former House Parliamentarian Lewis Deschler, for example, was a member of Speaker Sam Rayburn's "Board of Education." This was a group of the Speaker's House friends who would meet about sundown over drinks for political policy and strategy talks.[15]

Deschler drew key roles in preparing the 1957 civil rights bill for House consideration. He checked the draft bill to make sure the wording would permit it to be sent to a friendly committee. He checked committee changes in the measure to make sure the House germaneness rule still would bar certain types of unwanted floor amendments, and he cleared the special rule for the bill, readying it for floor action. Because civil rights advocates and opponents both had sought parliamentary advice from Deschler, he could warn the Speaker of an upcoming floor fight and could predict the mood of the House.

Evolution of the Office

Despite the importance of the parliamentarians, the origin of the office is uncertain. In the 19th century, presiding officers of the House and Senate either made their own parliamentary rulings or turned for advice to senior members or to senior clerks around the desk. Gradually it became a practice to rely on one of the clerks for advice on parliamentary matters. Finally, as sessions became longer and legislation — as well as congressional rules and precedents — became more complex, a separate position was created with sole responsibility for parliamentary matters. The House established the position of parliamentarian in 1927, the Senate in 1937. The office of the House parliamentarian was not formally established until 1977.

The position of parliamentarian is an ambiguous one, with few clearly defined responsibilities. The parliamentarians of the House and Senate, together with their assistants, do share some common functions. They advise the presiding officers on the always-changing parliamentary situation and on parliamentary procedures. The parliamentarian is present at all House and Senate sessions, sitting directly in front of the presiding officer in the Senate and just to his right in the House. The parliamentarians customarily are responsible for referring bills, resolutions and other communications to committees having the proper jurisdiction. The parliamentarians also prepare and maintain compilations of the precedents of each chamber.

The House parliamentarian is appointed by the Speaker; the Senate parliamentarian is appointed by the secretary of the Senate, who heeds the advice of the majority leader.

Influence of Parliamentarians

For a number of reasons, the House parliamentarian has emerged as a more influential figure than his Senate counterpart.

In part, the disparity is a matter of differing personalities of the men who have held the posts. House Parliamentarian Deschler, whose long tenure left an immense mark on the office, was an aggressive man, prepared to assume new functions and new responsibilities. His Senate counterparts, Charles L. Watkins and Floyd M. Riddick, were considered more self-effacing and less prone to seek additional duties. *(Comments on Deschler, box, p. 83)*

The disparity reflects basic differences in the power and composition of the House and Senate. In the Senate, power is diffused. There is no single overriding political position. Thus the parliamentarian, who serves the presiding officer, may find himself working with the vice president (the president of the Senate), the president pro tem or a senator picked as acting president pro tem. Furthermore, the vice president and the Senate majority may be of different political parties. As a result, the Senate parliamentarian lacks a firm base of political power from which to operate.

Quite a different situation exists in the House. There the parliamentarian is first, last and always the Speaker's man. And the Speaker is an important political power, regardless of varying personal operating styles. With the Speaker's political weight behind him, the parliamentarian can exercise some discretionary authority as the Speaker's representative.

The comparatively small size of the Senate, its greater continuity and its less restrictive regulations also contribute to the disparity. The value of an expert in procedural technicalities is enhanced when his constituency is a 435-member body that includes a sizable contingent of freshman and junior members and is governed by numerous, complex and restrictive rules and precedents.

As one representative put it: "[Y]ou are going to run into occasions when you have a bill of your own that's coming up and you want to explore whether or not it would be possible to bring it up under suspension of the rules or some other procedure.... Then you might want to dig in the rule book for that, but for the commonly accepted procedures the best way to learn is by watching and then when you see something you don't understand, ask an older member or ask [the parliamentarian]....

"He is available on the phone most of the day, and he is available on the floor of the House when the House is in session.... Rather than end up making what may appear to others to be a foolish point of order, it might perhaps be best to talk to [the parliamentarian] ahead of time and find out or get some notion. He won't make a ruling for you, but he will certainly give you a few notions of just what you are getting into." [16]

Parliamentarians and Legislation

The influence wielded by parliamentarians on the shape of legislation and the course of floor action is subtle but important. Does the White House or the House leadership want a certain committee to consider a certain bill? The parliamentarians can suggest how to word the measure so it will fall under that committee's jurisdiction. Is a Senate filibuster blocking action on a measure favored by the leadership? The Senate parliamentarian can guide the leadership in attempts to end the filibuster through Rule 22. Do potential House floor amendments threaten to unravel carefully worded compromises on a controversial bill? The House parliamentarian can protect the agreements through skilled application of the House germaneness rule — supported by judiciously selected precedents.

The public rarely sees the parliamentarian at work as adviser and tactician. These roles are carried out in private sessions, sometimes involving only the parliamentarian and a single member. Both sides are understandably reluctant

---

House, Senate Parliamentarians

Listed below are the men who have performed the functions of parliamentarian in the House and Senate. The House did not formally recognize the position of parliamentarian until 1927, the Senate not until 1937.

House

Charles R. Crisp	1891-95
Asher C. Hinds	1895-1911
Joel Bennett Clark	1911-15
Clarence Cannon	1915-21
Lehr Fess	1921-28
Lewis Deschler	1928-74
William H. Brown	1974-

Senate

Edward J. Hickey	(?)-1923
Charles L. Watkins	1923-65
Floyd M. Riddick	1965-74
Murray Zweben	1975-81
Robert B. Dove	1981-

The House parliamentarian presides over a staff of three assistants and a clerk, and in fiscal 1982 his annual budget was $305,000. His annual salary as of January 1982 was $60,000. The staff is housed in the Speaker's room, off the House chamber. The parliamentarian's own office is around the corner, also off the chamber and several steps closer to the floor than even the office of the Speaker.

Two assistants and a secretary comprise the Senate parliamentarian's staff. The parliamentarian, whose salary as of January 1982 was $58,500, and his staff share a first-floor Capitol office, a flight below the Senate chamber and the offices of the leadership.

Source: House and Senate Parliamentarians

to break this confidential relationship.

One example, drawn from the House side, shows Parliamentarian Deschler openly at work as adviser and tactician. In a 1969 dispute over seating Rep. Adam Clayton Powell, D-N.Y. (1945-67, 1969-71), the House leadership favored admitting Powell to the 91st Congress without any sanctions. Others sought to penalize the flamboyant member from Harlem, who had been excluded by the House from the 90th Congress for misusing public funds.

After Judiciary Committee Chairman Emanuel Celler, D-N.Y. (1923-73), had offered a leadership-backed resolution to swear in Powell, Speaker John W. McCormack, D-Mass. (1928-71), blocked a move by Powell's opponents to add a $30,000 fine and a forfeit of seniority. McCormack upheld a point of order offered by Celler against the opposition's amendment on the grounds that it failed to meet the House rule of germaneness even though the Powell debate was taking place before the House had adopted its rules for the new Congress.

McCormack quickly demonstrated that he had prepared himself for the obvious question of how he could invoke a House rule before it had been adopted. "The Chair anticipated that the question of germaneness would be raised and has had the precedents of the House thoroughly researched," the Speaker said. Then he sustained Celler's point of order. Citing a precedent based on a 1913 decision of Speaker Champ Clark, D-Mo. (1893-95, 1897-1921), McCormack explained: "While the House is governed by general parliamentary usage prior to the adoption of rules, the Speakers have been inclined to give weight to the precedents of the House in the interpretation of that usage." [17] Thus the leadership, through the help of Deschler's research and advice, won its point. But Powell's opponents won the battle when the House in a subsequent resolution agreed to seat Powell but to fine him $25,000 and to strip him of his seniority.

Codification of Precedents

Although the parliamentarians of both chambers shun publicity and attempt to avoid controversies, they are not always successful.

Deschler, for example, became involved in a political controversy over codifying House precedents. The precedents had last been codified in 1936. Precedents established since then were scattered through the pages of House debate in the *Congressional Record*.

Pressure to compile a new House codification and to keep it up to date developed among younger representatives. They frequently found themselves at odds with the leadership, particularly under Speaker McCormack, and often were caught off guard when forced to match precedents with Deschler. Deschler maintained a private file of post-1936 precedents, clipped from the Record and pasted in notebooks kept in his office.

Beginning in 1965, Congress provided money in the annual legislative branch appropriation bill specifically for codification. The 1970 Legislative Reorganization Act directed the Speaker to complete a compilation of the precedents by Jan. 1, 1977, and to prepare an updated version every two years thereafter. The task was completed shortly after Deschler's death in July 1976. *Deschler's Procedure in the House of Representatives* was published in March 1977. As of 1982, four volumes of *Deschler's Precedents* had been published.

In the Senate, where that body's more informal mode of operation renders precedents probably more important,

a compilation of precedents by Floyd M. Riddick, *Senate Procedures, Precedents and Practices*, was published in 1981 by the Government Printing Office (S Doc 97-2).

The *Congressional Record*

On Oct. 18, 1972, according to the *Congressional Record*, Majority Leader Hale Boggs, D-La. (1941-43, 1947-72), told the House: "In the next few minutes I would like to note for members the great amount of significant legislation enacted during the session." At the end of his speech, according to the Record, Boggs wished every member a Merry Christmas and Happy New Year.[18]

All of this was fiction. Hale Boggs was presumed to be dead on Oct. 18, the victim of a plane crash in Alaska two days before. As was routine, he had left behind in Washington a written speech to be published at the close of the congressional session. The fact that it was printed despite his death merely reflects the truth about the *Congressional Record* — it does not record verbatim what is said on the floor of the House and Senate but rather what members want the public to think has been said.

Until 1978 there was no way to differentiate the floor debate statements and remarks of members actually in attendance from the speeches written in some member's office and then submitted for publication in the Record.

1978 Change

According to the law, Title 44, Section 901, the *Congressional Record* "shall be substantially a verbatim report of proceedings" of Congress. But the Record would appear to fall short of honoring that mandate, even after the rules were tightened in 1978.

On March 1 of that year, the Government Printing Office (GPO), at the direction of the House and Senate, began using black dots, or bullets, to mark the beginning and end of speeches, articles and other material inserted in the Record without having been delivered in person.

However, despite that change in Congress' daily journal, readers of the *Congressional Record* still can be misled in trying to distinguish spoken remarks from undelivered speeches. A loophole in the 1978 change allows a member to avoid having his material "bulleted" by delivering a portion of his speech or remarks, even one sentence. In that case, the entire speech can be inserted in the Record, at the point in a debate or colloquy where the member wants it to appear, as though it were actually spoken.

Another divergence from the "verbatim report of proceedings" rule still is allowed: Members may liberally revise and edit the speeches and remarks they deliver during a floor debate before they are published in the Record.

Even if the Record for a particular day contains a member's remarks he does not like or feels to be inaccurate, he may still have them corrected for the permanent, bound edition published at the end of each session. This requires a unanimous consent request in the House, and the member is given two weeks from the day of the debate in question to make the request.

In 1979, with the advent of House telecasts of floor proceedings, Congress made another innovation in the Record: With the first issue for the 96th Congress, Jan. 15, 1979, the House section began to indicate the time of day, every 10 or 15 minutes, in its account of the day's floor debates. This made it easier to locate when a speech, vote or other business of the House took place. The time cues apply only to House action.

Criticisms of Edited Record

Some critics of the Record argue that the official source of Congress' debates ought to be an honest account. Others have a more specific reason: they worry that the existing goulash of speeches and insertions makes it difficult for executive agencies to determine what Congress actually intended to do in passing a law. "It allows you to have a legislative history that is warped, because it is not accurate," then-Rep. Steiger said in 1972. Steiger warned that sooner or later a federal agency was going to make a serious error by relying on the remarks of a member who was not even present during the debate.[19]

When legislation is debated in the House, a representative can even decide which position to support after a vote is taken. Since 1974 members have been required to sign their written insertions and present them within 15 minutes of the close of the day's business. But the rule enables a member to bring two opposing speeches into the chamber, remain silent until the vote is nearly completed, be recorded for the winning side, and then insert into the published debate a speech explaining his position.

Some corrections and additions are indeed necessary. Remarks made in heated debates may be judged offensive and edited out of the Record by a reporter or the member who made them. Grammar often is improved, and the transcripts often are polished.

Verbal Inflation

Verbal inflation on Capitol Hill paralleled the nation's economic inflation in the 1970s. The appropriation approved by Congress for its printing needs at the Government Printing Office in fiscal 1982 was $84,843,000. In fiscal 1979 that expense had been $73,961,000. These figures reflect the mounting printing costs and the increasing volume of congressional publications.

Included in the GPO's fiscal 1982 appropriation was $6.3 million to meet Congress' requests for copies of the Record. For the cost of printing copies for executive branch and non-government use, such as public libraries, another $16 million had to be appropriated. Approximately 32,000 copies of the *Congressional Record* are produced daily. GPO officials estimated the total cost of printing the Record in fiscal 1982 at $23,312,000, of which $731,000 was recouped through sales to the public.

The price of the Record to the public has increased steadily since 1970, when the subscription price was increased for the first time in 87 years. Until June 12, 1970, the price had been $1.50 a month. That June it was raised to $3.75 a month ($45 a year). It had increased to $75 a year by 1980 and to $135 between December 1980 and September 1981. The rate was raised to $208 on Oct. 1, 1981, and the price of a single copy was increased from 75 cents to $1. The big 1981 price jump was caused by Congress' decision the preceding June to end public subsidies for printing the Record. But members of Congress, the president and senior officials in the executive branch continue to get free copies.

In 1972 the Joint Committee on Printing, responding to a rise in the number of lengthy, undelivered insertions in the Record's Extensions of Remarks section, announced changes in the procedure by which senators and representatives are allowed to insert such speeches, newspaper articles and other printed material. In making the changes, the committee revived a procedure that had been repealed in 1968 requiring members planning to insert more than two pages of material in the Record to first obtain an estimate of the cost from the public printer. Even with the two-page limit on insertions, the size of the Record crept steadily upward.

In 1977 Congress cut in half the number of copies

Bolling on Deschler

In his 1966 book, *House Out of Order*, Rep. Richard Bolling, D-Mo., had this to say about then-Parliamentarian Lewis Deschler:

"The title [of parliamentarian] conjures up a vision of a dried, parchment-paper-like blinkered figure narrowly looking at the House through the prism of its general rules.

"Deschler is none of these things. He is a large-sized man with large-sized influence growing out of his encyclopedic knowledge. He cultivates anonymity. He never speaks to the press for quotation. There is little written about him. . . .

"And Lew Deschler does know the rules. He knows the practical application of them better than any group of members ever have and probably ever will. Deschler . . . has made himself the second most influential person in the House, during his service of more than three decades. Only the Speaker, at whose right hand he sits when the House is in session, has more influence. The word is 'influential,' rather than 'powerful,' because members who hold the power are influenced in their exercise of it by Deschler. The influence to a point, of course, is derivative. He has the Speaker's confidence. He knows the Speaker's mind. He can act on this.

"When consulted, Deschler can tell the inquiring member just what can be done under the rules. Then, as always, deferential, he may suggest how a desired purpose can be attained within the rules. Perhaps the timing is discussed, and lurking in the background is perhaps an implication that the purpose of the member may not really be a very good idea. . . .

"Deschler, the anonymous parliamentarian, is the catalyst that makes the House function, rent as it is by partisanship, faction, personal jealousies, logrolling, rivalries, and hearty dislikes. Each member in a position of leadership consults him about parliamentary procedure. So, too, does the perceptive member of whatever rank who wants to have an amendment adopted. Deschler is available. His 'open door' policy brings a flow of inquiring members."

Source: Richard Bolling, *House Out of Order* (New York: E. P. Dutton & Co., 1966), pp. 110-112.

Forerunners Of the 'Congressional Record'

1789-1790 — *The Congressional Register.* An early attempt to publish a record of congressional debates. Taken down in shorthand by Thomas Lloyd of New York. Four volumes.

1790-1825 — Debate in the House was reported in a haphazard way by some of the better newspapers. Senate debates scarcely were reported at all.

1834 — Publication of the first volume of *Annals of Congress.* Produced by Gales and Seaton. Brought together material from newspapers, magazines and other sources on congressional proceedings from 1st through 12th Congress. (March 3, 1789, to May 27, 1824). Forty-two volumes.

1824-1837 — *Register of Debate.* Produced by Gales and Seaton. This publication directly reported congressional proceedings.

1833-1873 — *The Congressional Globe.* Published by Blair and Rives; F. and J. Rives; F. and J. Rives and George A. Bailey. Covered 23rd through 42nd Congresses (Dec. 2, 1833, to March 3, 1873). Forty-six volumes.

1873 to Present — *Congressional Record.* Produced by the Government Printing Office since Dec. 1, 1873.

members receive. Each senator receives 50 free copies; each representative, 34 copies. In addition to the daily Record, each member received one subscription to what is called the "Greenbound Record," which is a semi-monthly bound compilation of the dailies. The permanent bound volume of the Record, printed on book paper, is published a few months after a session ends. Each member is allotted one complete set.

Record of Debates

Before 1825 debates in the House were not reported except in a haphazard way by some newspapers. Senate debates were seldom reported at all. Not until 1855 were reporters of congressional proceedings and debates paid at public expense, and only in 1863 were annual appropriations established in both chambers to cover reporting of the proceedings.

The debates were not published systematically before 1865, when the *Congressional Globe* — the forerunner of the Record — took on a form and style that later became standard. When the government contract for publication of the Globe expired in 1873, Congress passed an appropriations act providing that for the 43rd Congress, beginning later that year, the *Congressional Record* would be produced by the GPO. (*Forerunners of the* Congressional Record, *box, this page*)

Current Practice

Proceedings in both the Senate and House are taken down by separate staffs of reporters, eight in the Senate and seven in the House. The shorthand notes of the debates are recorded later and typed by a transcriber. The typed copy is then proofread by the reporters, given an appropriate heading and sent to the members for their own editing.

Reporting in the House is done on a half-hour schedule, requiring that each reporter spend five minutes of each half hour on the floor and the remaining time dictating, transcribing and correcting his notes. The Senate operates under the same procedures, but on an hourly basis. Each Senate reporter spends 10 minutes of each hour on the floor.

Corrected transcripts of debates have to be returned to the GPO by 9 p.m. the same day if they are to be included in the following day's Record.

The text of House and Senate floor debates and the listing of all votes and the material for the Extensions and Daily Digest sections are assembled by the GPO each night before printing. The size of the Record never can be accurately determined beforehand, because it depends on the length of the floor proceedings. The only known fact is that the Record must be printed and delivered by 8 a.m., regardless of its size or how late Congress remains in session. Occasionally, late House or Senate proceedings are held over for publishing in the next day's Record. Or a separate issue of the Record, covering the late action, is printed as "Part II" of the day's proceedings.

Production begins at 6:30 p.m., when "preparers" check incoming copy, note sections to be printed in specific type sizes and ascertain that the material is in proper sequential order. The copy is set, proofed, corrected and readied for printing by 2 a.m. Approximately 22 tons of paper are used to turn out the average issue of the Record. (*Government Printing Office, box, p. 560*)

About 100 copies are hand-delivered to the homes of members requesting such service in the Washington area. More than 200 are delivered to area libraries, offices and universities, and about 6,000 go to federal agencies.

Contents of the Record

The *Congressional Record* reports daily what is said on the floor of each chamber. Biweekly and hard-bound versions also are produced to provide a corrected and permanent record. The proceedings of the House and Senate alternately appear first in each daily printing of the Record.

The Record contains four separate sections: Proceedings of the House; Proceedings of the Senate; Extensions of Remarks; the Daily Digest.

Proceedings. The edited account of floor debate and other action on legislation in the House and Senate. A member may request "unanimous consent to extend my remarks at this point in the Record" at any time the member is able to gain recognition on the floor. When the request is granted, a member may include a statement, newspaper article or speech, and it will appear in the body of the Record where the member requested. And as long as he reads a few words from his speech or article, it will appear in the Record without bullets indicating it was submitted for publication rather than delivered in person.

Extensions of Remarks. Following the Record's account — actual or apparent — of floor debate in both chambers, senators and representatives are given additional space to extend their remarks. They may add such extraneous material as speeches given outside Congress, selected editorials, magazine articles or letters. Senators may add such material to the body of the Record; representatives must place it in the Extensions of Remarks section.

Daily Digest. The Legislative Reorganization Act of 1946 directed the Joint Committee on Printing, which controls the publication of the *Congressional Record,* to incorporate in the Record a list of congressional committee meetings and hearings, their places and subject matter. This section of the Record, titled the Daily Digest, summarizes the following material:

- Highlights of the day's congressional activities.
- Senate committee hearings, markup sessions and bills reported.
- Senate floor action.
- House committee hearings, markup sessions and bills reported.
- House floor action.
- Joint committee meetings and conference reports filed.
- Time and date of next Senate and House sessions and all committee meetings.

Friday issues of the Digest contain a listing of the congressional program for the coming week, including legislation scheduled for floor action by the House and Senate (if it has been announced) and all committee meetings.

At the beginning of each month the Digest publishes a résumé of congressional activity, providing statistical data for the preceding month on the following:

- Days Congress was in session.
- Number of pages of proceedings printed in the Record.
- Number of pages of extensions of remarks.
- Bills enacted into law.
- Measures reported by committees.
- Reports, quorum calls, votes taken and bills vetoed by the president.

The summary also provides information on the status of executive nominations.

Index. Published about twice a month, the index is the key to using the *Congressional Record.* It is a guide to the contents and a means of tracing floor action on legislation. The index consists of two parts: an index to the proceedings, which includes material both in the body and in the Extensions of Remarks section, and an index to the history of bills and resolutions.

Extensions of Remarks. One step further from the reality of House debate is the "Extensions of Remarks" section at the back of the *Congressional Record;* on a busy day this section alone can run to 80 pages or more. "Extensions of Remarks" is a misnomer. Nothing is extended because no remarks are made. This section is a collection of newspaper articles, outside speeches and other contributions, some related to legislative business, some to constituent matters, and some to hardly anything of general interest.

Occasionally, an economy-minded member of Congress is willing to say in public that the bulk of the material inserted in the extensions section is not worth what it costs. "Just take a look at the *Congressional Record* almost any day," complained Rep. Marjorie S. Holt, R-Md., in 1974. "It is bloated with tributes, memorials, and messages on every conceivable subject except the subjects under consideration by Congress on that day.... We often spend $15,000 to $20,000 a day on such effluvia. We could save millions every year if we could eliminate it." [20]

Additions to the proceedings or the extensions section do cost money. Sen. Robert M. La Follette, R-Wis. (1906-25), on May 5, 1914, inserted a 365-page speech on railroad rates. The cost of printing this extension, according to the Joint Committee on Printing, was $13,760.85. In 1935 a speech opposing the National Recovery Administration by Sen. Huey P. Long, D-La. (1932-35), took up 85 pages of the Record and cost $4,493. One of the longest Record insertions was by Rep. Royal C. Johnson, R-S.D. (1915-33), who listed 504 pages of names of World War I slackers. No calculations on the cost of this extension were made.

On May 24, 1972, the Joint Committee on Printing announced that members who planned inserting lengthy material to first obtain an estimate of the cost from the public printer. Members then were required, when seeking unanimous consent to extend their remarks, to state the probable cost of the material but not its content. [21]

Extensions have been known to cause trouble as well as expense. In the summer of 1974 false statements attributed to three representatives were placed in the Record, apparently as pranks. One, under the name of Rep. Earl F. Landgrebe, R-Ind. (1969-75), appeared a week after President Nixon resigned in disgrace. It proposed that President Ford nominate Nixon to be his vice president, and then resign the presidency to allow Nixon to accede to the office under the 25th Amendment.

Landgrebe was not amused by the prank, and neither was the House leadership. The Joint Committee immediately tightened the rules for submitting insertions for the Record, requiring the signatures of members on all written statements. [22]

Footnotes

1. Woodrow Wilson, *Congressional Government* (Cleveland: Meridian, 1956), p. 55.
2. George B. Galloway, *Congress at the Crossroads* (New York: Thomas Y. Crowell Co., 1946), p. 203.
3. *Congressional Quarterly Almanac 1973* (Washington, D.C.: Congressional Quarterly, 1974), p. 1074.
4. *National Small Shipments Traffic Conference Incorporated v. Civil Aeronautics Board,* 618 Fed. 2d 819. District of Columbia Circuit, 1980.
5. Clarence Cannon, *Cannon's Procedures in the House of Representatives* (Washington, D.C.: Government Printing Office, 1963), p. 220.
6. Ibid., p. 6.
7. Ibid., p. 221.
8. W. Holmes Brown, *Constitution, Jefferson's Manual and Rules of the House of Representatives,* 94th Cong., 1st sess., (Washington, D.C.: Government Printing Office, 1975), p. 611.
9. Walter J. Oleszek, *Congressional Procedures and the Policy Process* (Washington, D.C.: CQ Press, 1978), pp. 163-64
10. For a discussion of conference committees, see *Congressional Quarterly Weekly Report,* Feb. 8, 1975, p. 290 ff.
11. *Congressional Quarterly Almanac 1973,* p. 902.
12. *Congress and the Nation,* vol. 3 (Washington, D.C.: Congressional Quarterly, 1973), p. 382.
13. See *Congress and the Nation,* vol. 3, pp. 158, 167, for discussion of these complaints during 1970 dispute over development of a supersonic commercial airliner.
14. *Congressional Quarterly Almanac 1972* (Washington, D.C.: Congressional Quarterly, 1973), p. 361.
15. Neil MacNeil, *Forge of Democracy* (New York: David McKay Co., 1963), pp. 82-83.
16. Donald G. Tacheron and Morris K. Udall, *The Job of the Congressman* (Indianapolis: Bobbs-Merrill Co., 1966), p. 193; see also, pp. 231-33.
17. U.S., Congress, House, *Congressional Record,* 91st Cong., 1st sess., Jan. 3, 1969, p. 25.

18. *Congressional Quarterly Weekly Report,* March 15, 1975, p. 527.

19. Ibid., p. 528.

20. Ibid., p. 529.

21. *Congress and the Nation,* vol. 3, pp. 378 and 380.

22. *Congressional Quarterly Weekly Report,* Aug. 31, 1974, pp. 2382-83.

The Committee System

The most distinguishing characteristic of the legislative branch is the predominant role played by the committee system. Much of the business of Congress is done in committee. Modern law-making requires an understanding of many complex subjects, and the committee system provides a means by which members can attain a high degree of specialization in certain areas.

A committee that has subjected a bill to expert scrutiny traditionally has expected its decisions to be upheld on the floor. Committees, according to *Cannon's Procedure* of the House, "are not infallible, but they have had long familiarity with the subject under discussion, and have made an intimate study of the particular bill before the House and after mature deliberation have made formal recommendations and, other considerations being equal, are entitled to support on the floor." [1]

However, in the Congress of the 1980s many lawmakers no longer defer to committees on the details of legislation. There are more floor challenges to more committees as members gain the expertise and staff needed to make independent judgments.

Nevertheless, it is difficult — at times virtually impossible — to circumvent a committee that is determined not to act. A bill that has been approved by a committee may be amended when it reaches the House or Senate, but extensive changes generally are much more difficult to achieve at that stage. The actions of the committees more often than not give Congress its record of legislative achievement and failure.

"On Capitol Hill, the center stage of policy making is held by the committees and subcommittees," says political scientist Roger H. Davidson. "They are the political nerve ends, the gatherers of information, the sifters of alternatives, the refiners of legislative detail." [2]

So overriding has been the influence of committees in the legislative process that scholars over the years have called them "little legislatures" [3] and their chairmen, "petty barons." [4] Though the appellation "baron" may no longer apply in the more open and democratic Congress of today, committee chairmen — and increasingly subcommittee chairmen — wield great influence over the fate of legislation, and thus over government programs and operations.

Davidson and Walter J. Oleszek, both specialists on Congress with the Congressional Research Service of the Library of Congress, point out that the chairmen still are crucial to the legislative process: They "call meetings and establish agendas, hire and fire committee staff, arrange hearings, designate conferees, act as floor managers, control committee funds and rooms, chair hearings and markups [bill-drafting sessions], and regulate the internal affairs and organization of the committee.... The chairman has many procedural powers. Simply refusing to schedule a bill for a hearing may be sufficient to kill it. Or a chairman may convene meetings when proponents or opponents of the legislation are unavoidably absent. The chairman's authority derives from the support of a committee majority and a variety of formal and informal resources such as substantive and parliamentary experience and control over the committee's agenda, communications, and financial resources." [5]

While the diffusion of committee power ended the era of the autocratic chairmen, and made committee proceedings more accountable, the cost of those reforms was a marked slowdown in lawmaking. Younger and less experienced members began to demand a voice in policy making, and many became subcommittee chairmen. With more activist subcommittees came an increase in the volume of legislation, thus adding to the workload and the need for more staff.

The institutional changes of the 1970s pleased most members, many more of whom could now expect to become at least subcommittee chairmen of a committee during their congressional careers. But the underlying committee structure was left basically the same as it had been since enactment of the Legislative Reorganization Act of 1946. With Congress and the country facing new and more complex issues in the late 1970s and 1980s, that system was found wanting.

Nowhere were the obstacles to a coherent, smoothly run legislative program more apparent than in the energy field. When Congress was asked to respond to proposals to meet the 1970s energy crisis, the House leadership was confronted with the fact that there were more than 80 committees and subcommittees that claimed some jurisdiction over energy issues.

Less dramatic, but just as serious, overlapping of jurisdictions and committee rivalries were apparent in health, welfare, the economy, foreign policy and various other areas of legislative activity.

Though the problem was more acute in the House, efforts there to rationalize the committee structure were

Dates Standing Committees Were Established

Only committees in existence in 1981 are listed. Where committees have been consolidated, the date cited is that of the component committee that was established first. Names in parentheses are those of current committees where they differ from the original names.

House

1789—Enrolled Bills (House Administration)
1795—Commerce and Manufacturers
    (Energy & Commerce)
1802—Ways & Means (a select committee, 1795-1802)
1805—Public Lands (Interior & Insular Affairs)
1808—Post Office and Post Roads (Post Office & Civil
    Service)
1808—District of Columbia
1813—Judiciary
1813—Pensions and Revolutionary Claims (Veterans'
    Affairs)
1816—Expenditures in Executive Departments
    (Government Operations)

1820—Agriculture
1822—Foreign Affairs
1822—Military Affairs (Armed Services)
1822—Naval Affairs (Armed Services)

1837—Public Buildings and Grounds (Public Works
    and Transportation)

1865—Appropriations
1865—Banking & Currency (Banking, Finance &
    Urban Affairs)
1867—Education & Labor

1880—Rules
1887—Merchant Marine & Fisheries

1942—Select Small Business (Small Business)

1958—Science & Astronautics
    (Science & Technology)
1967—Standards of Official Conduct

1975—Budget

1977—Select Intelligence*

Senate

1789—Enrolled Bills (Rules & Administration)

1816—Commerce and Manufacturers
    (Commerce, Science & Transportation)
1816—District of Columbia (Governmental Affairs)
1816—Finance
1816—Foreign Relations
1816—Judiciary
1816—Military Affairs (Armed Services)
1816—Naval Affairs (Armed Services)
1816—Post Office and Post Roads (Governmental
    Affairs)
1816—Public Lands & Survey (Energy &
    Natural Resources)

1825—Agriculture (Agriculture, Nutrition & Forestry)
1837—Public Buildings and Grounds (Environment &
    Public Works)
1842—Expenditures in Executive Departments
    (Governmental Affairs)

1867—Appropriations
1869—Education & Labor (Labor & Human Resources)

1913—Banking & Currency (Banking, Housing &
    Urban Affairs)

1950—Select Small Business (Small Business)
1958—Aeronautical & Space Sciences (Commerce,
    Science & Transportation)

1970—Veterans' Affairs
1975—Budget
1976—Select Intelligence*

* Both the House and Senate Select Intelligence committees are permanent committees but for reasons relating to congressional rules on committee organization they are listed as select committees.

Source: George Goodwin Jr., *The Little Legislatures* (University of Massachusetts Press, 1970), and *Congressional Directories.*

less successful than in the Senate. Ambitious committee reorganization plans foundered in 1974, 1977 and 1980. Despite general dissatisfaction with the outmoded structure, members were unwilling to give up their newly won powers. The energy jurisdictional tangle, for example, which was a target of the 1974 proposals, remained unsolved in 1980 after another attempt to consolidate related committee jurisdictions met with little success. The House's answer that year was to paper over the problem by renaming the Interstate and Foreign Commerce Committee the Energy and Commerce Committee. Committee jurisdictions essentially stayed the same as before.

A 1977 Senate committee reorganization overhaul met with more success; six committees actually were abolished and a new Energy Committee, consolidating most energy-related jurisdictions except taxes, was established. That reorganization, said Sen. Adlai E. Stevenson III, D-Ill. (1970-81), who headed a study of the committee system, "democratizes the Senate, rationalizes jurisdictions and cuts far back on the multiple committee assignments which pull and haul senators into time conflicts every day."[6] Nevertheless, the final plan fell short of its sponsors' hopes, as committees with the most powerful special interests behind them emerged unscathed.

Erosion of the Chairman's Power

The innate power of the committee system often was exercised arbitrarily by committee chairmen. Until the changes of the 1970s took effect, committees usually were powers unto themselves. Strong party leadership in Congress might influence committee actions, but most committees — and their chairmen — had sufficient independence to operate pretty much as they wished. The chairmen's power was equaled only by a few party leaders who had great influence, such as Speaker Sam Rayburn, D-Texas (1913-61), or Senate Majority Leader Lyndon B. Johnson, D-Texas (1949-61).

A chairman's power resulted from the rigid operation of the seniority system, under which a person rose to a chairmanship simply through longevity in Congress. The unwritten seniority rule conferred a committee chairmanship on the member of the majority party with the longest continuous service on the committee. As long as his party retained control of Congress, he normally kept this position; if control passed to the other party, he changed places with the ranking member of the other party. *(Details, see Seniority chapter)*

However, there were limits to the benefits of seniority, even in the period before the 1970s reforms. It was an unwritten rule in both houses that a senator or representative could not be a chairman of more than one standing committee, regardless of seniority. In 1969 Richard B. Russell, D-Ga. (1933-71), became the senior senator on the Appropriations Committee upon the retirement of Carl Hayden, D-Ariz. (1927-69). Russell already was chairman of the Armed Services Committee. He decided to take the Appropriations chairmanship, but to do so he was forced to relinquish his control of Armed Services, which he had chaired since 1951.

Rule by seniority reigned supreme until the early 1970s. Then, changing circumstances caught up with it. The principal change was the election to Congress of dozens of new members — persons who had less patience with the admonition to newcomers, credited to Speaker Rayburn, that "to get along, go along." New members, who did not have much influence in the Senate or House, joined forces with disgruntled incumbents, who had chafed under the often heavy-handed rule of arbitrary chairmen. Thus, in the late 1960s and early 1970s began the revolt that was to undermine the seniority system and lead to numerous other procedural changes that redefined the role and power of committee chairmen.

Though the dramatic changes did not come until the 1970s, a portent of things to come occurred after the 1966 election defeat of Howard W. Smith, D-Va. (1931-67), the powerful chairman of the House Rules Committee. For the first time in its history the committee adopted a set of rules governing its procedures. The new regulations denied the chairman the right to set meeting dates, required the consent of a committee majority to table (kill) a bill and set limits on proxy voting. *(Details, box, p. 92)*

The 1970s revolt began in the House as membership turnover accelerated and the proportion of younger, first- and second-term members increased. These lawmakers demanded fundamental changes in the way Congress — and particularly the committees — operated. Major changes in Democratic Party caucus rules and, to a lesser extent, in the standing rules of the House and the Senate, diluted the authority enjoyed by committee chairmen and other senior members and redistributed the power among the junior members.

The single most important factor that undermined the chairmen's authority was the decision by Democrats in both chambers to require chairmen to be elected by the party's caucus. The change came gradually, beginning in 1971. By 1975 Democrats in both chambers had adopted rules requiring a secret-ballot election of the top Democrat on each committee at the beginning of every Congress. And in that year three House chairmen were ousted in caucus elections. *(Details, see Seniority chapter.)*

The election requirement made chairmen accountable to their colleagues for their conduct. Caucus election of committee chairmen was only one of a number of changes that restricted the chairmen's power. Committees were required under the 1970 Legislative Reorganization Act to have written rules. In 1973 House Democrats adopted a "bill of rights" that reinforced subcommittee autonomy.

In subsequent years, House Democrats gave members of each committee the power to determine the number of subcommittees their committee would have. And committees with more than 20 members were required to have at least four subcommittees.

Staffing prerogatives were extended to members other than the chairman. In the House subcommittee chairmen and ranking minority members were allowed to hire one staff person each to work on their subcommittees. In the Senate, junior members were allowed to hire up to three personal aides to work solely on a senator's committees. These changes made committee members less subservient to the chairman by giving them professional staff help on legislative issues.

Democrats in both chambers also limited the influence of chairmen and other senior members by restricting the number of chairmanships and committee slots that a member could hold. *(Details, box, p. 90)*

As the decade of the 1970s closed, the committee structure was still firmly entrenched in Congress, but much of the power and prestige that had been held by the full committees had been transferred to the subcommittees and a new, larger corps of chairmen. Subcommittees took on the institutional characteristics and vested interests of their parent committees. This led to a decentralization of power and to heavier legislative workloads for members of both houses.

So great was the proliferation of subcommittees that in 1979-81 House Democrats and the Senate moved to limit the number of units a committee was allowed to establish.

The Committee Structure

There are three principal classes of committees in Congress: standing committees, those with permanently authorized staff and broad legislative mandates; select or special committees, those that are supposed to be temporary in that they are authorized to operate for a specific period of time or until the project for which they are created has been completed (these committees' role usually is investigative rather than legislative); and joint committees, which have a membership drawn from both houses of Congress and usually are investigative or housekeeping in nature. Conference committees, a special variety of joint committee, serve only on an ad hoc basis to resolve differences in Senate and House versions of the same legislation. *(Box, p. 83)*

Below the committee level are a plethora of subcommittees, which are functional subdivisions of the committees. Like the full committees, they are composed of members of the majority and minority parties in roughly the same proportion as the party ratios on the full committees.

At the beginning of the 97th Congress in 1981 there were 298 committees (standing, special and select) and subcommittees:

• 20 Senate committees with 106 subcommittees.

• 25 House committees with 137 subcommittees (the subcommittee total did not include nine task forces of the Budget Committee and one policy group and one task force of the House Administration Committee).

• four joint committees with six subcommittees.

The Senate has 17 standing, or permanent, committees (including the Senate Select Intelligence Committee, which functions as a permanent committee) and the House, 23 (also counting the House Select Intelligence Committee as a permanent committee). The Senate in 1981 had only two more committees and the House only four more than the number in existence in 1947 — the first year following enactment of the 1946 Legislative Reorganization Act.

But that comparison was misleading. The difference was that the standing committees in 1981 had 232 subcommittees (102 in the Senate and 130 in the House), compared with 148 in 1947 (59 Senate and 89 House).

Standing Committees

The standing committees are at the center of the legislative process. Legislation usually must be considered and approved in some form at the committee level before it can be sent to the House or Senate for further action. *(Details, see Legislative Process chapter.)*

The Legislative Reorganization Act of 1946 organized the Senate and House committees along roughly parallel lines. One of the act's purposes was to eliminate confusing and overlapping jurisdictions by grouping together related areas. The legislative committees (as distinct from the Appropriations committees) generally were regrouped to follow the major organizational divisions of the executive branch.

Responsibility for overseeing the federal bureaucracy

was divided roughly as follows: Appropriations committees were to review the budget requests of the federal departments; the Expenditures committees (now House Government Operations and Senate Governmental Affairs) were to oversee the general economy and efficiency of government in administering federal policy and programs; and the legislative committees, along with their other responsibilities, were to oversee the administration of federal programs in their respective fields.

Committee Size. The size of the standing committees is fixed by the standing rules of the Senate and in the House by negotiations between the majority and minority parties and formal ratification by the full membership (except that the rules specify the size of the Budget and Select Intelligence committees). In the 97th Congress, House committees ranged in size from nine (District of Columbia) to 55 (Appropriations), Senate committees from 12 (Rules and Administration and Veterans' Affairs) to 29 (Appropriations).

Party Ratios. The Constitution and the standing rules of each chamber are silent on the matter of party ratios on committees. The Senate traditionally has more or less followed the practice of filling standing committees according to the strength of each party in the chamber.

The House, on the other hand, has been less inclined to allocate minority party representation on committees on the basis of the relative strength of the two parties. The majority party has felt little need to accommodate its political opposition, especially on important House committees.

In 1981 House Republicans tried to change the party ratios on four key committees: Appropriations, Budget, Rules and Ways and Means, to reflect the gains made by the party in the November 1980 congressional elections. The Democratic leadership refused, and the GOP then sought to get the ratios changed by amending the usually routine resolutions approving the standing rules, drawn up by the Democratic Caucus, and ratifying committee assignments. (Committee ratios traditionally have been established by the majority party and are not included in House rules.)

At the beginning of the 97th Congress the ratio of Democrats to Republicans in the House was about five to four; but the Democratic leadership had insisted on retaining a three-to-two ratio on the Appropriations and Budget committees, a more than two-to-one ratio on Rules and a ratio of slightly less than two-to-one on Ways and Means. Both Republican attempts were defeated on straight party-line votes, except for one Democratic defection.

Republicans then filed a lawsuit against the House leadership, charging the Democrats with unconstitutionally discriminating against GOP members and their constituents when they set the committee ratios.

The case was dismissed by the U.S. District Court for the District of Columbia on Oct. 8, 1981, but the decision was immediately appealed to the U.S. Court of Appeals in Washington, D.C. Republicans and Democrats alike promised to appeal future decisions in the case all the way to the Supreme Court.

Select and Special Committees

Select and special committees are established from time to time in both chambers to study special problems or concerns. Their size and life span usually are fixed by the resolutions that create them. Ordinarily they are not permitted to report legislation. Some of these committees,

Conference Committees:
The Final Arbiters of Legislation

The conference committee is an ad hoc joint committee appointed to reconcile differences between Senate and House versions of pending legislation. Before a bill can be sent to the president, it must be passed in identical form by both chambers. Whenever different versions of the same bill are passed, and neither chamber is willing to yield to the other, a conference becomes necessary to determine the final shape of the legislation. It is unusual for the Senate or House to reject the work of a conference committee, but this can be expected to occur on the average of once or twice a session.

As a rule, conference committees are composed of the senior members of the committees that handled the bill. They are appointed by the Speaker of the House and the presiding officer of the Senate upon the recommendations of the committee chairmen. There are no rules instructing which members must be appointed conferees. However, the residual power of appointment lies with the chamber as a whole. Although the chairmen, by tradition, pick the conferees in the House, under the rules of that chamber the Speaker retains the latent power to make the appointments, subject only to the restriction that he "shall appoint no less than a majority of Members who generally supported the House position as determined by the Speaker." Most chairmen today include members who are knowledgeable about the bill in question, whether or not they are considered senior members of the committee.

There need not be an equal number of conferees (or "managers" as they are called) from each house, because a majority vote determines the position of each house's delegation on all decisions made in the conference. Therefore, a majority of both the Senate and House delegations must agree before a provision emerges from conference as part of the final bill.

Both parties are represented on conference committees, with the majority party having a larger number, and a majority of conferees from each house must sign the conference report. In the past, conference committees met on the Senate side of the Capitol, with the most senior senator presiding, but this custom is no longer followed.

Until 1975 most conference committees met in secret. In November of that year both chambers amended their rules to require open meetings unless a majority of either chamber's conferees vote in open session to close the meeting for that day. In 1977 the House amended the rule to require open conference meetings unless the full House voted to close them. That rule was never adopted by the Senate, but in practice Senate conferees have always gone along with the representatives on those occasions — which have been limited to defense and intelligence agency bills — when the House has voted to close a conference committee.

After conferees reach agreement and their report is approved by one of the two houses, the conference committee automatically is dissolved. (If the second chamber were to disapprove the conference report, a new conference committee would have to be picked, although normally the same team of conferees would be appointed.)

The conference device, used by Congress since 1789, had developed its modern practice by the middle of the 19th century. (Current conference procedures, p. 64)

such as the permanent Select Aging Committee in the House and the Special Aging Committee in the Senate, have gone on from year to year. But in most cases, they remain in existence for only one or two Congresses.

Unlike most select committees, the Intelligence committees in both chambers consider and report legislation. But this is a special case, as the committees are permanent in everything but name. Because the panels' subject matter is narrower than that of most standing committees, they were designated as "select" rather than "standing" committees. (Details, box, p. 85)

Joint Committees

Joint committees are created by statute or by resolution, which also fix their size. Of the four functioning in 1982, none had the authority to report legislation. One of the four, the Joint Economic Committee, was directed to examine national economic problems and review the execution of fiscal and budgetary programs, but it depended on the standing committees to frame legislative proposals. It was the only joint committee having subcommittees.

The Joint Committee on Internal Revenue Taxation, made up of senior members of both parties from the House Ways and Means and Senate Finance committees, could make policy recommendations to those committees but it served chiefly to provide a professional staff on tax issues.

Chairmanships of joint committees offer a special situation. Although historically the chairmen of these panels tended to be drawn from the Senate, in recent years they have rotated from one chamber to another at the beginning of each Congress. When a senator serves as chairman, the vice chairman usually is a representative, and vice versa.

The last joint committee having legislative responsibilities was Joint Atomic Energy.

Protecting Committee Turf

The touchy problem of realigning committee jurisdictions was illustrated forcefully in January 1977 after the Senate Rules Committee decided to support a recommendation of a select committee on the Senate committee system, chaired by Sen. Adlai E. Stevenson III, D-Ill. (1970-81), that jurisdiction over the coastal zone management program be transferred from the Commerce Committee to a new Committee on Environment and Public Works.

When the committee convened Jan. 19 it was confronted by five angry members of the Commerce Committee demanding that the program be returned to them. Sen. Russell B. Long, D-La., the powerful Finance Committee chairman who also was a member of the Commerce Committee, accused Stevenson-plan backers of advocating "reshuffling just for the sake of reshuffling."

After a stormy hour, the Rules Committee by voice vote agreed to reconsider its action and then voted to transfer the program back to Commerce. It also agreed to the Commerce Committee members' demand that jurisdiction over oceans, weather and atmosphere and the National Oceanic and Atmospheric Administration be retained by the Commerce Committee.

Subcommittees

Subcommittees provide the ultimate division of labor within the committee system. Although they enable members of Congress to develop expertise in specialized fields, they often are criticized on grounds that they fragment responsibility, increase the difficulty of policy review and slow down the authorization and appropriation process.[7]

Subcommittees vary in importance from committee to committee. Some, especially the Appropriations subcommittees in both chambers, have well-defined jurisdictions and function with great autonomy. Much of their work — both on the House and Senate side — is routinely endorsed by the full committee without further review. Their importance was one reason that House Democrats in 1974 voted to make all Appropriations subcommittee chairmen subject to confirmation by the party caucus.

A few committees — such as the House Ways and Means and Senate Finance committees — resisted the creation of subcommittees, although there were logical subdivisions into which their work could be divided. Subcommittees were established by the Finance Committee in 1970 and by Ways and Means only in 1974 — after the Democratic Caucus voted to require them. The subcommittee requirement was established in part because of dissatisfaction with the power and performance of Ways and Means Chairman Wilbur D. Mills, D-Ark. (1939-77). *(Box, p. 96)*

The House and Senate Budget committees were among the few panels that had no subcommittees in the 97th Congress (both committees were exempted from the subcommittee requirement). The House panel, however, did have task forces.

Committee Rivalries

The standing committees of Congress, wrote Stephen K. Bailey in 1966, "exist to speed the work load; to facilitate meaningful deliberations on important measures and issues; to develop a degree of expertise among committee members and committee staff; and to serve as a convenient graveyard for inept proposals. They constitute the great baronies of congressional power. Many of them look outward in jealous competition with the president, with their opposite committee in the other house, and with the whole house of which they are a part." [8]

Jurisdictional Clashes. Jurisdictional disputes between and among committees have been evident since the inception of the standing committee system.[9] The Legislative Reorganization Act of 1946 attempted to eliminate the problem by defining each committee's jurisdiction in detail. But the 1946 act was not able to eliminate the problem.

As early as 1947 a fight broke out in the Senate over referral of the controversial armed forces unification bill. In the House the measure had been handled by the Committee on Executive Expenditures (now the Government Operations Committee), which had jurisdiction over all proposals for government reorganization. But in a Senate floor vote that chamber's Armed Services Committee successfully challenged the claim of the Expenditures Committee (now the Governmental Affairs Committee) to jurisdiction over the bill.

Such problems have continued to arise because the complexities of modern legislative proposals make it impossible to define jurisdictional boundaries precisely.

In the House the problem has been aggravated by a failure to restructure the committee system to meet changing developments and national problems. The need to consolidate jurisdictions became particularly acute in the energy field, an area that has become prominent only since the mid-1970s. As noted, many committees had inherited jurisdiction over some aspect of energy policy; when President Carter in 1977 submitted his comprehensive national energy program the impending jurisdictional tangle forced Speaker Thomas P. O'Neill Jr., D-Mass., to establish an ad hoc energy committee to guide it through the House.

O'Neill appointed 40 loyal Democrats, with a majority favorably disposed toward the Carter plan. Five House committees reviewed portions of the bill, but O'Neill set strict deadlines for them to conduct hearings and complete action on their sections. The ad hoc committee then reviewed the separate committees' work, proposed numerous strengthening amendments and sent the bill to the Rules Committee. That panel, an arm of the leadership, obeyed O'Neill's directions to protect the bill from crippling floor amendments. (The bill was passed by the House but ran into opposition in the Senate.)

Occasionally, when the opportunity arises, a bill is drafted in such a way that it will be referred to a committee favorable to it. Oleszek cites the classic example of the 1963 civil rights bill, which was worded somewhat differently in each chamber so that it would be referred to the Judiciary Committee in the House and the Commerce Committee in the Senate. Both panels were chaired by strong proponents of the legislation, while the chairmen of the House Interstate and Foreign Commerce Committee and the Senate Judiciary Committee were opposed to the legislation. "Careful drafting, therefore, coupled with favorable referral decisions in the House and Senate, prevented the bill from being bogged down in hostile committees." [10]

In the existing House committee setup, however, legislation usually is not so lucky as in the two examples cited above. Most bills are subject to strict jurisdictional interpretation and are not open to the legerdemain given the 1963 civil rights bill or the special handling the Speaker was able to give the 1977 energy bill. Oleszek observes that "committees guard their jurisdictional turfs closely, and the parliamentarians know and follow the precedents. It is only the rare case of genuine jurisdictional ambiguity that provides an opportunity for the draftsman and referral options for the Speaker and presiding officer of the Senate to bypass one committee in favor of another." [11] *(Parliamentarian's role, see Legislative Process chapter.)*

The desire to maintain existing committee jurisdictions figured prominently in the debate over establishment of a Senate Intelligence Committee in 1976. The committee was given exclusive legislative authority over the Central Intelligence Agency (CIA), but jurisdiction over the intelligence arms of the Federal Bureau of Investigation (FBI) and the Defense Department was shared with other committees — the Judiciary and Armed Services committees respectively. Those two committees vigorously resisted the transfer of intelligence jurisdiction from their purviews. In creating the panel, Congress required that two of its members be chosen from each of four committees that formerly held some jurisdiction over intelligence operations: Appropriations, Armed Services, Judiciary and Foreign Relations.

Multiple Referral. The more common solution to jurisdictional conflicts is to refer a bill to two or more committees, a practice called multiple referral. There are three types of multiple referrals: joint, when several committees consider a bill at the same time; sequential, when a bill is referred first to one committee, then to another and so on; and split, when parts of a bill are referred to different committees — this was the method O'Neill used for the Carter energy bill.

The House did not permit the practice of multiple referral, long in use in the Senate, until 1975. According to Davidson and Oleszek, about 200 measures in each Congress are referred to more than one committee in the Senate. On the House side, 1,241 measures (out of 10,397 introduced) were given multiple referral in the 96th Congress. [12]

Senate Appropriations Committee Chairman Mark O. Hatfield, R-Ore., (l) discusses the federal budget with Sen. John C. Stennis, D-Miss., at 1981 committee meeting. Seated is the panel's top-ranking Democrat, Sen. William Proxmire, Wis.

Appropriations and Authorizations. The relationships between the Appropriations committees and the legislative committees frequently provide striking illustrations of inter-committee rivalries. Legislative committees handle bills authorizing funds, but only the Appropriations committees are permitted to consider the actual funding for federal agencies and programs. This distinction is strictly observed by the legislative committees. The Appropriations committees, in turn, theoretically are barred by the standing rules from inserting legislative provisions in their appropriations bills, but they habitually do so and, despite grumbling from the legislative committees, are seldom overruled on the floor. (Details, see Legislative Process chapter.)

In the Senate, almost all senators on the 29-member Appropriations Committee also are members of various legislative committees and thus can participate in deliberations on authorization bills and oversight in their fields of interest. This reduces one area of conflict as far as the Senate is concerned. But in the House, the Appropriations Committee is defined as an "exclusive" committee by the Democratic Caucus, meaning that party members, as a rule, cannot also be on other standing and select committees.

The creation of the Budget committees in 1974 added yet another dimension to the potential for committee rivalries, especially on spending decisions.

Competition Between Chambers. Committees often are in competition with their counterparts in the other chamber as well. In 1962 the decorum of Congress was shattered when the House and Senate Appropriations committees, each headed by an octogenarian chairman, brought their long-smoldering differences into public view. At issue were questions about the Senate's right to initiate its own appropriations bills, whether the Senate could add funds to House-passed bills, who would chair the conference negotiations between the two chambers and where the conference meetings would be held. The dispute blocked conferences on appropriations bills for three months and temporarily bankrupted several government agencies. Although the deadlock finally was broken, the two committees never reached full agreement on their respective roles in the appropriations process. (Details, see Powers of the Purse chapter.)

Proposals to create new committees illustrate another problem in trying to rationalize the committee system in Congress. For years after the House had created a separate Veterans' Affairs Committee, the Senate Finance Committee refused to relinquish its jurisdiction over veterans' legislation. A Senate Committee on Veterans' Affairs finally was created in 1970. Similarly, a proposal to split the House Education and Labor Committee into two separate committees was one of the stumbling blocks to House action on the 1970 legislative reorganization.

It is very difficult to abolish a committee, once established, even though it no longer serves any purpose. Congress in 1952 created a Joint Committee on Immigration and Nationality Policy. The committee never met and never performed any function, yet it was not abolished until 1970.

Rules and Procedures

Neither house operates under a comprehensive code of committee procedure; general guidelines and restrictions are contained in Senate and House rules, which incorporate many of the provisions in the Legislative Reorganization Acts of 1946 and 1970 and other measures. Democratic Party Caucus rules have had an even greater impact on the committee structure.

One of the basic goals of the 1946 act was to standardize committee procedures in regard to holding regular meeting days, keeping committee records and votes, reporting legislation, requiring a majority of committee members to be in attendance as a condition of transacting committee business and following set procedures during hearings.

The 1946 rules were not uniformly observed by all committees, and continuing dissatisfaction with committee operations led, in the 1970 Reorganization Act, to further efforts to reform committee procedures, particularly to make them more democratic and accountable to the membership and the public.

Each Senate and House committee is required to establish and publish rules of procedure. These rules have stipulated that each chamber's standing committees must fix regular meeting days, though the rules authorize the chairman to call additional meetings. The rules also must contain procedures under which a committee majority may call a meeting if the chairman fails to do so.

Committees were required by the 1970 act to keep transcripts of their meetings and to make public all roll-call votes. In the House the rules require that information about committee votes be made available to the public at the committees' offices; the committees are directed to provide a description of each amendment, motion, order or "other proposition" voted on and the name of each committee member voting for or against the issue as well as those present but not voting. The rules also require that the results of all votes to report legislation be published in the committee reports (but the positions of each member do not have to be included).

In the Senate, the rules are less specific. They require that a committee's report on a bill include the results of roll-call votes on "any measure or any amendment thereto" unless the results have been announced previously by the committee. Senate rules require that in reporting roll-call votes the position of each voting member is to be disclosed.

The rules stipulate that it is the chairman's "duty" to see to it that legislation approved by his committee is reported. And there are procedures by which a committee majority may force a bill out of committee if the chairman fails to do so. The rules prohibit a committee from reporting any measure unless a majority of its members are actually present, and they place certain limits on proxy voting. Members are allowed time to file supplemental and minority views for inclusion in committee reports.

Although the regulations often are set aside, committees are supposed to announce hearings at least one week in advance, in most circumstances to hold meetings in open session, and to require witnesses to file written statements in advance. The rules allow minority party members to call witnesses during at least one day of hearings on a subject.

Committee Assignments

The rules of the House and Senate state that the membership of each house shall elect its members to committees. In practice, representatives of the two parties agree on committee assignments in advance and then submit their choices to the chambers, which simply ratify the parties' lists.

With some exceptions, the method currently in general use was adopted by the Senate in 1846 and by the House in 1911. The major difference involves the Democratic Party. Today the list of Democratic committee nominees is subject to prior approval by the party caucuses of the House and Senate.

The committee assignment procedure applies to all members and takes place at the beginning of every Congress. Barring a change in party control, however, the biannual practice usually affects only new members, who receive committee positions for the first time. Committee assignments also must be made from time to time during a session to fill vacancies caused by a member's death, resignation or voluntary transfer to another committee.[13]

At the beginning of a new Congress, resolutions are adopted by both houses containing the membership roster of the committees; the roster lists the names of the members submitted by the caucuses of the two parties. In the House, the majority party, usually after negotiations with the minority, sets the size of each committee in drawing up the membership roster that is presented to the House. (In the Senate, the size of the committees is established by the standing rules.) *(See also Party Ratios, p. 82)*

Although the procedural reforms of the 1970s established new methods for selecting committee chairmen, seniority still is rigidly adhered to in positioning members on committees and in filling vacancies, with new members being ranked at the bottom of his or her committees.

Members who stay on the same committee from one Congress to another are given the same seniority ranking they had in the previous Congress, unless a death, resignation or retirement on the committee allows them to move up a notch. But if a member, even a senior member, transfers from one committee to another, he is ranked at the bottom in seniority on his new committee.

As a rule, a member of Congress remains on his major committees throughout his career, gradually working his way up by longevity. And if he has done reasonably well, and not made a lot of enemies, he usually can expect to become the chairman or ranking minority member despite the changes in seniority since the early 1970s.

Many factors are involved in the decisions of the party leadership in assigning new members to committees, but once a member is assigned a committee, seniority remains the most important single factor in determining his advancement on that committee.

In the Senate, the Democratic committee roster is drawn up by the Democratic Steering Committee, headed by the party leader, who appoints the other Steering Committee members. The roster was first made subject to caucus approval in 1971. The Senate Republican committee roster is drawn up by the Republican Committee on Committees, which is appointed by the chairman of the Republican Conference (caucus), but the Republican Conference does not vote on the committee's nominations.

Resolutions containing each party's list of Senate committee assignments then go to the Senate, where approval is automatic, thus merely formalizing the committee appointments recommended by the two parties and the party ratios previously agreed upon.

In the House the Democratic committee roster is drawn up by the party's Steering and Policy Committee, whose nominations also are subject to caucus approval.

(From 1911 until 1975, Democratic committee assignments were made by the Democratic members of the Ways and Means Committee.) An exception applies to the Democratic members of the Rules Committee. In 1975 the Speaker was given the power to nominate all party members of that panel, again subject to ratification by the caucus.

Republican committee nominations in the House are determined by the party's Committee on Committees, made up of one representative from each state having at least one Republican in its House delegation. The committee is subdivided into an executive committee of about 15 members who cast as many votes as there are Republican members in their state delegations. This weighted voting permits big-state members of the executive committee to dominate assignments. The nominations first are submitted to the full Committee on Committees for approval. Unlike the Democratic Caucus, the House Republican Conference does not vote on all committee nominations. However, under a 1971 procedural change it does vote on the ranking Republican member of each committee.

The committee rosters prepared by the two parties then are incorporated in a single resolution, which must be adopted by the House. As in the Senate, this usually is a formality.

Factors in Assignments

Various factors govern the appointment of members to committees, including party loyalty, regional and state considerations, party ties and past loyalty, personal preferences of the leadership and previous experience.[14]

Some committees typically have an ideological bias or special-interest cast. The Agriculture committees, for example, are manned largely by members from farm states, the Interior committee by members from the Far West and Rocky Mountain states. The Armed Services committees usually have members from California, New York and the Deep South, where defense-related industries and shipbuilding plants are concentrated.

However, Davidson and Oleszek point out that since the 1970s "there have been concerted efforts to add people with different perspectives to panels whose ideological makeup is skewed in one direction. In 1971 two House committees dominated by conservatives — Appropriations and Armed Services — had liberal legislators appointed to them despite the protests of their respective chairmen." [15]

The Oversight Function

Congress has given the executive branch broad authority over the vast array of agencies and programs it has created. As the range of activities of the federal government has grown, so has the need for Congress to oversee how the executive branch administers the laws it has passed.

"A thoughtful, well-drafted law offers no guarantee that the policy intentions of legislators will be carried out," warns Oleszek. "The laws passed by Congress are general guidelines, sometimes deliberately vague in wording. The implementation of legislation involves development of administrative regulations by the executive agencies and day-to-day program management by agency officials. These are the subject of 'legislative oversight' — the continuing review by Congress of how effectively the executive branch is carrying out congressional mandates." [16]

1946 Mandate

Congress did not officially recognize its responsibility for oversight until enactment of the 1946 Legislative Reorganization Act. That law mandated that the House and Senate standing committees exercise "continuous watchfulness of the execution by the administrative agencies" of any laws under their jurisdiction.

Since that time, Congress has passed several measures affecting oversight activities.[17] In the 1970 Legislative Reorganization Act, Congress increased staff assistance to all House and Senate committees, recommended that committees ascertain whether programs within their jurisdiction should be funded annually, and required most committees to issue oversight reports every two years.

Congress acted in 1974 to improve its oversight procedures when it passed the Congressional Budget and Impoundment Control Act. That act strengthened the General Accounting Office's (GAO) role in acquiring fiscal, budgetary and program-related information from federal agencies, authorized the GAO to establish an office to develop and recommend methods by which Congress could review and evaluate federal programs and activities and authorized committees to assess the effectiveness of such programs and to require government agencies to carry out their own evaluations.

Oversight Committees

Related changes in committee practices adopted by the House in 1974 required committees with more than 15 members either to set up an oversight subcommittee or to require their legislative committees to carry out oversight functions. (In 1975 the minimum committee size needed to trigger the oversight requirement was raised to 20.)

Legislative subcommittees can carry out oversight only within their limited jurisdictions. On the other hand, most subcommittees set up specifically to conduct oversight usually can operate within the full committee's jurisdiction, a much broader mandate.

The House committee changes also gave seven committees — Budget, Armed Services, Education and Labor, Foreign Affairs, Interior and Insular Affairs, Science and Technology and Small Business — special oversight responsibilities that permitted them to cross jurisdictional lines in conducting investigations. In another step affecting oversight, the new procedures permitted committees to triple the size of their professional staffs.

On the Senate side, the 1977 committee reorganization granted several committees "comprehensive policy oversight" responsibilities, comparable to the special oversight mandate in the House. Committees were required to include in the reports accompanying legislation the regulatory impact of each bill or joint resolution.

Oversight Panels

In 1982 there were 11 House committees with oversight subcommittees: Armed Services; Banking, Finance and Urban Affairs; Energy and Commerce; Interior and Insular Affairs; Post Office and Civil Service; Public Works and Transportation; Science and Technology; Small Business; Veterans' Affairs; Ways and Means; and Select Intelligence. In addition to these panels, there were four committees whose function was implicitly oversight: Appropriations, Budget, District of Columbia and Government Operations.

There were five Senate committees with oversight sub-

committees as of 1982: Agriculture, Nutrition and Forestry; Environment and Public Works; Finance; Governmental Affairs (which had three oversight subcommittees); and Labor and Human Resources. As in the House, there were other Senate committees with implicit oversight functions: Appropriations and Budget.

Oversight Techniques

Oleszek has identified a variety of means by which Congress exercises its oversight functions:[18]

● Hearings and investigations, the most common and reoccuring form of oversight. The Justice Department's settlement of an anti-trust suit against American Telephone and Telegraph Co. (AT&T) in January 1982 prompted an oversight hearing by the Senate Commerce Committee to examine the terms of the settlement. A bill that had been passed by the Senate in 1981 was preempted by the settlement, and Sen. Larry Pressler, R-S.D., said the hearing was "a good forum to discuss how this agreement meets the goals of [the Senate-passed bill] and what legislative action needs to be taken at this point." Some committee members expressed doubt that the Justice Department had reflected the intentions of the Senate in drafting the settlement.

● Legislative veto of executive actions by one or both houses of Congress or by the committee with jurisdiction over the subject matter. For example, Congress used the legislative veto mechanism in 1982 to block implementation of a Federal Trade Commission (FTC) rule regulating sales of used cars that automobile dealers vigorously opposed. Congress had approved legislation in 1980 designed to curtail FTC regulations by means of the veto. That measure was one of about 200 laws containing more than 250 legislative veto provisions. (Legislative veto procedure, p. 69)

● Authorizations, especially annual authorizations that allow for frequent reviews of agency performance, and appropriations, which Oleszek describes as probably Congress' most effective oversight tool. With the disclosures in 1974-75 of improper activities by U.S. intelligence agencies, select committees of both the House and Senate, as well as a special presidential commission, investigated the Central Intelligence Agency and other sectors of the intelligence community.

Executive restructuring of the government's foreign intelligence operations and firmer congressional oversight of federal intelligence operations was accompanied by the creation of permanent Select Intelligence committees in the Senate (1976) and the House (1977). Both committees annually review the CIA's budget requests as well as oversee its clandestine operations.

● Nonstatutory controls, such as informal contacts between executive officials and committee members and staff, and statements incorporated in committee reports and conference reports, hearings and floor debates. According to Oleszek and Davidson, "non-statutory controls may be the most common form of congressional oversight. Administrators are well advised to consider carefully such informal instructions." [19] The authors add that the courts often rely on committee report language to interpret congressional intent. (See also court decision on custom of inserting congressional directives in committee and conference reports, p. 42)

● General Accounting Office audits of agencies and programs.

● Requirements that executive agencies submit to Congress periodic reports on program implementation.

● Informal groups within Congress and organizations outside Congress that inform members about specific problems in administering programs.

● The Senate confirmation process. The Senate's power to reject a president's nominee for a high-level administration position is a latent power that is seldom exercised either in committee or on the Senate floor. Usually the threat of its use is enough to deter presidents from nominating persons totally unacceptable to Congress. However, in the early days of the Reagan administration the Senate Foreign Relations Committee voted 13-4 to recommend that the Senate not confirm the nomination of Ernest W. Lefever as assistant secretary of state for human rights. Lefever withdrew his name from consideration before the nomination went to the Senate for a vote. Certain nominees in the past had been forced to withdraw in the face of a likely adverse committee vote, but according to committee experts the Lefever case was possibly the first in which the Foreign Relations Committee had taken the step of rejecting a presidential nominee.

● Program evaluation through the use of social science and management methodology, such as surveys, cost-benefit analyses and efficiency studies.

● Casework, the handling of constituent questions and problems regarding federal agency actions, by the staffs of individual members of Congress.

● Studies by congressional support agencies, including the Congressional Research Service, the Office of Technology Assessment and the Congressional Budget Office.

Effectiveness of Oversight

In the 1970s Congress began to express greater interest in oversight. This was attributed to several factors, such as "... dissatisfaction with big government; the rapid growth of congressional staff; revelations of executive abuses by agencies such as the FBI, CIA and IRS; the influx of new legislators skeptical of government's ability to perform effectively; and recognition that in a time of fiscal and resource scarcity Congress must make every dollar count." [20]

But some critics charged that congressional oversight remained largely ineffective. They cited the lack of institutional or political incentives to reward those members who conduct oversight; "sweetheart" alliances between the committees that have jurisdiction over the agencies that administer the programs being investigated; statutes with vague and imprecise language regarding program objectives, which thwart assessment; committee limitations, including unsystematic committee review of agency activities, inadequate coordination among committees sharing jurisdiction over the same agencies and programs, and congressional staffers' lack of understanding of programs approved by Congress because of frequent staff turnover. [21]

In addition, effective oversight requires the cooperation of the executive branch, and occasionally the federal bureaucracy or the White House has been recalcitrant in providing committees with materials they deem necessary to carry out their oversight responsibilities.

In 1981 the Oversight and Investigations Subcommittee of the House Energy and Commerce Committee, which was investigating the impact of Canadian investment and energy policy on American business, requested certain documents from the Interior Department. When the docu-

TV Cameras in Committee

All House and Senate committees allow television and radio coverage of hearings that are open to the public. Some committees permit markup sessions to be broadcast.

The Senate has a long tradition of allowing broadcast coverage of committee hearings. Senate rules leave to each committee the decision whether to admit radio and television coverage of a particular hearing. That decision usually is made by the committee chairman or, if there is an objection by a member, by a majority of the committee.

Until recent years the House was less hospitable to broadcasters than the Senate. After permitting a telecast of floor proceedings in 1947 — the first telecast of a congressional session — the House leadership closed the chamber to television and prescribed the same policy for committees. It was not until passage of the Legislative Reorganization Act of 1970 that the House sanctioned broadcast coverage of committee hearings.

In 1974, to permit television coverage of the Judiciary Committee's sessions on proposed articles of impeachment against President Nixon, the House amended its rules to allow broadcasting of markup meetings as well as hearings. Previously, rules had barred television and radio from markup sessions and other meetings.

While the Senate leaves decisions on broadcast coverage to its committees, the House incorporated in its standing rules a stringent set of standards that committees must follow when they allow broadcast coverage of their hearings or bill-drafting sessions. (Televising the House and Senate, box, p. 49)

ments were not forthcoming, the subcommittee subpoenaed Interior Secretary James G. Watt. The department nevertheless still refused to hand over some of the documents requested, and President Reagan claimed "executive privilege," citing sensitive foreign policy negotiations and deliberations in progress as justification for withholding the information.

Congress traditionally has looked askance at claims of executive privilege, charging that such immunity is an infringement of its legislative and oversight prerogatives. The subcommittee in the Canadian investment case voted to find Secretary Watt in contempt of Congress, an action that theoretically could have resulted in Watt's imprisonment if the House had agreed to the finding. The full committee also voted in favor of the contempt citation, but further House action was canceled when Interior surrendered the documents to the subcommittee. The compromise, according to subcommittee Chairman John D. Dingell, D-Mich, sustained the right of Congress to obtain executive documents.

Rules Governing Composition...

The following guidelines regulate the composition of congressional committees. In the House, they are determined by the Democratic Caucus and Republican Conference. In the Senate, they are set forth in the standing rules. *(Assignments procedures, p. 86)*

House

As the ruling party in 1983, the Democrats, through their caucus, divide the various House committees into three categories: exclusive, major and nonmajor. Exclusive committees are Appropriations; Ways and Means; and Rules. Major committees are Agriculture; Armed Services; Banking, Finance and Urban Affairs; Education and Labor; Foreign Affairs; Energy and Commerce; Judiciary; and Public Works and Transportation. Nonmajor committees are Budget; District of Columbia; Government Operations; House Administration; Interior and Insular Affairs; Merchant Marine and Fisheries; Post Office and Civil Service; Science and Technology; Small Business; and Veterans' Affairs. House select and joint committees remain within the purview of the House leadership, with the Speaker appointing the Democratic members and the minority leader the Republicans.

Democrats serving on an exclusive committee may not serve on any other standing committee; the only exception is that members of the Ways and Means and Appropriations committees may sit on the Budget Committee.

The party's caucus rules guarantee all Democrats a seat on one major or exclusive committee. No Democrat may serve on more than one major and one nonmajor, or on more than two nonmajor committees. Democrats are permitted a maximum of five subcommittee assignments. Another exception to the caucus rules allows Democrats to be assigned to either the District of Columbia or Judiciary committees regardless of other committee assignments.

Generally, Democrats are limited to one chairmanship — they may not simultaneously chair another full, select, permanent select, special, ad hoc or joint committee without the approval of the caucus. The only exceptions are that the Ways and Means Committee chairman may also serve as chairman of the Joint Committee on Taxation, and the House Administration Committee chairman may chair the Joint Printing Committee or the Joint Committee on the Library.

Committee chairmen may chair only one subcommittee of their committee and may not chair any subcommittee of another committee. No Democrat may chair more than one subcommittee of a committee with legislative jurisdiction, though Budget Committee members are exempt from this rule. The House Administration and Standards of Official Conduct committees as well as the joint committees are exempt from all caucus provisions regulating subcommittee chairmanships.

The Republican Conference dictates committee regulations for the minority party. The party's conference rules limit members of the party leadership to service on only one standing committee and prohibit them from serving as ranking minority member of any committee.

House Republicans tend to be less stringent than the Democrats in their committee regulations. The GOP defines major and minor committees essentially the same way as the Democrats, though the rules

---

A number of innovations have been recommended to make legislative oversight more effective, including the so-called "sunset" legislation considered in the late 1970s that would require Congress to re-establish various federal programs on a systematic basis, thus forcing Congress to take periodic affirmative action to keep federal programs in existence. There also have been proposals to require congressional committees to set forth in detail the goals legislation is designed to achieve and to specify the annual results expected. These proposals were never approved by Congress.

Early Use of Committees

Congressional committees became a major factor in the legislative process by evolution, not by constitutional design. The committee concept was borrowed from the British Parliament and transmitted to the New World by way of the colonial legislatures, most notably those of Pennsylvania and Virginia. But the committee system as it developed in Congress was modified and influenced by characteristics peculiar to American life.

In the early days of the Republic, when the nation's population was small and the duties of the central government were carefully circumscribed, Congress had little need for the division of labor that today's committee system provides. A people who viewed with grave suspicion the need to delegate authority to elected representatives in Washington were served by a Congress that only grudgingly delegated any of its own powers to committees.

In the early Congresses, legislative proposals were considered first in the Senate or House chamber, after which a special or select committee was appointed to work out the details of the legislation. Once the committee submitted its

...Of Congressional Committees

governing numbers and types of committee assignments are less precise. The Republicans' "blue ribbon" committees correspond to the Democrats exclusive committees, and it is rare for a Republican on a blue ribbon committee to sit on another committee.

Republicans may serve on one major committee and one minor committee, or on at least two minor committees. Except for certain rules for ranking committee members, the Republicans have no specific limitations on subcommittee assignments. No Republican may serve as the ranking member of more than one standing, select or ad hoc committee and of more than one subcommittee of any standing, select or ad hoc committee without the approval of the GOP Committee on Committees. No member may serve as ranking Republican member of more than two subcommittees of the standing, select and ad hoc committees on which he serves. And Republicans cannot be the ranking member on two subcommittees of the same committee. But this rule may be waived upon recommendation of the Committee on Committees.

Senate

Senate regulations dealing with the composition of committees were formalized in the 1977 committee reorganization plan. The Senate divides its standing committees into major and minor committees. Major ones are Agriculture, Nutrition and Forestry; Appropriations; Armed Services; Banking, Housing and Urban Affairs; Commerce, Science and Transportation; Energy and Natural Resources; Environment and Public Works; Finance; Foreign Relations; Governmental Affairs; Human Resources; and Judiciary. Minor committees are Rules and Administration; Veterans' Affairs; Aging; Intelligence; Small Business; the Joint Economic Committee; and the Joint Committee on Internal Revenue Taxation.

Senators — Democrats and Republicans — may sit on two major committees and one minor committee. Each senator is limited to membership on three subcommittees of each major committee on which he serves (the Appropriations Committee is exempt from the limit) and on two subcommittees of his minor committee. The chairman or ranking minority member of a committee may serve as an ex officio member without a vote on any subcommittee of that committee. There are numerous exceptions to these regulations that protect incumbent senators who would have been in violation of these rules at the time they took effect. By agreement of the majority and minority leaders, the limits on committee service may be ignored to maintain majority party control. Senate rules also permit a temporary addition of one or two members to committees above the official limits.

Though not part of the Senate rules, the 1977 committee reorganization suggested that no member of a committee receive a second subcommittee assignment until all members of the committee had received a first assignment.

A senator may serve as chairman of only one full committee at a time and may chair only one subcommittee of each committee on which he serves. The chairman of a major committee may serve as chairman of only one subcommittee of his major committees and one subcommittee of his minor committee. The chairman of a minor committee may not serve as chairman of any subcommittee on that committee; he may chair one subcommittee of each of his major committees.

---

report on the bill, it was dissolved. Approximately 350 such committees were created during the Third Congress alone.[22]

In the House, legislation first was considered in the Committee of the Whole House on the State of the Union — usually referred to merely as the Committee of the Whole — and then sent to an ad hoc, or select, committee. (The Committee of the Whole, another procedure borrowed from the British Parliament, is nothing more than the House operating under special rules to expedite business. During the early Congresses, when it was used to oversee the select committees, debate was unlimited. *Details, see Legislative Process chapter.*)

As legislation increased in volume and complexity, permanent (standing) committees gradually replaced select committees, and legislation was referred directly to the committees without first being considered by the parent body. This procedure gave the committees initial authority over legislation, each in its specialized jurisdiction, subject to subsequent review by the full chamber.

The First Standing Committees

The House led the way in the creation of standing committees. The Committee on Elections, created in 1789, was followed by the Claims Committee in 1794 and by Commerce and Manufacturers and Revision of the Laws in 1795. The number had risen to 10 by 1810. The next substantial expansion of committees did not occur until the administration of President James Monroe (1817-25). Between the War of 1812 and the Civil War the standing committee system became the standard vehicle for consideration of legislative business by the House, but it was not yet fully exploited as a source of independent power.[23]

The Senate was even slower in establishing standing committees. In the first 25 years of its existence, only four

Proxy Voting in Committee: The Bane of the Minority Party

Proxy voting in congressional committees permits one committee member to authorize another member to cast his votes for him in his absence. Though on first glance it appears to be an innocuous practice, it has been the bane of the minority party in Congress and a target of reformers for years.

Opponents contend that it encourages absenteeism and irresponsibility. Before the power of committee chairmen was diminished in the 1970s, it also was argued that proxy voting contributed to the domination of committees by the chairmen because the chairmen were in an ideal position to wrest proxies from committee members in return for the favors they could bestow.

And while chairmen no longer wield the power they once did, proxy voting, according to the minority party — particularly Republicans in the House — allows the majority to abuse the committee system.

Before 1970 the use of proxies was regulated either by custom or by guidelines established by individual committees; thus the practice differed from committee to committee. In some committees they never were allowed.

Proxy voting is not permitted on the floor of the Senate or House.

House

The Legislative Reorganization Act of 1970 was the first measure to address the criticisms leveled at proxy voting. That act prohibited the practice unless a committee's written rules specifically allowed it, in which case they were limited to a specific issue (a bill or an amendment or for procedural questions, for internal committee business, etc.). They also had to be in writing, designating the person on the committee authorized to use them.[1]

In October 1974 the House voted 196-166 to ban proxy voting entirely. But the ban did not last long, primarily because Democrats, who as the majority party controlled House operations, benefited from the use of proxies.

Republicans, a minority in the House for all but two Congresses since 1931, have argued that the Democrats' use of proxies allows them to extend their control over the committee system by scheduling numerous committee and subcommittee sessions at the same time.

Without proxy votes, the Democrats could not retain control of all committee business on all the committees because of scheduling conflicts.

The Democratic Caucus modified the ban at the beginning of the 94th Congress in 1975. The revision, which was added to the standing rules, once again gave committees the authority to decide whether to permit proxy voting. If a committee allowed proxies, they were to be used only on a specific amendment or procedural question. General proxies, covering all matters before a committee for either a specific time period or for an indefinite period, were prohibited. And, as before, they had to be in writing, with a member designated to cast the proxies. The proxy vote also had to be dated and could not be used to make a quorum.

Senate

For Senate committees, the 1970 act provided little restraint on the use of proxies. The law said proxy votes could not be used to report legislation if committee rules barred their use. If proxies were not forbidden on a motion to report a bill, they nevertheless could be used only upon the formal request of a senator who planned to be absent during a session.

Senate rules leave it up to individual committees to decide whether or not to allow proxies. To prevent the use of general proxies, Senate rules bar the use of a proxy if an absent member "has not been informed of the matter on which he is being recorded and has not affirmatively requested that he be so recorded." Proxies cannot be counted toward the quorum needed for reporting legislation.

In addition to proxy voting, some Senate committees permit polling, that is, holding an informal vote of committee members instead of convening the committee. Such votes usually are taken by sending a voting sheet to committee members' offices or by taking members' votes by telephone.

Because Senate rules require a quorum to be present for a committee to report legislation, polling is supposed to be restricted to issues involving legislation still pending before the committee, to matters relating to investigations and to internal committee business.

If polling is used to report legislation, any senator can challenge the bill.[2] Such was the case in December 1980 when opponents of a Carter nominee for a federal judgeship charged that the nomination had not been properly reported because the Judiciary Committee had approved it by a written poll of members.

The issue was dropped and the nominee was approved when Judiciary Chairman Edward M. Kennedy, D-Mass., gained Republican support by agreeing not to push other Carter judicial nominations pending in the committee.[3]

---

1. For a discussion of proxy voting in the House, see U.S., House, Select Committee on Committees, *Final Report*, 96th Cong., 2d sess. (1980), pp. 571-581.
2. For a discussion of proxy voting and polling in the Senate, see U.S., Senate, Office of Legal Counsel, *Manual of Senate Committee Procedure* (February 1981), pp. 31-38.
3. *Congressional Quarterly 1980 Almanac* (Washington, D.C.: Congressional Quarterly, 1981), pp. 16-A, 18-A.

standing committees were created, and all of them on the whole were more administrative than legislative. Most of the committee work fell to select committees, usually of three members, appointed as the occasion demanded and disbanded when their task was completed. These occasions were so frequent that during the session of 1815-16 between 90 and 100 select committees were appointed. Frequently, however, related legislation would be referred to special committees already in existence and the same senators appointed to deal with the related proposals.

In 1816 the Senate, finding inconvenient the appointment of so many ad hoc committees during each session, added 11 standing committees to the existing four. By 1863 the number had grown to 19.[24]

Committee Membership

Each chamber developed its own method of making appointments to the committees. The first rule established by the House in 1789 with respect to committee appointments reserved to the whole House the power to choose the membership of all committees composed of more than three members. That rule gave way in 1790 to a rule delegating this power to the Speaker, with the reservation that the House might direct otherwise in special cases. Eventually, however, the Speaker was given the right to appoint the members as well as the chairmen of all standing committees, a power he retained until 1911.

The principle that the committees were to be bipartisan, but weighted in favor of the majority party and its policies, was established early.[25]

In making committee appointments and promotions, certain principles governed the Speaker's choices. The wishes of the minority leaders in filling vacancies going to members of their party usually were respected. Generally, seniority — length of service on the committee — and factors such as geographical distribution and party loyalty were considered. But the Speaker was not bound by such criteria, and there were cases where none of those factors outweighed the Speaker's wishes. Despite complaints and various attempts to change the rule, the system remained in force until 1911, when the House again exercised the right to select the members of standing committees.

In the Senate, until 1823, assignment to a committee was made by vote of the entire membership. Members wishing to serve on a particular committee were placed on a ballot, with the choicest committee assignments going to those receiving the most votes. The senator with the largest number of votes served as chairman.

By the 1820s, however, a number of difficulties with the ballot system had become evident. The arrangement proved tedious and time consuming and provided no guarantee that the party in control of the chamber would hold a majority of seats on the committee or retain control of the committee chairmanships in the event of a vacancy. Several times in the ensuing years the Senate amended its rules to provide for appointment to committees by a designated official, usually the vice president or president pro tempore. However, abuse of the appointment power and a transfer of power between the two parties compelled the Senate to return to use of the ballot.

In 1823 a proposal that the chairmen of the five most important committees be chosen by the full Senate, and that the chairmen then have the power to make all other committee assignments, was rejected. The Senate instead amended the standing rules to give the "presiding officer" authority to make committee assignments, unless otherwise ordered by the Senate. Since Daniel D. Tompkins, vice president during the administration of James Monroe, scarcely ever entered the chamber, committee selection was left to the president pro tempore, who in effect had been chosen by and was responsible to the Senate majority leadership. But when the next vice president, John C. Calhoun, used the assignment power with obvious bias, the Senate quickly and with little dissent returned to the election method to fill committee vacancies.[26]

This time the chairmen were picked by majority vote of the entire Senate; then ballots were taken to select the other members of each committee, with members' rank on the committee determined by the size of their plurality. The Senate in 1828 changed the rules to provide for appointment to committees by the president pro tempore, but in 1833 it reverted to selection by ballot when control of the Senate changed hands. Since 1833 the Senate technically has made its committee assignments by ballot.

To avoid the inconveniences inherent in the ballot system, it became customary between 1833 and 1846 to suspend the rule by unanimous consent and designate an officer (the vice president, the president pro tempore or the "presiding officer") to assign members to committees.

The method of selecting committee members in use in 1982 was — with some modification — developed in 1846. In that year a motion to entrust the vice president with the task was defeated, and the Senate proceeded under the regular rules to make committee assignments by ballot. But after six chairmen had been selected, a debate ensued on the method of choosing the other members of the committees. At first, several committees were filled by lists — arranged in order of a member's seniority — submitted by the majority leader. After a number of committees had been filled in this manner, the ballot rule was suspended, and the Senate approved a list for the remaining vacancies that had been agreed upon by both the majority and minority leadership.[27]

Since 1846 the choice of committees usually has amounted to routine acceptance by the Senate of lists drawn up by special committees of the two major parties (today the Committee on Committees for the Republicans and the Steering Committee for the Democrats).

Committee Proliferation

The standing committee system, firmly established in the first half of the 19th century, expanded rapidly in the second half. During this period the committees developed into powerful, autonomous institutions, increasingly independent of the House and Senate and party control. Committee chairmen assumed ever greater powers over legislation. So great was their influence that Woodrow Wilson in 1885 could write: "I know not how better to describe our form of government in a single phrase than by calling it a government by the chairmen of the standing committees of Congress." [28]

The committee chairmen became even more powerful figures following the House "revolution" of 1909-10, which curtailed the powers of the Speaker and split up the House leadership. Committee seniority, already used extensively by the Speaker as a method for selecting the chairmen, was firmly established from that time on until the reforms of the 1970s.

The number of standing committees reached a peak in 1913, when there were 61 in the House and 74 in the Senate. The Appropriations, Ways and Means, Finance and Rules committees, in particular, exercised great influence; others were created and perpetuated chiefly to provide members with offices and clerical staff.

Committee Reorganization

Initial efforts to consolidate the House committee system were undertaken in 1909, when six minor committees were dropped. Two years later, when the Democrats took control, six superfluous committees were abolished. Up to that time, according to Galloway, "the reorganizations of 1910 and 1911 [were] the most spectacular and best known of any associated with Congress." [29]

Ten years later another committee reorganization took place. As a consequence of enactment of the Budget and Accounting Act of 1921, the House restored to its Appropriations Committee exclusive jurisdiction over all appropriations bills for federal departments and programs.

Before the creation of the Appropriations committees (1865 in the House and 1867 in the Senate), a single committee in each chamber had handled both revenue raising and appropriations legislation. In 1885 the House dispersed the powers of its Appropriations Committee among nine committees.[30] The Senate later followed the House example, and by 1914 eight of 14 annual appropriations bills were referred to committees other than the Appropriations panel.

Although this method allowed committees most familiar with each federal agency and its programs to consider their funding requirements, it resulted in a division of responsibility that did not permit congressional consideration or control of financial policy to be centralized. Accordingly, the House in 1920 and the Senate in 1922 restored exclusive spending powers to the Appropriations committees.

In 1921 the Senate reduced the number of its committees from 74 to 34. In many respects this rationalization of the committee structure simply was the formal abandonment of long-defunct bodies such as the Committee on Revolutionary Claims.[31] The House in 1927 reduced the number of its committees by merging 11 expenditures committees, those dealing mainly with oversight, into a single Committee on Expenditures in the Executive Departments.

1946/1970 Reorganization Acts

The next major overhaul of the committee structure took place in 1946 with enactment of the Legislative Reorganization Act. By dropping minor committees and merging those with related functions, the act achieved a net reduction of 18 in the number of Senate committees (from 33 to 15) and of 29 in the number of House committees (from 48 to 19). The act also defined in detail the jurisdictions of each committee and attempted to set ground rules for their operations.[32]

Between 1946 and a partial reorganization of Senate committees in 1977 only minor changes were made in the committee structure in Congress. During that period many of the achievements of the 1946 act were weakened by the gradual proliferation of subcommittees and by the creation of additional committees.

By the mid-1970s the standing committees still numbered only 21 in the House and 16 in the Senate, but by then there was a total of 268 subcommittees in both houses as well as seven joint committees and a growing number of select and special committees that had been set up to examine specific problems.

The Legislative Reorganization Act of 1970 changed some committee practices but made only minor revisions in the committee structure itself. It created a new Veterans' Affairs Committee in the Senate and made cosmetic changes such as renaming the Senate Committee on Banking and Currency the Banking, Housing and Urban Affairs Committee to reflect more accurately the committee's jurisdiction. The defunct Joint Committee on Immigration and Nationality Policy was formally abolished, and a Joint Committee on Congressional Operations was established.

The 1970 act marked the beginning of a decade of efforts in Congress to change the committee structure in the House and Senate.[33] But except for the 1977 changes in Senate committees, the modifications to the committee system had little impact. On the other hand, changes in House and Senate rules and in committee and parliamentary procedures had a significant impact on the way committees operated.

The principal changes affecting committee procedures required open committee hearings in most instances; required all roll-call votes taken in committee to be made available to the public; authorized radio and television coverage of House committee hearings (box, p. 89); authorized minority members of each House committee to select two of a committee's six permanent professional staff and permitted them to call witnesses of their choosing during at least one day of hearings on a bill; restricted newly elected senators to membership on only two major committees (and on only one of the following: Armed Services, Appropriations, Finance or Foreign Relations) and one minor, select or joint committee (committees classified as minor were District of Columbia, Post Office and Civil Service, Rules and Administration, and Veterans' Affairs; all other standing committees were considered major); and provided that a senator could not chair more than one full committee. (Current major and minor committees, box, p. 90)

House Committee Changes

An ambitious effort by the House in 1973-74 to consolidate and reorganize its committee structure met with limited success. A plan recommending broad changes in committees and committee jurisdictions was blocked by entrenched interests both in and out of Congress that benefited from the existing committee system.[34]

Subcommittee Bill of Rights

The House Democratic Caucus in January 1973 adopted a so-called subcommittee bill of rights. The new caucus rules created a party caucus for Democrats on each House committee and forced the chairmen to start sharing authority with other committee Democrats. Each committee caucus was granted the authority to select subcommittee chairmen (with members allowed to run for chairman based on their seniority ranking on the full committee), establish subcommittee jurisdictions, set party ratios on the subcommittees reflecting the ratio of the full committee, provide a subcommittee budget and guarantee all members a major subcommittee slot where vacancies made that possible. Each panel was authorized to hold hearings and set its own meeting times.

Under the "bill of rights," committee chairmen were required to refer designated types of legislation to each subcommittee within two weeks. They no longer could kill measures they opposed simply by pocketing them.

The Hansen Plan. The changes eventually adopted in 1974 came from a package of compromise recommendations proposed by Rep. Julia Butler Hansen, D-Wash. (1960-74), who headed the party's Committee on Organization, Study and Review.

The Hansen plan made some jurisdictional shifts — such as giving the Public Works Committee control over most transportation matters — but mainly it retained the existing committee structure dating from 1946.

Along with the minor committee adjustments came more procedural changes. Each standing committee's permanent staff, beginning in 1975, was increased from six to 18 professionals and from six to 12 clerks, with the minority party receiving one-third of each category. And in what would prove to be the most controversial provision, the plan gave the minority control of one-third of a committee's investigative staff funding. (The Democratic Caucus subsequently repealed the provision.)

In other changes, which also took effect in 1975, committees with more than 15 members (increased to more than 20 members by the Democratic Caucus in 1975) were required to establish at least four subcommittees. This change created an important precedent in that it institutionalized subcommittees for the first time. And committees with more than 15 members (increased to more than 20 in 1975 by the caucus) were required to set up an oversight subcommittee or to require their legislative subcommittees to carry out oversight functions.

Also affecting committees were new powers given the Speaker: he was authorized to refer bills that had been introduced to more than one committee at a time or to several committees in sequence. He also could split up bills and send the parts to different committees and set deadlines for committees to complete action and issue their report on legislation given multiple referral.

Proxy voting was banned in committee. (In 1975 proxy voting was partially restored by the Democratic Caucus: proxies were allowed on a specific issue or on procedural matters, and they had to be in writing and given to a member, among other requirements.)

Finally, the House was given a directive to organize itself for the next Congress in December of election years.

The Bolling Proposals. The Hansen plan was a substitute for a much broader bipartisan proposal, drafted by a special committee composed of five Democrats and five Republicans headed by Rep. Richard Bolling, D-Mo. The Bolling committee, which had been created in January 1973, submitted its reorganization proposals the following December.

Bolling proposed to consolidate related House committee jurisdictions within one committee. A frequent criticism of the existing committee setup was that it dispersed jurisdiction on related subjects among many panels. The plan would have reduced substantially the power and influence of the House Administration and Ways and Means committees. The latter, for example, would have lost its non-tax jurisdiction over foreign trade, unemployment compensation and health insurance. The plan also would have set up new committees on Energy and Environment, Public Works and Transportation, and Commerce and Health. Members would have been limited to membership on one of the 15 major committees in the plan.

Not surprisingly, the wholesale restructuring drew a flood of protest from chairmen and committee members who would have been adversely affected as well as from the lobbyists who dealt with those committees. The House Democratic Caucus shunted the plan to the Hansen committee, where it was watered down.

Both plans were brought to the House late in 1974, where the Bolling proposal was decisively rejected in favor of the Hansen substitute. Independent of the Hansen plan was the decision of the House to abolish the Internal Security Committee (until 1969 the House Un-American Activities Committee).

Caucus Actions Affecting Committees. Further changes in House committee operations unrelated to the Hansen plan were made in late 1974 and early 1975 by the Democratic Caucus. The impetus for these was the pickup of 43 additional seats by House Democrats in the November 1974 election, which gave the party a 291-144 majority.

Meeting in December 1974 to organize for the 94th Congress, Democrats decided to make a secret-ballot vote on the election of all committee chairmen automatic. In the past the procedure had been cumbersome. The new procedure allowed competitive nominations for chairmen if the original Steering Committee nominee was rejected. Democrats immediately made use of their new rule by deposing three committee chairmen. *(Details, Seniority chapter, p. 109)*

In other changes, the Democratic members of the Ways and Means Committee were stripped of their power to select the party's members of House committees; this authority was transferred to a revamped Democratic Steering and Policy Committee, whose members are appointed by the Speaker. At the same time, the caucus increased the size of the Ways and Means Committee from 25 to 37 members, a change aimed at giving the committee a more liberal outlook and thus more likely to support party-backed proposals on tax revision, health insurance and other issues. The caucus also required all committees to include a statement in their reports on a bill's impact on inflation and reports on appropriations measures to include information on changes in law made in the accompanying bill.

In actions affecting the independence of subcommittees, the caucus directed that the entire Democratic membership of each committee, rather than the chairmen alone, was to determine the number and jurisdiction of a committee's subcommittees. And the caucus specified that no member of a committee could become a member of a second subcommittee of that committee until every member of the full committee had chosen a subcommittee slot. (But a grandfather clause allowed sitting members on subcommittees to protect two subcommittee slots.) The one group of subcommittees that always had been semi-autonomous was the powerful units of the House Appropriations Committee. Thus the caucus decided that, along with full committee chairmen, all nominations for chairmen of these subcommittees would have to be approved by the Democratic Caucus. (Nominees for Appropriations subcommittee chairmen were selected by the membership of each subcommittee, with members bidding for subcommittee chairman in the order of their seniority on the subcommittee.)

The Speaker's powers were further buttressed by allowing him to select the Democratic members of the Rules Committee, subject to caucus approval.

All standing committees were given broad subpoena authority without the necessity of going to the House on each occasion to get approval. But subpoenas had to be

House Rules Committee Became . . .

The Rules Committee long has stood as a strategic gateway between the legislative committees and the floor of the House for all but the most routine legislation.

The power of the committee lies in its role of setting the rules or guidelines for floor debate on legislation. A "special rule" sets the time limit on general debate and regulates how the bill may be amended. It may forbid all amendments or, in some cases, all amendments except those proposed by the legislative committee that handled the bill. Thus the committee is able to structure the debate and the types of amendments that will be allowed on legislation or, on occasion, even prevent a bill from coming to the floor.

There have been frequent controversies throughout the history of the House over the function of the Rules Committee in the legislative process: whether it should be merely a clearinghouse, or traffic cop, for legislative business, the agent of the majority leadership, or a super-legislative committee editing the work of the other committees.

Defenders of the Rules Committee system of routing bills maintain it is the only feasible way to regulate the legislative flow efficiently in the 435-member House. And since the mid-1970s, in fact, the committee has returned to the role it performed until 1911 as an arm of the majority leadership.[1]

Changing Role of the Committee

The Rules Committee was established in 1789. Originally it was a select committee, authorized at the beginning of each Congress, with jurisdiction over House rules. However, since the rules of one Congress usually were readopted by the next, this function was not of great importance, and for many years the committee never issued a report.

In 1858 the Speaker was made a member of the committee, and in subsequent years the panel gradually increased its influence over legislation. The panel became a standing committee in 1880, and in 1883 it began the practice of issuing rules — special orders of business — for floor debate on legislation.

Other powers acquired by the committee over the years included the right to sit while the House was in session, to have its resolutions considered immediately (called privileged resolutions), and even to initiate legislation on its own, like any other legislative committee. Before 1910 the Rules Committee worked closely with the leadership in deciding what legislation could come to the floor. But in the Progressive revolt of 1909-10 against Speaker "Uncle Joe" Cannon, the committee was made independent of the leadership. Alternative methods of bringing legislation to the floor — the Discharge Calendar, Consent Calendar and Calendar Wednes-

day procedures — were added to the standing rules. And in 1910 a coalition of Democrats and insurgent Republicans succeeded in enlarging the Rules Committee and excluding the Speaker from it. (The ban on the Speaker was repealed in 1946, but subsequent Speakers have never sat on the committee.)

By the late 1930s the committee had come under the domination of a coalition of conservative Democrats and Republicans. From that time until the 1970s it repeatedly blocked or delayed liberal legislation.

Opposition to the obstructive tactics of the Rules Committee led, in 1949, to adoption of the "21-day rule." The rule provided that the chairman of a legislative committee that had approved a bill and requested a rule from the Rules Committee permitting the bill to be brought to the floor, could bring up the resolution if the committee failed to grant a rule within 21 calendar days of the committee's request. The rule required the Speaker to recognize the chairman of the committee wishing to call up the bill. Two years later, after the Democrats had lost 29 seats in the mid-term elections, the House repealed the 21-day rule. Although it had been used only eight times, the threat of its use was credited with prying other bills out of the Rules Committee.

House Revolt

At the beginning of the 86th Congress in 1959, a group of liberal Democrats dropped plans to seek a change in House rules that would break the conservative grip on the committee. Speaker Sam Rayburn, D-Texas (1913-61), assured them that bills reported from their committees would reach the House floor. However, the record of the 86th Congress showed that Rayburn often could not deliver on his promise. After the Rules Committee had blocked or delayed several measures that were to become key elements in the new Kennedy administration's legislative program, Democrats decided to act.

Accordingly, in 1961 the House by a narrow margin agreed to enlarge the committee from 12 to 15 members for the 87th Congress. That gave Rayburn and the administration a delicate 8-7 majority on most issues coming before the committee. By raising the number of Democrats to 10 from 8 (Republicans to 5 from 4), it permitted the appointment to the committee of two pro-administration Democrats. This enlargement was made permanent in 1963.

Nevertheless, dissatisfaction with the Rules Committee continued, and following the Democratic sweep in the 1964 elections the 21-day rule was revived. The new version of the rule, adopted by the House at the opening of the 89th Congress in 1965, did not require the Speaker to recognize a committee

... Arm of the Leadership in 1970s

chairman wishing to call up a 21-day resolution. Under the 1965 rule the Speaker retained discretion to recognize a committee chairman, so that it became highly unlikely for a bill to come up through this procedure without the approval of the House leadership. The new rule, which also was employed successfully only eight times, was abandoned in 1967 following Republican gains in the 1966 mid-term elections.

The House retained another rule, adopted in 1965, that curbed the committee's power to block conferences on legislation. Before 1965 most bills could be sent to a conference committee only through unanimous consent or adoption of a special rule issued by the Rules Committee. The 1965 change made it possible to send any bill to conference by majority vote of the House.

Despite repeal of the 21-day rule in 1967, the committee continued generally to pursue a stance more accommodating to the leadership. Several factors contributed to the committee's less conservative posture. First, it had lost its chairman of 12 years, Howard W. Smith, D-Va. (1931-67), who was defeated in a 1966 primary election. Smith was a skilled parliamentarian and the acknowledged leader of the House's conservative coalition — a voting alliance of Republicans and Southern Democrats. He was replaced as chairman by William M. Colmer, D-Miss. (1933-73). Although he also was a conservative, Colmer was unable to exert the high degree of control over legislation that Smith had exercised.

In addition, two liberal members had been added to the committee and a set of rules had been introduced to govern committee procedures. The rules took from the chairman the right to set meeting dates, a power Smith frequently had used to postpone or thwart action on bills he opposed. The consent of a majority was needed to kill a bill, and limits were placed on proxy voting.

The committee's latent powers of obstruction were obscured so long as it did not flaunt them, but in the closing days of the 1970 session the committee reverted to its old ways by refusing to approve several bills for House action.

Ally of Leadership

Liberal Democrats predicted a new era was at hand in 1973, when Colmer retired and was succeeded as chairman by Ray J. Madden, D-Ind. (1943-77). That same year, three Democrats considered loyal to the leadership were added to the committee.

The new makeup of the committee posed a different problem for the leadership. The panel approved for action a great deal of liberal legislation without regard to its chances of passage. The House itself, more conservative than the Rules Committee for the first time in years, began looking critically at the bills it scheduled for floor action and at the special rules under which they were to be debated.

Before 1973 the vast majority of the committee's special rules were approved with little opposition by the House. Between 1929 and 1972 rules issued by the committee were defeated on 50 occasions, but in 1973 alone the House rejected 13 rules.

In an attempt to strengthen the leadership's control over the committee, the Democratic Caucus voted in December 1974 to give the Speaker the power to nominate all Democratic members of the panel, subject to caucus approval. Using this power, Speaker Carl Albert, D-Okla. (1947-77), nominated liberals to fill two vacant positions.

But, although the committee was now allied with the leadership, the panel did not function immediately as an adjunct of the leadership. There were several reasons for this, according to political scientist Bruce I. Oppenheimer, including the fact that there was little assistance in that direction from Rules Chairman Madden or his successor, James J. Delaney, D-N.Y. (1945-47, 1949-78), who chaired the committee from 1977-78.[2]

Oppenheimer cited three new roles of the committee that began to take shape in the 94th Congress (1975-77): 1) expediting, rather than delaying, legislation for floor action; 2) providing a growing number of members having little experience in managing bills on the floor with a preview of what to expect in the House; and 3) assigning a few committee members the function of informing and advising the leadership on legislative matters.[3]

The Rules panel's gradual adjustment to its new position was manifested in several areas, according to Oppenheimer.[4] The first of these was the drafting of more complex rules, which provided greater leadership control of floor debate by resolving ahead of time some of the problems that resulted from the 1970s reforms, such as jurisdictional fights, unstructured floor debates and obstructive tactics.

A second area was the increase in legislative initiatives by the Rules Committee. The potential for such activity expanded significantly under Richard Bolling, D-Mo., who became chairman in 1979. Two standing subcommittees were created, and the committee's staff and budget were enlarged substantially.

A third area was the careful selection of party-oriented members to fill vacancies on the committee.

1. For a discussion, see Bruce I. Oppenheimer, "The Changing Relationship Between House Leadership and the Committee on Rules," in Frank H. Mackaman, ed., *Understanding Congressional Leadership* (Washington, D.C.: Congressional Quarterly Press, 1981), pp. 218-224.
2. Oppenheimer, "The Changing Relationship," p. 218.
3. Ibid., pp. 216-217.
4. Ibid., pp. 218-224.

approved by a majority of a committee.

Finally, reflecting their 1974 electoral gains, Democrats increased the party ratio on all House committees, except Standards of Official Conduct, to two Democrats to one Republican, plus one Democrat.

1977 Reorganization Plan

Another effort to restructure the committees was unsuccessful in 1977. In October of that year new recommendations for improving committee operations went down to defeat.[35] The House seemed to have had enough reform for the time being.

The Obey Commission. The new committee reorganization plan was drafted by the House Commission on Administrative Review, headed by Rep. David R. Obey, D-Wis. Included was a proposal to establish a select committee to suggest changes in committee practices. "Members have too many assignments, and jurisdictions are too confused for the strains and conflicts members currently endure to be substantially alleviated by piecemeal and procedural reform," a task force of the Obey commission had concluded. "The need for basic reform is crystal clear, and the House should act promptly to modernize the one instrument on which its effectiveness so critically depends — its committee system." [36]

Procedural Changes. In January 1977 the House approved a series of House rules changes affecting committee operations that had been endorsed by the Democratic Caucus in December 1976. In addition, it abolished the Joint Committee on Atomic Energy and stripped the House Committee on Standards of Official Conduct of its legislative jurisdictions.

In standing rules changes, committee privileges and powers were broadened; a quorum for conducting business, including bill-drafting sessions, was set at one-third of a committee's membership (for hearings, only two members need be present), and the subpoena power was extended to include subcommittees. All House-Senate conference committee meetings were required to be open to the public except when the House specifically voted to close a session (usually for national security reasons).

In a change that had been adopted by the Democratic Caucus in December 1976, the chairmen of the Ways and Means and Appropriations committees were stripped of their power to nominate the Democratic members of the Budget Committee; that power was transferred to the Democratic Steering and Policy Committee.

1979 Procedural Changes

The House Democratic Caucus, meeting in December 1978 to organize for the 96th Congress, further modified its rules on committee assignments and procedures.

The number of terms that Democrats were allowed to serve on the House Budget Committee was increased from two to three. (Under the two-term limit, seven committee members would have had to leave the 30-member committee.) Each House Democrat was limited to five subcommittee seats on House standing committees.

In a modification of a 1974 caucus rule, committees — except Appropriations — were required to allow each member to choose one subcommittee assignment before any member, without exception, could choose a second one. (In 1974 sitting members had been allowed to reserve two subcommittee positions.)

A committee chairman was prohibited from serving as chairman of any other standing, select, special or joint committee.

1980 Reorganization Failure

The House in March 1979 set up a Select Committee on Committees to once more recommend how to improve the House's internal organization and operations. But when the panel closed its doors in April 1980, it left behind barely a trace of its 13-month-long effort to change the House committee system.[37]

The panel had submitted five proposals: 1) that members be given space in the Capitol where they could work when floor action prevented them from returning to their offices; 2) that, to avoid scheduling conflicts in the House, committees be allowed to conduct business only on specified days; 3) that House Democrats be limited to five subcommittee assignments (a rule adopted in 1978 by the Democratic Caucus had applied only to subcommittee assignments on standing committees, not on select committees) and that, on a phased-in basis, each standing committee, except Appropriations, be limited to six subcommittees; 4) that one committee be designated as having primary responsibility for bills referred to more than one committee; and 5) that a separate standing committee on energy be created to untangle the existing overlapping committee jurisdictions dealing with energy-related legislation.

Of the five recommendations, none was adopted by the House. Only one — the plan to create an energy panel — went to the House floor, where the proposal was promptly gutted. In place of the select committee's plan, the House merely decided to rename its Commerce Committee the "Energy and Commerce" Committee and to designate that panel as its lead committee on energy matters.

In 1983, an additional change was made in the House rules. In response to concern about party loyalty, a rule was passed making continued assignment to House committees contingent upon members being members of their own party caucus. The change was made along with a change in the rules of the Democratic Caucus in December 1982 to throw a member out of the caucus if he or she switched parties.

Senate Committee Changes

While most of the attempts to reorganize the committee system in the 1970s were directed at the House, the Senate committee system was altered in 1977 by the first comprehensive committee consolidation in either house in 31 years. Earlier, in 1975, the Senate had adopted important procedural changes involving committees.

Senate Democrats that year voted to elect committee chairmen by secret ballot whenever one-fifth of the caucus requested it. Senate Republicans had decided in 1973 to choose their top-ranking committee members by conference votes.

Senate rules were changed to require most committee meetings, bill-drafting sessions as well as hearings, to be open to the public. A related rule change required Senate-House conference committees to be open to the public unless a majority of the conferees of either chamber voted in open session to close a meeting on a bill for that day. *(Conference committees, box, p. 83; related House rule, see above)*

Also in 1975, junior senators obtained committee staff

assistance for the first time. A new rule authorized them to hire up to three committee staffers — depending on the number and type of committee assignments they had — to work directly for them on their committees. In the past, committee staff members had been controlled by the chairmen and other senior committee members. *(Details, see Committee Staff chapter)*

1977 Committee Reorganization

The Senate in 1977 approved the first major restructuring of its committee system since the Legislative Reorganization Act of 1946. The changes were the product of a special committee that studied committee operations, chaired by Sen. Stevenson.[38]

The reorganization consolidated a number of Senate committees, revised jurisdictions of others, set a ceiling on the number of committees and subcommittees a senator can belong to or chair, gave minority members a larger share of committee staff and directed that committee hearings and other business be computerized to avoid scheduling conflicts.

One of the biggest organizational changes was the creation of a separate Energy Committee with authority over most aspects of energy policy except taxes.

The final result fell short of the Stevenson committee's goals for consolidating and merging committees. The original plan had called for abolition of all special, select and joint committees (except Select Intelligence) and of the District of Columbia, Post Office and Civil Service, Aeronautical and Space Sciences, and Veterans' Affairs committees.

But only six committees were abolished: District of Columbia, Post Office, and Space Sciences and the joint committees on Atomic Energy, Congressional Operations and Defense Production.

(The decision to end the joint committees was a unilateral Senate action. The House continued the Congressional Operations panel as a select committee for another two years.)

Special interest groups were able to preserve the Veterans' and Select Small Business committees, nearly preserved the Post Office and Civil Service Committee and thwarted plans to consolidate transportation legislation in one committee.

The 1977 changes established a committee structure consisting of 12 major committees, five minor committees and two joint committees, and committee jurisdictions and responsibilities were altered. *Major impact, box, p. 100)*

Changes also were made in Senate committee procedures. With certain exceptions, each senator was limited to membership on two major committees and one minor committee.

Each senator was limited to membership on three subcommittees of each major committee on which he served (the Appropriations Committee was exempted from this restriction). And each senator was limited to membership on two subcommittees of the minor committee on which he served.

Though it was not made a requirement, the Senate adopted language similar to the House's stating it to be the sense of the Senate that no member of a committee should receive a second subcommittee assignment until all members of the committee had received their first assignment.

The Senate also prohibited a senator from serving as chairman of more than one committee at the same time; prohibited a senator from serving as chairman of more than

one subcommittee on each committee of which he was a member; prohibited the chairman of a major committee from serving as chairman of more than one subcommittee on his major committees and as the chairman of more than one subcommittee on his minor committee, effective at the beginning of the 96th Congress; prohibited the chairman of a minor committee from chairing a subcommittee on that committee and prohibited him from chairing more than one of each of his major committees' subcommittees, which also took effect at the beginning of the the 96th Congress.

The Senate, in addition, banned any committee from establishing a subcommittee without approval of the full Senate, and required the Rules Committee to establish a central computerized scheduling service to keep track of meetings of Senate committees and subcommittees and House-Senate conference committees.

In a change related to staffing, the Senate required the staff of each committee to reflect the relative size of the minority and majority membership on the committee. On the request of the minority members of a committee, at least one-third of the staff of the committee was to be placed under the control of the minority party, except that staff deemed by the chairman and ranking minority member to be working for the whole committee would not be subject to the rule.

1981 Committee Changes

Few rules changes affecting the committee system were made at the outset of the 97th Congress. Party ratios on Senate committees were altered to reflect the GOP takeover of the Senate following the 1980 elections. But because of substantial Democratic electoral losses (resulting in many committee vacancies) only one surviving Democrat actually lost a committee assignment. *(House dispute over committee ratios, see p. 82)*

House Democrats, in a reversal of the 1970s trend, amended their caucus rules by voting to limit the number of subcommittees and similar committee sub-units that could be established by the House's standing committees. The change had been informally decided upon in 1979. Under the 1981 caucus change, the Rules and Ways and Means committees could have up to six subcommittees and Appropriations was allowed to retain all of its 13 panels. All other standing committees were restricted to a maximum of eight or the number it had as of 1981, whichever was fewer. The new rule affected four committees: Education and Labor, Agriculture, Budget and Banking — all of which had more than eight.

The caucus also waived a party rule limiting members of the Judiciary and District of Columbia committees to only one other legislative committee assignment.

Changing Subcommittee Role

The term "committee government" has long been used to describe the policy-making process on Capitol Hill. But as Davidson has observed, "[T]oday, the term 'subcommittee government' is nearer the mark."[39]

Subcommittees now handle most of the day-to-day legislative and oversight workload of Congress. The growth in the influence of subcommittees has been attributed to several factors:

"● the complexities of problems that require policy specialization;

1977 Senate Reorganization

Major changes in responsibility within Senate committees resulted from the 1977 reorganization.

The responsibilities of the Aeronautical and Space Sciences Committee were transferred to the Commerce, Science and Transportation Committee.

Matters under the jurisdiction of the District of Columbia and Post Office and Civil Service committees were transferred to the Governmental Affairs Committee.

Beginning in 1978, the functions of the Select Nutrition Committee were taken over by the Agriculture, Nutrition and Forestry Committee.

The responsibilities of the Joint Atomic Energy Committee were transferred to the Armed Services, Energy and Natural Resources, and Environment and Public Works committees.

The jurisdictions of the Joint Committee on Congressional Operations and the Select Committee to Study the Senate Committee System were transferred to the Rules Committee.

Other changes included:

Transfer of responsibility for school lunch legislation to the Agriculture Committee from the old Labor and Public Welfare Committee, now the Human Resources Committee.

A shift of foreign commerce and veterans' housing programs to the Banking Committee from the Commerce and Veterans' Affairs committees respectively.

A shift of responsibility for the naval petroleum reserves and the oil shale reserves in Alaska and for water power to Energy and Natural Resources from the Armed Services and Public Works committees respectively.

Transfer of responsibility for fisheries and wildlife, except for marine fisheries, to the Environment and Public Works Committee from the Commerce Committee.

"● the demands of interest groups calling for subcommittees . . . [to handle] their subject area;

"● the desires of members to chair subcommittees in order to initiate lawmaking and oversight, augment personal prestige and influence, gain staff and office space, and gain a national platform; and

"● the desire of majority Democrats in the early 1970s to circumscribe the power of committee chairmen."[40]

The trend toward "subcommittee government" came earlier in the Senate than in the House. The transformation has been described by Davidson as "relatively peaceful." The process was launched by the so-called Johnson Rule in 1953 when then-Majority Leader Lyndon Johnson initiated a plan whereby each freshman senator was given at least one major committee assignment. The process was expanded by the "open, benign leadership" of Mike Mansfield, D-Mont. (1953-77).[41]

The changeover in the House was much more difficult and acrimonious. A move to strengthen the autonomy of House subcommittees began in 1971 and culminated in decisions taken by the Democrats in the winter of 1974-75 that allowed subcommittee chairmen and ranking minority members to hire their own staffs and forced the Ways and Means Committee to establish subcommittees.

House Subcommittees

Until the early 1970s, House subcommittees generally did not play a dominant role in the legislative process. Major exceptions were the Appropriations subcommittees and the Banking Committee's housing subcommittee. The former were organized to parallel the executive departments and agencies, and most of the annual budget review was done at that level. The staggering size and complexity of the federal budget required each subcommittee to develop an expertise and an autonomy respected and rarely challenged by other subcommittees or by the full committee.

The housing subcommittee had a long tradition of independent operation. For many years it had control of its own budget and was able to hire and retain a widely respected staff.

Although the Legislative Reorganization Act of 1946 made drastic reductions in the number of House standing committees, it spawned an explosion at the subcommittee level. In the 80th Congress alone, the 19 standing committees that remained following the 1946 act's pruning spawned more than 100 subcommittees.

The creation of a larger network of subcommittees in the years following the 1946 act did not mean that power automatically gravitated there, however. Until the early 1970s, most House committees were run by chairmen who were able to retain much of the authority for themselves and a few trusted senior members, while giving little to junior members or subcommittees.

Those chairmen could dominate committees because they had the backing of Speaker Sam Rayburn and Speaker John W. McCormack, D-Mass. (1928-71), and the support, or at least the acquiescence, of their panels' members. They could pack subcommittees with members who would do their bidding, define the subcommittees' jurisdictions and what legislation they would consider, decide when they would meet and make the decisions on how much staff, if any, subcommittees could have.

Revival of the Democratic Caucus

The day of the dominant committee chairman began to wane with the revival of the House Democratic Caucus in 1969 and the retirement of McCormack as Speaker at the end of the 1970 session. With McCormack's departure, these chairmen lost a powerful ally at the top of the House leadership structure.

The caucus revival meant that moderate and liberal Democrats elected to the House in the 1960s, who were frustrated by the operation of a committee system that tended to freeze them out of power, at last had a vehicle to change House procedures. Their actions were directed at undercutting the power of committee chairmen and strengthening the role of the subcommittees, where the opportunity lay for them to gain a greater role and make an impact on the legislative process.

The drive had a sharp generational edge. Many middle-ranking Democrats elected in the late 1950s and 1960s were allied against the senior members and the leadership. Between 1958 and 1970, 293 Democrats entered the House. Between 1970 and 1974, another 150 Democrats were elected. From this group, many of whom tended to be more moderate or liberal than their predecessors, sprang the pressure for reform.

By the beginning of the 94th Congress (1975), Democrats who had been elected since 1958 held 108 of the 146 subcommittee chairmanships on House standing and select committees. Many of those members would have received subcommittee chairmanships even if the reforms had not been adopted, because they had accrued enough seniority. What the reforms did, however, was to give them real power when they finally took over a subcommittee.

Between 1971 and 1975, the old committee structure underwent many changes. During those four years a series of innovations was approved by the Democratic Caucus that guaranteed junior and middle-ranking Democrats greater power on subcommittees. The thrust of the changes was twofold: the authority of committee chairmen was curbed, and that of subcommittee leaders was strengthened. By 1976 subcommittees were displaying more independence, and subcommittee chairmen were playing a more active role in House floor action.

Committee Chairmen

The powers of the committee chairmen, the principal losers in the House power struggle, were pared in several ways: through changes in House rules and, more importantly, in the decisions adopted by the Democratic Caucus. All of the caucus innovations reordering committee operations were dependent, of course, on the Democratic Party remaining the majority in the House. The following decisions had the greatest impact on the committee system at this time:

1. No Democratic member could be chairman of more than one legislative subcommittee. That change made it possible to break the hold of the more conservative senior Democrats on key subcommittees, and it gradually made middle-level and even some junior Democrats eligible for subcommittee chairmanships. Adopted at the beginning of the 92nd Congress, that rule in its first year resulted in 16 relatively young Democrats — those elected since 1958 — getting their first subcommittee chairmanships on such key committees as Judiciary, Foreign Affairs and Banking, Currency and Housing.

2. Subcommittee members were protected by a "bill of rights" adopted by the caucus in 1973. The new rules established a Democratic caucus (the Democratic committee members) on each House committee and forced chairmen to begin sharing authority with the panel's other Democrats. That was made necessary because the committee caucus was given the authority to select subcommittee chairmen, establish subcommittee jurisdictions, set party ratios on subcommittees that reflected the ratios on the full committees and provide the budgets for running the subcommittees. Also, a caucus rule was added at this time promising more choice subcommittee assignments to younger Democrats.

Committee chairmen no longer could kill legislation by quietly pocketing it. They had to refer bills to subcommittees within two weeks, unless they were to be handled by the full committee.

3. All committees with more than 20 members were required to establish at least four subcommittees. This was directed at Ways and Means, which had operated without subcommittees during most of Wilbur Mills' 16-year chairmanship. It also established an important House precedent by institutionalizing subcommittees for the first time.

4. Another change was in subcommittee staffing. Subcommittee chairmen and the ranking minority members were authorized to hire one staff person each to work directly for them on their subcommittees.

5. Committees were required to operate through written rules. This also helped to check the arbitrary power of committee chairmen and to institutionalize subcommittees.

6. The Democratic Caucus in January 1975 specified that no Democrat could become a member of a second subcommittee on any full committee until every member of the full committee had chosen one subcommittee position. (Members on existing subcommittees, however, could protect two subcommittee slots. But this protection was eliminated in 1979.) The caucus decision was aimed principally at the House Appropriations Committee, where senior conservative Democrats dominated important subcommittees handling the budgets for defense, agriculture, labor, health, education and welfare programs.

7. In 1975 nominees for the subcommittee chairmanships of the Appropriations Committee were required to go before the caucus for approval.

8. In 1979 a caucus rule was adopted limiting each Democrat to five subcommittee seats on House committees. In addition, the caucus decided that the bidding for subcommittee chairmanships (except Appropriations) would be based on a member's seniority rank on the full committee. The procedure worked as follows: The majority party member with the most seniority would have the first crack at bidding for an open subcommittee chairmanship. If he did not receive a majority vote of the full committee, the member next in line in seniority could bid for the post. This procedure would continue down through the majority party membership until someone was elected. (Appropriations subcommittee chairmen are nominated by the members of each subcommittee. But unlike subcommittee chairmen on other committees, they must be confirmed by the Democratic Caucus.)

Impact of Subcommittee Changes

These reforms affected House committees differently. They had little effect on some, such as Agriculture, which had a tradition of largely autonomous subcommittees and good relations between the committee chairman and the membership.

The impact was much greater on those committees that had a tradition of strong central direction. In those cases — particularly Ways and Means, Interstate and Foreign Commerce (now Energy and Commerce), Interior and Insular Affairs, Foreign Affairs, Judiciary and Public Works (now Public Works and Transportation) were prime examples — the committees tended to become fragmented, with the chairman exercising much less control over the full committee, and the subcommittees assuming more independence over the legislative agenda.

Subcommittee chairmen also gained more influence on the House floor. In many cases, they began to replace the committee chairmen in managing legislation.

Increased Workload. The proliferation of subcommittees resulted in greatly increased demands on members. Subcommittees began holding more hearings, drafting more bills and handling more legislation on the floor. To meet the problem of subcommittee proliferation and to lessen members' workloads, both chambers in the late 1970s placed limits on the number of subcommittees each committee is allowed.

With the expansion of subcommittees came a steady increase in the amount of time members had to devote to subcommittee responsibilities. In 1947 the average senator served on two or three subcommittees; by 1976 he held 14 subcommittee assignments.

"Proliferation of committee panels means proliferation in assignments held by Senators. And the burdens and frustrations of too many assignments, whatever the benefits, produce inefficient division of labor, uneven distribution of responsibility, conflicts in the scheduling of meetings, waste of Senators' and staff time, unsystematic lawmaking and oversight, inadequate anticipation of major problems, and inadequate membership participation in committee decisions," stated a report of the Select Committee to Study the Senate Committee System, the panel that recommended the 1977 reorganization.[42]

As part of the 1977 reorganization, the Senate prohibited a senator from serving as chairman of more than one subcommittee on any committee on which he served. This, in effect, placed an indirect cap on subcommittee expansion by limiting the number of subcommittees of any committee to the number of majority party members on the full committee.

Senators also were allowed on only three subcommittees of each major committee on which they served (the Appropriations Committee was exempted from the limit) and on only two subcommittees of their minor committee.

The House Select Committee on Committees (the Patterson Committee) in a 1979 report emphasized the magnitude of the problem in the House: "On no other issue concerning committee system revision has the Select Committee on Committees found greater agreement on the part of a wider spectrum of Members, staffs, and students of Congress than that there are too many subcommittees in the House and that Members have too many subcommittee assignments."[43]

The Patterson committee said the proliferation of subcommittees had decentralized and fragmented the policy process and had limited members' capacity to master their work.

The number of subcommittees of House standing committees had increased from 69 in the 82nd Congress (1951-53) to 146 in the 96th Congress (1979-81). While the average number of committee/subcommittee assignments per member in 1979 was 6.2, a total of 223 members had seven or more committee/subcommittee assignments.

The Patterson committee proposed limiting each House member to a maximum of five subcommittee assignments, and — on a phased-in basis — limiting each House standing committee, except Appropriations, to a total of six subcommittees. The plan was approved by the Republican Conference, but the Democratic Caucus insisted on reviewing the proposal and it was never acted upon. The Democratic Caucus voted in December 1978 to limit Democrats to five subcommittee assignments on standing committees.

1981 Decisions Reverse Trend. In January 1981 the caucus limited the number of subcommittees or task forces that could be established by House standing committees in the 97th Congress. Under the caucus rules change, the Rules and Ways and Means committees were allowed to have up to six subcommittees while Appropriations could retain all 13 of its subcommittees. All other

standing committees were limited to no more than eight subcommittees or the number of subcommittees they had as of Jan. 1, 1981, whichever was fewer. Affected were the Education and Labor, Agriculture, Budget and Banking committees, all of which had more than eight subcommittees in the 96th Congress.

A committee with more than 35 members and fewer than six subcommittees could increase the number to six if it so desired.

Footnotes

1. Clarence Cannon, *Cannon's Procedure in the House of Representatives* (Washington, D.C.: U.S. Government Printing Office, 1963), p. 221.
2. Roger H. Davidson, "Subcommittee Government: New Channels for Policy Making," in Thomas E. Mann and Norman J. Ornstein, eds., *The New Congress* (Washington, D.C.: American Enterprise Institute for Public Policy Research, 1981), p. 99.
3. See George Goodwin Jr., *The Little Legislatures* (Amherst: University of Massachusetts Press, 1970).
4. Woodrow Wilson, *Congressional Government* (Cleveland: Meridian edition, 1956), p. 59.
5. Roger H. Davidson and Walter J. Oleszek, *Congress and Its Members* (Washington, D.C.: CQ Press, 1981) pp. 215-216.
6. *Congress and the Nation*, vol. 5, (Washington, D.C.: Congressional Quarterly, 1981), p. 881.
7. On subcommittees' role, see Goodwin, *The Little Legislatures*, pp. 50-59; Davidson, "Subcommittee Government," pp.99-133.
8. Stephen K. Bailey, *The New Congress* (New York: St. Martin's Press, 1966), p. 55.
9. On jurisdictional conflicts, see William L. Morrow, *Congressional Committees* (New York: Charles Scribner's Sons, 1969), p. 20.
10. Walter J. Oleszek, *Congressional Procedures and the Policy Process* (Washington, D.C.: CQ Press, 1978), pp. 55-56.
11. Ibid.
12. Davidson and Oleszek, *Congress and Its Members*, pp. 218-219.
13. Background and discussion of assignment process, see Goodwin, *The Little Legislatures*, pp. 69-100.
14. On selection of members, cf. Randall B. Ripley, *Congress: Process and Policy* (New York: W. W. Norton & Co., 1975), pp. 96 ff.; Davidson and Oleszek, *Congress and Its Members*, pp. 213-214.
15. Davidson and Oleszek, *Congress and Its Members*, p. 214.
16. Oleszek, *Congressional Procedures and the Policy Process*, p. 201.
17. Davidson and Oleszek, *Congress and Its Members*, p. 336.
18. Oleszek, *Congressional Procedures*, pp. 202-208.
19. Davidson and Oleszek, *Congress and Its Members*, p. 338.
20. Ibid.
21. Ibid., pp. 338-339.
22. George B. Galloway, *Congress at the Crossroads* (New York: Thomas Y. Crowell Co., 1946), p. 88.
23. On the evolution of the committee system, see Galloway, *Congress at the Crossroads*, pp. 127-131, and Goodwin, *The Little Legislatures*, p. 10.
24. Galloway, *Congress*, pp. 139-144; Goodwin, *The Little Legislatures*, pp. 11-12.
25. Galloway, *Congress*, pp. 127, 137.
26. George H. Haynes, *The Senate of the United States* (Boston: Houghton Mifflin Co., 1938), pp. 273 ff.
27. Ibid., p. 277.
28. Wilson, *Congressional Government*, p. 82.
29. Galloway, *Congress*, p. 135.
30. Ibid., pp. 129-130.
31. Haynes, *The Senate*, p. 284
32. For a concise discussion of the 1946 act, see Goodwin, *The Little Legislatures*, pp. 18-22.

33. For details on 1970 reorganization, see *Congress and the Nation,* vol. 3, (Washington, D.C.: Congressional Quarterly, 1973), pp. 382-396.

34. For details on 1974 House reforms, see *Congressional Quarterly Almanac 1974* (Washington, D.C.: Congressional Quarterly, 1975), pp. 634-641.

35. For details, see *Congressional Quarterly Almanac 1977* (Washington, D.C.: Congressional Quarterly, 1978), pp. 792-797.

36. House, Commission on Administrative Review, *Administrative Reorganization and Legislative Management; Vol. 2: Work Management,* 95th Cong., 1st sess., (Washington, D.C.: U.S. Government Printing Office, 1977), p. 38.

37. For details, see *Congressional Quarterly Almanac 1979* (Washington, D.C.: Congressional Quarterly, 1980), pp. 595-597, and *Congressional Quarterly Almanac 1980,* (Washington, D.C.: Congressional Quarterly, 1981), pp. 562-563.

38. For details, see *Congressional Quarterly Almanac 1977,* pp. 781-790.

39. Davidson, "Subcommittee Government," p. 99.

40. Davidson and Oleszek, *Congress and Its Members,* pp. 208-209.

41. Davidson, "Subcommittee Government," p. 107.

42. Senate, Temporary Select Committee to Study the Senate Committee System, *Structure of the Senate Committee System: Jurisdictions, Numbers and Sizes, and Limitations on Memberships and Chairmanships, Referral Procedures, and Scheduling,* 94th Cong., 2d sess. (Washington, D.C.: U.S. Government Printing Office, 1976), p. 6.

43. House, Select Committee on Committees, *Limitations on the Number of Subcommittees and Subcommittee Assignments,* Committee print, 96th Cong., 2d sess., 1980, p. 1.

Expansion of Committee Staff

Congressional committee staffs are responsible for much of the legislative work undertaken by Congress. The influence of the staff bureaucracy has grown over the years as many members, swamped with a workload of increasing bulk and complexity, rely on their aides for policy recommendations and professional expertise.

As the responsibilities of professional committee aides have changed, so has the type of staffer hired. One committee worker observed in 1979 that committee aides no longer come from political backgrounds. "Congress," he said, "is dominated by technocrats," issue-oriented individuals and specialists in numerous fields.[1]

The growing impact that committee staff is having on legislation has become a subject of concern. There is a feeling among some members that too many decisions are getting away from the persons who were elected to make them. Committee staff has grown in size as well as influence: The number of committee employees skyrocketed from fewer than 400 in 1946 to more than 3,000 in 1980, with much of this growth occurring in the 1970s.

A variety of factors accounted for this expansion: the increasing complexity and number of issues confronting Congress, a desire for independence from the executive branch and from other sources of power within Congress, the growth in the number of subcommittees and attempts to give junior and minority party members fairer treatment.

The extensive congressional staff structure that resulted, along with the greater expense of running the committee system, gradually began to worry senators and representatives. Responding to the Reagan administration's popular campaign to cut back government spending, Congress in 1981 acted to halt staff growth by cutting the operating budgets of many committees. Many Capitol Hill observers maintained, however, that Congress merely "retrenched" and that committee staffs would continue to grow in the 1980s.

Early Use of Staff

Senators and representatives were reluctant during the early years of Congress to admit that they required staff assistance, either in the committees or in their own offices. Thus, most chairmen handled committee matters themselves in the early part of the 19th century, although some committees occasionally hired clerks during heavy legislative periods.

Until the 1820s and 1830s there were very few standing committees. Congress rejected various requests to employ permanent committee clerks until about 1840 when, after pleas by the chairmen, some clerical assistance was permitted in emergencies on a per diem or hourly basis.

In 1856 the House Ways and Means and Senate Finance committees became the first to obtain regular appropriations for full-time clerks. Other committees followed, but their staffing generally was limited to persons hired for housekeeping duties, such as stenographers and receptionists. Members or their personal aides usually handled substantive committee work and bill drafting. But the number of committee employees increased very gradually. The first comprehensive pay bill authorizing appropriations for all legislative employees, including committee clerks, was enacted in 1924.

The Legislative Reorganization Act of 1946 attempted to separate the roles of committee and personal staffs. That law stated that professional committee staff members "shall not engage in any work other than committee business, and no other duties may be assigned to them." Nonetheless, committee and subcommittee staffers often handle personal and political work for the chairman of the panel to which they are attached.

The 1946 act was responsible for a number of substantial committee reforms. Under the act, the number of standing committees in the Senate was reduced from 33 to 15 and in the House from 48 to 19. The jurisdiction of each committee was more strictly defined. Early in the 1947 session, the Republican-controlled 80th Congress added four new select and special committees to the roster of standing (permanent) committees set up by the reorganization act.

In subsequent years other special committees were created, but the standing committee structure remained essentially unchanged. (Special and select committees are authorized for a specific issue or program — for example, to investigate an urgent national problem — and for a certain time period, after which they are supposed to be dissolved. But in some instances they have been given new leases on life and additional appropriations; some became firmly entrenched with large staffs, and a few even became permanent committees.)

The next change that had a significant effect on committee staffing procedures was provided by enactment of the Legislative Reorganization Act of 1970. That law increased to six, from four, the number of permanent professional staff employees authorized for each standing committee. Two of the six professional staffers, in addition to

Legislative Council Office

The Office of the Legislative Counsel, originally named the Legislative Drafting Service, was created in 1919 under the Revenue Act of 1918. The office was established, according to the act, to "aid in drafting public bills and resolutions or amendments thereto on the request of any committee of either House of Congress."

Each chamber has its own office, headed by a chief counsel, who is appointed by the Speaker of the House and by the president pro tempore in the Senate. Each counsel heads a staff of attorneys; in 1982 the House staff had 31 attorneys, the Senate, 17. Related support staff provide clerical help.

Under the 1918 statute, the Office of the Legislative Counsel was required to serve only the committees, but it traditionally also has provided assistance in drafting legislation to individual members. Title V of the Legislative Reorganization Act of 1970 reconstituted the House office, upgrading its responsibilities and making its services more readily available to members.

Members who want to introduce legislation rely on the lawyers in the Office of the Legislative Counsel to put the proposal into the appropriate legalese. The lawyers analyze and research the precedents, compare the bill with existing laws and sometimes suggest alternatives.

The office works closely with committee staffs as legislation is considered and marked up. Its assistance also is called upon during House-Senate conference committee negotiations.

Occasionally, attorneys from the office are assigned to committees or subcommittees for long periods, essentially serving as part of the committee staff.

Although the Office of the Legislative Counsel continues to perform important bill drafting services for Congress, there is a growing tendency on the part of the executive branch agencies and special interest groups to use their own specialists to draft the bill introduced on their behalf by members of Congress.

For fiscal 1982, the Senate and House authorized an appropriation of $3,410,600 for such services: $2,390,000 for the House office, and $1,010,600 for the Senate's.

Sources: Harrison W. Fox Jr. and Susan Webb Hammond, *Congressional Staffs* (New York: The Free Press, 1977), pp. 140-141; *Staff,* November/December 1981, 97th Congress/Issue 6 (Washington, D.C.: Committee on House Administration, 1981), p. 10.

one of six permanent clerical staffers provided under previous law, were to be reserved for the exclusive use of the committee's minority party members. That provision did not apply to the House and Senate Appropriations committees or to the House Committee on Standards of Official Conduct.

Staff Expansion Since 1946

Committee staffs expanded steadily following enactment of the 1946 Legislative Reorganization Act. In 1947 there were 399 aides on House and Senate committees; by 1982 the number had jumped to 3,278 — an increase of more than 650 percent. In the 1970s attempts to abolish a number of Senate and House committees met with near total failure because the chairmen, among others, lobbied for their retention.

A minor change incorporated in the 1970 Legislative Reorganization Act was supposed to rationalize committee funding procedures in the Senate by prohibiting certain subcommittees, which had operated semiautonomously, from submitting independent funding requests. The act required each committee to submit one funding estimate for the entire committee and its subcommittees. But this did little to stem the subcommittees' growing independence.

In 1973 the House Democratic Caucus adopted a "subcommittee bill of rights" stating that a majority caucus within each committee would determine subcommittee chairmen, jurisdictions and budgets. After that initiative by Democrats, who controlled the House, the power of subcommittees grew and, inevitably, so did their staffs. By the late 1970s the number of staffers working for subcommittees equaled the number assigned to full committees in the 1960s.[2]

A further change in House practices adopted in 1975 affected subcommittee staff growth. A rule was approved allowing subcommittee chairmen and the highest-ranking minority member on each panel to hire one staff person each to work directly for them on their subcommittee business.

The Senate in 1975 authorized an increase in committee staff in response to complaints of junior senators. That change (S Res 60) was intended to prevent a senator who already had staff on a committee from getting more staff for that committee. Thus, it benefited primarily junior senators who had been excluded from separate staff on their committees because of their low-seniority status. The plan cut into the traditional power base that senior members enjoyed through their control of committee staff and was opposed by many of them for that reason.[3]

Impact of Staff Growth

The impact of committee staff expansion was predictable. First, the cost of running committees ballooned. In fiscal 1976 Congress appropriated approximately $20.7 million for House committee expenses, including salaries, and $8.9 million for Senate committees. By fiscal 1982 House committee spending amounted to about $75.6 million. Senate committees were authorized approximately $41.9 million for the same period.[4]

Another result of greater staff was, not surprisingly, an increase in the volume of legislation. While more employees were hired to deal with the increasing workload, facing committee members, the additional staff created more work, necessitating still more staff.

Committee Staff Structure

Although the organization varies from committee to committee, most of them have dual staffs — one professional and one clerical. These generally are headed by a "staff director" and a "chief clerk," respectively.[5]

The distinctions between the professional and clerical staffs are blurred on many committees, but the duties of each can be separated roughly.

The clerical staff is responsible for the day-to-day running of the committee and assisting the members and professional staff. Some of its routine tasks include: keeping the committee calendar up to date, processing committee publications, referring bills that have been introduced to the appropriate departments and administration officials for comment, preparing the bill dockets, maintaining files, performing stenographic work, announcing hearings and contacting witnesses, and opening and sorting mail.

Professional staff members handle committee policy and legislative matters generally, including legal and other types of research, public relations, statistical and other technical work, and drafting and redrafting legislative language and amendments.

The clerical and professional aides just described are a committee's "statutory," or permanent, staff. Their positions are established by rules of the House or Senate or by law and are funded annually in the legislative branch appropriations bill. Committees also hire additional personnel for "investigative" work. These employees are considered temporary, but they often remain with the committees for extended periods of time.

Over the years, investigative employees have accounted for much of the increase in committee staff costs, as the budgets for these aides are flexible. In the House, funds for investigative staff are approved separately from statutory staff funds. The Senate, however, in 1981 eliminated the distinction for funding purposes. Senate committees now submit all funding requests in one budget document to the Rules and Administration Committee.

Recruitment and Tenure

Most committee employees are selected by the chairman, or the top-ranking minority party member, as a perquisite of office, subject only to nominal approval by the full committee.

From surveys and interviews with committee staff, one can make some generalizations about today's professional aides (as distinct from clerical aides). They are relatively young (average age, 40), and overwhelmingly male (89.2 percent according to a 1977 survey). Most committee professionals are residents of the District of Columbia metropolitan area, in contrast to members' personal office staff. Most of the aides have advanced degrees, particularly law degrees, and many bring previous experience in the executive branch to their committee positions. Many view their jobs as short-term commitments; few plan to make a career in Congress.[6]

The tenure of committee employees is subject to the chairman or member who hired them, and aides can be fired with or without cause. Congressional aides do not need to be reminded about the precarious nature of committee employment.

Salaries of committee employees increased dramatically after World War II. Some top staffers in 1981 earned almost as much as the members themselves. The highest paid committee aides received an annual salary of approximately $53,000.

Functions of Committee Staff

Committee aides, working within the jurisdiction of the committee and in close association with the members, generate and shape much of the legislation considered by Congress. The following list includes the important functions performed by aides on almost all House and Senate committees:

● Organizing Hearings. Staffers set up hearings on legislation and issues of interest to the committee leadership as well as on annual or periodic authorization measures on which the panel has jurisdiction. Aides select witnesses, prepare questions, inform the press, brief committee members and, occasionally, substitute for members or the chair if they cannot attend hearings.

● Oversight and Investigations. Much original research is conducted by staff members on issues that come before a committee. This usually involves a critique of existing legislation, court decisions and current practices.

● Bill Markup and Amendment Drafting. Staff aides assist in marking up bills by explaining technical provisions, outlining policy questions, analyzing proposed changes following committee decisions and incorporating the decisions in successive revisions of the bill. Although staff members may help in writing or rewriting proposed bills and amendments, they often serve as liaison between the Office of the Legislative Counsel (there is an office for each house), committee members, government agencies and special interest groups during the drafting of legislation. *(Office of the Legislative Counsel, box, p. 106)*

● Preparing Reports. Committee reports that accompany bills sent to the full chamber are almost entirely staff products. Often, the reports are the only reference available to non-committee members when a bill is considered by the House or Senate. Staff aides consult with the chairman or the majority party members to decide what should be emphasized in the report. Minority party members and opponents of the bill in question often may file "minority views," which as a rule are drafted by the committee's minority staff members. Then the staff writes the report, usually conforming to a standard format. Reports generally contain three major sections — the main body, which explains the bill and gives background and interpretation; the section-by-section analysis of the bill's provisions, and a written comparison of the bill with existing law. *(Further details, see Legislative Process chapter.)*

● Preparation for Floor Action. The top committee aides, those most familiar with the legislation, often accompany the committee chairman, or the bill's sponsor if not the chairman, when the bill is debated on the floor.

● Conference Committee Work. The staffs of corresponding committees in each house work together on the preparation of conference reports and in resolving differences in legislation initially considered by those committees and subsequently passed by the House and Senate.

● Liaison With Executive Branch, Special Interests. Staff aides communicate frequently with executive branch officials and lobbyists on pending legislative proposals. Some members regard this activity as the most consequential of all staff work. Lobbyists and representatives of special interest groups, particularly those that have Washington offices, often provide staff aides with detailed information and answers to questions.

● Press Relations. Committee staff perform a number of

press-related tasks. They alert reporters to upcoming hearings, markup sessions and floor action on committee-reported measures. Aides answer questions from the press and public, write press releases and provide background information on pending legislation and recent committee decisions.

Staff Partisanship

The party affiliation of committee employees has been and remains a controversial topic. For many years the chairman's prerogative prevailed in the selection of staff members. Thus most of the employees were from the majority party.

The 1946 Legislative Reorganization Act did not contain any provision for apportioning the professional staff of a committee between the chairman and the top-ranking minority member. The act simply stated that the "staff members shall be assigned to the chairman and ranking minority member of such committee as the committee may deem advisable." Committees interpreted that provision in various ways, and the whim of the chairman often determined the number of minority aides hired.

Several changes were made in minority staffing in the 1970s. The 1970 Legislative Reorganization Act provided that at least three full-time minority staff aides were to be assigned to most committees of the House and Senate.

In January 1971 the House voted to delete the provisions of the 1970 act providing that one-third of committee investigative funds — used to hire part-time professionals and to assist members — be allocated to the minority side.

The minority staffing issue surfaced again in late 1974, as representatives debated a proposal to reorganize House committees. That plan called for giving Republicans 10 of 30 staff members assigned to committees by statute and one-third of the investigative staff allotted to subcommittees by the House Administration Committee. But when the Democratic Caucus met in January 1975 it agreed to a compromise that allowed subcommittee chairmen and top-ranking minority members to hire one staff person each to work on their subcommittees — up to a maximum of six subcommittees — but dropped the one-third minority investigative staff guarantee.

The minority staffing compromise produced one of the most significant changes of the many revisions made in House rules during the 1970-75 period. As part of the 1975 change (S Res 60) made in committee staffing, all minority members were authorized to hire up to three personal committee aides.

In 1977 the Senate directed that committee staffs should be allocated in proportion to the number of majority and minority members on a standing committee.

Footnotes

1. Irwin B. Arieff, "The New Bureaucracy," *Congressional Quarterly Weekly Report,* Nov. 24, 1979, p. 2639.
2. Michael J. Malbin, "Delegation, Deliberation, and the New Role of Congressional Staff," in *The New Congress* (Washington, D.C.: American Enterprise Institute for Public Policy Research, 1981), p. 183.
3. *Congressional Quarterly Weekly Report,* June 14, 1975, pp. 1235-1236, and June 21, 1975, p. 1294.

4. For discussion of 1982 committee budgets, see *Congressional Quarterly Weekly Report,* March 20, 1982, pp. 635-636 and April 3, 1982, p. 734.
5. For a discussion of various staff patterns, see Davidson and Oleszek, *Congress and Its Members,* (Washington, D.C.: CQ Press, 1981), pp. 247-248.
6. See Fox and Hammond, *Congressional Staffs,* pp. 43-46, and Arieff, "The New Bureaucracy," pp. 2634-2635.

The Seniority System

Seniority — status based on length of service, to which are attached certain rights and privileges — pervades nearly all social institutions. But in no other political group has its sway been stronger than in the United States Congress.

As Barbara Hinckley pointed out in her 1971 study *The Seniority System in Congress*, " No other national legislative assemblies, no state legislatures use seniority as the sole criterion for choosing leaders."

In the same year the study was published, Congress made the rigid adherence to its "unique" practice obsolete. Both parties in the House of Representatives formally declared that seniority no longer was to be the sole criterion for choosing committee leaders. Shortly thereafter, Senate Democrats and Republicans adopted a similar directive.

These actions were part of a reform wave that began to build momentum in 1970, with passage of the Legislative Reorganization Act. The parties' declarations on seniority signaled a growing opposition to the unchecked power that committee chairmen enjoyed through the automatic advancement feature of the seniority system. Subsequent reforms — especially secret ballot elections by party members and major limitations on the number of top committee and subcommittee posts a member may hold — served to make the chairmen accountable both to their party leaders and the rank and file. The reforms weakened the seniority system but did not obliterate it.

After the reforms of the 1970s, the seniority system continued to dictate the assignment of office space and patronage privileges, as well as the election of the virtually powerless president pro tempore of the Senate. Seniority never had been the sole criterion for selection of the top leaders of Congress — the Speaker of the House and the floor leaders of both major parties.

Seniority operated most significantly on the committee level, and it was here that the reforms had their greatest impact. In 1973, when House Democrats decided that each chairman must stand for election by secret ballot, and in 1975, when the rank and file unseated three incumbent chairmen, the message was clear — the days of the autocratic chairman were over.

Congressional Seniority

Despite frequent references to a "seniority rule" and a "seniority system," Congress' observance of length of service never has been dictated by law or formal ruling. It developed as a tradition. The formal rules simply state that the House or Senate shall determine committee memberships and chairmen.

Seniority on Capitol Hill is based on the length of service in Congress, referred to as congressional seniority; or on the length of consecutive service on a committee, called committee seniority. As the system developed in both houses, it affected the assignment of office space, access to congressional patronage and deference shown members on the floor. But seniority was most apparent — and important — in the selection of committee chairman and in filling vacancies on committees, although state and regional considerations, party loyalty, legislative experience and a member's influence with his colleagues have always been important factors in making committee assignments.

At the beginning of each congressional session, members of each house are given a seniority ranking vis-á-vis their party colleagues. Senate rank generally is determined according to the official date of the beginning of a member's service, which is Jan. 3, except in the case of a new member sworn in after Congress is in session. For those elected or appointed to fill unexpired terms, the date of appointment, certification or swearing in determines the senator's rank.

When members are sworn in on the same date, custom decrees that those with prior political experience take precedence. Counted as political experience, in order of importance, are senatorial, House and gubernatorial service. Occasionally, a senator who resigned or was defeated for re-election might leave office a few days before the end of his term, allowing his successor to be appointed. The purpose was to give the newly elected member a few days' seniority over other freshman senators. In 1980, however, Senate Republicans and Democrats, acting separately, eliminated the principal advantages of this practice. Members appointed to fill out the remaining days of their predecessors' terms no longer were given an edge in obtaining their choice of committee assignments.

In the House, rank generally is determined according to the official date of the beginning of a member's service, which is Jan. 3 except in cases when representatives have been elected to fill a vacancy. In such cases, the date of election determines the rank. When members enter the

House on the same date, those with prior House service take precedence, starting with those with the longest consecutive service. Experience as a senator or governor is disregarded.

Committee Seniority

Once the party leadership has assigned its freshman members to committees, these lawmakers usually will stay on the committees throughout their congressional service. To switch to another committee means starting the climb to committee seniority all over again. Exceptions occur when a vacancy opens on one of the more powerful committees — usually the appropriations, budget and tax-writing committees — or when the party leaders need a reliable member on a less important committee.

Once on a committee, a member is not dropped except in unusual circumstances. The most junior members may be bumped from a committee if elections change party ratios. Members have been purged from committees (or lost seniority in some cases) when they switched party allegiance or openly bolted the party during a presidential election. *(Seating and discipline of members, p. 169)*

As members rise in rank on a committee, their chances of being heard, of asking witnesses questions and of handling major legislation increase. So, too, do their chances of heading a subcommittee, although today the senior member of a subcommittee is not necessarily selected to be chairman. (Until 1973 all subcommittee chairmen were appointed by the committee chairmen.) In the House, the Democratic Caucus adopted a rule directing the Democratic members of each standing committee to elect their subcommittee chairmen from the full committee membership. The rule varied for the more autonomous subcommittees of the House Appropriations Committee. For those panels, the caucus required subcommittee chairmen to be nominated from among the members of the subcommittee, with the vote on the nominees taken by the party caucus rather than by the committee.

Nevertheless, even after the reforms of the 1970s, seniority remained the normal path to becoming a committee or subcommittee chairman. A member next in line for a chairmanship usually could expect to be picked. But the reforms no longer made it automatic.

Two principal points are made in behalf of the seniority system's value to a well-functioning committee: the senior member's long experience with congressional procedures, customs and the legislative issues dealt with by the committee; and the system's neutrality, which prevents party-splintering struggles for power.

When the House Democratic Caucus for the first time unseated three incumbent chairmen in January 1975, it was the autocratic manner in which the chairmen had run their committees that was primarily responsible for their downfall.

Changes in Seniority System

From 1971 to 1977 a reform movement in Congress greatly altered the power structure, decentralizing legislative authority as never before while also strengthening the hand of the Speaker of the House. Chairmen of subcommittees assumed new importance, and committee chairmen were put on notice that they must act fairly with their colleagues or face loss of their positions.

Loosening the grip of seniority was seen as a crucial step toward changing committee operations with the issue treated strictly as a party matter. Democratic leaders feared that if seniority changes were proposed through legislation instead of through party rules, a bipartisan coalition could upset the majority party's control of the legislative program. When changes in seniority were offered as amendments on the floor of the House and Senate they consistently had been defeated.

The first successful blow to the seniority system in the post-World War II period was struck by a member of the Democratic leadership. In 1953 Senate Minority Leader Lyndon B. Johnson, D-Texas (1949-61), proposed, in what was to become known as the "Johnson Rule," that all Democratic senators be given a seat on one major committee before any Democrat was assigned to a second major committee. The proposal was a stunning blow to seniority, but it was approved by the Democratic Steering Committee, which makes Democratic committee assignments in the Senate. Later, Senate Republicans adopted the same party rule, first informally in 1959 and then through the Republican Conference in 1965.

In 1971, under renewed pressure to modify the seniority system, Senate Democrats and Republicans agreed to further changes. Sen. Mike Mansfield, D-Mont. (1953-77), who had become majority leader in 1961, announced a change in procedure: a meeting of the Democratic Party Caucus would be held at the request of any senator, and any senator would be free to challenge any Steering Committee nomination of a committee chairman. Republicans adopted a proposal that a senator could be the ranking minority member of only one standing committee. After the GOP took control of the Senate in 1981, Republicans applied the same rule to the selection of committee chairmen.

Changes Approved

The House Democratic Caucus established the Committee on Organization, Study and Review in 1970 to examine the party's organization and the seniority system. In January 1971 the caucus voted to adopt modest changes recommended by the committee.

The principal changes agreed upon were:
● The Democratic Committee on Committees, composed of the Democratic members of the Ways and Means Committee, would recommend to the caucus nominees for the chairmanship and membership of each committee, and such recommendations did not have to follow seniority. (The committee's power was transferred in December 1974 to the Steering and Policy Committee.)
● The Committee on Committees would make recommendations to the caucus, one committee at a time. Upon the demand of 10 or more caucus members, nominations could be debated and voted on.
● If a nomination were rejected, the Committee on Committees would submit another nomination.

In an important breakthrough for mid-career Democrats, the caucus decided that no member could chair more than one legislative subcommittee. That decision gave 16 Democrats who were elected to the House after 1958 their first subcommittee chairmanships, replacing more senior members.

House Republicans the same year agreed to allow all their members to vote on nominations for ranking minority members of each House committee. The Republican Conference adopted without change the recommendations of a task force on seniority headed by Barber B. Conable Jr., N.Y. The major change allowed the ranking Republican on each committee to be selected by vote, not automatically by seniority. If Republicans gained control of the House, the procedure also was to apply to selection of committee chairmen.

The Conable report set up a procedure for selecting ranking members. In nominating a member to be the top Republican on each committee, the Republican Committee on Committees was allowed to waive seniority and make the selection on some other basis. The Republican Conference then would have to vote, by secret ballot, on each nomination. If the nomination were rejected, the Committee on Committees would submit another nomination. The committee is composed of one representative from each state that has Republican members.

1973 Changes

Seniority still was under fire in the final days of the 92nd Congress (1971-73). Nevertheless, seniority survived new challenges in the early days of the 93rd Congress (1973-75). Although Senate Republicans and House Democrats had approved changes in the selection process, all the committee chairmanships and ranking minority positions were won by the members who would have held them automatically through seniority.

Senate Republicans attracted the most attention in January 1973 as they adopted one proposal to limit the seniority system. The plan permitted members of each standing committee to elect the top-ranking Republican on that committee, subject to approval by a vote of all Senate Republicans.

The final plan, approved by a 31-5 vote, was put forward by Sen. Howard H. Baker Jr., Tenn. It specifically asked that committees not use seniority as the sole criterion in choosing their top-ranking members. If a committee's choice was not accepted by the GOP Conference, the committee could drop the nomination and select another. All conference votes on nominees would be recorded and made available to the public.

Procedures for electing chairmen were changed to allow a secret ballot to be cast on any chairman's nomination if 20 percent of the caucus requested it. The result was that a vote was held on each nominated chairman.

The caucus also adopted a "bill of rights" for committee members that markedly reduced the chairmen's powers. It gave Democratic members of each committee the right to elect their subcommittee chairmen, whereas previously the committee chairmen could appoint the subcommittees and name the subcommittee chairmen, or refuse to appoint any subcommittees.

Several ranking committee members were challenged by their Republican colleagues in 1973, but, as with the Democratic chairmen, all those with top seniority prevailed.

1974-75: Reform and Revolt

When the House Democratic Caucus met in December 1974 to organize for the post-Watergate Congress beginning the following January, an innovation authorized by the committee changes of 1974 was in the wind. The November 1974 election had produced a group of 75 Democratic freshmen, most of them liberals. They soon showed their feistiness by asking all prospective committee chair-

men to appear before the freshmen and answer questions.

One of the caucus' first actions was to strengthen the weak Steering and Policy Committee by giving it the responsibility of making committee nominations — the power formerly held by the Ways and Means Democrats. The 24-member Steering Committee was chaired by the Speaker and consisted of the majority leader, the caucus chairman, 12 members elected by region and nine appointees of the Speaker.

The caucus made additional inroads in the committee seniority system. By 147-116, the caucus voted to make all subcommittee chairmen on the Appropriations Committee subject to election by the caucus. (At the same time, the caucus rejected a plan to make subcommittee chairmen on all committees, not just Appropriations, subject to caucus action.) Appropriations is a highly decentralized committee, with most of the important decisions made at the subcommittee level, and it was argued that the subcommittee chairmen were as powerful as most chairmen of the legislative committees.

The Democrats also made a secret-ballot vote on all nominations for chairmen automatic and gave the Speaker authority to nominate all Democratic members of the Rules Committee, subject to ratification by the caucus.

Finally, the caucus slightly refined its method of selecting committee chairmen by approving a proposal allowing competitive nominations in the caucus if the original selection of the Steering Committee was voted down. Existing rules had provided for a caucus vote on the next recommendation.

Two drastic suggestions for curbing the power of chairmanships were rejected. Democrats decided not to apply an age limit of 70 to all chairmen, and they rejected an effort to limit them to serving no more than three consecutive terms.

Rank-and-file Democrats in January 1975 asserted their new power by unseating three incumbent chairmen and narrowly re-electing another, whom the Steering Committee had proposed to drop. The three unseated chairmen were: W.R. Poage, Texas (1937-78), of the Agriculture Committee; F. Edward Hebert, La. (1941-77), chairman of the Armed Services Committee; Wright Patman, Texas (1929-76), chairman of the Banking and Currency Committee.

In the Senate there were no dramatic revolts against sitting chairmen, but Democrats for the first time created a system to make chairmen accountable to their colleagues. Democrats already had allowed any senator to call a meeting of the caucus to challenge a person nominated for a chairmanship by the party's Steering Committee. But, like a similar rule for House Democrats, this approach exposed a challenging senator to retribution by a chairman if the challenge failed.

In 1975 Democrats decided to select chairmen by secret ballot whenever one-fifth of the caucus requested it. The revised procedure provided that a list of nominees by the Democratic Steering Committee would be distributed to all Democrats. The Democrats would check off the names of the nominees they wished to subject to a secret ballot and would submit the list without signing it. If at least 20 percent of the caucus members wanted a vote on a nominee, it would be held automatically two days later.

Further Rebuffs to Seniority

In 1977 the Senate reorganized its committee system and, among other steps, further limited the number of committee and subcommittee spots a senator could hold. The effect was to make more leadership positions available to junior senators. *(Senate committee reorganization, p. 79)*

The November 1980 elections produced a big swing to the Republicans and the first GOP majority in the Senate since the 83rd Congress of 1953-55. The party picked up 12 Senate seats formerly held by Democrats, including those of four committee chairmen.

Three first-term senators became chairmen of standing committees and seven freshmen became subcommittee chairmen. Five of these chaired subcommittees of the powerful Appropriations Committee, an indication of how widely the "share the power" trend had spread. The strict limits that had been placed on senior members' subcommittee assignments in the 1970s were largely responsible for the freshmen's good fortune.

The seniority system also suffered more reversals on the House side. The Democratic Caucus in January 1977 for the first time rejected a sitting subcommittee chairman of the powerful Appropriations Committee. The victim was Robert L. F. Sikes, Fla. (1941-44, 1945-79), the longtime chairman of the Military Construction Subcommittee who had been reprimanded by the House the year before for conflicts of interest. Despite the support of Speaker Thomas P. O'Neill Jr., D-Mass., Sikes lost his bid to retain his chairmanship by a 93-189 vote. Two years later, seniority was rebuffed again as three junior House Democrats bumped more senior colleagues in committee elections for subcommittee chairmanships on the Commerce and Government Operations committees. In each case the winners were considered more liberal on legislative issues than the senior members they defeated. None of the three new chairmen previously had chaired the subcommittees at issue.

The shift in power to the subcommittee level was seen again in 1981, this time in the Foreign Affairs Committee. One subcommittee chairman was deposed in favor of a more "dynamic" member, and another member's bid for a chairmanship was rejected in favor of two colleagues who ranked just below him in seniority.

Pay and Perquisites

From the day newly elected members arrive in Washington to the day they leave Congress, lawmakers are presented with an array of perquisites that help to ease the pressures of congressional life.

A lawmaker's job is more difficult today than it was even a decade or two ago. In an era of ever-increasing complexity in the daily lives of Americans, staying on top of events and legislative issues requires a large professional staff and backup assistance.

In 1789 members were paid a flat rate of $6 per working day, from which they had to pay their living expenses, incidental expenses related to their congressional work and out-of-town living costs. Senators and representatives in the early years had no staff and no expense accounts.

Congressional salaries rose very gradually throughout the 19th century and were only as high as $10,000 a year by 1947. Since then, salaries have increased more than sixfold, to $69,800.

In 1982 the Tax Foundation, a Washington-based research organization, estimated that each senator annually cost the taxpayer $2.3 million and each representative cost $836,000. The cost of maintaining a congressional office goes well beyond a member's salary. The member is provided a large clerk-hire allowance for staff. Staff for the average legislator began to expand after World War I, changing Congress from a collection of one-man operations to a billion-dollar bureaucracy manned by thousands of employees.

Cost of Perquisites

Trying to calculate the amount of money Congress spends on itself can be very difficult. Some information is readily available in the semi-annual reports of the secretary of the Senate and quarterly reports of the clerk of the House. These publications list the salaries for all congressional employees and many expenditures made by members in their official duties. But the reports do not give the full picture.

It is difficult to attach a dollar value to many of the fringe benefits. Statutory perquisites provided by Congress include the franking privilege (free mail for official business) and use of free office space in federal buildings in a member's home state or district. In addition, each member receives an official expense allowance for travel, telephone and telegraph services, stationery, postage and newsletters and office expenses and equipment. Members also are allowed free storage of files and records, free office decorations, use of television and radio recording studios at less than commercial rates, authority to make certain patronage appointments, discounts at Capitol Hill shops, free or low-cost services and hundreds of free publications.

Members can receive various health protection plans and free emergency care while at work, life insurance and a generous retirement pension. Senators and representatives have access to elaborate computerized mailing and legislative analysis systems and the latest recreation facilities — swimming pools, saunas, masseurs and gymnasiums. Legislative counsels, legal counsels, chaplains, photographers and IRS advisers all stand by at the Capitol to assist the member. Attractive dining rooms, barber and beauty shops and convenient Amtrak and airline ticket offices are available in the Capitol and congressional office buildings.

Members and their staffs are not confronted with the daily hassle of finding a parking place in Washington. And they are exempt from various labor laws passed by Congress, including the Civil Rights Act of 1964 and the Equal Employment Act of 1972.

Finally, there is an ill-defined collection of informal fringe benefits and extra courtesies shown VIPs, as when an airline delays the departure of a plane to accommodate a member who arrives late. And if the member decides to drive to one of Washington's airports, there are convenient reserved parking spaces for him.

Advantages of Incumbency

While these special allowances may enable the member to better perform the role of public servant, from a political perspective they also conveniently help the incumbent to keep his or her name before the voters.

It is often difficult even for members to decide which perquisites come under the definition of official congressional business and which overlap into primarily political campaign work. For example, at what point does a series of computer-generated letters to constituents about a member's interest in the progress of health care legislation become more "political" than official?

With each new Congress, there invariably is friction between those members who want to increase their pay and perquisites and those who, for various reasons, resist additional layers of benefits and privileges. Proponents of ever more generous allowances say they are motivated by a desire to serve the public as efficiently as possible.

On the other hand, there are advocates — inside and outside Congress — who argue that Congress' appetite for self-largesse is greedy and redundant and that many perquisites are unnecessary to the accomplishment of members' legislative duties.

How Much Is Enough?

The modern Congress clearly needs a skilled staff, facilities and information systems to assist members in dealing with the mounting volume of legislation. But with so much money involved in extra allowances and expense accounts, inevitably some members have taken advantage of Congress' generosity.

To what extent are there abuses? It is difficult to tell. Probably the answer closest to the truth is that members abuse their privileges about as much as such privileges would be abused by the general public. Intentional, large-scale abuses are rare. In some cases, abuses result from genuine confusion over what is proper or improper. Abuses that seem to recur frequently are in employment of members' relatives as staff aides and in misuse of expense allowances or other funds. But even where such perquisites may be justified, they often are detrimental to Congress' public image.

Speaker Thomas P. O'Neill Jr., D-Mass., addressed this point in 1977 when the House debated the proposed House ethics code's limits on honoraria. "To allow us the privilege of continuing to earn outside income, no matter how stringent a provision of financial disclosure, creates in the public mind a suspicion of conflict, a suspicion of impropriety.... The issue is credibility, restoring public confidence in this Congress."

There remains the question of how much is enough. And under the separation of powers principle, it is the legislative branch — the collective membership of Congress — that sets its own salary and decides what perquisites to allow. Regulation of those perquisites also must remain a congressional function.

The Cost of Congress

The legislative branch, like any other government agency, must request funds for its own programs and activities in an annual budget. The process generally is the same as that for the executive branch departments: Proposed funding for Congress and related agencies is incorporated in a legislative appropriations bill, which must be approved by the House and Senate. There is one important difference, however. Neither chamber, as a general rule, delves into the requests and operations of the other.

In addition to the appropriations requirement, expenditures for some operations on Capitol Hill must first be authorized separately.

Each year congressional offices and agencies formulate their budget estimates. The clerk of the House and the secretary of the Senate are responsible for preparing appropriations requests for all the offices within their respective jurisdictions. In practice, they do little more than pass along the requests submitted to them by others. And at no point in the process is the overall legislative budget screened for duplication or waste.

Sovereign Chambers

The preliminary budget figures are forwarded to the president for inclusion in the overall federal budget that he submits to Congress at the beginning of each year. However, unlike executive branch expenses, the legislative branch figures are not subject to revision by the Office of Management and Budget in the Executive Office of the President. There is no outside agency that amends congressional funding decisions.

After passage of the first congressional budget resolution, the requests are considered in each house by the Legislative subcommittees of the Appropriations committees.

Hearings and markup sessions are held. The full committees then briefly consider the measure before sending the bill to the floor.

Since appropriations bills by tradition originate in the House, that chamber considers the congressional budget first. The House bill contains items for House expenditures, for joint committees and for various services and facilities used by both chambers such as the Capitol police, Capitol guides and the mail service, and for legislative support organizations and agencies such as the Congressional Research Service and the Office of Technology Assessment. Included in the legislative branch appropriations bill are funds for the Congressional Budget Office, the office of the Architect of the Capitol, Library of Congress, Botanic Gardens, Copyright Royalty Tribunal and several other offices.

Once the bill is passed by the House it is sent to the Senate, which adds appropriations for its own programs and operations. By custom, each branch maintains a "hands-off" policy toward the other's budget requests. Although the bill must be passed in identical form by both chambers, rarely does one house question the budget amounts added by the other. Occasionally, however, spending proposals are challenged. In 1978 the House deleted from the legislative appropriations bill $54.9 million approved by the Senate for construction of the Hart Senate Office Building.

The hands-off practice was broken again in 1981 when the Senate, in retaliation for the way the House had treated certain legislative budget items in an emergency appropriations bill, deleted all House budget items, leaving all programs in both chambers open to negotiations in conference. The dispute, dealing mainly with congressional pay, tax deductions and honoraria, subsequently was settled. *(See also members' pay, p. 115)*

As with the federal government in general, much of the legislative branch appropriations, such as salaries, are largely uncontrollable. And many allowances, such as members' official expense accounts, are determined in advance, and must be available to senators and representatives when needed.

Large congressional projects, such as construction of new office buildings, usually generate considerable controversy and opposition on Capitol Hill. And in the 1970s expenses that once were considered routine — such as mail allowances and funds for staff assistance — became controversial as voters grew disenchanted with the high cost of government.

Operating Costs

The cost of running Congress has grown dramatically. In 1960 the legislative budget — including the operations

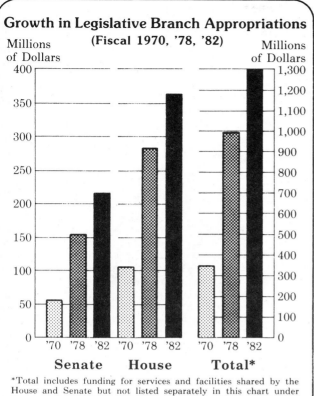

Growth in Legislative Branch Appropriations
(Fiscal 1970, '78, '82)

Millions of Dollars (left axis): 0, 50, 100, 150, 200, 250, 300, 350, 400

Millions of Dollars (right axis): 0, 100, 200, 300, 400, 500, 600, 700, 800, 900, 1,000, 1,100, 1,200, 1,300

Senate   House   Total*

*Total includes funding for services and facilities shared by the House and Senate but not listed separately in this chart under House or Senate (these joint items include mail costs under the franking privilege, expenses of the joint committees, the Capitol police, education of pages) as well as funding for the Library of Congress, Government Printing Office, General Accounting Office and other agencies under congressional jurisdiction.

Source: Congressional Appropriations Committees

PAY: PERENNIAL POLITICAL FOOTBALL

Article I, Section 6, of the Constitution provides that "Senators and Representatives shall receive a Compensation for their Services, to be ascertained by Law, and paid out of the Treasury of the United States."

The constitutional language settled one sensitive contemporary issue — whether a member's salary should be drawn from state or national funds — but it left the resolution of a far more delicate question up to Congress itself — deciding what that salary should be. The inevitable result was to make congressional salaries a political issue that has plagued Congress throughout its history.

In trying to minimize the adverse political fallout from periodically raising its own salary, Congress fell into the practice of incorporating such pay increases in general pay legislation granting raises for most government workers, including at times the judiciary and the president. But even that tactic often failed to blunt critical reaction.

Public opposition to congressional pay increases has been particularly strong at various times in the nation's history, leading to wholesale election defeats of members who voted for increases their constituents considered unwarranted. On two occasions, controversial salary increases were repealed by succeeding Congresses. Frequently, a few members refuse their pay raises, returning the increase to the Treasury or donating it to a public charity. Technically, all members must accept full pay. After receiving their salary, however, they may return any portion to the Treasury.

Despite the resistance both within and outside Congress, congressional pay has risen steadily, particularly in recent years. A member's pay in 1789 was $6 a day; in 1983 it stood at $69,800 for House members and $60,662 for Senate members annually. Although the salary of members remained unchanged for long periods, only rarely was it reduced.

In 1981 and 1982 members devised less direct methods of increasing their take-home pay, including an automatic annual cost-of-living adjustment. Members no longer have to face the politically sensitive issue of voting to raise their own pay, unless they seek an increase in basic salary.

Besides their salaries, members since 1946 have been eligible to participate in a retirement program. *(Retirement benefits, box, p. 123)*

Early Pay Legislation

During the Constitutional Convention of 1787, a principal question surrounding compensation of members was the source of the funds. Members of Congress under the Articles of Confederation had been paid by the states (members of the British Parliament at that time were not compensated). It was felt, however, that members of Congress under the Constitution should be paid, and paid by the national government.

Another question raised at the convention was whether senators and representatives should receive equal pay. Charles Pinckney of South Carolina twice moved "that no

of Congress and the related agencies — totaled $128.8 million; by 1981 that figure had jumped to approximately $1.25 billion. The increase reflected the growth of the legislative bureaucracy. In 1960 House and Senate employees numbered about 6,300; some 20 years later, that total exceeded 18,000. By one count, including "janitors, cooks, police, administrators, printers and support agency personnel, about 39,000 people worked for the legislative branch in 1981." [1]

In 1981, in line with the Reagan administration's call to cut government spending, the Republican-controlled Senate voted to slash its operating budget by 10 percent. The Democrat-controlled House voted to increase its budget, though by a smaller percentage than in previous years.

The legislative budget approved for fiscal 1982 (Oct. 1, 1981, through Sept. 30, 1982) totaled almost $1.3 billion — about 50 million more than the previous year's appropriation for Congress but almost $135 million below the amount originally requested. Major items included: $363.8 million for House activities; $214.4 million for the Senate; $275.7 million for joint and congressional support items, including the office of the Architect of the Capitol, the Capitol police and the Congressional Budget Office; and $445.6 million for related agencies.

Congressional Pay:
$6 a Day to $69,800 a Year

Year	Salary
1789-1795	$6 per diem
1795-1796	$6 per diem (House)
	$7 per diem (Senate)
1796-1815	$6 per diem
1815-1817	$1,500 per year
1817-1855	$8 per diem
1855-1865	$3,000 per year
1865-1871	$5,000 per year
1871-1873	$7,500 per year
1873-1907	$5,000 per year
1907-1925	$7,500 per year
1925-1932	$10,000 per year
1932-1933	$9,000 per year
1933-1935	$8,500 per year
1935-1947	$10,000 per year
1947-1955	$12,500 per year
1955-1965	$22,500 per year
1965-1969	$30,000 per year
1969-1975	$42,500 per year
1975-1977	$44,600 per year
1977-1980	$57,500 per year
1980-1982	$60,662 per year
1983-	$60,662 per year (Senate)
	$69,800 per year (House)

salary should be allowed" members of the Senate. "As this branch was meant to represent the wealth of the country," Pinckney asserted, "it ought to be composed of persons of wealth; and if no allowance was to be made, the wealthy alone would undertake the service." Pinckney's motion was seconded by Benjamin Franklin but twice was rejected, by votes of six states to five.[2]

Per Diem Compensation

One of the first, and most controversial, measures enacted by the new Congress in 1789 was a bill fixing the compensation of members. As originally approved by the House, representatives and senators alike were to be paid $6 a day. The proposal for equal pay developed into a dispute over whether senators, by reason of greater responsibilities and presumably higher qualifications, should receive a pay differential.

At the heart of the debate was an amendment by Rep. Theodore Sedgwick, Federalist-Mass., to lower House pay to $5 a day, thus creating a $1-a-day differential in favor of senators. But the amendment was defeated by voice vote. On Aug. 10, 1789, the House by a 30-16 roll call passed a bill providing for payment of $6 a day to members of both chambers.

In the Senate, the bill was amended to provide that senators be paid at the $6 rate until March 4, 1795, when their pay would be increased to $8 a day; the pay of representatives would remain at $6. The amended bill passed the Senate on Aug. 28, 1789.

After a House-Senate conference on the issue, the House on Sept. 11 by a 29-25 vote agreed to fix the pay of senators at $7 a day after March 4, 1795, and by a 28-26 vote set March 4, 1796, as the expiration date of the legislation. The Senate agreed to the House amendments on Sept. 12, and the bill was signed into law on Sept. 22, 1789, seven days before the end of the first session of Congress.

As enacted, the measure provided the first congressional perquisite: a travel allowance for senators and representatives of $6 for each 20 miles. It also provided a $6-a-day differential for the House Speaker (making his pay $12 a day) and compensation for a number of lesser House and Senate officials.

When a new pay law was enacted in 1796, only a glancing reference was made to continuing the differential for the Senate. Both the House and the Senate passed a bill equalizing the pay at $6 a day.

Short-Lived Salary Law

In 1816 Congress voted itself a pay increase and a shift from per diem compensation to an annual salary. An act of March 19, 1816, raised congressional pay to $1,500 a year and made the raise retroactive to Dec. 4, 1815, when the first session of the 14th Congress convened. The pay raise had been passed easily by both houses, but it was roundly condemned by the population at large. A number of members who had voted for the bill were defeated in the 1816 general election, and nine members resigned over the issue. One of the election victims was Rep. Daniel Webster, Federalist-N.H./Mass. He was not elected to Congress again until 1822.

The short session of the 14th Congress in 1817 repealed the $1,500 salary act, effective at the end of that Congress March 3, 1817. An act of Jan. 22, 1818, restored per diem compensation and set the rate at $8, retroactive to March 3, 1817.

Salaries, 1850s-1930s

Almost four decades after Congress had returned to per diem compensation, a successful conversion to annual congressional salaries finally was achieved. An act of Aug. 16, 1856, replaced the $8-a-day rate with a $3,000 annual salary, retroactive to the start of the 34th Congress Dec. 3, 1855. Another retroactive pay increase — to $5,000 — was approved July 28, 1866, and made effective as of Dec. 4, 1865, when the 39th Congress convened for its first session.

In the closing days of the 42nd Congress in 1873, still another retroactive pay raise was enacted, increasing salaries to $7,500. The higher salary was made retroactive to the beginning of the 42nd Congress, in effect providing members with a $5,000 windfall ($2,500 per year for the two preceding years). Despite precedents for making the increase retroactive, the size of the increase and the windfall effect boomeranged. Criticism of Congress already was at a high level because of the Crédit Mobilier scandal, and the pay increase was immediately condemned as a "salary grab" and a "back-pay steal." Some members returned their pay to the Treasury; others donated it to colleges or charities.

When the 43rd Congress opened in December 1873, scores of bills were introduced to repeal the increase. By an act of Jan. 20, 1874, congressional pay reverted to the previous $5,000 annual rate, where it stayed until a $7,500 salary was sanctioned in February 1907. A raise to $10,000 was approved in March 1925.

Government austerity was the byword as the Great Depression of the 1930s deepened. Salaries of federal employees were reduced, and members of Congress likewise had to take a pay cut. The Economy Act of June 30, 1932, provided for a 10 percent cutback in members' salaries, dropping them from $10,000 to $9,000. The cutback was increased another 5 percent, meaning a further drop to $8,500, by the Economy Act of March 20, 1933. Gradually the cutbacks were rescinded, and by the end of 1935 congressional salaries had been restored to the $10,000 level.

Postwar Salaries

Congress added to the Legislative Reorganization Act of 1946 a provision increasing congressional salaries from $10,000 to $12,500 and retaining an existing $2,500 nontaxable expense allowance for all members. The increase took effect at the beginning of the 80th Congress in 1947. A $15,000 annual salary and elimination of the expense allowance had been recommended in committee, but the legislation was amended in the House, and the House provision was retained in the final version of the act. The measure provided $20,000 salaries for the vice president and Speaker of the House.

Provision for the $2,500 expense allowance for representatives had been made in 1945 when the House Appropriations Committee included funding for it in a legislative branch appropriations bill. Although the bill did not so stipulate, the committee said the allowance probably would be tax-exempt. When the measure reached the House floor, opponents called the allowance an opening wedge for inflation and a pay increase by subterfuge. But a special rule drafted by the Rules Committee waived all points of order against the bill, thus thwarting efforts to eliminate the allowance on the floor. The legislation subsequently was adopted, 229-124. Other attempts to eliminate or change the proposal also failed, and the House approved the bill.

The Senate Appropriations Committee reported the bill after adding a $2,500 expense allowance for senators. But the committee amendment was defeated by the Senate, 9-43, and two compromise amendments also failed. An amendment to delete the House expense allowance was narrowly defeated, 22-28. The Senate thus passed the bill, which later was enacted, with the allowance for representatives but not for senators.

The question came up again during Senate action on a fiscal 1946 supplemental appropriations bill. The Senate Appropriations Committee offered an amendment to extend the expense allowance to senators, but the Senate again rejected the plan, 24-47. Senators ultimately received the $2,500 expense allowance in 1946 through the fiscal 1947 legislative branch appropriations bill.

End of Tax-Free Provision

In the Revenue Act of 1951 Congress eliminated the tax-free expense allowances, effective Jan. 3, 1952. Also made subject to taxation were the expense allowances of the president, vice president and Speaker of the House. The changes were approved 77-11.

Congress in 1953 created a Commission on Judicial and Congressional Salaries to study the salary question and make recommendations to Congress. As approved by the Senate, the commission would have been empowered to raise salaries. However, the measure was amended in the House to require congressional approval for any pay increase. The commission's report recommended a $10,000 salary boost, but Congress took no action. However, in 1955 Congress enacted legislation raising both congressional and judicial salaries. The bill increased members' salaries to $22,500 (from $12,500 plus the $2,500 expense allowance). It also provided $35,000 for the Speaker and the vice president (up from $30,000) and retained the existing $10,000 taxable expense allowance for both positions. The increases became effective March 1, 1955. *(Pay of congressional leaders, box, p. 6)*

The chief difference between the House and Senate bills was over the $2,500 expense allowance, which the House wanted to retain. But the Senate deleted it. Then the Senate rejected the final conference version because it retained an expense allowance provision. After that provision had been deleted, a second conference bill without the allowance was approved by Congress.

Congress again raised its own salaries, and those of other federal government employees, in 1964. Members' salaries were raised by $7,500, to $30,000. Salaries of the Speaker and the vice president were raised to $43,000. The bill was enacted after the House first killed a version of the bill raising congressional salaries by $10,000. The second measure was strongly backed by President Lyndon B. Johnson. Congress acted on the bill after most of the 1964 congressional primary elections had been held. It was passed in the House by 243-157 and in the Senate by 58-21.

Special Salary Commission

In 1967 Congress established a nine-member Commission on Executive, Legislative and Judicial Salaries to review the salaries of members of Congress, federal judges and top officers of the executive branch every four years and to recommend changes.

Creation of the commission plan was designed to relieve members of Congress of the politically risky task of periodically having to raise their own salaries. And it was hoped that the commission would set the salaries of top officials high enough to attract and keep the best qualified persons.

Three members of the commission were to be appointed by the president, two by the president of the Senate, two by the Speaker of the House and two by the chief justice. Beginning in fiscal 1969, the commission was to submit its recommendations to the president, who was to propose in his annual budget message the exact rates of pay "he deems advisable" for federal executives, judges and members of Congress. His recommendations could be either higher or lower than those of the commission, or he could propose that salaries not be altered. The recommendations were to take effect within 30 days unless Congress either disapproved all or part of the recommendations or enacted a separate pay measure.

The law did not work as well as its sponsors had hoped, although in its first test, in 1969, it worked as planned. Congressional salaries were increased from $30,000 to $42,500. But in 1973 President Nixon delayed naming a pay commission, and pay proposals were not sent to Congress until 1974, an election year. The Senate, uneasy about a pay raise at that time, killed the proposed increases.

Automatic Salary Increases

Congressional salaries were not increased again for almost seven years, during which period the cost of living had risen 47.5 percent. But in 1975 Congress, with sleight of hand, approved a cost-of-living increase for itself and other top officials of the government. The adjustment was tied to a government-wide pay raise. As part of the package, Congress opted to make itself and other top officials eligible for the annual October cost-of-living pay raise without having to vote on the raises. It would be received automatically unless members of the House or Senate decided not to take it.

The plan was worked out secretly over several months by congressional leaders in consultation with the Ford administration. It was cleared by Congress only five days after most members had first heard of it. One representative called the debate "vicious, one of the ugliest, most disgusting things I've ever seen.... Members who rarely say a thing during floor debate were shouting and screaming at each other, saying, 'Don't be a hero, you want this raise as much as we do.' It was ugly."[3]

The result was a 5 percent pay increase for members, bringing congressional salaries to $44,600 annually. It was much criticized by the voters, and in 1976 Congress decided it was prudent to pass up the automatic increase for that year. A provision denying the cost-of-living pay raise to members of Congress was added to the fiscal 1977 legislative branch appropriations bill.

1977 Pay Raise

Congress in 1977 made up for lost time by giving itself and other top government officials of the executive, legislative and judicial branches a $12,900 pay raise, increasing lawmakers' salaries to $57,500 annually. This amounted to a pay hike of about 29 percent. It was the first increase in basic pay since 1969.

The raise had been recommended by the third quadrennial Commission on Executive, Legislative and Judicial Salaries, chaired by businessman Peter G. Peterson. It conditioned its proposals for a salary increase upon adoption of a strong ethics code governing congressional conduct. And the panel called for public disclosure of members' financial worth, rigorous restrictions on outside earned income and on potential conflicts of interest, fully accountable expense allowances and publicly reported auditing of the ethics codes' provisions.

Members paid a price when they raised their salaries that year. Congress repealed the procedure that had allowed raises to take effect without a congressional vote. And the new ethics codes adopted by both chambers as part of the 1977 pay increase negotiations included a ban on so-called "slush funds" — unofficial office accounts maintained with cash gifts from members' friends and supporters — and tight limits on outside income. (In 1979, however, the Senate suspended those outside income limits for four years.)

Congress also denied itself the scheduled 1977 cost-of-living increase. Even so, criticism of the earlier raise that year was widespread.

In 1978 Congress also voted to forgo that year's cost-of-living increase. Also affected were the top congressional aides, judges and all other federal officials at or over the $47,500 pay level. Some 16,000 persons were affected. Other federal workers got the raise, which was 5.5 percent.

1977 Tax Break. Congress cleared legislation in July 1977 exempting members of Congress from paying income taxes in those jurisdictions where they lived while attending sessions of Congress. A similar bill was passed by Congress in 1976 but was vetoed by President Ford on grounds that it unfairly created a special class of citizens with special privileges.

In subsequent years the 1977 exemption was challenged in the courts, but on May 26, 1981, the Supreme Court upheld the income tax deduction.

As a practical matter, Maryland was the only state affected by the law because Virginia and the District of Columbia already had exempted members of Congress from their income tax laws. In 1977 there were about 125 members living in Maryland, and that number was estimated to be living there when the Supreme Court upheld the law in 1981.

The Court's action in *Maryland v. United States*[4] appeared to open the way for representatives and senators to seek refunds of taxes they paid Maryland in the past, although further litigation was expected to decide that question. The 1977 law included Senate language making the exemption retroactive, but it was never made clear precisely what the senators intended. At the time, a Senate Judiciary Committee spokesman suggested it would be up to the courts to decide whether members could seek refunds for taxes already paid to Maryland.

1978-79 Pay Raise Debates

The political volatility surrounding congressional pay surfaced once again in 1979 when the issue set off a Senate-House feud. That dispute forced the government to begin fiscal 1980 without spending authority for many federal agencies.

As 1979 began, members were earning $57,500 a year. Moreover, members were due for an automatic 7 percent pay hike that October under the cost-of-living pay procedures then in effect.

Besides the proposed 7 percent increase, members hoped to recoup the 5.5 percent comparability adjustment from 1978 that Congress had voted not to take in that election year. The 1978 hike had not been repealed; it had just been suspended for a year. Thus if Congress took no action on it members would receive both pay hikes, plus interest on the 5.5 percent raise, for a total increase of 12.9 percent, or more than $7,400.

With another election just a year away, however, a move was launched to limit or deny the congressional pay hikes altogether. Also caught up in the politics of the pay issue were federal judges and top-level executive branch bureaucrats making at least $47,500; past pay freezes had covered them as well.

The House Appropriations Committee recommended that the raise be limited to 7 percent, but in June the House knocked that limit down to 5.5 percent and then rejected the appropriations bill because it thought that increase too high.

Then, in late September, Congress became bogged down over an emergency stopgap funding bill that was being used as the vehicle for the pay hike. That measure was needed to fund agencies whose regular appropriations bills had not yet been approved. The House, in a non-recorded vote, accepted a compromise 5.5 percent hike. The Senate knocked that out and said "no raise."

But the House just two days before the new fiscal year was to begin insisted on the raise and adjourned for a

A Remedy for Absenteeism:
Paying Members Only by the Day

One suggestion as a way to curb absenteeism in Congress is to dock a member's pay for each day he fails to appear on the floor of the House or Senate. The Constitution makes no provision for this, saying only that "each House shall be the Judge of the Elections, Returns and Qualifications of its own Members, and a Majority of each shall constitute a Quorum to do Business; but a smaller Number may adjourn from day to day, and may be authorized to compel the Attendance of absent Members, in such Manner, and under such Penalties as each House may provide." (Article 1, Section 5)

Nevertheless, the first session of the First Congress in 1789 provided for an automatic docking of pay. Salaries were $6 a day for each day of attendance.

A law enacted in 1856 provided that "the Secretary of the Senate and the Sergeant at Arms of the House, respectively, shall deduct from the monthly payments of each member or delegate the amount of his salary for each day that he has been absent from the Senate or House, ... unless such member or delegate assigns as the reason for such absence the sickness of himself or of some member of his family."

Since then a few isolated attempts to compel attendance have cited this law. During the 53rd Congress (1894), after a ruling of the chair that the 1856 law was still in force, portions of some House members' salaries were withheld.

The 1894 incident was recalled in 1914 when the House adopted a resolution revoking all leaves of absence granted to members and directing the sergeant-at-arms to deduct members' pay for each day they were absent. The 1914 resolution was enforced stringently for a brief time.

But soon the practice of docking a member's pay for absenteeism was abandoned. The House parliamentarian's office argued there was no way of knowing when a member was away from his official duties.

In 1975 the Senate inserted a provision repealing the 1856 law in the fiscal 1976 legislative branch appropriations bill, but it was dropped from the final version of that bill.

In 1981 a U.S. district court judge rejected a California taxpayer's complaint that federal lawmakers should not be paid for days when they are absent from Congress without an excuse. In a brief opinion, Judge Spencer Williams of the Northern District of California dismissed the suit, ruling that merely being a taxpayer did not give the Californian sufficient standing to file the suit. Williams added that it would be "inappropriate for the courts to inquire into or supervise the attendance of members of a coordinate branch of government."

In a similar 1972 suit, a federal judge had dismissed a suit seeking to recover salaries and allowances paid several members of Congress who were away from Washington campaigning for the presidency.

week's recess, leaving the Senate with an unenviable choice: it could either approve the emergency funding resolution, thus keeping the government in business but also accepting the 5.5 percent pay increase, or kill the funding resolution, thus permitting the automatic 12.9 percent increase to go into effect but depriving most of the government of authority to spend money as of Oct. 1. An angry Senate voted to kill the resolution.

Finally, on Oct. 12, almost two weeks after the new fiscal year had begun and just before thousands of federal workers were about to be denied a paycheck, Congress approved an emergency funding measure that rolled back the 12.9 percent increase to 5.5 percent. The new raise brought congressional salaries up to $60,662.50 beginning in 1980.

While the increases for members of Congress and top executive branch officials were being rolled back, federal judges were able to retain the entire 12.9 percent pay hike because, under the Constitution, Congress is prohibited from reducing the compensation of judges during their term of office.

1980-81 Pay Controversies

In December 1980 Sen. Ted Stevens, R-Alaska, introduced legislation to provide a 17 percent increase in members' salaries — to $70,900 from $60,662. The amendment also proposed to increase the pay of judicial branch employees and some 34,000 top-level executive employees. The amendment was rejected handily by the Senate.

The next year, citing the need to cut federal spending, Congress rejected another large pay raise — amounting to 16.8 percent — for lawmakers and high-level government employees. (President Carter in 1980 had recommended a pay raise to $70,853 based on the recommendation of the Commission on Executive, Legislative and Judicial Salaries. President Reagan, who originally supported the increase, changed his mind, citing budgetary considerations.)

The proposed 1981 pay raise was debated amid disagreement between House and Senate members over the proper procedure for acting on proposed congressional salary hikes. The House and Senate each followed a different path in rejecting the pay raise. The Senate took a recorded vote on four separate resolutions of disapproval; the House merely took a voice vote on a resolution affirming "the sense of the House."

In 1977 Congress had amended the 1969 pay law by requiring each house to approve a presidential pay recommendation within 60 days in order for the proposed increase to take effect. The amendment stated that each chamber must take recorded votes on raising the pay of each branch of government. The approval of both chambers was required to raise the pay of employees in any of the three branches of government.

Future Automatic Pay Raises. Shying away from a vote on an outright pay increase for 1981, Congress that year devised indirect methods for achieving future pay hikes. It approved a procedure whereby members could receive the annual government-wide cost-of-living pay increase without either chamber having to vote on the raise. This automatic mechanism was scheduled to take effect at the start of fiscal 1983 (Oct. 1, 1982). The new cost-of-living pay procedure was approved in October 1981 as a rider attached to an emergency funding bill. While the final version of that legislation did not contain a 4.8 percent congressional pay raise for 1981 sought by House members, it did provide the mechanism for subsequent raises.

Since 1977, two years after Congress first voted to include itself in the annual cost-of-living pay raise program in effect for civil service employees, members had been required to vote on whether to take the pay hike. Four times — in 1977, 1978, 1980 and 1981 — members of Congress had voted to block the raise. In 1983 the House took the raise but the Senate rejected it. *(Raise, box, p. 3)*

1981 Tax Deductions. In the same 1981 emergency appropriations bill containing the automatic cost-of-living adjustment procedure, Congress approved a change in congressional tax laws that enabled senators and representatives to deduct from their income taxes the expenses they incurred while residing in Washington. Under a 1952 law, members had been allowed a maximum deduction of $3,000.

The Joint Taxation Committee estimated in 1981 that the change would cost the Treasury $3 million a year and provide a typical member in the 45 percent tax bracket with the equivalent of a $10,500 pay raise.

Though a similar proposal was pushed earlier in 1981 by House Appropriations Committee Chairman Jamie L. Whitten, D-Miss., it never came to a vote in the House. But Sen. Stevens won approval of the plan in the Senate. Besides the tax deduction change, Stevens had shepherded through to enactment measures increasing legislators' official perquisites, loosening restrictions on outside earnings by lawmakers and modifying provisions of the Senate's ethics code that placed strict limits on senators' honoraria. *(Congressional honoraria, p. 121)*

After the tax change had been enacted, it was discovered that the new deductions conflicted with a provision of a 1976 statute limiting the amount of deductions a person living alone could take on second homes used in connection with a trade or business.

Resolving Conflicting Statutes. Under the combined effect of the 1976 and 1981 laws, a member of Congress who lived alone while working in Washington could, in the same tax year, depreciate the cost of a second home in the capital area as well as deduct from his taxes his Washington housing expenses. But a member whose family resided with him in Washington for more than 14 days a year was not eligible for both tax breaks.

To remedy the situation, Congress in December 1981

tacked a nongermane tax provision onto a black lung benefits bill and passed that measure without a roll-call vote. The bill enabled members living with their families in Washington to claim the same tax benefits as members living alone. Congress also instructed the Treasury secretary to prescribe the "appropriate" business deduction a member could take for each day Congress was in session without actually having to substantiate his business expenses. *(Nongermane amendments, box, p. 67)*

Treasury Ruling for 1981. Regulations approved by the Treasury in January 1982 meant that the 1981 deduction would result in a saving of at least $19,200 for senators and $19,650 for House members. Since previous law allowed members a maximum deduction of $3,000 a year for their Washington expenses, the new legislation provided an additional deduction of at least $16,200 for senators and $16,650 for House members for that year. (The deduction would vary from year to year, depending on how many days each house is in session.)

A married member with two children and typical deductions who lived on his congressional salary alone during 1981 was able to keep about $7,000 that otherwise would have been paid in taxes, according to Congressional Quarterly calculations based on figures supplied by the Internal Revenue Service (IRS). Members with high Washington living expenses or with outside incomes in addition to their salaries could qualify for even bigger tax breaks.

The Treasury regulations were explained to members in a letter from Treasury Secretary Donald T. Regan. The letter said members of Congress could calculate their deductions for their Washington living expenses in one of three ways:

● They could deduct $75 for each "congressional day" during the year, without any substantiation of their actual expenses and whether or not they actually were in Washington all those days. That amount equaled the per diem payment in 1982 offered federal employees traveling to Washington on official business. A congressional day was defined as every day Congress was in session, plus weekends and similar breaks of up to four days in a row. Under this formula, there were 256 congressional days for senators and 262 for House members in 1981. A member choosing to deduct $75 per congressional day could also deduct additional expenses incurred outside Washington. For example, a member traveling outside of Washington on a day Congress was in session could deduct travel expenses as well as the $75.

● Members could deduct $50 a day plus the interest and taxes on their Washington homes. This option could be used by those members having big mortgages on expensive homes.

● Members could deduct their actual expenses so long as they were substantiated by proper records. This option could be used by members with expenses above $75 a day.

The increased deduction translated into substantial tax savings for members, according to a study prepared by the Congressional Research Service (CRS) and released by Sen. Dennis DeConcini, D-Ariz. For 1982, CRS estimated actual savings for a hypothetical member would range from about $5,000 to $10,000 a year, depending on the individual member's financial situation.

1982 Tax Deduction Repeal

The tax breaks provoked a public outcry. Taxpayers flooded Capitol Hill and the Internal Revenue Service with angry letters and phone calls protesting the new deductions. Common Cause, a citizens' lobby group, criticized the tax deductions as unjustified and inequitable and launched a nationwide "Give Taxpayers A Break" campaign to repeal the 1981 tax deduction. It pledged to get all representatives and senators to publicly disclose the amount of the deductions for Washington living expenses they took in 1981. According to Common Cause President Fred Wertheimer, "Congress' failure to provide regular cost-of-living adjustments for itself cannot justify enacting extravagant and unjustified tax breaks that turn members of Congress into a privileged class of taxpayers. This is bound to undermine public confidence in the fairness of our tax system."[5]

In response to the pressure, Congress in 1982 approved legislation repealing the 1981 deductions. The measure was enacted into law July 18, but was made retroactive to Jan. 1. It nevertheless allowed members to keep the lucrative deductions they took on their 1981 tax returns. The repeal restored the $3,000 annual limit on a member's deductions for Washington expenses — the limit that had been in force before 1981. The repeal, initiated by Sen. William Proxmire, D-Wis., was tacked on to a fiscal 1982 supplemental appropriations bill for federal agencies.

Earlier that year, the House threatened not to approve the repeal unless senators agreed to limit their outside earned income to the maximum allowed representatives. That dispute stalled final action on the spending bill/tax deduction repeal and exacerbated a bitter struggle between the House and Senate over the twin issues of members' tax breaks and honoraria. But the House backed down when it looked as if the honoraria provision might tie up the funding bill indefinitely.

Proposed Changes in Pay Procedure

In 1982 Sens. Proxmire and Strom Thurmond, R-S.C. introduced legislation to revise the way Congress handles congressional pay legislation, tax deductions and perquisites. The bill proposed to prohibit automatic cost-of-living adjustments and require members to provide item-by-item justifications of all congressional expenses for which tax deductions are claimed. In addition, any vote increasing pay, outside income or tax treatment affecting members would not go into effect until the next Congress. During the Constitutional Convention of 1787 a provision prohibiting members from raising their own pay without an intervening general election was debated but ultimately rejected.

Also under the senators' bill, changes in pay, tax treatment or outside earnings of members could not be attached to legislation that did not deal exclusively with those issues. The legislation would have to stand on its own and be subject to a recorded vote in the House and Senate. The proposal had not been considered by either house by the summer of 1982.

Honoraria Payments

For many years members of Congress have supplemented their income by delivering speeches, making public appearances and broadcasts, and publishing articles for fees and royalties. Payment of honoraria — money or anything of value — to senators and representatives is a time-honored way for private organizations and associations to get an "insider's view" of Washington. Besides the fee,

Top Honoraria Providers

Listed below are the 15 organizations that gave the most in honoraria to members of Congress in 1979. The figures in parentheses indicate the number of senators and representatives who received honoraria from each group.

Grocery Manufacturers of America (22)	$26,520
Chamber of Commerce of the U.S. (45)	26,290
Brookings Institution (74)	20,750
Food Marketing Institute (15)	19,500
National Association of Broadcasters (14)	18,000
Outdoor Advertising Association of America (17)	17,700
Pfizer Inc. (23)	17,250
American Bankers Association (16)	16,250
American International Group Inc. (9)	16,000
National Association of Home Builders (14)	14,250
Associated General Contractors of America (13)	13,000
Distilled Spirits Council of the U.S. (12)	12,500
American Mining Congress (8)	12,000
National Association of Realtors (12)	11,884
AFL-CIO (11)	11,500

members often receive expense-paid trips to the sites where the speeches are given as well as lodging and meals.

Much of the honoraria earned by members come from speeches to conventions held by trade associations and other business groups and labor unions. Other payments are given in return for briefings or addresses to education groups as well as schools and colleges, foreign policy associations, religious, ethnic and civic groups, and even the so-called single-issue organizations (such as the pro- and anti-abortion groups) that often have an ideological bias.

Honoraria also are used by a corporation's board of directors, or a small group of businessmen, lawyers and lobbyists for intimate meetings with members of Congress over dinner or lunch. These groups say a meal and a chat with a prominent senator or representative is worth the $1,000 or $2,000 payment because of the opportunity it provides for an off-the-record discussion of Washington goings-on.

Honoraria are perfectly legal, but many of the groups that provide such payments also have a personal or business stake in particular legislation pending in Congress.

One of the harshest criticisms leveled at honoraria payments is that they have become little more than legalized influence buying. Another charge is that the groups making such payments are more interested in gaining the friendship of elected officials, and easy access to them in the future, than in hearing members' opinions on current issues and developments in Washington.

Organizations that give honoraria — and members of Congress who accept them — deny any impropriety.

Many freely admit, however, that inviting a member of Congress to address a company's board of directors or a trade association's annual meeting — and paying him for his appearance — can have important benefits. It can give top management a better understanding of the Washington scene, provide an occasion to get to know an important member, ensure better access to the member in the future and provide an expert's assessment of the chances for passage of certain legislation of interest to the organization. It also can be used to let the member know he has the support of influential groups in his state or congressional district.

Until 1975 there were no restrictions on such earnings, and it was not unusual for prominent members of Congress to earn more from honoraria than from their salary.

Campaign Finance Laws

The era of completely unregulated honoraria payments ended on Jan. 1, 1975, when Congress' first campaign finance law took effect. That measure limited honoraria payments to members and other federal officials to $1,000 for a single speaking appearance or article and a total of $15,000 a year on all honoraria.

The restrictions were loosened considerably by provisions of the Federal Election Campaign Act Amendments of 1976. That law raised the ceiling on payments for a single speech or article to $2,000 and raised the annual amount permitted to $25,000.

The $25,000 was a net amount and did not include booking agents' fees, travel expenditures, subsistence and expenses for an aide or a spouse accompanying the member.

Though members were limited to $2,000 for one speaking engagement, some members managed to earn more than $2,000 from the same source by making repeat appearances.

For example, Sen. John Tower, R-Texas, has spoken to the American Bankers Association on several occasions since the mid-1970s. Although the $1,000 honorarium received by Tower on each occasion was well under the Senate's $2,000 annual limit, his total earnings from the ABA between 1975 and 1979 were $4,000.

The 1976 law permitted members to deduct any funds donated to charity or used to pay out-of-pocket expenses from their total yearly honoraria earnings for the purpose of complying with the $25,000 limitation. In addition, under the 1976 law House and Senate members could receive honoraria earned in previous years without applying those payments to their current year's limit.

Senate

Senators, having larger constituencies and receiving far more publicity than representatives, always have received more honoraria. Although senators have been required since 1969 to report their honoraria, they do not have to report how they use it. Some donate their honoraria to charitable institutions; others use the funds to cover office expenses and other official activities.

In 1973 senators collected nearly $1.1 million overall in honoraria. In 1974, the last year before the campaign finance law restrictions took effect, 77 senators reported honoraria totaling $939,619. In the first year under the new campaign finance law, 81 senators reported earning $637,893. The leading earner in 1975 was Sen. Herman E. Talmadge, D-Ga. (1957-81), who reported $14,980. In that year, colleges and universities spent more on honoraria — $136,172 given to 50 senators — than any other group.

In 1977, the first year in which the campaign act

amendments relaxing some of the honoraria limitations were in effect, 81 senators earned almost $1.1 million. In 1978 total Senate honoraria dropped slightly, but the amount earned by the 75 senators accepting honoraria averaged $14,600, compared to about $13,400 in 1977.

New Restrictions Delayed. A lower ceiling on the amount of money a senator could earn in outside income was to have gone into effect in 1979, but the Senate voted in March of that year to delay implementation of those requirements until 1983.

Total annual honoraria payments would have been limited to 15 percent of a senator's official salary. Those rules, which were part of the 1977 Senate ethics code, also reduced the maximum honorarium a senator could be paid for each speech or article to $1,000.

The delay had the effect of retaining a senator's maximum honorarium payment of $2,000 and annual honoraria earnings at $25,000 — the ceilings in the 1976 law.

At the time of the proposed 1979 rollback, senators were being paid $57,500 annually. Financial disclosure figures for 1978 showed that 59 senators in office in 1979 would have suffered a reduction in their total income under the 15 percent ($8,625) limit on outside earned income.

Total Senate honoraria payments in 1979 rose to $1,208,650, and were received by 86 senators, according to a report by the Democratic Study Group (DSG), a House organization of moderate and liberal Democrats. In 1980, 80 senators reported honoraria totaling $1,179,420.[6]

Repeal of Annual Honoraria Limit. In October 1981 the Senate repealed the $25,000 limit on honoraria. Sen. Stevens argued that since senators had an unlimited income from other sources they should be entitled to unlimited payments from speeches. That year 89 senators reported honoraria payments totaling $1,742,172, according to the DSG report. According to a Congressional Quarterly survey, the top five Senate honoraria collectors in 1981 were Robert Dole, R-Kan. ($66,850); Henry M. Jackson, D-Wash. ($56,250); Howard H. Baker Jr., R-Tenn. ($54,000); Steven Symms, R-Idaho ($40,700); and Jake Garn, R-Utah ($48,000). Those senators, with the exception of Jackson, gave all or part of their earnings to charity.

The Senate's 1981 action repealing the 1976 Federal Election Campaign Act Amendments affected senators' but not House members' honoraria ceiling. However, the related rule in the Senate Ethics Code was not repealed. Thus the lower ceiling that was delayed until 1983 still would take effect unless the Senate acted.

In June 1982 the House threatened to hold up final action on an emergency supplemental appropriations bill if the Senate did not reimpose the limit on outside earned income. But the House later relented on the funding bill without forcing the Senate to change its decision.

A continuing resolution passed in January 1983 repealed the honoraria ceiling. Senators currently are able to earn as much as they choose in outside income, including legal fees, business income and honoraria for speeches and articles. (See Congressional Pay Raise box, p. 3.)

House

Under the Federal Election Campaign Act Amendments of 1976, representatives were limited to $25,000 in annual honoraria payments and $2,000 for a single speech or article. But in its 1977 ethics code, the House placed a tighter restriction on outside earned income. Effective at the beginning of 1979, outside earned income, including

Life After Congress: Retirement Made Easier by Liberal Pensions

Members of Congress, like other federal employees, are excluded from participation in the Social Security program. Instead, they may participate in the Civil Service Retirement System, administered by the Office of Personnel Management (OPM).

Under the federal plan, a member, at his option, contributes 8 percent of his gross salary to a retirement fund; the government matches his contribution.

Pension Formula

A member becomes eligible for benefits upon retirement from Congress if he is 62 years of age with five years of congressional service (except in cases of disability); 60 years of age with 10 years of service; or 50 years of age with service in nine Congresses or 20 years of government service.

For each year of service, a retired member of Congress covered by the plan receives 2½ percent of his average salary earned in the three highest consecutive years. The amount cannot exceed 80 percent of a member's final congressional salary. Based on the 1983 Senate salary of $60,622.50, a member who had served for 32 years would receive about $48,500 annually. Cost-of-living adjustments in the pension are made once a year.

While the actual retirement income of former members is confidential under provisions of the Privacy Act, estimates indicate that many retired lawmakers receive handsome pensions. In 1980, for example, OPM calculated that two members defeated for re-election in 1980: 53-year-old Rep. John Brademas, D-Ind. (1959-81), and Sen. Frank Church, D-Idaho (1957-81), aged 54, would draw $30,840 and $39,500 a year, respectively, not including cost-of-living adjustments.

1946 Act Provisions

At the recommendation of a joint committee on congressional organization, Congress incorporated in the Legislative Reorganization Act of 1946 the provisions setting up the congressional retirement system for senators and representatives.

The 1946 act brought members of Congress under the Civil Service Retirement Act, permitting them, if they wished, to contribute 6 percent of their salaries to a retirement fund. Retirement annuities were to be calculated at 2½ percent of average salary multiplied by years of service, but could not exceed 75 percent of a member's final congressional salary.

Lawmakers who were retiring had to be at least 62 years old with a minimum of five years of congressional service to qualify for benefits.

Over the years Congress liberalized the pension law and also adjusted retirement benefits for Capitol Hill employees. A 1954 law maintained the basic contribution rate of 6 percent of salary but included the congressional expense allowance in the salary computation. It also provided for reduced retirement benefits at age 60 and made other minor changes in the program. In 1956 the contribution was raised to 7½ percent. Further changes were enacted in 1960, although the basic retirement benefits were left unchanged.

Benefits Liberalized in 1969

In 1969 retirement benefits were increased by specifying that the annuity computation formula would use an employee's average annual earnings during the highest consecutive three-year period, rather than during a five-year period, as had been required.

The method of computing annuities for congressional employees was liberalized by eliminating a 15-year limit on the number of years of service for which the annuity would be computed at 2½ percent of average pay. In addition, the contribution of members of Congress was increased from 7½ to 8 percent, and the contribution of congressional employees from 6½ percent to 7½ percent, beginning in January 1970.

'Kicker' Controversy

With enactment in 1969 of a law making modifications in the federal pension system, government retirees became eligible to receive a bonus in their pensions every time the cost-of-living went up by 3 percent over the previous base period for three consecutive months. In such situations, they became eligible for an extra 1 percent "kicker" payment.

The idea behind the kicker was to make up for the delay between the time the cost of living began to rise and the time it rose high enough to trigger a raise in pensions. However, because the kicker was then included in the base for the next raise, it had a multiplier effect, which critics charged went far beyond its intent.

Responding to criticism about the fairness of the 1969 bonus, Congress in September 1976 repealed the law authorizing the 1 percent "kicker" and replaced it with a system that would adjust the pensions automatically every six months without the 1 percent bonus.

Beginning in 1981, cost-of-living adjustments were made only once a year.

honoraria, was limited to 15 percent of a representative's annual salary. The code did not affect unearned income, such as dividends, interest payments, or rent from properties, and lawmakers with few holdings maintained the code discriminated in favor of the wealthier members.

A limit of $750 for each speech or article also was included in the 1977 ethics code. But that limit never was implemented since the ceiling was raised to $1,000 in January 1979, the date the honoraria limits took effect. The move came in response to a similar change in the Senate ethics code that had been made that same January at the request of Sen. Jacob K. Javits, R-N.Y. (1957-81). Javits, in arguing for the increase, said there was no reason the Senate should have the same limit on speaking fees as the House. The increase, he maintained, was justified to "try to preserve a measure of personal dignity for ourselves."

When Rep. Richard Bolling, D-Mo., proposed the same change in the House code, he said the report on the measure would justify the amendment with a single word, printed in boldfaced type: "Dignity."

The 1977 House ethics code defined outside earned income as "wages, salaries, professional fees, honorariums and other amounts (other than copyright royalties) received or to be received as compensation for personal services actually rendered."

But the code contained a major exception: "In the case of a member engaged in a trade or business in which the member or his family holds a controlling interest and in which both personal services and capital are income-producing factors, any amount received by such members [is exempt from the limit] so long as the personal services actually rendered by the member in the trade or business do not generate a significant amount of income."

That section was inserted to protect members from having to give up family farms and other small businesses. Members opposed to the exception questioned the phrase "significant amount of income," saying it was vague and subject to varying interpretations.

By 1978, the first year House members were required to disclose honoraria payments, 249 members listed earnings totaling about $1,180,000. The average of those accepting honoraria was $4,700.

Despite the earned income limit (15 percent of a representative's salary) that went into effect in 1979 under the ethics code, honoraria payments went up, with 287 representatives reporting $1,454,055.

According to the DSG, in 1980 269 representatives reported earning $1,065,452. And in 1981 honoraria payments to 320 members totaled $1,675,688.

After the Senate removed its annual honoraria limit in 1981, representatives complained that they deserved equal treatment.

In a surprise move, the House leadership on Dec. 15, 1981, brought to the floor and won approval of a change in House rules that increased House members' allowable outside earnings to 30 percent — from 15 percent — of their official salary. This change was given unanimous approval in less than half a minute. Only a handful of members were present.

At an annual salary of $69,800, House members could now earn up to $20,940 a year in honoraria, beginning in 1983. The continuing resolution passed in January 1983 that gave House members a $9,138 pay increase also continued to limit outside earnings for representatives to 30 percent of their annual salary. The salary for members of the Senate remained at $60,662.50.

PERQUISITES OF OFFICE: STAFF, EXPENSE ACCOUNTS

Along with power and prestige and a high salary, being elected to office today gives lawmakers a plethora of perquisites — benefits and privileges that go with the position.

The two most expensive perquisites are members' personal staff and office expense accounts. House and Senate office expense accounts today allow members to work and travel in style and comfort, to an extent undreamed of even a few short decades ago.

Staff aides multiply the member's arms, legs, eyes and ears, providing the assistance needed to allow the member to meet the many demands on his time. Properly used, a staff can function as the member's strongest ally. Misused, the staff becomes little more than a reservoir of wasted talents. And abused, a member's staff can turn traitor; like the gentleman and his valet, no member is a hero to his staff.

Personal Staff Allowance

For a century after ratification of the Constitution, no provision was made by either chamber for personal staff, except for chairmen of committees.

The Senate was the first to provide staff assistance. In 1885 senators were authorized to employ a clerk when Congress was in session. The rate was set at $6 per day. The House first authorized a clerk for each of its members in 1893 and provided him with a salary of $100 monthly.

Over the years the number of aides and their salaries increased steadily. And staff responsibilities expanded to include clerical and bureaucratic support skills and technical, legal and political skills. Personal staff members usually have to perform in all three areas. They also handle a member's constituent services, personal appearances, correspondence and public relations.

Office Staff

Most congressional offices are organized similarly, each containing an administrative assistant (AA), legislative assistants (LA), caseworkers and at least one press aide. The administrative assistant often serves as the member's alter ego and directs and supervises the office. The AA usually is in charge of the staff.

The office's daily legislative functions are handled by one or more legislative assistants, who work with the senator or representative on the member's committees and help draft bills and amendments and recommend policy initiatives and alternatives. They also may write the lawmaker's speeches and prepare position papers.

Members cannot handle the heavy congressional workload on their own. They need legislative assistants for substantive and political guidance because the daily congressional agenda is filled with complex, interdependent issues. There are more committee meetings than a member adequately can prepare for. Other members, federal officials, special interest groups and, sometimes, even the White House staff must be consulted before final decisions are made, and often there are lengthy floor debates going well into the evening. A member must rely heavily on staff at every major phase of the legislative process.[7]

Legislative assistants also monitor committee sessions that the member cannot attend. When Walter F. Mondale was a senator from Minnesota, D (1964-76), he resolved a scheduling conflict this way:

"As the hands of the clock opposite [his] desk neared 10 a.m., he faced a decision. Should he attend a meeting of the Senate Budget Committee? Should he go to the Senate Select Committee on Intelligence hearing? Or should he attend a Labor and Public Welfare subcommittee hearing on health manpower legislation? All three were to begin at 10 a.m.

" 'I think we may have some fireworks today,' said David Aaron, his top aide on the Intelligence Committee.

"Senator Mondale nodded and said: 'I think you're right.' Then returning to his Budget Committee aide, David Carp, he asked: 'How about the budget? How far are we likely to get on that today?'

" 'I think you can skip the morning,' replied Mr. Carp. 'I'll keep an eye on it.'

"Minutes later, accompanied by Mr. Aaron, Sen. Mondale headed for the intelligence hearing, Mr. Carp set out for the budget meeting and another staff aide was deployed to monitor the health manpower hearing."[8]

Caseworkers deal with constituent questions and problems (Social Security, veterans' pensions, federal loans for college students, etc.). Members also maintain offices in their district or state to help with the casework load. Salaries for district workers are included in members' staff allowance.

Committee Staff

In addition to their personal staffs, senior senators and representatives today are assisted on legislative matters by staffs of the committees and subcommittees on which they serve. In addition, all senators since 1975 have been authorized up to three aides to help them with their committee business. The chairman of a standing committee actually has two staffs. It is not unusual for an aide to do both committee work and personal casework for a member, no matter which payroll he or she is on. Senate employees in 1982, counting both personal and committee staffs, numbered approximately 6,800. The House had about 12,000 employees.[9] *(Details, see Committee Staff chapter.)*

Staff Growth

In 1946 the ceiling on personal staff was five for each House member and six for each senator. (A ceiling on the number of personal staffers a member could hire was first established in 1919.) These staffs have almost tripled in size since 1960 in both the House and Senate.

In August 1979 Sen. Proxmire gave his "Golden Fleece Award" to Congress "for the eruption in its staff and spending over the past decade."

Proxmire called for a halt to staff increases, arguing that "added staff is then used to justify new buildings, more restaurants, added parking spaces and greater support personnel, all of which has led to a quantum jump in congressional spending." He stated that in the preceding 10 years House and Senate staffs had increased by about 70 percent, from about 10,700 to 18,400 persons. And the cost of the staffs had risen by 270 percent, from $150 million to $550 million a year. (Proxmire gave his award regularly for what he regarded as "the biggest, most ironic, or most ridiculous example of excessive spending for the period.")

The staff explosion came about for a variety of reasons: a desire for congressional independence from the executive branch; the increasing volume and complexity of legislative issues faced by Congress; the decline of the congressional seniority system; a growing sense that the minority party in Congress should get fairer treatment; competition among committees and their members; election of more activist members; greater demands exerted by special interests; and an increase in mail and demands for services by constituents.

The modern congressional office often more closely resembles a customer service department of a large company than the typical legislative office of an earlier period.

Until World War I, a single clerk handled a member's entire correspondence. In those days, congressional mail usually involved awarding rural mail routes, arranging for Spanish-American War pensions, sending out free seeds and, occasionally, explaining legislation.[10]

Impact of Constituent Demands

Constituent demands expanded tremendously during the Vietnam War, according to Rep. Robert S. Walker, R-Pa., in 1979. "That has necessitated a great increase in the number of people needed to process the mail."

In 1981 constituents and interest groups sent approximately 196 million letters and post cards to members of Congress — an average of about 365,000 for each representative and 360,000 a senator. From 1971 to 1981 the volume of incoming mail had nearly quadrupled. During calendar year 1981, the House Post Office handled a record 160 million incoming pieces of mail, compared to 40 million in 1972. The Senate received about 36 million pieces of mail in 1981.[11]

The demand for constituent services — usually assistance with a constituent's problems with federal agencies — increased in the 1960s and 1970s as government became more involved in the daily lives of Americans. But members also helped to stimulate constituent demands. They expanded use of mobile offices, radio programs and newsletters to advertise the availability of their services and to garner political support.

Members nevertheless contend that large staffs are necessary to serve constituents as well as to properly carry out government oversight, which, it is argued, often saves taxpayers' money in the long run through better surveillance of the administration of the laws. "Congress is damned if you do and damned if you don't," stated Rep. David Obey, D-Wis. "If you don't increase your capability, you're ridiculed as being the sapless branch. If you do something, you're rapped for being a $1 billion Congress."[12]

Historically, liberals in Congress have tended to press for larger professional staffs while conservatives have sought staff cuts as one way to reduce the size of the federal government. But this is no longer necessarily true. In 1979 the Viguerie Communications Corp's newsletter "The New Right Report" scolded conservative senators who returned to the Treasury a portion of their staff allowance. A staff aide for a conservative member of Congress might cost the taxpayer $25,000 a year, the newsletter stated, "but he might help his boss save taxpayers billions of dollars."[13]

More Pay, More Flexibility

Hill staffers frequently are paid better or given greater responsibilities than they might expect in the executive branch because they don't face restrictions such as job experience requirements. In the executive branch, job qualifications, applications procedures, starting pay, and subsequent pay raises and promotions are rigidly regulated.

Congressional staff salaries are not linked to an established scale, such as the "General Schedule" (GS), that regulates the pay of most federal workers. Instead, salaries are determined by each congressional office, except in the few cases where a particular job and its salary are established by law. Although the legal minimum pay for congressional employees is lower than for executive branch workers, the legal maximum is higher in many cases.

GS rates as of 1982 began at $8,342. Employees of Congress could be paid annually as little as $1,200 in the House and $1,155 in the Senate, although the lowest pay generally is for interns.

With a few exceptions, top aides to representatives could be paid annual salaries in 1982 of up to $57,500 — the same as the maximum for the highest paid civil service employees (nonpolitical appointees) in the executive branch. The ceiling on staff salaries in the Senate was $57,000 in 1982. These House and Senate maximums also applied to persons employed by the clerk of the House and the secretary of the Senate, the House and Senate sergeants-at-arms, and the congressional leadership offices of each chamber.

Senate staffers on the average probably get higher salaries than their House counterparts, but there are no statistics on the extent of this disparity. "I don't know the percentage difference," commented Thomas E. Ladd, assistant to the clerk of the House in 1979, "but I know they [the Senate] pay their people more than we do."[14]

Most House and Senate employees qualify for the same annual cost-of-living raises as employees in the executive branch. Staff pay raises usually are tied to increases given other federal workers. Under existing law, a quadrennial commission reviews federal salaries and recommends increases. As revised in 1981, a recommended pay increase automatically goes into effect at the beginning of the next fiscal year unless Congress votes to disapprove it. *(Details, p. 115)*

The additional cost-of-living funds are not automatically included in congressional staffers' paychecks, however. Instead, they are added to the members' committee and personal payroll funds. A member or committee chairman can choose to give his employees the increase, use the money to hire more staffers or return the money to the Treasury at the end of the year.

House Staff Allowance

In 1982 the personal staff allowance of each House member was $352,536 a year, which members could use to hire up to 18 full-time and four temporary aides in their Washington and district offices. That allowance represented an increase of $125,266 since 1975. The increase in the staff allowance benefited mainly the junior members, who did not have the committee staff assistance enjoyed by their senior colleagues.

A maximum of $15,000 from a representative's unused House staff funds can be transferred to his official expense allowance for use in other categories, such as computer and related services.

Before 1979 the maximum number of personal aides a House member could hire was 18, with no exceptions. In July of that year the House approved a rules change permitting members to add up to four more staffers to their payrolls — without counting them toward the ceiling of 18 — if their jobs fit into one of five categories:

- a part-time employee, defined as one who works no more than 15 days a month and is paid $930 per month or less;
- a "shared" employee — a person employed by more than one congressional office;
- an intern in the members' Washington office, defined as an employee hired for up to 120 days and paid less than $9,600 on an annual basis;
- a person who temporarily replaces an employee on leave without pay, or
- a temporary employee, defined as a staff member hired for three months or less and assigned a specific task or function.

In 1976 the House Administration Committee instituted a series of reforms governing staff allowances in the aftermath of the sex-payroll scandal that forced Rep. Wayne L. Hays, D-Ohio (1949-76), to resign as Administration Committee chairman. At the same time, the House stripped the committee of its unilateral power to alter representatives' benefits and allowances. *(Hays scandal, see Ethics and Criminal Prosecutions chapter.)*

The committee's reforms required all representatives, including chairmen of committees and subcommittees, to certify monthly the salaries and duties of their staff and to disclose any kinships between staff employees and any House member. Quarterly reports detailing how House allowances are spent were required for the first time.

The reports of the clerk of the House are indexed by the name of the employee and by the member or House officer employing him, showing the employee's title and salary.

The House allowed the Administration Committee, without the need for further action by the House, to adjust the clerk-hire allowance to reflect federal government cost-of-living raises.

Senate Staff Allowance

The personal staff allowance of senators varies with the size of the member's state. For 1982 the annual allowance ranged from $621,054 for states with a population of fewer than two million residents to $1,247,879 for states with more than 21 million.[15]

Senators may hire as many aides as they wish within their allowance; typically, this ranges between 25 and 60, depending on the size of the state and the salary level. But only one aide may earn $57,000, the maximum annual salary allowed staffers. Five employees may not exceed $54,100 each per year, and three employees may not exceed $53,600 each per year. Senate staff allowances are cumulative within a fiscal year so that unused monthly allowances may be carried over.

Aside from annual cost-of-living adjustments and additional staff funds provided some senators as a result of a 1975 Senate rules change authorizing junior members to hire committee aides, the Senate clerk-hire allowance has remained essentially unchanged since 1968.

Under the 1975 action, senators were allotted a separate allowance to appoint up to three additional staffers to do specialized work on a senator's committees. The fiscal 1978 appropriations bill for the legislative branch com-

Growth in the Congressional Bureaucracy

The figures below are based on total Senate and House personal office staff, committee — including subcommittee — staff and support personnel. *(Committee staff, see p. 105)*

Year	Senate	House	Total	Year	Senate	House	Total
1955	1,962	3,623	5,585	1969	3,847	6,874	10,721
1956	2,342	3,965	6,307	1970	4,140	7,134	11,274
1957	2,378	4,005	6,383	1971	4,624	8,169	12,793
1958	2,516	4,082	6,598	1972	4,626	8,976	13,602
1959	2,700	4,217	6,917	1973	5,078	9,531	14,609
1960	2,643	4,148	6,791	1974	5,284	12,444	17,728
1961	2,713	4,774	7,487	1975	6,143	11,264	17,407
1962	2,889	4,968	7,857	1976	6,573	10,539	17,112
1963	2,982	4,952	7,934	1977	6,413	11,537	17,950
1964	3,071	5,020	8,091	1978	6,489	11,443	17,932
1965	3,219	5,672	8,891	1979	7,148	11,781	18,929
1966	3,294	6,190	9,484	1980	6,900	11,406	18,306
1967	3,587	6,365	9,952	1981	6,900	11,724	18,624
1968	3,632	6,446	10,078	1982	6,800	11,961	18,761

Source: U.S. Congress, House, Committee on Appropriations, *Legislative Branch Appropriations Bill, 1976*, H Rept 94-208, to accompany HR 6950, 94th Cong., 1st sess., 1975; Office of Personnel Management (1976-79 figures); 1982 estimates provided by the Senate Disbursing and House Finance offices.

bined this additional committee assistance allowance with senators' administrative and clerical allowance, so the annual Senate clerk-hire allowance actually consisted of two separate allowances. In 1982 each senator was authorized $192,624 for his legislative aides in addition to the regular clerk-hire allowance.

The original intent of the 1975 change was to give junior senators assistance in meeting their committee responsibilities. But because there no longer is any limit on the number of staffers that can be employed, a senator can use his legislative aides for either committee or personal staff work.

Impact of Large Staffs

So many aides have been recruited in recent years that the House and Senate have been forced to construct new office buildings as well as convert former hotels, apartments and federal buildings into temporary offices. Congress is not likely to return to the old days of small staffs.[16]

As Congress has grown, it has changed as an institution. What is most apparent is that the legislative branch has become more and more bureaucratic. With staff growth has come waste and duplication of effort. Some observers have charged that many of the newer congressional aides are interested in little more than self-aggrandizement and getting their bosses re-elected. They maintain that the availability of larger staffs is drawing Congress into areas where it has no business legislating. On the other hand, some Congress watchers argue that the larger congressional staff has better equipped lawmakers to deal with the complex and sensitive legislative issues they face.

Today's staffers are more highly qualified than ever before, and they come increasingly from professional rather than political backgrounds. As a result, Congress receives better information on which to base its decisions.

At the same time, many employees on Capitol Hill, especially those who have been there for a number of years, believe staffers often see their jobs as just way stations on the road to other prospects. Once, legislative work was a career, even a cause; today, the place is often compared to a corporation or a big government bureaucracy — better managed than before, with many competent people working hard, but impersonal. As one staffer put it: "It used to be a way of life. Now it's a job."

Sarah M. Martin, a staffer on Capitol Hill for 40 years, explained the change.

"When I first started work here, you got to know everybody on the Hill," she said. "We were almost one family, really. We helped each other out, no matter what the party affiliation."

Now, she said, "It's more time-consuming. The bigness — especially with the subcommittees — has broken up the closeness between members and their personal staffs and the committee staffs. People are out to advance themselves, to prove their worth, rather than to find a career. There's a lot of selfish motivation."[17]

As recently as the early 1970s, the administration of the congressional bureaucracy was much more informal. Before the Senate payroll was computerized in 1972, the Senate staff was paid by lining up in front of the Disbursing Office, where each employee was handed an envelope stuffed with his or her pay in cash. "You didn't even have to give them your name," recalled Chester Smith, a retired staff member of the Senate Rules Committee, who went to work on the Hill in 1946. "They knew who you were by your face. Now the pay-line would go all the way down to the Potomac [River] and back."

Problems of Nepotism

Nepotism has been a recurring problem in Congress. Some members occasionally have used their staff allowances to hire relatives and, in effect, supplement their own incomes.

On May 20, 1932, the House adopted a resolution providing that: "The Clerk of the House of Representatives is hereby authorized and directed to keep open for public inspection the payroll records of the disbursing officer of the House." The resolution was adopted without debate. Few members on the floor understood its import. On the next day, however, stories based upon examinations of the disbursing officer's records were published in the newspapers. They disclosed that 97 members of the House devoted their clerk-hire allowance, in whole or in part, to pay persons having the same names as their own. Presumably these persons were relatives. The names were published, and "nepotism in Congress" became a subject of wide public discussion. However, at that time nepotism was not illegal or even a violation of the standing rules.

Senate payroll information was not open for public inspection until 1959. On June 26, 1959, the Senate by voice vote adopted a resolution requiring the secretary of the Senate to make public the name, title, salary and employer of all Senate employees. The resolution was the outgrowth of critical newspaper stories on the withholding of payroll information, coupled with additional disclosures of congressional nepotism.

A January 1959 news story by Scripps-Howard staff writer Vance Trimble contained a lengthy list of relatives he said were employed in 1958 by members of Congress. Trimble had obtained the names by checking out similar names in public House and Senate records. He filed a court suit to gain access to Senate payroll records.

On Feb. 23, 1959, the Associated Press published a list of 65 representatives who had persons with "the same or similar family name" on their January payrolls. Three members who were on the AP list denied that their payroll namesakes were in any way related to them.

Nepotism also was a problem for Rep. Adam Clayton Powell Jr., D-N.Y. (1945-67, 1969-71).

Soon after his marriage in December 1960, Powell employed his Puerto Rican wife, Yvette Marjorie Flores, as a paid member of his congressional office staff. Mrs. Powell remained in Puerto Rico after the birth of a son in 1962, but she continued to draw a $20,578 annual salary as a clerk whose job was to answer mail from Spanish-speaking constituents.

The House in 1964 adopted a resolution aimed specifically at the Powell situation; it forbade members from hiring employees who did not work either in the member's home district or in the representative's Washington, D.C., office. (That provision was made permanent in 1976.) Mrs. Powell, however, continued to live in Puerto Rico. Following a select committee investigation of that and other charges against Powell, the House on March 1, 1967, voted to exclude him from the 90th Congress. However, the U.S. Supreme Court later ruled that the House action was unconstitutional, and Powell returned to Congress in 1969.

In 1967 Congress approved a measure to curb nepotism in federal employment. The measure, added to a

postal rate-federal pay bill, prohibited public officials, including members of Congress, from appointing or trying to promote the appointment of relatives in the agency in which the officials served. The ban covered all officials, including the president, but it did not cover relatives already employed. And it did not prevent an official in one agency or chamber of Congress from seeking to obtain employment for a relative in another agency or chamber.

The "Congressional Handbook," prepared for all members and updated periodically by the Senate Rules Committee and the House Administration Committee, lists 27 classifications of relatives whose employment by representatives and senators "is not permitted by [the 1967] law [5 U.S.C. 3110] under the staff allowances." Certification of an employee's relationship to a member of Congress must be made on payroll authorizations by the employing member or by the committee or subcommittee chairman.[18]

Misuse of Staff

In recent years the misuse of congressional staff for political gain has become a more common concern than nepotism. The celebrated sex-scandal in the mid-1970s involving Rep. Hays and one of his staffers resulted in a review of congressional perquisites. In July 1976, after Hays had been pressured to resign as chairman of the House Administration Committee, the House established a 15-member Commission on Administrative Review to study House accounting and personnel procedures and members' perquisites. It also stripped the House Administration Committee of its unilateral power to alter representatives' benefits and allowances. The committee already had approved a series of orders that revamped House perquisites and instituted controls over payroll and personnel procedures. *(Hays scandal, see Ethics and Criminal Prosecutions chapter, p. 191)*

Rep. Charles C. Diggs Jr., D-Mich. (1955-80), was censured by the House July 31, 1979, for misuse of his clerk-hire funds. Diggs had been convicted in 1978 and sentenced to a maximum of three years in prison for illegally diverting more than $60,000 of his congressional employees' salaries to his personal use.

Legislative Work vs. Politics. The issue of misuse of staff invariably comes up at election time. A member is accused by a political opponent of using employees on his congressional payroll in his re-election campaign.

When members return home to campaign they take with them the customary entourage of staff aides, who must juggle their political work with their status as government employees paid with federal tax dollars. There is no specific federal law against performing political duties, although the practice is somewhat limited by rules in the House and, to a lesser extent, in the Senate.

Using government-paid staff members to work on campaigns is not a new practice. But in light of recent payroll abuses, there have been signs that incumbents are trying to avoid the appearance of impropriety.

"Because of what has gone under the bridge in the past, people are more aware and more careful," said one legislative aide who took a 50 percent pay cut in 1978 to help his boss, Sen. Robert P. Griffin, R-Mich., in his unsuccessful effort to win a third term. "My sense is that everybody is overly sensitive and overly paranoid about it."[19]

In some cases, to avoid criticism from members' opponents, House and Senate staffers go on vacation or temporarily take themselves off the government payroll. Others try to mix their congressional job with election campaign duties and agree to a cut in pay to reflect the reduction in their congressional work. Others remain on the payroll so they don't lose benefits, but claim to put in a full day of constituent service at the member's district office before going to campaign headquarters to help their boss in his re-election bid.

So-called slush funds — leftover campaign contributions or donations to members of Congress — also were hotly criticized until they were banned in the late 1970s. For years senators and representatives used such money for staff and family travel as well as for dining with constituents, public meetings, parking fees, opinion polls, flowers for funerals, newsletter expenses, mailings of Christmas cards, office parties or just about any job-related expense not covered by the official congressional allowances.

In 1977 Congress banned contributions to unofficial office accounts and prohibited the conversion of campaign funds to personal use. Campaign contributions still could be used for official expenses.

Beginning in 1978, members were prohibited from maintaining unofficial office accounts. But until 1980 a loophole in the campaign finance law allowed a representative who was retiring from Congress to keep unused campaign funds for himself.

Supreme Court Ruling. In March 1981 the Supreme Court let stand an appeals court ruling that it was up to Congress to determine whether and under what restraints congressional aides may double as campaign workers while remaining on the public payroll.

The court's decision appeared to clear the way for a member of Congress to keep aides on the government payroll even when such aides are working almost exclusively on the member's re-election campaign.

The appeals court ruling came in a suit brought by former Federal Election Commission attorney Joel D. Joseph in 1977 against Sen. Howard W. Cannon, D-Nev., and Chester B. Sobsey, Cannon's $40,000-a-year administrative assistant. In the suit Joseph charged that Sobsey had remained on the Senate payroll from March 1975 through November 1976 even though he was working almost exclusively on Cannon's re-election campaign.·

The suit claimed that Cannon's approval of Sobsey's salary payments under those circumstances constituted a fraudulent claim against the government. But the appeals court refused to consider the substance of Joseph's complaint, holding that to judge the legality of Cannon's actions would violate the Constitution's separation of powers doctrine. Only the House and Senate can judge such "political questions," the appeals court ruled.

The appeals court based much of its ruling on a conclusion that Congress itself has set no hard-and-fast standard that would have enabled Cannon to determine where to draw the line between Sobsey's official duties and his political chores. Existing rules governing staff campaign work are lenient and subject to differing interpretations. In the past, both chambers have been extremely reluctant to police their members' use of staff in political campaigns. Congress never allowed its own staffers to be covered by the provisions of the Hatch Act — which prohibits federal government employees from participating in partisan political activities.

Under House regulations, staff members, while not permitted to contribute cash to a campaign, may assist a member's re-election effort so long as his assigned congressional duties also are being fulfilled. Those duties are set by each member, as is the amount of vacation time granted.

"If they are on their own time, they can do all the politicking they want," said a spokesman for the House Committee on Standards of Official Conduct.

Senate restrictions are even more lax. One House aide, who took himself off the payroll in 1978 to manage a Senate campaign, said: "The Senate rules have big wide holes in them large enough to let just about anybody work in the campaign from the federal staff."

The guiding document on the subject is a Senate Rules Committee report of Oct. 17, 1977, which states that "other than actual handling of campaign funds, the Senate has not imposed any restrictions on the participation of a member of a senator's staff in that senator's re-election campaign." Several weeks after the 1981 appeals court decision in the Cannon case, the Senate Select Ethics Committee proposed incorporating into the Senate ethics code a 1977 ruling by the committee declaring that senators should remove from their congressional payrolls staffers who undertake political work to the detriment of their official Senate duties. But the proposal was never acted on by the full Senate.

Flexibility of Staff Use. Unlike the House, which does not allow personal staff aides to solicit and receive campaign contributions, the Senate provides that two members of each staff may be designated for that purpose. In fact, in the Cannon Supreme Court case, the senator argued that he had designated Sobsey as one of the two staffers allowed to solicit and receive campaign funds.

The use of congressional staff on a campaign offers an enormous advantage to members over their challengers, who must use their own campaign funds to finance staff support. Critics of this practice have proposed that legislative aides' salary for hours spent politicking be counted against the limits on campaign spending. But this would be complicated because of the difficulty of assessing legislative work that is also usable in an election campaign. Some activities, such as managing a campaign, raising money and dealing with poll results, are clearly political. But case work, speech writing and preparation of responses on particular issues fall in a "gray" area.

Most of those engaged in campaign efforts at high levels are the administrative assistants — usually a member's top congressional aide and the one having the most political as well as legislative experience.

"The incumbent's staff allows him to attract and retain the nucleus of his personal political organization.... The incumbent fields a publicly paid team of experienced veterans to do a task they have succeeded in before, perhaps many times before, and which differs very little from their everyday jobs."[20]

In 1978 Tom E. Coker served as campaign manager for Sen. Maryon P. Allen, D-Ala. (1978) in the Alabama Democratic primary — lost by Allen — while continuing to receive his $44,000 annual pay as her administrative assistant. Coker said he did not try to hide his political activity. "I didn't feel there was anything wrong with the amount of time I was putting in on the campaign," which he estimated at about 40 percent of his working day.

For four years, Coker had been a chief political contact in the state for Sen. James B. Allen, D-Ala. (1969-78), working out of a third-floor office in the Capitol building. One source in the state Democratic Party said the 38-year-old Coker was "one of the best political operatives the state has ever seen." When Allen died in June and his widow, Maryon, took his seat and sought the remaining two years of his term, it was considered natural for Coker to head her effort.

Equal Rights in Congress

The U.S. Commission on Civil Rights in 1980 recommended that Congress bring itself under the laws protecting almost all other American workers from employment discrimination.

"All congressional employees should be guaranteed equal employment opportunities," the commission's July 4 report concluded.

Two years after that report had been issued, however, the commission's recommendations still had not been acted upon by either house of Congress.

Lack of Employment Protection

Congressional employees, the report noted, "lack the equal employment opportunity rights and protections afforded most other employees in the country." As a result, the report maintained, there were "disproportionately small numbers of minorities and women" working on Capitol Hill.

The report recommended that Congress set out a comprehensive scheme of administrative and judicial remedies for discrimination against Capitol Hill workers, and that it designate a legislative branch office headed by a presidential appointee to administer the program. The recommendations were prepared at the request of Sens. Birch Bayh, D-Ind. (1963-81) and Patrick J. Leahy, D-Vt., and Rep. Don Edwards, D-Calif.

When Congress wrote the 1964 Civil Rights Act, it exempted itself from that law's provisions. Since then, both the House and Senate have adopted rules prohibiting job discrimination. But the Senate never approved a mechanism for carrying out its rule, and the enforcement procedure set out by the House made complaints difficult to file and investigate.

Supreme Court Ruling

In a June 1979 decision (*Davis v. Passman*), the Supreme Court gave congressional workers the right to sue their employers for damages if they believed they were victims of job discrimination. (*Job discrimination, this page*)

Congress' female employees held fewer policy-making jobs and were paid less than their male counterparts, according to a 1980 survey conducted by the Capitol Hill Women's Political Caucus. For example, only 12 percent of the Senate's top legislative aides were women, according to the survey; in the House, only 37 percent were women.

On the other hand, lower paying jobs with little or no policy-making responsibility were held largely by women, according to the survey.

Asked if he had considered going off the government payroll, Coker said, "I didn't think too much about it. I felt the government had gotten more than their just due from me." He said he rarely had taken any time off, except for Sundays.

In Oregon, Republican Sen. Mark O. Hatfield's close friend and adviser, Gerald W. Frank, cut his staff salary from nearly $40,000 to $10,000 at the beginning of 1978 when he began to manage Hatfield's re-election campaign. His salary became the minimum that a Senate employee could earn and still be designated to receive campaign contributions in a Senate office. Because Frank said he spent more than half his time on official Senate business, he believed he should retain his ability to carry out campaign work.

Press secretaries often work on campaigns in the final weeks as media inquiries focus on politics. Joe Shafran, press aide to Rep. Marc L. Marks, R-Pa., was taken off the government payroll in 1978 because, Shafran said, Marks was exercising caution and didn't want any criticism from his opponent. "Frankly, if I'd stayed on the payroll, I get the feeling nobody would have cared," Shafran remarked.

In close races, however, it is not unusual to find a massive shift of personnel from congressional work to the campaign. Because this offers an obvious target for an opponent, staff members in these contests almost always leave the government payroll.

Rep. Abner J. Mikva, an Illinois Democrat (1969-73, 1975-79), won close elections in 1974 and 1976 and again in 1978. He had one of the most extensive House campaign operations in the country, one that included five campaign headquarters. Mikva began depleting his district office staff during the summer. Four staff persons working in his district, plus the campaign coordinator, were on the campaign payroll. And a legislative aide from his congressional office in Washington would leave Washington at the beginning of the year to work in Mikva's Skokie office and lay the groundwork for the campaign.

Former Rep. Frank M. Clark, D-Pa. (1955-74), was charged in 1978 with paying congressional salaries to 13 Pennsylvania residents who performed no official duties. Instead, they allegedly did personal or campaign work for Clark. He pleaded guilty in 1979 and served a prison sentence.

Job Discrimination

Although members of Congress have instituted voluntary rules to prohibit discrimination on Capitol Hill, they have exempted themselves from anti-job discrimination laws, including the Civil Rights Act of 1964, the Equal Employment Act of 1972 and the Equal Pay Act of 1963. (*Congressional exemptions, p. 139; equal rights for Capitol Hill employees, box, this page*)

A precedent-setting congressional job discrimination suit was settled out of court in 1979 for an undisclosed sum of money. The suit was filed in 1974 against former Rep. Otto E. Passman, D-La. (1947-77), by one-time aide Shirley Davis. The settlement was announced, but the amount of money paid Davis by Passman was never disclosed.

The suit established the constitutional right of a congressional employee who claims to be a victim of sex discrimination to sue a member of Congress for damages. However, the out-of-court settlement left undecided the question of whether the Constitution's 'speech or debate' clause provides a member of Congress with immunity from job discrimination suits in at least some circumstances.

The 'speech or debate' clause protects members from court suits for actions taken in Congress as part of their official duties.

The suit filed by Davis against Passman initially was thrown out of court by a federal district judge, who ruled that no law existed to provide Davis with protection from job discrimination by a member of Congress.

On appeal, however, the Supreme Court ruled that the Constitution itself gives individuals the right to sue members of Congress, regardless of the provisions of any particular statute, for alleged constitutional violations.

In its decision, the Supreme Court dealt only with Davis' right to sue Passman, not the merits of her complaint. The case was then sent back to the lower federal courts to be decided on the merits, but the out-of-court settlement was announced before the courts acted.

Special Allowances

The travel allowance provided in an act of Sept. 22, 1789, fixing the compensation of members of Congress was the first of what has become a plethora of special allowances lawmakers have created for themselves through the years.

One of the biggest today is the official expense allowance, which is separate from the clerk-hire allowance senators and representatives receive for staff assistance. The expense allowance covers domestic travel, stationery, newsletters, postage, telephone and telegraph service and office expenses in Washington, D.C., and in the member's congressional district or state.

In 1973 the Senate consolidated its allowances for stationery, postage, computer services, telephone and telegraph, travel, office expenses in their state and other official expenses, with no restrictions on the amount they could spend in any one category.

Until 1977 the House had nine separate special allowances, and representatives often had to adhere to certain limits on spending in each account. Special allowances generally were less generous and flexible for representatives than for senators.

Many House allowances had to be spent a month at a time, whereas Senate allowances usually were cumulative over an entire calendar year.

After the sex-payroll scandal that forced Rep. Wayne L. Hays, D-Ohio (1949-76), to resign as chairman of the House Administration Committee, the committee in 1976 instituted a number of changes in the administration of House perquisites, including the expense allowance and the staff allowance of representatives. *(Hays scandal, see Ethics and Criminal Prosecutions chapter.)*

House Expense Allowance

Provisions of the House Ethics Code approved in 1977 banned unofficial office accounts and replaced the separate allowances with a single "official expenses" allowance covering the costs incurred in running congressional offices, both in Washington and in members' home districts.

To implement the new code, the House Administration Committee drew up regulations providing members with two allowances: the official expense allowance and a staff, or clerk-hire, allowance. The consolidation was intended to simplify bookkeeping by members and House officers by making periodic transfers from one account to another unnecessary.

The consolidated account system replaced the nine separate special allowances for travel, office equipment leasing, district office leasing, telecommunications, stationery, constituent communications, postage, computer services and other official expenses.

The size of House members' official expense allowance was determined by combining expenses in six fixed categories. To that base, which was the same for each member, was added expenses for three variable allowances — travel, telephone and telegraph and district office rental, the amount of which depended upon the location of a member's district and its distance from Washington, D.C. According to the Administration Committee, the base figure for the official expense allowance in 1982 was $47,300. Although the total expense allowance available to each member varied, the average House allowance was $103,000 in 1982.[21] A California legislator, for example, received more than a New York legislator because the travel and telephone costs were higher.

One of the innovations made by the House reforms of 1976 was a requirement for quarterly reports detailing how members of Congress were using their expense allowance. When the first quarterly report was released in October 1977, the news media reported several controversial expenditures claimed by House members: entertainment, automobile insurance, a tuxedo rental, flowers, greeting cards and trophies. Less than a month later, the House Administration Committee adopted a set of guidelines that tightened restrictions on official expenses.

Under revised guidelines that took effect in January 1978, "official expenses" were defined as "ordinary and necessary business expenses incurred in support of the member's official and representational duties." House members could not charge sports trophies, flowers, television time or other potentially embarrassing expenditures to their office expense account, even if they thought these items were necessary for good public relations with constituents.

Although termed "guidelines" by the committee, staff members insisted the new restrictions would have the force of House rules. They said the House Administration Committee chairman would not sign vouchers for expenditures barred by the guidelines. If members labeled the proscribed expenditures as "political" and reported them as required by federal campaign statutes, they could pay for them with campaign contributions, according to a Federal Election Commission (FEC) official.[22]

1978 Guidelines. The committee's action was final and did not require approval by the House. Under the panel's guidelines, House members could not be reimbursed from their expense accounts for the following types of expenditures:

● Employment service fees, moving allowances and other expenses relating to hiring staff.

● Purchase or rental of items "having an extended useful life," such as the rental of a tuxedo. But members could charge office equipment relating to their duties to their official expense account.

● Greeting cards, flowers, trophies, donations and dues for groups, other than congressional organizations, approved by the Administration Committee. (Members who had claimed these expenses protested that constituents expected their representatives to send flowers to funerals, award sports trophies and join lodges.)

● Radio or television time or advertisements, except for

notices of meetings relating to congressional business.

● Tuition or fees for education and training unless a need for a special skill, relating to House activities, could be proved.

Flexibility of Allowance. Although funds still are earmarked for some types of official expenses, the House Administration Committee eliminated the requirement that separate records be kept for each category. Thus, all the money in the expense allowance can be used as each member sees fit, so long as it is spent for official expenses within the guidelines set by the committee. But even with the 1978 guidelines, expenses often are a matter of a member's interpretation.

To illustrate that point, *The Washington Post* in 1980 reported that some members had used their official expense account to pay for items such as meals and entertainment for constituents, visitors or staff assistants and sympathy cards for constituents, while others had purchased coffee and soft drinks for visitors, "free" blood pressure checks for constituents, films and photographs of members, letters to school graduates, dry cleaning, insurance, framing of mementos, newspapers, books, clipping services, lawn chairs, year-round rental cars, calendar cards, signs for offices, mobile telephones, message beepers and flags.[23]

With the consolidated system, it also is easier for members to use up their entire expense account funds each year since representatives may freely transfer funds from one category to another. And if the official expense account fund turns out to be insufficient, up to $15,000 of a member's clerk-hire funds may be transferred to the expense allowance.

Under House rules, members are required to submit documentation of expenses incurred in order to be reimbursed. The documentation is reviewed by the Clerk's Office but is not available for public inspection.

1979, 1981 Allowance Increases. In October 1979, acting virtually without public notice, the House Administration Committee increased the lump-sum basic allowance for official domestic travel and office equipment expenses by 21 to 26 percent. This was the first increase since 1977 and, according to the committee, reflected the cost of inflation. The increase, which did not require House approval, cost taxpayers about $5 million in fiscal 1980 and was added to members' expense allowance.

In May 1981 the House Administration Committee again increased the official expense account limit to cover inflationary increases in the cost of travel and office supplies, equipment and furnishings.

One survey estimated the cost of the 1981 increase at $4 million-$5 million a year for travel and office supplies and equipment. In addition, there was a one-time expenditure that year of approximately $3.5 million resulting from an increase in members' district office furniture allowance.[24]

The authority for the committee's 1979 and 1981 actions increasing the allowance was a little-noticed 1976 change in House rules that was intended to curtail the authority of the House Administration Committee to unilaterally increase allowances and staff without approval of the House. But the revised rule contained language permitting the committee alone to continue to adjust allowances to reflect increases in the cost of living.

Before the 1976 change, the committee was required to publish a notice in the *Congressional Record* when it ad-justed allowances and staff ceilings. The rules change did away with the public notice requirement.

Senate Expense Allowance

The amount of a senator's expense allowance, like that for a representative, varies. For a senator, it is determined by the size of his or her state and the distance between Washington, D.C., and the member's home state. In 1982 the allowance ranged from $33,000 annually for a senator from Delaware to $143,000 annually for a senator from Hawaii. The average Senate allowance in 1982 was $55,000.[25]

In 1977 senators' consolidated allowance was revised and renamed the Senate official office expense account. The dollar value of the allowance, payable from the contingent fund of the Senate, was determined by averaging the existing allowances for the two senators of each state, increasing that amount by 10 percent and rounding the number up to the nearest $1,000. This was designed to increase senators' expense allowances while providing the same amount for both senators from a state.

According to the 1980 "Senate Handbook," prepared by the Senate Rules and Administration Committee, the Senatorial Official Office Expense Account is a "multipurpose account" authorized each year. At the end of the year, any unused balance may not be carried over to the next year.

Before 1979 a senator was able to request reimbursement for office expenses on his signature alone. The senator merely had to sign his name beneath a statement printed on an itemized voucher that said "I certify that the above expenses were officially incurred."

Tightening the Rules. The Senate in August 1979 tightened its regulations on allowances by requiring senators to document each expense greater than $25. Expenses of $25 or less must either be itemized or documented. The new rule also required each voucher requesting reimbursement to be "personally signed" by a senator. This ended the practice of staff members signing senators' names to vouchers.

The 1979 change in the rules was drafted by Sen. Mark O. Hatfield, R-Ore., and cosponsored by all six members of the Select Ethics Committee. It grew out of that panel's investigation into charges of financial misconduct filed against Sen. Herman E. Talmadge, D-Ga. (1957-81). One of the charges against Talmadge was that he had filed vouchers with the Senate claiming reimbursement for expenses not incurred or not legally reimbursable. (*Talmadge case, see Ethics and Criminal Prosecutions chapter.*)

Until 1980 the Senate required its members to certify that payment of an official expense already had been made before reimbursement could be claimed. But in January of that year the Senate agreed to allow senators to be reimbursed for their official expenses upon presentation of an unpaid bill.

The Senate expense allowance may be used for official telegrams and long-distance phone calls and related services; phone calls incurred outside of Washington; stationery and office supplies purchased through the Senate Stationery Room for official business; any type of postal service or private mail delivery service relating to official business; district office expenses other than equipment and furniture; subscriptions to newspapers, clipping services and periodicals; official travel; expenses incurred by individuals selected by a senator to serve on panels or other bodies making recommendations on nominees to the service academies or federal judgeships; and "other official expenses as the senator determines are necessary."

There is no limit on the amount that can be spent in any one category, except for the latter category of "other official expenses." That discretionary allowance is unique to the Senate and was established under a provision of the fiscal 1978 legislative branch appropriations bill. The allowance permits a senator to spend up to 10 percent of his or her total available funds for any "official expenses."

Other changes in administrative practices adopted in 1980 were designed to eliminate several widely criticized perquisites senators enjoyed while providing greater flexibility in the use of official funds. Free shaving mugs, hairbrushes, combs and shipping trunks were eliminated, and various changes were made in travel regulations affecting senators. *(Travel allowances, this page)*

Definition of Official Expenses. Though the Senate spends millions of dollars annually on "official expenses," until 1980 it had never defined what was an official expense. This led some senators to request reimbursement for such items as chandeliers, sunglasses, paperweights and a contribution to a hospital located in Jerusalem. In 1979 the Senate Rules Committee put a hold on such reimbursement requests until there was agreement on what constituted an "official expense."

In April 1980 the Senate finally agreed on a definition after an earlier attempt in 1979 had foundered. Official expenses were defined as "ordinary and necessary business expenses incurred by a senator and his staff in the discharge of their official duties."

The following expenses specifically are excluded: commuting and commuter parking fees, greeting cards, flowers, trophies, awards or certificates, donations or gifts of any type (except gifts of flags flown over the United States Capitol and copies of an illustrated history book of Congress entitled "We, the People"), dues or assessments, broadcast or print advertising time except for help-wanted ads, expenses incurred by an individual who is not an employee, except those individuals selected by a senator to serve on panels or other bodies making recommendations on nominees to service academies or federal judgeships, salaries or compensation of employees, entertainment, meals, private automobile maintenance and employee moving expenses, including travel.

A 1980 revision of the definition, sponsored by Minority Whip Ted Stevens, R-Alaska, specified that the "official expenses" definition did not apply to the supplemental allowances — which are separate from the expense allowances — given the vice president, president pro tempore, majority and minority leaders and majority and minority whips. For fiscal 1983, those special leadership allowances were estimated at $10,000 each for the vice president, president pro tempore and the two leaders; the two whips each received $2,500.

Domestic Travel Allowance

The congressional travel allowance of 1789 came to $6 for each 20 miles. Needless to say, that figure has been altered on numerous occasions over the years to reflect the nation's increased mobility and, in recent years, escalating travel costs. In the early 1960s senators and representatives were allowed three government-paid trips home each year. The number was raised repeatedly in the following two decades so that by the late 1970s senators could take more

than 40 trips home and representatives were allowed 33.[26] By 1980 there were no limits on the number of trips that could be taken.

House. Until 1977 representatives received a separate travel allowance that permitted them 26 free round trips each year to and from their home district plus extra trips for their staffs. Members could choose to withdraw their travel allowance in cash, up to a maximum of $2,250 a year; any amount not used for travel could go toward members' personal expenses so long as they paid income taxes on it. As part of the changes it instituted in 1976, the House Administration Committee ended the "cash-out" option.

The House calculates a domestic travel allowance for each member and uses that figure in determining the official expense allowances. In 1982 that figure was the equivalent of 64 multiplied by the rate per mile (18 cents per mile for 3,000 miles or over, and 30 cents per mile for travel under 500 miles), multiplied by the mileage between the District of Columbia and the farthest point in the member's district, plus 10 percent. This works out to roughly 32 round trips a year. If a member's travel exceeds 32 round trips a year, other funds from the official expense allowance may be used. Members are reimbursed for the actual cost of travel, including rail and air fare, food and lodging. When a member travels in a privately owned or leased automobile, he is reimbursed at a rate of 24 cents a mile. Members also may be reimbursed for travel on official business that is in addition to visits to their home district or states. For official committee business, a member receives $50 per diem for domestic travel.

Members are allowed to accept free domestic transportation on non-commercial carriers — primarily company planes — under certain circumstances. If a member's trip is related to a scheduled appearance before a sponsoring group, transport is not considered a gift.

The Defense Department also provides members of Congress with free transportation in the line of official business. But department officials do not release figures on the cost of such special shuttle service.

A discount air fare program offered by some commercial air carriers is available to House members and staff traveling on official business.

Senate. Travel is one of several items authorized as part of senators' official expense accounts. Reimbursable travel expenses include:

● Per diem and actual transportation expenses. The maximum per diem within the continental United States in 1982 was $75 (the rate differed in Alaska and Hawaii). Covered by per diem expenses was food, lodging, tips, laundry and other incidental charges. There was no reimbursement for entertainment, nor could reimbursement for transportation (air and rail fare) exceed actual expenses. Under previous rules, reimbursement claims had been limited under certain circumstances to less than actual expenses.

● Privately owned automobile mileage not to exceed 20 cents per mile.

● Motorcycle mileage not to exceed 20 cents per mile.

● Airplane mileage not to exceed 45 cents per mile.

● Actual costs of parking fees, ferry fares and bridge, road, and tunnel tolls.

There is a statutory travel allowance for one round trip between a senator's home and Washington, D.C., which is paid to senators at the beginning of each regular session of Congress. Reimbursement for this travel is 20 cents per mile; mileage is calculated by the nearest route usually

Members' Allowances

Members of Congress have given themselves a variety of expense allowances. Today they are generally considered a necessary accessory to members' regular salary. They range from generous staff assistance and office space to free use of video recording facilities and sophisticated computer services. Congressional leaders receive additional remuneration. *(Box, p. 6)*

Listed below are the major allowances and, where available, the dollar value of those benefits as of 1982. No value is given to some of the allowances because of the difficulty in determining the range of reimbursed costs; this would be the case for travel and telephone usage, for example. Most of the allowances were transferable from one account to another.

	House	Senate
Washington office clerk-hire	$352,536	$621,054-1,247,879[1]
Committee legislative assistants	—[3]	$192,624
General office expenses	$47,300	$33,000-143,000[1]
Telephone/telegraph	15,000 long-distance minutes to district	—[2]
Stationery	—[2]	—[4]
Office space	2-3 room suites	5-8 room suites
Furnishings	provided	provided
Equipment	—[2]	provided
District/state offices		
Rental	2,500 sq. ft.	4,800-8,000 sq. ft.[1]
Furnishings/equipment	$35,000	$22,500-30,750[1]
Mobile office	—[2]	one
Communications		
Automated correspondence	—[2]	provided by Senate computer center
Audio/video recordings; photography	—[2]	—[2]
Travel	formula (min. $4,950-max. $38,500[5])	—[2]

1. Senators are allowed expenses based on a sliding scale linked to the state's population.
2. Expenses are covered through the general office expenses line item. In most cases supplies and equipment are charged at rates well below retail levels.
3. Provided for members of Appropriations, Budget, and Rules committees.
4. Senators pay for stationery out of their official expenses allowance and receive in addition allotments of white envelopes and letterheads, blank sheets and brown "public documents" envelopes based on the state's population.
5. Excluding Alaska, Hawaii and U.S. territories.

Source: Adapted from Davidson, Roger H., and Oleszek, Walter J. *Congress and Its Members.* Washington, D.C.: CQ Press, 1981. p. 124

traveled by a senator in going to his home state and returning to Washington. This reimbursement is automatic; it is not paid from the official office expense account, and no voucher is submitted.

The travel allowance for each senator used to be based on the cost of 40 round trips a year for states with fewer than 10 million people and 44 round trips for states with fewer than 10 million. A state's distance from Washington was figured in the computation. The travel allowance for senators no longer sets limits on the number of trips that can be taken each year. Senate regulations state that office staff must make round trips since the Senate will not pay the expenses of aides who relocate — for example, a staffer who moves to Washington after serving in a member's district office. (Although the House does not have any specific regulation governing round trips for staff, it also does not pay personnel relocation costs.)

In 1977 the Senate broadened the type of travel expenses that was reimbursable to include official travel anywhere within the United States (previous law had provided reimbursement only within a senator's home state). It also authorized per diem expenses for travel within a senator's home state. But neither the travel allowance nor the per diem allowance were permitted in the 60-day period immediately prior to a contested primary or general election in which the senator was a candidate for office. In addition, the Senate required senators to make public how they used the per diem and travel allowance funds.

A discount air fare program offered by some commercial air carriers is available to members and employees traveling on "official business only." Senators also can accept free domestic transportation from the Defense Department or company non-commercial carriers.

Stationery, Newsletters and Postage

House. A representative's funds for stationery, postage and newsletters come from his official expense account. There is no limit, within the account, on the amount he can spend on any one item. *(Current official expense account allowance, p. 131)*

Until recently, there were fixed allowances for each of these categories, but in 1977 the House Administration Committee merged them into one consolidated account.

A representative under the old system was allocated $6,500 a year to purchase stationery and office supplies. If he did not spend it all, a member could use the remainder to pay for publications or gifts for constituents or for personal expenses provided he paid income taxes on it. Representatives also were allowed $5,000 a year for the production of newsletters, questionnaires and any other correspondence eligible to be mailed under the frank.

Each representative's office also received a postage allowance for use on official mail that was ineligible for franking. In the 94th Congress, that annual allowance was $1,140. Unused allowance balances could not be accumulated. The previous allowances of $6,500 a year for stationery, $1,140 for special postage and $5,000 for newsletters and questionnaires were among the fixed categories used in 1977 to determine the base amount of the new consolidated account. Although the separate stationery, postage and newsletter allowances were used to determine the original base figure in 1977, there no longer are separate figures in the expense account for these items.

By 1982 the base amount of a representative's official expense account came to $47,300. (The size of the allowance varies from representative to representative, depending on distance between Washington and the member's congressional district.)

In addition to his expense account, each representative is allowed 40,000 "Public Document" envelopes a month without charge.

For many years, many lame-duck members have been criticized for taking their remaining expense account funds in the form of postage stamps. Critics have argued that lame-duck representatives do not need regular postage because they are allowed to use the frank for 90 days after they leave office to clean up all remaining official correspondence.

Senate. Funds for Senate stationery and postage come from the member's consolidated office expense account. Each senator also receives allotments of white envelopes and letterheads, blank sheets and brown "Public Document" envelopes, all based on the state's population.

Some services for printing and bulk mailing of newsletters, questionnaires, excerpts from the *Congressional Record* and other items are provided without charge by the Senate's Service Department.

Until 1980 reimbursement was authorized for air mail and special delivery stamps used on official mail. That year the Senate approved a rules change that permitted senators to be reimbursed for use of any type of postal service or private mail delivery service, even if the mail could be sent under a senator's frank at lower cost.

The 1980 change was intended to save time and money, according to the Senate Rules Committee in its report on the new rule. The committee added that the change "merely enlarges the range of delivery services" available to a senator. Another effect of that change, however, was to permit senators for the first time to claim reimbursement for the purchase of first-class postage stamps for letters that were eligible for the frank.

The use of first-class postage stamps was expected to cost additional money and make it more difficult for the Senate to enforce its franking rules. A member's signature on an envelope immediately identifies it as franked mail paid for with government funds. A stamped envelope, on the other hand, cannot be so identified.

Fund-raising letters, for example, cannot be mailed under the frank. If such letters were franked, they would be immediately recognizable as improperly mailed. But if that same letter were mailed with a stamp for which the senator later was reimbursed, there would be no way to determine if the franking rules had been violated.

Telephone and Telegraph Allowance

House. In computing the yearly telephone allowance for representatives in 1982, the following formula was used: the dollar equivalent of 15,000 multiplied by the highest long-distance telephone rate per minute from the District of Columbia to the member's district. A member may elect to use more than this amount on calls so long as total expenses in all official expense account categories do not exceed his or her established allowance.

The House Administration Committee in 1976 revised representatives' telephone and telegraph allowances to permit each member to have two wide-area telephone service (WATS) lines to reduce costs for long-distance calls. If a representative chose to use WATS lines, half the annual telecommunications allowance had to be given up. This rule was nullified in 1977 when the House adopted the consolidated office expense account.

Senate. Before the establishment of the consolidated account in 1973, the Senate Rules and Administration Committee fixed senators' telephone and telegraph rates. The allowance was based on a fixed number of long-distance calls totaling no more than a fixed number of minutes for calls to and from Washington. The committee used a complicated formula to determine the telegraph allowance, based on state population and Western Union rates from Washington. Both formulas were used to determine a senator's total consolidated allowance, now called the official office expense account.

FTS, WATS Allowances. Many members have access either to a nationwide Federal Telecommunications System (FTS) leased-line or a WATS line provided by the telephone companies. Each senator (including those from Alaska and Hawaii) are permitted two WATS lines in their Washington office, the cost of which is not charged against their official office expense account. FTS is available at a charge of $31 per month.

Office Allowances

House. The Washington office of a representative, typically a two- or three-room suite, is provided free of charge. Office furnishings and decorations, housekeeping and maintenance also are free. Additional storage space and trunks are available free of charge. Representatives pay for electrical and mechanical office equipment, including computers, from their official expense account.

In recent years, a handful of representatives have used their office expense account to pay for outside consultants to help them cope with the organizational demands of running a congressional office. Consultants have set up the Washington office of freshmen representatives, trained new staffers and improved mail flow, among other things. Neither the consulting firms nor the members are eager to advertise this use of the expense account since consultants are expensive. In 1979, Peat Marwick Mitchel, a Washington firm that performed management work for some members, estimated that setting up a new congressional office or working out a complete office reorganization plan cost between $5,000 and $10,000.[27]

In 1977 the House approved additional funds for district office expenses. The rental allowance for office space was increased to cover 2,500 square feet; the allowance previously had covered an office of 1,500 square feet. With rental costs varying across the country from $4 to $13.50 per square foot, the benefit to House members differed, although each benefited by at least several thousand dollars. Unused funds could be transferred within a member's consolidated office account and used for other office expenses.

The home offices are provided a maximum of $35,000 for furnishings and equipment.

An innovation of the 1970s was the "mobile district office" — a van with the member's name emblazoned on it that tours the district, carrying aides who hand out literature dealing with the member's activities, answer queries and process constituents' complaints and other matters. All expenses involved in leasing and operating a mobile office in the representative's district come from the member's official expense allowance.

Senate. The Washington office and furnishings for senators are provided free, as are housekeeping and maintenance services. Senators do not have allowances to buy or lease office equipment because it is provided by the sergeant-at-arms of the Senate.

In 1982 $6.5 million was requested by a Senate subcommittee to give the Senate office buildings a face-lift, including new paneling and doors. An additional $800,000 was requested for nine more X-ray units, which screen people entering the buildings.[28]

Congress is building a sixth office building to accommodate the expanding Senate bureaucracy. The nine-story structure, to be named after Sen. Philip A. Hart, D-Mich. (1959-76), was proposed in 1972 at an estimated cost of $48 million. In 1982 the estimated cost of the building had jumped to $137.7 million. The Senate that year requested $9.5 million for furnishings for the new building. An additional 47 policemen, at a cost of $869,000, and 80 employees for maintenance and service, also were requested.[29]

A Senator's home state office space is allocated according to the state's population. Within the allowed square footage there is no limit to the number of offices he may open.

Offices are provided free in federal buildings or leased from private owners at the General Services Administration (GSA) regional rate. Senators receive an aggregate furniture and equipment allowance. The minimum allowance of $22,500 for 4,800 square feet, which is the amount received by senators from the smallest states, is increased by $500 for each authorized increase of 200 square feet. All furnishings are provided through GSA. Each senator also is allowed to rent one mobile office for use throughout the state.

Rent and furnishings for senators' state offices are not chargeable to the official office account. These allowances also are provided through the GSA and are paid for by the Senate sergeant-at-arms.

Publications Allowance

In addition to their official expense allowance covering office operations, communications and travel, members of Congress receive a number of free publications. Some are used directly in the member's work, for example, a complete set of the U.S. Code and District of Columbia codes and supplements, four subscriptions to the *Federal Register*, and office copies of the *Congressional Record* and the *Congressional Directory*. All of these publications are printed by the United States Government Printing Office (GPO).

Besides three personal copies, representatives are allotted 34 subscriptions to the Record; senators are allotted 50. The cost of printing the Record in fiscal 1982 was estimated at approximately $476 per page.[30] (*Congressional Record*, see Legislative Process chapter.)

Until 1981 each member of Congress was entitled to a set of bound volumes of the Record, at a cost to the taxpayer of approximately $4,000 each.[31] A proposal by Rep. Dan Glickman, D-Kan., to eliminate this perk for representatives was adopted in 1981. Senators, however, still can receive the bound volumes free.

Glickman also proposed to eliminate memorial volumes of the Record. When a member of Congress dies, tributes spoken on the floor or submitted for publication first are printed in the daily Record, then reprinted, collated and bound in a memorial volume. Fifty copies are presented to the deceased's family, and another 250 are given to his or her successor. In a typical year, this printing and reprinting and binding of eulogies costs about $75,000, according to Glickman. Glickman also tried to reduce the

number of Record subscriptions allotted members — to 40 for each senator and 25 for each representative. These proposals were still pending in the House in August 1982.

All senators and representatives receive clothbound copies of the annual *Congressional Directory*, with their name engraved on it. Each senator's office receives 15 paperbound copies; an additional 40 copies may be distributed by each senator. Representatives receive 10 paperbound copies for their offices; they are permitted to distribute an additional 20 copies.

Members also receive allotments of special publications to send off to constituents. One of the most popular is the Yearbook of the Department of Agriculture. Each representative is allotted 400 copies, worth $2,800. Senators have an allotment of 550. Unused Yearbooks and certain other publications may be turned in to the Government Printing Office for exchange or credit toward other books or pamphlets.

Wall Calendars. Among other items members may choose to distribute are pamphlets on American history, the legislative process, historic documents and calendars, including "We, the People" wall calendars.

"We, the People" calendars are full-color, glossy photo calendars that carry the name of the congressman. They are published by the U.S. Capitol Historical Society and are a big hit with constituents. "No other comparable document receives such acclaim," said Rep. Joseph M. Gaydos, D-Pa., chairman of the House Administration Committee's Subcommittee on Contracts and Printing. "We print a very limited number. I wish we could double or triple it," Gaydos said.

In 1981 the House bought 950,000 calendars and the Senate bought 104,000, at a total cost of $590,000. Members no doubt will pressure the leadership to continue the practice of buying calendars, but because of inflation it is estimated that the cost will increase to $611,000 in 1983 — $22,000 more than the previous year.

In 1982, House members were allotted 2,500 free calendars; senators received 1,000. This allowance could be used for either the "We the People" or Government Printing Office (GPO) calendars.[32] Members also could buy additional calendars from their official expense account.

In 1980, the Americans for Democratic Action (ADA), an organization that lobbies for liberal causes, calculated that each representative was allowed about $7,369 worth of free publications.[33] But calculating an exact figure is not feasible because members receive and use hundreds of bills, annual reports from federal agencies, budget documents, manuals, published hearings and committee reports.

Goatskin-bound Volumes. Members are entitled to goatskin-bound copies of any one of some 25,000 different documents stocked by the Government Printing Office. In fiscal year 1980 one senator and 195 House members used this privilege, at a cost of nearly $30,880.[34]

Senators and representatives also receive an unabridged dictionary and stand as part of their office furnishings.

Additional Benefits

In addition to their pay, staff and expense allowances, remuneration for official foreign travel and franking privileges, members of Congress benefit from numerous services, courtesies and special favors that go along with the job. Because of the difficulty of defining and isolating types of benefits, it is not possible to compile a complete list or compute their precise value. Selected additional benefits are described below. *(See also members' retirement benefits, box, p. 123)*

Life Insurance

Regardless of a member's age or state of health, all senators and representatives receive $63,000 in term life insurance under the Federal Employees Group Life Insurance program. The government pays one-third of the premium of the basic plan. Additional $10,000 policies as well as coverage of from two to five times a member's annual pay are available, with the extra premiums determined by the age of the member. Family members also are eligible under these plans. Members pay the entire cost of the premiums for the additional policies.

Health Insurance

Under the Federal Employees Health Benefits Program, members are eligible for a variety of health insurance plans. The government contributions toward these plans vary, but they cannot exceed 75 percent of a member's insurance premium.

Capitol Hill Health Facilities

A staff of three doctors, 13 nurses, a pharmacist and other medical personnel stands by in the Capitol to give members free medical care while at work. The Office of the Attending Physician is staffed and operated by the Navy. Services available to members include physical examinations, laboratory work, electrocardiograms, periodic health preventive programs, physiotherapy, immunizations for foreign travel, ambulance service and supplies of prescription medicines. First aid stations in every House and Senate office building offer help to members, their staffs and visitors for minor ailments.

Library Services

The Library of Congress provides members with free research services and facilities, free speechwriting and free materials that can be sent to constituents or used to answer constituents' questions. About 800 employees in the Library's Congressional Research Service (CRS) work exclusively for members.

Surplus Books

The Library of Congress gives away to members and their staffs surplus books that are not suitable for the library's collections. Most of these volumes are duplicate copies of books already held by the library or discarded publications sent from various agencies or offices. Members may select and keep books for their own use or send volumes to libraries and schools in their districts or states. *(See also free publications, p. 136)*

Legislative Counsel

The Office of Legislative Counsel, with offices on both sides of Capitol Hill, assists members in drafting bills, resolutions and amendments. Its staff provides confidential help to committees and members on legislative matters only; it does not perform personal legal work for members. *(Office of the Legislative Counsel, box, p. 106)*

Legal Counsel

The Office of Senate Legal Counsel, created by the Ethics in Government Act of 1978, provides advice and handles legal matters relating to official work of Senate members, committees and staffers. Functions of the office include defending the Senate against outside suits; the filing of civil actions to enforce subpoenas; and the identification of pending legal proceedings that might affect congressional powers and responsibilities. The House counterpart to the Senate's Legal Counsel is the General Counsel in the office of the clerk.

In 1980 the Senate paid $124,351 in legal defense fees for William Proxmire, D-Wis., who had been sued for libel after he gave three federal agencies a "Golden Fleece" award to publicize what he considered examples of wasteful government grants.

Chaplains

Both the House and Senate have their own chaplain, who is responsible for opening each daily session with a prayer and for serving generally as spiritual counselor to members, their families and their staffs. The chaplains are officers of the House and Senate and in 1981 received salaries of $52,750. A group of taxpayers brought suit in 1980, charging that use of government money to pay the chaplains' salaries violated the First Amendment requirement that "Congress shall make no law respecting an establishment of religion." In 1982 the suit was pending at the appellate level.

Tax Preparation

The IRS maintains a temporary office in both the Senate and House between January and April each year to help members, staff and the general public prepare their income tax returns. The public criticism of the special services these offices provide for members and staff has resulted in demands that the IRS close these facilities.

Federal law allows members to deduct up to $3,000 a year for living expenses in Washington because they live in two places — their hometowns and Washington, D.C. The allowable deduction had been much higher in 1981 following enactment of legislation providing new tax breaks for members. That law was repealed in 1982. *(Details, see pay, p. 120)*

Recreation

Members of Congress have their own free health club, including a modern gymnasium in the Rayburn House Office Building and two exercise rooms in the Russell and Dirksen office buildings. Facilities include swimming pools, exercise machines and saunas as well as court facilities for volleyball, paddleball and basketball. The new Hart Senate Office Building contained a gym, but members rejected funds to complete it.

Capitol Hill Restaurants

Government subsidized food and eating facilities are available to members, staff and visitors. The Capitol and congressional office buildings contain five public restaurants and cafeterias; five restaurants for members, senior staff and their guests; and eight carry-out services. In addition, members may reserve several private dining rooms or arrange banquets and parties in caucus rooms with low-cost catering from the House and Senate restaurants.

Members' Recording Studios: 'Madison Avenue' on Capitol Hill

Nearly all the perquisites of members of Congress give incumbents certain campaign advantages over their challengers. For example, a member's staff, the franking privilege, and special allowances for travel, office expenses, stationery, newsletters, telephone and telegraph services — all at public expense — may improve members' chances of being re-elected. In addition, incumbents have an inherent news-making position that their opponents lack.

One of the greatest advantages — and perhaps a decisive one in an era of electronic campaigning — is the availability of radio and television recording facilities. The House Recording Studio, located in the Rayburn House Office Building, and the Senate Recording and Photographic Studio, located in a tunnel between the Capitol and the Russell Office Building, are available to all members.

House, Senate Facilities

Both recording studios are extensive. House facilities include four radio studios, one video and one film/video studio. The Senate maintains two radio studios, one video and one film/video studio.

In theory the recording studios are designed to help members communicate with their constituents. Radio or television tapes recorded at the studios can be mailed to local stations for use in local news or public affairs programming. Because licensed stations are required by the FCC to devote a percentage of their air time to public service broadcasts, they are often receptive to these tapes.

"Radio is an excellent way of combating the criticism that I'm off in Washington all the time and detached from the district," said Rep. Robert McClory, R-Ill., in 1979. "The surveys say more people get their news from local radio, and I have eight stations serving my district."

Increased Use

The use of the recording studios has significantly increased over the last 15 years. According to one estimate, in 1967 only 200 members of the House used the studios — less than 50 percent of the membership. In 1978 there were 352 members — over 80 percent — who used the facilities.[1]

Three of the most common programs produced by the studios are one-minute television commentaries for local news shows and 5-15 minute television interviews and regular talk shows.

The studios process color films for television, radio tapes and cassettes, usually within 24 hours.

Portable video equipment for documentaries is available, and senators can request remote shootings with a portable mini-camera. The studios also are equipped with speaker-phone service for two-way interviews with local radio or TV stations. In all cases, members must design their own programs and write their own scripts, but the studios provide such services as teleprompters and set makeup. Members are urged to make appointments for filming and taping on a regular basis.

Taping Floor Proceedings

Senate committee hearings can be taped by the Senate Recording and Photographic Studio at the request of a senator. The House Recording Studio is responsible for taping floor proceedings. House members may request copies of these tapes, which must be used for non-political purposes. (Televising congressional hearings, box, p. 89)

Studio productions are subsidized with public funds. Tapes and films are produced at cost, and representatives and senators may use their expense allowances to purchase audio and video tapes.

While services of the studios are for official business only, the ease with which members are able to be seen and heard over the airwaves gives them a certain built-in advantage at election time.

'Official Use' Only

The Senate Handbook, revised in November 1980, states: "Generally, the Recording Studio may not be used during the 60 days before the date of any primary or general election, whether regular, special or runoff, in which the Senator is a candidate for public office." The House does not restrict use of the studios during the campaign season so long as the programming qualifies as "official use."

The recording studios are a bargain, though the precise dollar value to members is difficult to calculate. Candidates running against incumbents are charged full rates by commercial recording studios. In 1982 the cost to members of a 15-minute radio program was $3. At a commercial studio such a program might cost $100.

---

1. Michael J. Robinson, "Three Faces of Congressional Media," in *The New Congress* (Washington: American Enterprise Institute for Public Policy Research, 1981), p.63.

Source: *Congressional Handbook: U.S. House of Representatives; Congressional Handbook: U.S. Senate*. Both printed November 1980.

The House restaurants operate from a "revolving fund," and all operating expenditures are paid from restaurant revenues. Senate restaurants also operate from a revolving fund, but some funds are appropriated each year for management employees and equipment maintenance. Congress provides the restaurants with the space, utilities, janitorial and other services, and the Government Printing Office prints the menus — all at no charge to the restaurants.

Merchandise Discounts

Stationery stores located in the House and Senate office buildings sell many gift items as well as normal office supplies, all at cost or slightly above. Members, their spouses and their staffs can buy such things as wallets, briefcases, pocket calculators and drinking glasses and ashtrays with the seal of either the House or the Senate. Christmas cards also are available at bargain prices.

Free Parking

Each representative gets a free Capitol Hill garage space for personal use, plus four additional spaces and one outside parking permit for staff use. Senators receive two parking spaces each, plus a limited number of outside permits for staff. By 1982 parking rates around Capitol Hill ranged from $35 to $84 a month, and parking spaces in prime business areas in Washington were rented for as high as $118 a month. Members may have their cars washed and waxed in the garages at discount prices. Free parking for an unlimited time period is provided for members at Washington-area airports (National, Dulles and Baltimore-Washington International).

Capitol Waiting Areas

Congress provides attractive waiting rooms in the Capitol for members' spouses and families. The Senate Ladies Lounge and the Members' Family Suite (House) are located near each chamber's galleries.

Grooming

The House and Senate provide six barber and beauty shops in the Capitol and office buildings that give haircuts to members and staff. While charges for haircuts formerly were at reduced rates, all of these facilities in 1982 maintained their prices were comparable to those in the Washington area.

Office Decorations

The U.S. Botanic Garden will loan to members' offices six potted plants per year and provide floral centerpieces for official functions. Members may request cut flowers as well.

Members may decorate their offices with free wall maps and charts, scenic photographs and reproductions of paintings and prints, all of which may be framed and installed at no cost to members. There are quotas on paintings and certain maps.

Ticket Offices

Two ticket offices run by the airlines in the Longworth (House) and Russell (Senate) office buildings and an Amtrak railroad ticket office in the Capitol make reservations and issue tickets for members. Special rates for rail travel are available for members traveling on official government business between Washington, D.C., and New York, N.Y. Congress provides these offices with operating space, utilities and janitorial services.

Park Service Lodges

Members of Congress also have access to five rustic lodges run by the National Park Service in the Grand Tetons, the Shenandoah National Park, Cape Hatteras, Catoctin Mountain Park and the Virgin Islands. The lodges are available both for vacation and business use, and prices range from $20 to $65 per day.

Photographs

Both the House and Senate provide official photographic services at public expense for members. Members may have photographs taken with constituents and at official functions or ceremonial events for news and publicity use. In 1982 the Senate spent approximately $290,000 for photographers; the House photographers' payroll was approximately $345,000.

The Senate and House have separate staff darkrooms. There are no longer separate studios for the Democrats and Republicans. One Senate photographer earned as much as $46,194 in 1982.[35]

Senators purchase photographic services through their expense accounts or excess campaign funds. The money is put into a photographic/recording studio revolving fund and is used to purchase photographic supplies. House funds are used to purchase cameras, film and supplies. *(Congressional recording studio, box, p. 138)*

Other Benefits

Miscellaneous services and perquisites available to members include:

● Special congressional license tags provided by the city permit unrestricted parking by members on official business anywhere in Washington.

● American flags flown over the Capitol and certified by the Architect may be purchased at cost and presented as gifts.

● Members and staff may have packages wrapped free of charge for mailing, a service used heavily during the Christmas season.

Exemptions From Statutes

Congress has exempted itself from the major labor laws enacted to protect virtually all other workers, including most federal employees.

Among labor laws that do not apply to the House and Senate are: the Civil Rights Act of 1964 and the Equal Employment Act of 1972, forbidding job discrimination on the basis of race, color, religion, sex or national origin; the Equal Pay Act, guaranteeing women salaries equal to those of men in similar jobs; the National Labor Relations Act, requiring recognition of unions and protection of workers from unfair labor practices; the Fair Labor Standards Act, setting minimum age, overtime and other standards; the Age Discrimination in Employment Act, protecting older workers; and the Occupational Safety and Health Act, setting standards for the work environment.

Congressional staffers lack seniority rights, job descriptions, salary structures, grievance procedures and guaranteed government-wide vacation, maternity and sick leave policies (each member sets his or her own policies regarding these employee benefits). Congress has also exempted itself from the Social Security System, Freedom of Information Act and the Privacy Act.

Two arguments traditionally have been used in defense of exempting Congress from the standards it has set for other employers.

One is the doctrine of separation of powers, which would be violated if an executive branch agency such as the Equal Employment Opportunity Commission were allowed to police congressional job practices. Critics of that argument point out that Congress could delegate authority to a new, independent agency outside the executive branch to enforce civil rights laws on Capitol Hill.

The other is that politicians and their employees need a loyal, compatible relationship that goes beyond the traditional labor-management situation. Thus members of Congress must have more freedom in hiring and firing, according to this argument. But critics point out that there are thousands of blue-collar workers on Capitol Hill who perform non-political tasks — cleaning personnel, policemen, waiters, janitors, groundskeepers, secretaries, technicians, mail clerks and elevator operators.

There are rules in both chambers (House Rule 43, Senate Rule 50) that ostensibly prohibit job discrimination by congressional employers. But the prohibitions are more form than substance because meaningful enforcement mechanisms are lacking.

The Franking Privilege

Every year millions of American households receive numerous pieces of mail that bear, in place of a stamp, a facsimile of the signature of a member of Congress. In election years the volume of franked mail handled by the Postal Service jumps dramatically, along with the cost to the American taxpayer. The mail may be addressed to an individual, or it may simply be sent to the "occupant," "resident" or "postal customer."

The envelope or package may contain a member's response to a query or request, a copy of a member's newsletter, a questionnaire, a packet of voting information, excerpts from the *Congressional Record*, government publications covering a variety of subjects such as energy, consumer or conservation issues, a brochure listing career or educational opportunities, a Department of Agriculture seed and agriculture report, or any of a wide variety of printed matter that relates in some way to the discharge of a legislator's "official duties."

Many students of Congress have cited the frank — the privilege of mailing letters and packages under one's signature without being charged for postage — as one of the most valuable and controversial of members' perquisites of office. The privilege actually is older than Congress itself. The first Continental Congress enacted a law in 1775 that accorded its members mailing privileges as a means of keeping their constituents fully informed of developments.

One of the first acts of Congress under the Constitution was to continue the practice. Except for a very brief time (the franking privilege was suspended for a few months in 1873), the practice remained virtually unchanged until 1973. That year, Congress updated the franking laws for the first time since the early 19th century and established machinery for self-policing franking practices.

In 1981 Congress cleared legislation further codifying

use of the frank and restricting its use in election years. But the privilege continues to be challenged by those who cite the political advantages accruing to incumbents by the free mailings allowed under the frank.

Franking Regulations

The regulations dealing with the franking privilege (Title 39, Section 3210, of the U.S. Code) limit the frank to correspondence "in which the Member deals with the addressee as a citizen of the United States or constituent." Members of Congress are not authorized to use the frank for letters that deal with personal business or friendships, pertain to the member's candidacy for political office or are used for partisan purposes. Originally, franking was allowed on mail received by members as well as on mail sent to members, but the latter has been prohibited for years.

Persons authorized to use the frank include the vice president, members and members-elect of Congress (senators, representatives, delegates and resident commissioners) and the officers of the House and Senate. In addition, the surviving spouse of a member who died during his term of office is permitted to use the frank for non-political correspondence relating to the death of the member. This authorization expires 180 days after the member's death.

Members and others vested with the franking privilege are entitled, on a restricted basis, to use the frank during the 90-day period immediately following the date on which they leave office. During this period, use of the frank is limited to matters directly related to the closing of the member's congressional office. Former members may not send newsletters, questionnaires and other mass-mailed material.

Mail of standing, select, special or joint committees of Congress, as well as subcommittees and commissions, may be sent under the frank of the chairman, ranking minority member or any other member of the committee. Excluded are "informal" or "ad hoc" groups of members — such as the House Democratic Study Group or the House Wednesday Group of Republicans — whose business relates to political, party policy or special interest matters.

The franking regulations prohibit a person entitled to use the frank from lending it to any non-member, private committee, organization or association. Use of the frank for the benefit of charitable organizations, political action committees, trade organizations and other groups is expressly forbidden. Nor may the frank be used for mail delivered to a foreign country. Violators can be punished.

What May Be Franked?

Despite those restrictions, a wide range of material may be sent out under the frank. The law states that the frank is designed to "assist and expedite the conduct of the official business, activities and duties of the Congress of the United States." The terms "official business and activities" are broadly defined to cover "all matters which directly or indirectly pertain to the legislative process or to any congressional representative functions generally, or to the functioning, working or operating of the Congress and the performance of official duties in connection therewith, and shall include, *but not limited to*, the conveying of information to the public, and the requesting of the views of the public, or the views and information of other authority of government, as a guide or a means of assistance in the performance of those functions." (Emphasis supplied)

Among the major categories of mail applicable to the

franking privilege are:

Newsletters and News Releases. The law authorizes use of the congressional frank for "the usual and customary congressional newsletter or press release, which may deal with such matters as the impact of laws and decisions on State and local governments and individual citizens; reports on public and official actions taken by Members of Congress; and discussions of proposed or pending legislation or governmental actions and the position of the Members of Congress on, and arguments for or against, such matters."

Examples of frankable material in newsletters or news releases include tabulations of a member's voting record; reports on a member's position on various legislative proposals; notices that a member will visit his or her district on official business; statements that are critical of administration or congressional policies — provided they are not presented in a partisan manner; invitations to meet and participate with another member in a public discussion or report on Congress if the meeting is not under political auspices; and a member's financial disclosure statement.

Questionnaires. Members may mail under the frank "the usual and customary congressional questionnaire seeking public opinion on any law, pending or proposed legislation, public issue, or subject." Members may not permit the frank to be used for the return of responses, but the results of the member's surveys may be included in a newsletter or other form of allowable franked correspondence.

Mailgrams. Members also may send Mailgrams under the frank, provided the material conforms to the same guidelines used in sending mail under the franking law.

Other Material. The regulations provide that the scope of the frank is not limited to the above categories. Members are advised to seek the opinion of the House Commission on Congressional Mailing Standards or the Senate Ethics and Rules committees, which are authorized to enforce the franking rules and laws.

Other materials that may be franked include mail to any individual or agency and to officials at any level of government regarding programs and proposed legislation; congressional committee and floor action and other related matters of public concern or public service; mail between members; mail from a member's Capitol Hill office to his congressional district offices (or between district offices) or from a member to a state or local legislator; non-partisan voter registration or election information or assistance; biographical or autobiographical material of a member or of his family that is mailed as part of a federal publication or in response to a specific request and is not intended for publicity purposes; and mail, including general mass mailings, that consists of federal laws or regulations, government publications or publications purchased with federal funds and publications containing items of general information.

Government publications include, among others, the Agricultural Yearbook, the *Congressional Directory,* Department of Agriculture pamphlets and reports and the *Congressional Record,* or a reprint of any part of the Record.

Prohibited Mail. In contrast to the broad scope of material that can be franked, the specific prohibitions on use of the frank are defined narrowly. They include "purely personal mailings;" mailings "laudatory and complimentary" of a member "on a purely personal or political basis;" expressions of condolence to a person who has suffered a loss or congratulations to a person who has achieved some personal distinction (expressions of congratulations to a person who has achieved some public distinction, such as election to public office or attainment of U.S. citizenship, may be franked); holiday greetings; reports on how a member spends time other than in connection with his legislative, representative or "other official functions;" and mailings "which specifically solicit political support."

In its summary of "Regulations on the Use of the Congressional Frank" the House Commission on Congressional Mailing Standards advises members that "personally phrased references ('I,' 'me,' 'the congressman') contained in a mass mailing generally should not appear more than eight times on each page of a mass mailing." The regulations also provide guidelines on use of photographs.

The U.S. Postal Service keeps records of all franked mail as it passes through the post office in Washington, D.C. Every three months it sends Congress a bill. The cost is computed by actual counts of pieces of mail and by weighing random samples. Members mailing newsletters and other mass mailings sent at bulk rate must submit mailing statements as to count and content; these are verified by the Postal Service. Funds to compensate the Postal Service for the cost of franked mail are contained in the annual legislative branch appropriations bills.

Franking Revisions

Neither the U.S. Postal Service nor its predecessor, the U.S. Post Office Department, inspect franked mail to determine whether any members abuse the practice by sending personal or political correspondence postage-free. Until 1968 the Post Office would issue rulings on specific charges of abuse if private citizens made official complaints; the Post Office could ask the offending members to make reimbursement. But the rulings were not binding, so some members refused to pay. In December 1968 the Post Office Department abandoned its attempts to collect from members who allegedly abused the frank. The Postal Service has continued that policy.

1973 Regulations. Before 1973 the only standards dealing with the franking privilege were those formulated by the Postal Service and the courts. Conflicting court decisions and a reluctance of many judges to rule on questions of congressional propriety resulted in general confusion about proper use of the frank. A number of disputes that arose during the 1972 election campaign convinced members that new regulations were necessary.

On Dec. 17, 1973, Congress approved a bill that established specific guidelines regarding the types of mail members could send under the frank, set up mechanisms to rule on individual cases, restricted the sending of mass mailings (defined as more than 500 pieces of identical mail) during the four weeks preceding congressional primary or general elections and, in the House, established a Commission on Congressional Mailing Standards, composed of three Republicans and three Democrats appointed by the Speaker, to resolve franking disputes arising under the law during general election campaigns. (The Senate Select Committee on Standards and Conduct — later renamed the Select Ethics Committee — was assigned a similar function.)

The bill's sponsor, Rep. Morris K. Udall, D-Ariz., succeeded in establishing definitions of the franking privilege that were acceptable to most members and that represented little change from established practices. Udall said the issue was whether Congress would define the privilege or whether "the judges are going to write the law for us."

House of Representatives
Franked Mass Mailings

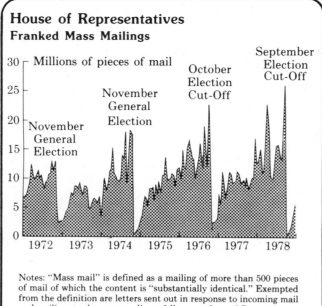

30 ┌ Millions of pieces of mail

September Election Cut-Off

October Election Cut-Off

November General Election

November General Election

Notes: "Mass mail" is defined as a mailing of more than 500 pieces of mail of which the content is "substantially identical." Exempted from the definition are letters sent out in response to incoming mail and mailings to the news media, to fellow members of Congress or to state, local or federal government officials.

Under the Constitution, the entire House of Representatives is elected every second year.

Source: Common Cause, et al., plaintiff, v. William F. Bolger, et al., defendants, Memorandum in Support of Plaintiffs' Motion for Summary Judgment, May 22, 1981.

The new regulations did not anticipate every kind of abuse. In 1975 Congress voted to close a loophole in the 1973 law that had allowed former Rep. Frank M. Clark, D-Pa. (1955-74), to send out a franked newsletter to his former constituents two months after his term had expired. The 1975 change permitted former members to use the frank for 90 days after leaving Congress, but only for mailings related to closing down the member's offices.

Restrictions Tightened in 1977. Use of congressional franking increased enormously in the 1970s. In 1970 members of Congress and others authorized to use the frank sent 190 million pieces of mail at a total cost of $11.2 million. By fiscal 1976 the volume had jumped to an estimated 322 million pieces and the cost to $46.1 million.

Early in 1977, when new ethics codes were passed, both chambers agreed to tighten restrictions on the franking privilege. The House amended its standing rules to impose new limitations on use of the "postal patron" designation — mail that does not include the recipient's name — to send franked mail. House rules in 1982 require franked postal-patron mail to be sent by the most economical means practicable — third-class bulk. The volume of postal-patron mail that a member could send annually under the frank was limited to an amount equal to six times the number of addresses in a member's district. All franked postal-patron mailing had to be submitted to the House Commission on Congressional Mailing Standards for an advisory opinion on whether the mailing met the restrictions on franked materials.

In addition, both the House and the Senate imposed new regulations on mass mailings — whether sent to a

postal-patron address or to a specific person. The 1977 rules prohibited any mass mailing under the frank unless preparation and printing costs were paid entirely from public funds. This was designed to end free political mailings and criticisms that mail printed for a member by special interest groups or political organizations was being sent at government expense. Members today are prohibited from mailing such materials under the frank, even if they state that it wasn't printed at government expense.

Such materials can be included in a mailing prepared and printed at private expense if they are of a "purely instructional or informational" nature. The 28-day pre-election cutoff in the 1973 law for sending mail under the frank was expanded in 1977 to 60 days before both primary and general elections in which the member sending the mail is a candidate.

In the House, any member who is a candidate for statewide office is barred from sending any franked mass mailing to residents outside his or her district. (Related regulations, box, p. 144)

In the Senate, rules incorporated in that chamber's ethics code required all mass mailings by a senator under the frank to be registered with the secretary of the Senate; the registration had to include a copy of the material, the number of pieces sent and a description of the groups receiving the mailing. The information was required to be available for public inspection.

The Senate also provided that its central computer facilities could not be used to store any political or campaign lists and that other mail-related uses of the computer would be subject to guidelines issued by the Senate Rules Committee.

However, neither the 1973 statute nor the restrictions in the 1977 ethics code succeeded in quieting criticisms that members used the frank to promote their re-election. Partly in response to those criticisms, both chambers in 1981 further amended the franking law. Some of the provisions broadened existing restrictions, but others relaxed certain requirements.

1981 Changes. For the first time, the franking regulations allowed senators to make statewide postal-patron mass mailings — a privilege House members within their districts were accorded under the original 1973 law. (However, the Senate Rules Committee, which has jurisdiction over franking, decided in February 1982 to postpone promulgating the new rules governing mass mailings, in effect suspending the postal-patron franking privilege for senators during the 1982 election year.)

The 1981 amendments to the franking law made permanent the 60-day pre-election cutoff on mass mailings. The prohibition applies to every member whose name appears on an official ballot for election or re-election to public office. (Exempted were committee chairmen in either chamber who were candidates in primary or general elections, provided the mailings related to routine committee business.)

The House Commission on Congressional Mailing Standards noted that "state election laws vary considerably. For example, in some states, if a member is unopposed in either the primary or general election, the member's name does not appear on the ballot. The member, therefore, would not be subject to the 60-day cutoff provision.

"In other states, however, a member's name may appear on the ballot whether or not the member has an opponent. Even if a member is unopposed, if the member's name is to appear on the ballot, the 60-day mass mailing prohibition *would* apply."

The 1981 amendments gave the Senate Select Ethics Committee and the House Commission on Congressional Mailing Standards statutory authority to enforce the franking rules and laws and to further regulate use of the frank. The jurisdiction of the House Mailing Standards Commission was extended to cover complaints against former members and House officials.

House members were required to submit to the commission a sample of each mass mailing in advance to determine whether it complied with the requirements of the franking law. In the Senate, it was left to the Ethics committee to decide whether senators also should be required to submit such samples in advance. (Although the committee did not mandate such a requirement for 1982, it urged members to obtain pre-mailing advice from the committee. Most senators did so, according to the committee's staff.)

Costs and Controversies

One of the most widely criticized aspects of the franking privilege has been the steady increase in the cost. By fiscal 1982 the expense came to about $75.1 million for more than 400 million pieces of mail. Some of the increase was due to rising postal rates, particularly for first-class mail. On occasion, Congress has renegotiated the status of certain types of its mail to reduce the franking charges. For example, in 1974 the *Congressional Record* was made eligible for less expensive second-class distribution instead of being sent first-class.

During hearings before the Senate Rules Committee in February 1982, Sen. Ted Stevens, R-Alaska, argued that a provision of the 1981 franking law allowing senators to make statewide postal-patron mailings actually would save money. He said the Postal Service charged a higher rate for individually addressed mass mail than for postal-patron mail, and that it charged 25 cents for each piece of incorrectly addressed mail that was returned to the Senate. Because postal-patron mail was not individually addressed, there would be no returns. Stevens, who drafted the 1981 law and helped to guide it through Congress, conceded that money would be saved only if the volume of Senate mail did not rise. But he predicted there would be no increase.

However, Senate Sergeant-at-Arms Howard S. Liebengood testified that if every senator made two statewide postal-patron mailings in 1982, along with the usual number of individually addressed letters, the total cost to the Senate in labor, printing, paper and postal charges would come to $49.9 million, an increase of $17.8 million over estimated Senate mailing expenditures under the existing practice. Four statewide mailings would cost about $89.1 million, he said. "The only way postal-patron mailing would be less expensive than the current individually addressed mail would be if senators were limited to sending 1.3 postal-patron mailings per year, and no individually addressed targeted mail were allowed," he concluded.[36]

Common Cause Suit

More controversial than the rising cost of the frank has been its impact on the political process. Neither the 1973 statute, nor the 1977 ethics code restrictions and the 1981 amendments quieted criticisms of the privilege.

One of the most persistent challenges to existing franking practices was a lawsuit filed in October 1973 by

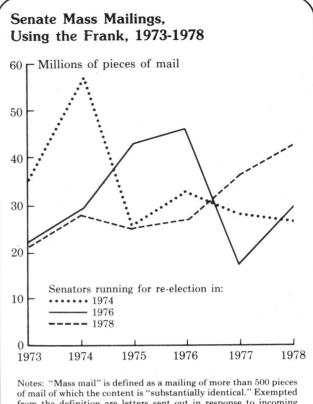

Senate Mass Mailings, Using the Frank, 1973-1978

Millions of pieces of mail

Senators running for re-election in:
- • • • • • • 1974
- —— 1976
- – – – – 1978

Notes: "Mass mail" is defined as a mailing of more than 500 pieces of mail of which the content is "substantially identical." Exempted from the definition are letters sent out in response to incoming mail and mailings to the news media, to fellow members of Congress or to state, local or federal government officials.

Under the Constitution, senators are divided into three classes, with one-third of the Senate elected every second year.

Source: Common Cause, et al., plaintiff, v. William F. Bolger, et al., defendants, Memorandum in Support of Plaintiffs' Motion for Summary Judgment, May 22, 1981.

Common Cause, a citizens' interest group. The suit charged that the frank was unconstitutional because the free mailing privilege aided the re-election of incumbents and therefore denied challengers equal protection of the law. After Congress approved the franking regulations in December 1973, Common Cause filed an amended complaint seeking a judgment that the law violated the Fifth Amendment by discriminating in favor of members of Congress who were candidates for public office "by conferring upon them a substantial political benefit not similarly conferred upon candidates who are not members of Congress."

After the suit was filed, congressional lawyers made repeated attempts to have the case thrown out of court. But those efforts failed, and oral arguments in the case were heard in September 1981 by a special three-judge panel of the U.S. District Court for the District of Columbia. Although litigation was completed, as of mid-1982 a judgment had not been handed down.

The criticisms in the Common Cause suit were directed at the advice given members regarding use of the frank; the practice of targeting mailings; the content of franked mail; the timing of franked mail to coincide with election cycles; and the impact of the frank on the political process in general.

Incumbency Insurance:
Employing the Extended Frank

When Indiana's Legislature drew a new congressional redistricting map in 1981, it did Rep. Elwood Hillis no favor. Although the map was a GOP product and Hillis was a six-term Republican incumbent, the new map stretched his once compact 5th District hundreds of miles from his home in Kokomo to the suburbs of Chicago in northwest Indiana.

Nearly 60 percent of the new electorate was not part of the old 5th that returned Hillis to office in 1980. The new district was strongly Republican, but no member of Congress likes to run in territory where he is unfamiliar.

Fortunately for those in office, there are ways of becoming familiar very fast. Voters in northwest Indiana already were receiving Hillis' newsletters and constituent services, even though they would remain in Democrat Floyd Fithian's 2nd District until January 1983. Before Hillis mounted his first general election campaign in his new district covering northwest Indiana, he was preceded by thousands of pieces of franked mail identifying him to the voters.

This "extended frank" is perfectly legal, and it is standard congressional practice. Legislation passed in 1973 specifically allowed free mailings to places members did not represent as long as they overlapped at least in part with the existing constituency. Hillis had as much right as anyone else to take advantage of the law.

"We have franking privileges up there, and we're using them," said a Hillis aide. "We feel it's part of our representation."

The same Indiana congressional map that gave Hillis nearly 300,000 new constituents also forced Reps. David W. Evans and Andrew Jacobs Jr. into a merged Indianapolis district, setting up a Democratic primary collision.

Evans blanketed the city with direct mail. "I am elected to serve you," he wrote in one newsletter, "and I intend to continue doing just that."

That was ordinary constituent communication, but in this case Evans was sending it to Jacobs' constituents, and leaving the impression that he, not Jacobs, was already their representative in Congress. All of it was legal, and all of it was free. The only problem for Evans was that it did not work. Jacobs won the May 1982 primary by more than 10,000 votes.

If there is no direct confrontation between incumbents, members normally are pleased to help each other campaign with the extended frank.

When congressional redistricting moves territory from one constituency to another, it is common practice for members to make a trade. The member who is gaining a few new counties begins providing constituent service for them as soon as the new map is approved. He turns the counties he is giving up over to the colleague who expects to represent them in the next Congress. Members like to say this provides for orderly transfer of constituent service. What they do not say is that it presumes the November election already has been held and the incumbents have been re-elected.

Jacobs was one incumbent who viewed the extended frank as an abuse. "It's very simple to explain," he said. "You pretend to represent an area that you'd like to represent. It's morally indefensible."

Jacobs was not the only member willing to suggest that the extended frank is a hard proposition to defend. Rep. Henry J. Hyde, R-Ill., found himself forced to run in 1982 in a district 95 percent new to him. Extended franking was the quickest — and cheapest — way to solidify his position in the areas where he was a stranger. After mulling it over, Hyde decided he could not go through with it. "I'm going to mass mail ... but I'm going to pay for it out of campaign money. What right have I got to frank a piece of mail in a district I don't represent?"

The fact is that Congress deliberately avoided solving the extended frank problem when it wrote the 1973 franking law.

Source: Adapted from Alan Ehrenhalt, "Incumbency Insurance: The Extended Frank," *Congressional Quarterly Weekly Report,* June 19, 1982, p. 1499.

In its memorandum on the case, Common Cause cited numerous instances where loopholes in the law worked to a member's political benefit. For example, although members are cautioned against mass mailings of *Congressional Record* reprints containing statements of praise by another member, the mailings may be prefaced by a colleague's comment on the member's "insightful analysis."

Besides franked newsletters reporting awards presented to members of Congress, Common Cause cited the political advantages derived from free mailing of material reflecting favorable ratings of members' voting records by various interest groups.

A common tactic, particularly in election years, is the use of targeted mass mailings sent out under the frank that tell a selected group of people what they want to hear and, probably just as important, avoid arousing groups thought to be unsympathetic. For example, farmers are told of a member's support for wheat exports, teachers are told of his support for education, doctors are told of his opposition to national health insurance. According to Common Cause, "This targeting tactic has two intended benefits for incumbents: It maximizes the chances of telling the voter something he will agree with and minimizes the chances of offending anyone else in the process. The net result is assistance to the incumbent's re-election, a gain derived solely from how the franking privilege is employed."[37]

Computers and the Frank

The Senate's central computer system facilitates the targeting of mass mailings, although House members may contract with outside computer firms to supply similar services. Although the 1977 rules barred the storage of lists of names and addresses identifying individuals as campaign workers or contributors or as members of any political party, a number of loopholes diminished the effectiveness of the restrictions. For example, to streamline correspondence to constituents, a senator might wish to put information on the central computer tape about a constituent's legislative interests or occupation, a bookkeeping device permitted under the rules. Some data can be helpful for both official and political purposes. Key demographic information provided by the Census Bureau such as an addressee's age, sex, race, income and homeownership, could be useful in predicting the person's legislative interests and political orientation.

Other data, however, could be used only for political gain. An addressee's political party affiliation, past voting patterns and past political contributions fall into this category and cannot be put into the Senate computer under the 1977 regulations.

Senate Practices. A provision of the fiscal 1978 legislative branch appropriations bill permits senators to spend up to 10 percent of their total expense allowance on whatever they deemed to be an "official expense." "Before the 1977 rules change, the senator purchased [computer mailing] lists with money from his own pocket," explained an aide to one senator. "That's why we pushed for the 10 percent discretionary fund. It was to permit us to buy mail lists for our newsletter." After the change, a number of senators began using their official expense allowance to purchase county-by-county or statewide voter registration lists. Because many states permit only elected officials to purchase such lists, challengers to incumbents in those states are not able to benefit from the wealth of computerized data on the lists.

Campaign consultants said they have advised senators to use those lists for statewide mailings as a way of keeping a senator's name before his constituents, to concentrate mail in precincts or counties in which the senator performed poorly in an earlier election and to "get out the vote" in precincts or counties in which the senator performed well in an earlier election.

Senate officials were among the first to admit there were ambiguities in the rules governing the frank and the use of computers. Whatever constraints the existing rules did have, according to Rules Committee officials, the centralized Senate computer is the key to their enforcement because it allows committee staffers to scrutinize everything going into and coming out of it.

House Procedures. House rules and procedures governing mailings are less strict than the Senate's and virtually unenforceable. While the Senate computer is centralized, House members are permitted to lease their own office computer facilities. That ensures complete confidentiality for members in the use of the computer. A 1975 rules change allows members to use funds from their office allowances to lease computers. *(Details, p. 131)*

House rules do not contain any restrictions on the source of electronic lists or the information that can be encoded on them when purchased or compiled with official funds. "It's not unusual for them to buy voter registration lists, motor vehicle lists or agency lists, such as a list from the Federal Aviation Administration of all licensed aviators, or from the Federal Communications Commission of all licensed ham radio operators in their state," a deputy director of the House Information Systems office pointed out.

House members also are free to buy mailing lists from their state and national political committees or from campaign consultants, so long as they are used for "official mailings." "If the mail had an information dissemination function, then there would be no prohibition on these kinds of mailings," according to the House official.

Making it easier for members to put a political slant on their mailings was a June 1974 ruling by the House Commission on Congressional Mailing Standards. The ruling upheld the right of a representative to ask a recipient's political affiliation in a constituent questionnaire mailed under the member's frank. The commission said knowing a constituent's party affiliation was relevant to a member's official duties.

A returned questionnaire signed, filled out with a return address, and marked with the constituent's political preference commonly has provided new members with the basis for their first electronic mailing list.

By 1982 it appeared that the marriage of the franking privilege with the modern computer age had resulted in a relationship of considerable potential political benefit to incumbents in Congress. At the very least, franked mass mail "reminds the electorate who the good old incumbent is, and even if his name is not on the material, the simple signature across the frank is enough to be a sort of political ad at that time of year," said Rep. John F. Seiberling, D-Ohio, in first proposing the 60-day election cutoff in 1973.

"The other side of this [is that] sometimes the poor incumbent is running against a millionaire who could buy the election if we didn't have this opportunity to communicate with our district," commented Rep. Charles H. Wilson, D-Calif. (1963-81), a member of the House Post Office and Civil Service Committee at the time of the hearings on the 1973 legislation.[38]

FOREIGN TRAVEL: BUSINESS AND PLEASURE

Special allowances are available to members of Congress who travel abroad on government business. According to William L. Safire in *The New Language of Politics*, "An overseas tour by a congressman or candidate is described by him as a fact-finding trip, and as a junket by his opponents, who usually add 'at the taxpayer's expense.' "[39]

A Congressional Quarterly survey published in August 1981 reported that 219 members of Congress had taken some 346 trips abroad at government expense during 1980. The trips by members and their personal and committee staffs cost a total of $2,803,966.85. The 1980 travel list was composed of 30 senators and 189 representatives, or 40.6 percent of the members.

Members generally undertake foreign travel on committee business or by executive request or appointment. Members traveling abroad on committee business or as delegates to meetings of various parliamentary groups are required by U.S. law to make public annually the cost of such trips. Public disclosure is not required for members' trips overseas that are funded by private sources or by executive branch agencies.

Pros and Cons of Foreign Travel

Ever since members of Congress have taken trips abroad at government expense, there have been opposing arguments on the value of such travel. Defenders say foreign travel enables members to develop insights they would not otherwise obtain and that such firsthand information is needed for intelligent legislating. Travel also helps members to overcome prejudices and provincialism and spreads goodwill for the United States, it is argued.

Opponents of overseas travel contend that such trips usually are a waste of the taxpayer's money. They contend that members traveling abroad spend only a minimal amount of time on official business, that they make unreasonable demands on U.S. embassy personnel in the countries they visit, that they sometimes damage American prestige through tactless acts or comments while abroad and that they often confound foreign officials by giving the impression that their comments reflect official U.S. policy.

Critics point to the use of "control rooms" as an example of extravagance and waste. Control rooms are set up by military escort officers in each hotel where members stay. They provide a place to assemble and have coffee in the morning or cocktails in the evening. Critics assert that this amounts to pampering Congress. But defenders of foreign travel respond that making lawmakers comfortable allows them to get more work done. They say that most members work hard and that the benefits of the trips far exceed the costs.

Even some members of Congress, however, question the value of foreign travel. "I have taken no junkets, and will not, because I believe they are an outrageous waste of the taxpayers' money. At a time when average Americans can hardly afford to take a weekend from home, it is terrible for politicians to be taking lush vacations at the people's expense," said Rep. Ron Paul, R-Texas, in 1981.

Critics of so-called "junketing" cite annual trips by members to meetings of the Interparliamentary Union and the North Atlantic Assembly — organizations that are intended to bring U.S. and foreign legislators together — and the Paris International Air Show, where aircraft manufacturers display their wares.

Even the congressional leadership is not immune from criticism for taking trips abroad. In April 1981 Speaker Thomas P. O'Neill Jr., D-Mass., and 14 other members flew to New Zealand and Australia for two weeks to hold discussions with those countries leaders on national security and economic issues. Many saw the trip, which came in the midst of a congressional battle over President Reagan's program to cut the federal budget, as a blatant example of wasteful spending. Some Democrats also criticized the sojourn, maintaining that the Speaker should have been in Washington lining up votes against the Reagan economic program.

One of the most celebrated junketeers in congressional history was Rep. Adam Clayton Powell Jr., D-N.Y. (1945-67,

Frequency of Members' Foreign Travel, 1970-80

From 1970 through 1980 the number of senators and representatives taking trips abroad on official business at government expense ranged from a low of 185 in 1974 to a high of 308 in 1975.

Year	Number of members taking government-paid trips	Number of trips taken at government expense[1]
1970	205	291
1971	274	447
1972	233	328
1973[3]	218	314
1974[2]	185	266
1975[2]	308	544
1976[4]	204	309
1977[4]	255	415
1978[4]	293	505
1979[4]	298	536
1980[5]	219	346

1. Trips in which any government funds were used are counted as government travel in CQ totals.
2. Totals based on incomplete information and disclosures supplied by congressional committees.
3. Totals based on CQ questionnaire response.
4. Totals based on CQ questionnaire response, State and Defense Department records and committee reports.
5. Totals based on committee reports and CQ responses.

Source: Congressional Quarterly surveys and questionnaires

1969-71). In one trip in 1962, Powell traveled through Europe for six weeks accompanied by two assistants — Corinne Huff, a receptionist in his office, and Tamara J. Wall, an associate labor counsel for the House Education and Labor Committee, of which Powell was chairman.

According to one report, Powell's itinerary included London, Rome, Paris, Vienna, Spain and Greece. He requested State Department assistance to obtain tickets to the Vienna film festival, reservations at various European nightclubs and a six-day cruise on the Aegean Sea.

Powell justified the trip on grounds that he and his two companions needed to study equal employment opportunities for women in the Common Market countries.

Rules on Lame-Duck Travel

Both houses of Congress adopted rules in 1977 forbidding foreign travel at government expense by members defeated for re-election. The rules also apply to members who have announced they are retiring. But the rules take effect only after the sine die adjournment of the second session of the Congress from which the member is retiring, or after the member's successor has been chosen in a general election. (Even if a member is defeated for renomination in a congressional primary, the rule does not apply until his successor is chosen in a general election.)

In 1980, 17 House members went overseas at government expense after announcing their retirements, but before Congress adjourned for the year.[40]

Efforts to Control Travel

Congress first initiated some control over members' foreign travel when it passed the Mutual Security Act of 1954, which allowed congressional committees to use foreign currencies for travel overseas. Members were required to make a full report to an appropriate oversight committee (House Administration, Senate Rules and Administration), indicating the amount of funds used and the purposes for which it was spent.

Public reporting in the *Congressional Record* first was required by the Mutual Security Act of 1958. Beginning in 1959, members who travel overseas have to submit itemized statements to their committee chairmen, showing the amount and dollar equivalent of the counterpart funds (foreign currencies) they spent and how the money was used, including lodging, meals, transportation and other expenses. Each committee was required to report this information on the previous year's travel to the proper oversight committee within the first 60 days of each session. The 1958 bill made the Senate Appropriations Committee, rather than Rules and Administration, responsible for handling the reports. Within 10 days of their receipt, the two committees had to publish the reports in the Record.

In 1961 Congress required mandatory publication in the Record of individual itemized expenditures. It also stipulated that appropriated U.S funds be reported along with counterpart funds.

In 1963 the House took further steps to curb foreign travel by allowing only five House committees to use appropriated funds and counterpart funds for travel abroad. Ten other committees were restricted to travel within the United States but could ask the Rules Committee for permission to travel abroad.

In 1967 the House Administration Committee banned the use of credit cards for transportation and accommodations and required uniform accounting and reporting by all House committees on a monthly basis. This action was taken after Rep. H. R. Gross, R-Iowa (1949-75), disclosed that on 12 occasions during a single trip in 1966, five members had collected per diem twice by traveling to two countries in the same day.

The Committee on Standards of Official Conduct issued a report in March 1968 calling for "clearer guidelines" regulating the use and reporting of expenditures. An immediate response of the House was to amend several committee travel authorizations to specifically make the per diem a one-time allowance, regardless of the number of countries visited in a single day.

Then in October 1973 Congress passed a State Department authorization bill that contained a provision eliminating the requirement for disclosure in the *Congressional Record*. The change was engineered by Rep. Wayne L. Hays, D-Ohio (1949-76), chairman of the Foreign Affairs Committee's State Department Subcommittee, where the bill originated. Hays also was chairman of the Committee on House Administration and a champion of generous perquisites for members.

Hays claimed he changed the old law to trim the size of the Record. "We decided we weren't going to spend eight or nine thousand dollars to let you guys [reporters] do your stories on congressional travel," he said. He said "there was no desire on anyone's part to cover up anything."

For a long time, Hays said, he had been trying to cut the size of the Record down" and that "this was just another useless bit of using up space in the Record." Nevertheless, the effect of the change was to substantially reverse two decades of reform efforts aimed at preventing abuses of foreign travel and providing full disclosure.

Under the revised law, the detailed breakdown of travel costs by committee and by member no longer was disclosed, and the two committees overseeing foreign travel no longer were required to make public a separate accounting of tax dollars spent on congressional travel. There was no way to check the dates of arrival and departure in various countries, making it impossible to tell how long senators and representatives stayed abroad. Also in the 1973 State Department bill, Congress voted itself a 50 percent increase in the per diem allowance for foreign travel — from $50 to $75.

Newspapers throughout the country printed stories about the change and editorialized against it. As a result, an amendment to the fiscal 1975 legislative branch appropriations bill reinstated language from the old law requiring that consolidated, detailed reports on foreign travel be made each year. But instead of being published in the Record, the amendment specified that the reports were to be made available to the public by the clerk of the House and the secretary of the Senate. The law was enacted in August 1974.

In amendments to the fiscal 1976 legislative branch appropriations bill, Congress specified that committee reports as well as parliamentary delegation reports had to be filed only with the secretary of the Senate and the House Administration Committee, not the clerk of the House. Rep. Hays thus gained control of the House foreign travel reports through his chairmanship of the committee. These changes did not affect the requirement that all consolidated reports be filed within 60 days of the beginning of each congressional session, but they did specify that the reports had to be open to public inspection. The changes became effective when the 1975 reports were filed in March 1976.

In 1976 the House added an amendment to a State Department authorization bill requiring that the annual foreign travel expense reports prepared by the House and Senate committees once again be printed in the Record. The House action was one of a number of reforms made in the aftermath of a sex-payroll scandal in which Hays, under pressure, resigned in June 1976 as chairman of the House Administration Committee. *(Details, see Ethics and Criminal Prosecutions chapter.)*

In 1978 Congress, in that year's foreign aid bill, required the chairman of each congressional committee to submit quarterly reports to the clerk of the House or the secretary of the Senate on the amounts spent by committee members and staff on foreign travel from foreign currencies and from congressionally appropriated funds.

Sources of Travel Funds

Annual reports published in the *Congressional Record* on travel by House committee members and other House delegations, such as those authorized by the Speaker, include the name of the members and committee aides, the time spent in each country and the amount spent on per diem, transportation and other expenses. The reports must be submitted to the clerk within 30 days from the date a trip is completed.

Senate foreign travel reports tend to be less specific. They often do not include the dates of the trips or the time spent in each country. The chairman's reports must be submitted to the secretary of the Senate within 30 days after the travel is completed.

In either case, the reports submitted by committees and printed in the Record rarely reveal the purpose of trips taken outside the United States or the sources of the travel funds. Those funds can come from various sources:

Appropriated Funds. Money is appropriated by Congress through the Mutual Security Act of 1954 to pay the expenses — including travel — of congressional committees for routine and special investigations. Certain committees, primarily the intelligence committees, may use some of their funds without making public disclosures as to their use.

Counterpart Funds. Members traveling abroad are allowed to use American-owned counterpart funds (foreign currencies held by U.S. embassies and credited to the United States as part of various foreign assistance programs; they can be spent only in the country of origin). Surplus foreign currency as of 1982 generally was disbursed on a $75 per diem basis by the embassies.

Representational Funds. American ambassadors overseas are allocated sums for official entertaining. These funds also can be used by members of Congress for the same purpose.

Agency Funds. Members of Congress can use funds of various government agencies when they speak on foreign policy issues at overseas posts. Such speaking arrangements can be the sole purpose of a member's trip abroad or part of a trip already planned. The departments of State and Defense are the agencies most called upon for such arrangements. For example, the International Communication Agency might ask a member to speak on an issue, whereupon the member or chairman of the committee will request the Defense or State departments to make the necessary travel arrangements.

Military Travel Subsidy. Members can travel on Military Aircraft Command planes, including cargo planes. These planes often are provided to members without charge.

PATRONAGE: WANING ADVANTAGE OF OFFICE

While the pay and perquisites of members and their staffs have grown enormously in recent years, political patronage has declined. Patronage is supposed to be one of the advantages of holding political office, but many members of Congress have regarded it as a nuisance.

Senators and representatives once pulled the political strings on thousands of federal jobs. On Capitol Hill and back home, a powerful member could place scores of persons in such jobs as local postmaster, health inspector, tax collector, welfare commissioner and even custodian of public morals. The congressional patronage empire thus provided members with a large payoff list for political supporters.

Today on Capitol Hill, the only jobs remaining under patronage are those that generally do not require special skills or technical knowledge, such as elevator operators, doorkeepers, mail carriers and clerks. All in all, a member now finds the available patronage jobs of little help in strengthening his political position or rewarding his campaign supporters back home.

"There was a time when the sergeant-at-arms was a sort of patronage baron," said Howard S. Liebengood, who became the 25th sergeant-at-arms of the Senate in 1981. "That was the historical perception. That has changed dramatically."[41]

Growth and Decline

Andrew Jackson was the first president to openly back political patronage. Convinced that political loyalty was of paramount importance, he made a clean sweep of the government and filled vacancies with his men at all levels. But when Jackson spoke out in favor of patronage, the number of government jobs requiring technical skills was not large. The few misfits given menial jobs through patronage appointments seemed to do little damage to the general efficiency of the government.

As the business of government grew more complex, and as it expanded, the inadequacies of a system that put a premium on loyalty rather than ability became glaringly apparent. Criticism of that method of appointment increased sharply after the assassination of President James A. Garfield by a disappointed job seeker in 1881. In response, Congress enacted the first major civil service reform in America. The 1883 Pendleton Act set up a three-man bipartisan board, the Civil Service Commission, and gave it authority to certify applicants for federal employment after they took competitive examinations. *(Civil Service history, box, p. 149)*

The 1883 act covered only about 10 percent of federal employees in the executive branch, but its key provision gave the president power to expand the civil service classifications by executive order. A series of such orders and additional legislation in the years that followed removed from politics nearly all non-policymaking jobs in the federal government.

While the value of patronage to members declined, Congress retained an influential voice in presidential appointments to high-level government positions. Today, jobs filled by the administration in that category include Cabinet and sub-Cabinet positions, the federal judiciary, major diplomatic and military posts and top positions on independent boards and regulatory agencies as well as some lesser positions exempt from the civil service.

Most of those appointments require Senate confirmation, although the administration is not required to consult with Congress before submitting its selections. The degree of influence a member has over those nominations generally depends on his personal relationship with the president and his power on Capitol Hill, rather than on his vote on confirmations.

The tradition of "senatorial courtesy" also affects many nominations.

In contrast to the executive branch, most congressional employees can be hired and fired at the whim of the members who employ them. They do not enjoy the elaborate job security provided by civil service regulations covering job qualifications, equitable application procedures, minimum starting salaries and the specific pay raise and promotion policies of the executive branch. *(See Expansion of Committee Staff Chapter, p. 105)*

Allocating Patronage Jobs

There are several hundred acknowledged patronage employees on Capitol Hill. They include chauffeurs, doorkeepers, elevator operators, pages and employees of the House and Senate post office. Most of the positions are supervised by the House doorkeeper and Senate sergeant-at-arms. Patronage privileges are meted out to members of Congress under a puzzling combination of written rules and traditions, which often contradict each other. The exceptions to the written procedures are so numerous and diverse that they have all but usurped the rules.

Of the two chambers, the House has the more clearly defined method for distributing patronage jobs among its members. The five-member patronage committee of the majority party controls all patronage jobs in the House. The committee assigns a small quota of the jobs to the minority party at the beginning of each session. These include such positions as clerk or page in the minority cloakroom. The remaining patronage jobs are allocated largely on the basis of seniority, though this is not a formal rule, and no seniority quota exists. In 1982 House Democrats in the New York State delegation were the only ones to pool their patronage slots to provide what they felt would be a more equitable distribution of the jobs.

The patronage committee was first established by a caucus of Democratic representatives in 1911. Three members of the Ways and Means Committee were chosen by the caucus to distribute patronage positions. Committee chairmen were excluded from the general distribution of patronage because they already had the power to make committee staff appointments.

When the Republicans won a majority in the House in 1918 they set up their own patronage committee, with rules that generally followed the Democrats' practice. In 1982 the majority committee responsible for patronage distribution, officially titled the House Democratic Personnel Committee, consisted of five members, and its counterpart, the Republican Personnel Committee, had eight members. But in the preceding decade, patronage distribution had become increasingly informal. The panels did not keep a list of patronage jobs and did not know how many existed at any one time.

In the Senate, patronage allocation is handled through the office of the secretary of the majority party, which gives the sergeant-at-arms a list of those senators entitled to patronage slots. As in the House, seniority is the general criterion used for distributing patronage. The minority party is entitled to fill one-third of the patronage positions; these are allocated through the office of the minority party secretary.

Current Practices

Today most support jobs on both sides of Capitol Hill are awarded on the basis of merit rather than patronage. The congressional empire has so dwindled that some senior members count themselves fortunate if they can appoint a few elevator operators or a mailman in the Senate or House post office.

The last blow to the system was dealt in 1969, when the Nixon administration decided to remove 63,000 postmaster and rural carrier appointments from politics. Instead, special boards were set up to select candidates for these positions. The Postal Reorganization Act of 1970, which established the U.S. Postal Service, put an end to patronage in the post office.

Patronage in the Capitol Police force was sharply reduced in the early 1970s. In 1971 patronage appointees constituted 25 percent of the total force. By 1975 there were no patronage police jobs on the Senate side and only 109 out of 627 positions on the House side. By 1982 the total number of patronage positions on the force had fallen to 45, and patronage appointees were required to meet the same standards and to undergo the same training as other members of the Capitol Police.

Many of the remaining jobs on Capitol Hill that used to be full-time patronage positions in 1982 were filled by college students and other persons in need of financial assistance. Students are thus able to work a shift as an elevator operator or chamber doorman and then go to

Civil Service History

American political patronage reached its peak in the post-Civil War era, when senators spent much of their time keeping track of patronage in their states and were allowed to dictate major appointments.

In 1881, for example, both of New York's senators resigned after President James A. Garfield refused to nominate their choice for the lucrative position of Collector of the Port of New York.

Both senators expected the New York Legislature to express its support by re-electing them. But before the Legislature could meet, Garfield was assassinated by a disappointed patronage seeker.

Public revulsion over the assassination and the excesses of patronage led two years later to passage of the Pendleton Act, the first major attempt at civil service reform in America.

The Pendleton Act set up a three-man bipartisan board, the Civil Service Commission, and empowered it to certify applicants for federal employment after competitive examinations.

The original act covered only about 10 percent of federal employees, but its key provision gave the president power to expand the civil service classifications by executive order. A series of such orders and additional legislation in the following years removed from politics nearly all nonpolicy-level jobs in the government.

The Civil Service received unexpected support from Garfield's successor, Chester Alan Arthur.

In 1884 the Pendleton Act produced one more disappointed office seeker — its sponsor, Sen. George H. Pendleton, D-Ohio. Pendleton was defeated for re-election by Henry Payne, an outspoken advocate of the patronage system.

classes. The turnover rate is high, but in most cases the efficiency of the operation is not affected because most of the patronage involves blue-collar slots requiring relatively unskilled labor.

The office of the doorkeeper is responsible for overseeing the largest number of patronage jobs in the House. Nearly all of the 376 positions authorized in 1982 by that office were filled through patronage. The doorkeeper supervises the officers of the press galleries, the doormen for the visitors' gallery and for the House chamber, the custodians, barbers, pages, and employees of the House Document room and the "folding room," which distributes newsletters, speeches and other materials for representatives.

The clerk of the House had 475 authorized positions in 1982, but relatively few were filled through patronage. However, of the 98 employees in the House post office nearly all were hired through patronage.[42]

A handful of other patronage jobs in the House, less clearly defined, are located in the offices of the majority and minority leaders, the parliamentarian, the minority sergeant-at-arms and the whips of both political parties.

The sergeant-at-arms of the Senate, who, along with the sergeant-at-arms of the House, has partial responsibility for the Capitol Police, also supervises a number of patronage employees. Of 1,213 Senate employees supervised by the sergeant-at-arms in 1982, 115 were strictly patronage appointments, although the remainder also could be appointed on that basis. The patronage positions included the Senate pages, doormen, elevator operators, custodians, officers of the Senate press galleries and employees of the Senate post office.

While patronage generally is restricted to non-skilled jobs, there is a group of Capitol Hill officials (technically not patronage employees, but many of whom oversee patronage positions) whose jobs depend on the influence of sponsors or on the party in control and the favor of the party leadership. The House doorkeeper, the House and Senate sergeants-at-arms, the secretary of the Senate and the clerk of the House work for all members of their respective houses, but they are elected by the members on strict party-line votes.

Appointments to Military Academies

One remnant of the patronage system has not only survived over the years but has continued to expand. Congressional appointees to the three major service academies account for more than three-fourths of these academies' combined enrollment. Although there have been proposals to remove all academy appointments from the patronage system, members of Congress have been reluctant to let the last sizable group in the congressional patronage system slip away from them.

Until 1902 the privilege of appointing candidates for admission to the academies was enjoyed only by representatives, the idea being to apportion academy enrollment on the basis of national population. Each congressional district was to supply one appointee every four years, thus giving each class maximum geographic variance and assuring equal distribution of appointments throughout the nation.

Eventually, senators and representatives alike were authorized to have as many as five appointees enrolled in each academy at one time. In 1982 the total enrollment at the U.S. Military Academy at West Point, N.Y., was set by law at 4,474. Of that number, 70 percent or more were congressional appointees. The maximum number of cadets at the U.S. Naval Academy at Annapolis, Md., was set at 4,425, 2,175 of whom could be appointed by Congress. Of about 4,500 cadets enrolled at the U.S. Air Force Academy at Colorado Springs, Colo., about 73 percent were congressional appointees.[43]

In appointing young men and women for cadetships at the academies, members of Congress have wide leeway in making their choices. Most senators and many representatives do not personally handle the screening of candidates. The job of selecting nominees usually falls to an administrative assistant in the senator's state office or the representative's home district.

In 1964 Congress set a quota of five cadet appointees in each academy at any one time per member of Congress. Either of two methods of selecting appointees may be used, the choice being left to the member.

●The general listing method allows for only minimal congressional influence in the selection. A list of as many as 10 candidates is submitted to each of the respective academies. Scholastic and physical tests are given the candidates, and the one making the best combined performance wins the appointment.

●The principal-alternate method allows the member far greater influence in the appointment process. Again, a list of as many as 10 candidates is submitted to the academy, but each candidate is ranked in order of the member's preference. If the first-preference candidate meets the academic and physical entrance requirements, then that candidate wins the appointment regardless of how well the other candidates perform. If the first-preference candidate does not fulfill the entrance requirements, then the first-alternate is considered and so on down the list until a qualified candidate is found.

The principal-alternate method may be used by a member when he feels that a particular young person has outstanding potential in some area that is not weighted heavily in the entrance requirements, such as creative talents or outstanding athletic ability. Of course, the method also can be use to ensure the appointment of a member's relative, if qualified, or the relative of a friend.

Before candidates can be considered for appointment, they must undergo scholastic, physical and medical testing. No candidate may be older than 21. He or she must be of "good moral character" and must never have been married. Candidates must also be United States citizens, unless they are entering one of the academies on a special program for foreigners. Persons already in military service who wish to attend one of the academies may take the annual competitive examination. If they score well they will be appointed.

A member of Congress also may nominate as many as 10 persons for appointment to the Merchant Marine Academy, Kings Point, N.Y. The candidates must take a nationally competitive examination to win appointment. No nominee on any member's list is guaranteed appointment. Instead, the highest-scoring candidates are appointed to the freshman class, regardless of who nominated them.

Members of Congress play no role in the selection of candidates to the U.S. Coast Guard Academy, New London, Conn.

Footnotes

1. Roger H. Davidson and Walter J. Oleszek, *Congress and Its Members* (Washington, D.C.: CQ Press, 1981), p. 237.

2. James Madison, *Notes of Debates in the Federal Convention of 1787,* with an Introduction by Adrienne Koch (Athens, Ohio: Ohio University Press, 1966), p. 198.
3. *Congressional Quarterly Weekly Report,* Aug. 9, 1975, p. 1803.
4. Certiorari denied May 26, 1981.
5. Common Cause press release, March 17, 1982.
6. U.S., Congress, House, Democratic Study Group, "The Outside Income Issue," Special Report No. 97-46, June 16, 1982, p. 7.
7. Davidson and Oleszek, *Congress and Its Members,* p. 237.
8. *The New York Times,* Nov. 4, 1975, p. 33.
9. Figures provided by Senate Disbursing Office and House Finance Office, June 1982.
10. Davidson and Oleszek, *Congress and Its Members,* p. 40.
11. Hearings for fiscal years 1970-83 before the House Legislative Branch Appropriations Subcommittee.
12. *The New York Times,* Jan. 16, 1977, p. 24.
13. Irwin B. Arieff, "Growing Staff System on Hill Forcing Changes in Congress," *Congressional Quarterly Weekly Report,* Nov. 24, 1979, p. 2638.
14. Brigette Rouson, "Hill Workers Often Receive High Pay, But Face Unemployment at Any Time, *Congressional Quarterly Weekly Report,* Nov. 24, 1979, p. 2644.
15. Figures provided by Senate Disbursing Office, June 1982.
16. Davidson and Oleszek, *Congress and Its Members,* p. 237.
17. Irwin B. Arieff, "Growing Staff System on Hill Forcing Changes in Congress," p. 2637.
18. U.S., Congress, Senate, Committee on Rules and Administration, *Congressional Handbook-U.S. Senate,* 96th Congress, 2d sess., November 1980, p. 19.
19. Christopher Buchanan, "Campaigning By Staff Aides Is Still a Common Practice," *Congressional Quarterly Weekly Report,* Oct. 28, 1978, p. 3116.
20. Richard F. Fenno, Jr., *Home Style: House Members in Their Districts* (Boston: Little, Brown & Co., 1978), p. 46.
21. Figure provided by House Administration Committee, July 1982.
22. "Committee Limits Spending From House Office Funds," *Congressional Quarterly Weekly Report,* Nov. 12, 1977, p. 2406.
23. *The Washington Post,* June 17, 1980, p. A10.
24. Irwin B. Arieff, "House Administration Panel Hikes Expense Allowances; First Increase Since 1979," *Congressional Quarterly Weekly Report,* May 16, 1981, p. 867.
25. Figure provided by Senate Disbursing Office, July 1982.
26. Davidson and Oleszek, *Congress and Its Members,* p. 125.
27. Irwin B. Arieff, "Packwood's Solution to Office Chaos," *Congressional Quarterly Weekly Report,* Nov. 24, 1979, p. 2640.
28. *Congressional Insight,* vol. VI, no. 18, (Washington, D.C.: Congressional Quarterly, April 30, 1982).
29. Ibid.
30. Figure provided by the office of Rep. Dan Glickman, D-Kan., July 1982.
31. Ibid.
32. Figures provided by the United States Capitol Historical Society, July 1982.
33. "ADA Special Report: Advantages of an Incumbent Seeking Re-Election" (Washington, D.C.: Americans for Democratic Action, December 1980).
34. "Judging A Perk By Its Cover," *Common Cause,* October 1981, p. 10.
35. U.S., Congress, Senate, *Report of the Secretary of the Senate from Oct. 1, 1981, to March 31, 1982,* (Washington, D.C.: U.S. Government Printing Office, 1982), p. 5.
36. Testimony of Howard S. Liebengood, Senate Sergeant-at-Arms, before the Senate Committee on Rules and Administration, Feb. 2, 1982.
37. Common Cause, et al., plaintiffs, v. William F. Bolger, et al., defendants, memorandum in support of plaintiffs' motion for summary judgment, filed in the U.S. District Court for the District of Columbia, May 22, 1981.
38. Irwin B. Arieff, "Computers and Direct Mail Are Being Married on the Hill to Keep Incumbents in Office," *Congressional Quarterly Weekly Report,* July 21, 1979, pp. 1445-1452.
39. William L. Safire, *The New Language of Politics: A Dictionary of Catchwords, Slogans and Political Usage,* rev. ed. (New York: Collier Books, 1972), p. 196.
40. Richard Whittle, "There May Be Foreign Travel Abuses, But Few Members Talk About Them," *Congressional Quarterly Weekly Report,* Aug. 22, 1981, pp. 1546-1547.
41. *The New York Times,* Nov. 9, 1981.
42. Figures from hearings for fiscal 1982 before the House Legislative Branch Appropriations Subcommittee and the Office of the Senate Sergeant-at-Arms.
43. Figures obtained from the Washington offices of West Point and the U.S. Air Force Academy, and from the superintendent's office at Annapolis.

Pressures on Congress

Congress writes laws for the entire nation. But members perform another duty, equally crucial in a representative assembly, as links between the American people and the federal government.

All senators and representatives are emissaries from states or congressional districts. Some come from booming resource-producing states and rural farming regions. Others represent populous industrial states or impoverished urban ghettos. As members of Congress, they are expected to voice their constituents' needs and views in the U.S. Capitol and before federal agencies as well.

The dual roles of Congress — making laws and responding to constituents' demands — were bound tightly together when the U.S. Constitution set up a legislature elected from states and from geographic districts. Since the First Congress formed in 1789, those two functions have forced members continually to balance great national issues with vital local concerns. As an ever-expanding legislative agenda made serving in Congress a full-time job, pressures have mounted on members to help constituents deal with a government that increasingly affects their daily lives.

But the voters are not the only group exerting pressures on Congress. Others include the media, members of Congress themselves, the president, the Supreme Court and lobbyists.

GOVERNMENT BY THE PEOPLE

The Constitution gives Congress specific legislative powers, but it does not spell out the duty of members to respond to constituent demands. That responsiblity nevertheless inevitably flows from the Constitution's requirement that the House of Representatives be elected directly by the people every two years — as well as from the 1913 amendment that substituted direct election to the Senate for selection by state legislatures. It has deep roots in the theory of representative government and in the American national experience.

The relationships between a member of Congress and his constitutents is the crux of self-government in the United States. The vitality of that relationship alone assures that government by laws enacted in Congress is also government by the people.

Prior to the American Revolution the colonists were English subjects who were represented, in theory, in the English Parliament. It was precisely the fictitious character of this representation against which the colonists rebelled. Having experienced government by their own elected representative in the colonial legislatures, their patience with remote rulers was limited. The frustrations imposed by a government in which they did not participate impressed upon Americans the importance of exercising continuous control over the government. They expected lawmakers to be dominated by their constituents because they were rebelling against a regime too independent of its subjects.

The framers of the Constitution constructed a bi-cameral national legislature to represent the states as well as the people. Constitutional provisions made the House the most representative unit of the federal government, with members elected for two-year terms directly by the voters. James Madison, writing in *The Federalist Papers*, maintained that the House was intended to have "an immediate dependence on, and an intimate sympathy with, the people."

But the founders responding to small states' fear that more populous regions would dominate the central government, insulated the Senate from the popular sentiments that the House would reflect. The Constitution therefore assigned two Senate seats to each state, set terms at six years and directed that senators be elected by state legislatures, not by the states' voters. Those provisions kept the Senate one step removed from the people.

Instruction of Representatives

In the first session of the First Congress, an amendment to the Bill of Rights was proposed that would have constitutionally guaranteed the right of the people "to instruct their representatives." Reps. Elbridge Gerry of Massachusetts and John D. Page of Virginia argued the case for instructions.

Much of the debate in the House centered on the question of whether instructions would be binding upon the representative. Yet, despite the inclusion of the princi-

ple of instructions in several state constitutions, the preponderance of opinion in the First Congress was that members should act as trustees for the whole nation, and not
merely as agents for their constituencies.

In its earliest years the House itself took up and debated most of the limitations that might legitimately be
placed on control of representatives by constituents even
though the people were recognized as sovereign. Many
arguments have been used to justify independence from
constituency pressures: The dangers of momentary popular
passion or caprice; the priority of considered popular
judgement expressed in the Constitution; the practical difficulties of establishing authentic constituent instructions,
and of reconciling conflicting ones; the information often
available to the representatives but not to constituents; the
need to deliberate, and to combine different viewpoints;
the sufficiency of the ballot box for controlling legislators;
and the priority of the national interest over local interests.

State Legislators and the Senate

But the Senate, elected by state legislatures, was more
responsive to instructions until the 20th century. The Senate was deliberately separated from the voters. Its constituents were not the people but the state governments, whose
legislators chose them. Senators came to the seat of government somewhat in the guise of ambassadors of semi-sover-
eign states. Their august name suggested the patrician
traditions of the Roman Senate; and the analogous upper
chamber in Great Britain, the House of Lords, was not
elected at all. The functions of senators included those of
an executive council — advice and consent in international
affairs and approval of presidential appointments. At first,
their debates were held in closed session, for they were not
responsible to the general electorate.

In the Constitutional Convention, the small states gave
vent to their fears of domination by the more populous
states. After it was determined that the House of Representatives would be chosen by popular election, the small
states made a stand for election of the second body of the
Congress, the Senate, by the state legislatures. The Great
Compromise shaped the function of the Senate by securing
equality of state representation in it.

Selection of senators by state legislatures posed no
problem for the majority of delegates in 1787. During the
American Revolution, the states entrusted their legislatures with paramount powers. The legislatures had elected
delegates to the Continental Congress, the Congress of the
Confederation and to the Constitutional Convention itself.

Selection of senators by the state legislators separated
senators from direct influence by the people — furthered
by giving senators six-year terms. Because the voters could
not show their preference for U.S. senators, the state legislators enjoyed great freedom in naming them and sometimes adopted the practice of instructing senators they
elected.

Insofar as the senator was considered an ambassador
of his state, the practice of giving instructions seemed
perfectly normal. The size and operation of the legislatures
made the practice of instruction a simple matter. To
strengthen the state's control over its senators, some urged
that legislatures be empowered to recall them. Legislatures
had enjoyed such power under the Articles of Confederation, and constitutional amendments to provide such recall were introduced frequently in the early years of the
Republic.

In the early years of Congress, senators generally
obeyed instructions received from state legislatures. State
legislatures, not surprisingly, were more inclined than the
senators themselves to consider their wishes binding on
their senators' actions. From the First Congress, some of
them sent instructions to the men they had chosen for the
Senate, a practice that reached a peak in the second quarter of the 19th century. The distinction between responsibility of senators and representatives to legislatures was
evident in the formula commonly used, of which one
adopted by the Tennessee General Assembly in 1940 serves
as an example: "That our Senators to Congress be *instructed* and our Representatives *requested* to vote against
the chartering by Congress of a National Bank." (Italics
added)

Direct Election of Senators

In 1913 the 17th Amendment, requiring direct election
of senators, entirely freed members of the upper house
from the constraints of legislative instructions. They were
thenceforth representatives of a different constituency —
the people of their states. Indeed, in many states they
could have claimed to represent the will of the people more
effectively than legislatures elected from malapportioned
districts. The shift to direct election did not imply, however, that the popular electorate would instruct senators as
legislatures had done.

Direct election confirmed that senators would have the
same freedom as House members to exercise independent
judgement on national issues. Although senators still
served for six-year terms, the requirement that they face
the voters also made them responsive to constituents' demands.

The extent of a senator's responsiveness, however, varied widely depending on the distance to the next elections
and the person's political popularity. In any case, senators
generally have enjoyed more independence than House
members.

Pork Barrel Politics

Most senators and representatives, even the most powerful, take care to justify their performance to the voters
who sent them to Congress. Even senior members who
spend most of their time on national issues craft images for
consumption back home to convince constituents that they
constantly watch out for state or district interests. Virtually all members try to protect their electoral bases through
the time-honored "pork barrel" politics by which Congress
distributes federal dams, military bases, grant and other
government benefits across the American landscape.

Congress cannot specify exactly where every dollar of
federal spending goes. Outlays for most programs are allocated by formulas written into law or by federal agencies
that decide where to build new facilities and award contracts for government purchases. But in federal public
works programs where spending is concentrated in local
areas Congress itself still designates the precise location of
projects through legislation.

In particular, Congress has kept a firm hold on the
distribution of federal water projects that dredge harbors
and build dams to control floods or store water. Those
projects are built and run by the Army Corps of Engineers
and by the Interior Department's Bureau of Reclamation
in the West. Typically, local officials and businessmen
conceive a water project; then congressional delegations

champion the plan in Congress. Even if a project's costs far outweigh its benefits, House and Senate logrolling usually assures support from other members who have their own projects to push.

Constituent Communications

Members of Congress have ample opportunity to demonstrate concern for their constituents. Despite the press of heavy House and Senate legislative agendas, senators and representatives also find time to keep their names before the voters back home in the states and districts.

The average House member makes 35 trips a year back to the district that elected him. Even in Washington, members spend just as much — if not more — time and effort working on constituent relations as in floor and committee sessions. Through an impressive array of resources — large staffs, media appearances, newsletters, mass mailings and travel — senators and representatives constantly cultivate what political scientist Richard F. Fenno Jr. identified in a 1978 study as "home style" that members present to constituents.

Members make use of a variety of channels in communicating with the people in their states and districts. Whatever roles senators and representatives adopt, they must know their constituents' views as they perform congressional duties. Members also seek to keep voters informed on national issues and their own committee and floor activities.

The volume of constituent contacts has mushroomed in the last few decades with technological change and sophisticated techniques for analyzing public opinion. Old-fashioned constituent mail from concerned voters still consumes the largest share of congressional staff time. More and more, however, members use taped television shows, computerized mailings, opinion polls and election returns surveys to assess constituent views and shape voter opinion.

Election returns are perhaps the most impressive indicators of constituent opinion. A member of Congress is highly conscious of the margins by which he and his predecessors have been elected. Because voting patterns are affected by so many factors, such as candidate personality, party affiliation and specific issues, the bare figure given only crudely hints of local sentiment. Breakdown of these figures by neighborhood may indicate which interest groups supported or opposed a member, and inferences can be drawn to explain the causes of that support or opposition. Shifts in population and voter registration within a district may indicate shifts in the strength of opinion on some issues. Ward-by-ward, precinct-by-precinct analysis of voting statistics assumes major significance when state legislatures redistrict House seats.

Americans also send members of Congress millions of letters and postcards each year, asking assistance or urging support for their positions on issues before the House and Senate. In turn, senators and representatives use their free franking privileges to send hundreds of millions of letters and newsletters a year — often using congressional computers to target the mail to particular groups they want to reach.

Constituents may come to Washington to contact their representatives or senators about legislation or to seek their assistance on individual matters. They may request help on business with a government agency, job hunting, a term paper, introductions to officials, or other matters. But the largest number of visitors from the home state or district are tourists who stop by the member's office. They may take advantage of the opportunity to make known their views or need, but they are more likely to seek information and aid as tourists in the nation's capital.

The staff welcomes constituents, knowing the importance of the direct impression they will take back to the district or state. Information about Washington tourist attractions and the federal government is provided in a variety of booklets and brochures; the office staff may prepare calendars of events as well. Passes to House and Senate visitors' galleries are handed out, and special tours of the White House and some executive agencies may be arranged.

For many Americans, the most memorable contact they have with Congress comes through "casework" that a member and his staff do to assist them in dealing with the government. Few members may relish that part of their work, but they all acknowledge that prompt and effective casework for constituents pays off in election support.

Most casework is handled by the staff. A telephone call to the appropriate agency is often sufficient, especially when the request is only for information. More complex matters, or those requiring a record of the transaction, are usually sent to the agency in writing. The constituent's letter, or a restatement of it by the senator or representative, may be used. A reply signed by the head of the agency is expected, and the member often forwards copies of it to the constituent.

Most members of Congress deal personally with difficult cases, or those involving personal friends, important supporters, influential figures in the district, or large numbers of constituents. When the member does intervene personally, he increases the chances of a prompt and favorable response. While some members will pursue cases to the point of appearing as counsel for constituents, many are reluctant to spend the time or exert the influence required to press individual matters that far.

THE MEDIA: OPEN TREND CONTINUES

Congress is an open institution. The House and Senate conduct most of the nation's business in public sessions, under scrutiny by all who watch. And the nation's news media, the press and radio-television journalists alike, cover Capitol Hill more thoroughly than they cover any other branch of government.

More than 4,000 reporters hold credentials to the House and Senate press galleries, and about 400 cover Congress exclusively.[1] At least a few watch every floor session from House or Senate press galleries, and some reporters sit in on most committee hearings and markup sessions. Media attention increased during the 1970s as Congress opened more of its activities than ever before to the press and public.

The trend toward open proceedings intensified the pressure that media coverage puts on members. As a result of changes in congressional rules and procedures, almost all House and Senate committees do their work, including the drafting of bills, in public sessions. Conference committees hammer out final decisions on compromise legislation with reporters and lobbyists crowding the rooms in which they work. And both the House and Senate now record members' votes on most questions of any importance during floor debate on legislation. In 1979, the House itself began televising floor proceedings.

In consequence, the press and constituents — as well as political opponents — watch members' actions more closely than ever before. After the Watergate scandal of the early 1970s, moreover, the Washington press corps stayed constantly on the alert for scandals and official misconduct, in Congress as well as the White House.

But the relationship between Congress and the press remains a two-way proposition, partly hostile but partly symbiotic. For senators and representatives, while coping with constant press scrutiny, also use news organizations that cover Capitol Hill to keep the public informed about their legislative accomplishments. And despite their post-Watergate toughness, journalists still rely on members to supply them with the news about government that reporters are paid to gather.

News media, in fact, play a vital if unofficial role in the way Congress and the entire federal government operate. Most members, as successful politicians, are skilled at courting journalists. Virtually all senators and representatives keep press secretaries on their Capitol office staffs to manage dealings with reporters and distribute releases to newspapers and to radio and television stations. Some members, most often senators, gain national prominence through major newspapers and television network news. And most members, in the House as well as the Senate, try to maintain cordial relations with reporters and editors from local press and radio stations that convey congressional news to constituents.

National Media

Most of the men and women accredited to the congressional press galleries spend relatively little time on Capitol Hill and many are technicians, photographers and other non-reporters. They work for a highly varied communications industry — newspapers, newsletters, magazines, and radio and television networks and stations — both national and local in focus. Newspapers, magazines and broadcasters in other nations assign an estimated 450 correspondents to Washington.

The national media not only report news about the federal government to readers and viewers. They also link different parts of the government, keeping policy makers informed on what other officials are doing. In exercising their discretion about which news developments to report and how much emphasis to give them, reporters and editors exert considerable impact on the governmental process. The national press, especially the television networks, pays more attention to the Senate than to the House. With fewer members, including well-known celebrities and presidential hopefuls, the Senate is considered more glamorous than the House. Few representatives, except for House leaders, committee chairmen and perhaps colorful mavericks, draw much attention from the national media.

But most members, in the House as well as the Senate, deal regularly with local media located in their states and districts. Nearly 10,000 newspapers and more than 10,000 periodicals are published in the United States, and nearly 9,000 radio stations and more than 1,000 television stations broadcast from cities all over the country. Nearly all carry some congressional news, but they usually rely on the wire services, networks or newspaper chain bureaus for most of their Washington coverage.

Most senators and representatives are eager to provide interviews and information to reach constituents through local media. To cover local stories, on the other hand, reporters from the local press and regional bureaus often rely on a few members and their staffs from the states and districts involved. As a result, members and reporters frequently stay on friendly terms; local media coverage is generally considered less aggressive than the national media's.

Historic Role of the Press

The nation's news media — and especially the Washington press corps — now assume significant power in the American governmental process. Their influence was not envisioned, however, by the men who founded the federal government after the 13 American colonies won independence.

The Constitutional Convention of 1787 — like the Continental Congress that ran the country during the Revolutionary War — met behind closed doors. As originally framed, the Constitution adopted in 1787 omitted any guarantee for freedom of the press or speech. But during its first decade in the 1790s, the fledgling government moved to assure that an independent press would scrutinize how it conducted the nation's business.

As first conceived, the American form of government provided no legal protection for a press bent on perusing the activities of government officials. This omission was criticized by Thomas Jefferson, who was in France at the time of the Constitutional Convention. In early 1787, Jefferson had written from Paris: "The people are the only censors of their governors; and even their errors will tend to keep these to the true principles of their institution. To punish these errors too severely would be to suppress the only safeguard of the public liberty. The way to prevent these irregular interpositions of the people is to give them full information of their affairs thru the channel of the public papers, & to contrive that those papers would penetrate the whole mass of the people. The basis of our government being the opinion of the people, the very first object should be to keep that right; and were it left to me to decide whether we should have a government without newspapers or newspapers without a government, I should not hesitate for a moment to prefer the latter." [2]

The main opposition to a guarantee of press freedom came from Alexander Hamilton, who wrote in *The Federalist* (No. 84): "What signifies a declaration that 'the liberty of the press shall be inviolably preserved'? What is the liberty of the press? Who can give it any definition which would not leave the utmost latitude for evasion? I hold it to be impracticable; and from this, I infer, that its security, whatever fine declarations may be inserted in any Constitution respecting it, must altogether depend on public opinion, and on the general spirit of the people and of the government." [3] At the Constitutional Convention, Hamilton had been able to repel attempts by James Madison and George Mason to add to the Constitution a Bill of Rights including a guarantee of freedom of the press.

Advocates of constitutional protection of freedom of the press finally won the struggle in 1791, when Virginia became the necessary 11th state to ratify a Bill of Rights consisting of 10 constitutional amendments. The first of the amendments provided: "Congress shall make no law respecting an establishment of religion, or prohibiting the free exercise thereof; or abridging the freedom of speech, or of the press; or the right of the people peaceably to assemble, and to petition the government for a redress of grievances."

Press Coverage of Congress

Like the concept of freedom of the press, newspaper coverage of Congress was not envisioned by the Founders of the Republic. Following the example of the British Parliament, which had never admitted reporters to its proceedings (and continued to exclude them until 1834), the U.S. House and Senate both adopted rules in 1789 excluding reporters. The rules were short-lived, however, as the House opened its proceedings to press coverage in 1790 and the Senate did the same in 1793.[4] In 1841, the Senate excluded reporters of local Washington newspapers to benefit the national party organs then prevalent in the capital. Since that time, neither chamber has sought to exclude correspondents, except from executive sessions. However, some individual reporters have been denied admission for misconduct or other violation of the standing rules of the press galleries.

The Capitol Hill press corps grew steadily to several hundred journalists during the 19th century and into the first decades of the 20th century. But the number of reporters covering Congress and federal agencies subsequently jumped dramatically during a 50-year period as the government took on vastly larger responsibilities.

Four congressional correspondents covered the House and Senate in 1813-14, and only 12 by 1823. By 1868 the number had risen to 58; by 1900, to 171; by 1930, to 251. The congressional press corps had climbed to 1,326 by 1960, however, and by 1980 stood at 1,450 correspondents holding House and Senate press gallery cards. Another 1,200 were accredited to the radio and television galleries and an equal number to the periodical press galleries.

Congress, mindful of the value of news reports to members, has been generous in setting up press facilities in the Capitol and in congressional office buildings. The House and Senate wings of the Capitol completed in 1857 included special press galleries. The House and Senate each set aside a long section of gallery, just above and behind the dais, for exclusive use by accredited correspondents. Unlike spectators sitting in public galleries above the other three sides of the chambers, journalists are permitted to take notes as they observe floor proceedings.

Rooms just outside the press galleries also are reserved for correspondents. Capitol press facilities provide typewriters, telephones and teletype machines, along with restrooms, coffee and candy machines and huge leather couches. Gallery staffers, paid by Congress, take messages, page reporters and provide other services to correspondents. Studios just off the House and Senate floors hold facilities for television and radio broadcasts and interviews.

House and Senate office buildings also contain press rooms for reporters to use when covering committee sessions or members' offices. Most congressional committees, especially those that draw major media attention, reserve press tables for reporters attending hearings or markup sessions. Committee staffs provide journalists with printed copies of testimony, members' remarks, draft bills and committee reports. A few committees are less accommodat-

ing. The House Rules Committee, for instance, has little room for reporters to crowd into its cramped meeting room near the House chamber.

Since early in the century, House and Senate committees have followed a policy of holding public hearings on most major legislation. Some exceptions are made, notably when panels hear testimony on classified matters from defense or intelligence officials. Before the 1970s, committee markup sessions in which members voted to amend or approve proposed bills were closed to press as well as the public. But House and Senate rules now require open markup sessions unless committee members vote specifically to bar reporters.

The House began regular televised sessions in 1979. The Senate in 1978 permitted radio broadcasts of its debates on the Panama Canal treaty. In 1981, after Republicans took control of the Senate, Majority Leader Howard H. Baker, R-Tenn., sponsored a resolution to authorize television coverage of Senate debates, but many senators remained opposed.

Vote Recording

In modern times, the *Congressional Record,* a nonpartisan publication of Congress, has provided a check for the press and public on the breakdown of roll-call votes. The *Record* has been unreliable, however, as a reference on congressional debates, because members are permitted to edit their remarks before the *Record* goes to the printer. In addition, the *Record* did not provide the breakdown of teller and standing votes, under which much important business was conducted in the House. However, the Legislative Reorganization Act of 1970 required that a breakdown of teller votes be recorded. Previously, the only check on members during a non-record vote was provided by teams of reporters who watched the vote and published the breakdown.

In the years since World War II, a further check on members has been made by Congressional Quarterly, which publishes breakdowns of all roll-call votes taken in the House and Senate and each year analyzes each member's voting record on the basis of party support and other considerations. In addition, CQ covers congressional debates, provides detailed provisions of bills, analyzes legislative strategy and lobbying campaigns and provides various other reports on congressional activities. In 1982, another news magazine, *National Journal* began its own vote analysis and rating system.

Congressional News Leaks

Many veteran Washington politicians, in both the executive and legislative branches, are masters of selectively leaking confidential information to the press. But Congress, historically more open in its dealings with reporters, may contribute more than its share of leaks.

Leaks can serve many purposes: to raise an alarm about proposed government action, to set the stage for further maneuvering, to take first credit for significant developments, or simply to embarrass the political opposition. As the media began covering Congress and the executive branch more intensively — and as more members of Congress gained access to secret or classified briefings and documents — Capitol Hill became fertile ground for journalists seeking inside information.

While representatives and senators frequently attempt to use news leaks for their own advantage, Congress has long been plagued by improper or injudicious release of information received in confidence. The Senate Watergate Committee, for one example, was plagued by leaks during its highly publicized investigation into the Nixon White House scandal.

Some members develop close ties with reporters who cover them. Leaders of both houses of Congress work especially hard to ensure that their own and their party's actions get favorable publicity. Through sensitive media relations, members can readily influence news coverage of Congress. But in the process the nation's media change the way that senators and representatives act, and indeed how the House and Senate function. At times, moreover, the press can exert an enormous impact on what issues members address and what Congress does about them.

Press Investigations of Members

Media investigations have also revealed misconduct by members of Congress — and prodded the House and Senate to tighten congressional codes of ethics.

In the past, the press customarily overlooked personal problems of members of Congress. Reporters drew a fine line between public officals' private lives and activities that abused the public trust or brought personal financial gain. During the 1970s, however, media coverage contributed to the downfall of several powerful senators and representatives involved in congressional scandals.

House Ways and Means Committee Chairman Wilbur D. Mills, D-Ark. (1939-77), once unquestioned master of congressional tax legislation, for instance, lost that post and eventually retired from public life after a series of highly publicized 1974 incidents involving an Argentine striptease dancer. Two years later, Rep. Wayne L. Hays, D-Ohio (1949-76), powerful chairman of the House Administration Committee and Democratic Congressional Campaign Committee, resigned after *The Washington Post* reported that he had kept a mistress on the House payroll.

Media attention to congressional ethics continued in the late 1970s and early 1980s. The press and television gave heavy coverage to a series of disclosures, notably the Korean lobbying and Abscam scandals, that cast doubt on congressional integrity. Those revelations, particularly on network news broadcasts that reached every member's constitutency, damaged the reputation of Congress.

MEMBERS GENERATE INTERNAL PRESSURES

Congress is composed of 535 men and women — 100 senators and 435 representatives — all forceful, politically minded individuals. Each represents a distinct part of the country, and all are besieged by intense pressures from constituents, lobbyists, the press and presidents. Yet the House and Senate generate their own internal pressures on members that powerfully influence the way Congress operates.

Internal pressures on members, both formal and unspoken, are essential for Congress to get its work done. They operate among colleagues, usually out of public view, at institutional, professional and social levels. The late

House Speaker Sam Rayburn, D-Texas (1913-61), summed up their significance when he advised House members that "to get along, you have to go along." [5]

Since Rayburn's day, the arm-twisting powers of House and Senate leaders have been eroded by changes that have made Congress a more democratic institution. The growing role of television in congressional campaigns — along with the rise of special-interest groups armed with political action funds for favored candidates — have diminished party allegiances. By the early 1980s, members found they could campaign more effectively for re-election by becoming independent-minded powers in their own right.

Still, even with a new and restless breed of member, congressional leaders can call on institutional loyalties and personal debts as they try to forge majorities on legislation. Other colleagues — committee and subcommittee chairmen, members of state delegations and regional and special-interest caucuses, and even personal friends — influence members' votes by offering specialized knowledge or personal advice on issues. Party allegiance and political horse-trading still play important roles, along with the time-honored traditions in both the House and Senate that members should observe unwritten codes of conduct to keep personal differences from disrupting congressional work.

Rules and customs of both houses of Congress place powerful weapons in the hands of the power structure to help it work its will. Members who cooperate often are rewarded with a choice committee assignment or a coveted public works project, or by a display of personal approval from the leadership — an act that enhances the member's prestige among his colleagues and his effectiveness as a legislator.

By the same token, members who have not supported party leaders on important issues have been relegated to minor committees, denied the benefits of "pork-barrel" appropriations and shunned by the leadership and even rank-and-file party colleagues. Their refusal to go along may make them so ineffective at serving their constituents' interests that their chances of re-election are endangered.

The price of acting independently of party leaders and committee chairmen was reduced in the 1970s by structural and procedural reforms that weakened the arbitrary power of senior party members, broadened the influence of subcommittees and made the committee assignment and chairmen selection processes more democratic. Nonetheless, members in the 1980s still had to contend with many formidable internal pressures when deciding how to cast their votes.

Party Pressures in Congress

The nation's Founding Fathers did not anticipate the role that political parties would come to play at all levels of the national government. The Constitution, in setting up the legislative branch, made no provision for partisan leaders to organize the House and Senate and discipline their members. Yet, through the nearly two centuries that Congress has operated, party affiliations have been the most important determinants of how members acquired power and used it.

Party pressures have weakened steadily during the 20th century but remain significant influences on senators and representatives. A representative's party identification — as a Republican or a Democrat — still is the single most reliable factor for predicting how a member votes and performs.

Speaker of the House

The Speaker, as top-ranking member of the party that controls the House, is normally the most powerful legislative leader. Nominated by his party's caucus or conference, then elected by the whole House in what is customarily a party-line vote, the Speaker can potentially mount extraordinary pressure on members to toe his party's line. While hardly the all-powerful leader that sometimes dominated the House, the Speaker still has authority that can nurture or thwart an individual member's congressional career.

The Speaker's duties, which spring from the Constitution and from rules and traditions of the House, include presiding over House sessions, recognizing members to address the House, deciding points of order, referring bills and reports to the appropriate committees and House calendars, appointing the House conferees for House-Senate conferences on legislation, and appointing members of select committees. The Speaker normally wields considerable influence within his party's committee on committees, which assigns party members to standing committees. Although the Constitution does not stipulate that the Speaker must be a member of the House, no non-member has ever been elected to the post. The Speaker, like any other member, may vote and may lead debate on the floor. Over the years, some Speakers have run the House with iron wills. Others have been dominated by House committee chairmen or influential members. More recently, Speakers have been forced to work hard to cater to independent-minded individual members as party discipline has faded.

Both the majority and minority parties of the House and Senate appoint officials to shape and direct party strategy on the floor. These officials, known as the majority and minority leaders, devote their efforts to tying together the loose alliances which compose their parties in hopes of shaping them into voting majorities to pass or defeat bills. Majority floor leaders have considerable influence over the scheduling of debate and the selection of members to speak on bills. The majority leader in the House ranks just below the Speaker in importance. In the Senate, the majority leader is the most powerful officer because neither the vice president nor the president pro tempore holds substantive powers over the chamber's proceedings. In both houses, the floor leaders are in a position to wield considerable pressure on members through their influence over the party apparatus.

Each party appoints a whip and a number of assistant whips to assist the floor leader in execution of the party's legislative program. The main job of the whip is to canvass party members on a pending issue and give the floor leader an accurate picture of the support or opposition he may expect for the measure. Whips also are responsible for making sure that party members are on hand to vote. At the direction of the floor leader, the whips also may apply pressure to ensure that party members follow the leadership line.

Changing Leadership Styles

Congressional leadership styles have changed with the times. In the process, congressional party leaders more and more have been forced to follow their members instead of the other way around. In both the House and Senate, leaders have nurtured control by sensing what most members thought and taking care of their political needs. Most congressional leaders in recent years have preferred to use tact and persuasion rather than overt pressure to win support for party measures.

When a congressional leader resorts to overt pressure tactics, one of the most effective methods is the "carrot-and-stick" approach of promising prestigious committee assignments for members who cooperate and undesirable ones for those who don't.

No other leader in the history of Congress was more proficient at this tactic than was Lyndon B. Johnson, D-Texas, when he served as Senate Democratic floor leader from 1953 through 1960 (minority leader 1953-54, majority leader 1955-60).

For years, Johnson and Speaker Sam Rayburn teamed up to protect Texas oil interests through careful assignment of members to the tax-writing Senate Finance and House Ways and Means committees.

Meanwhile, House reforms in the mid-1970s, while generally giving members more independence, strengthened the Speaker's control over committee assignments. In a December 1974 caucus, House Democrats transferred authority to assign committee seats among party members from the Democratic members of the Ways and Means Committee to the newly revived Democratic Steering and Policy Committee.

Distribution of Public Works

Another effective pressure method is the selective distribution of public works projects to members' states or districts. This can be a powerful lever in the hands of a congressional leader or committee chairman, because the political success or failure of members is based at least partly on how much "boodle" the member can win for his district.

Economists and environmentalists have long objected that congressional pork-barrel politics produce wasteful and destructive water projects. From time to time, presidents have tried to cut congressionally approved funding for public works only to run into vociferous House and Senate resistance. President Jimmy Carter for instance stirred stormy protests with his 1977 "hit list" of water projects slated for cancellation.

Congressional support for the system rests on the members' presumption that, over time, they can win approval for projects in their state and districts.

Committee Chairmen's Powers

House and Senate committee chairmen can wield strong pressures, both on members of their panels and on the full membership on the floor. Congressional reforms reduced their arbitrary powers in the mid-1970s, spreading some authority among subcommittee chairmen and concentrating others in the leadership. But full committee chairmen nonetheless are positioned to hold considerable sway over legislation within their purview.

During the post-World War II decades, committee chairmen often dominated Congress, especially the House. Chairmen brokered competing interests within their panels and usually won full House consent to committee recommendations. They scheduled committee meetings, set legislative agendas, appointed members and staff to subcommittees and managed committee legislation on the floor. But other House members, restless under the chairmen's sway, gradually chipped away at the power held by veteran committee leaders as they retired or died in office. That process culminated in reforms that House Democrats adopted in the 1970s to dilute the chairmen's control over legislation. *(Committee changes, p. 79)*

In the Senate as well, the growing prominence of subcommittees has dispersed power among many members. But full committee chairmen, especially experienced and knowledgeable congressional veterans, still carry important authority.

Logrolling as a Pressure Tool

Because of the diversity of interests in both the House and Senate, members must often trade their votes to get their pet bills enacted. Such maneuvering, known as "logrolling," has been practiced in Congress since the early days of the Republic and in state legislatures before that. Two examples of the practice:

● In 1868, Rep. Ransom Gillet, D-N.Y. (1833-37), recalled that the way to enact a tariff bill was to provide protection for the local interests of enough representatives to ensure the bill's passage.

● In 1964 liberal Democrats in the House voted for wheat and cotton subsidies in return for the support of rural conservatives for a new food stamp program. Both bills were passed April 8, the food stamp measure by a 229-189 roll-call vote and the wheat-cotton bill by a roll call of 211-203. The Johnson administration had arranged the trade after both bills appeared to be foundering in the House.[6]

Distribution of Campaign Funds

Congressional leaders also may exert pressure on members through promises of financial aid in the member's reelection campaign. Both the Democratic and Republican parties have Senate and House campaign committees that parcel out funds to party members for help in their campaigns.

The committees date from 1866 when the Democratic members of both houses, who were opposing the attempt by Radical Republicans to impeach President Andrew Johnson, appointed their own committees to run the midterm campaign.[7]

The committees do not participate in party primaries, only in the general elections. Their effectiveness as a pressure tool is limited, because party leaders rarely will threaten to cut off funds to a recalcitrant member if it might mean the election of a candidate of the opposition party. Thus while party leaders can offer the "carrot" of additional campaign money as an inducement to follow the party line, they scarcely can afford to employ the "stick" of cutting off funds altogether.

In particular, changes in federal campaign financing laws in the mid-1970s spawned the rapid spread of political action committees (PACs) armed with campaign funds to distribute among friendly legislators. Representing corporations, labor unions, professional, trade and myriad other interest groups, PACs by the 1980s were contributing millions of dollars to members of Congress in key positions to help their interests. The growth of PACs paralleled the spread of single-interest groups deeply involved in political campaigns on behalf of their own particular views. They contributed to the splintering of national party authority and gave members of Congress more freedom from internal party pressures.

Regional, Philosophic Alliances

Congress, as a representative institution, gives full play to the myriad regional, cultural, economic and ethnic differences that divide the American people. Members of the House and Senate, both Republicans and Democrats, frequently work together for common interests. As party discipline declined and special-interest groups took active political roles, senators and representatives began forming more coalitions, both informal and highly organized, to articulate and pursue particular goals they shared.

For nearly 50 years, a "conservative coalition" of Republicans and Southern Democrats has joined on the House and Senate floor to influence and occasionally dominate economic and social policy debates. Some state delegations, senators as well as representatives, traditionally have worked closely together to protect their state's most important needs. Since the 1970s, members increasingly have organized themselves into formal caucuses — defined along ethnic, sex, regional or economic lines — to form united fronts on behalf of blacks, women, Spanish Americans, the steel and textile industries, the Sun Belt and Frost Belt states and many other interests that make up larger parts of their constituencies.

Caucus Proliferation

Most congressional alliances are informal, and they come into play only when specific issues are before the House and Senate. But as party strength has fallen off in Congress, members have joined to form more organized groups that develop common stands on issues important to them and their constituents.

By 1981 senators and representatives had set up nearly 70 special-interest caucuses, known officially as legislative service organizations. Some, like the Democratic Study Group (DSG) that liberal and moderate Democrats established in the 1950s, shaped common stands on a host of issues over many years. Several groups, such as the DSG and its Republican counterparts, established formal links among political allies who often disagreed with their party leaders. Other caucuses, most notably the Congressional Black Caucus, organized members from minority groups. And, as regional rivalries intensified within the nation in the 1970s over energy and economic policy, caucus organizations proliferated around Capitol Hill to advance the cause of industrial states, energy producing regions, the steel, coal and textile industries and many other economic and social interests.

Caucus alliances have thrived in the House, where many members may feel isolated and anonymous, even within their own parties. Such groups operate outside official House and Senate procedures, and their impact on legislation is mixed. Some members complain that caucuses further disperse power in Congress, but others maintain that such groups provide a focus for issues that congressional leaders and committees might otherwise ignore.

Some groups, particularly in the Senate, are little more than a circle of lunch-table companions. Other groups have scores of members, assess regular dues, hire large staffs and use congressional telephones and office space. In 1981, 26 legislative service organizations had registered with the House, making them eligible to use congressional office facilities.

In 1981 the House Administration Committee cracked down on special caucuses that used House facilities but also accepted contributions from outside sources. Under the committee's regulations, legislative service organizations that relied on private funding sources would be required to work out of private offices without congressional funds. These groups were required to sever their official ties with the House by January 1983.

CONGRESS AND THE PRESIDENT

The president is the strongest source of pressure on Congress. Strong presidents have learned to lobby Congress directly, in person or through staff. They've influenced Congress indirectly, by focusing public opinion. They've used government jobs, contracts and other forms of patronage. They've threatened to veto bills, and — when all else has failed — they've gone ahead and vetoed them.

The president's role as lawmaker begins with his constitutional duty to "from time to time give to the Congress Information of the State of the Union, and recommend to their Consideration such Measures as he shall judge necessary and expedient." [8] To these bare bones Congress has attached other obligations. The president is required, for example, to send Congress an annual budget message, setting forth his plans for taxes and spending, and an economic report, giving his program for achieving, among other things, "maximum employment, production and purchasing power." [9]

The Constitution only hints at how a president is supposed to go about persuading Congress to pass his economic program, his tax and spending plan and the other measures he deems necessary and expedient. "He may, on extraordinary Occasions, convene both Houses, or either of them." And "he shall nominate, and by and with the Advice and Consent of the Senate, shall appoint Ambassadors, other public Ministers and Consuls, Judges of the supreme Court, and all other Officers of the United States, whose Appointments are not otherwise provided for, and which shall be established by Law: but the Congress may by Law vest the appointment of such inferior Officers, as they think proper, in the President alone, in the Courts of Law, or in the Heads of Departments." [10]

Finally, the Constitution gives the president the power to "return . . . with his Objections" any bill Congress has passed but that he disapproves of. This is the veto power. [11]

History of Presidential Lobbying

Since the birth of the Republic, presidents have lobbied Congress in person or through helpers. Careful of the form if not the substance of separate powers, early presidents kept their congressional lobbying subdued and their helpers few. In recent years, presidential lobbying has become more open and elaborate.

In this century, presidents have used a variety of tactics to court Congress. Woodrow Wilson kept his lobbying as discreet as possible. Franklin D. Roosevelt used White House aides to exert pressure on Congress. Because their official duties included drafting legislation, they were natural choices to lobby to get bills enacted. Like Roosevelt, Harry S Truman used White House assistants in part-time legislative liaison roles.

Beginning with Dwight D. Eisenhower, presidents have appointed full-time legislative liaison officers to their White House staff. In addition, all federal departments now have their own congressional liaison forces. The practice began in 1945, when the War Department created the office of assistant secretary for congressional liaison, centralizing congressional relations that had been handled separately by the military services.

President John F. Kennedy sought to beef up the liaison function, appointing his long-time associate Lawrence F. O'Brien as chief lobbyist and giving O'Brien full authority to speak for him on legislative matters.

Kennedy and O'Brien made extensive use of the congressional liaison offices of the Cabinet departments and executive agencies. When an administration bill was introduced in Congress, the department involved was given prime responsibility for getting the measure through subcommittee and committee. When the bill neared House or Senate floor action, O'Brien and his corps of White House lobbyists joined forces with the agency liaison teams.

The liaison system Kennedy nurtured paid dividends during the Lyndon B. Johnson administration. Loyal Democrats had picked up a working margin of seats in the 1964 election and with O'Brien still supervising the liaison job, almost all of the old Kennedy measures sailed through Congress. Even when Johnson appointed O'Brien postmaster general, he continued as chief White House lobbyist, after Johnson himself. [12]

Although President Richard Nixon sought to slow down the furious pace of legislation that had marked the Johnson years, he still relied on a large liaison staff to push key administration bills. As chief lobbyist, he named Bryce Harlow, who came back to the White House after eight years of lobbying for the Procter & Gamble Co. Harlow served Nixon until April 1974, four months before Nixon's resignation. Besides Harlow, William E. Timmons, who had served in both Senate and House offices, handled much of Nixon's day-to-day congressional liaison.

When Timmons resigned as chief liaison officer, President Gerald R. Ford promoted Max L. Friedersdorf to the position. A former newspaper reporter, Friedersdorf had been an administrative assistant to a House member and a congressional relations officer with the Office of Economic Opportunity.

President Jimmy Carter, a newcomer to Washington, got off to a bad start by appointing another Georgian and an equally inexperienced hand, Frank B. Moore, as his chief congressional lobbyist. Moore quickly offended congressional sensibilities by failing to return phone calls, missing meetings and neglecting to consult adequately about presidential appointments and programs.

Six months after taking office, Carter reorganized his liaison team by geography and added several Washington veterans, including William H. Cable, a respected House staffer who was put in charge of lobbying the House. Moore also adopted some of Lawrence O'Brien's techniques for pushing major bills through Congress, including close coordination of White House and department lobbyists and personal intervention by the president before key votes. The White House also began using computers to analyze past votes and target supporters for the future.

President Ronald Reagan got off to a better start than Carter by bringing back Max Friedersdorf to head his liaison staff. Friedersdorf's chief assistants, Powell E. Moore in the Senate and Kenneth M. Duberstein in the House, had substantial experience on Capitol Hill. Friedersdorf left the White House at the end of 1981 and turned his job over to Duberstein.

Going to the People

When even the most skillful direct pressure fails, presidents often turn to the public for help in moving Congress. Going over congressional heads to the people has always required cultivation of reporters and others responsible for gathering and transmitting the news. Today, radio and television permit a president to go over reporters' heads, too, in marshaling public opinion.

Woodrow Wilson began the practice of holding regular and formal press conferences but was the most effective in his direct appeals to the public. Several weeks after his inauguration, he issued a statement attacking the "extraordinary exertions" of special interest groups to change his tariff bill. Although Wilson succeeded in having his way with the tariff, the technique failed him in 1919 when he conducted a whistle-stop tour of the country to drum up support for the League of Nations. He was followed by a "truth squad" of senators opposed to the League. In the end, the Senate rejected the Treaty of Versailles, which contained the Covenant of the League. [13]

Probably no other president has used the news media so skillfully as FDR. He showered attention on White House reporters, holding 998 press conferences during his 147 months in office. [14] But radio was Roosevelt's most powerful tool for shaping public opinion and pressuring Congress. At the end of his first week in office, he had addressed a joint session of Congress and had gone on the radio to urge support for his banking reforms. His reforms were passed that very day.

Similar radio messages followed, and they became known as "fireside chats." As Arthur M. Schlesinger Jr. puts it, these radio talks were effective because they "conveyed Roosevelt's conception of himself as a man at ease in his own house talking frankly and intimately to neighbors as they sat in their living rooms." [15]

President Eisenhower permitted his news conferences to be filmed and then televised, after editing by the White House, and President Kennedy permitted live telecasts of his news conferences. For the first time, the public saw the actual questions and answers as they occurred, unedited. While these TV encounters with the press helped make Kennedy popular, they were not sufficient to pressure Congress into passing some of his programs.

President Johnson succeeded in getting both the public and Congress to accept his Great Society program at home. Johnson was master at moving congressmen in person. But his televised address to Congress on voting rights proved that he could move the people, too. The war in Vietnam finally soured both his public and his congressional relations.

President Nixon tried to go over the heads of the Washington press corps, which he regarded as hostile, by holding press conferences outside of the capital. He also tried to generate public support through TV, with mixed results.

President Ford took office promising an "open administration." [16] Indeed, at the end of 1975, the National Press Club praised him for conducting 24 news conferences in 19 months in office, compared with Nixon's 37 in 5½ years. But the club criticized Press Secretary Ron Nessen for being unprepared and devious in his briefings.

President Carter campaigned as a Washington outsider and continued to cultivate that populist image after he took office. Carter's inaugural parade up Pennsylvania Avenue, "town meetings," fireside chats and bluejeans — all conveyed to the people through television — failed, however, to generate enough support in the country to move his program through Congress.

President Reagan, a former actor, enjoyed early success with TV. In May 1981 Reagan made a televised address to a joint session of Congress to appeal for passage of his budget package, one that cut social spending and increased spending for defense. It was Reagan's first public appearance since an attempt on his life several weeks earlier, on March 30. A few days after his address, the Reagan budget easily passed the Democratic House.

Patronage: Favors for Voters

Another means for exerting pressure on Congress is patronage — the president's power to fill government jobs, award government contracts or do other political favors. Patronage can create a debt members repay by voting the president's way on legislation.

While the Constitution forbids a House or Senate member to hold another federal job, it does not forbid appointment of his friends, family and supporters. In this century, civil service and postal reform have reduced the number of jobs the president has to fill. But award of government contracts and other favors remains a powerful lever in the hands of presidents.

Thomas Jefferson initiated the "spoils system," which allows victors to appoint their own people to public office. But it was Andrew Jackson, 20 years later, who perfected and justified spoils. According to Martin and Susan Tolchin, Jackson was "the first to articulate, legitimize, and translate the spoils system into the American experience." [17]

President Lincoln used patronage to promote a constitutional amendment abolishing slavery. Unsure whether enough states would ratify the amendment, Lincoln sought to hasten the admission of a new state, Nevada. The Nevada bill was bogged down in the House, when Lincoln learned that the votes of three members might be up for bargaining. When Assistant Secretary of War Charles A. Dana asked Lincoln what the members expected in return for their votes, Lincoln replied: "I don't know. It makes no difference. We must carry this vote. . . . Whatever promises you make, I will perform." Dana made a deal with the three representatives, and Nevada entered the Union. The new state then voted for the 13th Amendment. [18]

Perhaps the most successful dispenser of patronage ever to hold the presidency was Woodrow Wilson, who made patronage an important instrument of his party leadership. Although patronage jobs had been cut back severely under President Grover Cleveland, as part of his civil service reform, Wilson used what patronage was left him with maximum effect.

The next Democrat in the White House, Franklin Roosevelt, also made effective use of his patronage power. His patronage chief, Postmaster General James A. Farley, asked job seekers such questions as "What was your preconvention position on the Roosevelt candidacy?" and "How did you vote on the economy bill?" If a member was asked to vote for a presidential measure against local pressures, the matter was put "on the frank basis of quid pro quo." [19]

The Eisenhower administration used patronage more as a stick than a carrot. The president's patronage dispenser, Postmaster General Arthur Summerfield, frequently set up shop in the office of House Minority Leader Charles A. Halleck, R-Ind. (1935-69), and berated Republican representatives who broke party ranks. Insurgents were warned that key jobs such as postmasterships might be cut back unless they got behind the president's program. [20]

Presidents Kennedy and Johnson both assigned the task of dispensing patronage to John Bailey, chairman of the Democratic National Committee. Although clever use of patronage swayed votes on several key bills, Kennedy preferred the pressure of direct lobbying. Johnson was a master at dispensing jobs and other favors. He invited congressmen to the White House for tete-a-tetes, danced with the wives, telephoned them on their birthdays and invited them to his Texas ranch. [21]

Richard Nixon presided over the dissolution of a large piece of the president's patronage empire when he signed a bill that converted the 141-year-old Post Office Department into the politically independent U.S. Postal Service. Although the main reason Congress passed the bill in 1970 was to solve the postal system's money problems, the measure ended the power of politicians to appoint or promote postmasters and other postal workers.

Veto: The Ultimate Threat

When other lobbying efforts fail to move Congress, a president may resort to his most powerful defensive weapon — the veto.

A president uses the veto not only to try to kill unpalatable bills but also to dramatize his policies and put Congress on notice that he is to be taken seriously. Short of a veto itself, a presidential threat to veto legislation is a powerful form of lobbying.

The Constitution says that any bill Congress passes must go to the president. The president must either sign it or send it back to Congress with his objections. A two-thirds vote of each house is required to override a veto. The Supreme Court ruled in 1919 that two-thirds of a quorum, rather than two-thirds of the total membership, is enough for an override. The veto is powerful because a president usually can muster the support of at least one-third plus one member of a House or Senate quorum.

Under Roosevelt, vetoes increased both in absolute numbers and in relation to the number of bills passed. Presidents Truman and Eisenhower continued to make extensive use of the veto. Truman used it to safeguard organized labor against industry and agriculture. When, during the coal and rail strikes of 1946, Congress passed a bill restricting strikes, Truman vetoed it, and Congress sustained the veto. The votes to sustain came mainly from members representing big cities. In 1947 Truman vetoed the Taft-Hartley Labor Act, claiming it was unfair to labor. By then, Republicans were in control of Congress, and the veto was overridden.

Eisenhower used the veto and the veto threat to defeat or limit social programs favored by the Democrats, who controlled Congress during six of his eight years in office. To fight liberal measures, Eisenhower put together a coalition of the Republican minority and conservative Southern Democrats. In 1959, for example, he vetoed two housing bills and another to promote rural electricity. Congress was unable to override either veto. That same year, Eisenhower used the threat of veto to defeat Democratic proposals for school aid, area redevelopment, a higher minimum wage and health care for the aged.

Presidents Kennedy and Johnson seldom had to use the veto or threaten it. They were activist presidents whose main interest lay in getting their programs through a Congress controlled by their own party. But in 1965 Johnson vetoed a military construction authorization bill that required advance congressional review of presidential decisions to close military bases.

Like Eisenhower, Presidents Nixon and Ford used the veto and its threat to prevent enactment of Democratic programs. [22] Nixon often justified his vetoes on grounds that the bills were inflationary. When Congress passed a Labor-HEW appropriations bill that exceeded his request by $1.1 billion, Nixon vetoed it on national radio and TV. The Democratic House upheld the veto. Congress also sustained him on his vetoes of bills authorizing funds for the war on poverty and for manpower training and public service jobs.

But in 1973 Congress approved legislation to limit the president's power to commit armed forces abroad without congressional approval. Nixon vetoed the bill but Congress overrode him. [23]

Ford vetoed 17 major bills in 1975 alone and was sustained in all but four of those. Seven of the 17 bills concerned energy and the economy. Not one of these vetoes was overridden. In 1975, both houses passed a consumer protection bill. The measure never went to conference, because Ford threatened to veto it.

Jimmy Carter was the first president since Truman to have a veto overridden by a Congress in the hands of his own party. In 1980, he disapproved a debt-limit bill that included a section killing an import fee he had imposed on foreign oil. Only a handful of senators and representatives, all Democrats, voted to sustain the veto. Later that year, Congress voted overwhelmingly to override Carter's veto of a bill to increase salaries of doctors at veterans hospitals.

During his first year, President Reagan vetoed two bills. In November 1981, he disapproved a continuing appropriations bill on grounds that it was "budget busting." Instead of trying to override the veto, Congress regrouped and sent Reagan a bill he could sign.

Reagan's second was a pocket veto of a bill that would have reduced bankruptcy fees. According to Reagan, the bill would have helped but one company.

THE SUPREME COURT AND JUDICIAL REVIEW

The Supreme Court can nullify an act of Congress. If the court finds that the law is in conflict with the Constitution, the nation's basic charter, the law is wiped off the books as if it had never been enacted.

This power — called judicial review — is a strong restraining influence on the national legislature. By virtue of this authority, the court can assure the country that Congress will not be able to dominate the government or put into effect laws violating the basic guarantees of the Constitution.

The Constitution did not expressly give the Supreme Court this power. Scholars disagree over whether or not the framers envisioned that the court would have the power of judicial review. The court, however, assumed this power early in its history, and in 1803 it exercised it for the first time to strike down as unconstitutional part of the very act of Congress that spelled out the Supreme Court's structure.

It was half a century before the court struck down another act of Congress. Although the power of judicial review has been exercised more frequently in the 20th century, the court has found relatively few acts of Congress unconstitutional overall. Only a few more than 100 acts have been declared unconstitutional, in almost 200 years of history. Most scholars agree that the primary significance of judicial review is the awareness of every senator and representative that the laws they pass can be vetoed by the Supreme Court if they run afoul of the Constitution.

The Court's Power

Unlike the rebels who framed the Declaration of Independence, the men who met at Philadelphia in 1787 to shape the U.S. Constitution represented conservative financial interests. These interests had suffered heavily during the period of national confederation following the Revolution, when state legislatures were controlled mostly by agrarian interests.

While the framers of the Constitution deprecated the excess of the legislatures, they held a high respect for the courts. Yet at the time the framers met judicial review was not a part of any government in the world. Despite considerable discussion of the need for some means to check the excesses of Congress, the idea of giving the courts the power to veto acts of Congress was never put to a direct vote. The closest the Convention got to considering such a scheme was when it rejected a plan establishing a Council of Revision, consisting of Supreme Court justices and the president, to consider the constitutionality of proposed acts prior to final congressional passage. As submitted to the state conventions for ratification, the Constitution left ambiguous the designation of the final arbiter of constitutional disputes.

In *The Federalist,* a series of essays written to promote adoption of the Constitution, Alexander Hamilton made clear that the framers expected the judiciary to rule on constitutional issues. In Number 78 of *The Federalist,* Hamilton wrote: "The complete independence of the courts of justice is peculiarly essential in a limited constitution. By a limited constitution, I understand one which contains certain specified exceptions to the legislative authority, such for instance, as that it shall pass no bills of attainder, no ex-post facto laws, and the like. Limitations of this kind can be preserved in practice no other way than through the courts of justice, whose duty it must be to declare all acts contrary to the manifest tenor of the Constitution void. Without this, all the reservations of particular rights or privileges would amount to nothing." [24]

The Court's Philosophy

The Supreme Court has tended through history to be a more conservative body than Congress, in part because Supreme Court justices are appointed for life and thus changes in the court and its philosophy come about more slowly and with less regularity than they do in Congress.

For most of the nation's first 150 years, for example, the court tended generally to defend property rights against government regulation. The court maintained this posture even into the 1930s, after the need had become evident for dramatic expansion of governmental power to deal with the severe economic problems facing the nation. In one of the most notable episodes in the history of judicial review, the court in 1935-36 struck down as unconstitutional 11 New Deal statutes — the heart of President Franklin D. Roosevelt's economic recovery program.

From 1937 on, the court has espoused a more flexible reading of the Constitution, and one that does not constrain the government's power over the economy. Since the New Deal, the court has dealt increasingly with issues of individual rights.

During the term of Chief Justice Earl Warren (1953-69), the court reached a series of landmark rulings that set off a number of revolutions — some quiet and some not so quiet — in American life. These rulings — on issues such as school segregation, school prayer, the rights of criminal suspects and the apportionment of legislative bodies — generated intense criticism from citizens and organizations across the country, criticism that was reflected in a spate of efforts in Congress to curb the Court's power.

Warren was succeeded as chief justice by Warren E. Burger in 1969, and although Burger was accurately described as a conservative, the court did not back off from the historic decisions of the 1950s and 1960s. In fact, although the court in the 1970s seemed to take a more limited view of the role of the courts in American life, it nevertheless moved ahead with a number of controversial rulings in areas such as abortion, women's rights, official immunity and freedom of expression.

Congress and the Court

Congress does not lack ways of influencing the court — or responding to what it finds to be ill-advised decisions. The Senate can refuse to confirm nominees to the court. Congress can actually reverse some of the court's decisions — either by statute or by approving a constitutional amendment that is then ratified by the states. This has happened three times, resulting in the 11th, 14th and 16th Amendments. And Congress can move to curb the jurisdiction of the court over certain matters.

Whatever the philosophy of the court, it always has had its share of congressional critics quick to accuse it of usurping undue power. The early Anti-Federalists (later known as Democratic-Republicans and finally as Democrats) thought the court was nullifying the Constitution with its rulings strengthening federal power at the expense of the states. New Deal Democrats more than a century later thought that the court was attempting to impose its own views of economic reality upon the nation with its decisions striking down the New Deal recovery program. And in more recent times conservatives have been driven virtually to despair by the court's rulings on civil rights, criminal law and electoral matters.

Each of these critical movements has produced efforts to curb the Supreme Court's power, through bills to 1) require that the court muster more than a majority vote to declare a law unconstitutional, 2) allow the removal of a justice if both Congress and the president agree in such action, or 3) redefine the court's jurisdiction by denying it the power to hear certain types of cases. None of these broad measures has been enacted, although just after the Civil War the Congress did for a time limit the court's jurisdiction over certain types of appeals.

Marbury v. Madison

In 1803 the court decisively claimed for itself the power to review acts of Congress. The doctrine of judicial review was first enunciated by the Supreme Court in the famous case of *Marbury v. Madison.* [25]

After Republican Thomas Jefferson had defeated Federalist John Adams for re-election in 1800 — but before the Republicans took office — Adams nominated a number of Federalists to judicial posts created by court-reform legislation passed by the lame-duck Federalist Congress. The nominations of 16 judges and some other officials were confirmed by the Senate and the commissions signed by Adams in the waning hours of his administration. When Adams' term expired at midnight on March 3, 1801, several of the commissions had not been delivered. Jefferson, who entered office at the stroke of midnight, ordered that these commissions be withheld.

One of the appointees whose commission had not been delivered was William Marbury, who had been named justice of the peace for the District of Columbia. Marbury sought to test Jefferson's power by filing suit in the Supreme Court asking for an order requiring Jefferson's secretary of state, James Madison, to deliver the commission. Marbury filed the suit under the Judiciary Act of 1789, which empowered the court to issue writs of mandamus compelling federal officials to perform their duties.

The chief justice was John Marshall, a staunch Federalist who had been secretary of state in the Adams administration and had been responsible in that capacity for delivering the commissions to Marbury and the other appointees.

Marshall, writing for the court, agreed that Marbury was entitled to his commission and that he should be granted the writ of mandamus so long as the court had jurisdiction over the case. Although the Judiciary Act of 1789 granted the Supreme Court the necessary jurisdiction, Marshall asserted that that part of the act was unconstitutional because Congress had no power to enlarge the court's original jurisdiction — its power to hear a case first before any other court.

Article III of the Constitution gave the Supreme Court original jurisdiction over "cases affecting ambassadors, other public ministers and consuls, and those in which a state shall be party." In other cases the Supreme Court was given only appellate jurisdiction "both as to law and fact, with such exceptions and under such regulations as the Congress shall make." Under the guise of handing his Jeffersonian foes a political victory, Marshall had laid the cornerstone of federal judicial power.

Dred Scott v. Sandford

It was not until the eve of the Civil War that the Supreme Court again held an act of Congress unconstitutional. It did so in the case of *Scott v. Sandford* in 1857, probably the court's most controversial and most criticized decision of all time.

Dred Scott, a slave, had been taken by his former master from the slave state of Missouri into territory made free by the Missouri Compromise. After returning to Missouri, Scott sued to establish his freedom on the ground that his sojourn in free territory had made him a free man. The Missouri supreme court held that he had indeed gained his freedom through being on free soil, but that he had lost it when he returned to the slave state of Missouri.

Because Scott's present master (Sandford) was a resident of New York, the case could now be considered by a federal court as a controversy between citizens who lived in different states, if Scott were a citizen of Missouri. When the case reached the U.S. Supreme Court, a majority of the justices decided that the case should not have been heard in federal court. Federal courts lacked jurisdiction over the

case, they said, because no Negro could be a U.S. citizen under terms of the Constitution and so the dispute between Scott and Sandford was not between citizens who lived in different states. But the court did not stop there. Chief Justice Roger Brooke Taney, who wrote what is considered the majority decision in the case (although nine separate opinions were filed by the justices), asserted that Scott was a slave because the Missouri Compromise, which had been repealed three years earlier by the Kansas-Nebraska Act, was unconstitutional. Congress, Taney declared, had no authority to limit the extension of slavery.

The *Dred Scott* decision aroused tremendous resentment in the North, especially among members of the newly organized Republican Party whose cardinal tenet was that Congress should abolish slavery in all of the territories. The decision eventually was reversed by the adoption of the 13th and 14th Amendments.

New Deal Legislation

The appointment in 1930 of Charles Evans Hughes to succeed William Howard Taft as chief justice of the United States seemed at the time to herald a new, less conservative era on the Supreme Court. In his six years as an associate justice (1910-16), Hughes had become known for his liberal attitude in the field of civil liberties. As it developed, however, the Hughes court became involved in an unprecedented clash with the legislative and executive branches over New Deal legislation. One after another, the court struck down Depression-born statutes passed by Congress at President Roosevelt's urging.

President Roosevelt, stung by the Supreme Court's piecemeal destruction of his legislative program, resolved after the 1936 elections to do something about it. In a surprise message to Congress, Feb. 5, 1937, he asked for legislation that would authorize the president, when any federal judge who had been in service for 10 years did not retire within six months after becoming 70 years old, to appoint an additional judge to the court in question. Such a law would have made it possible for Roosevelt to add six justices to the Supreme Court and thus presumably ensure a majority sympathetic to the New Deal.

Although the court had come under heavy fire for its anti-New Deal decisions, the court-packing plan ran into strong opposition within and outside of Congress. Hughes presented an able defense of the court before the Senate Judiciary Committee, which, on June 14, 1937, submitted an adverse report on the administration bill. A measure finally approved in August provided only for procedural reforms in the lower courts.

Judicial Review in Modern Times

In the 1970s and early 1980s, the Supreme Court continued to use its power of judicial review to nullify acts of Congress that ran afoul of constitutional guarantees. The laws invalidated in this period covered a wide range of issues.

Twice in the 1970s the court held that Congress had infringed upon states' rights. In 1970 the court held that Congress could not by statute lower to 18 the voting age for state and local elections. This decision was quickly rendered purely academic when Congress and the states approved the 26th Amendment lowering the voting age for all elections. [26]

Six years later, the court — for the first time since New Deal days — held that Congress had exceeded the reach of the power to regulate commerce. The justices in 1976 nullifed part of the 1966 amendments to the Fair Labor Standards Act, which required state and local governments to pay federal minimum wages to their employees and to compensate them for overtime work in line with the federal provisions. The court held in the case of *National League of Cities v. Usery* that the 10th Amendment barred federal interference with matters so close to the heart of state sovereignty. [27]

Court-Curbing Proposals

After Congress rejected the Roosevelt court-packing plan in 1937, the Supreme Court experienced a period of relatively placid relations with Congress until the Warren court launched on its course of judicial activism in the mid-1950s. Congressional attacks on the Warren court began in 1954, the year of the court's famous school desegregation decision, *Brown v. Board of Education of Topeka, Kansas.*

Congressional attacks on the court intensified in the early 1960s. The court in 1962 ruled unconstitutional the use of an officially prescribed prayer in New York state public schools.

Unhappiness with the Supreme Court's rulings allowing abortions, permitting the use of busing for school desegregation and forbidding prayer in public schools spurred congressional consideration of a number of bills in the 1970s and 1980s that would withdraw these subjects from the jurisdiction of the federal courts, including the Supreme Court.

Critics of the abortion and busing rulings tried — as had school prayer proponents earlier — to win approval of constitutional amendments overturning the court's decisions permitting abortion and busing. But the House in 1979 defeated an anti-busing constitutional amendment, 209-216. And three years earlier, in 1976, the Senate refused, 47-40, to debate an anti-abortion constitutional amendment. [28]

Late in the 1970s critics of these rulings tried a different tack, proposing legislation that would simply take away the court's authority to rule in these matters. Scholars disagreed over the scope of congressional power to impose such limits on the court's jurisdiction, but there was no denying that the Constitution does permit Congress to make "exceptions" to the Court's appellate jurisdiction.

LOBBYING BECOMES BIG BUSINESS

From Alaska lands to zero population growth, every conceivable issue has attracted the attention of competing interest groups, and across the country they and their lobbyists have become a potent force in the political process. Their ranks include the traditionally rich and powerful Capitol Hill lobbies, as well as the many grass-roots coalitions that derive power from their numbers and determination.

"America is no longer a nation. It is a committee of lobbies," wrote Charles Peters, editor-in-chief of *The Washington Monthly.* [29] The goals these groups espouse are diverse and, from their point of view, their causes are worthwhile.

Although their objectives may differ, the various groups pressuring Congress in the 1980s increasingly were using similar, often highly developed, strategies to get what they wanted. At one time lobbying may have meant a persuasive soloist pleading his case to a senator or representative; but as often as not the contemporary lobbyist depends far less than his predecessors on personal contacts and individualistic methods and more on coordinated, indirect techniques made possible by modern means of communication.

As it grew in size and sophistication, the lobbying profession lost much of the stigma attached to it from past scandals and the activities of unscrupulous influence peddlers. But concern lingered that some individuals and groups, despite their polish and adherence to laws and proprieties, might be having too much sway in Congress, to the detriment of the public interest.

Peters continued in his article to say that "Politicians no longer ask what is in the public interest, because they know no one else is asking. Instead they're giving each group what it wants. . . ."

In his farewell address to the nation delivered Jan. 14, 1981, President Jimmy Carter also expressed concern about the proliferation of single-interest groups, which he said was "a disturbing factor" that "tends to distort our purposes, because the national interest is not always the sum of all our single or special interests." [30]

Comments like these have produced little in the way of restrictions on lobbies or the way they operate. The dilemma for would-be reformers is that lobbying derives from basic American rights, and efforts to control it must avoid entanglements with those constitutional liberties.

Constitutional Protection

Lobbying has been recognized as a legitimate, protected activity from the earliest years of the United States. The First Amendment to the Constitution provided that "Congress shall make no law . . . abridging the freedom of speech or of the press; or the right of the people peaceably to assemble and to petition the Government for redress of grievances."

But there is a potential for corruption and conflict of interest inherent in protecting the rights of groups to petition, and James Madison was credited with foreseeing it. His classic statement in *The Federalist* (No. 10) defended the need for a strong federal government to act as an effective counterbalance: "Among the numerous advantages promised by a well-constructed union," he wrote, "none deserves to be more accurately developed than its tendency to break and control the violence of faction. . . . By a faction, I understand a number of citizens, whether amounting to a majority or minority of the whole, who are united and actuated by some common impulse of passion, or of interest, adverse to the rights of other citizens, or to the permanent and aggregate interests of the community." [31]

By the early 19th century, corruption and conflicts of interest were commonplace and, although they discomforted many, were taken as a matter of course. Abundant evidence accumulated that venal and selfish methods often were used to get legislative results. Chief among the indiscretions was bribery, where legislators traded influence for money.

Despite the deep and pervading sense of ambivalence that surrounded their profession, lobbyists continued to be attracted to Washington in the 20th century. Their legions grew steadily after the New Deal of the 1930s, paralleling the growth in federal spending and the expansion of authority into new areas. Over the next four decades the federal government became a tremendous force in the nation's life, thus expanding the areas where changes in federal policy could spell success or failure for special interest groups.

Then in the 1970s a series of congressional reforms opened up meetings, diminished the seniority system, forced more publicly recorded votes and increased the power of subcommittees. Power once concentrated in the leadership and committee chairmen was diluted to many members, as well as to the ranks of professional staffers that had swelled throughout the 1960s. Lobbyists found they had to influence more people, members and staffers alike, to get something accomplished.

Because of the unspecific — and some would say unenforceable — lobby registration laws, it was impossible to come up with an exact number of lobbyists in Washington. But whether they referred to themselves as political consultants, lawyers, foreign representatives, legislative specialists, consumer advocates, trade association representatives or government affairs specialists, there were an estimated 10,000 to 20,000 people lobbying in Washington in 1982 — either periodically or throughout the year. Even the lower end of this estimate showed a dramatic increase from the general figure of 4,000 cited in 1977.

Coalition Organizing

The concerted exercise of influence is as old as government itself, but most lobbyists agree that during the 1970s and into the 1980s coalition lobbying became a commonplace ritual in Washington. The ad hoc coalition, the working group, the alliance, the committee — these became the routine format of all but the most obscure lobbying campaigns.

The explosion of the lobbying business, aimed at comprehending and staunching the flow of government activism, meant many voices competing for the ear of Congress. One advantage for lobbyists and members alike was that collective lobbying allowed a sorting out of competing aims before going to Congress, almost like lawyers settling a case out of court.

By the 1980s a person with a cause found his first task was to persuade members of his own organization or group to support him, then to line up help from natural allies in other interest groups. These ad hoc lobby coalitions often are composed of a mix of corporate, association and business federation lobbyists, as well as unions and any other interests that can be enticed into a marriage of convenience. Allies on one issue sometimes become opponents on the next one.

By combining their knowledge and resources, members of coalitions improve their chances of overcoming the natural obstacles to new legislation, and they have a better chance of killing bills they oppose. In the early 1980s lobby coalitions increasingly were on the offensive to move legislation and to roll back existing laws.

Access Prerequisite

A lobbyist's strategy focuses on the interaction between his group and those on Capitol Hill and in the executive branch. To communicate with the power brokers, the advocate first needs access. So whether he is a partner in a Washington law firm or an in-house employee of a union, trade association or business, more often than not the lobbyist already has close ties with Congress. Many lobbyists have spent time as staff aides on Capitol Hill, and some were members of Congress.

Access is crucial, but knowledge and technique are just as critical because lobbyists traditionally have provided information as well as expertise to hard-pressed members and committees.

Direct lobbying most often begins at the committee or subcommittee level, as approval of a measure by a congressional panel usually ensures final passage. Except on highly controversial issues, committee decisions are almost always upheld by the full chamber. A thorough lobbyist provides to the committee and its professional staffers extensive background and technical information on the issue of interest, precise legislative language for a proposed bill or amendment, lists of witnesses for the hearings and the name of a possible sponsor for the bill.

The decentralization of power in Congress, resulting in the expansion in the number and importance of subcommittees, directly affected the lobbyist's job. As the number of people having power increased, so did the number of pressure points. It was advantageous for an interest group to have a supporter in power. Thus in the Congresses of the 1980s it was not unusual for a lobbyist to back a particular member for a slot on a favored committee, or for a leadership position on a panel.

Also, as "sunshine" laws and rules opened markup sessions, hearings and conferences to the public, the lobbyist no longer was left hovering outside the closed door excluded from the action; rather he could be right there watching every move — in many cases suggesting legislative language and compromise positions. This kind of help is especially useful during consideration of highly technical legislation. Recorded votes on amendments, and open knowledge of who introduced them, makes it easier for the lobbyist to monitor the action and apply pressure where most needed.

Grass-Roots Techniques

In conjunction with direct lobbying, many organizations seek to mobilize constituents into pressuring senators and representatives. High election turnovers gradually have created a Congress less wedded to old loyalties and more skittish about constituent pressures. This trend contributed to the current prominence of indirect, "grassroots" lobbying — inducing constituents back home to bring pressure on Congress.

Nearly every trade association or public interest group of any stature has developed its own grass-roots network to ensure that what its Washington lobbyists say is reinforced by an outpouring from back home. For those interests that do not have such a network, a thriving industry has grown up that promises clients it can take a whisper of public interest and amplify it into a roar of public pressure.

Traditional grass-roots pressure methods include maintaining a steady stream of correspondence with the lawmaker, even when not demanding a specific favor; arranging recess visits to local establishments; and dealing frequently and skillfully with local newspapers and television. These tools are not new to established groups; what is new is their magnitude and sophistication.

A fact of modern lobbying is that home-district pressure frequently does not spring spontaneously from the public. The genuine grass-roots support often is enhanced by the highly technical orchestration of a special-interest group, the more subliminal stimulation of a professional public relations campaign, and occasionally the persuasion of an employer or union.

Still the oldest and favorite instrument of the organized grass-roots lobbying campaign remains the postage meter. Computer technology and high-speed, low-cost telegram services enabled interest groups in the 1970s and 1980s to target mailings where they would do the most good.

Another grass-roots lobbying technique involves gaining attention through mass media campaigns — on the radio, television, or in newspapers and magazines. Thoughtful editorials in well-known or more obscure newspapers in members' districts often stimulate readers to write their congressman. John Shattuck, executive director of the American Civil Liberties Union (ACLU), said that many lobbyists underestimated the importance of developing close relationships with newspaper editors and editorial writers, whose influence upon constituents, and thereby upon members, could be pivotal on controversial issues.

Campaign Support

Campaign contributions to members of Congress serve two important functions for lobbying organizations. Political support not only can induce a congressman to back the group's legislative interests, but also can help to ensure that members friendly to the group's goals remain in office. While corporations have been barred since 1907, and labor unions since 1943, from making direct contributions to campaigns for federal office, contributors have found numerous ways to get around the restrictions. Labor pioneered in setting up separate political arms, such as the AFL-CIO's Committee on Political Education (COPE), that collect voluntary contributions from union members and their families and use the money to help elect senators and representatives favorable to their cause. It also is legal for unions to endorse candidates.

Similarly, corporations can organize political action committees (PACs) to seek contributions from stockholders and executive and administrative personnel and their families. Corporate PACs have proliferated, especially after the Federal Election Commission's SunPAC decision in 1975, and their influences have come to rival, if not surpass, those of labor. The SunPAC ruling allowed business PACs to solicit employees and not just stockholders, vastly expanding their potential to raise money.

Lobbying and the Law

Although lobbying is protected by the First Amendment guarantees of freedom of speech, and the right of citizens to petition the government for a redress of grievances, abuses led to periodic efforts by Congress to regulate lobbying. The principal method of regulation was disclosure rather than actual control. In four laws, lobbyists were required to identify themselves, who they represented and their legislative interests. In one law, lobbyists also were required to report how much they and their employers spent on lobbying. But definitions were unclear, enforcement minimal. As a result, the few existing disclosure laws produced only limited information, and their effects were questionable.

One reason for the relative lack of limitations on lobbies was the difficulty of imposing effective restrictions without infringing on the constitutional rights of free speech, press, assembly and petition. Other reasons included a fear that restrictions would hamper legitimate lobbies without reaching more serious lobby abuses, the consolidated and highly effective opposition of lobbies, and the desire of some members to keep open avenues to a future lobbying career. Congress succeeded in enacting two major lobbying laws, the Foreign Agents Registration Act of 1938 and the Federal Regulation of Lobbying Act of 1948.

The political spending of pressure groups also was the object of numerous campaign finance bills enacted over the years by Congress. The ability to promise electoral support or opposition gave pressure groups one of the most effective devices in their attempts to influence Congress on legislation. Precisely for this reason, Congress attempted on several occasions to limit campaign contributions made by corporations, organizations and individuals in connection with federal elections. The limitations were intended to prevent those with great financial resources from using them to dominate the selection of members of Congress and thereby its legislative decisions.

Lobbying Investigations

Over the years investigations of lobbying practices stemmed from a wide range of motives. Lobby investigations were used to respond to intense public concern about lobbying, to gather information on the workings of existing regulatory legislation and to help prepare the way for, and to shape, proposed new regulatory legislation.

The most recent case of lobby investigation began on Oct. 24, 1976, when *The Washington Post* disclosed that the Justice Department was probing reports that South Korean agents dispensed between $500,000 and $1 million a year in cash and gifts to members of Congress to help maintain "a favorable legislative climate" for South Korea.

Tongsun Park, a Washington-based Korean businessman and socialite, was named as the central operative. Park fled to London shortly after the story appeared. He stayed there until August 1977, then went to Korea. He later returned to the United States to testify at House and Senate hearings on Korean influence-peddling.

By 1978 the House and Senate ethics committees had ended their probes without recommending any severe disciplinary action against colleagues linked to the scandal. The House investigation, which began in early 1977 with reports that as many as 115 members of Congress had taken illegal gifts from South Korean agents, ended in October 1978 with the House voting its mildest form of punishment, a "reprimand," for three California Democrats: John J. McFall (1957-78), Edward R. Roybal and Charles H. Wilson (1963-81).

Two former representatives were prosecuted for taking large sums of money from Tongsun Park: Richard T. Hanna, D-Calif. (1963-74), pleaded guilty to a reduced charge and went to prison, and Otto E. Passman, D-La. (1947-77), was acquitted in 1979.

Footnotes

1. Roger H. Davidson and Walter J. Oleszek, *Congress and Its Members*, (Washington, D.C.: CQ Press, 1981), pp. 7, 112-113.

2. Quoted in George H. Haynes, *The Senate of the United States,* 2 vols. (Boston: Houghton Mifflin Co., 1938), vol. 2, p. 1026.

3. *The Federalist Papers,* with an Introduction by Clinton Rossiter (New York: Mentor, 1961), No. 84, p. 514.

4. Robert O. Blanchard, ed., *Congress and the News Media* (New York: Hasting House Publishers, 1974), p. 7.

5. Richard Bolling, *House Out of Order* (New York: E.P. Dutton & Co., 1965), p. 48. A slightly different version of the quotation ("If you want to get along in the House, go along.") appears in Neil MacNeil, *Forge of Democracy* (New York: David McKay Co., 1963), p. 75.

6. Randall B. Ripley, *Party Leaders in the House of Representatives* (Washington, D.C.: Brookings Institution, 1967), pp. 132-35.

7. Hugh A. Bone, *American Politics and the Party System,* 3rd ed. (New York: McGraw-Hill, 1965), pp. 127-28.

8. The Constitution, Article II, Section 3 and Section 2, Clause 2.

9. Employment Act of 1946, Section 2.

10. The Constitution, Article II, Section 3 and Section 2, Clause 2.

11. Ibid., Article I, Section 7, Clause 2.

12. John Deakin, *The Lobbyists* (Washington, D.C.: Public Affairs Press, 1966), pp. 45-46.

13. James E. Pollard, *The Presidents and the Press* (New York: Macmillan Co., 1947), p. 147.

14. James E. Pollard, *The Presidents and the Press: Truman to Johnson* (Washington, D.C.: Public Affairs Press, 1964), p. 27.

15. Arthur M. Schlesinger Jr., *The Coming of the New Deal* (Boston: Houghton-Mifflin Co., 1958), p. 559.

16. *Presidency 1974* (Washington, D.C., Congressional Quarterly, 1975), p. 76-A.

17. Martin Tolchin and Susan Tolchin, *To the Victor: Political Patronage From the Clubhouse to the White House* (New York: Random House, 1971), p. 323.

18. DeAlva Stanwood Alexander, *History and Procedure of the House of Representatives* (Boston: Houghton-Mifflin Co., 1916), pp. 378-379.

19. Wilfred E. Binkley, *President and Congress* (New York: Vintage Books, 1962), p. 301.

20. MacNeil, *Forge of Democracy,* p. 265.

21. Roger H. Davidson and Walter J. Oleszak, *Congress and Its Members* (Washington, D.C.: CQ Press, 1981), p. 300.

22. *Congress and the Nation,* vol. 3, (Washington, D.C.: Congressional Quarterly, 1973), pp. 101A-105A.

23. *Congressional Quarterly Almanac 1973,* pp. 28, 905.

24. *The Federalist Papers,* with an Introduction by Clinton Rossiter (New York: New American Library, Mentor Books, 1961), No. 78, p. 466.

25. *Marbury v. Madison,* 1 Cr 137 (1803).

26. *Oregon v. Mitchell,* 400 U.S. 112 (1970).

27. *National League of Cities v. Usery,* 426 U.S. 833 (1976).

28. *Congress and the Nation,* vol. 5, (Washington, D.C.: Congressional Quarterly 1981), p. 801; vol 4, p. 366.

29. Charles Peters, "The Solution: A Rebirth of Patriotism," *Washington Monthly,* October 1978, p. 37.

30. *Historic Documents of 1981* (Washington, D.C.: Congressional Quarterly, 1982), p. 33.

31. Alexander Hamilton, John Jay and James Madison, *The Federalist Papers* (New York: New American Library, 1961), pp. 77-78.

Seating and Disciplining

In laying down the authority of Congress to seat, unseat and punish its members, the Constitutional Convention of 1787 drew inspiration from its favorite concept: checks and balances. The Constitution, while empowering Congress to pass judgment on the qualifications of members, put bounds on that power by listing certain mandatory qualifications. In carrying out the concept of a balance of power among the branches of the federal government, the judicial branch has been called on at various times to interpret the authority of Congress under the constitutional clauses on membership qualifications and on punishment of members' misconduct.

The power of Congress to determine whether a member-elect fulfills the requirements for service as a national legislator has come into conflict, over the years, with the right of voters in each state to decide who shall represent them. When Congress rules on controversies such as disputed elections, the uncertain citizenship of a member-elect, or other questions of competence, senators or representatives from all parts of the country are, in effect, deciding whether the citizens of a state may or may not be represented in Washington by the person selected by those citizens as their choice.

Although Congress has often had to determine the winner in contested elections, the clear choice of the voters has been rejected, for lack of the requisite qualifications, in fewer than 20 cases since 1789. Congress also has infrequently used its constitutional power to punish or expel members for disorderly or improper conduct. As of 1982, eight senators, 20 representatives and one territorial delegate have been formally censured by their colleagues for misconduct. There have been 15 expulsions in the Senate and four in the House.

The authority of Congress to judge the qualifications of members and to punish those who behave improperly rests on two clauses in Article I of the Constitution. The first is Clause 1 of Article I, Section 5, which reads in part: "Each House shall be the Judge of the Elections, Returns and Qualifications of its own members...." This clause would appear to give each house carte blanche in the validation of elections and the seating of members-elect. However, the election of members of Congress is regulated elsewhere in Article I and in the 17th Amendment that provides for direct election of senators. In addition, the Constitution specifically lists the qualifications required for membership in Congress.

The second clause on seating, unseating, and punishment of members is Clause 2 of Article I, Section 5, reading: "Each House may determine the Rules of its Proceedings, punish its Members for disorderly Behavior, and, with the Concurrence of two thirds, expel a Member." The original draft of this clause did not include the words "with the concurrence of two thirds." When the clause was considered in the Constitutional Convention, Aug. 10, 1787, James Madison of Virginia said that the right of expulsion was "too important to be exercised by a bare majority of a quorum, and in emergencies might be dangerously abused." [1] He proposed requiring a two-thirds vote for expulsion.

Gouverneur Morris of Pennsylvania opposed Madison's proposal. He said: "This power may be safely trusted to a majority. To require more may produce abuses on the side of the minority. A few men from fractious motives may keep in a member who ought to be expelled." [2] But Edmund Randolph and George Mason of Virginia and Daniel Carroll of Maryland spoke in support of Madison's proposal, and it was adopted by a vote of 10 states in favor, one (Pennsylvania) divided and none opposed.

Litigation on the seating and disciplining of members of Congress reached the Supreme Court in the latter part of the 19th century in suits focused mainly on legalistic questions such as the power of Congress to subpoena witnesses when considering the qualifications of members. These suits afforded the court an opportunity to indicate bases upon which to judge the qualifications of members and to suggest the scope of punishment that may be imposed on members. In cases argued during the present century, the court has ruled more directly on the nature of the power of Congress to exclude members-elect and to punish or expel sitting members.

The constitutional clause on the qualifications of members-elect has raised more questions of interpretation than has the authority to punish members. One of the most serious issues is whether exclusion of a member-elect deprives a state unwarrantedly, even for a short time, of its constitutionally guaranteed representation in Congress. The Supreme Court in 1969 said a state may send to Congress anyone it chooses, if that person meets the qualifications in the Constitution and is legally elected. Earlier, in 1926, the court ruled that William S. Vare of Pennsylvania had not been legally elected to a Senate seat because of corruption in the election campaign. The court ruling said

172 How Congress Works

that exclusion in such a case did not violate a state's rights. In 1969, the court reversed the the House of Representatives' exclusion of Adam Clayton Powell Jr. because Powell met the basic constitutional requirements. *(Details, Vare, this page and 178; Powell, p. 176)*

Right to Punish Members

The Supreme Court, in its 1880-81 term, handed down a decision that upheld the right of Congress to punish its members. Although the case, *Kilbourn v. Thompson* (103 U.S. 168) directly involved only private persons under investigation by the House, it occurred at a time when the Crédit Mobilier scandal had aroused suspicions of financial misdeeds by several members of the House, including Speaker James G. Blaine, R-Maine.

This moved the court to go beyond its ruling on private citizen Kilbourn and to discuss the power to punish members of Congress. Speaking in the context of calls for punishment of members accused of unethical financial involvement in the business under investigation, it said:

● "The Constitution expressly empowers each House to punish its own members for disorderly behavior. We see no reason to doubt that this punishment may in a proper case be imprisonment."

● "Each House is by the Constitution made the judge of the election and qualifications of its members. In deciding on these it has an undoubted right to examine witnesses and inspect papers, subject to the usual rights of witnesses in such cases; and it may be that a witness would be subject to like punishment at the hands of the body engaged in trying a contested election, for refusing to testify, that he would if the case were pending before a court of judicature."

In a later case, *In re Chapman* (166 U.S. 66), decided in 1897, the court reaffirmed the right of Congress to compel testimony on matters within its jurisdiction.[3] It also defined the circumstances under which either chamber might expel one of its members: "The right to expel extends to all cases where the offense is such as in the judgment of the Senate is inconsistent with the trust and duty of a member."

Automatic Expulsion

The reference to expulsion in the court's opinion of 1897 was supplemented in an opinion handed down in 1906 interpreting an act of Congress approved June 11, 1864. The act provided that any senator or representative found guilty of illegally receiving compensation for services provided in connection with a claim, contract or other proceeding before a government agency "shall . . . be rendered forever thereafter incapable of holding any office . . . under the government of the United States."[4] Sen. Joseph R. Burton, R-Kan. (1901-06), had been convicted under this law. In fighting to keep his seat, Burton's lawyers contended that the 1864 law violated the constitutional right of the Senate to decide on expulsion of its members.

In the court's decision May 21, 1906, Justice John M. Harlan, said: "The final judgment of conviction did not operate, *ipso facto*, to vacate the seat of the convicted senator nor compel the Senate to expel him or to regard him as expelled by force alone of the judgment" (*Burton v. United States*, 202 U.S. 344). On the following day, the Senate asked its Committee on Privileges and Elections to recommend what action, if any, should be taken. Burton resigned on June 4, 1906, before the committee reported.

Primary Election Misconduct

Misconduct by a member-elect provided the next major case for the Supreme Court to rule on congressional power to judge members' qualifications. This case came from the Federal Corrupt Practices Act of June 25, 1910, as amended Aug. 19, 1911. The two laws limited the amount of money that a candidate for Congress could spend on a campaign.

Truman H. Newberry, R-Mich. (1919-22), and 16 others were found guilty of conspiring to violate the corrupt practices legislation in the Democratic senatorial primary election of Aug. 27, 1918, in Michigan. Newberry's opponent was Henry Ford.

Acting on Newberry's appeal, *Newberry v. United States* (256 U.S. 232), the Supreme Court ruled that Congress did not have power to control in any way a state's party primaries or conventions for designating candidates for the Senate or House.

Twenty years after *Newberry*, the Supreme Court reversed itself on the right of Congress to legislate on primary elections. In a decision May 26, 1941, *United States v. Classic* (313 U.S. 299), the court said that the power to regulate national elections, assigned by the Constitution to Congress, "includes the authority to regulate primary elections when, as in this case, they are a step in the exercise by the people of their choice of representatives in Congress."

Denial of Representation

The court did not have to rule until 1929 on the question of whether exclusion of a member-elect by Congress deprives a state, even temporarily, of its right to representation. The issue was before the justices only peripherally, but they decided the matter anyway.

The case concerned the Nov. 2, 1926, Senate election of Pennsylvania Republican William S. Vare (House 1912-27), which the Senate voided because of corruption. The court, in *Barry et al. v. United States ex rel. Cunningham* (279 U.S. 597), said the Senate had authority "to exclude persons asserting membership who either had not been elected or, what amounts to the same thing, had been elected by resort to fraud, bribery, corruption, or other sinister methods having the effect of vitiating the election."

The court then went on to the key issue of representation. The justices said the Article V equal representation language prohibited a state from being deprived of its equal suffrage in the Senate. The court said this was "a limitation upon the power of amendment," and did not apply in the Vare situation.

"The temporary deprivation of equal representation" from not seating a person while an election controversy is resolved, the court said, "is the necessary consequence of the exercise of a constitutional power, and no more deprives the state of its 'equal suffrage' in the constitutional sense than would a vote of the Senate vacating the seat of a sitting member or a vote of expulsion."

The Vare case was significant for one other question answered by the Supreme Court: whether Congress, in judging election cases, violated the principle of separation of powers by exercising a judicial function. The court said that the Constitution, by authorizing Congress to be the judge of its members' qualifications, conferred on each house "certain powers which are not legislative but judicial in character," including the power "to render a judgment which is beyond the authority of any other tribunal to review."

Basic Membership Standards

The Supreme Court in 1969 acknowledged that a chamber could expel a member for misconduct, but limited the grounds for refusing to seat a member-elect to those specified in the Constitution. The issue arose when the House in 1967 refused to seat New York Democrat Adam Clayton Powell Jr., on the grounds that he had misappropriated public funds. Powell and 13 voters in his district brought suit against the officers of the House. *(Details of Powell case, p. 176)*

The central legal issues in the Powell suit were:

● Could the House add to the Constitution's three qualifications for House membership? Those three standards required the member be at least 25 years old, have been a U.S. citizen for at least seven years and, when elected, be an inhabitant of the state from which he was elected.

● Did the courts have the power to examine the actions of the House?

U.S. District Judge George L. Hart Jr. ruled April 7, 1967, that he had no jurisdiction in the case and dismissed the suit.

The U.S. Court of Appeals for the District of Columbia on Feb. 28, 1968, affirmed Hart's action. The Court of Appeals stated that the case involved a political question, which, if decided, would constitute a violation of the separation of powers and produce an embarrassing confrontation between Congress and the courts.

While the case was before the Supreme Court, the next Congress seated Powell, who had been re-elected again in 1968. But the court decided that the issues, including Powell's claim for back pay, required settlement. By a 7-1 vote on June 16, 1969, the Supreme Court reversed the lower court. Chief Justice Earl Warren, delivering the opinion of the court, said that the House had improperly excluded Powell because he met the constitutional requirements of age, residence and citizenship.

On the question of the court's jurisdiction, Warren acknowledged that five members of Congress who were defendants (the Speaker of the House, the majority and minority leaders and the ranking members of the committee that investigated Powell) were immune under the speech or debate clause of the Constitution. However, three other defendants, functionaries of the House who had withheld Powell's pay and denied him such perquisites as an office and staff, were liable for action, the court said.

A claim for back pay was sent back to a lower court but Powell never pursued the matter.

CHALLENGING THE RIGHT TO A SEAT

The Constitution provides in Article VI that senators and representatives "shall be bound by Oath or Affirmation, to support this Constitution."

Congress has enacted laws, adopted rules and made ad hoc decisions under this provision. It has prescribed the form of the oath and procedures for administering it, and has grappled with such questions as whether a challenged

---

Constitutional Standards For Members of Congress

● A senator must be at least 30 years old and have been a citizen of the United States not less than nine years (Article I, Section 3, Clause 3).

● A representative must be at least 25 years old and have been a citizen not less than seven years (Article I, Section 2, Clause 2).

● Every member of Congress must be, when elected, an inhabitant of the state that he or she is to represent (Article I, Section 2, Clause 2, and Section 3, Clause 3).

● No one may be a member of Congress who holds any other "Office under the United States" (Article I, Section 6, Clause 2).

● No person may be a senator or a representative who, having previously taken an oath as a member of Congress to support the Constitution, has engaged in rebellion against the United States or given aid or comfort to its enemies, unless Congress has removed such disability by a two-thirds vote of both houses (14th Amendment, Section 3).

---

member-elect should take an oath before the dispute is settled. The ad hoc decisions have gone both ways.

The congressional oath of office was prescribed by an act of June 1, 1789: "I, A B, do solemnly swear (or affirm) that I will support the Constitution of the United States." [5] In the light of Civil War experience, this language was expanded in 1868, to read: "I, A B, do solemnly swear (or affirm) that I will support and defend the Constitution of the United States against all enemies, foreign and domestic; that I will bear true faith and allegiance to the same; that I take this obligation freely, without any mental reservation or purpose of evasion; and that I will well and faithfully discharge the duties of the office on which I am about to enter. So help me God." [6]

Before the first meeting of each Congress, Senate and House officials compile lists of members-elect on the basis of certifications signed by the state governors and secretaries of state. At the first meeting of each house in a new Congress, the presiding officer (the Speaker in the House and the vice president in the Senate) administers the oath orally in the form of a question beginning, "Do you solemnly swear (or affirm). . .?" and the answer by each new member is "I do." New members chosen between regular elections are sworn in the same way.

The number of new members who are sworn together has varied. In the Senate, the oath was administered in some Congresses to groups of four and in later Congresses to all new members at once; since 1927, the oath has been administered to groups of four. In the House, the oath was administered for many years by state delegations, but since 1929, to all new members at once.

Challenge Procedure

A member's right to take the oath and be seated may be challenged by an already seated member or by a private individual or group. A member-elect whose right to a seat is questioned presents himself in the usual way to take the oath. The presiding officer, either on his authority or, more often, on the basis of a motion, may ask the individual to stand aside while the oath is administered to other members-elect. Sometimes, a member-elect takes the oath without prejudice and a resolution to investigate his right to the seat is introduced later.

A member-elect who has stood aside still may go onto the chamber floor. The House in particular has allowed a challenged member to argue his claim to the seat. House Rule 32, which lists those who may be "admitted to the Hall of the House," includes "contestants in election cases during the pendency of their cases in the House."

The Senate rule on floor access doesn't mention persons involved in election contests. Traditionally, however, contestants have been present during consideration of their cases.

A disputed seat controversy ususally is sent to a committee. Sometimes, a select committee is established for this purpose; at other times, the question is referred to the Senate Rules or House Committee on Administration or another standing committee. The committee often holds hearings and usually presents a report and a draft resolution incorporating its recommendations.

Qualification Controversies

Until the Powell case, Congress had acted from time to time as if it were entitled to add qualifications as well as to wink at failure to meet them.

Alexander Hamilton in No. 60 of *The Federalist* wrote: "The qualifications of the persons who may ... be chosen are defined and fixed in the Constitution, and are unalterable by the legislature." [7]

Later authorities, including a House committee in 1900 considering the seating of a Mormon convicted of polygamy, argued that the Constitutional Convention intended to empower Congress to add qualifications. The committee concluded that if the Convention meant to restrict qualifications to the three in the Constitution, it would have phrased them affirmatively. For example, the framers would have written: "Every member of the House of Representatives shall be of the age of 25 years at least," rather than deliberately using supposedly more flexible negative phrasing: "No person shall be a Representative who shall not have attained to the age of 25 years."

The qualifications issue was a dilemma. If Congress followed only the three requirements, it had to seat individuals regarded as obnoxious. If it excluded such individuals, it could be charged with exceeding its powers. The Civil War turmoil focused the issue.

Both houses added a qualification for membership in 1862 known as the "Ironclad Oath Law" or the "Test Oath Law." It required members to swear, before taking the oath of office, that they had never voluntarily borne arms against the United States or aided, recognized, or supported a jurisdiction hostile to the United States. This law remained in effect until the 14th Amendment was ratified in 1868.

Cases Occurring in the Senate

Only three senators-elect have been denied seats for lack of the requisite qualifications:

(1) Albert Gallatin, born in Geneva, became a U.S. citizen in 1785. When elected to the Senate by the Pennsylvania Legislature in 1793, he had not been a citizen nine years as required by the Constitution. He contended that every man who had taken part in the Revolution was a citizen according to the law of reason and nature. The Senate on Feb. 28, 1794, by a vote of 14 to 12, disagreed and said his election was void. [8]

(2) James Shields, a native of Ireland, was elected a senator from Illinois in 1848. Shields had been naturalized Oct. 21, 1840, but would not be a citizen until Oct. 20, 1849. He appeared March 5, 1849, to take his seat. Although Shields was seated on March 6, the Senate on March 15 adopted a resolution declaring his election void on the ground of insufficient years of citizenship. Shields then was elected to fill the vacancy thus created and was allowed to serve from Oct. 27, 1849.

(3) Phillip F. Thomas of Maryland had given $100 to his son when the son entered Confederate military service. When Thomas was elected a U.S. senator by the Maryland Legislature in 1866, he was charged with being disloyal for giving aid and comfort to the enemy. The Senate voted 27 to 20 to exclude Thomas.

Exclusion proceedings based on the age qualification for senators were avoided, in two cases, by different means. When Henry Clay, D-R-Ky., arrived in Washington to take his seat, he lacked five months of the required 30 years. The Senate tacitly ignored this fact, and he was sworn in, Nov. 19, 1806. Rush D. Holt, D-W.Va. (1935-41), also had not reached the age of 30 when the time came for him to enter the Senate in 1935. He delayed the presentation of his credentials until his 30th birthday and was then admitted. The Senate later rejected, 62-17, a proposal to declare Holt's election invalid on the ground of age.

Exclusion Cases Rejected

Exclusion proceedings have not always blocked a member from taking a seat.

Severe illness prevented John M. Niles, D, in 1843 from taking the Senate seat to which the Connecticut Legislature had elected him. Because Niles showed signs of mental strain when he arrived in April 1844, the Senate appointed a committee to consider his case. The committee reported that Niles was "laboring under mental and physical debility, but is not of unsound mind." It said there was "no sufficient reason why he be not qualified and permitted to take his seat," which he did within a month. [9]

Hiram R. Revels, R-Miss., a former slave who was elected to the Senate in 1870, was challenged because he had not become a citizen until 1868, when the 14th Amendment was ratified. The Senate ruled that the amendment made Revels retroactively a citizen and seated him.

Reed Smoot, R-Utah (1903-33), a senator-elect in 1903, was challenged by Utah citizens who said that as a Mormon he favored polygamy and opposed the separation of church and state. Smoot was given the oath on a tentative basis and his eligibility was then studied by the Committee on Privileges and Elections. The committee later concluded that Smoot was not entitled to his seat. When the issue came to a vote in 1907, Sen. Philander C. Knox, R-Pa. (1904-09; 1917-21), argued that a two-thirds vote was required because the action involved expulsion rather than

Senate Cases Involving Qualifications for Membership

Congress	Session	Year	Member-elect	Grounds	Disposition
3rd	1st	1793	Albert Gallatin, D-Pa.	Citizenship	*Excluded*
11th	1st	1809	Stanley Griswold, D-Ohio	Residence	Admitted
28th	1st	1844	John M. Niles, D-Conn.	Sanity	Admitted
31st	Special	1849	James Shields, D-Ill.	Citizenship	*Excluded*
37th	2nd	1861	Benjamin Stark, D-Ore.	Loyalty	Admitted
40th	1st	1867	Phillip F. Thomas, D-Md.	Loyalty	*Excluded*
41st	2nd	1870	Hiram R. Revels, R-Miss.	Citizenship	Admitted
41st	2nd	1870	Adelbert Ames, R-Miss.	Residence	Admitted
59th	2nd	1907	Reed Smoot, R-Utah	Mormonism	Admitted*
69th	2nd	1926	Arthur R. Gould, R-Maine	Character	Admitted
74th	1st	1935	Rush D. Holt, D-W.Va.	Age	Admitted
75th	1st	1937	George L. Berry, D-Tenn.	Character	Admitted
77th	2nd	1942	William Langer, R-N.D.	Character	Admitted*
80th	1st	1947	Theodore G. Bilbo, D-Miss.	Character	Died before Senate acted

* Senate decided that a two-thirds majority, as in expulsion cases, would be required for exclusion. The resolution proposing exclusion did not receive a two-thirds majority.

Source: U.S., Congress, Senate, Committee on Rules and Administration, Subcommittee on Privileges and Elections, *Senate Election, Expulsion and Censure Cases from 1793 to 1972*, compiled by Richard D. Hupman, S Doc 92-7, 92nd Cong. 1st sess., 1972.

exclusion. Knox said, "There is no question as to Sen. Smoot's possessing the qualifications prescribed by the Constitution, and therefore we cannot deprive him of his seat by a majority vote." [10] The two-thirds requirement was approved, but it never mattered. In voting, the Senate rejected motions to expel and exclude Smoot by 24-43 and 28-42 votes.

When Arthur R. Gould, R-Maine (1926-31), was elected to the Senate in 1926, a controversy arose over an accusation that some 14 years earlier he had been involved in bribery. In the committee's hearings on the matter, Gould contended that denying him a seat denied the right of Maine's citizens to select their own senator. The committee reported that Gould's alleged part in the bribery case had not been proved.

In 1941 William Langer's, R-N.D. (1941-59), claim to a Senate seat was challenged over alleged misconduct during his service as governor of North Dakota and in other posts in that state's government. When an investigating committee recommended that Langer be excluded, the Senate added a two-thirds requirement, as it had done in the case of Reed Smoot, and then on March 27, 1942, voted down the proposed resolution.

The most recent exclusion case involving a senator-elect arose in January 1947 over Theodore G. Bilbo, D-Miss. (1935-47). Bilbo had been accused of fraud, violence in preventing blacks from voting, and other offenses. He was asked to stand aside when other senators-elect took the oath. He died in August 1947 before the question of his right to his seat had been settled.

Cases Occurring in the House

Ten members-elect have been excluded from the House of Representatives as not qualified to serve.

John Bailey of Massachusetts was the first excluded. He was challenged on the ground that he was not a resident of the district that he purported to represent. The House, by a resolution of March 18, 1824, declared that Bailey was not entitled to his seat. He returned home, was elected to fill the vacancy created by his exclusion, and was seated Dec. 13, 1824.

In 1867, Southern states elected to Congress four citizens whom the House found to be tainted with acts of disloyalty during the Civil War. They were Democrats John Y. Brown and John D. Young of Kentucky, and independents W. D. Simpson of South Carolina and John A. Wimpy of Georgia.

South Carolina had another representative-elect excluded three years later. Benjamin F. Whittemore, a Republican, was censured by the House in 1870 for selling appointments to the U.S. Military Academy and resigned on Feb. 24 of that year. When Whittemore was re-elected to the same Congress, Rep. John A. Logan, D-Ill., discussed his case on the House floor: "It is said that the constituency has the right to elect such member as they deem proper. I say no. We cannot say that he shall be of a certain politics, or of a certain religion, or anything of that kind; but, Sir, we have the right to say that he shall not be a man of infamous character." [11] The House on June 21, 1870, excluded Whittemore by a vote of 130 to 76.

The House based two exclusions on polygamy. George Q. Cannon was elected in 1872 as a delegate from the Utah Territory. In the first and second sessions of the 43rd Congress, the question of his eligibility was raised and was settled in his favor. Cannon served in the House until 1881 without being challenged, but in 1882 the issue arose again. The House, taking account both of Cannon's practice of polygamy and of doubts about the validity of his election, declared the seat vacant, in effect excluding Cannon.

In 1900, members of the House questioned the right of Brigham H. Roberts, elected as a representative from Utah, to take his seat. Roberts had been found guilty some years earlier of violating an 1882 law that prohibited polygamy. This was the case, mentioned earlier, in which an investigating committee argued that the Founding Fathers had not foreclosed the right of Congress to establish qualifications for membership other than those mentioned in the Constitution. The House refused to seat Roberts, 268-50.

In the 20th century, only Victor L. Berger, Wisconsin Socialist, and Adam Clayton Powell Jr. *(see below)* have been excluded from the House.

Berger had been convicted in 1919 of violating the Espionage Act of June 15, 1917, by publishing anti-war statements. While an appeal was pending, he was elected to the 66th Congress. By resolution of the House, Nov. 10, 1919, Berger was declared "not entitled to take the oath of office as a representative." [12] He was re-elected during the same Congress and excluded again on Jan. 10, 1920. But after the Supreme Court had reversed Berger's conviction, he was elected to the House three more times, in 1922, 1924 and 1926, and was seated without question.

Cases in which House proceedings on exclusion ended in admission of the representative-elect evoked various memorable exchanges on the floor. An example is the case of John C. Conner, D-Texas, who was accused of having whipped black soldiers under his command in 1868 and of having boasted in 1869 that he would escape conviction by a military court by bribing witnesses. Rep. James A. Garfield, R-Ohio, speaking in the House on March 31, 1870, raised a constitutional question on this case: "Allow me to ask . . . if anything in the Constitution of the United States . . . forbids that a 'moral monster' shall be elected to the Congress?" [13] Rep. Ebon C. Ingersoll, R-Ill., replied: "I believe the people may elect a moral monster to Congress if they see fit, but I believe that Congress has a right to exclude that moral monster from a seat if they see fit." [14] A resolution allowing Conner to take his seat was adopted the same day.

The Powell Case

One of the stormiest episodes in congressional history was the precedent-shattering case of Rep. Adam Clayton Powell Jr., D-N.Y. (1945-67; 1969-71).

It was Powell's exclusion from the House that led to the Supreme Court decision prohibiting Congress from adding to the constitutional qualifications for membership in Congress.

In 1937 Powell succeeded his father as pastor of the Abyssinian Baptist Church in Harlem, one of the largest congregations in the country. The new pastor was elected

to the 79th Congress in 1944 with the nomination of both the Democratic and Republican parties. He took his seat with the Democrats, was re-elected regularly by large majorities, served as chairman of the House Committee on Education and Labor from 1961 to 1967, and was considered by many observers the most powerful black in the United States. Throughout his legislative career, he retained his pastorate.

Powell's troubles stemmed in part from his flamboyant personality and his apparent disregard for the law. On the eve of Powell's 1952 re-election bid, the Internal Revenue Service said that he had underestimated his 1945 income tax by $2,749. A 1960 trial for criminal tax evasion resulted in a hung jury, and Powell eventually paid $27,833 in back taxes and penalties. Meanwhile he lost two suits brought by a widow in his district, Esther James, whom he had described in a television interview as a "bag woman" or graft collector for New York City police.

While in legal difficulties Powell was held in contempt of court on four occasions.

In the 1950s and the early 1960s, Powell repeatedly went on costly pleasure trips at government expense. In addition, he incurred criticism for taking a staff member, Corinne A. Huff, on many trips to Bimini Island in the Bahamas. Out of government funds, he paid his wife $20,578 a year as a clerk while she lived in Puerto Rico. She was ordered dropped from the payroll in 1967.

The preceding year Powell was stripped by his committee colleagues of his powers as chairman of the House Education and Labor Committee. He had angered committee Democrats by his long absences which delayed House action on President Johnson's anti-poverty bill. By a vote of 27 to 1, the committee Sept. 22, 1966, adopted new rules, one of which provided that if the chairman failed to bring a bill to the floor, one of the six subcommittee chairmen could do so.

The House Democratic Caucus on Jan. 9, 1967, removed Powell from the chairmanship of the Committee on Education and Labor for the duration of the 90th Congress. This was the first time since 1925 that a committee chairman had been deposed in either house of Congress. Powell, who attended the caucus, called the action "a lynching, northern style." [15] A day later, Powell was embroiled in a challenge to his seat in the House.

When members of the House convened Jan. 10, 1967, a resolution submitted by Morris K. Udall, D-Ariz., proposed that Powell be sworn in, pending the result of a 60-day investigation of his conduct by a select committee. Udall contended that stripping Powell of his chairmanship was punishment enough because his malfeasance was based on his misuse of that position. But the resolution was rejected on a 126-305 vote.

The House then adopted a resolution offered by Minority Leader Gerald R. Ford, R-Mich. (1949-73), which denied Powell his seat pending an investigation. The vote was 363 to 65.

House Judiciary Committee Chairman Emanuel Celler, D-N.Y. (1923-73), was chairman of the select committee appointed to investigate Powell's qualifications for his seat. The committee conducted hearings beginning Feb. 8, 1967. Its report, submitted Feb. 23, included a recommendation, unprecedented in congressional history, that Powell be fined. The committee proposed that he be sworn in; that his seniority be based on the date of his swearing in; that he be censured for "gross misconduct" through misuse of funds of the Committee on Education and Labor,

House Cases Involving Qualifications for Membership

Congress	Session	Year	Member-elect	Grounds	Disposition
1st	1st	1789	William L. Smith, Fed-S.C.	Citizenship	Admitted
10th	1st	1807	Philip B. Key, Fed-Md.	Residence	Admitted
10th	1st	1807	William McCreery, —Md.	Residence	Admitted
18th	1st	1823	Gabriel Richard, Ind-Mich. Terr.	Citizenship	Admitted
18th	1st	1823	John Bailey, Ind-Mass.	Residence	*Excluded*
18th	1st	1823	John Forsyth, D-Ga.	Residence	Admitted
27th	1st	1841	David Levy, R-Fla. Terr.	Citizenship	Admitted
36th	1st	1859	John Y. Brown, D-Ky.	Age	Admitted
40th	1st	1867	William H. Hooper, D-Utah Terr.	Mormonism	Admitted
40th	1st	1867	Lawrence S. Trimble, D-Ky.	Loyalty	Admitted
40th	1st	1867	John Y. Brown, D-Ky.	Loyalty	*Excluded*
40th	1st	1867	John D. Young, D-Ky.	Loyalty	*Excluded*
40th	1st	1867	Roderick R. Butler, R-Tenn.	Loyalty	Admitted
40th	1st	1867	John A. Wimpy, Ind-Ga.	Loyalty	*Excluded*
40th	1st	1867	W. D. Simpson, Ind-S.C.	Loyalty	*Excluded*
41st	1st	1869	John M. Rice, D-Ky.	Loyalty	Admitted
41st	2nd	1870	Lewis McKenzie, Unionist-Va.	Loyalty	Admitted
41st	2nd	1870	George W. Booker, Conservative-Va.	Loyalty	Admitted
41st	2nd	1870	Benjamin F. Whittemore, R-S.C.	Malfeasance	*Excluded*
41st	2nd	1870	John C. Conner, D-Texas	Misconduct	Admitted
43rd	1st	1873	George Q. Cannon, R-Utah Terr.	Mormonism	Admitted
43rd	2nd	1874	George Q. Cannon, R-Utah Terr.	Polygamy	Admitted
47th	1st	1881	John S. Barbour, D-Va.	Residence	Admitted
47th	1st	1882	George Q. Cannon, R-Utah Terr.	Polygamy	Seat vacated[1]
50th	1st	1887	James B. White, R-Ind.	Citizenship	Admitted
56th	1st	1899	Robert W. Wilcox, Ind-Hawaii Terr.	Bigamy, treason	Admitted
56th	1st	1900	Brigham H. Roberts, D-Utah	Polygamy	*Excluded*
59th	1st	1905	Anthony Michalek, R-Ill.	Citizenship	Admitted
66th	1st	1919	Victor L. Berger, Socialist-Wis.	Sedition	*Excluded*
66th	2nd	1920	Victor L. Berger, Socialist-Wis.	Sedition	*Excluded*
69th	1st	1926	John W. Langley, R-Ky.	Criminal misconduct	Resigned
70th	1st	1927	James M. Beck, R-Pa.	Residence	Admitted
71st	1st	1929	Ruth B. Owen, D-Fla.	Citizenship	Admitted
90th	1st	1967	Adam C. Powell Jr., D-N.Y.	Misconduct	*Excluded*[2]
96th	1st	1979	Richard A. Tonry, D-La.	Vote fraud	Resigned

1. Discussions of polygamy and an election contest led to a declaration that the seat was vacant.
2. Supreme Court June 16, 1969, ruled that the House had improperly excluded Powell.

Source: Hinds and Cannon, *Precedents of the House of Representatives of the United States,* 11 vols. (1935-41); Joint Committee on Congressional Operations, *House of Representatives Exclusion, Censure and Expulsion Cases from 1789 to 1973,* committee print, 93rd Cong., 1st sess., 1973.

refusal to pay the judgment against him, and non-cooperation with House investigating committees; and that he be fined $40,000, to be paid to the clerk of the House in the form of a monthly deduction of $1,000 from Powell's salary, in order to "offset any civil liability of Mr. Powell to the United States." [16]

The House on March 1, 1967, rejected the committee's proposals and adopted instead a resolution excluding Powell from the 90th Congress — the first exclusion since Victor L. Berger was barred in 1919 and 1920. On the select committee's proposals, the vote was 202 in favor, 222 against; on the exclusion resolution, 307 in favor, 116 against.

As in his ouster from his committee chairmanship, Powell ascribed his downfall to racism. It is possible that racial feeling played a part in the vote to exclude Powell. Celler said on television and on the House floor that he saw "an element of racism in the vote." Arlen J. Large, a Washington correspondent, wrote in *The Wall Street Journal,* March 22, 1967: "Disclaimers of race as a factor in Mr. Powell's exclusion don't jibe with the nearly solid anti-Powell votes of Southern congressmen, reflecting the bitterly worded letters from white voters back home."

In his appearances before the select committee, Powell responded only to questions relating to the constitutional requirements for House membership — his age, citizenship and inhabitancy. These were the only questions that the House could properly inquire into, Powell and his lawyers claimed. Upon his exclusion by the House, Powell filed suit. The case eventually reached the Supreme Court, which on June 16, 1969, ruled that the House had improperly excluded Powell, a duly elected representative who met the constitutional requirements for membership.

His district re-elected Powell in a special election April 11, 1967, but he did not apply to the House to be seated while appealing his exclusion to the courts. Re-elected in 1978, Powell was sworn in and seated but subjected to loss of seniority and fined $25,000. In the voting on the resolution imposing these penalties, there were 254 yeas, 158 nays.

Although he had won the right to be seated, Powell rarely attended Congress, preferring instead his retreat in Bimini. In 1970 Charles B. Rangel successfully challenged Powell in the Democratic primary and went on to win the general election. Powell died in Miami, Fla., April 4, 1972.

Contested Elections

Decentralization of control over elections in the United States may have strengthened participatory democracy, but it has led frequently to controversy over election results. Losing candidates and their supporters believe in many cases that more voters were on their side than the official count showed. Floyd M. Riddick wrote in *The United States Congress: Organization and Procedure:* "Seldom if ever has a Congress organized without some losing candidate for a seat in either the Senate or House contesting the right of the member-elect to be senator or representative, as the case might be, as a result of the election in which the losing candidate participated." [17]

To avert partisanship, a 1798 law established procedures to settle contested House elections. The law expired in 1804. A new law was passed in 1851 and amended in 1873 and 1875. These laws sought to give a judicial rather than partisan character to contested election proceedings, but party loyalty usually governed the outcomes.

The Federal Contested Election Act of 1969 superseded the earlier legislation. The new law, which also applied only to House contests, prescribed procedures for instituting a challenge and presenting testimony but did not establish criteria to govern decisions. It was more restrictive than earlier laws because it allowed only candidates on the ballot or *bona fide* write-in candidates to contest election results. Previously, anyone having an interest in a congressional election could initiate proceedings.

Senators were chosen by state legislatures until the adoption in 1913 of the 17th Amendment to the Constitution, which provided for direct popular elections. Before then, contested senatorial elections often involved accusations of corruption in the legislatures. Congress never passed a law on contested Senate elections comparable to that for the House.

The number of contested congressional elections since 1789 probably is in the hundreds, most experts agree. But an exact number has never been determined because students of the subject disagree on what constitutes a contested election. George B. Galloway of the Legislative Reference Service stated in 1953 that there had been 136 election contests in the Senate from 1789 to 1952. John T. Dempsey, in an unpublished 1956 University of Michigan doctoral dissertation, counted 125 in the Senate from 1789 to 1955. (It appears that Galloway included, and Dempsey excluded, contested appointments made by state governors to fill seats vacated by death or otherwise.) In these same time periods, Galloway counted 541 House election contests while Dempsey put the number at 546.

Senate Cases

Lorimer. Three contested Senate elections in the 20th century illustrate the complexity of such proceedings. William Lorimer, R-Ill. (1895-1901, 1903-09; Senate 1909-12), was elected a senator by the Illinois Legislature and took his seat on June 18, 1909. In May 1910 he requested that the Committee on Privileges and Elections examine press reports of bribery and corruption in the election. The Senate on March 1, 1911, rejected 40-46 a resolution declaring that Lorimer had not been "duly and legally elected." [18]

The case was reopened in the next Congress and the decision reversed after a specially appointed committee heard more testimony. While the committee majority favored dropping the charges, the minority pressed to overturn Lorimer's election. On June 13, 1912, the Senate adopted a resolution, 55-28, declaring the election invalid. Throughout the proceedings on Lorimer his Republican Party held almost a 2 to 1 majority in the Senate.

Vare. Corruption also was the central issue in the case of Republican William S. Vare in Pennsylvania. During the primaries in 1926, newspapers reported illegal activities by Vare supporters to aid their candidate. Vare won the primary and the November election.

The Senate meanwhile, on May 19, 1926, had appointed a committee to investigate Pennsylvania's senatorial primaries and the fall election. Vare's Democratic rival, ex-Secretary of Labor William B. Wilson, charged that Vare's victory was won illegally. When Congress met, Vare was asked to stand aside while other senators-elect were sworn in.

Proceedings dragged on for two years. The Senate received a series of reports on the case, including one from a special committee, Feb. 22, 1929, that said Vare, because of excessive use of money to get nominated and elected, was not entitled to a seat. On Dec. 5, the Senate Committee on Privileges and Elections reported that Vare had received a plurality of the legal votes cast in the election. But the Senate the following day voted 58-22 to deny Vare a seat and 66 to 15 that Wilson had not been elected. The Pennsylvania governor later appointed Joseph R. Grundy, R (1929-30), to the vacant Senate seat. Republicans controlled the Senate throughout the proceedings on Vare.

Wyman-Durkin Contest. The closest Senate election since popular voting for the Senate was instituted in 1913 occurred Nov. 5, 1974, in New Hampshire, where Republican Louis C. Wyman (House 1963-65, 1967-74; Senate 1974-75) led Democrat John A. Durkin (Senate 1975-80) by only two votes.

The election spawned a long, bitter and embarrassing dispute in the Senate covering seven months and 41 roll-call votes which ended when the Senate for the first time declared a vacancy due to its inability to decide an election contest.[19]

The dispute began when final unofficial returns gave Wyman a 355-vote margin over Durkin. A recount then found Durkin the winner by 10 votes. The state ballot commission examined the recount and found Wyman the winner by two votes.

(Wyman actually served for a short period. His predecessor, Sen. Norris Cotton, R (House 1947-54; Senate 1954-74), who was retiring, resigned late in December 1974 to take advantage of a special early-retirement pension bonus. The New Hampshire governor appointed Wyman to fill the remaining 60 hours of Cotton's term, until noon Jan. 3, 1975. Had Wyman been seated, the few extra hours would have helped establish seniority rights over other newly elected senators.)

Durkin filed a petition of contest with the Senate Dec. 27, 1974, challenging Wyman's right to the seat and defending the validity of his own recount victory. Wyman Jan. 5, 1975, filed a petition in the Senate urging that Durkin's petition be dismissed. He also asked that the seat be declared vacant, to open the way for a new election in New Hampshire. Wyman and his supporters feared Durkin would win if the Senate, with its 61-38 Democratic majority, reviewed the ballot commission findings as the Democratic candidate requested.

The first skirmish occurred soon after the Senate convened. On Jan. 28, the Senate turned aside Republican attempts to seat Wyman temporarily and to declare the seat vacant and voted, 58-34, to send the dispute to the Senate Rules and Administration Committee. The Senate thus accepted the arguments of Senate Majority Leader Mike Mansfield, D-Mont. (House 1943-53; Senate 1953-77), and Rules Chairman Howard W. Cannon, D-Nev., who cited the constitutional provision that each house of Congress should be the judge of its own elections and said the Rules Committee should at least try to determine who won before calling for a new election.

Democrats also said that the conflicting rulings of the New Hampshire authorities precluded seating either of the contestants, even though Wyman had the most recent certification. Republicans claimed that precedent dictated temporary seating of Wyman, without prejudice to Durkin's challenge. But the motion to temporarily seat Wyman failed on a 34-58 vote, while a motion to declare the seat vacant lost, 39-53.

The Rules Committee agreed to examine and recount the ballots in dispute. By April 25 nearly 1,000 ballots had been examined. But the committee failed to agree on 27 of the ballots, splitting on four-to-four tie votes. Tie votes also occurred on eight legal and procedural issues. The eight issues and 27 ballots were sent to the Senate floor to be resolved.

Floor consideration of the disputed election began June 12 with a second attempt by the Republicans to declare the seat vacant. The motion was defeated, 43-55, and a filibuster by Republicans and several Southern Democrats supporting the Republican position began. An unprecedented six attempts were made to invoke cloture (shut off debate) but they all failed to obtain the required 60 votes. An attempt to settle one of the eight disputed issues in Wyman's favor July 15 was defeated on a 44-49 vote. After this loss, the Republicans charged that a Democratic "steamroller" was in operation and refused to allow a vote on any other issue.

The Senate began to spend less and less time each day on the New Hampshire dispute and returned to debate on substantive legislation. But neither side appeared ready to compromise. In the absence of any definitive Senate action, public pressure mounted for a vacancy to be declared and a new election held.

Finally, Durkin relented and asked for a new election. Durkin's change of mind was a surprise to the Senate Democratic leadership, but there was a feeling of relief that the impasse had been broken. The Senate June 30 voted 71-21 to declare the seat vacant as of Aug. 8.

Durkin won the special Sept. 16 election with 53.6 percent of the vote and was sworn in Sept. 18, 1975.

House Cases

William F. Willoughby stated flatly in *Principles of Legislative Organization and Administration* in 1934: "The whole history of the handling of election contests by the House has constituted one of the major scandals of our political system." [20] Willoughby noted that after enactment of the 1851 law on procedures for adjudicating elections "for many years the House made little or no pretense of settling election contests on any basis of equity, political considerations in practically all cases determining the decision reached." In 1955, John T. Dempsey, a doctoral candidate at the University of Michigan, made a case-by-case examination of the 546 contested election cases he had counted in the House. He found that only on 47 occasions, less than 10 percent of the total, did the controlling party award a contested seat to a member of the minority party.

Mississippi Dispute. Perhaps the most dramatic election dispute settled by the House in recent years was that of the Mississippi Five in 1965. The governor of Mississippi certified the election to the House in 1964 of four Democrats and one Republican. The Democrats were Thomas G. Abernethy (1943-73), William M. Colmer (1933-37), Jamie L. Whitten (still a member in 1982) and John Bell Williams (1947-68); the Republican was Prentiss Walker (1965-67).

Their right to be seated in the House was contested by a biracial group, the Mississippi Freedom Democratic Party (M.F.D.P.), formed originally to challenge the seating of an all-white delegation from the state to the 1964 Democratic National Convention. This group, when unsuccessful in getting its candidates on the 1964 congressional election ballot, conducted a rump election in which Annie Devine, Virginia Gray and Fannie L. Hamer were the winners.[21]

The three women, when they sought entrance to the House floor, were barred. However, Speaker John W. McCormack, D-Mass. (1928-71), asked the regular Mississippi representatives-elect to stand aside while the other members of the House were sworn in. Rep. William F. Ryan, D-N.Y. (1961-72), sponsor of the challenge, contended that the regular congressional election in Mississippi was invalid because blacks had been systematically prevented from voting. A resolution to seat the regular Mississippi delegation was adopted on Jan. 4, 1965, by a voice vote.

Later that year Congress enacted the Voting Rights Act of 1965, which contained strict sanctions against states which practiced discrimination against minority voters.

DISCIPLINING ERRANT MEMBERS

For offenses of sufficient gravity, each house of Congress may punish its members by expulsion or censure (the words "condemn" and "denounce" have been used as synonyms for censure). Of the two degrees of punishment, censure is milder and requires a simple majority vote while expulsion requires a two-thirds majority. Censure also has the advantage of not depriving constituents of their elected senators or representatives. Grounds for disciplining members usually consist of a member's action during service in Congress. Both houses have seldom used their power to punish a member for offenses committed prior to an election and have been shy about punishing misdeeds committed during a previous Congress.

For minor transgressions of the rules, the presiding officer of either house may call a member to order, without a formal move to censure. For example, on Jan. 14, 1955, Sen. Russell B. Long, D-La., while presiding over the Senate, called Sen. Joseph R. McCarthy, R-Wis. (1947-57), to order when McCarthy questioned the motives of some senators who had voted on a resolution continuing an investigation of communists in government. Long said: "The statement of the junior senator from Wisconsin was that other senators were insincere. In making that statement, the senator from Wisconsin spoke contrary to the rules of the Senate. . . . He must take his seat." [22] Later on the same day, Long again called McCarthy to order.

In recent years, Congress has turned to other methods when it wants to discipline members yet wants to avoid the strong measure of censure or expulsion. These methods have included denial of the member's right to vote, fines, stripping of chairmanships and reprimand.

Expulsion

Fifteen senators have been expelled, one in 1797 and 14 during the Civil War. Formal expulsion proceedings in the Senate have been instituted nine times since the Civil War, always without success. (Chart, p. 181)

In the House, only four members have been expelled, three in 1861 and one in 1980. Ten representatives were censured as a lesser form of punishment during expulsion proceedings against them. (Chart, p. 183)

Conspiracy against a foreign country (the 1797 case in the Senate) and support of a rebellion (the Civil War cases of 14 senators and three representatives) were the only grounds on which a member of Congress was expelled until the Abscam corruption scandal of 1980. In a few cases, a member escaped expulsion by resigning; the most recent was Sen. Harrison A. Williams Jr., D-N.J. (House 1953-57; Senate 1959-82) in 1982.

Grounds for Expulsion

In the successful expulsion cases, the grounds were conspiracy, disloyalty or corruption. The unsuccessful cases were concerned with the killing of a representative in a duel, the assaulting of a senator or a representative, treasonable or offensive utterances, sedition, corruption and Mormonism.

Prior Offenses. The most important question raised about the validity of grounds for expulsion has been whether a member of either house may be expelled for offenses committed prior to his election.

John Quincy Adams, while serving in the Senate, submitted a committee report supporting the Senate's power to expel a member for pre-election conduct that came to light after he had taken his seat. The case was that of John Smith, D-Ohio, who allegedly had been connected with Aaron Burr's conspiracy to separate several of the Western states from the Union. Adams' committee, in its report of Dec. 31, 1807, said: "When a man whom his fellow citizens have honored with their confidence on the pledge of a spotless reputation has degraded himself by the commission of infamous crimes, which become suddenly and unexpectedly revealed to the world, defective, indeed, would be that institution which should be impotent to discard from its bosom the contagion of such a member." [23]

The expulsion case against Smith was lost by a single vote on April 9, 1808, when 19 yeas, not enough to make up the required two-thirds, were cast for expulsion, against 10 nays. Later Congresses that debated proposals to unseat members repeatedly took up the question of whether acts committed prior to the member's election furnished legitimate grounds for expulsion.

Incompatible Office. The Constitution, in Article I, Section 6, provides: "[N]o Person holding any Office under the United States, shall be a Member of either House during his Continuance in Office." When a senator or representative has accepted appointment to another "Office under the United States," he has jeopardized but not always lost his privilege of remaining in Congress, depending on the type of office he accepted and the attitude of the house in which he was serving. If he lost his post in Congress by accepting another office, he is not considered to have been expelled; his seat is treated as having been vacated.

Cases arising in the Civil War and subsequent wars in which members of Congress served in the armed forces generally did not result in vacating of their seats. In the war with Spain, a House committee appointed to investigate the question recommended adoption of a resolution declaring vacant the seats of four representatives who had accepted commissions in the Army to serve in the war with Spain. "No mere patriotic sentiment," it said, "should be permitted to override the plain language of the fundamental written law." [24] On March 2, 1899, the House, by a vote of 77 yeas and 163 nays, declined to consider the proposed resolution.

Cases of Expulsion in the Senate

Congress	Session	Year	Member-elect	Grounds	Disposition
5th	2nd	1797	William Blount, Ind-Tenn.	Anti-Spanish conspiracy	*Expelled*
10th	1st	1808	John Smith, D-Ohio	Disloyalty	Not expelled
35th	1st	1858	Henry M. Rice, D-Minn.	Corruption	Not expelled
37th	1st	1861	James M. Mason, D-Va.	Support of rebellion	*Expelled*
37th	1st	1861	Robert M. Hunter, D-Va.	Support of rebellion	*Expelled*
37th	1st	1861	Thomas L. Clingman, D-N.C.	Support of rebellion	*Expelled*
37th	1st	1861	Thomas Bragg, D-N.C.	Support of rebellion	*Expelled*
37th	1st	1861	James Chestnut Jr., States Rights-S.C.	Support of rebellion	*Expelled*
37th	1st	1861	Alfred O. P. Nicholson, D-Tenn.	Support of rebellion	*Expelled*
37th	1st	1861	William K. Sebastian, D-Ark.	Support of rebellion	*Expelled*[1]
37th	1st	1861	Charles B. Mitchel, D-Ark.	Support of rebellion	*Expelled*
37th	1st	1861	John Hemphill, State Rights D-Texas	Support of rebellion	*Expelled*
37th	1st	1861	Louis T. Wigfall, D-Texas[2]	Support of rebellion	Not expelled
37th	1st	1861	Louis T. Wigfall, D-Texas	Support of rebellion	*Expelled*
37th	1st	1861	John C. Breckinridge, D-Ky.	Support of rebellion	*Expelled*
37th	1st	1861	Lazarus W. Powell, D-Ky.	Support of rebellion	Not expelled
37th	2nd	1862	Trusten Polk, D-Mo.	Support of rebellion	*Expelled*
37th	2nd	1862	Jesse D. Bright, D-Ind.	Support of rebellion	*Expelled*
37th	2nd	1862	Waldo P. Johnson, D-Mo.	Support of rebellion	*Expelled*
37th	2nd	1862	James F. Simmons, Whig-R.I.	Corruption	Not expelled
42nd	3rd	1873	James W. Patterson, R-N.H.	Corruption	Not expelled
53rd	1st	1893	William N. Roach, D-N.D.	Embezzlement	Not expelled
58th	3rd	1905	John H. Mitchell, R-Ore.	Corruption	Not expelled
59th	2nd	1907	Reed Smoot, R-Utah	Mormonism	Not expelled
65th	3rd	1919	Robert M. La Follette, R-Wis.	Disloyalty	Not expelled
73rd	2nd	1934	John H. Overton, D.-La.	Corruption	Not expelled
73rd	2nd	1934	Huey P. Long, D-La.	Corruption	Not expelled
77th	2nd	1942	William Langer, R-N.D.	Corruption	Not expelled
97th	2nd	1982	Harrison A. Williams Jr., D-N.J.	Corruption	Not expelled[3]

1. The Senate reversed its decision on Sebastian's expulsion March 3, 1877. Sebastian had died in 1865 but his children were paid an amount equal to his Senate salary between the time of his expulsion and the date of his death.

2. The Senate took no action on an initial resolution expelling Wigfall because he represented a state that had seceded from the Union; three months later he was expelled for supporting the Confederacy.

3. Facing probable expulsion, Williams resigned March 11, 1982.

Source: U.S., Congress, Senate, Committee on Rules and Administration, Subcommittee on Privileges and Elections, *Senate Election, Expulsion and Censure Cases from 1793 to 1972,* compiled by Richard D. Hupman, S Doc 92-7, 92nd Cong., 1st sess., 1972.

Members of both houses have been appointed to serve as commissioners to negotiate peace and arbitrate disputes, as members of "blue ribbon" boards of inquiry, and so forth, without losing their seats in Congress. The House in 1919 authorized members who had been absent on military service to be paid their salaries minus the amount they were paid for military service. Judge Gerhard A. Gesell of the U.S. District Court for the District of Columbia ruled April 2, 1971, that the 117 members who held commissions in military reserve units were violating the incompatible-office clause of the Constitution. The decision reached the Supreme Court which ruled June 25, 1974, that the plaintiffs — present and former members of the reserves opposed to the Vietnam War — did not have legal standing to make the challenge. *(Schlesinger v. Reservists Committee to Stop the War,* 418 U.S. 208)

Civil War Cases

After the Senate's expulsion of William Blount, Ind-Tenn., in 1797 for conspiracy to incite members of two Indian tribes to attack Spanish Florida and Louisiana, the only successful expulsion cases were those resulting from the Civil War.

On Jan. 21, 1861, Jefferson Davis, D-Miss., like a number of other Southern senators before and after that date, announced his support of secession and withdrew from the Senate. On March 14, 1861, 10 days after Lincoln's inauguration, the Senate adopted a resolution ordering that inasmuch as the seats of these Southerners had "become vacant, . . . the Secretary be directed to omit their names respectively from the roll." [25] Although Davis and the five other Southern senators had left voluntarily, they had not formally resigned. Hence the Senate's action bore some resemblance to expulsion.

Senate Expulsions. On a single day, July 11, 1861, the Senate actually expelled 10 members, two each from Arkansas, North Carolina, Texas and Virginia, and one each from South Carolina and Tennessee, for failure to appear in their seats and for participation in secession. The vote was 32 in favor of expulsion, 10 against. Sen. John C. Breckinridge, D-Ky., who had been vice president of the United States from 1857 to 1861, was expelled Dec. 4, 1861, by the following resolution: "Whereas John C. Breckinridge, a member of this body from the State of Kentucky, has joined the enemies of his country, and is now in arms against the Government he had sworn to support: Therefore, Resolved, That said John C. Breckinridge, the traitor, be, and he hereby is, expelled from the Senate." [26] On this resolution the vote was 37 to 0.

Of the 10 expulsions voted by the Senate on July 11, 1861, one was later annulled. In 1877, the Committee on Privileges and Elections reviewed the expulsion of Sen. William K. Sebastian, D-Ark., decided that the Senate had a right to reverse its earlier action and recommended such reversal. The Senate on March 3, 1877, adopted the committee's recommendation, which was based on its findings that the charges made against Sebastian in 1861 were "occasioned by want of information, and by the overruling excitement of a period of great public danger." [27] Sebastian had remained loyal to the Union throughout the war.

In 1862, the Senate expelled three senators, all for disloyalty to the government: Missouri Democrats Trusten Polk and Waldo P. Johnson and Indiana Democrat Jesse D. Bright. Polk was accused of stating in a widely published letter his hopes that Missouri would secede from the Union. Johnson reportedly held similar feelings and did not appear to take his Senate seat. Bright was charged with treason for giving an arms salesman a letter of introduction to Confederate President Jefferson Davis.

House Expulsions. On July 13, 1861, the House expelled a member-elect, John B. Clark, D-Mo., who had not yet taken the oath. After a brief debate on Clark's entrance into the Confederate forces, and without referring the case to a committee, the House adopted the expulsion order by slightly more than a two-thirds vote, 94 to 45.

Two other representatives were expelled in December 1861: John W. Reid, D-Mo., for taking up arms against the country, and Henry C. Burnett for open rebellion against the federal government.

More than 100 years later the House expelled a member, only the fourth such event. Rep. Michael "Ozzie" Myers, D-Pa. (1976-80), one of seven members of Congress caught in the FBI's Abscam trap, was expelled on Oct. 2, 1980. The vote was 376-30. Videotapes made by the FBI had shown Myers accepting a bribe of $50,000 in cash and boasting of his familiarity with Philadelphia officials and the Mafia. Two other Abscam participants found guilty in court resigned from the House to avoid expulsion proceedings: Reps. John W. Jenrette Jr., D-S.C. (1975-80), and Raymond F. Lederer, D-Pa. (1977-81).

Recent Expulsion Efforts

Sen. Robert M. La Follette, R-Wis. (House 1885-91; Senate 1906-25), made a speech at St. Paul, Minn., Sept. 20, 1917, decrying American participation in the war in Europe. On the basis of that speech, Minnesota's Public Safety Commission petitioned the Senate to expel La Follette for sedition. The Senate by a 50-21 vote dismissed the petition on Jan. 16, 1919.

In 1932-34, the two senators from Louisiana, Huey P. Long (1932-35) and John H. Overton (House 1931-33; Senate 1933-48), both Democrats, were accused of fraud and corruption in connection with their nomination and election. The Committee on Privileges and Elections investigated but eventually asked to be taken off the cases. The Senate did so on June 16, 1934, in effect burying expulsion resolutions that had been introduced.

Charges of corruption against Sen.-elect William Langer, R-N.D. (1941-59), prompted an effort to block his admission or to expel him should he be seated. On March 27, 1941, the Senate first rejected a resolution, 37-45, stating that the case did not fall within the constitutional provisions for expulsion. It then rejected, 30-52, a resolution declaring that Langer was not entitled to his seat.

The only senator caught in the Abscam net, New Jersey Democrat Harrison A. Williams Jr., was convicted of accepting stock in a titanium mining company in return for his promise to get government contracts for the mine's output. On Aug. 24, 1981, the Senate Ethics Committee unanimously recommended that the Senate expel Williams. After numerous delays, the Senate began debate on the committee's resolution March 3, 1982. On March 11, when it was clear to all that over two-thirds of the senators would vote for expulsion, Williams resigned his Senate seat. *(Abscam investigation, p. 207)*

Censure

In the entire history of Congress, the Senate has censured eight of its members while the House has censured 20 of its members.

In the Senate, censure proceedings are carried out with a degree of moderation typical of that chamber's proceedings. The alleged offender, for example, is granted the privilege of speaking in his own behalf.

In the House, the treatment of an offender is more harsh. The House often has denied the privilege of speaking to a representative accused of wrongdoing. In most cases in the House, a censured member is treated like a felon; the Speaker calls the person to the bar of the House and makes a solemn pronouncement of censure.

For example, Speaker Frederick H. Gillett, R-Mass. (House 1893-25; Senate 1925-31), on Oct. 27, 1921, directed the sergeant at arms to bring to the bar of the House Rep. Thomas L. Blanton, D-Texas (1917-29). The Speaker then made the following statement:

"Mr. Blanton, by a unanimous vote of the House —

Cases of Expulsion in the House

Congress	Session	Year	Member-elect	Grounds	Disposition
5th	2nd	1798	Matthew Lyon, Anti-Fed-Vt.	Assault on representative	Not expelled
5th	2nd	1798	Roger Griswold, Fed-Conn.	Assault on representative	Not expelled
5th	3rd	1799	Matthew Lyon, Anti-Fed-Vt.	Sedition	Not expelled
25th	2nd	1838	William J. Graves, Whig-Ky.	Killing of representative in duel	Not expelled
25th	3rd	1839	Alexander Duncan, Whig-Ohio	Offensive publication	Not expelled
34th	1st	1856	Preston S. Brooks, State Rights Dem.-S.C.	Assault on senator	Not expelled
34th	3rd	1857	Orsamus B. Matteson, Whig-N.Y.	Corruption	Not expelled
34th	3rd	1857	William A. Gilbert, Whig-N.Y.	Corruption	Not expelled
34th	3rd	1857	William W. Welch, American-Conn.	Corruption	Not expelled
34th	3rd	1857	Francis S. Edwards, American-N.Y.	Corruption	Not expelled
35th	1st	1858	Orsamus B. Matteson, Whig-N.Y.	Corruption	Not expelled
37th	1st	1861	John B. Clark, D-Mo.	Support of rebellion	*Expelled*
37th	1st	1861	Henry C. Burnett, D-Ky.	Support of rebellion	*Expelled*
37th	1st	1861	John W. Reid, D-Mo.	Support of rebellion	*Expelled*
38th	1st	1864	Alexander Long, D-Ohio	Treasonable utterance	Not expelled*
38th	1st	1864	Benjamin G. Harris, D-Md.	Treasonable utterance	Not expelled*
39th	1st	1866	Lovell H. Rousseau, R-Ky.	Assault on representative	Not expelled*
41st	2nd	1870	Benjamin F. Whittemore, R-S.C.	Corruption	Not expelled*
41st	2nd	1870	Roderick R. Butler, R-Tenn.	Corruption	Not expelled*
42nd	3rd	1873	Oakes Ames, R-Mass.	Corruption	Not expelled*
42nd	3rd	1873	James Brooks, D-N.Y.	Corruption	Not expelled*
43rd	2nd	1875	John Y. Brown, D-Ky.	Insult to representative	Not expelled*
44th	1st	1875	William S. King, R-Minn.	Corruption	Not expelled
44th	1st	1875	John G. Schumaker, D-N.Y.	Corruption	Not expelled
48th	1st	1884	William P. Kellogg, R-La.	Corruption	Not expelled
67th	1st	1921	Thomas L. Blanton, D-Texas	Abuse of leave to print	Not expelled*
96th	2nd	1980	Michael "Ozzie" Myers, D-Pa.	Corruption	*Expelled*

*Censured after expulsion move failed or was withdrawn.

Source: Hinds and Cannon, *Precedents of the House of Representatives of the United States,* 11 vols. (1935-41); Joint Committee on Congressional Operations, *House of Representatives Exclusion, Censure and Expulsion Cases from 1789 to 1973,* committee print, 93rd Cong., 1st sess., 1973; *Congressional Quarterly Almanac 1980.* (Washington, D.C.: Congressional Quarterly, 1981).

yeas, 293; nays, none — I have been directed to censure you because, when you had been allowed the courtesy of the House to print a speech which you did not deliver, you inserted in it foul and obscene matter, which you knew you could not have spoken on the floor; and that disgusting matter, which could not have been circulated through the mails in any other publication without violating the law, was transmitted as part of the proceedings of this House to thousands of homes and libraries throughout the country, to be read by men and women, and worst of all by children, whose prurient curiosity it would excite and corrupt. In accordance with the instructions of the House and as its representative, I pronounce upon you its censure." [28]

Censure by the Senate

Timothy Pickering, Fed-Mass., was the first member to be censured by the Senate. In December 1810, he had read aloud in the chamber secret documents relating to the 1803 convention with France for the cession of Louisiana. The Senate on Jan. 2, 1811, adopted the following resolution of censure: "Resolved, That Timothy Pickering, a Senator from the State of Massachusetts, having, ... whilst the Senate was in session with open doors, read from his place certain documents confidentially communicated by the President of the United States to the Senate, the injunction of secrecy not having been removed, has, in so doing, committed a violation of the rules of this body." [29] Twenty senators voted for the resolution; seven, against it.

Benjamin Tappan, D-Ohio, was similarly censured on May 10, 1844, when the Senate adopted a two-part resolution concerning his release to the press of confidential material relating to a treaty for the annexation of Texas. The first part, adopted 35 to 7, censured Tappan for releasing the documents in "flagrant violation" of the Senate rules. The second, adopted 39 to 3, accepted Tappan's apology and said that no further censure would "be inflicted on him." [30]

Threatened violence was involved in the next censure case in the Senate. On the Senate floor April 7, 1850, Thomas H. Benton, D-Mo., made menacing gestures and advanced toward Henry S. Foote, Unionist-Miss., while Foote was making a speech. Foote drew a pistol from his pocket and cocked it. Before any damage was done, other senators intervened and restored order. A committee appointed to consider the incident said in its report, July 30, that what the two men had done was deplorable. The committee recommended that Foote be censured, but the Senate took no action. This was the only Senate case in which an investigating committee's recommendation of censure was not adopted.

More than half a century later, on Feb. 22, 1902, while the Senate was debating Philippine affairs, Sen. Benjamin R. Tillman, D-S.C. (1895-1918), made a statement questioning the integrity of Sen. John L. McLaurin, D-S.C. (1897-1903). When McLaurin branded it as "a willful, malicious and deliberate lie," [31] Tillman advanced toward McLaurin, and they engaged in a brief fist-fight. After they had been separated, the Senate by a vote of 61 to 0 declared them to be "in contempt of the Senate" and referred the matter to the Committee on Privileges and Elections for a report on any further action that should be taken.

The committee on Feb. 27 reported a resolution recommending censure and the Senate adopted the resolution by a vote of 54 to 12.

The censure case of Sen. Hiram Bingham, R-Conn. (1924-33), occurred in 1929 when he placed on the Senate payroll, as a member of his staff, Charles L. Eyanson, a secretary to the president of the Connecticut Manufacturers' Association, to assist him in dealing with tariff legislation. Sen. George W. Norris, R-Neb. (1903-13; Senate 1913-43), introduced a resolution declaring that Bingham's action was "contrary to good morals and senatorial ethics." [32]

During consideration of the resolution on Nov. 4, 1929, the Senate agreed to add language stating that Bingham's actions were "not the result of corrupt motives." [33] The resolution was then adopted by a vote of 54 to 22, with 18 senators (including Bingham) not voting.

McCarthy Case. The sixth member of the Senate to be censured — "condemned" was the actual language used by the Senate — was Joseph R. McCarthy, R-Wis. (1947-57). Proceedings on this case began in the 82nd Congress (1951-52) and were concluded in the 83rd (1953-54). Sen. William Benton, D-Conn. (1949-53), in August 1951 offered a resolution calling on the Committee on Rules and Administration to investigate, among other things, McCarthy's participation in the defamation of Sen. Millard E. Tydings, D-Md. (House 1923-27; Senate 1927-51), during the Maryland senatorial campaign, to determine whether expulsion proceedings should be instituted against McCarthy. On April 10, 1952, McCarthy submitted a resolution calling for investigation by the same committee of Benton's activities as assistant secretary of state, campaign contributions Benton had received, and other matters. The Rules Committee's Privileges and Elections Subcommittee, after conducting an investigation, submitted an inconclusive report on Jan. 2, 1953.

In the spring of 1954, the Senate Permanent Investigations Subcommittee conducted hearings on mutual accusations of misconduct by McCarthy and Army officials.

Sen. Ralph E. Flanders, R-Vt. (1946-59), on July 30 introduced a resolution censuring McCarthy. Among Flanders' reasons for pressing censure were McCarthy's refusal to testify before the Rules subcommittee in 1952, refusal to repudiate the "frivolous and irresponsible" conduct of Investigations Subcommittee Counsel Roy M. Cohn and consultant G. David Schine on their 1953 subversion-seeking trip to Europe, and "habitual contempt for people." [34] The Senate on Aug. 2 adopted, by a vote of 75 to 12, a proposal to refer Flanders' censure resolution to a select committee. Three days later, Vice President Richard Nixon appointed the select committee.

The Select Committee to Study Censure Charges held hearings from Aug. 31 to Sept. 13, 1954. McCarthy, in defending himself before the committee, contended that the Senate cannot punish a member for what he did in a previous Congress. The committee rejected that contention and on Sept. 27 submitted a 40,000-word report unanimously recommending that the Senate adopt a resolution censuring McCarthy.

After a recess during the congressional election campaign, the Senate reconvened Nov. 8 to consider the censure proposal. Proceedings in the next few weeks led to modifications of that proposal and substitution of the word "condemned" for "censured." (Historians nonetheless count McCarthy's rebuke as a censure; Sen. Herman E. Talmadge's 1979 "denunciation" by the Senate, however, was considered an action short of censure.)

The Senate adopted the resolution of condemnation on Dec. 2 by a vote of 67 to 22. Republicans split evenly, 22 favoring and 22 opposing the resolution. All 44 Democrats, together with Sen. Wayne Morse, R-I-D-Ore. (1945-69),

Censure Proceedings in the Senate

Congress	Session	Year	Member-elect	Grounds	Disposition
11th	3rd	1811	Timothy Pickering, Fed-Mass.	Breach of confidence	*Censured*
28th	1st	1844	Benjamin Tappan, D-Ohio	Breach of confidence	*Censured*
31st	1st	1850	Thomas H. Benton, D-Mo.	Disorderly conduct	Not censured
31st	1st	1850	Henry S. Foote, Unionist-Miss.	Disorderly conduct	Not censured
57th	1st	1902	John L. McLaurin, D-S.C.	Assault	*Censured*
57th	1st	1902	Benjamin R. Tillman, D-S.C.	Assault	*Censured*
71st	1st	1929	Hiram Bingham, R-Conn.	Bringing Senate into disrepute	*Censured*
83rd	2nd	1954	Joseph R. McCarthy, R-Wis.	Obstruction of legislative process, insult to senators, etc.	*Censured*
90th	1st	1967	Thomas J. Dodd, D-Conn.	Financial misconduct	*Censured*
96th	1st	1979	Herman E. Talmadge, D-Ga.	Financial misconduct	*Denounced*

Source: U.S., Congress, Senate, Committee on Rules and Administration, Subcommittee on Privileges and Elections, *Senate Election, Expulsion and Censure Cases from 1793 to 1972*, compiled by Richard D. Hupman, S Doc 92-7, 92nd Cong., 1st sess., 1972; *Congressional Quarterly Almanac 1979* (Washington, D.C.: Congressional Quarterly, 1980).

voted for the resolution. In January 1955, when control of Congress passed to the Democrats, McCarthy lost his committee and subcommittee chairmanships. His activities thereafter attracted less public attention, and he died May 2, 1957.

Dodd Case. House Speaker Sam Rayburn, D-Texas (1913-61), often said that the ethics of a member of Congress should be judged not by his peers but by the voters at re-election time.

By the mid-1960s, it had become clear that neither Congress nor the public felt this was enough. In 1964, the Senate was jolted by publicity over charges that Robert G. "Bobby" Baker had used his office as secretary to the Senate majority to promote his business interests. To allay public misgivings, the Senate on July 24 of that year established a Select Committee on Standards and Conduct with responsibility for investigating "allegations of improper conduct" by senators and Senate employees. In September, however, the Senate assigned jurisdiction over the Baker case to the Rules and Administration Committee. *(Baker case, p. 201)*

The new select committee's first inquiry, begun in 1966, concerned the Dodd case. On Jan. 24, 1966, and later dates, columnists Drew Pearson and Jack Anderson accused Sen. Thomas J. Dodd, D-Conn. (House 1953-57; Senate 1959-71), of having (1) used for personal expenses funds contributed to him to help meet the costs of his campaign for re-election in 1964, (2) double-billed the government for travel expenses, and (3) improperly exchanged favors with Julius Klein, a public relations representative of West German interests. On the last charge, the columnists said that Dodd had gone to Germany for the purpose of interceding with Chancellor Konrad Adenauer on behalf of Klein's accounts, although the trip was supposedly made

on Senate business.

Dodd on Feb. 23, 1966, requested the Select Committee on Standards and Conduct to investigate his relationship with Klein. The committee conducted hearings on all three of the Pearson-Anderson charges in June-July 1966 and March 1967. Dodd testified in his own defense.

● On the first charge, Dodd said he "truly believed" the proceeds from the testimonial dinners "to be donations to me from my friends." [35]

● The second charge, he said, stemmed from "sloppy bookkeeping" by Michael V. O'Hare, who had been an employee of Dodd. O'Hare and other former Dodd employees reportedly had taken documents from Dodd's files and made copies of them available to the committee. In the course of the hearings, Dodd called O'Hare a liar. [36]

● On charge three, Dodd denied that he had been a mere errand boy for Klein on the trip to Europe.

The committee on April 27, 1967, submitted its report on the Dodd case. It recommended that Dodd be censured for spending campaign contributions for personal purposes and for billing seven trips to both the Senate and private organizations. The committee dropped the third charge, saying that while Dodd's relations with Klein were indiscreet, there was not sufficient evidence of wrongdoing.

Voting on the committee's recommendations, June 23, 1967, the Senate censured Dodd on the first charge, by a vote of 92 to 5, but refused by a vote of 45 yeas to 51 nays to censure him on the second charge. The resolution as adopted recorded the judgment of the Senate that Dodd, "for having engaged in a course of conduct . . . from 1961 to 1965 of exercising the influence and favor of his office as a United States Senator . . . to obtain, and use for his personal benefit, funds from the public through political testimonials and a political campaign, deserves the censure of

Senate Condemnation Of Joseph R. McCarthy

Resolution relating to the conduct of the Senator from Wisconsin, Mr. McCarthy. [S Res 301, 83rd Cong., 2nd sess., adopted Dec. 2, 1954.]

Section 1. Resolved, that the Senator from Wisconsin, Mr. McCarthy, failed to cooperate with the Subcommittee on Privileges and Elections of the Senate Committee on Rules and Administration in clearing up matters referred to that Subcommittee which concerned his conduct as a Senator and affected the honor of the Senate and, instead, repeatedly abused the Subcommittee and its Members who were trying to carry out assigned duties, thereby obstructing the constitutional processes of the Senate, and that this conduct of the Senator from Wisconsin, Mr. McCarthy, is contrary to Senatorial traditions and is hereby condemned.

Section 2. The Senator from Wisconsin (Mr. McCarthy), in writing to the chairman of the Select Committee to Study Censure Charges (Mr. Watkins) after the Select Committee had issued its report and before the report was presented to the Senate charging three members of the Select Committee with "deliberate deception" and "fraud" for failure to disqualify themselves;

In stating to the press on Nov. 4, 1954, that the special Senate session that was to begin Nov. 8, 1954, was a "lynch party";

In repeatedly describing this special Senate Session as a "lynch bee" in a nationwide television and radio show on Nov. 7, 1954;

In stating to the public press on Nov. 13, 1954, that the chairman of the Select Committee (Mr. Watkins) was guilty of "the most unusual, most cowardly thing I've ever heard of" and stating further: "I expected he would be afraid to answer the questions, but didn't think he'd be stupid enough to make a public statement"; and in characterizing the said Committee as the "unwilling handmaiden," "involuntary agent," and "attorneys-in-fact" of the Communist party and in charging that the said Committee in writing its report "imitated Communist methods — that it distorted, misrepresented, and omitted in its efforts to manufacture a plausible rationalization" in support of its recommendations to the Senate, which characterizations and charges were contained in a statement released to the press and inserted into the *Congressional Record* of Nov. 10, 1954, acted contrary to Senatorial ethics and tended to bring the Senate into dishonor and disrepute, to obstruct the constitutional processes of the Senate, and to impair its dignity.

And such conduct is hereby condemned.

the Senate; and he is so censured for his conduct, which is contrary to accepted morals, derogates from the public trust expected of a Senator, and tends to bring the Senate into dishonor and disrepute." [37] The preponderance of affirmative votes was the largest in the history of censure proceedings in the Senate.

Dodd declined to seek the Democratic nomination for senator from Connecticut in 1970 but ran in the general election as an independent. He placed third, with 24 percent of the votes, while the Democratic nominee lost to Republican Lowell P. Weicker Jr., 34 percent to 42 percent. Dodd died May 24, 1971.

His son, Christopher J. Dodd, D-Conn., was elected to the House in 1974 and served there until his election to the Senate in 1980.

Talmadge Case. Twelve years after the censure of Thomas Dodd the Senate voted to discipline Georgia veteran Herman E. Talmadge, D (1957-81), for financial misconduct. Talmadge was formally "denounced" — a punishment regarded as slightly less severe than censure.

In 1978 both a federal grand jury and the Senate Ethics Committee (by then a permanent, standing committee) began investigating reports of financial irregularities by Talmadge that first arose during his divorce proceedings. The charges, reported extensively by *The Washington Star*, stemmed principally from Talmadge's ex-wife Betty and his former administrative assistant Daniel Minchew, a member of the Interstate Commerce Commission. Campaign expenses and office accounts were the focus of the investigations.

Financial information made public during his bitterly contested divorce settlement revealed that Talmadge had written only one check to "cash" during the entire period 1970-76.

Talmadge said he was able to live without cashing checks because he accepted small amounts of cash from his constituents, friends and supporters throughout his public career. He also admitted to accepting meals, lodging and most of his clothes.

"Wherever I go [in Georgia], people entertain me, lodge me, give me small amounts of money," Talmadge told *The Washington Star* in May 1978.

Talmadge also acknowledged that he had not reported the money, goods or services as "income" or as campaign contributions because they were "gifts." A spokesman said the senator was unable to remember a single individual who had given him such gifts of cash and goods.

During a one-day appearance before the Ethics Committee in 1979 Betty Talmadge, told the committee that her husband had for years kept a roll of cash, most of it in hundred dollar bills, in his overcoat pocket in a closet of their Washington residence. Talmadge denied it.

At the committee hearings which began April 30, 1979, Talmadge delivered an unsworn statement that called the bulk of the charges against him "trivial" and "petty" and said the remaining, serious charges were untrue or due to negligence. For example, the failure in his initial 1974 campaign report (a year when he was re-elected) to list campaign receipts and expenditures was due to "confusion" by his staff, he said.

Although he was reimbursed "around $12,000" by his campaign committee in January 1975 for his 1974 expenses — a total not reported to the Federal Election Commission until 1978 — Talmadge told the Ethics panel that "there is not the slightest basis for concluding that those errors were due to anything but inadvertence and confusion."

Talmadge said the fact that he repaid the Senate more than $37,000 in 1978 for expenses that were claimed in prior years, but were not reimbursable under Senate rules, should put that charge to rest. He laid the improper claims to his staff.

Talmadge reserved his harshest words for former aide Minchew, whom he called "a proven liar, cheat and embezzler."

In June Minchew testified for eight days before the committee. He said his role in laundering campaign contributions and Senate expense funds through a secret Washington bank account was to provide the senator with "insulation" and "deniability" in case the scheme ever was uncovered. By the end of his testimony several committee members and the special counsel expressed doubts of Minchew's credibility, which was shaken by questioning from Talmadge's attorney.

On Oct. 3 the Ethics Committee issued a report recommending that the Senate denounce Talmadge for financial misconduct. The committee rejected a censure proposal. Instead, the committee resolution said Talmadge's conduct "is reprehensible and tends to bring the Senate into dishonor and disrepute and is hereby denounced."

The committee skirted the question of Talmadge's direct involvement in the financial misconduct. Instead, it said "Talmadge either knew, or should have known, of these improper acts and omissions, and, therefore, by the gross neglect of his duty to faithfully and carefully administer the affairs of his office, he is responsible for these acts and omissions." Talmadge called the committee's action "a personal victory" and said the findings "support my basic contention ... that I was negligent in the oversight of my office, but that I have committed no intentional wrongdoing."

The committee said that Talmadge:
- Improperly collected $43,435.83 in reimbursements after submitting false, unsigned expense vouchers from 1973 to 1978;
- Filed inaccurate reports and failed to file other reports in a timely fashion in accounting for the use of funds during his 1974 Senate race;
- Filed "inaccurate" Senate financial disclosure reports for 1972 through 1977;
- Failed to report more than $10,000 in campaign contributions deposited in the secret Washington bank account.

The committee said that allegations of improper conduct by Talmadge in real estate transactions were "without foundation." It also said that charges of non-payment of gift taxes were "not substantiated."

On Oct. 11, 1979, the Senate voted 81-15 to denounce Talmadge as recommended by the committee. Despite the overwhelming vote, many senators gave testimonials to Talmadge's service in the Senate, where he was fifth in seniority, chairman of the Agriculture and Forestry Committee and ranking Democrat on the Finance Committee.

In May 1980 the Justice Department announced it had completed its investigation of Talmadge's financial affairs and decided not to seek an indictment. The senator was defeated in his 1980 try for re-election.

Censure by the House

The House in 1789 adopted a rule which, as amended in 1822 and 1880, is still in effect (Rule 14, Section 4). It reads: "If any member, in speaking or otherwise, transgress the rules of the House, the Speaker shall, or any member may, call him to order; ... and if the case require it, he

Censure for Dueling Withheld

The killing of one representative by another in a duel in 1838 went uncensured by the House. Rep. Jonathan Cilley, Jackson D-Maine, had made statements on the floor reflecting on the character of James W. Webb, prominent editor of a New York City newspaper which was a Whig organ. When Webb sent Cilley a note by the hand of Rep. William J. Graves, Whig-Ky., demanding an explanation of the statements, Cilley refused to receive the note. Further correspondence led to a challenge by Graves and agreement by Cilley to a duel with rifles.

The duel took place on Feb. 24, 1838, on the Marlboro Pike in Maryland, close to the District of Columbia. Graves and Cilley each fired twice, with no result. In the third volley, Cilley was shot fatally in the abdomen. Four days later, the House appointed a committee to investigate the affair. A majority of the committee recommended on April 21 that Graves be expelled from the House and that the seconds in the duel, Rep. Henry A. Wise, Tyler D-Va., and George W. Jones (a member of the Tennessee House of Representatives who served in the national House of Representatives, 1843-59), be censured. One of the minority group on the committee, Rep. Franklin H. Elmore, State Rights Dem-S.C., observed that dueling by members had been frequent and generally had gone unnoticed by the House. A motion to lay the committee's report on the table and to print the testimony was agreed to May 10, and an attempt on July 4 to take up the report was unsuccessful. Graves was not expelled and Wise and Jones were not censured.

shall be liable to censure or such punishment as the House may deem proper." [38] The censure clause of this rule has been invoked 33 times, and censure has been voted 20 times, two-thirds of them in the 1860s and 1870s. Grounds for censure have included assault on a fellow member of the House, insult to the Speaker, treasonable utterance, corruption and other offenses. In the 20th century three representatives have been censured. (Chart, p. 189)

The first censure motion in the House was introduced following a physical attack in January 1798 by Rep. Matthew Lyon, Anti-Fed-Vt., on Rep. Roger Griswold, Fed-Conn., who had taunted Lyon on his allegedly poor military record. The censure motion failed. In the following month, Lyon and Griswold engaged in an affray with tongs and cane. Both fracases occurred on the House floor. Following the second incident, a motion was introduced to censure both members. The motion failed.

The first formal censure by the House was imposed in 1832 on William Stanbery, D-Ohio, for saying, in objection to a ruling by the chair, "The eyes of the Speaker [Andrew

Stevenson, D-Va.] are too frequently turned from the chair you occupy toward the White House." [39] There were 93 votes for censuring Stanbery; 44 were opposed. Censure for unacceptable language or offensive publication was imposed in seven other cases. For example, Rep. John W. Hunter, Ind-N.Y., was censured on Jan. 26, 1867, for saying, about a statement made by a colleague, "So far as I am concerned, it is a base lie." [40]

In 1842, censure was considered and rejected in the case of one of the most distinguished representatives in American history, John Quincy Adams, a former president of the United States. Adams had presented to the House, for 46 of his constituents, a petition asking Congress to dissolve the Union and allow the states to go their separate ways. A resolution proposing to censure him for this act was worded so strongly that Adams asserted his right, under the Sixth Amendment to the Constitution, to a trial by jury. He succeeded in putting his opponents on the defensive, and the resolution was not put to a vote.

Rep. Lovell H. Rousseau, R-Ky., during the evening of June 14, 1866, assaulted Rep. Josiah B. Grinnell, R-Iowa, with a cane in the portico on the East Front of the Capitol. On the House floor, earlier in the month, Grinnell had imputed cowardice to Rousseau. A committee appointed to report on the case recommended that Rousseau be expelled. That recommendation was rejected, but the House voted on July 17, 1866, that he "be summoned to the bar of this House, and be there publicly reprimanded by the Speaker for his violation of its rights and privileges." [41] The order was carried out July 21, despite Rousseau's announcement that he had sent his resignation to the governor of Kentucky.

Corruption was the basis for censure or proposed censure in a number of cases. The House on Feb. 27, 1873, by a vote of 182 to 36, censured Reps. Oakes Ames, R-Mass., and James Brooks, D-N.Y., for their part in a financial scandal involving Crédit Mobilier stock given to members of Congress. Three years later, Speaker James G. Blaine, R-Maine, was accused of involvement in that scandal as well as of receiving excessive payments from the Union Pacific Railroad Co. for bonds sold to the company. Two months before the convention at which Blaine hoped to be chosen the Republican candidate for president, he spoke in the House on the charges against him. By selective reading of a series of allegedly incriminating letters, Blaine managed to confuse the evidence sufficiently to rout the proponents of censure.

In one instance, the House rescinded part of a censure resolution. During debate on a bill in 1875, Rep. John Y. Brown, D-Ky., referred to Rep. Benjamin Butler, R-Mass., as "outlawed in his own home from respectable society; whose name is synonymous with falsehood; and who is the champion, and has been on all occasions, of fraud; who is the apologist of thieves; who is such a prodigy of vice and meanness that to describe him would sicken imagination and exhaust invective." [42]

Brown was censured Feb. 4, 1875, for that insult and for lying to the Speaker in order to continue his insulting speech. But a year later, on May 2, 1876, the House agreed to rescind that portion of the censure resolution condemning Brown for lying to the Speaker. The charge of insulting another member remained, however. [43]

The three years 1978-80 produced the first committee-approved censure resolutions in the House since 1921. Two representatives were censured — Charles C. Diggs Jr., D-Mich., and Charles H. Wilson, D-Calif. — and the punishment of another — Edward R. Roybal, D-Calif. — was reduced to a reprimand. Diggs and Wilson were the 19th and 20th members of the House to be censured.

Diggs Case. Rep. Charles C. Diggs Jr., D-Mich. (1955-80), was censured by the House July 31, 1979, for misuse of his clerk-hire funds. An attempt to expel him from the House was rejected.

Diggs had been convicted Oct. 7, 1978, on 29 felony counts centering on charges that he illegally diverted more than $60,000 of his congressional employees' salaries to his personal and official use. He was re-elected to the House in November 1978 despite the conviction.

When Congress convened Jan. 9, 1979, House Republicans announced they would seek to expel Diggs from the House as a convicted felon. The House Standards of Conduct Committee began an investigation of his case but moved too slowly to satisfy Rep. Newt Gingrich, a freshman Republican from Georgia.

If Diggs chose to vote despite his conviction, Gingrich informed Diggs in a Feb. 22 letter, Gingrich would move to expel Diggs from the House. Existing House rules recommended — but did not require — that convicted House members refrain from voting unless they were re-elected after their conviction.

On the House floor Feb. 28, Diggs voted "yea" on a bill to increase the public debt limit. The next day, Gingrich offered a resolution to expel Diggs from the House. Majority Leader Jim Wright, D-Texas, immediately moved to refer the resolution to the Standards Committee, and this carried, 322-77.

The committee filed formal charges against Diggs for violating House rules and negotiated with him for an admission of guilt. On June 27 Diggs sent a letter to the committee admitting to some of the charges. He agreed to be censured by his colleagues in return for ending the committee's investigation into his financial affairs.

In the letter, Diggs admitted he had padded his office payroll and accepted kickbacks from five present and former employees. He said his personal gain from the kickbacks totaled $40,031.66. Diggs offered to repay the sum with interest. Diggs said he thought the agreement with the committee would help his pending appeal of his conviction. (It did not. The appeal was turned down by the Supreme Court in June 1980, and Diggs resigned from Congress the next day and began serving his three-year jail sentence.)

In recommending censure rather than expulsion, the committee explained in its July 19 report that it had "considered his admission of guilt of serious offenses against the House rules, his apology to the House therefor, his agreement to make restitution of substantial amounts by which he was unjustly enriched, and the nature of the offenses charged."

On July 30, 1979, a move by a Republican group of representatives trying to force a vote on an expulsion resolution was tabled — and thus killed — by a 205-197 vote. The next day censure of Diggs was approved by a vote of 414-0, with four members voting present.

Wilson Case. Rep. Charles H. Wilson, D-Calif. (1963-81), was censured by the House June 10, 1980, for financial misconduct. The action came just a week after Wilson lost his bid for renomination in the June 3 California primary. The House approved the censure resolution on a voice vote after rejecting 97-308 a move to reduce Wilson's punishment from a censure to a reprimand.

Following the vote, Wilson was called to the front of the chamber, where House Speaker Thomas P. O'Neill Jr.,

Censure Proceedings in the House

Congress	Session	Year	Member-elect	Grounds	Disposition
5th	2nd	1798	Matthew Lyon, Anti-Fed-Vt.	Assault on representative	Not censured
5th	2nd	1798	Roger Griswold, Fed-Conn.	Assault on representative	Not censured
22nd	1st	1832	William Stanbery, D-Ohio	Insult to Speaker	*Censured*
24th	1st	1836	Sherrod Williams, Whig-Ky.	Insult to Speaker	Not censured
25th	2nd	1838	Henry A. Wise, Tyler Dem.-Va.	Service as second in duel	Not censured
25th	3rd	1839	Alexander Duncan, Whig-Ohio	Offensive publication	Not censured
27th	2nd	1842	John Q. Adams, Whig-Mass.	Treasonable petition	Not censured
27th	2nd	1842	Joshua R. Giddings, Whig-Ohio	Offensive paper	*Censured*
34th	2nd	1856	Henry A. Edmundson, D-Va. }	Complicity in assault on senator	Not censured
34th	2nd	1856	Laurence M. Keitt, D-S.C. }		*Censured*
36th	1st	1860	George S. Houston, D-Ala.	Insult to representative	Not censured
38th	1st	1864	Alexander Long, D-Ohio	Treasonable utterance	*Censured*
38th	1st	1864	Benjamin G. Harris, D-Md.	Treasonable utterance	*Censured*
39th	1st	1866	John W. Chanler, D-N.Y.	Insult to House	*Censured*
39th	1st	1866	Lovell H. Rousseau, R-Ky.	Assault on representative	*Censured*
40th	1st	1867	John W. Hunter, Ind-N.Y.	Insult to representative	*Censured*
40th	2nd	1868	Fernando Wood, D-N.Y.	Offensive utterance	*Censured*
40th	3rd	1868	E. D. Holbrook, D-Idaho[1]	Offensive utterance	*Censured*
41st	2nd	1870	Benjamin F. Whittemore, R-S.C.	Corruption	*Censured*
41st	2nd	1870	Roderick R. Butler, R-Tenn.	Corruption	*Censured*
41st	2nd	1870	John T. Deweese, D-N.C.	Corruption	*Censured*
42nd	3rd	1873	Oakes Ames, R-Mass.	Corruption	*Censured*
42nd	3rd	1873	James Brooks, D-N.Y.	Corruption	*Censured*
43rd	2nd	1875	John Y. Brown, D-Ky.	Insult to representative	*Censured*[2]
44th	1st	1876	James G. Blaine, R-Maine	Corruption	Not censured
47th	1st	1882	William D. Kelley, R-Pa.	Offensive utterance	Not censured
47th	1st	1882	John D. White, R-Ky.	Offensive utterance	Not censured
47th	2nd	1883	John Van Voorhis, R-N.Y.	Offensive utterance	Not censured
51st	1st	1890	William D. Bynum, D-Ind.	Offensive utterance	*Censured*
67th	1st	1921	Thomas L. Blanton, D-Texas	Abuse of leave to print	*Censured*
95th	2nd	1978	Edward R. Roybal, D-Calif.	Lying to House committee	Not censured
96th	1st	1979	Charles C. Diggs Jr., D-Mich.	Misuse of clerk-hire funds	*Censured*
96th	2nd	1980	Charles H. Wilson, D-Calif.	Financial misconduct	*Censured*

1. Holbrook was a territorial delegate, not a representative.
2. The House later rescinded part of the censure resolution against Brown.

Sources: Hinds and Cannon, *Precedents of the House of Representatives of the United States,* 11 vols. (1935-41); Joint Committee on Congressional Operations, *House of Representatives Exclusion, Censure and Expulsion Cases from 1789 to 1973,* committee print, 93rd Cong., 1st sess., 1973; *Congressional Quarterly Almanac 1978, 1979, 1980* (Washington, D.C.: Congressional Quarterly, 1979, 1980, 1981).

Assault on Sumner

Sen. Charles Sumner, R-Mass., in a speech on the Senate floor, May 20, 1856, denounced in scathing language supporters of the Kansas-Nebraska Act of 1854, which repealed the Missouri Compromise of 1820 and permitted the two new territories to decide whether slavery would be allowed there.

Two days later, while Sumner was seated at his desk on the Senate floor after the day's session had ended, he heard his name called. Looking up, he saw a tall stranger, who berated him for his speech and then struck him on the head repeatedly with a heavy walking stick, which was broken by the blows. Sumner fell bleeding and unconscious to the floor. He was absent from the Senate, because of the injuries suffered in the assault, for three and a half years, until Dec. 5, 1859.

The attacker was Rep. Preston S. Brooks, State Rights Dem.-S.C., nephew of one of those whom Sumner had excoriated — Sen. A. P. Butler, State Rights Dem.-S.C. Expulsion proceedings against Brooks failed, on a strictly party vote. He resigned his House seat, July 15, 1856, but was elected to fill the vacancy caused by his resignation.

Rep. Laurence M. Keitt, D-S.C., was censured by the House on July 15, 1856, for having known of Brooks' intention to assault Sumner, for having taken no action to discourage or prevent the assault, and for having been "present on one or more occasions to witness the same." Keitt resigned, July 16, 1856, and was elected to fill the vacancy caused by his resignation. A resolution similar to the one censuring Keitt but directed against Rep. Henry A. Edmundson, D-Va., had failed of adoption, July 15, 1856.

D-Mass., read the censure resolution to him. Wilson then turned and quickly left the chamber.

In voting to censure Wilson, the House found him guilty of improperly converting almost $25,000 in campaign funds to his personal use and accepting $10,500 in gifts from an individual with a direct interest in legislation before Congress.

The House action was the second time in two years that Wilson had been disciplined by the House. The California Democrat was reprimanded in October 1978 after he first denied — and then acknowledged — receiving wedding gifts, including $600 in cash, from South Korean businessman Tongsun Park.

The individual the committee said was placed on Wilson's payroll and who allegedly had kicked back to the California Democrat was Lee Rogers, president of a Los Angeles mail order firm called the American Holiday Association.

At Standards Committee hearings a committee lawyer produced a letter from Wilson to Rogers boasting that the representative's "strong opposition" to a bill opposed by Rogers had killed the legislation in subcommittee. "You may be certain that I will work with you to see it stays buried in the subcommittee," the letter concluded.

After the censure vote a new Democratic rule forced Wilson to give up his chairmanship of a House postal subcommittee. In May House Democrats had voted to automatically deprive censured members of their chairmanships.

Roybal Case. The House Standards Committee conducted highly publicized hearings in 1977-78 into reports of congressional lobbying by agents of the South Korean government and of lavish gifts to representatives by Korean businessman Tongsun Park. The investigations ended with slaps on the wrist to three members of Congress, John J. McFall (1957-78), Edward R. Roybal and Charles H. Wilson (above), all California Democrats. The committee charged McFall and Roybal with failing to report campaign contributions from Park and Wilson with failing to report, on a committee questionnaire, wedding gifts from Park that included $600 in cash. The recommended punishment was a reprimand for McFall and Wilson and censure for Roybal because the committee concluded he had lied to it.

On the House floor Oct. 13, 1978, the resolution to censure Roybal was rejected on a 219-170 vote and he was reprimanded instead, as were McFall and Wilson. Several Roybal supporters suggested that as a Hispanic he was a victim of bias. (Details, p. 206)

Other Forms of Discipline

As lesser forms of punishment than expulsion or censure, the House has from time to time reprimanded members or forced them to give up chairmanships. Members who remained in the House after criminal indictments or convictions have been urged to refrain from voting.

Reprimands

Chairman John J. Flynt Jr., D-Ga. (1954-79), of the House Committee on Standards of Official Conduct, said in 1976 that he saw no real difference between reprimand and censure. In the case of a reprimand, however, no further action is taken against a member. When censured, a member must stand in the well of the House and be publicly admonished by the Speaker.

Flynt's statement came after his committee recommended a reprimand for Rep. Robert L. F. Sikes, D-Fla. (1941-44, 1945-79), for failing to disclose financial holdings in defense business and a conflict of interest. Sikes was the first member of Congress investigated by the Standards Committee.

The complaint against Sikes was filed by the self-styled public affairs lobby Common Cause and forwarded to the committee by 44 representatives. After collecting information and testimony from Sikes and his counsel, the committee recommended a formal reprimand.

On July 29, 1976, the House approved the reprimand by a vote of 381-3. The following January the House Democratic Caucus voted 189-93 to unseat Sikes as chairman of the Appropriations Subcommittee on Military Construction.

At the culmination of the lengthy investigation of

South Korean government attempts to influence U.S. members of Congress, the House voted on Oct. 13, 1978, to reprimand three California representatives. *(Roybal case, above)*

Loss of Chairmanship

Depriving members of chairmanships became in recent years a common form of punishment:

● It was one of several disciplinary actions taken against Rep. Adam Clayton Powell Jr. in 1966-67. *(p. 176)*

● Rep. Wayne L. Hays, D-Ohio (1949-76), in mid-1976 gave up the chairmanship of both the Democratic Congressional Campaign Committee and the House Administration Committee after it was alleged that he had kept a mistress on the latter committee's payroll. Hays was pressured to resign the posts by the House Democratic leadership, and it was evident that the Democratic Caucus would have forced him to do so if he had not stepped aside voluntarily. Hays resigned from Congress Sept. 1, 1976. *(Hays case details, p. 195)*

● Rep. Robert L. F. Sikes, D-Fla. (1941-44, 1945-79), lost his appropriations subcommittee chairmanship in 1977. *(above)*

● In January 1979 House Democratic leaders convinced Rep. Charles C. Diggs Jr., D-Mich. (1955-80), to resign as chairman of the Africa Subcommittee of the House Foreign Affairs Committee after his conviction for taking kickbacks. Diggs voluntarily gave up his chairmanship of the Committee on the District of Columbia. He was later censured by the House. *(p. 188)*

The House Democratic Caucus May 29, 1980, changed its rules to take away automatically a committee or subcommittee chairmanship from any party member who was censured by the House, or indicted or convicted of a felony carrying a sentence of at least two years. Democrats backed the revision in caucus rules because of their concern about the precedent in a pending resolution to censure Rep. Charles H. Wilson, D-Calif. (1963-81), that also stripped him of a subcommittee chairmanship. Democrats feared that letting the entire House vote on a chairmanship would rob the party caucuses of an important prerogative.

The previous year the caucus had turned down a proposal to allow the full caucus, rather than committee members alone, to vote on subcommittee chairmanships of members reprimanded by the House. Instead, the proposal applied only to members censured or convicted of a felony liable to a prison term of two years or more.

By the end of 1980, three members had been stripped of their chairmanships under the new rules: Wilson, John M. Murphy, D-N.Y. (1963-81), and Frank Thompson Jr., D-N.J. (1955-81). Murphy and Thompson lost their full committee chairmanships following their indictments in the Abscam investigation. *(Abscam scandal, p. 207)*

Suspension

In 1972 the House began a move to formalize an unwritten rule that a member indicted for or convicted of a crime should refrain from voting on the House floor or in committee. Prior to 1972, the last time a member voluntarily refrained from voting was in 1929 when, under indictment in the District of Columbia, Frederick N. Zihlman, R-Md. (1917-31), did not vote on the floor and temporarily turned over his chairmanship of the House Committee on the District of Columbia to the committee's ranking member.

The move to formalize that unwritten rule was prompted by the case of John Dowdy, D-Texas (1952-73), who was convicted Dec. 31, 1971, of charges arising from acceptance of a bribe, conspiracy and perjury. While Dowdy appealed his conviction, the ethics committee reported a resolution May 3, 1972, stating that any House member convicted of a crime for which he could receive a sentence of two or more years in prison should not participate in committee business or House votes. The maximum sentence for the crimes Dowdy was convicted of was 40 years in prison and a $40,000 fine.

Because the Rules Committee failed to act, the resolution was not enacted. But Dowdy, in a June 21, 1972, letter to Speaker Carl Albert, D-Okla. (1947-77), promised he would refrain from voting.[44] He retired from the House at the beginning of 1973.

Not until April 16, 1975, did the House enact a resolution similar to the one proposed in 1972. Under the 1975 rule, the voluntary prohibition against voting would apply during an appeal of the conviction but would end on reversal or when the member was re-elected subsequent to conviction, even if the verdict was upheld on appeal. The new rule was adopted by the House April 16, 1975, by a vote of 360-37. Later, it was incorporated in the House Code of Official Conduct.

Diggs took advantage of the rule's leniency in 1979 until he was censured on July 31 of that year. Diggs had been convicted of taking kickbacks in October 1978 but was re-elected by his Detroit constituents in November. He continued to vote in the House until the censure resolution passed.

Footnotes

1. Asher C. Hinds and Clarence Cannon, *Hinds' and Cannon's Precedents of the House of Representatives of the United States* (Washington, D.C.: U.S. Government Printing Office, 1935-41), vol. 1, p. 525.
2. Ibid.
3. Ibid., vol. 2, p. 1075.
4. Ibid., vol. 2, p. 847.
5. Ibid., vol. 1, p. 84.
6. Ibid.
7. *The Federalist Papers*, with an Introduction by Clinton Rossiter (New York: Mentor, 1961), No. 60, p. 371.
8. U.S. Congress, Senate, Committee on Rules and Administration, *Senate Election, Expulsion and Censure Cases*, S. Doc. 92-7, 92nd Cong. 1st sess., 1971, p. 1.
9. Ibid., p. 12.
10. Hinds, *Precedents*, vol. 1, p. 588.
11. William F. Willoughby, *Principles of Legislative Organization and Administration* (Washington, D.C.: The Brookings Institution, 1934), p. 270.
12. Hinds, *Precedents*, vol. 6, p. 58.
13. Ibid., vol. 1, p. 489.
14. Ibid.
15. Kent M. Weeks, *Adam Clayton Powell and the Supreme Court* (New York: Dunellen, 1971), p. 79.
16. Ibid., p. 134.
17. Floyd M. Riddick, *The United States Congress: Organization and Procedure* (Washington, D.C.: National Capitol Publishers, 1949), p. 12.
18. George H. Haynes, *The Senate of the United States* (Boston: Houghton-Mifflin Co., 1938), p. 131.
19. For more background, see *Congressional Quarterly Almanac 1975* (Washington, D.C.: Congressional Quarterly, 1976), p. 699.
20. William Willoughby, *Principles*, p. 277.
21. For more background, see *Congressional Quarterly Almanac*

1965 (Washington, D.C.: Congressional Quarterly, 1966), p. 609.

22. *Congressional Record,* 84th Cong., 1st sess., Jan. 14, 1955, p. 373.
23. Hinds, *Precedents,* vol. 2, p. 817.
24. Ibid., vol. 1, p. 613.
25. *Senate Election, Expulsion and Censure Cases,* p. 29.
26. Ibid., p. 31-32.
27. John T. Dempsey, *Control by Congress Over the Seating and Disciplining of Members* (Ph.D. dissertation, University of Michigan, 1956), p. 294.
28. Hinds, *Precedents,* vol. 6, p. 404-405.
29. *Senate Election, Expulsion and Censure Cases,* p. 6.
30. Ibid., p. 14.
31. Ibid., p. 96.
32. Ibid., p. 128.
33. Ibid.
34. *Congressional Record,* 83rd Cong., 2nd sess., July 30, 1954, p. 12730.

35. U.S. Congress, Senate, Committee on Standards and Conduct, *Investigation of Senator Thomas J. Dodd, Hearings before the Select Committee on Standards and Conduct,* 89th Cong., 2nd sess., 1966, p. 846.
36. Ibid., p. 847.
37. *Senate Election, Expulsion and Censure Cases,* p. 157.
38. Hinds, *Precedents,* vol. 5, p. 103.
39. Ibid., vol. 2, p. 799.
40. Ibid., p. 801.
41. Ibid., p. 1134.
42. Ibid., p. 802.
43. Ibid., vol. 4, p. 26.
44. Dowdy actually voted three times by proxy in the House District of Columbia Committee June 22 after he had said he would not vote in committee or on the floor. Dowdy explained the votes by saying that he had given his proxy to the committee for use at a meeting scheduled on June 21 which was postponed until June 22 without his knowledge. Dowdy's pledge to refrain from voting was made the evening of June 21. For details, see *Congressional Quarterly Almanac,* p. 796.

Ethics and Criminal Prosecutions

Under the Constitution, each house of Congress has the power to punish members for misconduct. Article I, Section 5 states:

Each House may determine the Rules of its Proceedings, punish its Members for disorderly Behavior, and with the concurrence of two thirds, expel a Member.

It is a power Congress historically has been reluctant to use.

Only 15 senators and four representatives have been expelled (although others have resigned to avoid expulsion) and almost all such cases arose during the Civil War. Lesser disciplinary actions — censure and reprimands — have been almost as rare. *(Details, p. 171)*

This reluctance has stemmed from a variety of reasons. There is a belief among some that, except in cases where a member's actions are illegal and punishable by the courts, the electorate, not the person's colleagues, must be the ultimate judge of his behavior.

Loyalty among members, especially of the same party, and toward Congress as an institution is another factor.

The difficulty of agreeing on what constitutes a conflict of interest and misuse of power has also clouded the question.

The reluctance to punish fellow members was apparent in the 1960s when a series of scandals led to the formation of ethics committees to oversee the conduct of members of Congress. Until 1976, the ethics panels were frequently derided by critics as "do-nothing" committees.

Scandals in the 1960s involved Sens. Thomas J. Dodd, D-Conn. (House 1953-57; Senate 1959-71), and Daniel B. Brewster, D-Md. (House 1959-63; Senate 1963-69), Secretary to the Senate Majority Bobby Baker and several representatives, including Adam Clayton Powell Jr., D-N.Y. (House 1945-67, 1969-71), who was almost expelled from the House.

The Powell case and several criminal prosecutions of members of Congress produced notable court rulings on the exclusion of members and the extent of their immunity from prosecution.

The power of each house of Congress to judge the elections and qualifications of its own members and the power to punish members for disorderly behavior are essential to the functioning of Congress as a co-equal branch of the government, free from harassment and domination by the other branches.

They are reinforced by the speech or debate clause of the Constitution (Article I, Section 6), which has been broadly interpreted by the courts as granting members of Congress immunity from prosecution for nearly all actions related to their legislative functions. *(Congressional immunity, p. 200)*

Post-Watergate Reforms

The Watergate affair, whose central crime was abuse of power in the White House, also focused attention on influence-buying in the federal government. Among the key findings were the milk lobby's deal with President Nixon and illegal campaign contributions from powerful corporations.

Several years after Watergate a foreign government, the Republic of South Korea, was found guilty by congressional investigating committees of spending hundreds of thousands of dollars, often as campaign contributions, to influence Congress.

In what became known as the post-Watergate period, Congress first strengthened markedly the public disclosure law on election campaign contributions and then turned to its own ethical standards. Meanwhile the Justice Department began to give more attention to "white collar crime," including alleged misdeeds by individual members of Congress.

The result in the 1970s was the most wide-ranging congressional movement toward ethics reform in U.S. history.

Like most waves of reform it was followed by countermovements and some backsliding, but its major achievements remained historical: for the first time the law required full disclosure to the public of major campaign contributions and the financial holdings of top officers and employees of all three branches of government.

Whether Congress on its own would show more determination to punish unethical practices by its members remained somewhat in doubt.

The "Koreagate" investigations (1977-78) resulted in little more than wrist-slapping of several members involved.

But the Abscam trials (1980-81), in which seven members of Congress were prosecuted by the Justice Department and found guilty by juries, produced the first expulsion of a member of Congress since the Civil War. The other six members either resigned from Congress or were turned out of office by their constituents before their probable expulsion could occur.

The Abscam cases were the first involving a bloc of members of Congress since the Crédit Mobilier scandal of 1872.

CODES OF CONDUCT: LONG PASSAGE TO A LAW

Throughout its history Congress has shown a natural reluctance to investigate its own members and punish them. The executive branch, through its Justice Department, occasionally has brought suit against a member of Congress, often for income tax evasion, but in the main it has been the press, and since the 1960s, television, that has put a spotlight on congressional scandals.

Ban on Nepotism

In a move that surprised most members of Congress and reporters, the House voted in 1967 to prohibit nepotism by federal officials, including senators and representatives. The proposal was offered by Rep. Neal Smith, D-Iowa, as a floor amendment to the postal rate and federal pay bill of 1967 and was adopted by a 49-33 standing vote. The Senate accepted the Smith proviso, with language extending it to less immediate relatives (sons-in-law, for example), and the ban was written into permanent law.

In explaining his amendment, Smith said it was aimed in particular at postmasters in small post offices who were inclined to hire their wives as post office clerks.

But nepotism by members of Congress — the hiring of wives, children, brothers and other close relatives for work on a member's own staff — was a frequent source of critical press comment. Columnists over the years had charged certain members with padding their official staffs or district offices with relatives who did no work for their government paycheck.

The nepotism ban prohibited officers or employees of the federal or District of Columbia governments from appointing, or recommending for appointment or promotion, a relative to serve in the same agency or department as the official.

Thus, as an outgrowth of stories on congressional nepotism and withholding of payroll information, the Senate in 1959 began to make public payroll information on all Senate employees. Similar information had been available in the House since 1932. And, beginning in 1960, critical stories on congressional junkets led to a series of curbs on travel expense by congressmen.

Congress took no effective action, however, on sweeping conflict-of-interest problems: for instance, the ethical limits on outside employment and income, dealings with regulatory agencies, voting on matters in which the member had a personal stake, relations with lobbyists and campaign contributors.

No formal code of ethics for members existed until 1958, when a code applying throughout the government was adopted. *(Box, p. 199)*

The code was part of the reaction to the 1957-58 investigation of Sherman Adams, chief of staff to President Eisenhower. Adams accepted gifts from a businessman, Bernard Goldfine, who it turned out was seeking favorable treatment from federal agencies. In the aftermath Adams resigned.

The code of ethics was hortatory. It had no legal force.

Ten years later the House and Senate separately adopted new rules that it was hoped would help prevent conflicts of interest in Congress. The new rules were largely a response to the internal investigations of Sen. Dodd, Secretary to the Senate Majority Baker and Rep. Powell. *(Baker, p. 201; Powell, p. 176)*

Special committees on ethics also were established. After seeing the partisan bickering during the Senate Rules and Administration Committee's investigation of Bobby Baker, senators in 1964 voted to set up a strictly bipartisan committee to investigate allegations of improper conduct by senators and Senate employees. The Select Committee on Standards and Conduct had as its first chairman a respected elder, Sen. John Stennis, D-Miss. Its first case was the investigation and censure of Thomas Dodd.

The new Senate rules declared that a senator should use the power and perquisites entrusted to him by the people "only for their benefit and never for the benefit of himself or of a few." They also:

● Spelled out conditions under which senators could accept money from fund-raising events and the uses to which contributions could be put. In addition to campaign expenses, contributions could be used for travel and printing or broadcasting of reports to constituents. These accounts were popularly known as "slush funds."

● Prohibited all except designated Senate employees from soliciting or distributing campaign funds.

● Required senators and employees above a certain income to file confidential financial disclosure statements annually with the U.S. comptroller general. Contributions received at fund-raisers and honoraria of $300 or more were to be made public.

The House in 1967, after the Powell case, established a 12-member bipartisan Committee on Standards of Official Conduct to recommend a code of conduct for representatives and the powers it might need to enforce it. The first chairman was Rep. Melvin Price, D-Ill.

The committee recommended two new rules to the House in 1968, one a Code of Official Conduct, the other a requirement for financial disclosure. In adopting these the House also made the committee permanent and gave it investigative and enforcement powers.

The new code, among other things, declared that a

member may "accept no gift of substantial value, directly or indirectly, from any person, organization or corporation having a direct interest in legislation before the Congress" or accept an honorarium for a speech or article "in excess of the usual and customary value for such services."

The House rule on financial disclosure, unlike the Senate's, required that the information be available to the public. The Senate had rejected a similar requirement by a vote of 40-44. Representatives were told to list financial interests of more than $5,000 or income of more than $1,000 from companies doing substantial business with the government or regulated by the government, and their sources of income for services exceeding $5,000 annually.

In 1970, the House broadened the public disclosure requirements to include two new items — the source of each honorarium of $300 or more earned in one year, and the names of creditors to whom $10,000 or more was owed for 90 days or longer without the pledge of specific security.

1976 Scandals

Until 1976 the House committee proved reluctant to make any public investigation of misconduct. For example, *Life* magazine on Aug. 9, 1968, raised charges of wrongdoing against Rep. Cornelius E. Gallagher, D-N.J. (1959-73), calling him a "tool and collaborator" of a reputed Mafia figure in New Jersey. The Committee on Standards of Official Conduct, after looking into the *Life* allegations, chose not to release any information on its inquiry and no action against Gallagher was taken by the committee. Chairman Price said that "there was no proof of any violation of the code [of ethics] which the committee had adopted.

In 1972 Gallagher was indicted for income tax evasion, perjury and conspiracy to hide kickbacks. He pleaded guilty to the tax charge and was sentenced to two years in prison. In 1978, during the "Koreagate" hearings, Tongsun Park testified that among his payments to members of Congress in the early 1970s was $211,000 to then Rep. Gallagher.

Eight years after its establishment as a permanent committee, the House Committee on Standards of Official Conduct undertook its first investigation of a member. And within weeks after it launched an investigation of Robert L. F. Sikes, D-Fla. (1941-44, 1945-79), in May 1976 — which resulted in the House reprimanding Sikes — it began a probe of Wayne L. Hays, D-Ohio (1949-76). Hays' sex scandal came on the heels of the escapades of striptease dancer Fanne Foxe and Rep. Wilbur Mills, D-Ark. (1939-77), the influential chairman of the Ways and Means Committee. Publicity about the Mills-Foxe affair began Oct. 9, 1974, when Foxe jumped out of Mills' car and into the Potomac River tidal basin and was rescued by a policeman. It culminated in December when Mills resigned his chairmanship, acknowledged his alcoholism and decided not to seek re-election.

Besides the Sikes and Hays cases, five criminal proceedings against members of Congress in 1976 helped create the climate for the ethics codes of 1977:

● Rep. Andrew J. Hinshaw, R-Calif. (1973-77), was convicted Jan. 26, 1976, of two bribery charges stemming from his previous service as assessor of Orange County, Calif.

● Rep. James R. Jones, D-Okla., pleaded guilty Jan. 29, 1976, of failing to report a cash campaign contribution from Gulf Oil Corp. in 1972, a misdemeanor, not a felony.

● Rep. Henry J. Helstoski, D-N.J. (1965-77), was indicted June 2, 1976, on charges he accepted money in return for introducing private bills in Congress to permit certain aliens to remain in the United States. *(p. 205)*

● Rep. Allan T. Howe, D-Utah (1975-77), was convicted July 23, 1976, in Salt Lake City for soliciting two policewomen posing as prostitutes.

● Rep. James F. Hastings, R-N.Y. (1969-76), was convicted in December 1976 of taking payroll kickbacks from his congressional employees.

The Sikes and Hays cases resulted in discipline of the two members by their colleagues in the House.

Sikes Case

Sikes was formally reprimanded by the House July 29, 1976, when it accepted by a vote of 381-3 the Standards Committee's findings that he was guilty of financial misconduct. Sikes, the longtime chairman of the House Subcommittee on Military Construction Appropriations, was found in three instances to "have violated standards of conduct applicable to all members of Congress."

Sikes was charged with failing to disclose his investments in a defense contractor, Fairchild Industries, in a bank he helped establish on a naval base in his district, and in parcels of Florida lands whose value he sought to upgrade through legislation.

The complaint against Sikes was transmitted to the ethics committee by 44 House members, an unprecedented action at the time, and was based on information developed by Florida newspaper reports and groups outside Congress. After an initial inquiry the committee voted May 12 to hold a formal investigation of Sikes' actions. By elevating the probe from the status of an inquiry to an investigation, the panel gave itself the authority to subpoena financial records and question witnesses under oath.

Hays Case

Less than a month after undertaking the Sikes investigation, the ethics committee began a probe of a sex-and-public payroll scandal involving Ohio Rep. Hays, the powerful chairman of the House Administration Committee and House Democrats' fund-raising committee, the Democratic National Congressional Committee. In a story which broke in *The Washington Post* May 23, 1976, Elizabeth Ray accused Hays of giving her a $14,000-a-year job on the House Administration Committee in exchange for sexual favors.

Hays at first denied the Ray charge but then admitted to the House May 25 that he had had a "personal relationship" with Ray. However, he denied that he had hired her to be his mistress.

On May 25, Hays asked the ethics committee to investigate the matter. The same day 28 House members, in a letter to ethics Chairman John J. Flynt Jr., D-Ga. (1954-79), asked the committee to take up the Hays case. On June 2, the committee voted 11-0 to begin an immediate investigation into the charges.

The Justice Department and FBI had entered the case soon after Ray made her charges, and by May 26, a federal grand jury in Washington, D.C., began hearing testimony relating to her allegations.

Pressure built up quickly in the House to oust Hays from his leadership positions. On June 3 he relinquished his chairmanship of the Democratic Congressional Campaign Committee. Hays won renomination to his House seat in a close Democratic primary in Ohio's 18th District June 8. Then, bowing to pressure from the House Democratic leadership, Hays resigned the chairmanship of the House Administration Committee June 18 and on Aug. 13 announced he would not run for re-election to Congress in 1976. On Sept. 1 Hays resigned from Congress. The ethics panel then voted, 12-0, to end its investigation of Hays.

House, Senate Codes

In 1977 the House and Senate adopted separate, but largely similar, codes of ethics for their members and employees. The following year Congress passed a law, the Ethics in Government Act, to enforce the codes and to apply their financial disclosure requirements to the other two branches of government. *(Ethics Act, p. 198)*

The impetus for the 1977 codes of conduct came from the congressional scandals of 1976, a special post-Watergate concern for integrity in government and the recommendations of two public commissions. One was the quadrennial Commission on Executive, Legislative and Judicial Salaries, chaired in 1976-77 by businessman Peter G. Peterson, a former Secretary of Commerce. The other was a special Commission on Operations of the Senate, headed by former Sen. Harold E. Hughes, D-Iowa (1969-75).

Both commissions recommended pay increases for Congress provided effective codes of ethics were adopted. The Hughes commission, saying the Senate had "insufficient safeguards against conflicts of interest," urged adoption of a ban on honoraria and full financial disclosure by members of the Senate and top employees.

The Peterson commission also called for financial disclosure plus additional steps — a limit on the outside income members could earn in addition to their congressional salaries, accountable expense allowances and public audits of compliance with the conflict of interest restrictions. The commission was regarded as having significant influence because it was the originating body for salary increases at the highest levels of government, including Supreme Court justices and Cabinet members.

Pay and Ethics

President Gerald R. Ford, with the concurrence of President-elect Jimmy Carter, approved the commission recommendations for pay increases and a congressional code of ethics and forwarded them to Congress on Jan. 17, 1977. Under the proposal congressional salaries would rise 28.9 percent, from $44,600 to $57,500. Other officials, including the top grades of the civil service, would get comparable increases.

Congressional leaders moved swiftly to put the twin proposals for Congress on track. Keenly aware of public opinion, House Speaker Thomas P. O'Neill Jr., D-Mass., and Senate Majority Leader Robert C. Byrd, D-W.Va., made passage of strong ethics codes a condition for approval of salary increases for Congress and top executive branch officials, which they believed were sorely needed. Both leaders said that a limit on outside income that members could earn beyond their salary was essential to a strong code; O'Neill called the provision "the heart and soul of the entire package" of ethical standards. It became the most bitterly fought section of the code in each house.

It did not apply to "unearned" income such as dividends and capital gains.

O'Neill assigned responsibility for drawing up an ethics code to a bipartisan Commission on Administrative Review headed by Rep. David R. Obey, D-Wis., which began work in late 1976. The commission released a proposed code on Feb. 7, 1977, and the House passed it, after heated debate on the outside income issue, by a vote of 402-22 March 2.

The Senate used the Obey Commission's work as the basis for a Senate code that paralleled the House code in most respects. It passed the Senate April 1 after two weeks of debate and action on 64 amendments.

The 86-9 vote in favor of passage by no means reflected the depth of feeling in the Senate against elements of the new code. Sen. Gaylord Nelson, D-Wis., the floor manager for the code, said after the vote that many of those senators who voted for the measure did so out of fear of the political hazards of a negative vote.

Nevertheless, Nelson said, Senate acceptance of full financial disclosure was a "milestone" because past efforts to force senators to make public their financial operations had been hotly contested.

In both chambers the earned income limit produced the bitterest opposition, but in each case it was approved by lopsided margins. The House vote was 344-79 and the Senate's was 62-35. It continued to be attacked, however, both before and after its Jan. 1, 1979, effective date. In March 1979 the Senate voted 54-44 to defer imposing the limit on senators for four years, to 1983.

Code Provisions

The limit on outside earned income — set at 15 percent of the congressional salary, or $8,625 at the salary level existing in 1977 — was directed at conflict-of-interest problems raised by large honoraria given by interest groups and at the continuing but declining practice of members carrying on as private lawyers or insurance agents while supposedly working full time as members of Congress. The source and amount of this income had to be reported.

The codes also abolished office accounts, which put an end to the last remaining device by which members could accept unreported contributions from organizations or individuals and use the funds for virtually any purpose. Members also were faced with new restrictions on their use of the franking privilege to send mail.

And finally, the idea that a member's personal financial activities were nobody's business but his own was put to rest. As passed, the codes required members to make public data on their income, gifts received, financial holdings, debts, securities, commodity transactions and real estate dealings. Spouses had to report much the same information.

Members were not required to report the exact value of their holdings of different kinds but only a range of value — the scale ran from not more than $5,000 to greater than $5 million (later reduced to $250,000 and over). In the 1978 Ethics in Government Act Congress applied roughly the same disclosure rules to high officials of the executive and judicial branches. *(Major provisions, p. 198)*

Both codes prohibited members and employees from accepting gifts of $100 or more from lobbyists and foreign nationals and forbade the conversion of testimonial or campaign funds to personal use. They also set a maximum amount a member could accept as an honorarium. *(See below)*

Rules Governing Members' Conduct:
Constitution, Hill Rules and Criminal Laws

Concern for the ethical conduct of members of Congress is reflected in the Constitution, federal statutes and Senate and House rules. Some key provisions affecting members' conduct follows:

Constitutional Provision

"Each House may determine the Rules of its Proceedings, punish its Members for disorderly Behavior, and, with the Concurrence of two thirds, expel a Member." (Article I, Section 5, Clause 2)

". . . They shall in all Cases, except Treason, Felony and Breach of the Peace, be privileged from Arrest during their Attendance at the Session of their respective Houses, and in going to and returning from the same; and for any Speech or Debate in either House, they shall not be questioned in any other Place." (Article I, Section 6, Clause 1)

"No Senator or Representative shall, during the Time for which he was elected, be appointed to any civil Office under the Authority of the United States, which shall have been created, or the Emoluments whereof shall have been encreased during such time; and no Person holding any Office under the United States, shall be a Member of either House during his Continuance in Office." (Article I, Section 6, Clause 2)

"No Title of Nobility shall be granted by the United States; And no Person holding any Office of Profit or Trust under them, shall, without the Consent of the Congress, accept of any present, Emolument, Office, or Title, of any kind whatever, from any King, Prince, or foreign State." (Article I, Section 9, Clause 8)

"The Senators and Representatives before mentioned . . . shall be bound by Oath or Affirmation, to support this Constitution. . . ." (Article VI, Clause 3)

Criminal Statutes

A series of laws in Title 18 of the U.S. Code make it a federal crime for members of Congress to engage in certain actions. Prohibited acts, excluding those relating to campaign spending, include:

Soliciting or receiving a bribe for the performance of any official act, for the violation of an official duty or for participating in or permitting any fraud against the United States. The penalty is a $20,000 fine or three times the monetary equivalent of the thing of value, whichever is greater, or imprisonment for not more than 15 years, or both, plus possible disqualification from holding office. (18 USC 201c)

Soliciting or receiving anything of value for himself or because of any official act performed or to be performed by him. The penalty is a $10,000 fine or imprisonment for not more than two years, or both. (18 USC 201g)

Soliciting or receiving any compensation for services in relation to any proceeding, contract, claim, controversy, etc., in which the United States is a party or has a direct and substantial interest, before any department, agency, court martial, officer or civil or military commission. The penalty is a $10,000 fine and imprisonment for not more than two years, or both, plus disqualification from holding office. (18 USC 203a)

Practicing in the Court of Claims. The penalty is a $10,000 fine and imprisonment for not more than two years, or both, plus disqualification from holding office. (18 USC 204)

Receiving, as a political contribution or otherwise, anything of value for promising use of or using influence to obtain for any person an appointive office or place under the United States. The penalty is a $1,000 fine, or imprisonment for not more than one year, or both. (18 USC 211)

The campaign laws prohibit buying a vote, promising employment, soliciting political contributions from federal employees and threatening the job of a federal employee who fails to give a campaign contribution. (18 USC 597-606)

Chamber Rules

Prior to the adoption of ethics codes in 1968, the chief ethical curbs on members' activities related to voting. *(Provisions of codes, this page and p. 196)*

In 1801, when he was Vice President and presiding over the Senate, Thomas Jefferson wrote in *Jefferson's Manual:*

"Where the private interests of a Member are concerned in a bill or question he is to withdraw. And where such an interest has appeared, his voice has been disallowed. . . . In a case so contrary, not only to the laws of decency, but to the fundamental principle of the social compact, which denies to any man to be a judge in his own cause, it is for the honor of the House that this rule of immemorial observance should be strictly adhered to."

Jefferson's rule gave rise to Rule 8 of the House, which requires each member present to vote "unless he has a direct personal or pecuniary interest in the event of such question." In most cases this decision has been left to the member. Under an 1874 ruling, a representative may vote for his private interests if the measure is not for his exclusive benefit, but for that of a group.

Under Rule 12 senators may be excused from voting, provided they give their reasons for abstaining, and senators have been excused in the past because of such a direct interest in the outcome.

The Senate code contained three significant sections not in the House code. One was a provision to prohibit senators or employees from engaging in a professional practice, such as law, for compensation. Strom Thurmond, R-S.C., the Republican floor manager of the code, had proposed the flat ban in committee, arguing that senators had "no business" practicing other professions. It was modified on the floor to permit senators and employees to practice a profession so long as they were not affiliated with any firm and so long as their work was not carried out during Senate office hours. *(Description of legal practice by members, p. 202)*

The Senate code also prohibited former senators from lobbying in the Senate for one year after leaving office and prohibited former staff members for a senator or committee from lobbying their former employer or committee member and staff for one year.

Unlike the House code the Senate code declared that no member, officer or employee could refuse to hire an individual, discharge an individual or discriminate with respect to promotion, pay or terms of employment on the basis of race, color, religion, sex, national origin, age, or state of physical handicap.

Ethics in Government Act

In October 1978 Congress enacted the Ethics in Government Act, which gave legal force to the financial disclosure requirements of the House and Senate ethics codes (slightly amended) and required the same disclosures by high-ranking members of the executive and legislative branches. The new law set civil penalties for violations of these requirements.

It contained other strong conflict-of-interest provisions covering executive employees who leave the government (known as "revolving door" restrictions) but did not apply those constraints to members and employees of the legislative branch.

President Carter had given impetus to these new precautions even before he assumed the presidency. He required his appointees to meet guidelines for financial disclosure, divestiture of holdings that could create conflicts between private and government interests, and post-government employment restrictions, and asked Congress to enact them into law.

As a direct outgrowth of the Watergate investigations the Ethics in Government Act established procedures for court appointment of a special prosecutor to substitute for Justice Department prosecutors whenever a high-ranking federal official was accused of criminal action. The Watergate special prosecutor had been appointed under the attorney general's general authority to name special counsel. The new law set forth a step-by-step process for initiating and carrying out such an investigation.

The act also set up an office in the executive branch to monitor compliance and an office of legal counsel in the Senate to represent that body and its members in court. The House decided not to be covered by this new office.

The basic elements of the Ethics in Government Act having been debated in Congress since 1976, a consensus was clear by the time the House debated the Senate-passed bill in September 1976.

The final version of the legislation was signed by President Carter Oct. 26, 1978.

Major Provisions

The ethics act:
● Wrote into law the financial disclosure provisions of the Senate and House ethics codes adopted by both chambers in 1977. Those codes were enforceable only by internal penalties such as a reprimand; writing the codes into law allowed violations to be enforced with fines. However, the final bill provided only civil penalties; criminal penalties were dropped.

● Applied the same disclosure requirements to the president, vice president, top-level executive branch officials, Supreme Court justices, federal judges and other top employees of the judicial branch.

● Also applied the disclosure requirements to candidates for federal office.

● Required disclosure of earned income, by source, type and amount, unearned income by categories of value (such as $5,000-$15,000 and $15,000-$50,000) and honoraria totaling $100 or more in a year. In addition, certain information about gifts had to be disclosed.

Also required disclosure by category of value of information about property holdings, debts and interests in trades or businesses.

● Required disclosure of certain information about finances of a spouse and dependent children.

● Provided civil but not criminal penalties for disclosure violations. Maximum penalties would be $5,000.

● Required that the public have access to the information disclosed.

● Required the reports to be filed by May 15 of each year with the first reports under the law due in 1979 for calendar year 1978.

● Established an Office of Government Ethics in the Office of Personnel Management, which was created in 1978 by President Carter's reorganization proposal splitting the Civil Service Commission in two. The new ethics office would develop rules and regulations on government conflicts of interest and other ethical problems, and monitor and investigate compliance with federal ethics laws.

● Placed new restrictions on business activities of federal workers who left the government. These "revolving door" restrictions prohibited former officials from representing anyone before their old agencies in connection with a matter on which they participated personally and substantially while in office. Senior officials received a broader prohibition; they were banned for one year from any representation before their former agency.

● Established a mechanism for court appointment of a special prosecutor to investigate criminal allegations against high-level government officials, including the president, vice-president and Cabinet-level officers. The attorney general was to conduct a preliminary investigation and request a special prosecutor if the allegations appeared to have merit. As a precaution, a majority of members of either political party on the Judiciary Committees could request the attorney general to apply to the court for a special prosecutor. The prosecutor (a temporary appointee) was assigned all investigative and prosecutorial functions of the Justice Department and his independence was assured by allowing his removal from office only for extraordinary impropriety or severe disability.

Income Limit Raised

The Senate's action early in 1979, deferring the limit on senators' outside income for four years, to 1983, created bitter resentment among House members. It enabled senators to collect honoraria up to a total of $25,000 per year and $2,000 per speech while representatives were limited to earning no more than $9,099 beyond their salaries and $1,000 per honorarium. (Because of a cost-of-living raise moving congressional salaries in 1979 up to $60,662.50, the 15 percent cap on representatives' outside earned income rose to $9,099 from the previous $8,625.)

Two years later the Senate poured more salt into representatives' wounds. It voted 45-43 on Sept. 24, 1981, to remove entirely the $25,000 ceiling on honoraria. That galvanized the House Rules Committee to approve a resolution raising the earnings limit to 40 percent of representatives' salaries. When brought to a roll-call vote on the House floor, however, the resolution was defeated 147-271 Oct. 28. Six weeks later House leaders arranged a quiet flipflop without a recorded vote.

The change in the House's earned income rule occurred Dec. 15 with surprising swiftness and little warning. During a lull in House business, John P. Murtha, D-Pa., rose and asked for unanimous consent to approve a resolution increasing the ceiling on House members' outside earnings from 15 percent of their official salary to 30 percent. When no one objected, Murtha returned to his seat. The entire process took about 10 seconds.

Supporters of the move said privately that it was necessary because members needed higher pay — either directly or indirectly — but were unwilling to go on record for it for fear of a public outcry. They compounded their public relations problems the next day, however, when both houses increased the congressional tax deduction for Washington, D.C., living expenses. And in December 1982, House members raised their annual salary to $69,800.

The doubling of representatives' earned income limit raised it to $20,940 while senators remained free of any limit. When financial disclosure reports for 1981 were filed they revealed that the top honoraria earner in the House, Ways and Means Committee Chairman Daniel Rostenkowski, D-Ill., had received $52,600 for speeches and articles and had given $38,100 of that to charity. His tax-writing counterpart in the Senate, Robert Dole, R-Kan., chairman of the Finance Committee, led the Senate list with $66,850. Dole gave $30,500 of his honoraria to charity.

Honoraria

Congress first limited how much its members could earn from honoraria in the 1974 campaign finance law. For 1975, senators and representatives could receive no more than $15,000 annually for giving speeches and writing articles and were limited to $1,000 per item.

Under pressure from the Senate, that ceiling was raised in the 1976 amendments to the campaign law to allow members of Congress to receive $2,000 per individual event and an aggregate amount of $25,000 a year. However, the $25,000 limit was a net figure because members were allowed to deduct certain expenses.

The 1977 House and Senate ethics codes, with their 15 percent limit on earned income, cut the ceiling on total honoraria to less than $10,000 and the limit on a single honorarium to $1,000. But the Senate subsequently put off its income limit and repealed the $25,000 honorarium ceiling, keeping only the campaign law's $2,000 per speech maximum. Critics said senators were placing themselves in bond to interest groups willing to pay generous honoraria. Supporters replied that without the opportunity to earn

honoraria the Senate would become even more a rich man's club.

The principal purpose of the limits on earned income and honoraria was to reduce potential conflicts of interest. It was recognized that organizations often gave honoraria

Government's Code of Ethics

Congress in 1958 approved the following Code of Ethics (H Con Res 175, 85th Congress, 2d session) for all government employees, including members of Congress.*

Any person in Government service should:

1. Put loyalty to the highest moral principles and to country above loyalty to persons, party, or Government department.

2. Uphold the Constitution, laws, and legal regulations of the United States and of all governments therein and never be a party to their evasion.

3. Give a full day's labor for a full day's pay; giving to the performance of his duties his earnest effort and best thought.

4. Seek to find and employ more efficient and economical ways of getting tasks accomplished.

5. Never discriminate unfairly by the dispensing of special favors or privileges to anyone, whether for remuneration or not; and never accept, for himself or his family, favors or benefits under circumstances which might be construed by reasonable persons as influencing the performance of his governmental duties.

6. Make no private promises of any kind binding upon the duties of office, since a Government employee has no private word which can be binding on public duty.

7. Engage in no business with the Government, either directly or indirectly, which is inconsistent with the conscientious performance of his governmental duties.

8. Never use any information coming to him confidentially in the performance of government duties as a means for making private profit.

9. Expose corruption wherever discovered.

10. Uphold these principles, ever conscious that public office is a public trust.

* The report of the House Committee on Standards of Official Conduct, *In the Matter of a Complaint Against Rep. Robert L. F. Sikes* (H Rept 94-1364, July 23, 1976) stated the following: "Although the Code of Ethics for Government Service was adopted as a concurrent resolution, and as such, may have expired with the adjournment of the 85th Congress, the standards of ethical conduct expressed therein represent continuing traditional standards of ethical conduct to be observed by Members of the House at all times, which were supplemented in 1968 by a specific Code of Official Conduct."

Immunity in Washington

Members of Congress apparently were no longer to be immune from arrest in Washington, D.C., for crimes such as drunk driving and soliciting prostitutes, according to a 1976 Justice Department ruling.

Reports occasionally would appear in the press of such incidents in Washington involving a member of Congress. Invariably, once police confirmed that the suspect was a member, action against the person would be dropped.

The Justice Department ruling, which had been requested by the D.C. chief of police, stemmed from a case involving Rep. Joe D. Waggonner Jr., D-La. (1961-79). Waggonner had been arrested after he allegedly solicited a District of Columbia policewoman posing as a prostitute. He was released when police identified him as a member of Congress.

The Justice Department ruling was announced on July 23, 1976. Based on the ruling, D.C. police said, members "and all other elected and appointed federal, state, and local officials are subject to arrest for the commission of criminal offenses to the same extent and in the same manner as all other citizens." An exception would be continued for most parking violations by private automobiles bearing congressional license plates.

The non-arrest policy, which had been in effect for more than 100 years, had been based on "a misinterpretation of the meaning" of the Privilege from Arrest Clause in Article I, Section 6 of the Constitution, a police spokesman said.

At least since *Williamson v. United States* (207 U.S. 425, 446) in 1908, this language was believed to have been inserted in the Constitution to prevent political harassment through civil arrest. The more sweeping policy against arrest was thought to have been aimed at not offending the legislators, who controlled the D.C. Police Department budget.

---

effect. After the limit was doubled late in 1981, 18 representatives reported receiving over $15,000 in honoraria, but 26 senators got more than $25,000. (Transfers to charity brought totals down to the law's limits.)

Under House and Senate ethics rules a member must report gifts of transportation, food, lodging or entertainment aggregating $250 or more from any one source during the preceding calendar year. The rule applies to individuals and groups that do not have a direct interest in legislation.

But the codes specifically bar members and employees from accepting gifts aggregating more than $100 during a calendar year from persons with direct interests in legislation, or from foreign nationals. Both houses defined persons with direct interests in legislation as lobbyists (even if they are not registered lobbyists) and businesses, labor unions and organizations which maintain political action committees.

Subsequent advisory opinions, however, made it clear that a member may accept from a lobbying group more than $100 in food, lodging, transportation and other "necessary expenses" as long as the member "renders personal services sufficient to constitute 'equal consideration' for the expenses provided by the sponsoring organization."

As long as the service performed "is more than perfunctory in nature," the payment is considered an honorarium.

Any travel provided to the member in connection with speechmaking is counted as a reimbursement, and not a gift, the codes state.

In other words, according to a House Standards Committee aide, if a member goes to "a company's moose hunting lodge for the weekend, that's a gift." However, if the member "goes to the lodge to make a speech," then the member should disclose his food, lodging and transportation as a reimbursement, the aide continued.

In addition, lobbying groups can treat members to expense-paid "fact-finding trips," as long as the organization pays only "necessary expenses" and the trip is directly related to the member's official duties.

HILL IMMUNITY: SHIELDING LEGISLATORS

The concept of congressional immunity from certain legal actions was a well-established principle in England when it was added to the American Constitution. Article I, Section 6 provides that senators and representatives "shall in all cases, except Treason, Felony and Breach of the Peace, be privileged from Arrest during their Attendance at the Session of their respective Houses, and in going to and returning from the same; and for any Speech or Debate in either House, they shall not be questioned in any other Place."

The privilege-from-arrest clause has become practically obsolete, as various court decisions have excluded more and more acts and proceedings from the protection of the clause. As presently interpreted, the clause applies only to arrests in civil suits, such as non-payment of debts or breach of contract; and most state constitutions or statutes prohibit arrest generally in such actions. Civil arrests were

---

to members of Congress serving on committees that handled legislation sought by the donor organization. Getting legislators to speak to a conference and mingle with organization representatives could be an effective lobbying technique.

Senate Majority Leader Robert C. Byrd, D-W.Va., arguing for the limit on earned income in 1977, said the "honoraria circuit" heightened public concern about congressional ethics when interest groups "pay extremely large sums of money for a short speech by a senator." He called the $25,000 a year ceiling on honoraria "intolerably high."

Congressional Quarterly reported that 12 senators and seven representatives earned $25,000 or more in honoraria in 1978, before the House limit on earned income took

Congressional Aides Misuse Power

Misuses of power and conflicts of interest have not been limited to members of Congress. Occasionally congressional aides have used their positions and their employers' prestige for personal gain. Following are two of the most famous cases.

Bobby Baker

Bobby Baker began his Capitol Hill career as a teenage page in the Senate. Ambitious and aggressive, Baker rose to the position of secretary to the Senate majority, making himself right-hand man to his mentor, Majority Leader Lyndon B. Johnson, D-Texas (House 1937-49; Senate 1949-61), in the late 1950s.

When he quit his post under fire, Baker on paper was worth $2 million, most of it gained, the subsequent court records showed, from combining law practice with influence peddling. The notoriety caused by the Baker case is credited with moving the Senate to create an ethics committee.

Baker resigned his Senate job in 1963 after a civil suit was brought against him, charging that he used his influence to obtain contracts for a vending machine concern in which he had a financial interest. Senate investigations conducted over the next two years concluded that Baker was guilty of "gross improprieties." The investigating committee recommended that the Senate require full financial disclosures by senators and top employees of the Senate.

Baker meanwhile was brought to trial on charges of income tax evasion, theft and conspiracy to defraud the government. He was found guilty in January 1967; after appeals had been exhausted, he began his prison term four years later. The major charge on which he was found guilty was that he had collected more than $99,000 from a group of California savings and loan executives, ostensibly as campaign contributions, but that in reality he had kept about $80,000 of the total for himself.

At the trial two of the California executives testified that in 1962 they gave Baker about $66,000 for campaign contributions to seven senators and one House member, Ways and Means Committee Chairman Wilbur D. Mills, D-Ark. (1939-77). Mills and one of the senators, Foreign Relations Committee Chairman J. W. Fulbright, D-Ark. (1945-74), testified that they had received none of the funds. Defense counsel stipulated that none of the other six senators had received any of the funds. One of the savings and loan executives testified that Baker told him the California savings and loan associations could improve their standing in Congress with a "very impressive" contribution to certain senators and House members and could "win friends" in Congress at a time when a bill was pending to increase taxes on the associations.

Baker testified he turned the money over to Sen. Robert S. Kerr, D-Okla. (1949-63), a power on the Senate Finance Committee, for his re-election campaign. Kerr was dead by the time Baker told his story.

Sweig and the Speaker's Office

A congressional scandal which attracted nationwide attention when it was revealed in 1969 involved influence-peddling in the office of Speaker John W. McCormack, D-Mass. (1928-71). In the end, one of his top aides, Dr. Martin Sweig, was convicted July 9, 1970, of perjury, and Jan. 28, 1972, of misusing the Speaker's office to influence government decisions.

Sweig, who had worked for McCormack 24 years and was drawing an annual salary of $36,000 in 1969, was implicated with Nathan M. Voloshen, New York City lawyer-lobbyist and longtime McCormack friend. On June 17, 1970, Voloshen pleaded guilty to charges of conspiring to use the Speaker's office to influence matters before federal government agencies and to three counts of lying to a federal grand jury about the charges.

---

more common at the time the Constitution was adopted.

Long v. Ansell (293 U.S. 76) in 1934 and *U.S. v. Cooper* (4 Dall. 341) in 1800 declared that the clause does not apply to service of process in civil or criminal cases; nor does it apply to arrest in any criminal case. Furthermore, *Williamson v. United States* (207 U.S. 425, 446) in 1908 interpreted the phrase "treason, felony, or breach of the peace" as excluding all criminal offenses from the privilege's coverage.

The speech or debate clause has been cited more frequently by members seeking immunity from actions against them. Various court decisions have broadly interpreted the phrase "speech or debate" to include virtually everything a member does in carrying out his legislative responsibilities.

'Speech or Debate' Broadly Construed

The first Supreme Court interpretation of the speech or debate clause occurred in 1881 in *Kilbourn v. Thompson* (103 U.S. 168). The case is also widely cited for its ruling on the limits of congressional investigations.

It involved a contempt of Congress citation against Hallet Kilbourn, manager of a real estate pool, for refusing to answer questions before the House Select Committee on the Real Estate Pool and Jay Cooke Indebtedness. The

Members of Congress...

Until World War II, to be a member of Congress was to hold a part-time job. Consequently, certain occupations which demand almost full-time attention — running a business or teaching school, for example — sent few representatives to Congress while others, notably the law, sent many. For years more than half of all members of Congress have been lawyers, while few have been active businessmen (though many have been retired businessmen).

Legal Practice and Past Scandals

Lawyers have never been forbidden to practice law while holding congressional office, but the combination of the two professions has led to numerous scandals.

Sen. Daniel Webster's retainer from the Bank of the United States is familiar to many. What is not so well known is that Webster's professional relationship with the bank was no secret; he represented the bank in 41 cases before the Supreme Court. It was not an unusual arrangement for the time; neither was it universally condoned. John Quincy Adams, for example, as a member of Congress declined to practice before federal courts.

It was not until the 1850s that members were forbidden to represent claimants against the U.S. government. This restriction grew out of a scandal surrounding senator, and later secretary of the Treasury, Thomas Corwin of Ohio. Corwin successfully recovered half a million dollars (an enormous sum for those days) in a mining case; scandal erupted when it was revealed that both the claimant and silver mine were frauds.

Legal practice played a supporting role in the great railroad robbery known as the Crédit Mobilier scandal of the Grant administration. In that case, as brought out in a congressional hearing, promoters of the Union Pacific Railroad used stock in Crédit Mobilier, a joint stock company they controlled, to bribe members of Congress to keep up federal subsidies to the railroad.

The early 1900s again brought congressional ethics to a low spot in public opinion. Heavily promoted by publisher William Randolph Hearst, a series of articles by David Graham Phillips called *Treason of the Senate* alleged corrupt behavior by 21 senators. The series played a major role in promoting direct election of senators.

Only one of the 21 senators replied publicly to Phillips' charges. He was Sen. Joseph W. Bailey, D-Texas (1901-13), who had received more than $225,000 in legal fees for several months' services to a Texas oilman. Bailey vehemently defended his practice of law while serving in the Senate: "I despise those public men who think they must remain poor in order to be considered honest. I am not one of them. If my constituents want a man who is willing to go to the poorhouse in his old age in order to stay in the Senate during his middle age, they will have to find another senator. I intend to make every dollar that I can honestly make without neglecting or interfering with my public duty." [1]

Bar Association Actions

The legal profession moved to discourage congressional law practice in the late 1960s. The move

---

House ordered Kilbourn jailed for contempt. He won release on a writ of habeus corpus and sued the Speaker, members of the investigating committee and Sergeant at Arms John G. Thompson for false arrest. The Supreme Court sustained Kilbourn's claim, on the grounds that it was not a legitimate investigation.

The court decided the case on the basis of Congress' investigatory powers. But the defendants, in the course of their arguments, raised the speech or debate clause as a defense, and the court also commented on this issue in its opinion. The court said the protection of the clause was not limited to words spoken in debate, but also was applicable to written reports, to resolutions offered, to the act of voting, and to all things generally done in a session of the House by one of its members in relation to the business before it.

Legislative Acts Protected

The Supreme Court on Feb. 24, 1966, held in a 7-0 decision that in prosecuting a former member of Congress the executive branch may not constitutionally inquire into the member's motives for making a speech on the floor, even though the speech was made for a bribe and was part of an unlawful conspiracy.

The holdings in *United States v. Johnson* (383 U.S. 169) left members immune from prosecution for their words and legislative deeds on the floor of Congress, with one exception reserved by the court — prosecution under a "narrowly drawn" law enacted by Congress itself "to regulate the conduct of its Members." Members of Congress already were immune from libel suits for speeches made on the floor.

Johnson was the first case of its kind. The court was unable to find among the English or American cases any direct precedent. The court did discuss cases holding that legislators were protected from private suits for their legislative words and deeds; and it cited approvingly a Supreme Court decision, the force of which appeared to extend the *Johnson* doctrine to state legislators.

The *Johnson* case arose out of the conviction of former

...And the Practice of Law

came after a series of scandals which involved, sometimes indirectly, congressional law practices. Among those cases (discussed elsewhere in this chapter) were those of Rep. Thomas F. Johnson, D-Md., Senate Majority Secretary Bobby Baker, Sen. Thomas J. Dodd, D-Conn. and Rep. Cornelius Gallagher, D-N.J.[2]

The American Bar Association revised its canons in 1969. Its new Code of Professional Responsibility provided that the name of a public official should not be used in the name of a law firm or in the firm's professional notices "during any significant period in which he is not actively and regularly practicing law as a member of the firm."[3]

Most state bar associations adopted the code, as well as a number of state supreme courts, thus clearing the way for formal grievance proceedings if violated.

In an extensive study of congressional ethics, conducted in 1967-69, a special committee of the Association of the Bar of the City of New York made several recommendations on congressmen and the legal profession. The committee recommended that members of Congress voluntarily refrain from any form of law practice, except for first-termers who foresaw little prospect for re-election. The committee also recommended that Congress enact legislation to forbid "double door" law partnerships (under which the law partner of a member of Congress engages in federal agency practice prohibited by law to the member) and to forbid members from appearing for compensation in the courts.[4] The longtime chairman of the House Judiciary Committee, Emanuel Celler,

D-N.Y. (1923-73), was a practitioner of a "double door" partnership.

In 1978 Rep. Joshua Eilberg, D-Pa. (1967-78), was indicted on charges he illegally received legal fees for helping a Philadelphia hospital get a federal construction grant. The House Standards Committee said he received more than $100,000 from his law firm under circumstances suggesting he was influenced in "the performance of his government duties." Eilberg was defeated for re-election that fall and pleaded guilty to reduced charges in 1979.

Income from Law Practices

In financial disclosure reports for the year 1975, 53 representatives reported at least $1,000 in income from a law practice. Nineteen of those were freshmen in the 94th Congress. Eight members of the House noted on their disclosure forms that they had withdrawn from practice.[5]

Disclosure reports on 1980 income gave approximately the same figures on present and withdrawn legal practice, but the ethics code's limit on outside earned income appeared to have reduced the 20 practicing lawyers' income considerably.[6]

---

1. James C. Kirby, *Congress and the Public Trust; Report of the Association of the Bar of the City of New York Special Committee on Congressional Ethics* (New York: Atheneum, 1970), pp. 81-82.
2. For details on the involvement of law practices in these cases, see *Congress and the Public Trust*, pp. 83-85.
3. Ibid., p. 103.
4. Ibid., pp. 234-235.
5. *Congressional Quarterly Weekly Report*, July 31, 1976, p. 2053.
6. *Congressional Quarterly Weekly Report*, Sept. 5, 1981, p. 1690.

Rep. Thomas F. Johnson, D-Md. (1959-63), on June 13, 1963, by a federal jury in Baltimore. The government charged that Johnson, former Rep. Frank W. Boykin, D-Ala. (1935-63), and two officers of a Maryland savings and loan company then under indictment, J. Kenneth Edlin and William L. Robinson, entered into a conspiracy whereby Johnson and Boykin would approach the Justice Department to urge a "review" of the indictment and Johnson would make a speech on the floor of the House defending savings and loan institutions. Johnson made the speech June 30, 1960, and it was reprinted by the indicted company and distributed to the public. Johnson and Boykin allegedly received money in the form of "campaign contributions." Johnson's share was more than $20,000.

Johnson was convicted on seven counts of violating the federal conflict-of-interest law and on one count of conspiring to defraud the United States; the others were convicted of the same charges. President Johnson Dec. 17, 1965, granted Boykin a full pardon.

The 4th Circuit Court of Appeals Sept. 16, 1964, set

aside Johnson's conspiracy conviction on grounds that it was unconstitutional under provisions of Article I, Section 6: "...for any Speech or Debate in either House, they [senators and representatives] shall not be questioned in any other Place." The court ordered a new trial on the other counts on grounds that evidence taken about Johnson's speech on the conspiracy count "infected" the entire case.

The Supreme Court affirmed the lower court's ruling, thus foreclosing further protection on the conspiracy count but permitting retrial on the other counts. In the majority opinion, Justice John Marshall Harlan said the purpose of the speech or debate clause was "prophylactic," that it was adopted by the Constitutional Convention (without discussion or opposition) because of the English experience with efforts of the Crown to intimidate and punish Parliament. The clause was intended to protect the independence and integrity of Congress, the justice said, and to reinforce the separation of powers by preventing an "unfriendly" executive and a "hostile" judiciary appointed by the executive from reaching into congressional activity for evidence of criminality.

The government's theory, rejected by Justice Harlan, was that Johnson's criminal act — acceptance of a bribe and entering into a conspiracy — predated his floor speech. Justice Harlan said the indictment particularized the speech as part of the conspiracy charged, and evidence about the speech was taken at trial.

On Jan. 26, 1968, Johnson was convicted for a second time on the conflict-of-interest charges by the U.S. District Court in Baltimore. He was sentenced to six months in prison.

Immunity Protection Narrowed

On June 29, 1972, the Supreme Court in effect narrowed the category of protected actions under the immunity clause. The court's ruling was issued in a case involving former Sen. Daniel B. Brewster, D-Md. (House 1959-63; Senate 1963-69).

A federal grand jury Dec. 1, 1969, indicted Brewster, Spiegel Inc., a Chicago mail-order firm, and Cyrus T. Anderson, a lobbyist for the firm, on charges of violating federal bribery laws. The indictment charged that Brewster received $24,500 from Spiegel Inc. and Anderson to influence his "action, vote and decision" on postal rate legislation.

The grand jury said the payments were made in five installments between Jan. 10, 1966, and Jan. 31, 1968. Brewster was a member of the Senate Post Office and Civil Service Committee during a 1967 debate on postal rate increases for regular third-class mail. Spiegel was a major user of such rates. Brewster had been defeated for re-election in 1968.

Ten months after Brewster's indictment, a U.S. district court judge dismissed it on the grounds that the senator was immune from prosecution because of the speech or debate clause.

The government took an appeal directly to the Supreme Court, which issued a decision June 29, 1972, narrowing the category of protected actions under the immunity clause. A six-man court majority ruled: "Taking a bribe is, obviously, no part of the legislative process or function." (United States v. Brewster, 408 U.S. 501)

Chief Justice Warren E. Burger, writing the opinion, continued: "The illegal conduct is taking or agreeing to take money for a promise to act in a certain way. There is no need for the government to show that [Brewster] fulfilled the alleged illegal bargain ... for it is taking the bribe, not performance of the illicit compact, that is a criminal act." Importantly, the court upheld the validity of the indictment because it would not be necessary for the government to inquire into legislative acts or their motivations in order to prove a violation of the bribery statute. Brewster was ordered to stand trial and was convicted Nov. 17, 1972.

In its verdict, the jury found Brewster guilty of a lesser bribery charge, that of accepting an unlawful gratuity. Following the verdict, Spiegel Inc. pleaded guilty. Brewster was sentenced to two-to-six years in prison and fined $30,000. In August 1974 a federal appeals court reversed the conviction on grounds the jury had not been given proper instructions. A new trial was scheduled for August 1975. But on June 25, 1975, Brewster pleaded no contest to a felony charge of accepting an illegal gratuity while he was a senator.

Protected Acts Specified

On June 29, 1972, the Supreme Court took the unusual step of specifying in some detail certain acts of a legislator that were protected by the immunity clause. The case involved Sen. Mike Gravel, D-Alaska (1969-81), and his actions in releasing portions of the then-classified Pentagon Papers history of United States' involvement in the Vietnam War.

During the controversy over publication of the Pentagon Papers in 1971 by The New York Times, The Washington Post and several other newspapers, Gravel on June 29, 1971, convened a special meeting of the Public Works Subcommittee on Public Buildings, of which he was chairman. With the press and the public in attendance, Gravel read classified documents from the Pentagon Papers into the subcommittee record. Subsequently, the senator arranged for the verbatim publication of the subcommittee record by Beacon Press, the non-profit publishing arm of the Unitarian-Universalist Association.

In August 1971 a federal grand jury in Boston, investigating the release of the Pentagon Papers, ordered an aide to Gravel, Leonard S. Rodberg, to appear before it. Rodberg had been hired the night Gravel called the session of his subcommittee to read excerpts from the secret documents. Rodberg subsequently helped Gravel edit and make arrangements for publication of the papers. The grand jury also subpoenaed several persons associated with Beacon Press who were involved in publication of the papers.

Rodberg moved to quash the subpoena on the grounds he was protected from the questioning by congressional immunity, contending such immunity extended to staff members. Gravel filed a motion to intervene on Rodberg's behalf, claiming Rodberg was acting under the senator's orders, which were immune from judicial inquiry.

The Justice Department, in a brief filed in the case Sept. 8, 1971, said no immunity existed for either Rodberg or Gravel. While not saying so directly, the department's action left open the possibility it might subpoena Gravel himself to testify.

A lower court ruled in October 1971 that the grand jury could not question any witness about Gravel's conduct at the special meeting or about his preparation for the meeting. The grand jury also was prohibited from questioning Rodberg about his own actions taken at Gravel's direction relating to the meeting.

In January 1972 the court of appeals held that Gravel could be questioned about the subsequent publication of the subcommittee record by Beacon Press but not about the subcommittee meeting itself. The same immunities extended to Gravel were also to be applied to Rodberg, the court ruled. But third parties, the court ruled, could be questioned about any of their own actions regarding the publication and the ad hoc committee session.

In a 5-4 decision on June 29, 1972, the Supreme Court specifically enumerated the activities of Gravel and Rodberg that were protected by the immunity clause (Gravel v. United States, 408 U.S. 606).

The court said no witness could be questioned concerning: 1) the conduct of Gravel or his aides at the meeting of the Subcommittee on Public Buildings and Grounds of the Senate Public Works Committee on June 29, 1971; 2) the motives and purposes behind the conduct of Gravel or his aides at the June 29 meeting; 3) communications between Gravel and his aides during the terms of their employment and related to the June 29 meeting or any other legislative act of the senator; 4) any act, in itself not criminal, performed by the senator or by his aides in the course of their employment in preparation for the subcommittee meeting, except as it proved relevant to investigating possible third-party crime.

The ruling held that Gravel's constitutional immunity did not shield him or his aides from grand jury questioning regarding their activities not directly related to their legislative responsibilities. "While the Speech or Debate Clause recognizes speech, voting and other legislative acts as exempt from liability that might attach," the court stated, "it does not privilege either senator or aide to violate an otherwise valid criminal law in preparing for or implementing legislative acts."

The court concluded that the immunity of Gravel's aide was identical to that of his employer and defined the latter's as immunity from "prosecutions that directly impinge upon or threaten the legislative process."

The court majority concurred with the lower court ruling that the negotiations leading to the unofficial publication of the committee record were outside the protection of the speech or debate clause; further, however, it also held that both Gravel and Rodberg were vulnerable to grand jury questioning and possible liability regarding their roles in the Pentagon Papers publication.

Legislative Protection Restated

The Supreme Court on Oct. 9, 1973, upheld an appellate court ruling that had reversed five of eight conspiracy, bribery and perjury convictions against former Rep. John Dowdy, D-Texas (1952-73), on grounds that they violated the immunity clause.

A federal grand jury in Baltimore, Md., March 31, 1970, indicted Dowdy. The indictment alleged he had accepted a $25,000 bribe at the Atlanta, Ga., airport on Sept. 22, 1965, to intervene in a federal and District of Columbia investigation of the Monarch Construction Co. of Silver Spring, Md.

Dowdy was convicted on Dec. 30, 1971, in U.S. District Court in Baltimore of crossing a state line to receive a bribe, conspiracy to obstruct justice, conspiracy to violate conflict of interest statutes, and five counts of perjury. He was sentenced to 18 months in prison and fined $25,000.

On March 13, 1973, the Fourth Circuit Court of Appeals reversed five of the eight convictions and reduced Dowdy's sentence to six months in prison and a $3,000 fine. Convictions on three counts of perjury were sustained. (*Dowdy v. United States,* 479 F.2d 213)

The court held that evidence used in the trial that violated Dowdy's immunity "was an examination of the defendant's actions as a congressman, who was chairman of a subcommittee investigating a complaint, in gathering information in preparation for a possible subcommittee investigatory hearing."

Although the alleged criminal act — bribery — was the same in both the Dowdy and Brewster cases, the major difference, which resulted in one case being upheld and one case being reversed, was the source of the evidence. In Brewster's case there was sufficient evidence available outside of Brewster's legislative activities to permit the case to go forward. In Dowdy's case so much of the evidence was based on Dowdy's legislative activities that the court reversed five of the eight convictions.

On Oct. 9, 1973, the Supreme Court upheld the ruling of the lower court (*Dowdy v. United States,* 414 U.S. 866).

After losing a bid to stay out of prison for health reasons, Dowdy began his term Jan. 28, 1974.

1979 Rulings

In June 1979 the Supreme Court released two decisions concerning congressional immunity.

In *United States v. Helstoski,* the court forbade federal prosecutors to use any evidence of past legislative actions in prosecuting former Rep. Henry Helstoski, D-N.J. (1965-77). He was indicted in 1976 on charges he accepted money in return for introducing private bills allowing certain aliens to remain in the United States. As a result of the decision the prosecutors dropped seven bribery-related counts against Helstoski and sought reindictment of him on remaining obstruction of justice counts. The district judge, however, dismissed these counts also, ruling they were "tainted" by Helstoski's legislative actions.

In *Hutchinson v. Proxmire,* the court held that congressional immunity did not protect Sen. William Proxmire, D-Wis., from being sued for libel by a scientist who charged that he had been injured by Proxmire's remarks ridiculing his research. The allegedly libelous remarks were made on the Senate floor in 1975 and then published in a press release and newsletter. The court ruled that only the remarks on the floor were protected by the Speech or Debate clause.

Proxmire was sued by Dr. Ronald Hutchinson, a researcher at the Kalamazoo, Mich., State Hospital, after the Wisconsin Democrat gave the National Aeronautics and Space Administration and the Office of Naval Research his Golden Fleece Award. Those agencies had awarded Hutchinson $500,000 in grants for research into how monkeys exhibit aggression. Proxmire garnered considerable publicity by periodically giving Golden Fleece Awards to spotlight what he considered outstanding cases of government waste.

Proxmire made an out-of-court settlement with Hutchinson, announcing the settlement in a March 24, 1980, speech on the Senate floor. Although he did not say so in the speech, the senator agreed to pay the scientist $10,000 in return for ending further litigation. Proxmire used the 1980 Senate floor speech to "clarify" his 1975 Golden Fleece statements, which had led to the suit in the first place.

Although Hutchinson paid his own legal fees in the lengthy suit, the $124,351 tab for Proxmire's defense was picked up by the Senate.

CRIMINAL PROBES: SPUR TO ETHICS ACTIONS

The creation of ethics committees in the House and Senate institutionalized the legislature's responsibility to police itself. It was an unpopular task, and the committees often proved reluctant to investigate a fellow member unless criminal proceedings had already started.

Critics of this approach argued that the congressional ethics codes spelled out higher standards of behavior than just avoidance of criminal activity. They suggested that members must be answerable to their colleagues for questionable legislative actions that could not be prosecuted in court because of the Constitution's immunity clause.

The procedures followed by the committees, in which they acted as investigator, prosecutor and jury, came under criticism. And members were reluctant to serve on the committees, so turnover was rapid and their caliber as a whole not widely respected in Congress. "It's a thankless responsibility" was the inevitable reaction of those picked to serve on the committees.

Two major investigations were undertaken by the ethics committees between 1977 and 1982, one centering on the South Korean government's long effort to buy influence in Congress and the other a follow-up to the FBI's Abscam net for corrupt legislators.

Korean Influence Buying

On Oct. 24, 1976, *The Washington Post* broke the story that the Justice Department was probing "the most sweeping allegations of congressional corruption ever investigated by the federal government."

The *Post* said that South Korean agents dispensed between $500,000 and $1 million a year in cash and gifts to members of Congress to help maintain "a favorable legislative climate" for South Korea.

Tongsun Park, a South Korean businessman operating in Washington, was named as the principal dispenser of favors.

Follow-up reports said an influence-buying plan had been hatched in the Blue House, the South Korean equivalent of the White House, at a meeting in late 1970 or early 1971 of President Park Chung Hee, Tongsun Park, high Korean Central Intelligence Agency (KCIA) officials and Pak Bo Hi, later a chief aide to Korean evangelist Sun Myung Moon.

President Park reportedly was concerned about a Nixon administration plan to withdraw about a third of the U.S. troops in Korea. Growing opposition in the United States to the war in Vietnam also raised fears in Korea that a pullout would lessen American ability to protect it against another invasion from North Korea. Continued U.S. congressional support therefore became a high priority of the Park regime.

The House Committee on Standards of Official Conduct began a slow-moving investigation of the involvement of representatives in the South Korean scheme in January 1977. The Senate Ethics Committee also conducted an investigation of senators' reported roles and a House Foreign Affairs subcommittee looked into the South Korean government's alleged plot.

Soon after the initial Post story, Tongsun Park fled the country. Indicted by the U.S. government Sept. 6, 1977, Park stayed in Korea while lengthy negotiations were carried out by his government and the U.S. Justice Department. Finally he agreed to testify before the House ethics committee if granted immunity from prosecution.

The indictment charged Park with 36 counts of conspiracy to defraud the United States, bribery, mail fraud, failure to register as a foreign agent and making illegal political contributions.

Former Rep. Richard Hanna, D-Calif. (1963-74), was named as an unindicted co-conspirator, as were former KCIA directors Kim Hyung Wook and Lee Hu Rak.

The indictment charged that Park and Hanna, around 1967, concocted a scheme to collect large commissions from sales of U.S. rice to South Korea and to use some of that money to buy friends for Korea in Congress. The KCIA directors were alleged to have cooperated in the scheme. Park, a lavish party-giver in Washington, reportedly received more than $9 million in commissions on rice sales from 1969 to 1976.

Hanna had retired from Congress in 1974 after serving six terms. As a sponsor of the Asian Development Bank, he had made numerous trips to Asia and to Korea. He was later indicted and in March 1978 pleaded guilty to one count of conspiracy to defraud the government. He admitted that he had agreed to use his office to help Tongsun Park and had received $200,000 for his efforts between 1969 and 1975. He began serving a 2½-year prison term in May 1978.

Before holding hearings both ethics committees drew up questionnaires asking members of the two houses to report what, if any, contacts they had with South Korean government representatives and any gifts or political contributions received from Tongsun Park or others.

Park's testimony before the House ethics committee began Feb. 28, 1978, and ran for more than a week. While he named members to whom he had given contributions, he denied being a representative of the South Korean government or conspiring to buy influence in Congress. He did, however, describe the help he had received from then-Rep. Otto E. Passman, D-La. (1947-77), in retaining his lucrative commissions on sales of rice to South Korea. As chairman of the House Appropriations subcommittee that dealt with rice and other Food for Peace commodity sales abroad, Passman was in a good position to help his rice-growing constituents as well as Park. (Passman was defeated for re-election in the 1976 congressional primary, indicted in 1978 for bribery and conspiracy to defraud the U.S. government, but acquitted of all charges the next year.)

During his testimony, Park said that most of his payments went to three former House members — Passman, who Park testified received cash and gifts of between $367,000 and $407,000; former Rep. Hanna, who allegedly received $262,000; and former Rep. Cornelius Gallagher, D-N.J. (1959-73), who Park said got $211,000. (Hanna admitted receiving $200,000.)

Four sitting representatives became the objects of disciplinary hearings by the House ethics committee. They were three California Democrats, John J. McFall (1957-78), Edward R. Roybal and Charles H. Wilson (1963-81), and Rep. Edward J. Patten, D-N.J. (1963-81). The committee's report said McFall had converted a $3,000 campaign contribution from Park to his personal use, Roybal had done the same with a $1,000 contribution and then lied under oath about it, Wilson had denied receiving money from Park despite the latter's testimony that he gave Wilson $1,000 as a wedding gift, and Patten had forwarded a contribution he received from Park as a personal contribution to a New Jersey political organization.

The committee cleared Patten, and recommended reprimands for McFall and Wilson and censure of Roybal for deliberately lying under oath. The probe ended in October 1978 when the House voted to reprimand all three Californians, its mildest form of punishment. (*Censure, p. 190*)

The Senate Ethics Committee concluded its Korean investigation in October 1978 with a report that recommended no disciplinary action against any incumbent or former senator.

The third committee investigating U.S.-Korean relations concluded that the South Korean government sought to bribe U.S. officials, buy influence among journalists and professors, extort money from American companies and rig military procurement contracts to win support for what the panel called the "authoritarian" government of President Park Chung Hee. In its final report, released in November 1978, the House International Relations Subcommittee on International Organizations said that the South Korean government's illegal activities went beyond its legal and extra-legal lobbying efforts. The 450-page report, which outlined the history of U.S.-Korean relations, indicated that the South Koreans frequently pursued policies antithetical to U.S. interests. The most notable of those incidents involved South Korean efforts to develop nuclear weapons, a project the subcommittee said was abandoned by 1975.

Abscam Investigation

An FBI undercover operation known as Abscam, a combination of the words Arab and scam (a con man's trick), in 1980 implicated seven members of Congress in criminal wrongdoing.

By May 1981, juries had convicted the seven — six House members and one senator — for their role in the affair, and by March 11, 1982, none of the seven was still in Congress.

The House members were John W. Jenrette Jr., D-S.C. (1975-80), Richard Kelly, R-Fla. (1975-81), Raymond F. Lederer, D-Pa. (1977-81), John M. Murphy, D-N.Y. (1963-81), Michael "Ozzie" Myers, D-Pa. (1976-80), and Frank Thompson Jr., D-N.J. (1955-81). Another House member, John P. Murtha, D-Pa., was named an unindicted co-conspirator and testified for the government in the trial of Murphy and Thompson. The senator was Harrison A. Williams Jr., D-N.J. (House 1953-57, Senate 1959-82).

In summary, Abscam led to the following congressional actions with respect to the convicted seven:

● Ozzie Myers was expelled from the House of Representatives on Oct. 2, 1980, only the fourth representative ever expelled and the first since the Civil War.

● Three others — Jenrette, Lederer and Williams — resigned from Congress to avoid almost certain expulsion.

● Kelly, Murphy and Thompson were defeated by their constituents before being convicted in court.

The unindicted conspirator, Murtha, was cleared by the House ethics committee over the objections of the committee counsel.

Two elements made Abscam far more than a routine corruption case. One was the FBI's use of videotapes to record the meetings of phony sheiks, members of Congress and others — a development that allowed the public to see one representative stuffing money into bulging pockets. The other unusual element was the prominence of three of those convicted — senior committee chairmen, two of whom (Thompson and Williams) were generally considered leaders within their party.

The Scam

According to published accounts and subsequent court evidence, an undisclosed number of members of Congress had been approached by intermediaries who offered to introduce them to representatives of wealthy Arabs interested in making investments in their districts. The representatives were actually undercover FBI agents. Some of the members were asked if they could use their Hill positions to help the Arabs obtain U.S. residency. Others were asked to use their influence in government to obtain federal grants and gambling licenses or to arrange real estate deals.

Five of the accused — Williams, Kelly, Lederer, Myers and Thompson — were videotaped accepting cash or stock. Jenrette was tape-recorded saying he had been given the cash by an associate. Murphy allegedly told an associate to accept the cash.

The defendants' claim that the government had entrapped them won support in some legal and congressional circles, and leaks to the press were generally condemned.

Although Attorney General Benjamin Civiletti asked congressional committees to hold up investigations until the criminal trials were completed, both the Senate Select Ethics Committee and the House Committee on Standards of Official Conduct began their own investigations.

In the end, the House committee waited until Myers, Jenrette and Lederer had been convicted in court before taking final action. Using court evidence as the basis for its probe, the panel recommended that Myers be expelled, and the full House agreed. *(See p. 182)*

Jenrette resigned from the House just as the Standards Committee was ready to hand down a recommendation for his expulsion. Lederer resigned in 1981 after the committee recommended his expulsion.

Because Kelly, Murphy and Thompson were defeated for re-election, no congressional disciplinary action against them was taken.

The Senate committee unanimously recommended in August 1981 that Williams be expelled. After numerous delays the Senate debated the recommendation for five days in March 1982 before Williams submitted his resignation.

The Court Cases

Myers and three co-defendants were convicted Aug. 30, 1980, of bribery, conspiracy and interstate travel to aid racketeering. The co-defendants were Camden, N.J., Mayor Angelo J. Errichetti, Philadelphia attorney Howard L. Criden, and Louis C. Johanson, a member of the Philadelphia City Council and a partner in Criden's law firm.

Videotapes seen by the jurors showed Myers accepting an envelope with $50,000 in cash from an agent.

The government charged that Myers took the money in return for promises to introduce a private immigration bill to help the agent's supposed Arab employer gain permanent U.S. residence.

Myers then boasted of his familiarity with Philadelphia government officials and members of the Mafia and agreed to accept an additional $85,000.

On the stand, Myers acknowledged that he had accepted money from the undercover agents. However, he maintained he was not bribed because he had never intended to do anything in return for the money.

Following a five-week trial, Jenrette was convicted Oct. 7, 1980, on two counts of bribery and a single count of conspiracy. Convicted with him was a business associate, John R. Stowe. During the trial, government prosecutors charged that Jenrette and Stowe had accepted $50,000 in cash from an undercover FBI agent. Prosecutors described the payment as the first installment of a $100,000 bribe to be paid the two men in return for a promise from Jenrette to introduce a private immigration bill on behalf of the agent's supposed Arab employer.

"I've got larceny in my blood," jurors saw Jenrette say during a videotaped meeting with the agent.

Jenrette was defeated in the November 1980 election. In December the ethics committee recommended that the House discipline him and on Dec. 10 he resigned just before the committee was to vote on his expulsion.

Murphy and Thompson on Dec. 3, 1980, became the third and fourth members of Congress to be convicted for their involvement in Abscam.

After their indictments both men were required by House rules to yield their committee chairmanships until the criminal charges were resolved. Murphy was chairman of the House Merchant Marine and Fisheries Committee and its Merchant Marine Subcommittee. Thompson chaired the House Administration Committee, the Education and Labor Committee's Subcommittee on Labor-Management Relations and the Joint Committee on Printing.

According to the indictment, Thompson was introduced to the undercover agents by Philadelphia attorney Howard L. Criden at an October 1979 meeting in Washington. At that meeting, Thompson agreed to use his official position to help a group of Arab businessmen — the agents' supposed employers — on "an immigration matter," the indictment alleged. At a second meeting, Thompson and Criden were given $50,000, the indictment said, which they shared with "others."

The indictment said Thompson then agreed to introduce the agents to other members of Congress willing to take bribes. He subsequently met with Murphy, the indictment said, after which Murphy and Criden met with two FBI agents in a hotel near New York's Kennedy International Airport, where they were given $50,000 in return for Murphy's promise of help on the immigration matter. The cash was shared among Murphy, Thompson, Criden and "others," the indictment said.

Thompson then introduced Criden to Murtha, the indictment said. In a subsequent meeting with the FBI agents, Criden was given an additional $50,000 payment which he shared with Thompson and Murphy, according to the indictment. The indictment said Murtha agreed to use his official position to help the Arab businessmen gain United States residency, but he did not share in the cash payments.

The indictment further alleged that Murphy agreed to find investment opportunities in shipping companies for the agents' supposed employers, and to use his position as chairman of the Merchant Marine Committee to advance those companies' interests. The indictment said that Murphy and an unnamed associate intended to benefit both directly and indirectly from the investments.

Thompson also sought investments from the Arab businessmen, the indictment said. It added that benefits from the investments were to accrue to Thompson as well as to unnamed former law partners.

During the trial, Thompson took the stand to deny he had ever received any bribe money. However, Murtha, who was not indicted in the case, testified that Thompson had approached him on the House floor during 1979 to tell him he could share with Thompson and Murphy $50,000 in "walking around" money in return for meeting with the undercover agents. Murtha subsequently met with the agents but accepted no cash from them.

Murphy did not testify in his own defense.

Both Thompson and Murphy were convicted by a Brooklyn, N.Y., jury of conspiracy and acceptance of unlawful gratuity. Thompson also was convicted of bribery but Murphy was exonerated of that charge.

The convictions came a month after the two lost their re-election bids.

Kelly, the only Republican caught by Abscam, was convicted Jan. 26, 1981, of bribery and conspiracy. He had lost his re-election bid in the Sept. 9, 1980, Florida primary.

The July 15 indictment alleged that Kelly accepted $25,000 in cash from an FBI undercover agent in return for agreeing to use his influence to help people emigrate to the United States. The indictment alleged further that Kelly was later to have received $75,000 as part of the conspiracy.

When Kelly's name surfaced in February news accounts of the Abscam probe, he admitted to reporters that he took $25,000 in FBI money. But Kelly said it was part of his own investigation of "shady characters."

During the trial, Kelly was seen on videotape at a Washington home rented by the FBI stuffing money into his pockets and asking before he left whether the money made visible bulges in his clothing.

Lederer was convicted Jan. 9, 1981, in a Brooklyn, N.Y., federal district court, of bribery, conspiracy, accepting an illegal gratuity, and interstate travel to aid racketeering. His indictment, handed down May 28, 1980, charged that Lederer in September 1979 accepted a $50,000 bribe in a hotel room near Kennedy Airport in New York from an undercover FBI agent who said he represented Arab businessmen. Lederer promised to introduce private bills to give the Arabs permanent U.S. residency, the indictment said.

Lederer shared the $50,000 payment with Errichetti, Criden and Johanson (convicted with Myers), the indictment charged.

As the only Abscam figure re-elected to the House in 1980, Lederer faced disciplinary action by the new Congress. Supported by the Philadelphia Democratic organization, he had easily won his primary election over six opponents April 22 and was re-elected in November with 55 percent of the vote.

On April 28, 1981, the Standards Committee recommended that Lederer be expelled from the House. The following day Lederer announced that he would resign from the House May 5.

Senator Williams

Williams was convicted May 1, 1981, of all nine counts brought against him. They included bribery, conspiracy, accepting outside compensation for the performance of official duties and aid to a racketeering enterprise.

Standing seventh in seniority among Senate Democrats, Williams was chairman of the Senate Labor and Human Resources Committee until Republicans gained control of the Senate in 1981. He also was ranking member of the Banking Committee, former chairman of its Securities Subcommittee, and a member of the Rules and Administration Committee.

He was only the fourth senator convicted of criminal wrongdoing while in office.

Like the other Abscam defendants, he was convicted of promising to introduce a private immigration bill for what turned out to be a phony sheik (actually an FBI agent in disguise).

Williams Was 4th Senator Convicted in Office

Sen. Harrison A. Williams Jr., D-N.J. (1959-82), was the fourth senator to have been convicted of criminal wrongdoing while in office.

Prior to Williams, the last sitting senator to be convicted was Truman H. Newberry, R-Mich. (1919-22), found guilty in March 1920 of election irregularities.

Newberry's conviction was reversed by the Supreme Court in May 1921. But he resigned his seat in November 1922 after realizing that despite the Supreme Court's finding, "his position could never be other than uncomfortable," according to "Senate Election, Expulsion and Censure Cases" (S Doc 92-7).

The other two sitting senators to have been convicted were:

• John H. Mitchell, R-Ore. (1873-79, 1885-97, 1901-05), convicted in July 1905 on charges of accepting compensation for services rendered before a U.S. department. He died in late 1905 while his conviction was on appeal.

• Joseph R. Burton, R-Kan. (1901-06), convicted in November 1905 for allegedly using the mails for fraudulent purposes and accepting compensation for services rendered before a U.S. department. Burton's conviction was upheld by the Supreme Court in May

1906, and in June he resigned from the Senate and served five months in prison.

Indicted But Not Convicted

Congressional Quarterly found records of four other senators indicted while in office but not convicted. They were:

• John Smith, D-Ohio (1803-08), indicted in 1806 along with Vice President Aaron Burr for treason. He was found not guilty.

• Charles H. Dietrich, R-Neb. (1901-05), indicted in December 1903 on bribery and conspiracy charges in connection with the appointment of a postmaster and the leasing of a post office. The charges were dropped on a technicality in January 1904.

• Burton K. Wheeler, D-Mont. (1923-47), indicted in April 1924 on a bribery charge. Wheeler was acquitted.

• Edward J. Gurney, R-Fla. (House, 1963-69; Senate, 1969-74), indicted in April 1974 for alleged election law violations. The indictment was dismissed in May 1974. Gurney was again indicted in July 1974, this time on charges of perjury and soliciting bribes. He was acquitted on the bribery solicitation charge in August 1975 and on the perjury charge in October 1976.

Unlike the others he was not charged with accepting a large cash payment but with accepting shares in a titanium mine in return for a promise to help the enterprise get government contracts. Prosecutors said the stock certificates omitted Williams' name in order to conceal his interest in the mine. The stock was in the name of a close associate who was an unindicted co-conspirator in the case. The "scam" concerned a scheme to secure a $100 million loan to the mine and processing facility in Piney River, Va., from the supposed sheik.

Denying the charges, Williams said he had intended only to help friends who owned the mine to obtain a loan from a wealthy Arab.

Williams also acknowledged that he had boasted of his influence with high government officials "to an uncomfortable degree" in the presence of the bogus Arab and that he had accepted stock in the mine. But he said he believed the stock certificates to be worthless.

After his conviction Williams continued to vote on the Senate floor while pursuing an appeal to higher courts. He followed a precedent set in 1924 by Sen. Burton K. Wheeler, D-Mont. (1923-47), after his indictment for bribery. The Montana senator, however, was never convicted.

Wheeler at the time of the indictment headed a special committee investigating the failure of the Warren G. Harding administration to prosecute federal officials suspected of influence-peddling in the Teapot Dome scandal.

Wheeler maintained he had been framed by the very officials he was investigating.

Rather than keep off the floor, Wheeler demanded the right to speak to declare his innocence and to ask the Senate to investigate the charge. During the ensuing probe, he continued to vote.

Wheeler subsequently was cleared of any wrongdoing both by the Senate and by a federal jury. Since then, indicted senators have remained active in Senate affairs until they either were cleared or left the Senate.

House rules urged — but did not require — a convicted member to refrain from voting in committee and on the floor until the member either was cleared or re-elected.

The Senate Ethics Committee, after reviewing the evidence in the court case and hearing Williams present his defense again, voted unanimously Aug. 24, 1981, to recommend that the Senate expel him. That would have been the 16th expulsion from the Senate and the first since the Civil War. *(Box, p. 181)*

After numerous delays the Senate began debating the recommendation March 3, 1982. Noting Williams' claim that the government tried "to manufacture crime out of nothing," Ethics Vice Chairman Howell Heflin, D-Ala., a former judge, argued that the evidence upheld the case against Williams regardless of the government's conduct.

"At any point in this drawn out, sordid affair," Heflin said, "Senator Williams could have said, 'Wait a minute.

What you're proposing is wrong. That is not what I had in mind. I can't be involved in this.' But he didn't. He stayed; he discussed; he agreed; he promised; he pledged — to abuse his office, his public trust, for which now he must be expelled."

The Democratic Whip, Alan Cranston, D-Calif., worked on Williams' behalf to reduce the punishment to a censure motion. But when closer friends of Williams reluctantly endorsed expulsion, it became clear that Cranston's motion would fail and that well over the required two-thirds of the Senate was ready to vote to expel Williams.

On March 11, 1982, he resigned from the Senate. His colleagues then voted to create a special committee to examine the FBI's conduct in the Abscam cases. Entrapment was the most important issue raised by the Abscam defendants in appealing their convictions. Eventually the Supreme Court would have to rule on the validity of the government's procedures, it was believed.

Index